Glencoe

INTERACTIVE

Teacher Edition

Read and Write

English Learner

AMERICAN LITERATURE

The McGraw·Hill Companies

 Glencoe

Send all inquiries to:
Glencoe/McGraw-Hill
8787 Orion Place
Columbus, OH 43240-4027

ISBN: 978-0-07-889573-9
MHID: 0-07-889573-1

Printed in the United States of America.
1 2 3 4 5 6 7 8 9 10 079 14 13 12 11 10 09 08

Contents

Contents (continued)

Contents (continued)

Overview

Glencoe's *Read and Write* for English learners provides additional language and concept support for students using the *Glencoe Literature* program. This resource may be used to preteach the selections or as a parallel instruction to the whole group.

The *Read and Write* student edition follows the organization of the *Glencoe Literature* program, with instruction and support provided for the following features:

- Literary Element
- Reading Strategy
- Vocabulary

Helping English Learners to Improve Proficiency

One of the major concerns of teachers of English learners (ELs) is how to move students beyond basic interpersonal communicative skills to academic language proficiency. Research shows that the most effective way for ELs to develop this proficiency—and to build content knowledge and improve language learning—is to focus them on *active engagement* in learning and to use *metacognitive and cognitive learning strategies*. Monitoring comprehension, building background, making inferences about possible meanings of new vocabulary—systematic instruction in all these strategies helps ELs become more proficient.

The *Read and Write* philosophy of learner interaction, strategic intervention, and academic language development aligns with current linguistic thinking and best practices for teaching English learners. *Read and Write* offers comprehensible instruction that is cognitively demanding and contextually embedded. Side notes, for instance, explain reading strategies and literary elements in a clear, interactive format, providing concrete examples for abstract concepts, such as drawing conclusions.

Using the Student Edition

The *Read and Write* student edition uses "considerate text" to provide a variety of interactive EL strategies that engage students at all levels of proficiency.

Before You Read

The features **Connect to the Genre, Literary Element**, and **Reading Strategy** are introduced before students read the selection and parallel the instruction of the *Glencoe Literature* program, using an accessible approach for English learners.

Vocabulary

- **Selection Vocabulary** parallels the vocabulary taught in *Glencoe Literature*, but modified definitions and example sentences provide systematic vocabulary instruction and additional context for accessing words' meanings.
- **Content Vocabulary** provides additional illustrated vocabulary words that are:
  - essential to understanding the selection
  - likely to be used again throughout the school year
  - multidisciplinary
- **Vocabulary Practice** activities appear in the back of the student book for each lesson. These activities are leveled to meet students' varying proficiency levels. **Activity A** provides vocabulary practice for Beginning/Early Intermediate students; **Activity B** provides vocabulary practice for Intermediate students; and **Activity C** provides vocabulary practice for Early Advanced students. The **Vocabulary Check** after reading offers the same scaffolded practice.

- **Pronunciation Key** Refer students to the **Pronunciation Key** on page 348 for help in pronouncing new vocabulary words.

During Reading

Students are able to access selection text at their proficiency level:

- **Beginning/Early Intermediate** Beginning and Early Intermediate students are able to access selection text by focusing on a unique **To Sum Up** feature that summarizes each selection page in an easy-to-read format. By reading these features, students will be able to access the essential meaning of the story.
- **Intermediate** Intermediate students are able to access the selection text at their proficiency level by reading the boxed portions of the selection. By focusing on these selected portions of text, students will be able to access the essential elements of the story, including plot development, characterization, literary elements, and text features.
- **Early Advanced** Early advanced students are able to read the entire selection to access the text at their proficiency level. Additional interactive side-margin notes challenge these students at a deeper level to make meaning from the entire text.

Interactive side margin notes ensure students' active participation in applying strategies such as analyzing, identifying, defining, explaining, and critiquing. This interactive approach encourages students to be engaged as active speakers and listeners by using partner-talk and other tools, such as sentence frames, that guide their use of language. Students at different proficiency levels are able to explore questions and prompts together. This highly-structured opportunity promotes language use in a non-threatening way among peers.

- **Literary Element** offers practice in an interactive format for the literary element introduced before reading.
- **Background Information** provides additional relevant context to build background.
- **Content Vocabulary** is defined and illustrated at point of use in context.
- **Idioms and figurative language** are defined at point of use for student interpretation.
- **Comprehension Check** allows students to periodically check their comprehension of the selection in an interactive format.
- **To Sum Up** summarizes each selection page for Beginning and Early Intermediate students.
- **Reflect** allows students to practice the Reading Strategy. A partner icon signals to students to discuss their opinions and thoughts with a classmate. This opportunity allows students to demonstrate a range of speaking skills and strategies for paired activities or flexible small-group instruction.
- **Note Taking** gives students a structure for taking notes while they read nonfiction. A process for taking notes is particularly useful in understanding informational text, and research shows that students who take good notes perform better on tests. Using this process, drawn from the Cornell note-taking system, students will record notes, recap what they've learned, and summarize their notes.

After You Read

Students apply what they've learned in a cumulative review after reading in **Vocabulary Check** and **Comprehension Check**. A **four-domain activity** after each lesson allows students to practice speaking, listening, reading, and writing within the context of the selection, using a fun, interactive format. Some of these after reading activities appear in the back of the student book.

Using the Teacher Edition

The *Read and Write* Teacher Edition presents comprehensive guidance for teachers in providing effective, efficient instruction for English learners. The lessons are easy to navigate—labeled sections correspond to each feature of the student page. Lessons give teachers optimal opportunities to scaffold instruction and check for understanding, using a variety of instructional techniques for content, vocabulary acquisition, and language development, including:

- Oral Language and Building Background
- Interactive Question-Response
- Modeling
- Differentiated Instruction
- Vocabulary Routines
- Academic Vocabulary
- Writing Links
- Fluency
- Oral Assessment
- Comprehension
- Word Study
- Grammar Links

Oral Language and Building Background Differentiated instruction for each lesson opener develops students' oral language and builds background at these levels of proficiency: Beginning/Early Intermediate, Intermediate, and Early Advanced.

Interactive Question-Response Each lesson is explored through a research-proven interactive approach, called *Interactive Question-Response,* which helps teachers coach English learners in using language to make connections and meaning. This conversational, interactive instruction creates context and provides opportunities for students to see how information builds and connects. This type of instruction provides ample opportunities for students to talk and use new language. It helps teachers ask the right kind of questions that focus on the basic meaning of the text and build overall understanding. Interactive teacher modeling helps students to use what they already know as they add new knowledge. It also allows numerous opportunities for using role-play and movement activities to enhance vocabulary meaning. These techniques make instruction engaging and memorable for students.

Modeling Modeling is the process of demonstrating a thinking process. To model, the teacher reads aloud the interactive prompt as students follow along. Then, in everyday language, the teacher reasons aloud. The purpose of modeling is for students to understand the steps that readers follow to solve a reading problem or analyze text. The goal is to have students apply similar reasoning procedures during their own reading processes. To complete the modeling cycle, individual students should think aloud, with a partner or with the class, to demonstrate their own thinking processes as they employ the reading strategy or skill. Reasoning aloud makes students more aware of what they do as they read. Listening to a student think aloud shows the teacher how the student's abilities are developing and where the student needs support and guidance in applying the strategy. Teachers should use the scripting in *Read and Write* as a springboard for modeling in their own words to sound as natural as possible.

Differentiated Instruction Differentiated instruction throughout the lessons provides the means to clarify difficult text for students at these proficiency levels: Beginning/Early Intermediate, Intermediate, and Early Advanced.

Vocabulary Routines To provide teacher-directed instruction for vocabulary development, vocabulary routines appear for each lesson: Words are defined in a new way, additional sentences show the words in different contexts, and students define, explain, and compare and contrast vocabulary in their own words.

Academic Vocabulary Lessons feature academic vocabulary words. Academic vocabulary words represent a research-based collection of words that are commonly used in academic texts. Direct instruction presents students with the basics of a working academic vocabulary, one that will prove useful in reading, writing, and research in many areas of study.

Writing Link Each lesson suggests a writing assignment related to the selection to provide context for student writing that serves an intended purpose. See page T14 of this teacher edition for a Writing Checklist that students may use to evaluate their own writing.

Fluency Students practice oral reading skills throughout the program by choral reading and reading aloud individually. These fluency lessons provide instruction and practice for reading aloud narrative and expository text fluently and accurately and with appropriate pacing, intonation, and expressions. See the Program Scope and Sequence on page T10 for an overview of the fluency skills covered in this teacher edition. See also pages T15 and T16 for best practices of fluency development and Oral Reading Guidelines to evaluate students' oral reading performance.

Oral Assessment An oral assessment at the end of each selection allows teachers to evaluate students' level of language output. Teachers use five selection-related questions to prompt oral responses that demonstrate students' proficiency levels. The same questions are used for all students, so teachers may wish to incorporate additional strategies for beginners, such as using gestures or pictures to help elicit responses. For early advanced students, teachers may wish to prompt expanded responses by asking students to expand, elaborate, or clarify their answers. See page T17 of this teacher edition for an Oral Assessment Rubric to evaluate students' proficiency levels.

Comprehension Blackline Masters Students start a graphic organizer at the beginning of each selection and complete it as they read to reinforce skills, such as identifying and analyzing. The graphic organizers for all lessons begin on page A1 at the back of this teacher edition.

Word Study Blackline Masters Word study instruction occurs throughout these lessons and feature words from the selections to illustrate particular word study topics, such as analogies, metaphors, similes, and word origins and derivations. Word study activities that reinforce instruction begin on page A1 at the back of this teacher edition. See the Program Scope and Sequence on page T10 for an overview of the word study topics in this program.

Grammar Link Blackline Masters Throughout the program, teachers are referred to grammar, sentence structure, and punctuation lessons that begin on page A1 at the back of this teacher edition. The instruction and practice features characters and topics from the selections to provide meaningful context as students apply concepts. See the Program Scope and Sequence on page T10 for an overview of the grammar, sentence structure, and punctuation topics.

Program Scope and Sequence

Selection	Literary Element	Reading Strategy	Writing
Comparing Literature **The Sky Tree** *Joseph Bruchac* **How the Leopard Got His Claws** *Chinua Achebe and John Iroaganachi* **Prayer to the Pacific** *Leslie Marmon Silko*	Oral Tradition	Question]	Paragraph
Upon the Burning of Our House *Anne Bradstreet* **To My Dear and Loving Husband**	Metaphor	Draw Conclusions About Author's Beliefs	Extended Metaphor
TIME: How They Chose These Words *Walter Isaacson*		Determine the Main Idea and Supporting Details	Fact Sheet
Letter to John Adams *Abigail Adams*	Description	Recognize Author's Purpose	Letter
Comparing Literature ***from* Civil Disobedience** *Henry David Thoreau* **On the Eve of Historic Dandi March** *Mohandas K. Gandhi* ***from* Long Walk to Freedom** *Nelson Mandela*	Argument	Evaluate Evidence	Speech
The Pit and the Pendulum *Edgar Allan Poe*	Suspense	Identify Sequence	Interview
Comparing Literature ***from* My Bondage and My Freedom** *Frederick Douglass* **Frederick Douglass** *Robert Hayden* **In Texas Grass** *Quincy Troupe*	Autobiography	Analyze Cause and Effect	Mission Statement
And Ain't I a Woman? *Sojourner Truth*	Oratory	Evaluate Argument	Speech
***from* Mary Chesnut's Civil War** *Mary Chesnut*	Journal	Distinguish Fact and Opinion	Journal Entry

Fluency	Grammar	Word Study
	Irregular Verbs: *Have, Do,* and *Go*	Antonyms/Synonyms
	Past Time Expressions	
	The Simple Past Tense: Time Clauses with *Before* and *After*	
	The Present Perfect Tense of *Be: For* and *Since*	
Expression and Intonation: Bring out Meaning	Spelling of Regular Past Tense Verbs; Pronunciation of *–ed: /t/, /d/,* and */id/*	Negative Prefixes: *un-, im-, in-, il-, dis-, a-,* and *ir-*
Expression and Intonation: Punctuation (exclamation point)	The Simple Past Tense: Irregular Verbs	Root Words and Word Origins AND Denotations and Connotations
	Future Time Clauses with *Before, After,* and *When*	Context Meaning
	Object Pronouns	
Expression and Intonation: Punctuation (comma)	Possessive Pronouns	Multiple Meaning Words

Selection	Literary Element	Reading Strategy	Writing
I Hear America Singing *Walt Whitman* **When I Heard the Learn'd Astronomer**	Free Verse	Paraphrase	Poem
If you were coming in the Fall *Emily Dickinson* **My Life closed twice** **The Soul selects**	Rhyme	Analyze Sound Devices	Journal Entry
The Celebrated Jumping Frog of Calaveras County *Mark Twain*	Dialect	Analyze Comic Devices	Graphic Story
A Wagner Matinée *Willa Cather*	Point of View	Identify Sequence	Advice Column
Douglass *Paul Laurence Dunbar* **We Wear the Mask**	Rhyme Scheme	Clarify Meaning	Blog
The Love Song of J. Alfred Prufrock *T. S. Eliot*	Allusion	Connect to Cultural Context	Anecdote
The Jilting of Granny Weatherall *Katherine Anne Porter*	Stream of Consciousness	Draw Conclusions About the Protagonist	Character Sketch
When the Negro Was in Vogue *Langston Hughes*	Juxtaposition	Analyze Concrete Details	Blog
The Rockpile *James Baldwin*	Foil	Make Generalizations About Characters	Editorial
The Crucible, Act I *Arthur Miller*	Dialogue	Draw Conclusions About Characters	Journal Entry
Comparing Literature **Ambush** *Tim O'Brien* **The Gift in Wartime** *Tran Mong Tu* *from* **Stay Alive, My Son** *Pin Yathay with John Man*	Mood	Analyze Concrete Details	List
Snow *Julia Alvarez*	Indirect Characterization	Connect to Contemporary Issues	Paragraph
Salvador Late or Early *Sandra Cisneros*	Imagery	Analyze Sound Devices	Song
Thoughts on the African-American Novel *Toni Morrison*	Essay	Determine Main Idea and Supporting Details	Essay
Functional Documents		Analyze Expository Text	Travel Directions

Fluency	Grammar	Word Study
	While and *When* with Past Time Clauses	
Pacing: Meaningful Phrases		
Expression and Intonation: Dialogue	Pronouns and Antecedents	Figurative Language: Idioms and Similes
Expression and Intonation: Punctuation (period)	Commas before *and, but,* and *or*	
Pacing: Phrasing	Word Order of Adjectives	
Expression and Intonation: Punctuation (question mark)	Sentence Fragments	Base Words
Pacing: Phrasing	Comparitive Form of Adjectives: *-er* and *more*	
	Run-on Sentences	
Intontation and Pacing: Smooth Reading	Interrogative AND Exclamatory and Imperative Sentences	Homophones
	Adjectives and Adverbs	
	Comparative and Superlative Forms of Adverbs: *-er* and *more*	

Writing Checklist

1. I followed the directions for writing.

2. My writing shows that I read and understood the article.

3. I capitalized the names of people and the proper names of places and things.

4. I put a punctuation mark at the end of each sentence.

5. I read my writing aloud and listened for missing words.

6. I used a dictionary to check words that didn't look right.

Check off the things on the list that you have done for each writing assignment.

Selection Titles	Checklist Numbers ✔					
	1	2	3	4	5	6
The Sky Tree; How the Leopard Got His Claws; Prayer to the Pacific						
Upon the Burning of Our House; To My Dear and Loving Husband						
TIME: How They Chose These Words						
Letter to John Adams						
from Civil Disobedience; On the Eve of Historic Dandi March; from Long Walk to Freedom						
The Pit and the Pendulum						
from My Bondage and My Freedom; Frederick Douglass; In Texas Grass						
And Ain't I a Woman?						
from Mary Chesnut's Civil War						
I Hear America Singing; When I Heard the Learn'd Astronomer						
If you were coming in the Fall; My Life closed twice; The Soul selects						
The Celebrated Jumping Frog of Calaveras County						
A Wagner Matinée						
Douglass; We Wear the Mask						
The Love Song of J. Alfred Prufrock						
The Jilting of Granny Weatherall						
When the Negro Was in Vogue						
The Rockpile						
The Crucible, Act I						
Ambush; The Gift in Wartime; from Stay Alive, My Son						
Snow						
Salvador Late or Early						
Thoughts on the African-American Novel						
Functional Documents						

Best Practices for Fluency Development

Glencoe's *Read and Write* for English learners provides differentiated instruction for fluency practice of the following skills:

Expression and Intonation
- Punctuation
- Bring Out Meaning
- Dialogue

Pacing
- Phrasing
- Meaningful Phrases
- Smooth Reading

Why Fluency Is Important for English Learners Slow, disfluent reading is associated with poor comprehension and inefficient reading overall. If reading proceeds haltingly, it is difficult for readers to make connections, activate background knowledge, acquire new information, or find deeper meaning in text. It's important for secondary students to understand the role fluency plays in the reading process. As students become aware of their oral and silent reading behaviors, they will be able to monitor their fluency.

Strategies for Developing Fluency

Oral Reading One of the most effective ways to help students build fluency is by having them listen to good oral readers and then practice oral reading themselves. Research shows that when a student hears the fluent reading of a text while simultaneously reading silently, fluency as well as vocabulary and comprehension improve.

Repeated Reading When students have difficulty with phrasing or inappropriate chunking of words, they need repeated practice in order to infer phrasing boundaries. Through repeated oral readings, the reader learns to transfer this knowledge of phrase patterns to other, unfamiliar passages.

Paired Reading Pair students and allow them to practice reading orally to one another. A partner may choose to read one paragraph at a time to the other, or the more fluent reader may read a long passage while the partner follows along silently.

Choral Reading Choral reading is a technique that allows students to use their voices in unison to convey meaning. This practice allows shy or insecure students to practice fluency in a safe environment.

By using these strategies, students will improve:

- Phrasing: the ability to chunk text into syntactically appropriate units
- Smoothness: the ability to read without hesitation or inappropriate pauses
- Prosody: the ability to portray the intonation, rhythm, and vocal stress in speech

Read and Write calls out passages in the selections that are appropriate for practicing certain fluency skills. Following is an effective sequence for presenting these lessons:

- Tell students they will be doing a choral reading of the passage.
- Read aloud the passage twice, demonstrating phrasing, smoothness, and prosody.
- Allow students to read the passage silently, practicing the fluency elements.
- Have students practice reading aloud the passage with a partner before choral reading.
- Students may join in the choral reading one at a time, until they are all reading together, or teachers may choose to have all students read together at the same time.

Teachers may want to evaluate students individually, using the Oral Reading Guidelines on page T16. Teachers may choose to keep records of students' oral readings to be able to show students' fluency improvement after repeated oral readings.

Oral Reading Guidelines

This guide will help you evaluate students' oral reading performances. In each of the five categories listed, score a student's fluency, using a scale of 1 to 4. After the evaluation in each category, average the five scores and record an overall score.

	Score 1 Poor	Score 2 Fair	Score 3 Good	Score 4 Excellent
Accuracy	Word Recognition is poor (below 85%); the reader attempt to decode but is usually unsuccessful.	Word recognition is marginal (86–90%); the reader often self-corrects but unsuccessfully.	Word recognition is good (91–95%); the reader often self-corrects successfully.	Word recognition is excellent (96% or above); self-corrections are necessarily few and usually successful.
Rate	The reading rate is slow and laborious.	The reading rate is somewhat slow and inappropriately fast.	The reading rate is adequate but sometimes unevenly fast or slow.	The reading rate is consistently conversational and appropriate.
Phrasing	The reader reads word-by-word in one tone, often not recognizing phrases, clauses, or ends of sentences.	The reader reads in groups of two or three words, often not recognizing phrases, clauses, or ends of sentences.	The reader has good expression but may pause in mid-sentence.	The reader reads expressively, showing understanding by recognizing phrases, clauses, and ends of sentences.
Smoothness	The reader pauses, hesitates, and repeats words many times.	The reader pauses and hesitates when encountering challenging parts.	The reader encounters occasional breaks in reading due to specific words; the reading is generally smooth.	The reader encounters very few breaks; the reading is smooth and even.
Prosody	The reader ignores punctuations and reads each word with equal emphasis.	The reader pays attention to punctuation, but reads in a monotone.	The reader uses expression appropriately to facilitate meaning.	The reader appropriately employs expression to enhance the text, using intonation, rhythm, and vocal stress to clarify meaning.

Name _____ Overall Score_____

Class_____ Percentage Score_____%

Student _____ **Date** _____

Selection _____ **Page** _____

Oral Assessment Rubric

Read the questions from the selection-specific Oral Assessment as you evaluate students' levels of language output. Place a checkmark in the box that reflects the type of student response to each question. Then tally the types of responses to determine students' proficiency levels.

Questions	Beginning Non-verbal response	Beginning/ Early intermediate 1- or 2-word answer(s)	Early intermediate/ Intermediate Phrase(s)	Intermediate/ Early Advanced Short sentence(s)	Early advanced Complete sentence(s)
Question 1					
Question 2					
Question 3					
Question 4					
Question 5					

Total responses _____ _____ _____ _____ _____

Proficiency Level _____

Teaching the Objectives

The following abbreviated curriculum is a suggestion for addressing those objectives that students commonly encounter on standardized tests. You may use it as a guide for prioritizing instruction in preparation for the tests

Selections/Lessons	Pacing/ Days	Genre	Where to Find the Instruction	Commonly Tested Objectives
Comparing Literature: The Sky Tree AND How the Leopard Got His Claws AND Prayer to the Pacific	3–7	Myths AND Poetry	pp. 1–16, 306	**Literary Study:** Analyzing oral tradition. **Reading:** Questioning. **Reading:** Comparing works across time and place.
Upon the Burning of Our House AND To My Dear and Loving Husband	1–4	Poetry	pp. 17–24, 307–308	**Literary Study:** Analyzing metaphor. **Reading:** Drawing conclusions about author's beliefs. **Reading:** Understanding synonyms.
TIME: How They Chose These Words	2–6	Historical Essay	pp. 25–36, 309–310	**Reading:** Determining the main idea and supporting details.
Letter to John Adams	1–4	Letter	pp. 37–44, 311–312	**Literary Study:** Analyzing description. **Reading:** Recognizing author's purpose. **Reading:** Understanding analogies.
Comparing Literature: *from* Civil Disobedience AND On the Eve of Historic Dandi March AND *from* Long Walk to Freedom	4–17	Essay AND Speech AND Autobiography	pp. 45–78, 313–315	**Literary Study:** Analyzing argument. **Literary Study:** Analyzing political assumptions. **Literary Study:** Comparing persuasive messages. **Reading:** Evaluating evidence **Reading:** Understanding antonyms
The Pit and the Pendulum	3–9	Short Story	pp. 79–98, 316	**Literary Study:** Analyzing suspense. **Reading:** Identifying sequence. **Reading:** Understanding word origins.
Comparing Literature: *from* My Bondage and My Freedom AND Frederick Douglass AND In Texas Grass	2–7	Autobiography AND Poetry	pp. 99–114, 317	**Literary Study:** Analyzing autobiography. **Reading:** Analyzing cause and effect. **Reading:** Comparing literature. **Reading:** Understanding denotation and connotation.
And Ain't I a Woman	1–4	Speech	pp. 115–122, 318	**Literary Study:** Analyzing oratory. **Reading:** Evaluating argument. **Reading:** Understanding word usage.
from Mary Chesnut's Civil War	2–5	Memoir	pp. 123–132, 319	**Literary Study:** Analyzing journal. **Reading:** Distinguishing fact and opinion. **Reading:** Understanding context clues.
I Hear America Singing AND When I Heard the Learn'd Astronomer	1–3	Poetry	pp. 133–138, 320–321	**Literary Study:** Analyzing free verse. **Reading:** Paraphrasing.

Selections/Lessons	Pacing/Days	Genre	Where to Find the Instruction	Commonly Tested Objectives
If you were coming in the Fall AND My Life closed twice AND The Soul selects	1–4	Poetry	pp. 139–146, 322–323	Literary Study: Analyzing rhyme. Reading: Analyzing sound devices.
The Celebrated Jumping Frog of Calaveras County	3–7	Short Story	pp. 147–158, 324	Literary Study: Analyzing dialect. Reading: Analyzing comic devices. Reading: Understanding word origins.
A Wagner Matinée	2–6	Short Story	pp. 159–170, 325–326	Literary Study: Analyzing point of view. Reading: Identifying sequence. Reading: Understanding analogies.
Douglass AND We Wear the Masks	1–4	Poetry	pp. 171–178, 327	Literary Study: Analyzing rhyme scheme. Reading: Clarifying meaning. Reading: Understanding denotation and connotation.
The Love Song of J. Alfred Prufrock	2–5	Poetry	pp. 179–188, 328–329	Literary Study: Analyzing allusion. Reading: Connecting to cultural context. Reading: Understanding antonyms.
The Jilting of Granny Weatherall	2–7	Short Story	pp. 189–202, 330–331	Literary Study: Analyzing stream of consciousness. Reading: Drawing conclusions about the protagonist. Reading: Understanding context clues.
When the Negro Was in Vogue	2–5	Autobiography	pp. 203–212, 332–333	Literary Study: Analyzing juxtaposition. Reading: Analyzing concrete details. Reading: Understanding synonyms.
The Rockpile	2–7	Short Story	pp. 213–226, 334–335	Literary Study: Analyzing foil. Reading: Making generalizations about characters. Reading: Understanding analogies.
The Crucible, Act I	4–13	Drama	pp. 227–254, 336–337	Literary Study: Analyzing dialogue. Reading: Drawing conclusions about characters. Reading: Understanding word parts.
Comparing Literature: Ambush AND The Gift in Wartime AND from Stay Alive, My Son	3–7	Short Story AND Poetry AND Memoir	pp. 255–268, 338–339	Literary Study: Analyzing mood. Reading: Analyzing concrete details. Comparing literature. Reading: Understanding word origins.
Snow	1–4	Short Story	pp. 269–276, 340	Literary Study: Analyzing indirect characterization. Reading: Connecting to contemporary issues. Reading: Understanding word parts.
Salvador Late or Early	1–3	Short Story	pp. 277–282, 341–342	Literary Study: Analyzing imagery. Reading: Analyzing sound devices.

Teaching the Objectives

Selections/Lessons	Pacing/Days	Genre	Where to Find the Instruction	Commonly Tested Objectives
Thoughts on the African-American Novel	2–6	Essay	pp. 283–294, 343	**Literary Study:** Analyzing an essay. **Reading:** Determining main idea and supporting details. **Reading:** Identifying and understanding word parts.
Functional Documents	2–6	Functional Documents	pp. 295–305, 344–346	**Reading:** Analyzing expository texts.
	48–150 days			

Why Use This Book?

Read for Fun and Read to Learn!

The notes and features of *Read and Write* will help you read and understand each literature and nonfiction selection. As you use these notes and features, you practice the skills and strategies that good readers use when they read.

Before You Read

Connect

Before you read, think about your own experiences. Share your knowledge and opinions.

Literary Element and Reading Strategy

Learning about literary elements helps you to learn about important features of literature. Reading skills help you develop good strategies to understand what you read.

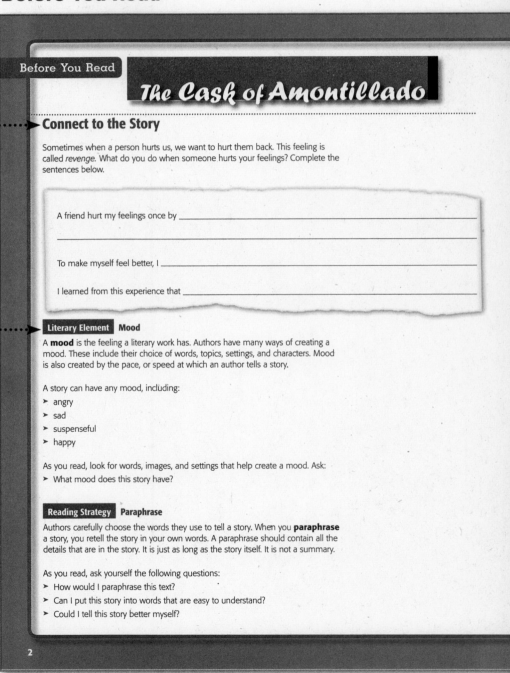

Before You Read

The Cask of Amontillado

Connect to the Story

Sometimes when a person hurts us, we want to hurt them back. This feeling is called *revenge*. What do you do when someone hurts your feelings? Complete the sentences below.

A friend hurt my feelings once by _____

_____

To make myself feel better, I _____

I learned from this experience that _____

Literary Element   Mood

A **mood** is the feeling a literary work has. Authors have many ways of creating a mood. These include their choice of words, topics, settings, and characters. Mood is also created by the pace, or speed at which an author tells a story.

A story can have any mood, including:
➤ angry
➤ sad
➤ suspenseful
➤ happy

As you read, look for words, images, and settings that help create a mood. Ask:
➤ What mood does this story have?

Reading Strategy   Paraphrase

Authors carefully choose the words they use to tell a story. When you **paraphrase** a story, you retell the story in your own words. A paraphrase should contain all the details that are in the story. It is just as long as the story itself. It is not a summary.

As you read, ask yourself the following questions:
➤ How would I paraphrase this text?
➤ Can I put this story into words that are easy to understand?
➤ Could I tell this story better myself?

2

Selection Vocabulary

precluded (pri klōō′ ded) *v.* stopped or prevented; made impossible (p. 4)
*The wind and the rain **precluded** our picnic.*

impunity (im pū′ nə tē) *n.* no punishment, harm, or danger (p. 4)
*Jack skips class every day with **impunity**.*
➤ Cognate (Spanish) **impunidad**

accosted (ə kôs′ ted) *v.* rudely and aggressively spoke to (p. 5)
*The angry crowd **accosted** the criminal.*

explicit (eks plis′ it) *adj.* extremely clear (p. 6)
*Sally was **explicit** about how to wash the dog.*
➤ Cognate (Spanish) **explícito**

implore (im plôr′) *v.* to beg (p. 9)
*I **implore** you to speak more quietly.*
➤ Cognate (Spanish) **implorar**

Content Vocabulary

carnival (kär′ nə vəl) *n.* a festival or season of celebration (p. 5)
*We watched people in costumes sing and dance at the **carnival**.*

bargain (bär′ gən) *n.* a cheap price (p. 5)
*The car was a **bargain** at just two hundred dollars.*

For Sale $200

mask (mask′) *n.* something that covers the face (p. 6)
*The actor wore a **mask** that covered his face.*
➤ Cognate (Spanish) **máscara**

orbs (orbz′) *n.* spheres or round objects, such as eyes (p. 6)
*Your eyes are two beautiful **orbs**.*
➤ Cognate (Spanish) **orbe**

For more practice, see page 324. ➔

Read, Respond, Interact

Notes support you as you read. Interact with and respond to the text by answering questions and reading information.

During Reading

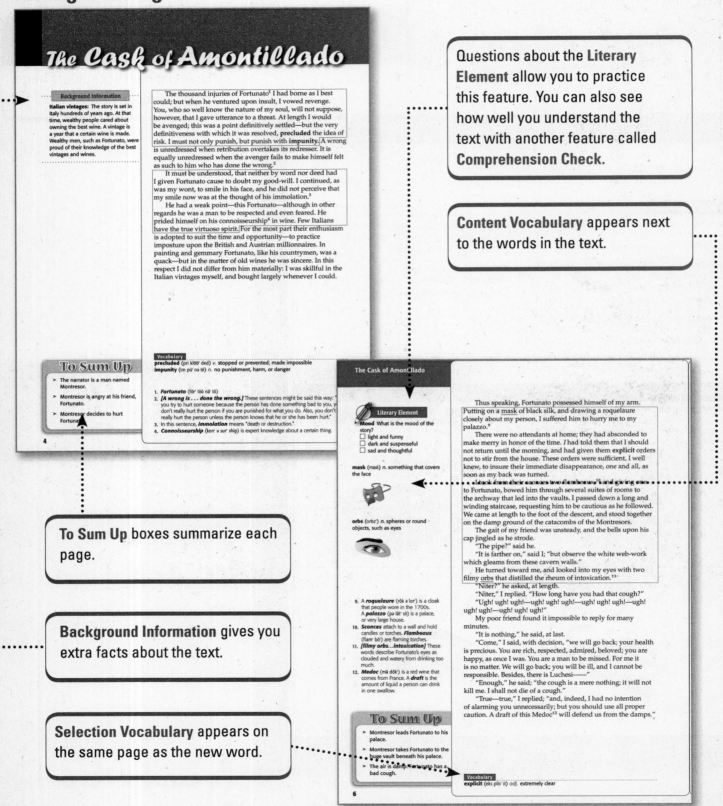

The Cask of Amontillado

Background Information

Italian vintages: The story is set in Italy hundreds of years ago. At that time, wealthy people cared about owning the best wine. A vintage is a year that a certain wine is made. Wealthy men, such as Fortunato, were proud of their knowledge of the best vintages and wines.

The thousand injuries of Fortunato[1] I had borne as I best could; but when he ventured upon insult, I vowed revenge. You, who so well know the nature of my soul, will not suppose, however, that I gave utterance to a threat. At length I would be avenged; this was a point definitively settled—but the very definitiveness with which it was resolved, **precluded** the idea of risk. I must not only punish, but punish with **impunity.** A wrong is unredressed when retribution overtakes its redresser. It is equally unredressed when the avenger fails to make himself felt as such to him who has done the wrong.[2]

It must be understood, that neither by word nor deed had I given Fortunato cause to doubt my good-will. I continued, as was my wont, to smile in his face, and he did not perceive that my smile now was at the thought of his immolation.[3]

He had a weak point—this Fortunato—although in other regards he was a man to be respected and even feared. He prided himself on his connoisseurship[4] in wine. Few Italians have the true virtuoso spirit. For the most part their enthusiasm is adopted to suit the time and opportunity—to practice imposture upon the British and Austrian millionaires. In painting and gemmary Fortunato, like his countrymen, was a quack—but in the matter of old wines he was sincere. In this respect I did not differ from him materially: I was skillful in the Italian vintages myself, and bought largely whenever I could.

Vocabulary
precluded (pri klōō´ ded) v. stopped or prevented; made impossible
impunity (im pū´ na tē) n. no punishment, harm, or danger

1. **Fortunato** (fôr´ tōō nä´ tō)
2. **[A wrong is . . . done the wrong.]** These sentences might be said this way: you try to hurt someone because the person has done something bad to you, you don't really hurt the person if you are punished for what you do. Also, you don't really hurt the person unless the person knows that he or she has been hurt.
3. In this sentence, **immolation** means "death or destruction."
4. **Connoisseurship** (kon´ a sur´ ship) is expert knowledge about a certain thing.

To Sum Up
- The narrator is a man named Montresor.
- Montresor is angry at his friend, Fortunato.
- Montresor decides to hurt Fortunato.

4

Questions about the **Literary Element** allow you to practice this feature. You can also see how well you understand the text with another feature called **Comprehension Check.**

Content Vocabulary appears next to the words in the text.

The Cask of Amontillado

Literary Element

Mood What is the mood of the story?
- ☐ light and funny
- ☐ dark and suspenseful
- ☐ sad and thoughtful

mask (mask) n. something that covers the face

orbs (ôrbz´) n. spheres or round objects, such as eyes

9. A **roquelaure** (rôk a lor´) is a cloak that people wore in the 1700s. A **palazzo** (pä lät´ sō) is a palace, or very large house.
10. **Sconces** attach to a wall and hold candles or torches. **Flambeaux** (flam´ bō´) are flaming torches.
11. **[filmy orbs...intoxication]** These words describe Fortunato's eyes as clouded and watery from drinking too much.
12. **Medoc** (mä dôk´) is a red wine that comes from France. A **draft** is the amount of liquid a person can drink in one swallow.

Thus speaking, Fortunato possessed himself of my arm. Putting on a **mask** of black silk, and drawing a roquelaure closely about my person, I suffered him to hurry me to my palazzo.[9]

There were no attendants at home; they had absconded to make merry in honor of the time. I had told them that I should not return until the morning, and had given them **explicit** orders not to stir from the house. These orders were sufficient, I well knew, to insure their immediate disappearance, one and all, as soon as my back was turned.

I took from their sconces two flambeaux, and giving one to Fortunato, bowed him through several suites of rooms to the archway that led into the vaults. I passed down a long and winding staircase, requesting him to be cautious as he followed. We came at length to the foot of the descent, and stood together on the damp ground of the catacombs of the Montresors.

The gait of my friend was unsteady, and the bells upon his cap jingled as he strode.

"The pipe?" said he.

"It is farther on," said I; "but observe the white web-work which gleams from these cavern walls."

He turned toward me, and looked into my eyes with two filmy **orbs** that distilled the rheum of intoxication.[11]

"Niter?" he asked, at length.

"Niter," I replied. "How long have you had that cough?"

"Ugh! ugh! ugh!—ugh! ugh! ugh!—ugh! ugh! ugh!—ugh! ugh!—ugh! ugh! ugh!"

My poor friend found it impossible to reply for many minutes.

"It is nothing," he said, at last.

"Come," I said, with decision, "we will go back; your health is precious. You are rich, respected, admired, beloved; you are happy, as once I was. You are a man to be missed. For me it is no matter. We will go back; you will be ill, and I cannot be responsible. Besides, there is Luchesi——"

"Enough," he said; "the cough is a mere nothing; it will not kill me. I shall not die of a cough."

"True—true," I replied; "and, indeed, I had no intention of alarming you unnecessarily; but you should use all proper caution. A draft of this Medoc[12] will defend us from the damps."

To Sum Up
- Montresor leads Fortunato to his palace.
- Montresor takes Fortunato to the huge vault beneath his palace.
- The air is damp. Fortunato has a bad cough.

Vocabulary
explicit (eks plis´ it) adj. extremely clear

6

To Sum Up boxes summarize each page.

Background Information gives you extra facts about the text.

Selection Vocabulary appears on the same page as the new word.

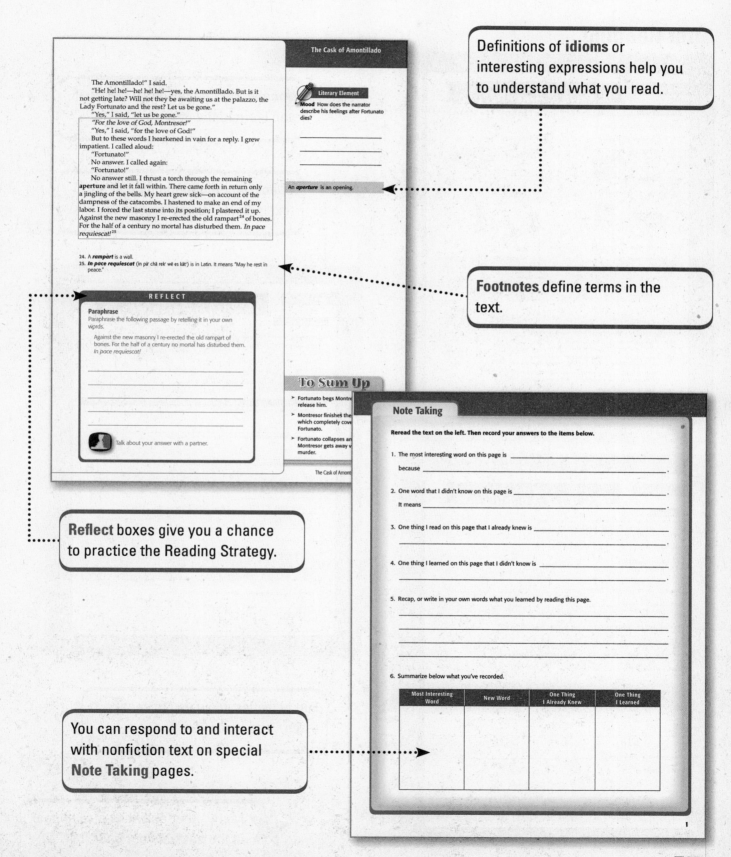

The Cask of Amontillado

The Amontillado!" I said.

"He! he! he!—he! he!—yes, the Amontillado. But is it not getting late? Will not they be awaiting us at the palazzo, the Lady Fortunato and the rest? Let us be gone."

"Yes," I said, "let us be gone."

"*For the love of God, Montresor!*"

"Yes," I said, "for the love of God!"

But to these words I hearkened in vain for a reply. I grew impatient. I called aloud:

"Fortunato!"

No answer. I called again:

"Fortunato!"

No answer still. I thrust a torch through the remaining **aperture** and let it fall within. There came forth in return only a jingling of the bells. My heart grew sick—on account of the dampness of the catacombs. I hastened to make an end of my labor. I forced the last stone into its position; I plastered it up. Against the new masonry I re-erected the old rampart[24] of bones. For the half of a century no mortal has disturbed them. *In pace requiescat!*[25]

24. A **rampart** is a wall.
25. **In pace requiescat** (in pär chä rek' wē es kät') is in Latin. It means "May he rest in peace."

REFLECT

Paraphrase
Paraphrase the following passage by retelling it in your own words.

Against the new masonry I re-erected the old rampart of bones. For the half of a century no mortal has disturbed them. *In pace requiescat!*

_____

_____

_____

_____

_____

Talk about your answer with a partner.

Literary Element

Mood How does the narrator describe his feelings after Fortunato dies?

_____

_____

_____

An *aperture* is an opening.

To Sum Up

➤ Fortunato begs Montre... release him.

➤ Montresor finishes the... which completely cove... Fortunato.

➤ Fortunato collapses an... Montresor gets away w... murder.

The Cask of Amonti...

Note Taking

Reread the text on the left. Then record your answers to the items below.

1. The most interesting word on this page is _____
   because _____.

2. One word that I didn't know on this page is _____
   It means _____.

3. One thing I read on this page that I already knew is _____
   _____

4. One thing I learned on this page that I didn't know is _____
   _____

5. Recap, or write in your own words what you learned by reading this page.
   _____
   _____
   _____
   _____

6. Summarize below what you've recorded.

Most Interesting Word	New Word	One Thing I Already Knew	One Thing I Learned

1

Definitions of **idioms** or interesting expressions help you to understand what you read.

Footnotes define terms in the text.

Reflect boxes give you a chance to practice the Reading Strategy.

You can respond to and interact with nonfiction text on special **Note Taking** pages.

Show What You Know

After reading activities help you focus your understanding of the text.
Here, you apply the skills and strategies you practiced during reading.

After Reading

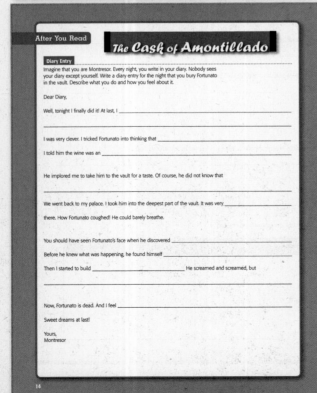

Vocabulary Check shows how well you learned the new vocabulary.

Check your understanding of the text in **Comprehension Check**.

Fun activities allow you to speak, listen, read, and write.

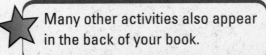

Many other activities also appear in the back of your book.

The SKY **TREE**

by Joseph Bruchac

How the LEOPARD Got His Claws

by Chinua Achebe and John Iroaganachi

Prayer to the Pacific

by Leslie Marmon Silko

Learning Objectives

For pages 1–16, 306

In studying these texts, you will focus on the following objective:

Literary Study: Comparing cultural context.

Reading: Questioning and comparing works across time and place.

Oral Language

Build Background

Read aloud the titles and authors. Explain that students will read *The Sky Tree,* a Huron myth; *How the Leopard Got His Claws,* a West African folktale; and "Prayer to the Pacific," a Native American poem. **Ask:**

- What do the titles of these selections have in common? *(They are all about nature.)*

- What do you think the stories will be about? *(They might explain something or tell how something happened.)*

Talk About the Myths

Explain that the first story tells how mud from the bottom of the ocean becomes Earth. The second story tells how the animals became enemies. The third selection explains where rain comes from.

Beginning/Early Intermediate Have you ever wondered how the rain began, or where the stars came from? (yes/no) Have students draw a picture of one thing in nature they would like to know more about.

Lesson at a Glance

Oral Language
- Build Background
- Talk About the Myths

Vocabulary
- Content Vocabulary

Literary Element
- Oral Tradition

Reading Strategy
- Question

Writing Link
- Paragraph

Comprehension
- BLM

Word Study
- Antonyms and Synonyms BLM

Grammar Link
- Irregular Verbs: *Have, Do,* and *Go* BLM

Technology
- Student Works™ Plus
- Teacher Works™ Plus
- Listening Library Audio CD
- Classroom Presentation Toolkit
- Glencoe Visual Vocabulary
- Skill Level Up!™ A Skill-Based Language Arts Game

Interactive Question-Response

Connect to the Myths

Read aloud Connect to the Myths. Show students pictures of mountains, oceans, rivers, forests, or other natural landscapes. **Model** *Mountains are huge and rocky. The ocean is deep and full of fish and other sea animals.* Have students follow your example, then discuss with their partners reasons why nature is important to people.

Literary Element
Oral Tradition

Read aloud Literary Element. **Ask:** What stories have you heard? Have students think of stories they heard. These might be fairy tales or fables, family stories, or favorite bedtime stories. Allow students to tell some of the stories they know from memory.

Reading Strategy Question

Read aloud the Reading Strategy. Then tell students a story from memory, such as "The Three Little Pigs." Provide students with examples of questions such as *What does "I'll huff and I'll puff" mean? Why did the wolf want the pigs to open the door? Why did the first pig's house fall down? What happened at the end of the story?* Remind students that questions often start with *Who, What, Why, When,* or *Where.*

The SKY TREE
How the LEOPARD Got His Claws
Prayer to the Pacific

Connect to the Myths

Think about mountains, oceans, rivers, and forests. Picture them in your mind. Describe them to your partner. Then talk with your partner about why nature is important.

Literary Element   Oral Tradition

Some stories are written down. Other stories are told from one person to another. These stories are part of a culture's **oral tradition**. Stories may be passed on for many years before they are written in a book.

As you read, ask yourself: Why did people want to pass on these stories?

Reading Strategy   Question

Reading is more than knowing the words. It is important to understand how the words work together. One way to make sure you understand what you are reading is to **question**. This means stopping often to ask yourself questions. It also means stopping when you don't understand something.

As you read, stop after each paragraph and write down any questions you have. You can answer your questions by doing one of the following:

- rereading
- continuing to read
- using a dictionary
- asking another person

Comparing Literature

A **myth** is a traditional story. Myths usually explain a belief, a custom, or a force of nature. The stories of many cultures often contain the following elements:

- supernatural forces or beings with special powers
- personification of animals, that is, having animals act like people
- beginning of the world

As you read, look for the elements of myth found in these stories.

Content Vocabulary			
soil (soil) *n.* dirt (p. 4) *We planted the flowers in the soil.*	**plots** (pläts) *n.* small areas of land (p. 6) *The land was divided into several plots for growing food.*	**shelter** (shel' tər) *n.* something that provides protection from the weather, such as a building (p. 7) *A tent is a shelter used for camping.* 	**seized** (sēzd) *v.* took away suddenly; grabbed (p. 8) *The child seized the piece of candy.*
salute (sə lut') *v.* to honor someone with a gesture of respect (p. 10) *Soldiers have to salute their leaders.* ➤ Cognate (Spanish) **saludar**	**contempt** (kən tempt') *n.* disliking something because you think it is worthless (p. 11) *The girl looked at her vegetables with contempt.*	**staggered** (stag ərd') *v.* walked unsteadily, nearly falling (p. 12) *The tired runner staggered across the finish line.* 	**waded** (wād ed') *n.* walked in shallow water (p. 13) *The children waded into the ocean to collect shells.* ➤ Cognate (Spanish) **vadeó**

For more practice, see page 306. ➡

Vocabulary Routine

To introduce the vocabulary, read aloud the words and definitions in the student book and have students repeat after you. Discuss how the pictures illustrate the words or sentences. Then follow the vocabulary routine below.

Content Vocabulary

Define: If a child's shoe has **soil** on it, it has dirt on it. Example: We put *soil* into the flower pot. Ask: Describe a place you would find soil. DESCRIPTION

If someone owns several **plots** of land, they own several small areas of land. *The garden was made of many plots.* If you had a plot in a garden, what would you plant? EXPLANATION

Shelter is a place that is protected from the weather. *When the rain started, we ran to the shelter.* What kinds of shelter do people build? EXAMPLE

If you **seized** something, you picked it up suddenly. *We were so hungry, we each seized two sandwiches.* What is another word for *seized*? SYNONYM

When people **salute,** they honor someone with a sign of respect. *The sailors salute their captain.* Describe what a salute looks like. DESCRIPTION

If you feel **contempt** for something, you think it is worthless. *The musician looked at the broken guitar with contempt.* What is the opposite of *contempt*? ANTONYM

If a man **staggered** as he walked, he walked unsteadily. *The man staggered under the weight of the large box.* What could happen to a person if they staggered on a busy street? EXPLANATION

If a girl **waded** into the river, she walked into the shallow water. *We waded across the stream to have a picnic.* What would happen to your shoes if you waded with them on? EXPLANATION

Vocabulary Practice Have students complete the vocabulary practice activity on p. 306.

The SKY TREE

Interactive Question-Response

Comparing Literature

If students are having difficulty responding, read aloud the note. Then have a student volunteer read aloud the first two sentences of the story. **Ask:** *What you learn in these sentences? (The story is about "the beginning;" at that time, Earth was covered with water; people lived in Sky Land.)* **Model** thinking about the literary element: *I know that many stories in the oral tradition are myths. Myths are often stories about the beginning of the world. Since this story starts with "in the beginning," it is probably one of those stories.*

Content Vocabulary

Read aloud the word and its definition. Focus students on the sentence "Bring up soil from the bottom, and place it on my back." **Ask:** *Where does Turtle want the animals to get the soil? (the bottom of the water) How do you think the animals will get the soil? (They will dive down in the water to the bottom; they will carry it up.)*

Comparing Literature

Reread the boxed text at the beginning of the page. Underline the words that tell you this is a story about how the world began.

soil (soil) *n.* dirt

To Sum Up

➤ Only fruit from the Sky Tree can heal the sick old chief.

➤ Aataentsic cuts down the tree to get the fruit. She falls through a hole in the sky.

➤ Turtle tells the sea animals to dive into the water to bring up soil.

4

In the beginning, Earth was covered with water. In Sky Land, there were people living as they do now on Earth. In the middle of that land was the great Sky Tree. All of the food which the people in that Sky Land ate came from the great tree. The old chief of that land lived with his wife, whose name was Aataentsic,[1] meaning "Ancient Woman," in their longhouse[2] near the great tree. It came to be that the old chief became sick and nothing could cure him. He grew weaker and weaker until it seemed he would die. Then a dream came to him and he called Aataentsic to him.

"I have dreamed," he said, "and in my dream I saw how I can be healed. I must be given the fruit which grows at the very top of Sky Tree. You must cut it down and bring that fruit to me."

Aataentsic took her husband's stone ax and went to the great tree. As soon as she struck it, it split in half and toppled over. As it fell a hole opened in Sky Land and the tree fell through the hole. Aataentsic returned to the place where the old chief waited.

"My husband," she said, "when I cut the tree it split in half and then fell through a great hole. Without the tree, there can be no life. I must follow it."

Then, leaving her husband she went back to the hole in Sky Land and threw herself after the great tree.

As Aataentsic fell, Turtle looked up and saw her. Immediately Turtle called together all the water animals and told them what she had seen.

"What should be done?" Turtle said.

Beaver answered her. "You are the one who saw this happen. Tell us what to do."

"All of you must dive down," Turtle said. "Bring up soil from the bottom, and place it on my back."

1. **Aataentsic** was Mother Earth in myths told by the Huron people. The Huron believed they were Aataentsic's children.
2. A **longhouse** was a Native American home. It had space for more than one family. It also had rooms for tribal ceremonies.

Comprehension

To support students as they read the selection, have them begin the graphic organizer on page A2.

Immediately all of the water animals began to dive down and bring up soil. Beaver, Mink, Muskrat, and Otter each brought up pawfuls of wet soil and placed the soil on the Turtle's back until they had made an island **of great size.** When they were through, Aataentsic settled down gently on the new Earth and the pieces of the great tree fell beside her and took root.

Something *of great size* is very big.

Background Information

The Huron believed that Earth was an island. They thought this island grew on the back of a great turtle. The Huron called themselves Wendat, which means "islanders."

REFLECT

Question
Reread "The Sky Tree." As you read, jot down questions that you have about the story. With a partner, discuss the questions and try to answer them.

_____
_____
_____
_____
_____

Talk about your answer with a partner.

To Sum Up

➤ Aanaentsic and the tree land on the soil.
➤ The tree and the earth begin to grow.

Interactive Question-Response

Background Information

Read aloud the note. Ask students to think about why this story was important to the Huron people. **Ask:** *Why did the Huron people call themselves "islanders"? (They believed that they lived on an island.)* **Model** *I think this story was important to the Huron people because it helped explain where they came from. People want to know where they came from.*

Reflect

Partner Talk After students reread the text on their own, have them take turns reading the text aloud to practice fluency.

To Sum Up

Beginning/Early Intermediate Have students work in pairs to read all of the To Sum Up statements. Then have students list some of the characters in the story. (*the chief, Aatentsic, Turtle, the water animals*) Have them tell one thing these characters did in the story. (*The chief had a dream. Aataentsic chopped down the tree. Turtle saw what happened. The water animals got soil.*)

Interactive Question-Response

Comparing Literature

If students have difficulty responding, write the words *When* and *Where* on the board. Ask a student to read aloud the first sentence of *The Sky Tree.* Write "In the beginning" under "When," and "in the forest" under "Where." Then have another student read the first sentence of *"How the Leopard Got His Claws."* **Ask:** *What should I write under "When"?(In the beginning) What should I write under "Where"? (the Earth, covered with water)*

Content Vocabulary

Have a student read aloud the word *plots* and its definition. **Ask:** *Which do you think is a plot—a garden or a road? (a garden) How do the animals use their plots? (They farm them; they grow food.)*

Comparing Literature

Reread the first sentence of "The Sky Tree." Then read the first sentence of this story. Underline the part that is the same. Circle the part that is different.

Came round means "began."

---

plots (pläts') *n.* small areas of land

To Sum Up

➤ The leopard was king of the forest animals.

➤ The dog was the only animal with big, sharp teeth.

➤ The animals worked hard on their farms.

6

If you look at the world in terms of storytelling, you have, first of all, the man who agitates, the man who drums up the people—I call him the drummer. Then you have the warrior, who goes forward and fights. But you also have the storyteller who recounts the event, and this is the one who survives, who outlives all the others. It is the storyteller who makes us what we are, who creates history. The storyteller creates the memory that the survivors must have; otherwise, their surviving would have no meaning.

—Chinua Achebe

In the beginning... all the animals in the forest lived as friends. Their king was the leopard. He was strong, but gentle and wise. He ruled the animals well, and they all liked him.

At that time the animals did not fight one another. Most of them had no sharp teeth or claws. They did not need them. Even King Leopard had only small teeth. He had no claws at all.

Only the dog had big, sharp teeth. The other animals said he was ugly, and they laughed at him.

"It is foolish to carry sharp things in the mouth," said the tortoise.

"I think so, too," said the goat.

The monkey jumped in and began to tease the dog.

"Don't worry, my dear friend," said the monkey. "You need your teeth to clear your farm."

The animals laughed at the monkey's joke.

When the farming season **came round,** King Leopard led the animals to their farmland. They all worked hard to prepare their plots. At the end of the day they returned home tired. They sat on log benches in the village square. As they rested they told stories and drank palm wine.[1]

---

1. **Palm wine** is made from the sap, or watery part, of the palm tree.

But soon it would be the rainy season, and the animals would have no shelter from the rain.

The deer took this problem to King Leopard. They talked about it for a long time. King Leopard decided to call the animals together to discuss it.

One bright morning…King Leopard beat his royal drum. When the animals heard the drum, they gathered at the village square. The tortoise was there. The goat was there, too. The sheep, the grass-cutter,[2] the monkey, the hedgehog,[3] the baboon, the dog and many others were there.

King Leopard greeted them and said, "I have called you together to plan how we can make ourselves a common shelter."

"This is a good idea," said the giraffe.

"Yes, a very good idea," said many other animals.

"But why do we need a common house?" said the dog. He had never liked King Leopard.

"The dog has asked a good question," said the duck. "Why do we need a common shelter?"

"We do need somewhere to rest when we return from our farms," replied King Leopard.

"And besides," said the goat, "we need a shelter from the rain."

"I don't mind being wet," said the duck. "In fact, I like it. I know that the goat does not like water on his body. Let him go and build a shelter."

"We need a shelter," said the monkey, jumping up and down in excitement.

"Perhaps we need one, perhaps we don't," said the lazy baboon sitting on the low fence of the square.

The dog spoke again. "We are wasting our time. Those who need a shelter should build it. I live in a cave, and it is enough for me." Then he walked away. The duck followed him out.

"Does anyone else want to leave?" asked King Leopard. No one answered or made a move to go.

"Very well," said King Leopard. "Let the rest of us build the village hall."

The animals soon scattered about to find building materials. The tortoise copied the pattern on his back and made the plan of the roof. The giant rat and mouse dug the foundations. Some animals brought sticks, some ropes, others made roof-mats.

As they built the house, they sang many happy songs. They also told many jokes. Although they worked very hard, everyone was merry.

After many weeks they finished the building.

It was a fine building. The animals were pleased with it. They agreed to open it with a very special meeting.

2. A **grass-cutter** is a kind of rodent.
3. A **hedgehog** is a small, hairy animal. Some hedgehogs have quills, or hard spines.

---

shelter (shel' tar) *n.* something that provides protection from the weather, such as a building.

✎ **Comprehension Check**

What elements of myth are in this story so far?

☐ supernatural forces or beings
☑ personification of animals
☑ beginning of the world

To Sum Up

➤ Some animals plan to build a shelter.

➤ The dog does not want to build a shelter

➤ The dog and the duck do not help build the shelter.

Interactive Question-Response

Content Vocabulary

Read aloud the word *shelter* and its definition. Have students draw pictures of different kinds of shelter such as houses, tents, and caves.

Comprehension Check

If students have difficulty responding, review the mythical elements that are listed. Explain that "supernatural" means "greater than natural." This could include special powers, great strength, or magical abilities. **Ask:** *Does anyone in the story have special strength or magical powers? (no)* Explain that "personification of animals" means talking about animals as if they can do things people do. **Ask:** *Do the animals in this story act like people? (Yes, they talk and farm.)*

Interactive
Question-Response

Content Vocabulary

Read aloud the word and definition of *seized*. Place an eraser on a table. Pick it up slowly. **Ask:** *Did I seize the eraser? (no)* Place the eraser back on the table. This time, grab it suddenly. **Ask:** *Did I seize the eraser? (yes)*

Comprehension Check

If students have difficulty responding, have them read aloud the sentences that describe the deer. As they read, list details about the deer *(he is at the shelter; he is surprised; he talks to the dog; he cries in pain.)* Guide students in identifying details from this list that make the deer seem human.

seized (sēzd) *v.* took away suddenly; grabbed

 Comprehension Check

How does the deer feel and act like a person?

- ☑ He feels surprised.
- ☐ He runs.
- ☑ He talks.

To Sum Up

- ➤ It begins to rain. The animals go to the shelter.
- ➤ The dog's cave begins to flood, so he goes to the shelter.
- ➤ The dog throws all the animals out of the shelter.

8

On the opening day the animals, their wives and children gathered in the hall. King Leopard then made a short speech. He said: "This hall is yours to enjoy. You worked very hard together to build it. I am proud of you."

The animals clapped their hands and gave three cheers to their king.

From that day they rested in their new hall whenever they returned from their farm.

But the dog and the duck kept away from the hall.

One morning the animals went to their farms as usual. King Leopard went to visit a chief in another village.

At first the sun was shining. Then strong winds began to blow. Dark clouds hid the sun. The first rain was coming. The songbirds stopped their singing. The humming insects became quiet. Lightning flashed across the dark clouds. Claps of thunder sounded. The rain poured and poured.

The animals in their farms saw the rain coming and began to hurry to the village hall.

The dog also saw the rain coming and returned to his cave. But it was a very, very heavy rain. Water began to enter the cave. Soon it was flooded.

The dog ran from one end of his cave to the other. But the water followed him everywhere. At last he ran out of the cave altogether and made straight for the hall of the animals.

The deer was already there. He was surprised to see the dog enter the hall.

"What do you want here?" said the deer to the dog.

"It is none of your business," replied the dog.

"It is my business," said the deer. "Please go out, this hall is for those who built it."

Then the dog attacked the deer and bit him with his big, sharp teeth. The deer cried with pain. The dog seized him by the neck and threw him out into the rain.

The other animals came in one after the other.

The dog barked and threw each of them out. They stood together shivering and crying in the rain. The dog kept barking and showing his teeth.

Then the deer cried out:

O Leopard our noble king,
Where are you?
Spotted king of the forest,
Where are you?
Even if you are far away
Come, hurry home:

The worst has happened to us
The worst has happened to us…
The house the animals built
The cruel dog keeps us from it,
The common shelter we built
The cruel dog keeps us from it,
The worst has happened to us
The worst has happened to us…

The cry of the deer rang out loud and clear. It was carried by the wind. King Leopard heard it on his way back from his journey and began to run toward the village hall.

As he got near, he saw the animals, wet and sheltering under a tree. They were all crying. As he got nearer still, he could see the dog walking up and down inside the hall.

King Leopard was very angry. "Come out of the hall at once," he said to the dog. The dog barked and rushed at him. They began to fight. The dog bit the leopard and tore his skin with his claws. King Leopard was covered with blood. The dog went back to the hall. He stood at the door barking and barking. "Who is next? Who! Who!" he barked.

King Leopard turned to the animals and said: "Let us go in together and **drive out the enemy.** He is strong, but he is alone. We are many. Together we can drive him out of our house."

But the goat said: "We cannot face him. Look at his strong teeth! He will only tear us to pieces!"

"The goat is right," said the animals. "He is too strong for us."

Drive out the enemy means "force the enemy to leave."

Comprehension Check

What does King Leopard want the animals to do? Underline words that tell you his plan.

REFLECT

Question
Think about King Leopard and the dog. Write one question about King Leopard and one question about the dog.

Will the animals help King Leopard force the dog to leave?

Why is the dog cruel to the other animals?

_____

_____

_____

 Talk about your answer with a partner.

To Sum Up

➤ King Leopard tells the dog to come out of the shelter.

➤ The dog attacks King Leopard.

➤ The other animals are afraid. They do not want to help fight the dog.

How the Leopard Got His Claws **9**

Interactive
Question-Response

Comprehension Check

Have students share the words that they underlined. Then ask student volunteers to paraphrase the leopard's plan. **Ask:** *Why does the leopard want the animals to work together, instead of alone? (None of the animals can fight the dog alone. Together they might be able to beat him.)*

Reflect

Partner Talk Have students work in pairs to write their questions. To get them started, have students describe King Leopard and the dog, and give one or two details about what has happened to each character so far. Explain that students might have questions about what *has* happened, *why* it happened, or what *will* happen in the future.

Word Study   [BLM]

Synonyms and Antonyms

Remind students that **synonyms** are words that have the same (or similar) meanings and that **antonyms** are words that have opposite (or nearly opposite) meanings. Ask students to identify synonyms for *cruel (mean)* and *angry (upset)*. Ask students to identify two antonym pairs on the page (*alone/many* and *up/down*).

Then have students practice recognizing and using synonyms and antonyms by completing the activity on page A3.

Interactive
Question-Response

Content Vocabulary

Have a student read aloud the word and definition of *salute*. **Ask:** *Have you ever seen a soldier salute? What does a salute look like?* Allow students to demonstrate. **Ask:** *Why do people give a salute? (to show respect)*

To Sum Up

| Beginning/Early Intermediate | Have students work in pairs to read all of the To Sum Up statements so far in the story. Then have students use words such as *first, after that, next,* and *then* to orally retell the major events of the story so far.

salute (sə lüt′) *v.* to honor someone with a gesture of respect

His heart was heavy means "he was very sad."

The tortoise stood up and said: "I am sure we are all sorry about what has happened to the leopard. But he was foolish to talk to the dog the way he did. It is foolish to annoy such a powerful person as the dog. Let us make peace with him. I don't know what you others think. But I think he should have been our king all along. He is strong; he is handsome. Let us go on our knees and salute him."

"Hear! Hear!" said all the animals. "Hail the dog!"

Tears began to roll down the face of the leopard. **His heart was heavy.** He loved the animals greatly. But they had turned their backs on him. Now he knew they were cowards. So he turned his back on them and went away. Because of his many wounds he was weak and tired. So he lay down after a while to rest under a tree, far from the village.

The animals saw him go. But they did not care. They were too busy praising their new king, the dog. The tortoise carved a new staff for him. The toad made a new song in his praise:

The dog is great
The dog is good
The dog gives us our daily food.
We love his head, we love his jaws
We love his feet and all his claws.

The dog looked round the circle of animals and asked, "Where is the leopard?"

"We think he has gone away, O King," said the goat.

"Why? He has no right to go away," said the dog. "Nobody has a right to leave our village and its beautiful hall. We must all stay together."

"Indeed," shouted the animals. "We must stay together! The leopard must return to the village! Our wise king has spoken! It is good to have a wise king!"

The dog then called out the names of six strong animals and said to them: "Go at once and bring back the leopard. If he should refuse to follow you, you must drag him along. If we let him go, others may soon follow his wicked example until there is no one left in our village. That would be a very bad thing indeed. It is my duty as your king to make sure that we all live together. The leopard is a wicked animal. That is why he wants to go away and live by himself. It is our duty to stop him. Nobody has a right to go away from our village and our beautiful hall."

To Sum Up

➤ The animals decide to make the dog their king.

➤ The leopard goes away.

➤ The dog orders the leopard to come back to the village.

"Nobody has a right to go away from the village," sang all the animals as the six messengers went to look for the leopard.

They found him resting under the tree beyond the village. Although he was wounded and weak he still looked like a king. So the six messengers stood at a little distance and spoke to him.

"Our new king, the dog, has ordered you to return to the village," they said.

"He says that no one has a right to leave the village," said the pig.

"Yes, no one has a right to leave our village and its beautiful hall," said the others.

The leopard looked at them with <u>contempt</u>. Then he got up slowly. The six animals **fell back.** But the leopard did not go toward them. He turned his back on them and began to go away—slowly and painfully. One of the animals picked up a stone and threw it at him. Then all the others immediately picked up stones and began to throw. As they threw they chanted: "No one has a right to leave our village! No one has a right to leave our village!"

Although some of the stones hit the leopard and hurt him, he did not turn round even once. He continued walking until he no longer heard the noise of the animals.

The leopard traveled seven days and seven nights. Then he came to the house of the blacksmith. The old man was sitting at his forge. The leopard said to him: "I want the strongest teeth you can make from iron. And I want the most deadly claws you can make from bronze."

The blacksmith said: "Why do you need such terrible things?" The leopard told his story. Then the blacksmith said: "I do not blame you."

The blacksmith worked a whole day on the teeth, and another full day on the claws. The leopard was pleased with them. He put them on and thanked the blacksmith. Then he left and went to the house of Thunder.

The leopard knocked at the door and Thunder roared across the sky.

"I want some of your sound in my voice," said the leopard. "Even a little bit."

"Why do you want my sound in your voice?" asked Thunder. "And why have you got those terrible teeth and claws?"

The leopard told his story. "I do not blame you," said Thunder. He gave the sound to the leopard. "Thank you for the gift," said the leopard. And he began his journey home.

contempt (kan tempt') *adv.* disliking something because you think it is worthless

Fell back means "moved backwards."

✏️ **Comparing Literature**

The leopard gets claws and teeth from a blacksmith. He gets sound from Thunder. Which elements of myth are in this part of the story?
- ☑ supernatural forces or beings
- ☑ personification of animals
- ☐ beginning of the world

To Sum Up

➤ A blacksmith makes claws and teeth for the leopard.

➤ Thunder gives his sound to the leopard.

Interactive Question-Response

Content Vocabulary

Read the definition of *contempt* aloud. Then have a student read the sentence containing the word *contempt.* Have students demonstrate facial expressions that show contempt. **Ask:** *Why does the leopard feel contempt for the other animals? (Possible answer: The other animals are only doing what the dog wants them to do; they are not thinking for themselves.)*

Comparing Literature

Explain that a blacksmith is a person who makes things out of metal. A blacksmith uses a *forge*—a furnace or very hot fire—to soften or melt the metal. **Ask:** *Is the blacksmith a supernatural being? (no)* Explain that thunder is the sound that follows a flash of lightning. **Ask:** *Is the character Thunder a supernatural being? (yes)*

Differentiated Instruction

Clarify the Text

Beginning/Early Intermediate As these students read the To Sum Up text, they may not understand that Thunder is a character in the story. Explain that thunder is usually a sound, but in this story Thunder is the character who gives the leopard his sound. **Ask:** *What do you think Thunder looks like? (Answers will vary.) What sound does the leopard make when he has Thunder's sound? (He may have a loud roar.)*

Interactive Question-Response

Content Vocabulary

Read the definition of *staggered* aloud. Then have a student demonstrate what staggered means. Have students take turns making up simple sentences that use the word *staggered*.

Comparing Literature

If students have difficulty responding, read aloud the last paragraph of the story, pausing after each sentence to have a student paraphrase. Then read the check-box options, and ask students to decide whether each question is answered in the story.

staggered (stag ard') *v.* walked unsteadily, nearly falling

 Comparing Literature

Reread the last paragraph of the story. What questions about the world does this story try to answer?

- ☑ Why do animals fight each other?
- ☐ Why do people eat meat?
- ☑ Why do hunters keep dogs?
- ☑ Why does the leopard have claws?
- ☐ Why do animals live on farms?

To Sum Up

➤ The leopard uses his claws and teeth to force the dog to leave.

➤ The leopard makes the animals pull apart their shelter.

➤ The dog runs away and becomes the hunter's slave.

➤ The animals are no longer friends. They are enemies.

The leopard journeyed for seven days and seven nights and returned to the village of the animals. There he found the animals dancing in a circle round the dog. He stood for a while watching them with contempt and great anger. They were too busy to notice his presence. He made a deep, terrifying roar. At the same time he sprang into the center of the circle. The animals stopped their song. The dog dropped his staff. The leopard seized him and bit and clawed him without mercy. Then he threw him out of the circle.

All the animals *trembled*.

But they were too afraid to run. The leopard turned to them and said: "You miserable worms. You shameless cowards. I was a kind and gentle king, but you turned against me. From today I shall rule the forest with terror. The life of our village is ended."

"What about our hall?" asked the tortoise with a trembling voice.

"Let everyone take from the hall what he put into it," said the leopard.

The animals began to weep as they had wept long ago in the rain. "Please forgive us, O Leopard," they cried.

"Let everyone take from the hall what he put into it," repeated the leopard. "And hurry up!" he thundered.

So the animals pulled their hall apart. Some carried away the wood, and some took the roofmats. Others took away doors and windows. The toad brought his talking drum and began to beat it to the leopard and to sing:

Alive or dead the leopard is king.
Beware my friend, don't twist his tail.
But the leopard roared like thunder and the toad dropped his drum and the animals scattered in the forest.

The dog had already run a long way when the leopard roared. Now he ran faster and faster. His body was covered with blood, and he was very, very weak. He wanted to stop and rest a little. But the fear of the leopard was greater than his weakness. So he staggered and fell and got up and staggered on and on and on…

After many days the dog came to the house of the hunter.

"Please protect me from the leopard," he cried.

"What will you do for me in return?" asked the hunter.

"I will be your slave," said the dog. "Any day you are hungry for meat I shall show you the way to the forest. There we can hunt together and kill my fellow animals."

"All right, come in," said the hunter.

Today the animals are no longer friends, but enemies. The strong among them attack and kill the weak. The leopard, full of anger, eats up anyone he can lay his hands on. The hunter, led by the dog, goes to the forest from time to time and shoots any animals he can find. Perhaps the animals will make peace among themselves someday and live together again. Then they can keep away the hunter who is their common enemy.

Prayer to the Pacific

I traveled to the ocean
    distant
                from my southwest land of sandrock
                  to the moving blue water

5 Big as the myth of origin.

Pale

pale water in the yellow-white light of
                    sun floating west
                      to China
10   where ocean herself was born.
Clouds that blow across the sand are wet.

Squat in the wet sand and speak to the Ocean:
    I return to you   turquoise   the red coral you sent us,
            sister spirit of Earth.
15 Four round stones in my pocket   I carry back the ocean
            to suck and to taste.

Thirty thousand years ago
    Indians came riding across the ocean
    carried by giant sea turtles.
20 Waves were high that day
    great sea turtles <u>waded</u>   slowly out
              from the gray sundown sea.
Grandfather Turtle rolled in the sand   four times
        and disappeared
25   swimming into the sun.

✏️ Comparing Literature

What elements of myth does this poem include? List them.

1. supernatural forces or beings:

sister spirit of Earth

2. personification of animals:

Grandfather Turtle

3. beginning of the world:

myth of origin; ocean herself

was born

---

waded (wād′ ed) *v.* walked in shallow water

To Sum Up

➤ The speaker goes to the ocean and thinks about how it began.

➤ The speaker remembers how Indians rode across the ocean. They rode on the backs of giant sea turtles.

Interactive Question-Response

Comparing Literature

If students have difficulty responding, read aloud chunks of 5 lines at a time. After each chunk, have students evaluate if any of the three mythical elements listed are in that chunk. Suggest that, if they are unsure, they underline possible answers. After you are done reading, have students share what they underlined.

Content Vocabulary

Read aloud the word *waded* and its definition. Then have students find this word in the poem. Invite them to read aloud line 21, then draw a picture of the image: "great sea turtles waded slowly out."

Interactive Question-Response

Comparing Literature

If students have difficulty responding, have them read aloud the last two stanzas of the poem. Have them circle the words *rain* and *raindrops*.

Reflect

Partner Talk If students don't get all the definitions from their classmates, have them look up words in the dictionary.

Comparing Literature

Where does the poem say rain comes from? Underline the lines that tell where rain comes from.

And so   from that time
        immemorial,[1]
                                    as the old people say,

30   rain clouds drift from the west
                gift from the ocean.

Green leaves in the wind
Wet earth on my feet
        swallowing raindrops
                clear from China.

To Sum Up

➤ The speaker says that rain is a gift from the ocean.
➤ The speaker says that the rain falling on her comes from China.

14

REFLECT

Question
Reread the poem. List words you don't know. Then with your partner, ask classmates to provide definitions.

_____

_____

_____

_____

_____

Talk about your answer with a partner.

Oral Assessment

Observe individuals' responses to the following prompts. See the Oral Assessment Rubric on page T17 to determine students' levels of language output.

1. In "The Sky Tree," why did Aataentsic chop down the tree?

2. In "How the Leopard Got His Claws," why did the leopard want claws?

3. In "Prayer to the Pacific," what does the ocean give to the speaker?

4. Which two selections were about animals that talked?

5. How does each selection talk about a beginning?

The SKY TREE
How the LEOPARD Got His Claws
Prayer to the Pacific

Vocabulary Check

A. Circle the picture that best answers the question.

1. Which picture shows **soil**?

3. Which person is in a **shelter**?

2. Which picture shows a **shelter**?

B. Circle the letter of the word that answers each question correctly.

4. Who would **salute** a general?
   a. a farmer   b. a student   c. a soldier

5. If you **seized** a cactus, what would happen?
   a. You would laugh.   b. You would feel pain.   c. You would fall asleep.

6. If you **waded** into a lake, where might you be?
   a. at a beach   b. in a house   c. at a store

C. Circle the letter of the sentence that uses the boldface word correctly.

7. a. Several **plots** were sold at the grocery store.
   b. Flowers grew in several of the **plots**.

8. a. The angry woman looked at the poor man with **contempt**.
   b. The happy woman felt **contempt** for the poor man.

9. a. The tired man **staggered** through the door.
   b. The car **staggered** in the deep snow.

Vocabulary Check

B. **Intermediate**

Have students clarify the meanings of *general*, *cactus*, and *waded* by looking these words up in a dictionary. Then read each question and options *a*, *b*, and *c* aloud. Have students answer *yes* or *no* to questions such as *"Would a farmer salute a general?" If you seized a cactus, would you laugh?" "Where would you find a lake?"*

Grammar Link   BLM

Irregular Verbs: *Have, Do,* and *Go*

Prepare students to complete the activity on page A4. Read the grammar instruction with students, and complete the first item with them to help them get started.

Comprehension Check

C. Early Advanced

Explain that in myths, the last part of the story often explains why the story is important. Have students review the ending of each selection before answering the question.

The SKY TREE
How the LEOPARD Got His Claws
Prayer to the Pacific

Comprehension Check

A. 1. Why did Aataentsic cut down the Sky Tree?

Aataentsic cut down the Sky Tree because   Possible answer: she wanted to heal her husband

2. What happened when she cut it down?

After she cut down the sky tree,   Possible answer: it fell through a hole in Sky Land   .

3. Draw a picture of Aataentsic and the Sky Tree on Turtle's back.

B. 4. Each selection makes animals seem like people. Use the graphic organizer below to compare the animals in the three selections.

	Animals	Personification
The Sky Tree	Turtle, Beaver, Mink, Muskrat, Otter	The animals speak and work together to solve a problem.
How the Leopard Got His Claws	Leopard, Dog, Deer, Duck, Goat, Tortoise, Toad	The animals speak, farm, persuade, make jokes, sing songs, drink wine.
Prayer to the Pacific	Turtle	The turtle is called "Grandfather Turtle"

C. Answer the questions to compare The Sky Tree, How the Leopard Got His Claws, and Prayer to the Pacific.

5. Think about the myths. Then complete the sentences. Each of the selections talks about a beginning.

The Sky Tree talks about the beginning of   Possible answer: Earth.

How the Leopard Got His Claws talks about how animals began to   Possible answers: fight; be enemies.

Prayer to the Pacific talks about the beginning of   Possible answer: rain.

Which myth explains how the animals became enemies?   How the Leopard Got His Claws.

All three of the myths have animals who   Possible answer: talk or act   like people.

Writing Link

Paragraph

In the West African tale "How The Leopard Got His Claws," the animal leaders—both the wicked dog and the good leopard—use violence to seize and hold power. Have students write a paragraph in which they identify and evaluate the lesson that this tale makes about the effect of violence on the life of a community. Tell them to be sure to use evidence from the tale in showing what the lesson is. Set a limit of 150–200 words.

An effective paragraph should:

- identify the lesson of the story.

- evaluate the lesson.

- use evidence from the story.

- stay within the space limit.

Learning Objectives

For pages 17–24, 307–308

In studying these texts, you will focus on the following objectives:

Literary Study: Analyzing metaphor.

Reading: Drawing conclusions about author's beliefs.

Upon the *Burning* of Our House *and*
To My Dear and Loving Husband

by Anne Bradstreet

Upon the Burning of Our House *and* To My Dear and Loving Husband **17**

Oral Language

Build Background

Read the title and author. Explain that students will read two poems, "Upon the Burning of Our House" and "To My Dear and Loving Husband," by Anne Bradstreet, a Puritan poet who lived in the 1600s. **Ask:**

- **What do you think these poems are about based on the titles?** *(the poet's house burning down and the poet's husband)*

- **What kind of woman do you think Anne Bradstreet was?** *(emotional, strong, loving, kind, educated)*

Talk About the Poems

Explain that the first poem is about the poet's house burning down and that the second is a love poem.

Intermediate Ask: *What would it be like to have a fire in your home?* Have students describe the damage a fire could cause.

You could lose _____ in a fire. (your stuff, your home) A fire could hurt _____. (your family, your pets)

Lesson at a Glance

Oral Language
- Build Background
- Talk About the Poems

Vocabulary
- Selection Vocabulary
- Content Vocabulary
- Academic Vocabulary

Literary Element
- Metaphor

Reading Strategy
- Draw Conclusions About Author's Beliefs

Writing Link
- Extended Metaphor

Comprehension
- BLM

Grammar Link
- Past Time Expressions BLM

Technology
- Student Works™ Plus
- Teacher Works™ Plus
- Listening Library Audio CD
- Classroom Presentation Toolkit
- Glencoe Visual Vocabulary
- Skill Level Up!™ A Skill-Based Language Arts Game

Interactive Question-Response

Connect to the Poems

Read aloud Connect to the Poems. Draw a two-column chart on the board. **Model** *If I lost my CD collection, I would have no music to listen to. I would get bored.* Model writing your response in the chart, and have students suggest other responses. Then have students fill in their own charts.

Literary Element Metaphor

Read aloud the Literary Element. Explain, using drawings, that a metaphor compares two things. Draw on the board a butterfly and the word *love.* **Model** *Love is a butterfly because love makes me feel happy and light. A butterfly looks happy and light.* Draw other examples of metaphors on the board *(big cities are forests or jungles, chocolate is heaven, the moon is a guide at night).* Ask students to explain why they think these things are similar. Then ask the class to think of other things they could compare.

Reading Strategy Draw Conclusions About Author's Beliefs

Read aloud the Reading Strategy. Explain to students that drawing conclusions about an author's beliefs will help them to understand what a reading selection means. **Ask:** *What is something important that happened to you? What did you think about what happened? How does this show what you believe?* Model a response for the students. **Model** *I bought a gift for my friend. I bought this gift because I think my friend is nice. I believe that people should do nice things for their friends.* Prompt students to share their own stories and tell what their stories show about their beliefs

Connect to the Poems

Think about the important people in your life and the things you own. Make a list of these people and things. Write down how you would feel to lose these people and things.

People/Things	Feelings
my pet dog	I would be very sad.

Literary Element Metaphor

A **metaphor** is a figure of speech that compares two very different things. For example, if you said, "Love is a butterfly," you would be using a metaphor. Love and butterflies are different. But when you compare love to a butterfly, you are saying that love is beautiful and pleasant, like a butterfly.

As you read, look for comparisons between two different things. What metaphors does the author use?

Reading Strategy Draw Conclusions About Author's Beliefs

When you **draw a conclusion**, you make a statement about what you have read. As you read, stop and think about what you have read. Draw conclusions about the author's beliefs by asking yourself these questions:

- What happens in the poem?
- What does the author think about what happens in the poem?
- What does the author believe?

18

Selection Vocabulary

bereft (bi reft') *adj.* without something needed or wanted (p. 20)
*The bad weather left him **bereft** of his good mood.*

chide (chīd) *v.* to find fault with or to blame (p. 21)
*The teacher will **chide** the student if he does not finish his homework.*

recompense (rek'əm pens') *n.* something given in return for something else (p. 22)
*The students asked for **recompense** for their hard work at the car wash.*
➤ Cognate (Spanish) **recompensa**

Content Vocabulary

dreadful (dred' fəl) *adj.* very bad (p. 20)
*We stayed in the house during the **dreadful** storm.*

consume (kən sōōm') *v.* to eat up (p. 20)
*The birds will **consume** any crumbs on the ground.*
➤ Cognate (Spanish) **consumir**

sufficient (sə fish' ənt) *adj.* as much as is needed (p. 20)
*The family had **sufficient** food to last the entire week.*
➤ Cognate (Spanish) **suficiente**

repay (ri pā') *v.* to pay back or give back (p. 22)
*I will **repay** Jennifer for buying my lunch.*

For more practice, see page 307. ➡

Upon the Burning of Our House *and* To My Dear and Loving Husband **19**

Vocabulary Routine

To introduce the vocabulary, read aloud the words and definitions in the student book and have students repeat after you. Discuss how the pictures illustrate the words or sentences. Then follow the vocabulary routine below.

Selection Vocabulary

Define: When you are **bereft** of something, you don't have that thing anymore. Example: The shopping trip left Gus *bereft* of money. Ask: What is another example of something that could leave you *bereft* of money? EXAMPLE

When you **chide** someone, you tell them that they did something wrong. *Jill will chide her dog if he chews on her shoes again.* Describe a time when you should *chide* someone. DESCRIPTION

You might give someone **recompense** if they helped you fix something. *After Logan helped Kerry find a job, Kerry gave Logan a gift as recompense.* When would you give *recompense* for something? EXPLANATION

Content Vocabulary

A very bad thing is **dreadful.** *Juan had a scary dream last night that was dreadful.* How are *dreadful* and *wonderful* different? ANTONYM

When you **consume** something, you use it up. *The fire will consume the fuel.* How are the words *consume* and *eat* different? How are they the same? COMPARE AND CONTRAST

When you have a **sufficient** amount of something, you have enough of it. *We had a sufficient amount of gas to drive to the movie theater.* What would be a sufficient amount of snow to make a snowman? EXPLANATION

When you **repay** someone, you return what they gave you. *You should repay someone when you borrow money.* Describe a time when you had to repay someone. DESCRIPTION

Vocabulary Practice Have students complete the vocabulary practice activity on p. 307.

Upon the *Burning* of Our House

Interactive Question-Response

Comprehension Check

Ask students to share what they underlined in the text. **Ask:** *What was the narrator doing when the fire started? (sleeping) How do you know? (because she says she was "wakened") What woke her up? (a "thund'ring noise")*

Thund'ring is the word "thundering" with the letter *e* removed. *Thundering* means "rumbling loudly during a storm."

Oft is a shorter way to say "often."

Comprehension Check

Reread the boxed text on this page. Underline the words that tell what the speaker is doing when the fire starts.

In silent night when rest I took
For sorrow near I did not look
I wakened was with **thund'ring** noise
And piteous shrieks of <u>dreadful</u> voice.
5   That fearful sound of "Fire!" and "Fire!"
Let no man know is my desire.
I, starting up, the light did spy,
And to my God my heart did cry
To strengthen me in my distress
10 And not to leave me succorless.[1]
Then, coming out, beheld a space
The flame <u>consume</u> my dwelling place.
And when I could no longer look,
I blest His name that gave and took,[2]
15 That laid my goods now in the dust.
Yea, so it was, and so 'twas just.
It was His own, it was not mine,
Far be it that I should repine;[3]
He might of all justly **bereft**
20 But yet sufficient for us left.
When by the ruins **oft** I past
My sorrowing eyes aside did cast,
And here and there the places spy
Where oft I sat and long did lie:
25 Here stood that trunk, and there that chest,
There lay that store I counted best.

To Sum Up

➤ The speaker's house is on fire.
➤ The speaker believes that God has a reason for burning her house.
➤ The speaker has lost her things. She believes God will take care of her family.

Vocabulary

bereft (bi reft') *adj.* without something needed or wanted

1. *Succorless* means "helpless."
2. The line refers to the Bible verse Job 1:21, ". . . the Lord gave, and the Lord hath taken away; blessed be the name of the Lord."
3. *Repine* means "to express unhappiness" or "to complain."

Comprehension

To support students as they read the selection, have them begin the graphic organizer on page A5.

My pleasant things in ashes lie,
And them behold no more shall I.
Under thy roof no guest shall sit,
30 Nor at thy table eat a bit.
No pleasant tale shall e'er be told,
Nor things recounted done of old.
No candle e'er shall shine in thee,
Nor bridegroom's voice e'er heard shall be.
35 In silence ever shall thou lie,
Adieu, Adieu,⁴ all's vanity.⁵

Then straight I 'gin my heart to **chide,**
And did thy wealth on earth abide?
Didst fix thy hope on mold'ring dust?
40 The arm of flesh didst make thy trust?
Raise up thy thoughts above the sky
That dunghill mists away may fly.
Thou hast a house on high erect,
Framed by that mighty Architect,
45 With glory richly furnished,
Stands permanent though this be fled.
It's purchased and paid for too
By Him who hath enough to do.
A price so vast as is unknown
50 Yet by His gift is made thine own;

There's wealth enough, I need no more,
Farewell, my **pelf,** farewell my store.
The world no longer let me love,
My hope and treasure lies above.

---

4. **Adieu** (a dōō) is a French word that means "good-bye."
5. The line refers to the Bible verses from Ecclesiastes 1:2 and 12:8, "Vanity of vanities: all is vanity." **Vanity** means "having too much pride in one's looks."

REFLECT

Draw Conclusions About Author's Beliefs
Reread lines 13–15 on page 20. What conclusions can you draw about Bradstreet's faith in God from those lines?

Possible answer: She believes that God is responsible for all

things, good and bad, and that she must trust God's will.

 Talk about your answer with a partner.

Pelf means "money" or "wealth."

Literary Element

Metaphor Who is the "mighty Architect"? Check one.
☑ God
☐ the speaker's husband

Comprehension Check

Reread the last box of text on this page. Underline the words that tell where the speaker's real wealth is.

Vocabulary ....

chide (chīd) v. to find fault with or to blame

To Sum Up

➤ All of the speaker's things have burned.
➤ God has built a house for the speaker in heaven.
➤ The speaker's real wealth is in heaven.

Interactive Question-Response

Literary Element   Metaphor

If students have difficulty responding, **Ask:** *When the author says, "Thou hast an house on high erect," where would a "house on high" be? (heaven) When the author says, "Framed by that mighty Architect," what is an architect? (someone who designs buildings) If the "mighty Architect" is in heaven, who is the architect? (God) What does God build for the author? (a home in heaven)*

Comprehension Check

Ask students to share what they underlined in the text. **Ask:** *When the author says, "lies above," where is above? (heaven) What are the author's "hope and treasure"? (true happiness and eternal life) Why would the author's true happiness be only in heaven? (The author believes that there is no happiness in material possessions and wealth. True happiness can be found only in heaven.)* If students have trouble answering the last question, discuss with them the common religious belief that spiritual happiness is more valuable than earthly happiness.

Reading Strategy   Reflect

Partner Talk If students have difficulty responding, explain that the author "blest" (blessed) God's name even though He "gave and took" things away.

Interactive Question-Response

Comprehension Check

Ask students to share what they underlined in the text.
Ask: *How rich does the author think the East is? (Very rich) Why might the author compare her love to gold and riches? (to say that her love is more important than being rich)*

Selection Vocabulary

Have students read the word and definition for *recompense.* Then have them read the line, "Nor ought but love from thee, give / recompense." **Ask:** *What does the author want in return from her husband? (Nothing but love) What is the author giving to her husband? (Her love)*

Reflect

Partner Talk If students have difficulty responding, have then rewrite line 10 in their own words by completing the following sentence frame:

I pray that _____ [anno: the heavens] reward you _____ [anno: in many ways.].

Comprehension Check
Reread the first stanza. Underline the words that tell how much the speaker values her husband's love.

Nor ought but love from thee means "nothing but your love."

In love let's so persevere means "let's never give up on our love."

Vocabulary
recompense (rek′ m pens′) *n.* something given in return for something else

To Sum Up

➤ The speaker says her love is more valuable than gold and riches.

➤ She values her husband's love. She expects nothing in return from him but love.

➤ She wants his love for her to be rewarded in heaven. She wants their love to continue after they have died.

If ever two were one, then surely we.
If ever man were loved by wife, then thee;
If ever wife was happy in a man,
Compare with me, ye women, if you can.
5 I prize thy love more than whole mines of gold
Or all the riches that the East doth hold.
My love is such that rivers cannot quench,
Nor ought but love from thee, give **recompense.**

Thy love is such I can no way repay,
10 The heavens reward thee manifold,[1] I pray.
Then while we live, **in love let's so persevere[2]**
That when we live no more, we may live ever.[3]

1. **Manifold** means "in many different ways."
2. In the 1600s, the word **persevere** was pronounced *per sé ver.* The word rhymes with **ever** in the next line with this pronunciation.
3. Here, **ever** is a shorter way to say "forever."

REFLECT

Draw Conclusions About Author's Beliefs
Reread lines 9–10. How does Bradstreet's description of her love for her husband reflect her religious beliefs?

Possible answer: Only God, or the heavens, has the power to reward her husband appropriately.

 Talk about your answer with a partner.

Oral Assessment

Provide the following prompts to one student at a time. Observe students' responses. See the Oral Assessment Rubric on page T17 to determine students' levels of language output.

1. What happened to the speaker's house?
2. Who has a reason for burning the speaker's house?
3. Where is the speaker's real wealth?
4. Why does the speaker compare her love to gold and riches?
5. Why will the husband and wife's love last forever?

Upon the *Burning of Our House* and *To My Dear and Loving Husband*

Vocabulary Check

A. Circle the picture that best answers the question.

1. Which picture shows **dreadful** traffic?

3. Which picture shows a **sufficient** amount of water to fill a swimming pool?

2. Which picture shows someone **consuming** something?

4. Which person is **repaying** someone?

B. Match the word to its synonym.

c.	5. chide	a. horrible
d.	6. recompense	b. enough
a.	7. dreadful	c. blame
b.	8. sufficient	d. reward

C. Which statement uses the word correctly? Circle the letter of the correct sentence.

9. (a) She was left **bereft** of possessions.
   b. The fire left the house **bereft**.

10. (a) The speaker says she should **chide** herself for being sad after the fire.
    b. The speaker says the fire will **chide** her if she does not escape the house.

11. (a) The poet wants love from her husband as **recompense** for her love.
    b. The poet does not need **recompense** from her husband.

Grammar Link BLM

Past Time Expressions

Prepare students to complete the activity on page A6. Read the grammar instruction with students, and complete the first item with them to help them get started.

Vocabulary Check

A. Beginning/Early Intermediate

Read each question aloud. Then point to the first picture. Ask students to answer with yes or no. If they say no, point to the next picture. Then, turn the question into a statement and have students repeat it as you point to the word and picture. For example, **Ask:** *Which picture shows dreadful traffic? This traffic looks dreadful.*

Academic Vocabulary

Write the following sentence on the board: *Anne Bradstreet walks by the* **site** *of her former home and thinks about her life there.*

Then write the following possible meanings for *site* on the board.

a. ability to see

b. Internet address

c. place where something is located

d. quote as an authority or example

Ask students to choose the correct meaning for *site* in the example sentence. Students should be able to determine that *c* is the correct definition. Explain that *site* is an academic vocabulary word that they can use to name a location. Explain that *b* is also correct, but an Internet site represents a specialized use of the word. Point out that two other words, *sight* and *cite*, sound just like *site* but mean different things. Ask students to pick out the correct definitions for the other two words. (*a. is* sight; *d. is* cite.)

Comprehension Check

A. Beginning/Early Intermediate

Read each item aloud. Encourage students to offer answers to fill in the blanks. If students have trouble answering, use gestures and facial expressions to demonstrate possible responses. For example, to demonstrate *sad,* frown or pretend to cry.

After Reading

Have students complete the after reading activity on page 308.

Upon the *Burning* of Our House *and* *To My Dear and Loving Husband*

Comprehension Check

A. Fill in the blanks to show how the speaker feels in the poems.

1. The poet feels _____Possible answers: sad, afraid, horrified_____ when her house is on fire.

2. After her house burns down, the poet blames herself for being sad and begins to feel
   _____Possible answer: hopeful_____.

3. In "To My Dear and Loving Husband," the speaker _____Possible answer: loves_____ her husband.

B. The poet uses metaphor in "Upon the Burning of Our House." Fill in the boxes with the things that the poet compares.

Metaphor

God	=	Architect

C. Answer the questions about metaphor in "Upon the Burning of Our House."

4. Near the end of the poem, what two things does the poet compare?
   God and an architect

5. Where is the "house on high"?
   heaven

6. Why does the author feel better at the end of the poem?
   God has a house for her in heaven.

For more practice, see page 308. ➡

24

Writing Link

Extended Metaphor

Have students choose a person, place, object, or idea to describe by using an extended metaphor. Suggest that students begin by choosing two things to compare. Students can set up their comparison in a Venn diagram, listing the differences in the outer circles and the similarities in the place where the two circles intersect. For example, if students were to compare the mind or brain to a sponge in an extended metaphor, they might say that both absorb things; liquid or knowledge, both can be washed, and both dry out when not in use. The differences might include that one is living material and the other dead; one is encased or protected and the other stands alone; and one is living and the other is dead.

TIME How They Chose These Words

by Walter Isaacson

Oral Language

Build Background

Read the title and author. Explain that students will read "How They Chose These Words" by Walter Isaacson, a magazine article that talks about the words of the Declaration of Independence. **Ask:**

- **Do you know what the Declaration of Independence is?** *(yes/no; It is an important historical document stating America's freedom from the rule of England.)*

- **Based on the title, what do you think this article will be about?** *(the writers of the Declaration of Independence)*

Talk About the Article

Explain that many people worked together to write and edit the Declaration of Independence.

Early Advanced **Ask:** *Why do you think it was important for the Americans to write a statement about independence? (The Declaration explained the actions of the Americans. They wrote down the reasons for what they did. Without it, people would not have understood why they disobeyed the king of England.)*

Lesson at a Glance

Oral Language
- Build Background
- Talk About the Article

Vocabulary
- Content Vocabulary

Reading Strategy
- Determine the Main Idea and Supporting Details

Writing Link
- Fact Sheet

Comprehension
- BLM

Grammar Link
- The Simple Past Tense: Time Clauses with *Before* and *After* BLM

Technology
- Student Works™ Plus
- Teacher Works™ Plus
- Listening Library Audio CD
- Classroom Presentation Toolkit
- Glencoe Visual Vocabulary
- Skill Level Up!™ A Skill-Based Language Arts Game

TIME How They Chose These Words

Interactive Question-Response

Connect to the Article

Read aloud Connect to the Article. Reproduce the list on the board: **Model** *I always check to make sure that my words are spelled correctly.* Model writing your response in the list, and have volunteers suggest other responses. Then have individuals fill in their own lists.

Reading Strategy Determine Main Idea and Supporting Details

Read aloud the Reading Strategy. Tell students that if they are able to determine the main idea and supporting details, then they will be able to better understand the author's message. They will also remember the article more easily and be able to form their own opinions about the article. Tell students that sometimes the main idea is not stated directly. Students may have to look at the details in the article to figure out the main idea. All of the details should point to one idea that is more important than everything else. Have students read the title, the *deck* (the sentence that appears in large type below the title), and the headings for clues to the subject of the article. Ask them to keep these clues in mind as they read.

Connect to the Article

When you edit your writing, you make changes to it. How do you edit your writing? What kinds of changes do you make when you edit?

Partner Talk Discuss these questions with a partner. Then make a list of five things you can edit in a piece of writing. The first one has been done for you as an example.

Things to edit:
1. Make sure all sentences are complete.
2. Possible answers: Check for misspelled words,
3. take out sentences you don't need,
4. choose better words,
5. fix punctuation

Reading Strategy   Determine the Main Idea and Supporting Details

Every article or paragraph has one important idea that the author wants readers to understand. The most important idea in an article or paragraph is the **main idea**.

Details are the smaller parts that make up a whole. An author uses supporting details to show why the main idea is important. A **supporting detail** might be:

- an example
- a description
- an event
- a quotation

As you read, ask yourself, What is this article about? Then use a graphic organizer like the one below to write the main idea and some examples of supporting details from the article.

Main Idea:
Supporting Details:
1. Thomas Jefferson wrote the first draft of the document.
2.
3.

Note Taking

This selection will help you take notes. You take notes for a number of reasons. Notes can help you understand and remember what you read. You can also use what you learn about taking notes in other classes. Good notes help you study for tests, too.

This article has special pages to help you take notes. You will use four skills as you take notes:

Skill	Description
Reread	Look back over the pages you have read.
Record	Write down your answers to the questions you are given.
Recap	Briefly review in your own words.
Summarize	Briefly state the main points.

Content Vocabulary

committee (kə mit'ē) *n.*
a group of people who work together on a project (p. 28)
*The **committee** planned the holiday party.*
➤ Cognate (Spanish) **comité**

document (däk'yə mənt) *n.* something written or printed that gives information about a subject (p. 28)
*The student signed a **document** to get a driver's license.*
➤ Cognate (Spanish) **documento**

compose (kəm pōz') *v.* to create, such as a piece of writing or music (p. 28)
*Marcos will **compose** a letter to his grandmother.*

console (kən sōl') *v.* to comfort someone who feels sad (p. 34)
*When Andrea's cat died, her friend went to **console** her.*
➤ Cognate (Spanish) **consolar**

For more practice, see page 309. ➡

Vocabulary Routine

To introduce the vocabulary, read aloud the words and definitions in the student book and have students repeat after you. Discuss how the pictures illustrate the words or sentences. Then follow the vocabulary routine below.

Content Vocabulary

Define: A **committee** is a group who gets together and works on a project. Example: The committee made plans for a new library building. Ask: What are some actions that a *committee* might do? EXPLANATION

A **document** is something written that has information. *The document has information about how to open a bank account.* What are some examples of *documents?* EXAMPLE

If you **compose** something, then you create it. *The writer plans to compose her first novel by the end of the year.* How are the words *compose* and *write* alike? How are they different? COMPARE AND CONTRAST

When you **console** someone, you help him or her feel better. *I went to console my friend because she was having a bad day.* Describe a time when you might *console* someone. DESCRIPTION

Vocabulary Practice Have students complete the vocabulary practice activity on page 309.

Interactive
Question-Response

Content Vocabulary

Read aloud the word and definition for *committee*. **Ask:** *Who was on the committee to draft the declaration? (Benjamin Franklin, Thomas Jefferson, John Adams, Roger Sherman, and Robert Livingston)*

Background Information

Read aloud the note. Review with students the stages of the writing process *(prewrite, draft, revise, edit, publish)*. Remind students that a *draft* is the first form of a piece of writing. As students read, ask them to think about each of these stages. Remind students that even these great American leaders revised, edited, and had others look over their writing.

Content Vocabulary

Read aloud the sentence containing the word document. **Ask:** What document did Jefferson help write? (The Declaration of Independence)

Read aloud the sentence containing the word *compose*. **Ask:** *What is another word that describes what Jefferson does in this sentence? (writes; creates)*

---

committee (kə mit'ē) *n.* a group of people who work together on a project

Background Information

On July 4, 1776, a group of Americans called the Continental Congress voted to be free of the rule of England. The Declaration of Independence is a document that states this desire to be free.

document (däk'yə mənt) *n.* something written or printed that gives information about a subject

compose (kəm pōz') *v.* to create, such as a piece of writing or music

To Sum Up

➤ In 1776, the Continental Congress called for a document that would explain why America wanted to be free from England.

➤ Thomas Jefferson and Benjamin Franklin helped to write this document.

➤ Jefferson wrote the first draft.

28

As the continental congress prepared to vote on the question of American independence in 1776, it appointed a committee for a job that no one at the time thought was very important. The task, however, would turn out to be a momentous one: drafting a declaration that explained the decision. The committee included Benjamin Franklin, of course, and Thomas Jefferson and John Adams, as well as Connecticut merchant Roger Sherman and New York lawyer Robert Livingston.

How was it that Jefferson, at age 33, got the honor of drafting the document? His name was listed first on the committee, signifying that he was the chairman, because he had gotten the most votes and because he was from Virginia, the colony that had proposed the resolution. His four colleagues had other committee assignments that they considered to be more important. None of them realized that the document would eventually come to be viewed as a cornerstone of American politics. As for Franklin, he was still laid up in bed with boils and gout when the committee first met.

And thus it fell to Jefferson to compose, on a little lap desk he had designed, some of the most famous phrases in history while sitting alone in a second-floor room of a house on Market Street in Philadelphia just a block from Franklin's house. "When, in the course of human events . . . ," he famously began.

Comprehension BLM

To support students as they read the selection, have them begin the graphic organizer on page A7.

Note Taking

Reread the text on the left. Then record your answers to the items below.

1. The most interesting word on this page is _____

   because _____.

2. One word that I didn't know on this page is _____

   It means _____.

3. One thing I read on this page that I already knew is _____

   _____.

4. One thing I learned on this page that I didn't know is _____

   _____.

5. Recap, or write in your own words what you learned by reading this page.

   _____

   _____

   _____

   _____

6. Summarize below what you've recorded.

Most Interesting Word	New Word	One Thing I Already Knew	One Thing I Learned

Note Taking

To help students get started, you might want to model your thinking process for completing one of the items.

Interactive Question-Response

Comprehension Check

Ask students to share what they underlined in the text. Then, ask students to read the boxed text on page 32. Explain the differences between the words *sacred*, which means "given by God," and *self-evident*, which means "understood through reason." **Ask:** *Why is this edit important? (It shows that the Americans were acting with reason and were protecting their rights.)*

A **bill of particulars** is a list of complaints.

Comprehension Check

Reread the paragraph at the bottom of the page. Underline the words that describe the most important edit Franklin made.

To Sum Up

➤ Jefferson and Franklin had different writing styles.

➤ When Jefferson finished the first draft, he gave it to Franklin.

➤ Franklin edited the draft and made some changes.

Taking a Page from Franklin

The document Jefferson drafted was in some ways similar to what Franklin would have written. It contained a highly specific **bill of particulars** against the British. It also recounted, as Franklin had often done, the details of America's attempts to make peace despite England's unbending attitude. Indeed, Jefferson's words echoed some of the language that Franklin had used, earlier that year, in a draft resolution that he never published: "Whereas, whenever kings, instead of protecting the lives and properties of their subjects, as is their bounden duty, do endeavor to perpetrate the destruction of either, they thereby cease to be kings, become tyrants, and dissolve all ties of allegiance between themselves and their people."

Jefferson's writing style, however, was different from Franklin's. It was graced with rolling rhythms and smooth phrases, soaring in their poetry and powerful despite their polish. In addition, Jefferson drew on a depth of philosophy not found in Franklin. He echoed both the language and grand theories of English and Scottish Enlightenment thinkers. Having read John Locke's Second Treatise on Government at least three times, Jefferson was most notably influenced by Locke's concept of natural rights. And Jefferson built his case, in a manner more sophisticated than Franklin would have, on a contract between government and the governed that was founded on the consent of the people. Jefferson also, it should be noted, borrowed freely from the phrasings of others, including the resounding Declaration of Rights in the new Virginia constitution. Today, this kind of borrowing might lead to accusations of plagiarism, but back then it was considered not only proper but learned.

When he had finished a draft and included some changes from Adams, Jefferson sent it to Franklin on the morning of Friday, June 21. "Will Doctor Franklin be so good as to peruse it," he wrote in his cover note, "and suggest such alterations as his more enlarged view of the subject will dictate?" People were much more polite to editors back then.

Change for the Better?

Franklin made only a few changes, some of which can be viewed written in his hand on what Jefferson referred to as the "rough draft" of the Declaration. The most important of his edits was small but significant. He crossed out, using the heavy backslashes that he often employed, the last three words of Jefferson's phrase "We hold these truths to be sacred and undeniable." Franklin changed them to the words now enshrined in history: "We hold these truths to be self-evident."

Note Taking

Reread the text on the left. Then record your answers to the items below.

1. The most interesting word on this page is _____

   because _____ .

2. One word that I didn't know on this page is _____ .

   It means _____ .

3. One thing I read on this page that I already knew is _____

   _____ .

4. One thing I learned on this page that I didn't know is _____

   _____ .

5. Recap, or write in your own words what you learned by reading this page.

   _____

   _____

   _____

   _____

6. Summarize below what you've recorded.

Most Interesting Word	New Word	One Thing I Already Knew	One Thing I Learned

Note Taking

To help students get started, you might want to model your thinking process for completing one of the items.

Interactive Question-Response

To Sum Up

Beginning/Early Intermediate ➤ Have students work in pairs to reread all the To Sum Up statements from the beginning of the article on page 28. Then have students decide together which three details are the most important so far. Provide the following sentence frame for students to complete.

The most important details are

when _____,

when _____,

and when _____.

(The most important details are when the Continental Congress wanted a Declaration of Independence, when Jefferson wrote the first draft, and when Franklin made important edits.)

Axiom are truths that are understood by most people.

Inalienable rights are freedoms that everyone should have.

To Sum Up

➤ Franklin used the word *self-evident* to describe truths that can be understood through reason.

➤ The document now focused more on reason, not religion.

The idea of "self-evident" truths drew on the rational view of the world held by Isaac Newton and Franklin's close friend David Hume. The great Scottish philosopher Hume had developed a theory that distinguished between truths that describe matters of fact (such as "London is bigger than Philadelphia") and truths that are declared so through reason and definition ("the angles of a triangle total 180 degrees"; "all bachelors are unmarried"). He referred to the latter type of **axioms** as "self-evident" truths. By using the word sacred, Jefferson had implied, intentionally or not, that the principle in question—the equality of men and their endowment by their creator with **inalienable rights**—was a matter of religion. Franklin's edit turned it instead into a matter of reason and rationality.

Franklin's other edits were less suitable. He changed Jefferson's "reduce them to arbitrary power" to "reduce them under absolute despotism," and he took out the literary flourish in Jefferson's "invade and deluge us in blood" to make it more sparse: "invade and destroy us." And a few of his changes seemed stodgy and unnecessary. "Amount of their salaries" became "amount and payment of their salaries."

Note Taking

Reread the text on the left. Then record your answers to the items below.

1. The most interesting word on this page is _____

   because _____ .

2. One word that I didn't know on this page is _____

   It means _____ .

3. One thing I read on this page that I already knew is _____

   _____ .

4. One thing I learned on this page that I didn't know is _____

   _____ .

5. Recap, or write in your own words what you learned by reading this page.

   _____

   _____

   _____

   _____

6. Summarize below what you've recorded.

Most Interesting Word	New Word	One Thing I Already Knew	One Thing I Learned

Note Taking

To help students get started, you might want to model your thinking process for completing one of the items.

Interactive Question-Response

Content Vocabulary

Read aloud the sentence in which the word *console* appears. **Ask:** *Why did Franklin console Jefferson? (Jefferson was unhappy because the Continental Congress had cut out many parts of his draft.)*

Reflect

Partner Talk Have students work in pairs to answer. Have students look at each paragraph or section and ask themselves, What is this paragraph or section about? Once students determine the main idea of the paragraph or section, ask them which of the three sentences it supports. Have them continue until they are able to determine the main idea. **Model** *In the first paragraph, the Continental Congress wants someone to write about independence. I'm not sure which sentence is the main idea yet, so I'll go on to the next paragraph.* Write the following sentence frame on the board to help students organize their thoughts.

In this paragraph/section, _____.

Not insensible to these mutilations means that Jefferson was hurt because some of his writing was cut.

console (kən sōl´) *v.* to comfort someone who feels sad

Famous flourish means that Hancock signed with such a wavy style that his signature became famous.

To Sum Up

➤ The Continental Congress made more edits and cuts to the document.

➤ Jefferson was upset by the cuts, but Franklin helped him feel better.

➤ On August 2, 1776, the members of the Continental Congress signed the Declaration of Independence.

Congress Makes Cuts

After the Continental Congress voted for independence from England, it formed itself into a committee to consider Jefferson's draft Declaration. The members were not so light in their editing as Franklin had been. Large sections were sliced out, most notably the one that criticized the king for continuing the slave trade. Congress also, to its credit, cut by more than half the draft's final five paragraphs, in which Jefferson had begun to ramble in a way that detracted from the document's power. Jefferson was upset. "I was sitting by Dr. Franklin," he recalled, "who perceived that I was **not insensible to these mutilations.**" Franklin did his best to console him.

At the official signing of the parchment copy on August 2, John Hancock, the president of the Congress, penned his name with his **famous flourish.** "There must be no pulling different ways," he declared. "We must all hang together." Supposedly, Franklin replied, "Yes, we must, indeed, all hang together, or most assuredly we shall all hang separately." Their lives, as well as their sacred honor, had been put on the line.

—*Updated 2005, from TIME, July 7, 2003*

REFLECT

Determine the Main Idea and Supporting Details

A. Place a check next to the sentence that best describes the main idea of the article.

___ Editing is an important part of any writing assignment.

✓ The writing process played an important part in the writing of the Declaration of Independence.

___ The authors of the Declaration had to work together to gain America's independence.

B. Explain why you think your choice is the best answer.

Possible answer: Each paragraph discusses some part of the

writing process and how it affected the creation of the final

version of the Declaration of Independence.

 Talk about your answer with a partner.

Oral Assessment

Provide the following prompts to one student at a time. Observe students' responses. See the Oral Assessment Rubric on page T17 to determine students' levels of language output.

1. What is the Declaration of Independence?

2. What role did Thomas Jefferson play in writing the Declaration?

3. What role did Benjamin Franklin play in writing the Declaration?

4. Why did the Continental Congress make cuts to the Declaration?

5. How was the writing process important to the Declaration of Independence?

Note Taking

Reread the text on the left. Then record your answers to the items below.

1. The most interesting word on this page is _____

   because _____.

2. One word that I didn't know on this page is _____

   It means _____.

3. One thing I read on this page that I already knew is _____

   _____.

4. One thing I learned on this page that I didn't know is _____

   _____.

5. Recap, or write in your own words what you learned by reading this page.

   _____

   _____

   _____

   _____

6. Summarize below what you've recorded.

Most Interesting Word	New Word	One Thing I Already Knew	One Thing I Learned

Note Taking

To help students get started, you might want to model your thinking process for completing one of the items.

Vocabulary Check

A./B.

Beginning/Early Intermediate/Intermediate

Read each word aloud. Encourage students to point to the correct picture or answer with yes or no as you point to first to the word and then to each picture.

Comprehension Check

C. **Early Advanced**

Remind students that all details in the article must support the main idea, but they can also help answer questions about the article. Tell students to look for supporting details in the text that answer each of the questions.

Writing Link

Fact Sheet

Students should research the Declaration of Independence and the people and events that led to its creation. Have them create a "Did You Know" fact sheet listing information about the document. They should include the names of the people involved in drafting and editing it, the signers, significant events that led to the desire for independence, and other interesting facts that they discover during their research.

After Reading

Have students complete the after reading activity on page 310.

Vocabulary Check

A./B. Match each word to the correct picture.

1. document   2. compose   3. console

C. Think about what you read in the article. Complete each sentence with a vocabulary word from below.

> committee   compose

4. Thomas Jefferson's job was to _____compose_____ the Declaration, and Benjamin Franklin's job was to edit it.

5. The _____committee_____ to draft the Declaration of Independence included Jefferson, Franklin, and others.

Comprehension Check

A./B. Complete the sentences.

6. The Declaration of Independence was a document that explained why America wanted _____
   Possible answer: freedom from England
   .

7. Franklin helped Jefferson when he Possible answer: edited the first draft _____

8. Jefferson was upset when the Continental Congress Possible answer: cut out many parts of his draft

C. Answer the questions below.

9. What book influenced Jefferson as he wrote the Declaration? How did this book influence his beliefs?
   Locke's Second Treatise on Government influenced Jefferson's belief in natural rights and the idea
   that government should come from the will of the people.

10. What criticism of the king did the Continental Congress cut from the Declaration?
    The Congress cut the criticism of the slave trade.

For more practice, see page 310. ➡

36

Grammar Link   BLM

The Simple Past Tense: Time Clauses with *Before* and *After*

Prepare students to complete the activity master on page A8. Read the grammar instruction with students, and complete the first item with them to help them get started.

Letter to John Adams

by Abigail Adams

Learning Objectives

For pages 37–44, 311–312

In studying this text, you will focus on the following objectives:

Literary Studies: Analyzing description.

Reading: Recognizing author's purpose.

Oral Language

Build Background

Read the title and author. Explain that students will read "Letter to John Adams" by Abigail Adams, his wife. **Ask:**

- Do you write letters? What other forms of communication do you use? *(letters, email, text messages.)*

- Abigail Adams wrote this letter in 1776. Why do you think she did not use a different form of communication? *(In 1776, letters were the main form of communication across distances.)*

Talk About the Letter

Explain that John Adams was the first vice president and second president of the United States. Abigail Adams, his wife, is known for writing interesting letters and for supporting equal rights for all.

Abigail Adams wrote this letter to her husband on March 31, 1776, right after the British retreated from Boston. America was on its way to winning the Revolutionary War.

Beginning/Early Intermediate ▶ Tell students that after America became free, the Congress, which included John Adams, had to write laws. Show them a picture of the Constitution or Bill of Rights.

Lesson at a Glance

Oral Language
- Build Background
- Talk About the Letter

Vocabulary
- Selection Vocabulary
- Content Vocabulary

Literary Element
- Description

Reading Strategy
- Recognize Author's Purpose

Writing Link
- Letter

Comprehension
- BLM

Grammar Link
- Present Perfect Tense of Be: *For* and *Since* BLM

Technology
- Student Works™ Plus
- Teacher Works™ Plus
- Listening Library Audio CD
- Classroom Presentation Toolkit
- Glencoe Visual Vocabulary
- Skill Level Up!™ A Skill-Based Language Arts Game

Interactive Question-Response

Connect to the Letter

Read aloud Connect to the Letter. Reproduce the sentence stem and write-on lines on the board. **Model** *I think it's important to talk with friends and relatives who live far away, because it's important to know what's happening in their lives. Also we can tell them news about what's happening in our lives, such as having a new class or a new friend.* Model writing your response on a write-on line, and have volunteers suggest other responses. Then have individuals complete the sentence on their own.

Literary Element   Description

Read aloud Literary Element. On the board, draw a five-column chart with the heads *sight, sound, smell, taste,* and *touch.* Tell students you will use descriptive language to describe the classroom. **Model** *I see lots of colorful posters on the walls. I will write* colorful posters *in the column labeled* sight. Have students add other descriptive words that describe the classroom.

Reading Strategy   Recognize Author's Purpose

Read aloud Reading Strategy. Tell students that if they know an author's purpose, they will understand why she uses certain words and details. Explain that if an author's purpose were to tell readers that baseball is a great sport, then he or she might use words like *great, fun,* and *exciting.* **Ask:** *What words might you use if your purpose were to tell readers that baseball is a bad sport?* (slow, boring, dull). Remind students that as they read, they should think about how the details help the author achieve her purpose.

Letter to *John Adams*

Connect to the Letter

Do you think it's important to talk with friends or relatives who live far away? Why? Explain your answer on the lines below.

It's important to talk with friends and relatives who live far away because

1. Possible answer: we can find out about their lives.
   _____
   _____
   _____

2. Possible answer: we can tell them stories or news.
   _____
   _____
   _____

Literary Element   Description

Description is the use of words that create a picture in your mind. Good descriptive writing appeals to all five senses: sight, sound, smell, taste, and touch. It helps bring people, places, and things to life when you read.

As you read, look for details that help you imagine colonial Boston. Ask yourself: What do these details tell me about the time and place of the letter?

Reading Strategy   Recognize Author's Purpose

The **author's purpose** is the reason that he or she writes. Most authors write to inform, to explain, to entertain, to persuade, or to describe. As you read, think about the details that Adams includes. Ask yourself:

- Does this detail inform, explain, entertain, persuade, or describe?
- How does this detail help me understand the purpose of the letter?

Selection Vocabulary

vassals (va slz) *n.* servants or slaves (p. 40)
*The **vassals** plowed the land for their master.*
➤ Cognate (Spanish) **vasallos**

deprive (di prv) *v.* to take away from; to stop someone
from having or enjoying (p. 40)
*The dry weather will **deprive** the earth of rain.*
➤ Cognate (Spanish) **privar**

tyrants (t mts) *n.* rulers who use power in an unfair way
(p. 41)
*The cruel kings were **tyrants**.*
➤ Cognate (Spanish) **tiranos**

foment (f ment) *v.* to help grow or develop (p. 41)
*One way to **foment** change is to elect new leaders.*
➤ Cognate (Spanish) **fomentar**

Content Vocabulary

defense (di fens) *n.* ability to resist an attack (p. 40)
*The castle's walls created a strong **defense** against
enemies.*
➤ Cognate (Spanish) **defensa**

passion (pash n) *n.* strong liking of or desire for
something (p. 40)
*He became a chef because of his **passion** for food.*
➤ Cognate (Spanish) **pasión**

generous (jen r s) *adj.* very giving (p. 41)
*The **generous** couple donated money to the museum.*
➤ Cognate (Spanish) **generoso**

dispute (dis pūt') *n.* argument; difference of opinion
(p. 42)
*The two brothers had a **dispute** over who should get the
last slice of pizza.*
➤ Cognate (Spanish) **generoso**

For more practice, see page 311. ➡

Letter to John Adams   39

Vocabulary Routine

To introduce the vocabulary, read aloud the words and
definitions in the student book and have students repeat
after you. Discuss how the pictures illustrate the words
or sentences. Then follow the vocabulary routine below.

Selection Vocabulary

Define: A person who serves someone else is a ***vassal.***
Example: The *vassal* cleaned the house for the master.
Ask: What is another word for a *vassal?* SYNONYM

When you ***deprive*** someone, you prevent him or her
from having something. *The strict laws deprive the
citizens of freedom.* How are the words *deprive* and
give different? ANTONYM

Tyrants are rulers who abuse their power. *The tyrants
made their people suffer.* What words would you use
to describe a *tyrant?* DESCRIBE

To ***foment*** means to help something get started.
*They wrote letters to their senator in order to foment
change.* How might you *foment* change in your school
or community? EXPLANATION

Content Vocabulary

If you put up a strong ***defense,*** you can stop an attack.
The goaltender is an important part of a team's defense.
How might a sports team put up a strong *defense?* EXPLAIN

If you have a ***passion*** for something, you feel very
strongly about it. *The pilot has a passion for flying
airplanes.* How would you describe someone who has
a *passion* for learning? DESCRIBE

A ***generous*** person gives a lot. *The generous boss
gave all of her employees a raise.* How are the words
generous and *giving* similar? How are they different?
COMPARE AND CONTRAST

When two people have a ***dispute,*** they disagree.
*The children had a dispute about who should do the
chores.* What is another word for *dispute?* SYNONYM

Vocabulary Practice Have students complete
the vocabulary practice activity on p. 311.

Letter to John Adams

Interactive Question-Response

Content Vocabulary

Read aloud the word and definition for *defense*.

Focus students on the first paragraph. **Ask:** *Why would Virginia need to put up a defense? (to protect itself during the war) If America did not have a strong defense, what might have happened? (America might have lost the war.)*

Content Vocabulary

Read aloud the word and definition for *passion*. Ask students to name someone in history who had a passion for freedom. **Model** *Someone with a passion for freedom feels strongly that all people should be free. Abraham Lincoln had a passion for liberty. He helped free the slaves in the Civil War.*

Background Information

Read aloud the note. Explain that since Abigail Adams was living with her children in Braintree, she had to send someone else to watch her house in Boston.

Comprehension Check

Ask students to share what they underlined in the text. **Ask:** *How do you think John Adams will react when he hears this news about his home? (relieved)*

To Sum Up

> **Beginning/Early Intermediate** Read the statements in the To Sum Up box aloud with students. Then have them complete the following sentence about the author:

Two words that describe Abigail Adams are _____ and _____. (curious, fair)

---

defense (di fens) *n.* ability to resist an attack

passion (pa shn) *n.* strong liking of or desire for something

---

Background Information

In 1774, the Adams family moved to Braintree because Boston had become too violent.

 Comprehension Check

Reread the boxed text in the middle of the page. Underline the words that tell about the Adams' home in Boston.

To Sum Up

➤ Adams wants to know about her husband and his work.

➤ Adams thinks that all people should have freedom.

➤ Adams says that her home has not been badly damaged in the war.

Braintree, March 31, 1776

I wish you would ever write me a letter half as long as I write you; and tell me if you may where your fleet are gone? What sort of <u>defense</u> Virginia can make against our common enemy? Whether it is so situated as to make an able defense? Are not the gentry[1] lords and the common people **vassals**? Are they not like the uncivilized natives Britain represents us to be? I hope their rifle men,[2] who have shown themselves very savage and even bloodthirsty, are not a specimen of the generality of the people.

I am willing to allow the colony great merrit for having produced a Washington, but they have been shamefully duped by a Dunmore.[3]

I have sometimes been ready to think that the <u>passion</u> for liberty cannot be equally strong in the breasts of those who have been accustomed to **deprive** their fellow creatures of theirs. Of this I am certain: that it is not founded upon the generous and Christian principle of doing to others as we would that others should do unto us.

Do not you want to see Boston; I am fearful of the small pox, or I should have been in before this time. I got Mr. Crane to go to our house and see what state it was in. I find it has been occupied by one of the doctors of a regiment, <u>very dirty, but no other damage has been done to it. The few things which were left in it are all gone.</u> Crane has the key, which he never delivered up. I have wrote to him for it and am determined to get it cleaned as soon as possible and shut it up. I look upon it a new acquisition of property, a property which one month ago I did not value at a single shilling, and could with pleasure have seen it in flames.

Vocabulary

vassals (va' salz) *n.* servants or slaves
deprive (di priv') *v.* to take away from; to stop someone from having or enjoying

1. **Gentry** means the upper class.
2. **Rifle men** are British soldiers and Loyalists fighting against American forces.
3. **The Earl of Dunmore** was Virginia's last governor from England. He promised freedom to slaves who would fight for England. This angered American who were fighting against England.

Comprehension BLM

To support students as they read the selection, have them begin the graphic organizer on page A9.

The town in general is left in a better state than we expected, more owing to a precipitate[4] flight than any regard to the inhabitants, though some individuals discovered a sense of honor and justice and have left the rent of the houses in which they were for the owners and the furniture unhurt, or if damaged sufficient to make it good.

Others have committed abominable ravages. The mansion house of your president[5] is safe and the furniture unhurt, whilst both the house and the furniture of the Solicitor General have fallen a prey to their own merciless party. Surely the very fiends feel a reverential awe for virtue and patriotism, whilst they detest the parricide[6] and traitor.

I feel very differently at the approach of spring to which I did a month ago. We knew not then whether we could plant or sow with safety, whether when we had toiled we could reap the fruits of our own industry, whether we could rest in our own cottages, or whether we should not be driven from the sea coasts to seek shelter in the wilderness, but now we feel as if we might sit under our own vine and eat the good of the land.

I feel a gaieté de coeur[7] to which before I was a stranger. I think the sun looks brighter, the birds sing more melodiously, and nature puts on a more cheerful countenance. We feel a temporary peace, and the poor fugitives are returning to their deserted habitations.

Though we felicitate ourselves, we sympathize with those who are trembling lest the lot of Boston should be theirs. But they cannot be in similar circumstances unless pusillanimity[8] and cowardice should take possession of them. They have time and warning given them to see the evil and shun it.—I long to hear that you have declared an independency—and by the way, in the new Code of Laws which I suppose it will be necessary for you to make, I desire you would remember the ladies, and be more <u>generous</u> and favorable to them than your ancestors. Do not put such unlimited power into the hands of the husbands. Remember, all men would be **tyrants** if they could. If particular care and attention is not paid to the ladies, we are determined to **foment** a rebellion, and will not hold ourselves bound by any laws in which we **have no voice,** or representation.

Vocabulary ....

tyrants (tī′rants) *n.* rulers who use power in an unfair way
foment (fō′ ment′) *v.* to help grow or develop

4. *Precipitate* means "sudden."
5. John Hancock was the ***president*** of the Continental Congress. When the British occupied Boston, General William Howe took over Hancock's house.
6. Here, ***parricide*** means "a person who commits the crime of treason, or betraying one's country."
7. *Gaieté de couer* (gä a tä d ə koer′) is a French idiom that means "having a light heart" or "playfulness."
8. *Pusillanimity* (pyü′ s ə l ə ni′ mə tē) means "being a coward."

✏️ **Literary Element**

Description Reread the boxed text near the top of the page. Underline the details that describe the writer's hopefulness?

generous (jen r s) *adj.* very giving

A law in which you **have no voice** is a law that does not include your ideas or opinions.

To Sum Up
➤ Adams feels safe and hopeful now that British have left Boston.
➤ Adams wants her husband to "remember the ladies" when writing new laws.

Interactive Question-Response

Literary Element Description

If students have difficulty responding: **Model** *Descriptive words help us sense what we read. Which words in this paragraph can I sense? I can see the words* rest in our cottages; *they paint a picture of someone sleeping in a cozy bed near a fireplace.* **Ask:** *Can you see the words* eat the good of the land? *(yes) Describe what you see. (Answers will vary.)*

Content Vocabulary

Read aloud the word and definition for *generous.* Ask students to name someone they know who is generous. **Model** *I can think of someone who is generous. Every time I visit my grandmother, she cooks me a delicious meal. She probably spends days preparing all the food. She is generous with her time.*

To Sum Up

Beginning/Early Intermediate Have students work in pairs to read the statements in the To Sum Up box. **Ask:** *Is Adams worried about women's rights or men's rights? (women's) Which words tell you that she is worried about women's rights? ("remember the ladies")*

Interactive Question-Response

Content Vocabulary

Read aloud the word and definition for *dispute.* Point out that Adams says she has "no dispute" with the idea that all men are tyrannical. **Ask:** *If you have "no dispute" with something, do you agree or disagree with it? (agree)* Explain that Adams agrees with the idea that all men are tyrants.

To Sum Up

Beginning/Early Intermediate Have students work in pairs to read the statements in the To Sum Up box. **Ask:** *Does Adams think men are better than women? (no) Does she think women are better than men? (no)* Prompt students to explain that Adams thinks men and women are equal.

Reflect

Partner Talk Have students work in pairs to answer. **Model** *To answer this, I would think about what Adams is saying. Adams is telling her husband that women should be treated like equals. Then I would think about why she is saying it. She is saying it because she knows her husband is helping to write the new laws for the nation. It seems like she wants to convince him to write fair laws.* Write the following sentence frame on the board to help students organize their thoughts:

Adams' purpose is to _____. I know this because she tells her husband _____ and _____.

---

dispute (dis pūt′) *n.* argument; difference of opinion

That your sex are naturally tyrannical is truth so thoroughly established as to admit no <u>dispute</u>, but such of you as wish to be happy willingly give up the harsh title of master for the more tender and endearing one of friend. Why, then, not put it out of the power of the vicious and the lawless to use us with cruelty and indignity with impunity. Men of sense in all ages abhor those customs which treat us only as the vassals of your sex. Regard us then as beings placed by providence under your protection, and in imitation of the Supreme Being, make use of that power only for our happiness.

Abigail

To Sum Up

➤ Adams believes that men should be women's friends, not their masters.

➤ Adams believes that men and women should be treated equally.

42

REFLECT

Recognize Author's Purpose
In the last paragraph, is the author's purpose to inform, to explain, to entertain, to persuade, or to describe? Explain your answer.

Possible answer: The author's purpose is to persuade her
husband to give women equal rights.
_____
_____
_____

 Talk about your answer with a partner.

Oral Assessment

Provide the following prompts to students one at a time. Observe students' responses. See the Oral Assessment Rubric on page T17 to determine students' levels of language output.

1. Tell me about Abigail Adams.

2. Where is John Adams when Abigail writes her letter?

3. What does Abigail tell her husband about Boston?

4. How is Abigail feeling about the war?

5. What does Abigail think about the nation's new laws?

Letter to John Adams

After You Read

Vocabulary Check

A. Circle the picture that best answers the question.

1. Which picture shows **defense**?

3. Which person is being **generous**?

2. Which person has a **passion** for art?

B. Circle the letter of the word that answers each question correctly.

4. What might you say during a **dispute**?
   a. "I disagree."
   b. "I agree."
   c. "I think you're right."

5. How might you **deprive** someone of your attention?
   a. spend lots of time with him
   b. go on a trip or vacation with him
   c. avoid him whenever you can

C. Circle the letter of the sentence that uses the boldface word correctly.

6. a. The **tyrants** invited everyone to the feast.
   b. The **tyrants** made the people work very hard.

7. a. The unhappy citizens will **foment** change.
   b. The content worker will **foment** a protest against the employer.

8. a. The **vassals** worked for the ruling class.
   b. The ruling class worked for the **vassals**.

Vocabulary Check

A. Beginning/Early Intermediate

Read each question aloud. Encourage students to point to the right answer. Then turn the question into a statement and have students repeat as you point to the word and picture. For example: *Which picture shows defense? This picture shows defense.*

Grammar Link BLM

The Present Perfect Tense of *Be*: *For* and *Since*

Prepare students to complete the activity on page A10. Read the grammar instruction with students, and complete the first item with them to help them get started.

Comprehension Check

B. [Intermediate]

Direct students' attention to the fourth paragraph on page 41. Remind them that descriptive language appeals to the five senses. **Ask:** *Which words in this paragraph can you see? Which words in this paragraph can you hear?*

After Reading

Have students complete the after reading activity on page 312.

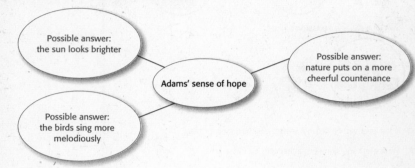

Letter to John Adams

Comprehension Check

A. List two things that Abigail Adams tells her husband in her letter.

1. Abigail Adams tells her husband that __Possible answer: she would like to hear from him more often.__ .

2. She also tells him that __Possible answer: she is feeling hopeful.__ .

B. Abigail Adams uses descriptive writing to explain how hopeful she feels about the young nation. In the web below, write examples of the descriptive language she uses.

- Possible answer: the sun looks brighter
- Adams' sense of hope
- Possible answer: nature puts on a more cheerful countenance
- Possible answer: the birds sing more melodiously

C. Answer the questions about the use of description in "Letter to John Adams."

6. Did Adams's descriptions bring colonial Boston to life for you? Why or why not?

   Answers will vary.

   _____

7. What descriptive language does Adams use to describe her feelings as spring approaches? Based on this language, how do you think she feels?

   Possible answer: Adams says "the sun looks brighter, the birds sing more melodiously, and nature

   puts on a more cheerful countenance." These descriptions show that she is filled with hope.

8. What descriptive words does Adams use in the last two paragraphs? How do they help her make her arguments?

   Possible answer: Adams says that women might "foment a rebellion" if they are not given equality.

   This makes her argument sound very serious.

For more practice, see page 312. ➡

Writing Link

Letter to Abigail Adams

Students should imagine that John Adams has received his wife's letter and decided to write back. Have students work in small groups to list two topics his letter would address. Then have them write the letter. Remind students to use standard letter format, including a salutation, body, closing, and signature. If necessary, show them how to set up a friendly letter with these features.

FROM
CIVIL DISOBEDIENCE
by Henry David Thoreau

On the Eve of
Historic Dandi March
by Mohandas K. Gandhi

FROM
LONG WALK TO FREEDOM
by Nelson Mandela

Learning Objectives

For pages 45–78, 313–315

In studying these texts, you will focus on the following objectives:

Literary Studies: Comparing cultural context. Comparing themes. Analyzing argument.

from Civil Disobedience/On the Eve of Historic Dandi March/*from* Long Walk to Freedom   **45**

Oral Language

Build Background

Read the titles and authors. Explain that students will read and compare three essays that deal with responses to unjust situations. **Ask:**

- The word *disobedience* has the word *obedience* as its root. What does *obedience* mean? *(to obey)*

- How does adding *dis–* to obedience change its meaning? *(disobedience is the opposite of obedience)*

Talk About the Essay

Explain that each essay discusses the things people do to support their ideas or beliefs.

Beginning/Early Intermediate ▶ **Ask:** *Have you ever seen people protesting something? (yes/no)* Gesture carrying a picket sign to help students understand what a protest is.

Intermediate ▶ Explain that people use different techniques to stand up for what they believe in and to promote change. Have students list some different methods used to promote change.

People can promote change against an unfair situation by ___. (marching, petitioning, writing articles or letters, organizing boycotts)

Lesson at a Glance

Oral Language
- Build Background
- Talk About the Essay

Vocabulary
- Content Vocabulary
- Academic Vocabulary

Literary Element
- Argument

Reading Strategy
- Evaluate Evidence

Writing Link
- Speech

Fluency
- Expression and Intonation: Bring Out Meaning

Comprehension [BLM]
- BLM

Word Study [BLM]
- Negative Prefixes: *un–, im–, in–, il–, dis–, a–,* and *ir–*BLM

Grammar Link [BLM]
- Spelling of Regular Past Tense Verbs: Pronunciation of *–ed: /t/, /d/,* and */id/* BLM

Technology
- Student Works™ Plus
- Teacher Works™ Plus
- Listening Library Audio CD
- Classroom Presentation Toolkit
- Glencoe Visual Vocabulary
- Skill Level Up!™ A Skill-Based Language Arts Game

Interactive Question-Response

Connect to the Essay

Read aloud Connect to the Essay. Reproduce the chart on the board. **Model** *I think that freedom of speech is important. I would go to court to fight for my freedom of speech.* Model writing your response in the chart, and have volunteers suggest other responses. Then have individuals fill in their own charts.

Literary Element Argument

Explain that an argument uses reasons and evidence to logically support a point. Read aloud the Literary Element. Then, write on the board: School cafeterias should not provide sugary snacks. Have students provide reasons and evidence that could be used to support this point.

Reading Strategy Evaluate Evidence

Read aloud the Reading Strategy. Tell students that separating fact from opinion is an important step in deciding how good an argument is. Make two columns on the board, one for facts and one for opinions. Ask students to provide facts about their school. Then ask them to provide opinions.

Comparing Literature

Compare Cultures Read aloud the Comparing Literature note. Point out to students that the writers came from different countries. Thoreau lived in the United States, Gandhi lived in India, and Mandela lived in South Africa. **Ask:** *How do you think the authors overcame the challenges that they faced? (through their actions and words: by writing, by marching, by speaking, by leading)*

Comparing Literature

FROM CIVIL DISOBEDIENCE
On the Eve of Historic Dandi March
FROM LONG WALK TO FREEDOM

Connect to the Essay

What ideas are important to you? What risks would you take to support those ideas? Fill in the chart below to think about how you would stand up for your ideas.

What I Believe	What I Would Do
1. I believe that Possible answer: my family is important.	2. I would Possible answer: fight to protect my family.
2. I believe that Possible answer: people should be treated equally.	2. I would Possible answer: join a march for equal rights.

Literary Element Argument

Authors use **arguments** to persuade readers that their point of view is correct. A good argument uses

- evidence
- reasons
- logicn

For example, in "Civil Disobedience," Thoreau argues that the government should have less power than it does. As you read the essay, ask yourself: What reasons and evidence does Thoreau use to support his argument?

Reading Strategy Evaluate Evidence

When you **evaluate evidence**, you ask whether the author's main points have solid support. One way to evaluate evidence in an argument is to decide whether the author is presenting facts or opinions.

- Facts are true statements that can be proven.
- An example of a fact is "It is forty degrees outside today."
- Opinions are statements of an author's beliefs. Opinions cannot be proven.
- An example of an opinion is "Cold weather is better than warm weather."

As you read "Civil Disobedience," ask yourself: What facts does Thoreau present? Which of his statements are opinions?

Comparing Literature Compare Cultures

Thoreau, Gandhi, and Mandela all lived at different times in different parts of the world. Each of them faced a challenge that was created by the specific culture in which they lived. Each of them responded to the challenge in a way that reflects that specific culture. As you read, ask yourself: How did the specific time and place in which each writer lived affect him? What effect did the culture have on what he did?

Content Vocabulary

strained (strānd) *v.* pressed or poured through a device with holes for filtering (p. 52) *We **strained** the pasta before we served it for dinner.* 	**individual** (in' də vij' ōō əl) *n.* a single person (p .58) *I saw an **individual** wearing a green hat.* ➤ Cognate (Spanish) **individuo**
authority (ə thôr' ə tē) *n.* power to tell someone what to do (p. 58) *The teacher has the **authority** to assign homework.* ➤ Cognate (Spanish) **autoridad** 	**boycott** (boi' kot) *v.* to protest by refusing to participate (p. 62) *The boys plan to **boycott** the school dance this year.* ➤ Cognate (Spanish) **boicot**
victorious (vik tôr ē əs) *adj.* winning (p. 64) *Our team lost last week, but this week we were **victorious**.* ➤ Cognate (Spanish) **victorioso** 	**extraordinary** (iks trôr' r də ner' ē) *adj.* very unusual (p. 66) *The pumpkin was featured on the news for its extraordinary size.* ➤ Cognate (Spanish) **extraordinario**
domination (dom' ə nā' shən) *n.* the state of controlling someone or something (p. 68) *A wolf pack recognizes the **domination** of its leader.* ➤ Cognate (Spanish) **dominación**	**illusion** (ĭ lōō' zhən) *n.* something that misleads or deceives (p. 72) *The magician produced the **illusion** that the woman was cut in half.* ➤ Cognate (Spanish) **ilusión**

For more practice, see page 313. ➡

Vocabulary Routine

To introduce the vocabulary, read aloud the words and definitions in the student book and have students repeat after you. Discuss how the pictures illustrate the words or sentences. Then follow the vocabulary routine below.

Content Vocabulary

Define: Something is **strained** if it is pressed or poured through a device with holes that filters it. Example: After we cooked the sauce, we *strained* it. Ask: Give an example of something that might be *strained*. EXAMPLE

An **individual** is a single person. *I told my family that I wanted to be treated as an individual.* What word is similar in meaning to *individual*? SYNONYM

Authority is the lawful power to do something. *Teachers have the authority to keep students after school.* How do people gain *authority*? EXPLANATION

A **boycott** is a protest against an organization by refusing to deal with it. *The group organized a boycott of the hotel chain.* Why would someone want to hold a *boycott*? EXPLANATION

When people are **victorious,** they have won something. *Our swim team was victorious at the meet.* What is the opposite of *victorious*? ANTONYM

Something **extraordinary** is very special. *The young actor's performance was extraordinary.* Describe a time when you saw something *extraordinary*. DESCRIPTION

Domination is having control over someone or something weaker than you are. *Smaller companies were forced out of business by the domination of the big corporation.* What word means the opposite of *domination*? ANTONYM

An **illusion** is a misleading impression. *I acted under the illusion that Jacqueline disliked me.* A *delusion* is a false belief that a person continues to believe in spite of evidence. How are the words *illusion* and *delusion* the same? How are they different? COMPARE AND CONTRAST

Vocabulary Practice Have students complete the vocabulary practice activity on page 313.

FROM
CIVIL DISOBEDIENCE

Interactive Question-Response

Background Information

Read the note aloud. Point out that *opposed* means that Thoreau was against the war. **Ask:** *Do you know any words that have the same root as opposed? (opponent)*

Literary Element Argument

If students have trouble responding: **Model** *I know that authors often give examples to support their arguments. Examples usually come after a statement of the main argument. Thoreau argues against government in the second paragraph. The last sentence of the second paragraph mentions the Mexican War. So he is probably using that war as an example to support his argument.* **Ask:** *Why does Thoreau think that the Mexican War supports his argument? (because the people as a whole would not support this war)*

A *standing army* is an army that stays together during peacetime.

Background Information

The Mexican-American War was fought from 1846 to 1848. Thoreau opposed it in part because he believed that it would spread slavery.

Literary Element

Argument What example does Thoreau give of a problem caused by government?
- [ ] Vietnam War
- [ ] Revolutionary War
- [x] Mexican War

If you *bend something to your will*, you make it do what you want.

Wooden gun refers to a toy gun made out of wood. A toy does not provide protection.

To Sum Up

➤ Thoreau believes that less government is better than more government.

➤ He thinks the Mexican War is an example of the problems government causes.

➤ He says that government doesn't do valuable things. People do valuable things.

I heartily accept the motto, "That government is best which governs least"; and I should like to see it acted up to more rapidly and systematically. Carried out, it finally amounts to this, which also I believe—"That government is best which governs not at all"; and when men are prepared for it, that will be the kind of government which they will have. Government is at best but an expedient;[1] but most governments are usually, and all governments are sometimes, inexpedient. The objections which have been brought against a **standing army**, and they are many and weighty, and deserve to prevail, may also at last be brought against a standing government. The standing army is only an arm of the standing government. The government itself, which is only the mode which the people have chosen to execute their will, is equally liable to be abused and perverted before the people can act through it. Witness the present Mexican war, the work of comparatively a few individuals using the standing government as their tool; for, in the outset, the people would not have consented to this measure.

This American government—what is it but a tradition, though a recent one, endeavoring to transmit itself unimpaired to posterity,[2] but each instant losing some of its integrity? It has not the vitality and force of a single living man; for a single man can **bend it to his will.** It is a sort of **wooden gun** to the people themselves. But it is not the less necessary for this; for the people must have some complicated machinery or other, and hear its din,[3] to satisfy that idea of government which they have. Governments show thus how successfully men can be imposed on, even impose on themselves, for their own advantage. It is excellent, we must all allow. Yet this government never of itself furthered any enterprise, but by the alacrity[4] with which it got out of its way. *It* does not keep the country free. *It* does not settle the West. *It* does not educate. The character inherent in the American people has done all that has been accomplished; and it would have done somewhat more, if the government had not sometimes got in its way. For government is an expedient by

1. **Expedient** means "something employed to bring about a desired result" or "a means to an end."
2. **Posterity** means "the generations of people to come in the future."
3. A **din** is a loud noise that lasts for a while.
4. **Alacrity** means "speed."

Comprehension BLM

To support students as they read the selection, have them begin the graphic organizer on page A11.

Note Taking

Reread the text on the left. Then record your answers to the items below.

1. The most interesting word on this page is _____

   because _____ .

2. One word that I didn't know on this page is _____ .

   It means _____ .

3. One thing I read on this page that I already knew is _____

   _____

4. One thing I learned on this page that I didn't know is _____

   _____

5. Recap, or write in your own words what you learned by reading this page.

   _____

   _____

   _____

   _____

6. Summarize below what you've recorded.

Most Interesting Word	New Word	One Thing I Already Knew	One Thing I Learned

Note Taking

To help students get started, you might want to model your thinking process for completing one of the items.

Interactive Question-Response

Comprehension Check

Ask students to share their answers. **Ask:** *Thoreau believes that majority rule is not based on justice. Why do you think that he believes this? (A position is not right just because a majority of people agree with it. Thoreau might point to the example of slavery to show that majority rule does not always lead to justice.)*

---

which men would fain[5] succeed in letting one another alone; and, as has been said, when it is most expedient[6], the governed are most let alone by it. Trade and commerce, if they were not made of india-rubber, would never manage to bounce over the obstacles which legislators are continually putting in their way; and if one were to judge these men wholly by the effects of their actions and not partly by their intentions, they would deserve to be classed and punished with those mischievous persons who put obstructions on the railroads.

But, to speak practically and as a citizen, unlike those who call themselves no-government men, I ask for, not *at once* no government, but at once a better government. Let every man make known what kind of government would command his respect, and that will be one step toward obtaining it.

After all, the practical reason why, when the power is once **in the hands** of the people, a majority are permitted, and for a long period continue, to rule, is not because they are most likely to be **in the right,** nor because this seems fairest to the minority, but because they are physically the strongest. But a government in which the majority rule in all cases cannot be based on justice, even as far as men understand it. Can there not be a government in which majorities do not virtually decide right and wrong, but conscience?—in which majorities decide only those questions to which the rule of expediency is applicable? Must the citizen ever for a moment, or in the least degree, resign his conscience to the legislator? Why has every man a conscience then? I think that we should be men first, and subjects afterward. It is not desirable to cultivate a respect for the law, so much as for the right. The only obligation which I have a right to assume is to do at any time what I think right. It is truly enough said that a corporation has no conscience; but a corporation of conscientious men is a corporation *with* a conscience. Law never made men a whit[7] more just; and, by means of their respect for it, even the well-disposed are daily made the agents of injustice....

Some years ago, the State met me in behalf of the Church, and commanded me to pay a certain sum toward the support of a clergyman whose preaching my father attended, but never I myself. "Pay," it said, "or be **locked up** in the jail." I declined to pay. But, unfortunately, another man **saw fit** to pay it. I did not see why the schoolmaster should be taxed to support the priest, and not the priest the schoolmaster: for I was not the State's schoolmaster, but I supported myself by voluntary subscription. I did not see why the lyceum[8] should not present its tax-bill, and have the State to back its demand, as well as the Church. However, at the request of the selectmen,[9] I condescended to make some such statement as this in writing: "Know all men by these presents, that I, Henry Thoreau, do

---

In the hands of means "belonging to."

If you are *in the right,* you are correct.

Comprehension Check

Reread the first two sentences of the second full paragraph. Underline the phrase that shows what Thoreau thinks about majority rule.

Someone who has been *locked up* has been put in jail.

To *see fit* to something is to think that it is worth doing.

To Sum Up

➤ Thoreau doesn't want to end government. He wants to change it.

➤ He thinks that obeying your sense of right and wrong is more important than following the law.

➤ He once refused to pay a church tax. Someone else paid it for him.

---

5. *Fain* means "gladly," "willingly," or "happy to do it."
6. *Expedient* means "something that is easy to do for a certain purpose."
7. A *whit* is a very small amount.
8. A *lyceum* is a group that organizes educational events.
9. *Selectmen* are people who are elected to run a town.

Differentiated Instruction

Clarify the Text Support students in understanding Thoreau's ideas about conscience and the law.

Beginning/Early Intermediate Read aloud the second bullet in To Sum Up. **Ask:** *Which is more important to Thoreau: what you believe is right or what you are told to do? (what you believe is right)*

Intermediate Have partners read aloud the boxed text on page 50. Then have them complete these sentence frames. *Thoreau believes that everyone has a ____. (conscience) He thinks that the only requirement he must follow is to ____. (do what he thinks is right)*

Early Advanced Point out that Thoreau uses rhetorical questions to make his point that people should obey their conscience. Ask students to reread the second full paragraph on page 50. Have them identify Thoreau's rhetorical questions and then restate them as declarative sentences.

Note Taking

Reread the text on the left. Then record your answers to the items below.

1. The most interesting word on this page is _____

   because _____ .

2. One word that I didn't know on this page is _____ .

   It means _____ .

3. One thing I read on this page that I already knew is _____

   _____ .

4. One thing I learned on this page that I didn't know is _____

   _____ .

5. Recap, or write in your own words what you learned by reading this page.

   _____

   _____

   _____

   _____

6. Summarize below what you've recorded.

Most Interesting Word	New Word	One Thing I Already Knew	One Thing I Learned

Note Taking

To help students get started, you might want to model your thinking process for completing one of the items.

Interactive Question-Response

Content Vocabulary

Read aloud the word and definition for *strained*. Ask students to remember a time that they have seen food strained: **Model** *If I boil vegetables, I don't want to serve them with the water. I pour the water and vegetables through a strainer with holes in it. The water goes through the strainer, but the food stays inside. When I'm finished, the vegetables have been strained.*

To Sum Up

> **Beginning/Early Intermediate** ▶ Have students work in pairs to reread all the To Sum Up features from the beginning of the story on page 48. **Ask:** *What are two things that Thoreau believes? (Government should be limited; People should follow their conscience) How does he stand up for his beliefs? (He is willing to go to jail.)*

If you **sign on** to something, you agree to participate in it.

strained (strānd) *v.* pressed or poured through a device with holes for filtering

After my own fashion means "in the way that I want."

Someone who offers a choice between *"your money or your life"* will kill you unless you give up your money.

To Sum Up

➤ Thoreau also refused to pay a poll tax. He was put in jail for one night.

➤ He felt free even though he was in jail.

➤ He says that the state can never force you to change what you believe.

---

not wish to be regarded as a member of any incorporated society which I have not joined." This I gave to the town clerk; and he has it. The State, having thus learned that I did not wish to be regarded as a member of that church, has never made a like demand on me since; though it said that it must adhere to its original presumption that time. If I had known how to name them, I should then have signed off in detail from all the societies which I never **signed on** to; but I did not know where to find a complete list.

I have paid no poll-tax[10] for six years. I was put into a jail once on this account, for one night; and, as I stood considering the walls of solid stone, two or three feet thick, the door of wood and iron, a foot thick, and the iron grating which strained the light, I could not help being struck with the foolishness of that institution which treated me as if I were mere flesh and blood and bones, to be locked up. I wondered that it should have concluded at length that this was the best use it could put me to, and had never thought to avail itself of my services in some way. I saw that, if there was a wall of stone between me and my townsmen, there was a still more difficult one to climb or break through, before they could get to be as free as I was. I did not for a moment feel confined, and the walls seemed a great waste of stone and mortar. I felt as if I alone of all my townsmen had paid my tax. They plainly did not know how to treat me, but behaved like persons who are underbred. In every threat and in every compliment there was a blunder[11]; for they thought that my chief desire was to stand the other side of that stone wall. I could not but smile to see how industriously they locked the door on my meditations, which followed them out again without let[12] or hindrance, and they were really all that was dangerous. As they could not reach me, they had resolved to punish my body; just as boys, if they cannot come at some person against whom they have a spite, will abuse his dog. I saw that the State was half-witted, that it was timid as a lone woman with her silver spoons, and that it did not know its friends from its foes, and I lost all my remaining respect for it, and pitied it.

Thus the State never intentionally confronts a man's sense, intellectual or moral, but only his body, his senses. It is not armed with superior wit or honesty, but with superior physical strength. I was not born to be forced. I will breathe **after my own fashion**. Let us see who is the strongest. What force has a multitude? They only can force me who obey a higher law than I. They force me to become like themselves. I do not hear of *men* being *forced* to live this way or that by masses of men. What sort of life were *that* to live? When I meet a government which says to me, **"Your money or your life,"** why should I be in haste to give it my money? It may be in a great strait, and not know what to do: I cannot help that. It must help itself; do as I do. It is not worth the while to snivel about it. I am not responsible for the successful working of the machinery of society.

10. A ***poll-tax*** is money that people must pay in order to vote. Today, poll-taxes are illegal in the United States.
11. A ***blunder*** is a serious mistake. Someone who makes a blunder is careless or confused.
12. ***Let*** in this sentence means "something that blocks movement."

Note Taking

Reread the text on the left. Then record your answers to the items below.

1. The most interesting word on this page is _____

   because _____ .

2. One word that I didn't know on this page is _____

   It means _____ .

3. One thing I read on this page that I already knew is _____

   _____ .

4. One thing I learned on this page that I didn't know is _____

   _____ .

5. Recap, or write in your own words what you learned by reading this page.

   _____

   _____

   _____

   _____

6. Summarize below what you've recorded.

Most Interesting Word	New Word	One Thing I Already Knew	One Thing I Learned

Note Taking

To help students get started, you might want to model your thinking process for completing one of the items.

Interactive Question-Response

Reflect

Partner Talk Have students work in pairs to answer. To help students get started: **Model** *To answer this question, I would start by asking what statements of Thoreau's could be proven. For example, he says that the rooms were whitewashed once a month. Someone who wanted to check that statement could find out whether the rooms really were whitewashed once a month. So this is a fact. On the other hand, I would look for Thoreau's own beliefs to find opinion statements. For example, the first sentence of the paragraph says that the night in jail was interesting. Other people might feel very differently about spending a night in jail. This is Thoreau's own opinion.*

Write the following sentence frames on the board to help students organize their thoughts.

Another statement that can be definitely proven is _____. Another statement of Thoreau's own beliefs is _____.

In their shirt-sleeves means "wearing a shirt without a coat."

In my turn means "when my turn came."

Someone who is honest **as the world goes** is honest compared to most people.

To Sum Up

➤ Thoreau thought that his night in jail was interesting.

➤ Thoreau's roommate showed him how things were done in jail. Thoreau liked him.

➤ The roommate was in jail for burning a barn. Thoreau believes he is innocent.

I am not the son of the engineer. I perceive that, when an acorn and a chestnut fall side by side, the one does not remain inert to make way for the other, but both obey their own laws, and spring and grow and flourish as best they can, till one, perchance, overshadows and destroys the other. If a plant cannot live according to its nature, it dies; and so a man.

The night in prison was novel and interesting enough. The prisoners **in their shirt-sleeves** were enjoying a chat and the evening air in the doorway, when I entered. But the jailer said, "Come, boys, it is time to lock up"; and so they dispersed, and I heard the sound of their steps returning into the hollow apartments. My room-mate was introduced to me by the jailer as "a first-rate fellow and a clever man." When the door was locked, he showed me where to hang my hat, and how he managed matters there. The rooms were whitewashed once a month; and this one, at least, was the whitest, most simply furnished, and probably the neatest apartment in the town. He naturally wanted to know where I came from, and what brought me there; and, when I had told him, I asked him **in my turn** how he came there, presuming him to be an honest man, of course; and, **as the world goes,** I believe he was. "Why," said he, "they accuse me of burning a barn; but I never did it." As near as I could discover, he had probably gone to bed in a barn when drunk, and smoked his pipe there; and so a barn was burnt. He had the reputation of being a clever man, had been there some three months waiting for his trial to come on, and would have to wait as much longer; but he was quite domesticated and contented, since he got his board for nothing, and thought that he was well treated.

REFLECT

Evaluate Evidence
Reread Thoreau's description of the jail. Write down two facts and two opinions that Thoreau provides in this description.

Possible answer: Facts: The prisoners in their shirt-sleeves

were enjoying a chat; the rooms were whitewashed once

a month; Opinions: The night in prison was novel and

interesting; the roommate was an honest man.

_____

 Talk about your answer with a partner.

Differentiated Instruction

Clarify the Text Support students in understanding Thoreau's night in jail.

Beginning/Early Intermediate Read aloud the third bullet in To Sum Up. **Ask:** *Does Thoreau think that his roommate is guilty of burning down a barn? (no)*

Intermediate Have partners read aloud the boxed text on page 54. **Ask:** *What does Thoreau's roommate show him? (where to put his hat and how things are done) How does Thoreau think the barn burned down? (He thinks his roommate accidentally set fire to it while drunk.)*

Early Advanced Explain to students that authors sometimes use irony, or the reversal of expectations, to make a point. **Ask:** *What is surprising about Thoreau's description of the jail? (Everyone seems friendly and in a good mood.) What point do you think Thoreau is trying to make? (The jail is more civilized than the town outside.)*

Note Taking

Reread the text on the left. Then record your answers to the items below.

1. The most interesting word on this page is _____

   because _____.

2. One word that I didn't know on this page is _____.

   It means _____.

3. One thing I read on this page that I already knew is _____

   _____.

4. One thing I learned on this page that I didn't know is _____

   _____.

5. Recap, or write in your own words what you learned by reading this page.

   _____

   _____

   _____

   _____

6. Summarize below what you've recorded.

Most Interesting Word	New Word	One Thing I Already Knew	One Thing I Learned

Note Taking

To help students get started, you might want to model your thinking process for completing one of the items.

Interactive Question-Response

Comprehension Check

If students have difficulty responding: **Model** *In order to answer this question, I would look for the place in the text where he talks about getting out of jail. In the beginning of the last full paragraph, Thoreau writes, "When I came out of prison—for someone interfered, and paid that tax. . ." For can be used to mean "because." So Thoreau is explaining why he got out of jail. I remember that he was put in jail for not paying his tax. So it makes sense that he got out when someone else paid it for him.*

Someone who has ***broken out*** from prison has escaped.

Something ***printed in a circular form*** has been printed so that it can be passed around among a small group.

If you ***pump someone dry***, you ask for as much information from that person as you can.

Green here means "inexperienced."

Comprehension Check

Why is Thoreau set free from the jail?

Possible answer: Somebody

pays his tax for him.

_____

_____

_____

To Sum Up

➤ Thoreau sees his town from the jail window. It looks different to him.

➤ The next morning his roommate goes to work. Thoreau is released.

➤ Thoreau sees life differently after his night in jail.

56

He occupied one window, and I the other; and I saw that if one stayed there long, his principal business would be to look out the window. I had soon read all the tracts[13] that were left there, and examined where former prisoners had **broken out,** and where a grate had been sawed off, and heard the history of the various occupants of that room; for I found that even here there was a history and a gossip which never circulated beyond the walls of the jail. Probably this is the only house in the town where verses are composed, which are afterward **printed in a circular form,** but not published. I was shown quite a long list of verses which were composed by some young men who had been detected in an attempt to escape, who avenged themselves by singing them.

I **pumped my fellow prisoner as dry as I could,** for fear I should never see him again; but at length he showed me which was my bed, and left me to blow out the lamp. It was like traveling into a far country, such as I had never expected to behold, to lie there for one night. It seemed to me that I never had heard the town clock strike before, nor the evening sounds of the village; for we slept with the windows open, which were inside the grating. It was to see my native village in the light of the Middle Ages, and our Concord was turned into a Rhine[14] stream, and visions of knights and castles passed before me. They were the voices of old burghers[15] that I heard in the streets. I was an involuntary spectator and auditor[16] of whatever was done and said in the kitchen of the adjacent village inn—a wholly new and rare experience to me. It was a closer view of my native town. I was fairly inside of it. I never had seen its institutions before. This is one of its peculiar institutions; for it is a shire town.[17] I began to comprehend what its inhabitants were about.

In the morning, our breakfasts were put through the hole in the door, in small oblong-square tin pans, made to fit, and holding a pint of chocolate, with brown bread, and an iron spoon. When they called for the vessels again, I was **green** enough to return what bread I had left; but my comrade seized it, and said that I should lay that up for lunch or dinner. Soon after he was let out to work at haying in a neighboring field, whither he went every day, and would not be back till noon; so he bade me good-day, saying that he doubted if he should see me again.

When I came out of prison—for some one interfered, and paid that tax—I did not perceive that great changes had taken place on the common, such as he observed who went in a youth and emerged a tottering and gray-headed man; and yet a change had to my eyes come over the scene—the town, and State, and country—greater than any that mere time could effect. I saw yet more distinctly the State in which I lived….

13. ***Tracts*** are pamphlets or booklets about politics or religion.
14. The ***Concord*** refers to the Concord River in Massachusetts. The Rhine River is located in Germany and Holland.
15. ***Burghers*** are people who live in a city.
16. Here, ***auditor*** means "someone who hears," or "someone who listens."
17. A ***shire town***, or county town, is the main town in a particular area.

Word Study [BLM]

Negative Prefixes: *un-, im-, in-, il-, dis-, a-,* and *ir-*

Point out the word *involuntary* in the text. Explain to students that negative prefixes such as *un-, im-, in-, il-, dis-, a-,* and *ir-* change root words to their antonyms. Examples include *happy/ unhappy, legal/illegal,* and *natural/unnatural.*

Then have students practice adding negative prefixes to other words by completing the activity on page A12.

Note Taking

Reread the text on the left. Then record your answers to the items below.

1. The most interesting word on this page is _____

   because _____ .

2. One word that I didn't know on this page is _____ .

   It means _____ .

3. One thing I read on this page that I already knew is _____

   _____ .

4. One thing I learned on this page that I didn't know is _____

   _____ .

5. Recap, or write in your own words what you learned by reading this page.

   _____

   _____

   _____

   _____

6. Summarize below what you've recorded.

Most Interesting Word	New Word	One Thing I Already Knew	One Thing I Learned

Note Taking

To help students get started, you might want to model your thinking process for completing one of the items.

Interactive Question-Response

Literary Element Argument

If students have difficulty responding: **Model** *In order to answer this question, I would look carefully at the sentence where Thoreau talks about monarchy and democracy. In the first part of the sentence, he says that moving from monarchy to democracy is progress. In the second part of the sentence, he says that the positive change is respect for the individual. So a democracy has more respect for an individual than a monarchy does.* **Ask:** *Why might Thoreau think that a democracy has more respect for the individual than a monarchy does? (individuals in a democracy have more power to shape the laws that they must obey)*

Content Vocabulary

Read aloud the word and definition for *individual*. Ask students to list some rights that individuals have in the United States. **Model** *I could look in the Constitution to see what rights individuals have. For instance, I have the right to speak freely. I also have the right to a fair trial if I am accused of a crime.*

Have a student read aloud the word and definition for *authority*. Ask students to read the sentence containing the word *authority* in "*from* Civil Disobedience" and work in pairs to paraphrase the sentence.

Reflect

Partner Talk Have students work in pairs to answer. To help students get started: **Model** *To answer this, I would reread the paragraph and the footnotes to clarify my understanding of the text.* Write the following sentence frame on the board to help students organize their thoughts.

Thoreau argues that _____. (the State must respect the individual)

Thoreau supports his argument by _____. (referencing thoughts put forth by Confucius)

In an ***absolute monarchy***, the king or the queen has complete power. In a ***limited monarchy***, the king or the queen shares power with others.

Literary Element

Argument What quality separates a monarchy from a democracy, according to Thoreau's argument?

_____

_____

_____

individual (in′ də vij′ oo əl) *n.* a single person

The ***rights of man*** are the basic freedoms that every person should have.

authority (ə thôr′ ə tē) *n.* power to tell someone what to do

Here, ***bore this kind of fruit*** means "developed people like this."

To Sum Up

➤ Thoreau wonders whether democracy is the best kind of government.

➤ He thinks the best government would treat everyone with respect.

The authority of government, even such as I am willing to submit to—for I will cheerfully obey those who know and can do better than I, and in many things even those who neither know nor can do so well—is still an impure one: to be strictly just, it must have the sanction[18] and consent of the governed. It can have no pure right over my person and property but what I concede to it. The progress from an **absolute to a limited monarchy,** from a limited monarchy to a democracy, is a progress toward a true respect for the <u>individual</u>. Even the Chinese philosopher[19] was wise enough to regard the individual as the basis of the empire. Is a democracy, such as we know it, the last improvement possible in government? Is it not possible to take a step further towards recognizing and organizing the **rights of man?** There will never be a really free and enlightened State until the State comes to recognize the individual as a higher and independent power, from which all its own power and <u>authority</u> are derived, and treats him accordingly. I please myself with imagining a State at least which can afford to be just to all men, and to treat the individual with respect as a neighbor; which even would not think it inconsistent with its own repose[20] if a few were to live aloof from it, not meddling with it, nor <u>embraced</u> by it, who fulfilled all the duties of neighbors and fellow-men. A State which **bore this kind of fruit,** and suffered it to drop off as fast as it ripened, would prepare the way for a still more perfect and glorious State, which also I have imagined, but not yet anywhere seen.

18. ***Sanction*** means "approval" or "support."
19. The ***Chinese philosopher*** is Confucius (c. 551–479 B.C.).
20. ***Repose*** means "peace of mind."

REFLECT

Evaluate Evidence
Reread the closing paragraph of "Civil Disobedience." What is one fact that Thoreau uses to support his argument?

_____

_____

_____

_____

_____

 Talk about your answer with a partner.

Note Taking

Reread the text on the left. Then record your answers to the items below.

1. The most interesting word on this page is _____

   because _____ .

2. One word that I didn't know on this page is _____ .

   It means _____ .

3. One thing I read on this page that I already knew is _____

   _____ .

4. One thing I learned on this page that I didn't know is _____

   _____ .

5. Recap, or write in your own words what you learned by reading this page.

   _____

   _____

   _____

   _____

6. Summarize below what you've recorded.

Most Interesting Word	New Word	One Thing I Already Knew	One Thing I Learned

Note Taking

To help students get started, you might want to model your thinking process for completing one of the items.

Interactive Question-Response

Comparing Literature

Compare Cultures If students have difficulty answering: **Model** *I would answer this question by process of elimination. For example, both Thoreau and Gandhi talk about being arrested for what they believe. I also remember that Thoreau was against the Mexican War. Gandhi is against violence, so he is also probably against war. On the other hand, Gandhi talks about a sacred river in the first paragraph of the essay. I don't remember Thoreau talking about sacred rivers, and rivers are not usually considered sacred in the United States.* **Ask:** *What does the idea of a sacred river suggest about how Indians view nature? (They have great respect for nature.)*

Comparing Literature

Which phrase expresses a difference between Gandhi and Thoreau's cultures?

☑ sacred river
☐ imprisoned for beliefs
☐ against war

A **breach of peace** is a violent or disorderly event.

Every **nook and corner** means "everywhere."

To **sit still** is to sit without moving.

To Sum Up

➤ Gandhi is speaking to his followers before they march.
➤ He reminds them that they believe in nonviolence.
➤ Gandhi asks them to break the salt laws if he is arrested.

In all probability this will be my last speech to you. Even if the Government allow me to march tomorrow morning, this will be my last speech on the sacred banks of the Sabarmati.[1] Possibly these may be the last words of my life here.

I have already told you yesterday what I had to say. Today I shall confine myself to what you should do after my companions and I are arrested. The program[2] of the march to Jalalpur[3] must be fulfilled as originally settled. The enlistment of the volunteers for this purpose should be confined to Gujarat[4] only. From what I have seen and heard during the last fortnight, I am inclined to believe that the stream of civil resisters will flow unbroken.

But let there be not a semblance of **breach of peace** even after all of us have been arrested. We have resolved to utilize all our resources in the pursuit of an exclusively nonviolent struggle. Let no one commit a wrong in anger. This is my hope and prayer. I wish these words of mine reached **every nook and corner** of the land. My task shall be done if I perish and so do my comrades. It will then be for the Working Committee of the Congress[5] to show you the way and it will be up to you to follow its lead. So long as I have not reached Jalalpur, let nothing be done in contravention to the authority vested in me by the Congress. But once I am arrested, the whole responsibility shifts to the Congress. No one who believes in nonviolence, as a creed, need, therefore, **sit still.** My compact with the Congress ends as soon as I am arrested. In that case there should be no slackness in the enrolment of volunteers. Wherever possible, civil disobedience of salt laws should be started. These laws can be violated in three ways. It is an offense to manufacture salt wherever there are facilities for doing so. The possession and sale of contraband salt, which

1. The **Sabarmati** is a river in western India.
2. **Program** here means "mission."
3. **Jalalpur** is a city in India. It was the last stop on Gandhi's march to Dandi.
4. **Gujarat** is a state in western India.
5. The **Congress** is the Indian National Congress. Gandhi led this political party in the 1920s and 1930s.

Fluency

Expression and Intonation: Bring Out Meaning

Intermediate/Early Advanced ➤ Tell students that they will be doing a choral reading of the first two lines on this page. Remind students to read with expression and tone that matches the emotion, meaning, tone, or mood of the passage. Model the fluency skill as you read the text at a moderate tempo. Then have one student read a sentence. Have another student join in, and a third, and so on. When students reach the end of the passage, have pairs of students reread to each other. To assess individual fluency, use the Oral Reading Guidelines on page T16.

Beginning/Early Intermediate ➤ Have these students choral read only the first paragraph of the passage. Before they begin, model the pronunciation of the text. Then have students practice reading the paragraph in pairs before the choral reading.

Note Taking

Reread the text on the left. Then record your answers to the items below.

1. The most interesting word on this page is _____

   because _____ .

2. One word that I didn't know on this page is _____

   It means _____ .

3. One thing I read on this page that I already knew is _____

   _____ .

4. One thing I learned on this page that I didn't know is _____

   _____ .

5. Recap, or write in your own words what you learned by reading this page.

   _____

   _____

   _____

   _____

6. Summarize below what you've recorded.

Most Interesting Word	New Word	One Thing I Already Knew	One Thing I Learned

Note Taking

To help students get started, you might want to model your thinking process for completing one of the items.

On the Eve of Historic Dandi March

Interactive Question-Response

Content Vocabulary

Read aloud the word and definition of *boycott.* **Ask:** *Why does Gandhi want people to boycott the law courts? (to pressure the government into granting India independence)*

If you have a *free hand*, you are allowed to do what you want.

All and sundry means "everyone."

boycott (boi′ kot) *v.* to protest by refusing to participate

Shoulder to shoulder means "together."

To Sum Up

➤ Gandhi lists the things people can do to break the salt laws.

➤ He also suggests other ways that people can protest the government.

➤ He wants his followers to stop working with the government in any way..

62

---

includes natural salt or salt earth, is also an offense. The purchasers of such salt will be equally guilty. To carry away the natural salt deposits on the seashore is likewise violation of law. So is the hawking of such salt. In short, you may choose any one or all of these devices to break the salt monopoly.

We are, however, not to be content with this alone. There is no ban by the Congress and wherever the local workers have self-confidence other suitable measures may be adopted. I stress only one condition, namely, let our pledge of truth and nonviolence as the only means for the attainment of Swaraj[6] be faithfully kept. For the rest, every one has a **free hand.** But, that does not give a license to **all and sundry** to carry on on their own responsibility. Wherever there are local leaders, their orders should be obeyed by the people. Where there are no leaders and only a handful of men have faith in the program, they may do what they can, if they have enough self-confidence. They have a right, nay it is their duty, to do so. The history of the world is full of instances of men who rose to leadership, by sheer force of self-confidence, bravery and tenacity. We too, if we sincerely aspire to Swaraj and are impatient to attain it, should have similar self-confidence. Our ranks will swell and our hearts strengthen, as the number of our arrests by the Government increases.

Much can be done in many other ways besides these. The liquor and foreign cloth shops can be picketed. We can refuse to pay taxes if we have the requisite strength. The lawyers can give up practice. The public can boycott the law courts by refraining from litigation. Government servants can resign their posts. In the midst of the despair reigning all round people quake with fear of losing employment. Such men are unfit for Swaraj. But why this despair? The number of Government servants in the country does not exceed a few hundred thousand. What about the rest? Where are they to go? Even free India will not be able to accommodate a greater number of public servants. A Collector then will not need the number of servants he has got today. He will be his own servant. Our starving millions can by no means afford this enormous expenditure. If, therefore, we are sensible enough, let us bid goodbye to Government employment, no matter if it is the post of a judge or a peon. Let all who are cooperating with the Government in one way or another, be it by paying taxes, keeping titles, or sending children to official schools, etc., withdraw their cooperation in all or as many ways as possible. Then there are women who can stand **shoulder to shoulder** with men in this struggle.

You may take it as my will. It was the message that I desired to impart to you before starting on the march or for the jail. I wish that there should be no suspension or abandonment of the war that commences tomorrow morning or earlier, if I am arrested before that time. I shall eagerly await the news that ten batches are ready as soon as my batch is arrested. I believe there are men in India to complete the work begun by me.

---

6. *Swaraj* means "home rule." The Indians wanted to rule themselves. They did not want to be ruled by the British any longer.

Differentiated Instruction

Clarify the Text Support students in understanding Gandhi's speech to his followers.

Beginning/Early Intermediate ▶ Read aloud the third bullet in To Sum Up. **Ask:** *What does Gandhi want his followers to stop doing? (working with the government)*

Intermediate ▶ Have partners read aloud the boxed text on page 62. Have them complete the following sentence frames. *Gandhi tells his followers to picket ____. (liquor stores and foreign cloth shops) If he is arrested, he wants his followers to ____. (continue the struggle)*

Early Advanced ▶ Point out that Gandhi makes an argument in the second full paragraph about people who are afraid of becoming unemployed. Have students paraphrase the conclusion of this argument and the reasons that Gandhi gives to support his conclusion.

Note Taking

Reread the text on the left. Then record your answers to the items below.

1. The most interesting word on this page is _____

   because _____ .

2. One word that I didn't know on this page is _____ .

   It means _____ .

3. One thing I read on this page that I already knew is _____

   _____ .

4. One thing I learned on this page that I didn't know is _____

   _____ .

5. Recap, or write in your own words what you learned by reading this page.

   _____

   _____

   _____

   _____

6. Summarize below what you've recorded.

Most Interesting Word	New Word	One Thing I Already Knew	One Thing I Learned

Note Taking

To help students get started, you might want to model your thinking process for completing one of the items.

On the Eve of Historic Dandi March

victorious (vĭk tôr ē əs) *adj.* winning

If you **turn a deaf ear,** you refuse to listen.

Your **inner voice** is your conscience, or your sense of right and wrong.

I have faith in the righteousness of our cause and the purity of our weapons. And where the means are clean, there God is undoubtedly present with His blessings. And where these three combine, there defeat is an impossibility. A Satyagrahi,[7] whether free or incarcerated, is ever victorious. He is vanquished only when he forsakes truth and nonviolence and **turns a deaf ear** to the **inner voice.** If, therefore, there is such a thing as defeat for even a Satyagrahi, he alone is the cause of it. God bless you all and keep off all obstacles from the path in the struggle that begins tomorrow.

7. A **Satyagrahi** is someone who believes in nonviolence. He or she works for justice in the world without using violent methods.

To Sum Up

➤ Gandhi believes that he and his followers will win.

➤ He tells them that the government cannot defeat them.

➤ He says that they can only defeat themselves. The people must be true to their beliefs.

64

REFLECT

Evaluate Evidence
Reread the text on page 64. Is Gandhi expressing facts or opinions in this paragraph?

Possible answer: Gandhi is expressing his opinion. He

believes that he and his followers will succeed.

How do you know?

Possible answer: He uses words such as "I believe" and

"I have faith." These words are used to express an opinion.

Talk about your answer with a partner.

Interactive Question-Response

Content Vocabulary

Have a student read the word and definition for *victorious.* **Ask:** *According to Gandhi, what makes a person victorious? (staying true to one's beliefs)*

To Sum Up

Beginning/Early Intermediate ➤ Have students work in pairs to reread the To Sum Up boxes from the beginning of the selection on page 60. Then ask students to decide what the three most important points are in Gandhi's speech. Have them fill in this outline:

Gandhi's most important points to his followers are that they should

A. *(remain nonviolent)*

B. *(avoid cooperating with the government)*

C. *(stay true to their beliefs)*

Reflect

Partner Talk Have students work in pairs to answer. To help students get started: **Model** *To answer this, I would reread the paragraph on this page and the Reading Strategy on page 46. The Reading Strategy says that opinions are statements of an author's beliefs and cannot be proven. In the passage, I see that Gandhi uses words such as "I believe" and "I have faith," which show that he is expressing his opinion. He is hopeful that he and his followers will succeed.* Write the following sentence frame on the board to help students organize their thoughts.

Gandhi uses words such as _____, (I believe and I have faith) which show that he is expressing _____. (his opinion)

Note Taking

Reread the text on the left. Then record your answers to the items below.

1. The most interesting word on this page is _____

   because _____ .

2. One word that I didn't know on this page is _____ .

   It means _____ .

3. One thing I read on this page that I already knew is _____

   _____ .

4. One thing I learned on this page that I didn't know is _____

   _____ .

5. Recap, or write in your own words what you learned by reading this page.

   _____

   _____

   _____

   _____

6. Summarize below what you've recorded.

Most Interesting Word	New Word	One Thing I Already Knew	One Thing I Learned

Note Taking

To help students get started, you might want to model your thinking process for completing one of the items.

Interactive Question-Response

Content Vocabulary

Read the word and definition for *extraordinary*. Point out that Mandela describes apartheid in South Africa as an "extraordinary human disaster." **Ask:** *What is another way to say extraordinary human disaster? (terrible tragedy for people)*

A *rainbow gathering* is a group of people with many different ethnic backgrounds.

extraordinary (iks trôr′ r də ner′ ē) *adj.* very unusual

On our own soil means "in our country."

A *common victory* is a victory that people have won together.

May 10 dawned bright and clear. For the past few days, I had been pleasantly besieged by arriving dignitaries[1] and world leaders who were coming to pay their respects before the inauguration.[2] The inauguration would be the largest gathering ever of international leaders on South African soil.

The ceremonies took place in the lovely sandstone amphitheater formed by the Union Buildings in Pretoria.[3] For decades, this had been the seat of white supremacy, and now it was the site of a **rainbow gathering** of different colors and nations for the installation of South Africa's first democratic, nonracial government.

On that lovely autumn day I was accompanied by my daughter Zenani. On the podium, Mr. de Klerk[4] was first sworn in as second deputy president. Then Thabo Mbeki[5] was sworn in as first deputy president. When it was my turn, I pledged to obey and uphold the constitution and to devote myself to the well-being of the republic and its people. To the assembled guests and the watching world, I said:

Today, all of us do, by our presence here…confer[6] glory and hope to newborn liberty. Out of the experience of an extraordinary human disaster that lasted too long, must be born a society of which all humanity will be proud.

…We, who were outlaws not so long ago, have today been given the rare privilege to be host to the nations of the world **on our own soil.** We thank all of our distinguished international guests for having come to take possession with the people of our country of what is, after all, a **common victory** for justice, for peace, for human dignity.

We have, at last, achieved our political emancipation.[7] We pledge ourselves to liberate all our people from the continuing bondage of poverty, deprivation, suffering, gender, and other discrimination.

Never, never, and never again shall it be that this beautiful land will again experience the oppression of one by another…. The sun shall never set on so glorious a human achievement.

Let freedom reign. God bless Africa!

To Sum Up

➤ Nelson Mandela is going to a ceremony in South Africa.

➤ He will become the leader of South Africa's first nonracial government.

➤ He says that South Africa must set an example for the rest of the world.

1. **Dignitaries** are people who hold important positions.
2. An **inauguration** is a kind of ceremony. It celebrates the beginning of someone's term as an official.
3. **Pretoria** is the capital of South Africa.
4. **F. de Klerk** was the president of South Africa from 1989 to 1994.
5. **Thabo Mbeki** is a South African leader. He became president of South Africa in 1999.
6. **Confer** means "to give an honor."
7. **Emancipation** is the process of becoming free from control.

Differentiated Instruction

Clarify the Text Support students in understanding Mandela's speech.

Beginning/Early Intermediate Read aloud the three bullets in To Sum Up. **Ask:** *Who is the new leader in South Africa? (Nelson Mandela)*

Intermediate Have partners read aloud the boxed text on page 66. **Ask:** *Who has come to the inauguration? (dignitaries and world leaders) What does Mandela think is a glorious human achievement? (the end of racial oppression in South Africa)*

Early Advanced Have students imagine that they are newspaper reporters covering Mandela's inauguration. Ask them to write a brief news item summarizing Mandela's speech.

Note Taking

Reread the text on the left. Then record your answers to the items below.

1. The most interesting word on this page is _____

   because _____.

2. One word that I didn't know on this page is _____.

   It means _____.

3. One thing I read on this page that I already knew is _____

   _____.

4. One thing I learned on this page that I didn't know is _____

   _____.

5. Recap, or write in your own words what you learned by reading this page.

   _____

   _____

   _____

   _____

6. Summarize below what you've recorded.

Most Interesting Word	New Word	One Thing I Already Knew	One Thing I Learned

Note Taking

To help students get started, you might want to model your thinking process for completing one of the items.

Interactive Question-Response

Content Vocabulary

Have a student read aloud the word and definition for *domination*. Then have students read the sentence from the passage containing *domination*. **Ask:** *Who set up the system of domination? (South African whites) How did they treat blacks in South Africa? (They treated them unfairly.)*

To Sum Up

Beginning/Early Intermediate ▶ Have students work in pairs to reread the To Sum Up features on pages 66 and 68. **Ask:** *What change does Mandela's election represent? (the end of racial government in South Africa) Did Mandela achieve this change by himself or did he have help? (He had help.)*

Lifted our eyes means "looked up."

Days gone by means "in the past."

If you *know something by heart*, you have memorized it.

People who *patch up their differences* agree to get along.

domination (dom′ a nā′ shan) *n.* the state of controlling someone or something

To Sum Up

➤ Black and white South Africans sing their national songs at the ceremony.

➤ Mandela thinks about the racist system that he helped end.

➤ He remembers the courage of the people that helped him change South Africa.

A few moments later we all **lifted our eyes** in awe as a spectacular array of South African jets, helicopters, and troop carriers roared in perfect formation over the Union Buildings. It was not only a display of pinpoint precision and military force, but a demonstration of the military's loyalty to democracy, to a new government that had been freely and fairly elected. Only moments before, the highest generals of the South African Defense Force and police, their chests bedecked[8] with ribbons and medals from **days gone by,** saluted me and pledged their loyalty. I was not unmindful of the fact that not so many years before they would not have saluted but arrested me. Finally a chevron of Impala jets[9] left a smoke trail of the black, red, green, blue, white, and gold of the new South African flag.

The day was symbolized for me by the playing of our two national anthems, and the vision of whites singing *"Nkosi Sikelel' iAfrika"* and blacks singing *"Die Stem,"* the old anthem of the republic. Although that day, neither group knew the lyrics of the anthem they once despised, they would soon **know the words by heart.**

On the day of the inauguration, I was overwhelmed with a sense of history. In the first decade of the twentieth century, a few years after the bitter Anglo-Boer War[10] and before my own birth, the white-skinned peoples of South Africa **patched up their differences** and erected a system of racial domination against the dark-skinned peoples of their own land. The structure they created formed the basis of one of the harshest, most inhumane societies the world has ever known. Now, in the last decade of the twentieth century, and my own eighth decade as a man, that system had been overturned forever and replaced by one that recognized the rights and freedoms of all peoples regardless of the color of their skin.

That day had come about through the unimaginable sacrifices of thousands of my people, people whose suffering and courage can never be counted or repaid. I felt that day, as I have on so many other days, that I was simply the sum of all those African patriots who had gone before me. That long and noble line ended and now began again with me. I was pained that I was not able to thank them and that they were not able to see what their sacrifices had wrought.[11]

The policy of apartheid created a deep and lasting wound in my country and my people. All of us will spend many years, if not generations, recovering from that profound hurt. But the decades of oppression and brutality had another, unintended effect, and that was that it produced the Oliver Tambos, the Walter Sisulus, the Chief Luthulis, the Yusuf Dadoos, the Bram Fischers, the Robert Sobukwes[12] of our time—men of such extraordinary courage, wisdom, and generosity that their like may never be known again. Perhaps it requires such depth of oppression to create such heights of character. My country is rich in the minerals and gems that lie beneath its soil, but I have always known that its greatest wealth is its people, finer and truer than the purest diamonds.

8. *Bedecked* means "decorated" or "clothed."
9. A *chevron* is a V-shaped pattern. An *Impala jet* is a fighter plane.
10. The *Anglo-Boer War* (1899–1902) was fought between the British and the Boers. The Boers are South Africans who came from Holland.
11. *Wrought* means "made."
12. *Oliver Tambo, Walter Sisulu, Chief Luthuli, Yusuf Dadoo, Bram Fischer,* and *Robert Sobukwe* are people who also fought to change South Africa.

Note Taking

Reread the text on the left. Then record your answers to the items below.

1. The most interesting word on this page is _____

   because _____.

2. One word that I didn't know on this page is _____.

   It means _____.

3. One thing I read on this page that I already knew is _____

   _____.

4. One thing I learned on this page that I didn't know is _____

   _____.

5. Recap, or write in your own words what you learned by reading this page.

   _____

   _____

   _____

   _____

6. Summarize below what you've recorded.

Most Interesting Word	New Word	One Thing I Already Knew	One Thing I Learned

Note Taking

To help students get started, you might want to model your thinking process for completing one of the items.

Interactive Question-Response

Comparing Literature

Compare Cultures If students have difficulty responding: **Model** *To answer this question, I would begin by thinking about the main goal of Mandela's struggle. Mandela says on this page that he was trying to bring about a great transformation. That transformation was the end of apartheid in South Africa. I can look back at the other essays to see the goals of the other authors. Thoreau talks about the importance of the individual throughout his essay. The last page states that government should protect individual rights. Gandhi and his followers are marching to make India independent.*
Ask: *Does anything connect the different goals of Thoreau, Gandhi, and Mandela? (All of them fought systems that treated people unequally: slavery in the United States, colonialism in India, and apartheid in South Africa)*

Time and again means "often."

Comparing Literature

Mandela talks about giving one's life for an idea. What idea did Mandela fight for? How was it different from what Thoreau and Gandhi fought for?

Possible answer: Mandela

fought for a nonracial South

Africa, Thoreau fought for

the rights of the individual,

and Gandhi fought for an

independent India.

If you are **pushed to your limits**, you are treated as badly as you can withstand.

With our eyes wide open means "with complete awareness."

To Sum Up

➤ Mandela learned how to be brave from the people he worked with.
➤ He always had faith that his side would win. He believed that people were good.
➤ He was ready to give up things for the struggle. His family suffered as well.

It is from these comrades in the struggle that I learned the meaning of courage. **Time and again,** I have seen men and women risk and give their lives for an idea. I have seen men stand up to attacks and torture without breaking, showing a strength and resiliency that defies the imagination. I learned that courage was not the absence of fear, but the triumph over it. I felt fear myself more times than I can remember, but I hid it behind a mask of boldness. The brave man is not he who does not feel afraid, but he who conquers that fear.

I never lost hope that this great transformation would occur. Not only because of the great heroes I have already cited, but because of the courage of the ordinary men and women of my country. I always knew that deep down in every human heart, there is mercy and generosity. No one is born hating another person because of the color of his skin, or his background, or his religion. People must learn to hate, and if they can learn to hate, they can be taught to love, for love comes more naturally to the human heart than its opposite. Even in the grimmest times in prison, when my comrades and I were **pushed to our limits,** I would see a glimmer of humanity in one of the guards, perhaps just for a second, but it was enough to reassure me and keep me going. Man's goodness is a flame that can be hidden but never extinguished.

We took up the struggle **with our eyes wide open,** under no illusion that the path would be an easy one. As a young man, when I joined the African National Congress,[13] I saw the price my comrades paid for their beliefs, and it was high. For myself, I have never regretted my commitment to the struggle, and I was always prepared to face the hardships that affected me personally. But my family paid a terrible price, perhaps too dear a price for my commitment.

In life, every man has twin obligations—obligations to his family, to his parents, to his wife and children; and he has an obligation to his people, his community, his country. In a civil and humane society, each man is able to fulfill those obligations according to his own inclinations and abilities. But in a country like South Africa, it was almost impossible for a man of my birth and color to fulfill both of those obligations. In South Africa, a man of color who attempted to live as a human being was punished and isolated. In South Africa, a man who tried to fulfill his duty to his people was inevitably ripped from his family and home and was

13. The **African National Congress (ANC)** is a South African political party founded by blacks in 1912.

Note Taking

Reread the text on the left. Then record your answers to the items below.

1. The most interesting word on this page is _____

   because _____ .

2. One word that I didn't know on this page is _____ .

   It means _____ .

3. One thing I read on this page that I already knew is _____

   _____ .

4. One thing I learned on this page that I didn't know is _____

   _____ .

5. Recap, or write in your own words what you learned by reading this page.

   _____

   _____

   _____

   _____

6. Summarize below what you've recorded.

Most Interesting Word	New Word	One Thing I Already Knew	One Thing I Learned

_____

Note Taking

To help students get started, you might want to model your thinking process for completing one of the items.

Interactive Question-Response

Content Vocabulary

Have a student read the word and definition for *illusion*. Draw on the board two lines of equal length, one ending with concave arrows and the other ending with convex arrows (also known as the Mueller-Lyons arrow illusion). Ask students which line is longer. Show them that the two lines are the same length. **Ask:** *Why is this an example of illusion? (because the length of the lines is deceptive)*

Reflect

Partner Talk Have students work in pairs to answer. To help students get started: **Model** *To answer this question, I would start by asking which of Mandela's statements could be proven. For example, Mandela says he began to want freedom as a young man. Whether someone feels a certain way is a matter of fact, proven by what they say or how they act. When Mandela says that he wanted freedom as a young man, his statement is factual. But it is closely related to a statement of opinion. If Mandela said, "Freedom matters most," that would be a statement of his own personal belief.*

Write the following sentence frames on the board to help students organize their thoughts.

Another statement that can be definitely proven is ___. This statement is closely related to Mandela's personal belief that ___.

To gain something ***at the expense of*** someone else is to gain from his or her loss.

If your voice ***trails off***, it slowly gets softer.

---

illusion (ĭ lōō′ zhən) *n.* something that misleads or deceives

---

To Sum Up

➤ Mandela felt free when he was a child. He lived freely in his village.

➤ The only rules he had to follow were the rules of his family and tribe.

➤ Mandela realized that he was not really free when he was a young man.

---

forced to live a life apart, a twilight existence of secrecy and rebellion. I did not in the beginning choose to place my people above my family, but in attempting to serve my people, I found that I was prevented from fulfilling my obligations as a son, a brother, a father, and a husband.

In that way, my commitment to my people, to the millions of South Africans I would never know or meet, was **at the expense of** the people I knew best and loved most. It was as simple and yet as incomprehensible as the moment a small child asks her father, "Why can you not be with us?" And the father must utter the terrible words: "There are other children like you, a great many of them…" and then one's voice **trails off.**

I was not born with a hunger to be free. I was born free—free in every way that I could know. Free to run in the fields near my mother's hut, free to swim in the clear stream that ran through my village, free to roast mealies[14] under the stars and ride the broad backs of slow-moving bulls. As long as I obeyed my father and abided by the customs of my tribe, I was not troubled by the laws of man or God.

It was only when I began to learn that my boyhood freedom was an illusion, when I discovered as a young man that my freedom had already been taken from me, that I began to hunger for it. At first, as a student, I wanted freedom only for myself, the transitory freedoms of being able to stay out at night, read what I pleased, and go where I chose. Later, as a young man in Johannesburg, I yearned for the basic and honorable freedoms of achieving my potential, of earning my keep, of marrying and having a family—the freedom not to be obstructed in a lawful life.

14. A ***mealie*** is an ear of Indian corn.

REFLECT

Evaluate Evidence
Reread Mandela's description of his early life. Identify one statement that presents a fact. How could you rewrite that statement to present an opinion?

Possible answer: Fact: I wanted the freedom to stay out at

night; Opinion: I believe I should have the freedom to stay

out at night.

 Talk about your answer with a partner.

Reread the text on the left. Then record your answers to the items below.

1. The most interesting word on this page is _____

    because _____ .

2. One word that I didn't know on this page is _____ .

    It means _____ .

3. One thing I read on this page that I already knew is _____

    _____ .

4. One thing I learned on this page that I didn't know is _____

    _____ .

5. Recap, or write in your own words what you learned by reading this page.

    _____

    _____

    _____

    _____

6. Summarize below what you've recorded.

Most Interesting Word	New Word	One Thing I Already Knew	One Thing I Learned

Note Taking

To help students get started, you might want to model your thinking process for completing one of the items.

Interactive Question-Response

Comparing Literature

Compare Cultures If students have difficulty responding: **Model** *To answer this question, I would think about the points that Mandela makes on this page. He says that he could not be free until his people were free. He also says that the system in South Africa hurt the people in power as well as the people it oppressed. When I think back to the other selections, I remember that Thoreau emphasizes how he was always free, even in jail. So he would probably not agree that Mandela was not free. On the other hand, Gandhi doesn't talk about the people in power. He is concerned throughout his speech with his followers, the oppressed. So he never makes the point that an unjust system also hurts the people in power.* **Ask:** *What contrast between South Africa and the United States is suggested by the different points of view of Thoreau and Mandela? (The United States focuses more on the individual than South Africa does.) What difference between Gandhi's struggle and Mandela's do the different points made in their selections reflect? (Mandela's struggle took place within one country, while Gandhi was fighting an external power.)*

Comparing Literature

Compare Cultures Underline an idea on this page that is not expressed by Thoreau. Underline an idea on this page that is not expressed by Gandhi.

To **cast off** is to throw away.

To Sum Up

➤ Mandela joined the fight to win equal rights for his people.

➤ He wasn't just fighting for his people. The old system was bad for everyone.

➤ The victory that he has won is just the beginning of real freedom.

But then I slowly saw that not only was I not free, but my brothers and sisters were not free. I saw that it was not just my freedom that was curtailed, but the freedom of everyone who looked like I did. That is when I joined the African National Congress, and that is when the hunger for my own freedom became the greater hunger for the freedom of my people. It was this desire for the freedom of my people to live their lives with dignity and self-respect that animated my life, that transformed a frightened young man into a bold one, that drove a law-abiding attorney to become a criminal, that turned a family-loving husband into a man without a home, that forced a life-loving man to live like a monk. I am not more virtuous or self-sacrificing than the next man, but I found that I could not even enjoy the poor and limited freedoms I was allowed when I knew my people were not free. Freedom is indivisible; the chains on any one of my people were the chains on all of them, the chains on all of my people were the chains on me.

It was during those long and lonely years that my hunger for the freedom of my own people became a hunger for the freedom of all people, white and black. I knew as well as I knew anything that the oppressor must be liberated just as surely as the oppressed. A man who takes away another man's freedom is a prisoner of hatred, he is locked behind the bars of prejudice and narrow-mindedness. I am not truly free if I am taking away someone else's freedom, just as surely as I am not free when my freedom is taken from me. The oppressed and the oppressor alike are robbed of their humanity.

When I walked out of prison, that was my mission, to liberate the oppressed and the oppressor both. Some say that has now been achieved. But I know that is not the case. The truth is that we are not yet free; we have merely achieved the freedom to be free, the right not to be oppressed. We have not taken the final step of our journey, but the first step on a longer and even more difficult road. For to be free is not merely to **cast off** one's chains, but to live in a way that respects and enhances the freedom of others. The true test of our devotion to freedom is just beginning.

Differentiated Instruction

Clarify the Text Support students in understanding Mandela's reflections about freedom.

Beginning/Early Intermediate ➤ Read aloud the three bullets in To Sum Up. **Ask:** *Has Mandela reached the end of his fight for freedom? (no)*

Intermediate ➤ Have partners read aloud the boxed text on page 74. Have them complete the following sentence frames. *If I try to take away your freedom, I am ___. (a prisoner of hatred myself) Freedom from oppression is not complete freedom, but just ___. (the freedom to be free)*

Early Advanced ➤ Have students summarize Mandela's argument that injustice is bad for oppressors as well as oppressed. Then ask them to write two or three sentences stating whether they agree with Mandela's argument.

Note Taking

Reread the text on the left. Then record your answers to the items below.

1. The most interesting word on this page is _____

   because _____ .

2. One word that I didn't know on this page is _____ .

   It means _____ .

3. One thing I read on this page that I already knew is _____

   _____ .

4. One thing I learned on this page that I didn't know is _____

   _____ .

5. Recap, or write in your own words what you learned by reading this page.

   _____

   _____

   _____

   _____

6. Summarize below what you've recorded.

Most Interesting Word	New Word	One Thing I Already Knew	One Thing I Learned

Note Taking

To help students get started, you might want to model your thinking process for completing one of the items.

Interactive Question-Response

To Sum Up

Beginning/Early Intermediate ▶ Have students work in pairs to reread the To Sum Up features from the beginning of the selection on page 66. Then ask students to decide what the three most important points are in Mandela's essay. Have them fill in this outline:

Mandela's main points in his essay are

A. *(South Africa can set an example for the world)*

B. *(the struggle to end injustice in South Africa took courage and sacrifice)*

C. *(the fight for freedom involves everyone and is just beginning)*

Reflect

Partner Talk Have students work in pairs to answer. To help students get started: **Model** *To answer this, I would reread the paragraph on this page and the Reading Strategy on page 46. The Reading Strategy says that facts are true statements that can be proven. Mandela says that he has "walked the long road to freedom," in other words, he has reached the goal of attaining freedom for his country. His statement is true and can be proven by the work that he has done and his inauguration as a South African leader. But he realizes that there is still work to be done to attain freedom for all people.* Write the following sentence frame on the board to help students organize their thoughts.

Mandela has _____. (walked the long road to freedom) He has reached his goal _____. (by the work that he has done)

If you *steal a view*, you look in a secretive way.

I walked that long road to freedom. I have tried not to falter; I have made missteps along the way. But I have discovered the secret that after climbing a great hill, one only finds that there are many more hills to climb. I have taken a moment here to rest, to **steal a view** of the glorious vista[15] that surrounds me, to look back on the distance I have come. But I can rest only for a moment, for with freedom come responsibilities, and I dare not linger, for my long walk is not yet ended.

15. **Vista** in this context means "a broad look at history."

To Sum Up

➤ Mandela compares his life to climbing a hill.

➤ When you climb a hill, you see other hills when you reach the top.

➤ Mandela has reached one goal. But he wants to win more freedom for all people.

76

REFLECT

Evaluate Evidence
Reread page 76. What facts does Mandela state on this page?

Possible answer: Mandela says, "I have walked that long road to freedom." But he knows that there is more work to be done because he "finds that there are many more hills to climb" and his "long walk is not yet ended."

_____

_____

 Talk about your answer with a partner.

Oral Assessment

Provide the following prompts to one student at a time. Observe students' responses. See the Oral Assessment Rubric on page T17 to determine students' levels of language output.

1. What does Thoreau believe about government?

2. Why was Thoreau sent to jail?

3. What steps does Gandhi want his followers to take if he is arrested?

4. What ceremony is Nelson Mandela attending on May 10?

5. What did Mandela think about freedom when he was a child?

Note Taking

Reread the text on the left. Then record your answers to the items below.

1. The most interesting word on this page is _____

   because _____ .

2. One word that I didn't know on this page is _____ .

   It means _____ .

3. One thing I read on this page that I already knew is _____

   _____ .

4. One thing I learned on this page that I didn't know is _____

   _____ .

5. Recap, or write in your own words what you learned by reading this page.

   _____

   _____

   _____

   _____

6. Summarize below what you've recorded.

Most Interesting Word	New Word	One Thing I Already Knew	One Thing I Learned

Note Taking

To help students get started, you might want to model your thinking process for completing one of the items.

Comprehension Check

B. Intermediate

Point out to students that they should consider both what Gandhi and Mandela believed and what they did when comparing the two. Suggest that they reread corresponding parts of the selections as they fill in the chart.

Writing Link

Speech

Have students consider which selection influenced their thinking the most and challenged them to think in a new way. Have students who selected the same selection work as partners. Partners can discuss and jot down the points they find the most compelling and that they would like others to believe. Then have each student write a persuasive speech designed to sway others to their thinking. You may wish to have students present their speeches to the class.

Students' speeches should:

- present a unified argument
- use persuasive techniques, such as emotional and logical appeals
- support points with evidence

After Reading

Have students complete the after reading activities on pages 314 and 315.

FROM CIVIL DISOBEDIENCE
On the Eve of Historic Dandi March
FROM LONG WALK TO FREEDOM

Comprehension Check

A. Answer these questions about the selection from "Civil Disobedience" by Henry David Thoreau.

1. Why was Thoreau put in jail? Possible answer: He did not pay his poll-tax.

2. How did Thoreau feel while he was in jail? Possible answer: he felt free

B. Nelson Mandela was inspired in his struggle by Gandhi. However, Mandela and Gandhi were different in some ways. These differences were due in part to their different cultures. Fill in this chart to compare and contrast Mandela and Gandhi.

	Similarities	Differences
Mandela & Ghandi	3. Nelson Mandela and Mohandas K. Gandhi were similar because Possible answer: they both fought against injustice.	4. Nelson Mandela and Mohandas K. Gandhi were different because Possible answer: Gandhi stressed nonviolent practices.
South Africa & India	5. South Africa and India were similar because Possible answer: they both treated their people unfairly.	6. South Africa and India were different because Possible answer: India was a British colony, while South Africa was independent.

C. Answer the questions about the arguments made by Thoreau and Mandela.

7. Why does Thoreau believe that government should be limited?

Possible answer: Thoreau argues that government, especially by majority rule, limits the freedom of the individual.

8. Why does Mandela believe that freedom for everyone is important?

Possible answer: Mandela argues that no one is truly free unless everyone is free.

For more practice, see pages 314 and 315.

Grammar Link BLM

Spelling of Regular Past Tense Verbs: Pronunciation of –ed: /t/, /d/, and /id/

Prepare students to complete the activity on page A13. Read the grammar instruction with students, and complete the first item with them to help them get started.

The Pit and the Pendulum

by Edgar Allan Poe

The Pit and the Pendulum **79**

Oral Language

Build Background

Read the title and author. Explain that students will read "The Pit and the Pendulum" by Edgar Allan Poe, an author who wrote many stories of horror and suspense. **Ask:**

- What is a pit? *(a hole in the ground, either natural or made by humans)*

- A pendulum is an object that hangs from something and swings back and forth. Have you ever seen a pendulum? *(Students may have seen clocks with pendulums in real life or in film.)*

Talk About the Story

Explain that this story takes places in the early 1800s in Spain. A religious court called the Inquisition gave harsh sentences to people who did not agree with certain beliefs. Explain that this story is about someone who has been placed in a dungeon, which is a dark, underground prison.

Beginning/Early Intermediate ▶ Ask students to use words to describe what a dungeon would be like. *(dark, scary, lonely, cold)*

Early Advanced ▶ **Ask:** *Do you think a court like the Inquisition could exist today in the U.S.? Why or why not?*

Lesson at a Glance

Oral Language
- Build Background
- Talk About the Short Story

Vocabulary
- Selection Vocabulary
- Content Vocabulary
- Academic Vocabulary

Literary Element
- Suspense

Reading Strategy
- Identify Sequence

Writing Link
- Interview

Fluency
- Expression and Intonation: Punctuation

Comprehension BLM
- BLM

Word Study BLM
- Root Words and Word Origins BLM
- Denotations and Connotations

Grammar Link BLM
- The Simple Past Tense: Irregular Verbs BLM

Technology
- Student Works™ Plus
- Teacher Works™ Plus
- Listening Library Audio CD
- Classroom Presentation Toolkit
- Glencoe Visual Vocabulary
- Skill Level Up!™ A Skill-Based Language Arts Game

Interactive Question-Response

Connect to the Story

Read aloud Connect to the Story. Reproduce the sentence starters on the board. Point out that the words *fear, scare,* and *afraid* are closely related in meaning. **Model** *Many people are afraid of heights. People fear heights because they think they might fall by accident.* Write your response on the board, and have volunteers suggest other responses. Then have individuals fill in their own sentences.

Literary Element **Suspense**

Read aloud the Literary Element. Ask students if they have ever watched a scary movie or crime drama on television. Maybe they have read a book that was so good that they did not want to put it down. Ask students to explain how those shows, movies, or books made them feel. Explain, using body language, that suspense makes people feel like they are *on the edge of their seats.* Explain that this idiom means that something is so interesting that it is as if a person is sitting with their shoulders tense and their body straining forward so as to better hear or read what happens next.

Reading Strategy **Identify Sequence**

Read aloud the Reading Strategy. Tell students that if they track the order of events, then they will be able to better understand what is happening in a story. Ask students to think about what they did after they woke up this morning. Then ask students to share with a partner what they did in the morning. After students have shared with a partner, ask them what common *signal* words they used to describe their morning. *(first, next, then, after, before)* **Model** *After I got up, I brushed my teeth. Then I took a shower and got dressed. After I got dressed, I ate breakfast.*

Connect to the Story

What are some things that people are afraid of? Why? What are some things that you are afraid of? Talk with a partner about the things that scare people. Then complete the sentences below.

Many people are afraid of Possible answers: spiders, **and** heights, or flying   .
People fear these things because   Possible responses: People are scared of things
or situations that are unfamiliar or strange. They may become afraid when they feel
out of control.
Some things that scare me are: Responses will vary.

Literary Element   Suspense

Suspense is a feeling of curiosity or uncertainty about what will happen next. Writers may create suspense in a story by having something threaten the main character. Writers may also give clues about what might happen. Sometimes you may even feel fearful for the main character.

As you read, pay attention to:
- events in the story that make you think about what will happen next
- clues the writer gives about what is to come

Ask yourself: Am I curious about what will happen next? If so, then why?

Reading Strategy   Identify Sequence

Sequence is the order of events. To show sequence, writers often use signal words and phrases, such as:
- *before*
- *next*
- *earlier that morning*
- *after that*

As you read this story, look for signal words that help you understand the sequence of events.

Selection Vocabulary

deduce (di dōōs', dūs') *v.* to come to a conclusion (p. 84)
The clues helped us deduce the answer to the trick question.
➤ Cognate (Spanish) **deducir**

impede (im pēd') *v.* to slow or block action (p. 85)
Road construction will impede travel this summer.
➤ Cognate (Spanish) **impedir**

lethargy (leth' ar jē) *n.* not moving; the state of being slow or tired (p. 88)
Dad told Bill to be active and get over his lethargy.
➤ Cognate (Spanish) **letargo**

proximity (prok sim' ə tē) *n.* closeness in space or time; nearness (p. 91)
Our house is in close proximity to the shopping mall.

Content Vocabulary

descent (di sent') *n.* movement from a higher level to a lower level (p. 83)
After it reached the top of the hill, the roller coaster made a fast descent.
➤ Cognate (Spanish) **descenco**

ravenous (rav' ə nəs) *adj.* very hungry (p. 89)
The ravenous student ate three sandwiches, two apples, and a large bowl of soup.

fatigue (fə t ē g') *n.* weakness due to tiredness (p. 86)
Because Mary stayed up late the night before, she felt fatigue during the race.
➤ Cognate (Spanish) **fatiga**

despair (di spār') *n.* loss of hope (p. 91)
Kimberly felt despair due to all of her homework.
➤ Cognate (Spanish) **desesperanza**

For more practice, see page 316. ➡

Vocabulary Routine

To introduce the vocabulary, read aloud the words and definitions in the student book and have students repeat after you. Discuss how the pictures illustrate the words or sentences. Then follow the vocabulary routine below.

Content Vocabulary

Define: ***Descent*** means "going down." Example: We took the elevator in our *descent* to the ground floor. Ask: If you are making a *descent*, where might you be going? EXAMPLE

If you feel ***fatigue,*** it may be difficult to stay awake. *Marta did not sleep well during the storm, so the next day she felt fatigue.* Describe a time when you felt *fatigue*. DESCRIPTION

A ***ravenous*** person wants to eat as much as possible. *Vicki's father ate seven pancakes because he felt ravenous.* Why might you feel *ravenous*? EXPLANATION

When people feel ***despair,*** they are unhappy because they have no hope. *After she lost her dog, Shannon felt despair.* What is another word for *despair*? SYNONYM

Vocabulary Practice Have students complete the vocabulary practice activity on p. 316.

Selection Vocabulary

Define: When you ***deduce*** something, you use reasoning to draw a conclusion based on information you know or assume. Example: From her sad expression, we *deduced* that she did not win the race. Ask: What would you deduce had recently happened if you looked out the window and saw that the street and sidewalks were wet? EXAMPLE

When you ***impede*** something, you hinder or block its progress or action. *Heavy traffic impeded me from getting to the concert on time.* Describe a time when you were impeded from doing something. DESCRIPTION

Lethargy is sluggish inactivity or drowsiness. *His lethargy was caused by a poor diet and lack of sleep.* What words can you think of that mean the opposite of lethargy? ANTONYM

Proximity means "closeness" or "nearness." *The proximity of our house to public transportation was a strong selling point to buyers.* Why would the proximity of a hospital be an advantage if you were seriously injured or sick? EXAMPLE

When something is ***diffused,*** it is spread out or scattered over an area. *The air became diffused with smoke from many campfires.* Describe a room that is diffused with light. DESCRIPTION

The Pit and the Pendulum

Interactive Question-Response

Background Information

Read aloud the note. Explain to students that people are sometimes afraid of those who are different. This fear may cause them to behave cruelly or unjustly, as was the case with the Inquisition. Ask students what this beginning reveals about that narrator. *(He might have different religious beliefs.)* Ask students to think of other situations in which people are treated poorly or unjustly because they are different. *(Students should discuss situations of discrimination against people of different races or religious beliefs.)*

A *sentence* is a punishment given by a judge to someone who is guilty of a crime.

> **Background Information**
>
> This story is set during the last years of the Spanish Inquisition (1478–1834). It was begun by the Roman Catholic Church. The Inquisition was a court that arrested people who did not believe in the Church's teachings. Many people were given sentences of death by the Inquisition.

To Sum Up

➤ The narrator remembers standing before black-robed judges.

➤ The judges sentence him to death.

I was sick—sick unto death with that long agony; and when they at length unbound me, and I was permitted to sit, I felt that my senses were leaving me. The **sentence**—the dread sentence of death—was the last of distinct accentuation which reached my ears.

After that, the sound of the inquisitorial voices seemed merged in one dreamy indeterminate hum. It conveyed to my soul the idea of *revolution*—perhaps from its association in fancy with the burr of a millwheel. This only for a brief period; for presently I heard no more. Yet, for a while, I saw; but with how terrible an exaggeration! I saw the lips of the black-robed judges. They appeared to me white—whiter than the sheet upon which I trace these words—and thin even to grotesqueness;[1] thin with the intensity of their expression of firmness—of immovable resolution—of stern contempt of human torture. I saw that the decrees of what to me was Fate, were still issuing from those lips. I saw them writhe with a deadly locution.[2] I saw them fashion the syllables of my name; and I shuddered because no sound succeeded. I saw, too, for a few moments of delirious horror, the soft and nearly imperceptible waving of the sable draperies which enwrapped the walls of the apartment. And then my vision fell upon the seven tall candles upon the table. At first they wore the aspect of charity, and seemed white slender angels who would save me; but then, all at once, there came a most deadly nausea over my spirit, and I felt every fiber in my frame thrill as if I had touched the wire of a galvanic battery,[3] while the angel forms became meaningless specters,[4] with heads of flame, and I saw that from them there would be no help. And then there stole into my fancy, like a rich musical note, the thought of what sweet rest there must be in the grave. The thought came gently and stealthily, and it seemed long before it attained full appreciation;

1. **Grotesqueness** means "not natural in shape or look."
2. **Locution** is a way of speaking.
3. The narrator feels as if he has received an electric shock.
4. **Specters** are ghosts.

Comprehension

To support students as they read the selection, have them begin the graphic organizer on page A14.

but just as my spirit came at length properly to feel and entertain it, the figures of the judges vanished, as if magically, from before me; the tall candles sank into nothingness; their flames went out utterly; the blackness of darkness supervened; all sensations appeared swallowed up in a mad rushing <u>descent</u> as of the soul into Hades.[5] Then silence, and stillness, and night were the universe.

I had **swooned**; but still will not say that all of consciousness was lost. What of it there remained I will not attempt to define, or even to describe; yet all was not lost. In the deepest slumber—no! In delirium—no! In a swoon—no! In death—no! even in the grave all *is not* lost. Else there is no immortality[6] for man. Arousing from the most profound[7] of slumbers, we break the gossamer web of *some* dream. Yet in a second afterward, (so frail may that web have been) we remember not that we have dreamed. In the return to life from the swoon there are two stages; first, that of the sense of mental or spiritual; secondly, that of the sense of physical, existence. It seems probable that if, upon reaching the second stage, we could recall the impressions of the first, we should find these impressions eloquent in memories of the gulf beyond. And that gulf is—what? How at least shall we distinguish its shadows from those of the tomb? But if the impressions of what I have termed the first stage, are not, at will, recalled, yet, after long interval, do they not come unbidden, while we marvel whence they come? He who has never swooned, is not he who finds strange palaces and wildly familiar faces in coals that glow; is not he who beholds floating in midair the sad visions that the many may not view; is not he who ponders over the perfume of some novel[8] flower—is not he whose brain grows bewildered with the meaning of some musical cadence which has never before arrested his attention.

Amid frequent and thoughtful endeavors to remember; amid earnest struggles to regather some token of the state of seeming nothingness into which my soul had lapsed, there have been moments when I have dreamed of success; there have been brief, very brief periods when I have conjured up remembrances which the lucid reason of a later epoch assures me could have had reference only to that condition of seeming unconsciousness. These shadows of memory tell, indistinctly, of tall figures that lifted and bore me in silence down—down—still down—till a hideous dizziness oppressed me at the mere idea of the interminableness[9] of the descent. They tell also of a vague horror at my heart, on account of that heart's unnatural stillness. Then comes a sense of sudden motionlessness throughout all things; as if those who bore me (a ghastly train!) had outrun, in their descent, the limits of the limitless, and paused from the wearisomeness of their toil. After this I call to mind flatness and dampness; and that all is *madness*—the madness of a memory which busies itself among forbidden things.

5. In Greek myth, **Hades** is the underground place of the dead.
6. **Immortality** is life without end.
7. **Profound** means "complete" or "deep."
8. A **novel** flower is new and different.
9. **Interminableness** means "without end."

descent (di sent′) *n.* movement from a higher level to a lower level

Swooned means "fainted."

To Sum Up
➤ The narrator faints.
➤ People pick him up and carry him down into a strange place.

Interactive Question-Response

Content Vocabulary

Read aloud the word and definition for *descent*. Then ask a student to read aloud the three sentences that begin with "These shadows of memory." Ask students to observe that the vocabulary word has been used twice. Explain to students that the narrator is remembering what happened to him after he fainted in the courtroom. People are carrying him. **Ask:** *What repeated word shows where they are going? (down–down–still down) How does the narrator describe the kind of descent that the people are making? (They are going so far down that it seems as if it will never end.) How would you feel if you were in the narrator's situation? (Students might say that it would be scary to be carried so far underground. It might make them feel trapped.)*

Interactive Question-Response

Comprehension Check

Ask students to share what they underlined in the text. **Ask:** *From the context clues in this sentence, what do you think the word aghast means? (fearful, amazed, or shocked) Can you use your own words to restate the meaning of this sentence? (I wasn't afraid that I would be in complete darkness.) Why is the narrator afraid of this? (Students may say that it is scarier to be in total darkness because you cannot know what is around you. If you have light, then you can see what is coming.)*

Selection Vocabulary

Explain that *deduce* means "to draw a conclusion from something known." As students read, ask them to notice how the narrator deduces things about the dungeon. **Ask:** *What is the narrator trying to deduce at this moment? (He is trying to deduce where he is and what has happened to him.)*

Comprehension Check

Reread the boxed text on this page. Underline the words that tell what the narrator fears.

Very suddenly there came back to my soul motion and sound—the tumultuous motion of the heart, and, in my ears, the sound of its beating. Then a pause in which all is blank. Then again sound, and motion, and touch—a tingling sensation pervading my frame. Then the mere consciousness of existence, without thought—a condition which lasted long. Then, very suddenly, *thought*, and shuddering terror, and earnest endeavor to comprehend my true state. Then a strong desire to lapse into insensibility.[10] Then a rushing revival of soul and a successful effort to move. And now a full memory of the trial, of the judges, of the sable draperies, of the sentence, of the sickness, of the swoon. Then entire forgetfulness of all that followed; of all that a later day and much earnestness of endeavor have enabled me vaguely to recall.

So far, I had not opened my eyes. I felt that I lay upon my back, unbound. I reached out my hand, and it fell heavily upon something damp and hard. There I suffered[11] it to remain for many minutes, while I strove to imagine where and *what* I could be. I longed, yet dared not to employ my vision. I dreaded the first glance at objects around me. It was not that I feared to look upon things horrible, but that I grew aghast lest there should be *nothing* to see. At length, with a wild desperation at heart, I quickly unclosed my eyes. My worst thoughts, then, were confirmed. The blackness of eternal night encompassed me. I struggled for breath. The intensity of the darkness seemed to oppress and stifle me. The atmosphere was intolerably close. I still lay quietly, and made effort to exercise my reason. I brought to mind the inquisitorial proceedings,[12] and attempted from that point to **deduce** my real condition. The sentence had passed; and it appeared to me that a very long interval of time had since elapsed. Yet not for a moment did I suppose myself actually dead.

Such a supposition, notwithstanding what we read in fiction, is altogether inconsistent with real existence;—but where and in what state was I? The condemned to death, I knew, perished usually at the *autos-da-fé*,[13] and one of these had been held on the very night of the day of my trial. Had I been remanded to my dungeon, to await the next sacrifice which would not take place for many months? This I at once saw could not be. Victims had been in immediate demand. Moreover, my dungeon, as well as all the condemned cells at Toledo, had stone floors, and light was not altogether excluded.

To Sum Up

➤ The narrator opens his eyes to find himself in complete darkness.

➤ He tries to understand what has happened to him.

Vocabulary

deduce (di dōōs′, dūs′) *v.* to come to a conclusion

10. The narrator wishes that he could not feel or think.
11. Here, **suffered** means "allowed."
12. During the Inquisition, a person who did not confess was thought to be guilty.
13. People who were sentenced by the Inquisition were often burned alive in ceremonies called **autos-da-fé** (ó tóz′ da f ā′). This phrase is Portuguese for "acts of faith." The Inquisitors had faith that the sentenced people were guilty.

Differentiated Instruction

Clarify the Text Support students in understanding the narrator of the story.

Beginning/Early Intermediate Remind students that a narrator is the person telling the story. **Ask:** *Who is the narrator and what is his name? (The author does not give him a name. The reader does not know much about his past.)*

Intermediate Ask students to think about what they know about the narrator. **Ask:** *What do we know about the narrator's past? (The narrator must have done something that the court of the Inquisition did not like. We do not know who he is or what he did.)*

Early Advanced **Ask:** *What kind of thoughts does the narrator have about his imprisonment? (The narrator seems very upset. He is unsure about what is happening. He is afraid.)* **Ask:** *Why do you think the author does not tell the name of the narrator? (The narrator's anonymity makes it easier for the reader to imagine being in that position.)*

A fearful idea now suddenly drove the blood in torrents upon my heart, and for a brief period, I once more relapsed into insensibility. Upon recovering, I at once started to my feet, trembling convulsively in every fiber. I thrust my arms wildly above and around me in all directions. I felt nothing; yet dreaded to move a step, lest I should be **impeded** by the walls of the *tomb*. Perspiration burst from every pore and stood in cold big beads on my forehead. The agony of suspense grew at length intolerable, and I cautiously moved forward, with my arms extended, and my eyes straining from their sockets, in the hope of catching some faint ray of light. I proceeded for many paces; but still all was blackness and vacancy. I breathed more freely. It seemed evident that mine was not, at least, the **most hideous of fates.**

And now, as I still continued to step cautiously onward, there came thronging upon my recollection a thousand vague rumors of the horrors of Toledo. Of the dungeons there had been strange things narrated—fables I had always deemed them—but yet strange, and too ghastly to repeat, save in a whisper. Was I left to perish of starvation in the subterranean[14] world of darkness; or what fate, perhaps even more fearful, awaited me? That the result would be death, and a death of more than customary bitterness, I knew too well the character of my judges to doubt. The mode and the hour were all that occupied or distracted me.

Vocabulary

impede (im pēd′) *v.* to slow or block action

14. **Subterranean** describes things below the earth's surface.

REFLECT

Identify Sequence

What happens after the narrator hears his sentence of death? Number the following events in the order in which they occur.

_6_ The narrator tears off a part of his robe and sets it down.

_1_ The narrator is carried down to a strange place.

_5_ The narrator finds the wall.

_4_ The narrator stands and stretches out his arms.

_3_ The narrator finds that he is in complete darkness.

_2_ The narrator is afraid to open his eyes.

Talk about your answer with a partner.

Most hideous of fates means the worst thing that could happen to someone.

Literary Element

Suspense Reread the boxed text on this page. Underline the words that tell how the narrator reacts to the feeling of suspense.

To Sum Up

➤ The narrator extends his arms in front of him and begins to move carefully.

Interactive Question-Response

Literary Element   Suspense

Ask students to share what they underlined. Explain that the word *intolerable* describes something you cannot bear any longer and *agony* means "great mental or physical pain." **Ask:** *Why does the narrator begin to move forward? (Even though he is afraid, the suspense of not knowing what is around him is too much for him.) How does the narrator's feeling of suspense affect the reader? (The reader feels suspense with the narrator. Like the narrator, the reader wants to know more about the dungeon.)*

Reflect

Partner Talk Have students work in pairs to answer. To help students get started: **Model** *To answer this, I would think about the first thing that happened after the narrator heard the sentence of death. OK, first he fainted and he was not sure what was happening. Then, he remembers people carrying him down somewhere. So that would be the number 1.* Write the following sentence frames on the board to help students organize their thoughts.

The first thing that happens is _____.

Then, the next thing that happens is _____.

Interactive Question-Response

Content Vocabulary

Read aloud the word and definition of *fatigue*. Explain that the word *prostrate* means "lying face down" or "lying flat" and *excessive* means "more than normal." **Ask:** *What is the effect of the narrator's excessive fatigue?* (He stumbles and falls. He is too tired to get up and continue walking, so he falls asleep.)

Literary Element Suspense

Tell students that the first signal phrase is *upon awakening* because it means "after I woke up." Tell students to find other signal words and phrases in the paragraphs that begin "Upon awakening" and "I had little object." Once students have completed the activity, ask them to share what they underlined. Then ask them to share their response about suspense. **Ask:** *How does the sequence of events add to the suspense in the story?* (With each event, the reader feels a growing sense of danger for the narrator.)

---

fatigue (fə tēg′) *n.* weakness due to tiredness

 Literary Element

Suspense Reread the two paragraphs that begin "Upon awakening" and "I had little object." Underline the signal words and phrases that show the sequence of events. Why is this part of the story suspenseful?

Possible response: The reader

is afraid of what the narrator

will find in the dark. It could be

something scary.

_____

I could not help supposing means "I had no choice except to suppose." The narrator sees no other possibility.

To Sum Up

➤ The narrator reaches a stone wall.

➤ He tears off a piece of his robe and sets it on the ground. The cloth will help him find his starting place.

➤ He learns that the dungeon is large. He decides to cross the room.

86

My outstretched hands at length encountered some solid obstruction. It was a wall, seemingly of stone masonry—very smooth, slimy, and cold. I followed it up; stepping with all the careful distrust with which certain antique narratives had inspired me. This process, however, afforded me no means of ascertaining the dimensions of my dungeon; as I might make its circuit, and return to the point whence I set out, without being aware of the fact; so perfectly uniform seemed the wall. I therefore sought the knife which had been in my pocket, when led into the inquisitorial chamber; but it was gone; my clothes had been exchanged for a wrapper of coarse serge. I had thought of forcing the blade in some minute crevice of the masonry, so as to identify my point of departure. The difficulty, nevertheless, was but trivial; although, in the disorder of my fancy, it seemed at first insuperable.[15] I tore a part of the hem from the robe and placed the fragment at full length, and at right angles to the wall. In groping my way around the prison I could not fail to encounter this rag upon completing the circuit. So, at least I thought: but I had not counted upon the extent of the dungeon, or upon my own weakness. The ground was moist and slippery. I staggered onward for some time, when I stumbled and fell. My excessive <u>fatigue</u> induced me to remain prostrate; and sleep soon overtook me as I lay.

<u>Upon awakening</u>, and stretching forth an arm, I found beside me a loaf and a pitcher with water. I was too much exhausted to reflect upon this circumstance, but ate and drank with avidity.[16] <u>Shortly afterward,</u> I resumed my tour around the prison, and with much toil, came at last upon the fragment of the serge. <u>Up to the period when</u> I fell I had counted fifty-two paces, and <u>upon resuming</u> my walk, I counted forty-eight more;—when I arrived at the rag. There were in all, then, a hundred paces; and admitting two paces to the yard, I presumed the dungeon to be fifty yards in circuit. I had met, however, with many angles in the wall, and thus I could form no guess at the shape of the vault; for vault **I could not help supposing** it to be.

I had little object—certainly no hope—in these researches; but a vague curiosity prompted me to continue them. Quitting the wall, I resolved to cross the area of the enclosure. <u>At first</u> I proceeded with extreme caution, for the floor, although seemingly of solid material, was treacherous with slime. <u>At length</u>, however, I took courage, and did not hesitate to step firmly; endeavoring to cross in as direct a line as possible. I had advanced some ten or twelve paces in this manner, when the remnant of the torn hem of my robe became entangled between my legs. I stepped on it, and fell violently on my face.

In the confusion attending my fall, I did not immediately apprehend a somewhat startling circumstance, which yet, in a few seconds afterward, and while I still lay prostrate, arrested my attention. It was this—my chin

15. Something that is **insuperable** cannot be overcome.
16. **Avidity** is interest and excitement.

Word Study BLM

Root Words and Word Origins

Point out the word *obstruction* in the first sentence. Explain that, if students did not know this word, they could use their knowledge of word parts and word origins to help them figure out its meaning: **Model** *Obstruction* has three word parts: the prefix *ob-* "in the way, against;" the Latin root *struct* "built up" (from *structus,* past participle of *struere*); and the noun-forming suffix *–ion*. Together, they mean "something built up in the way." **Ask:** If you were unfamiliar with the meaning of the Latin root *struct*, where could you find it? (in the etymology of the dictionary entry for the word *obstruction*.)

Then have them practice applying their knowledge of word parts and word origins by completing the activity on page A15.

rested upon the floor of the prison, but my lips and the upper portion of my head, although seemingly at a less elevation than the chin, touched nothing. At the same time my forehead seemed bathed in a clammy vapor, and the peculiar smell of decayed fungus arose to my nostrils. I put forward my arm, and shuddered to find that I had fallen at the very brink of a circular pit, whose extent, of course, I had no means of ascertaining at the moment. Groping about the masonry just below the margin, I succeeded in dislodging a small fragment, and let it fall into the abyss.[17] For many seconds I hearkened to its reverberations as it dashed against the sides of the chasm in its descent; at length there was a sullen plunge into water, succeeded by loud echoes. At the same moment there came a sound resembling the quick opening, and a rapid closing of a door overhead, while a faint gleam of light flashed suddenly through the gloom, and as suddenly faded away.

I saw clearly the doom which had been prepared for me, and congratulated myself upon the timely accident by which I had escaped. Another step before my fall, and the world had seen me no more. And the death just avoided, was of that very character which I had regarded as fabulous and frivolous[18] in the tales respecting the Inquisition. To the victims of its tyranny, there was the choice of death with its direst physical agonies, or death with its most hideous moral horrors. I had been reserved for the latter. By long suffering my nerves had been unstrung, until I trembled at the sound of my own voice, and had become in every respect a fitting subject for the species of torture which awaited me.

Shaking in every limb, I groped my way back to the wall; resolving there to perish rather than risk the terrors of the wells, of which my imagination now pictured many in various positions about the dungeon. In other conditions of mind I might have had courage to end my misery at once by a plunge into one of these abysses; but now I was the veriest of cowards. Neither could I forget what I had read of these pits—that the *sudden* extinction of life formed no part of their most horrible plan.

Agitation of spirit kept me awake for many long hours; but at length I again slumbered. Upon arousing, I found by my side as before, a loaf and a pitcher of water. A burning thirst consumed me, and I emptied the vessel at a draught. It must have been drugged; for scarcely had I drunk, before I became irresistibly drowsy. A deep sleep fell upon me—a sleep like that of death. How long it lasted of course, I know not; but when, once again, I unclosed my eyes, the objects around me were visible. By a wild sulphurous luster, the origin of which I could not at first determine, I was enabled to see the extent and aspect of the prison.

In its size I had been greatly mistaken. The whole circuit of its walls did not exceed twenty-five yards. For some minutes this fact occasioned me a world of vain trouble; vain indeed! for what could be of less

17. **Abyss** (a bis') means "a very deep hole."
18. Here, **fabulous** means "imaginary" and frivolous means "silly."

Shaking in every limb means that the narrator is so scared that his arms and legs are shaking.

To Sum Up

➤ As the narrator walks, he trips on his robe and falls. He almost falls into a pit in the center of the dungeon.

➤ He is scared and goes back to the wall.

➤ After he sleeps, he wakes up to see some light. He sees that the dungeon is smaller than he thought.

Interactive Question-Response

To Sum Up

Beginning/Early Intermediate ➤ Have students work in pairs to reread all the To Sum Up statements from the beginning of the story on page 82. Then have students think about how the narrator reacts to what happens to him. Provide the following sentence frame for students to complete two times.

When _____, the narrator _____.

Model *When the court sentences him to death, the narrator faints.*

Other responses: 1) he wakes up in darkness, is afraid; 2) he is curious about the size of the dungeon, uses part of his robe to measure the size; 3) he tries to cross the room, almost falls into the pit.

Interactive Question-Response

Selection Vocabulary

Read aloud the word and definition of *lethargy*. Invite a volunteer to pantomime lethargy. Then have students read the sentence containing the word *lethargy* ("In feeling my way around I had found many angles, and thus deduced an idea of great irregularity; so potent is the effect of total darkness upon one arousing from lethargy or sleep!"). **Ask:** *What happens because of the narrator's lethargy? (He misjudges the size and shape of his dungeon.)* **Ask:** *Have you ever woken up from great lethargy? How did you feel? Did you make mistakes?*

importance, under the terrible circumstances which environed[19] me, than the mere dimensions of my dungeon? But my soul took a wild interest in trifles, and I busied myself in endeavors to account for the error I had committed in my measurement. The truth at length flashed upon me. In my first attempt at exploration I had counted fifty-two paces, up to the period when I fell; I must then have been within a pace or two of the fragments of serge; in fact, I had nearly performed the circuit of the vault. I then slept, and upon awaking, I must have returned upon my steps—thus supposing the circuit nearly double what it actually was. My confusion of mind prevented me from observing that I began my tour with the wall to the left, and ended it with the wall to the right.

I had been deceived, too, in respect to the shape of the enclosure. In feeling my way around I had found many angles, and thus deduced an idea of great irregularity; so potent is the effect of total darkness upon one arousing from lethargy or sleep! The angles were simply those of a few slight depressions, or niches, at odd intervals. The general shape of the prison was square. What I had taken for masonry seemed now to be iron, or some other metal, in huge plates, whose sutures or joints occasioned the depression. The entire surface of this metallic enclosure was rudely daubed in all the hideous and repulsive devices[20] to which the charnel[21] superstitions of the monks has given rise. The figures of fiends in aspects of menace, with skeleton forms, and other more really fearful images, overspread and disfigured the walls. I observed that the outlines of these monstrosities were sufficiently distinct, but that the colors seemed faded and blurred, as if from the effects of a damp atmosphere. I now noticed the floor, too, which was of stone. In the center yawned the circular pit from whose jaws I had escaped; but it was the only one in the dungeon.

All this I saw distinctly and by much effort: for my personal condition had been greatly changed during slumber. I now lay upon my back, and at full length, on a species of low framework of wood. To this I was securely bound by a long strap resembling a surcingle.[22] It passed in many convolutions about my limbs and body, leaving at liberty only my head, and my left arm to such extent that I could, **by dint of** much exertion, supply myself with food from an earthen dish which lay by my side on the floor. I saw, to my horror, that the pitcher had been removed. I say to my horror; for I was consumed with intolerable thirst. This thirst it appeared to be the design of my persecutors to stimulate: for the food in the dish was meat pungently seasoned.

Looking upward I surveyed the ceiling of my prison. It was some thirty or forty feet overhead, and constructed much as the side walls. In one of its panels a very singular figure riveted my whole attention. It was the painted figure of Time as he is commonly represented, save that, in lieu of[23] a scythe, he held what, at a casual glance, I supposed to be the

By dint of means "by force of" or "by using."

Vocabulary ....

lethargy (leth′ ər jē) *n.* not moving; the state of being slow or tired

To Sum Up

➤ The narrator learns that he has been tied to a piece of wood.

➤ He can reach a bowl of meat next to him.

19. To **environ** is to surround.
20. Here, **devices** are designs.
21. Here, **charnel** means "deathlike."
22. A **surcingle** is a belt or band used to hold a saddle on a horse.
23. **In lieu** (in l o͞o) of means "in place of."

Differentiated Instruction

Clarify the Text Support students in understanding the narrator's state of mind.

Beginning/Early Intermediate ➤ Read aloud the sentence that begins "By long suffering." **Ask:** *How does the narrator feel if he trembles, or shakes, at the sound of his own voice? (He feels nervous, scared, and unable to control himself.)*

Intermediate ➤ Ask students to look for clues in the story that show the narrator's state of mind. *(One clue is that the narrator is stays awake for many hours after he discovers this pit. This shows that he is nervous and scared.)*

Early Advanced ➤ Point out that the narrator is nervous and terrified, but he also uses his reason. Ask students to find examples of both states of mind. *(He is too afraid to open his eyes when he first finds himself in the dungeon. He measures the size of the dungeon.)*

pictured image of a huge pendulum such as we see on antique clocks. There was something, however, in the appearance of this machine which caused me to regard it more attentively. While I gazed directly upward at it (for its position was immediately over my own) I fancied that I saw it in motion. In an instant afterward the fancy was confirmed. Its sweep was brief, and of course slow. I watched it for some minutes, somewhat in fear, but more in wonder. Wearied at length with observing its dull movement, I turned my eyes upon the other subjects in the cell.

A slight noise attracted my notice, and, looking to the floor, I saw several enormous rats traversing it. They had issued from the well, which lay just within view to my right. Even then, while I gazed, they came up in troops, hurriedly, with ravenous eyes, allured by the scent of the meat. From this it required much effort and attention to scare them away.

It might have been half an hour, perhaps even an hour, (for I could take but imperfect note of time) before I again cast my eyes upward. What I then saw confounded and amazed me. The sweep of the pendulum had increased in extent by nearly a yard. As a natural consequence, its velocity was also much greater. But what mainly disturbed me was the idea that it had perceptibly *descended*. I now observed—with what horror it is needless to say—that its nether extremity[24] was formed of a crescent of glittering steel, about a foot in length from horn to horn; the horns upward, and the under edge evidently as keen as that of a razor. Like a razor also, it seemed massy and heavy, tapering from the edge into a solid and broad structure above. It was appended to a weighty rod of brass, and the whole *hissed* as it swung through the air.

I could no longer doubt the doom prepared for me by monkish ingenuity[25] in torture. My cognizance of the pit had become known to the inquisitorial agents—*the pit* whose horrors had been destined for so bold a recusant[26] as myself—*the pit*, typical of hell, and regarded by rumor as the Ultima Thule[27] of all their punishments. The plunge into this pit I had avoided by the merest of accidents, and I knew that surprise, or entrapment into torment, formed an important portion of all the grotesquerie of these dungeon deaths. Having failed to fall, it was no part of the demon plan to hurl me into the abyss; and thus (there being no alternative) a different and a milder destruction awaited me. Milder! I half smiled in my agony as I thought of such application of such a term.

REFLECT

Identify Sequence

What happens after the narrator walks around the dungeon? Number the following events in the order in which they occur.

_3_ The narrator discovers the pit in the center of the dungeon.

_1_ The narrator tries to walk across the dungeon.

_2_ The narrator trips and falls.

_4_ The narrator wakes up and finds himself tied to a piece of wood.

 Talk about your answer with a partner.

---

ravenous (rav′ ə nəs) *adj.* very hungry

Cast my eyes means "look in a direction."

Comprehension Check

Check all of the correct answers that could complete this sentence. The narrator sees that the pendulum:

- ☑ has sped up.
- ☐ has slowed down.
- ☑ has steel edges.
- ☑ has moved closer to him.
- ☑ is descending.
- ☐ makes no sound.
- ☑ makes a hissing sound as it swings.

24. The pendulum's **nether extremity** is its lower end.
25. **Ingenuity** (in′ jə noo̅′ ə tē) is being creative and clever to solve problems.
26. A **recusant** (re′ kyə zənt) is someone who does not obey.
27. Here, **Ultima Thule** (ul′ tə mə thoo̅′ lē) means "greatest amount." *Ultima Thule* was once thought to be the place in the world that was farthest north.

To Sum Up

➤ The narrator sees a pendulum that swings above him.

➤ Large rats come near the meat, and the narrator tries to keep them away.

➤ The narrator sees that the pendulum has sharp steel edges. It is moving faster, and it is slowly dropping toward him.

Interactive Question-Response

Content Vocabulary

Have a student read aloud the word and definition of *ravenous.* **Ask:** *Why does the author write that the rats have* ravenous *eyes? How would a person with* ravenous *eyes look? (The rats are very hungry and they are looking at the meat as if they want to eat. Someone with ravenous eyes would look at food as if they cannot wait to eat it.)*

Comprehension Check

Ask students to share which boxes they checked. Explain that *terror* means "something that causes extreme fear." **Ask:** *How does this second terror differ from the first? (The first involves a fall into a deep, dark pit. The second has a person trapped while he waits for a sharp-edged pendulum to drop and kill him.) How does the pendulum harm the mind, as well as the body? (The narrator must watch and wait as the pendulum slowly descends.)*

Reflect

Partner Talk Have students work in pairs to answer. To help students get started: **Model** *To answer this, I would think about the first thing that happens after the narrator walks around the dungeon. He tries to walk across the dungeon. So that would be number 1.* Write the following sentence frames on the board to help students organize their thoughts.

The first thing that happens is _____.

Then, the next thing that happens is _____.

Interactive Question-Response

Literary Element Suspense

If students struggle to understand how and why the pendulum will eventually kill the narrator, have a volunteer lie on the floor. Use a pencil as a pendulum. Swing it closer and closer to the student's chest. **Model** *If I were on the floor, I'd be nervous. I know the pendulum is eventually going to touch me. It will cut through my clothes, and then it will cut me. But I don't know how much time will pass before then. I almost wish the pendulum would cut me now, so I wouldn't have to wait.* **Ask:** *How does the slowness of the pendulum make the punishment worse? (The narrator has no choice but to watch and wait.)*

The narrator calls his captors **demons** because the punishments seem like the torments of hell.

Fraying of my robe means that the pendulum will first tear the edge of the narrator's robe.

Literary Element

Suspense How is the pendulum going to kill the narrator? Underline the words that tell you.

To Sum Up

➤ The narrator sees that the pendulum is moving toward his heart.

➤ He watches the pendulum descend and thinks about what to do.

What boots it[28] to tell of the long, long hours of horror more than mortal, during which I counted the rushing vibrations of the steel! Inch by inch—line by line—with a descent only appreciable at intervals that seemed ages—down and still down it came! Days passed—it might have been that many days passed—ere it swept so closely over me as to fan me with its acrid breath. The odor of the sharp steel forced itself into my nostrils. I prayed—I wearied heaven with my prayer for its more speedy descent. I grew frantically mad, and struggled to force myself upward against the sweep of the fearful scimitar.[29] And then I fell suddenly calm, and lay smiling at the glittering death, as a child at some rare bauble.[30]

There was another interval of utter insensibility; it was brief; for, upon again lapsing into life there had been no perceptible descent in the pendulum. But it might have been long; for I knew there were **demons** who took note of my swoon, and who could have arrested the vibration at pleasure. Upon my recovery, too, I felt very—oh, inexpressibly sick and weak, as if through long inanition.[31] Even amid the agonies of that period, the human nature craved food. With painful effort I outstretched my left arm as far as my bonds permitted, and took possession of the small remnant which had been spared me by the rats. As I put a portion of it within my lips, there rushed to my mind a half formed thought of joy—of hope? Yet what business had I with hope? It was, as I say, a half formed thought—man has many such which are never completed. I felt that it was of joy—of hope; but I felt also that it had perished in its formation. In vain I struggled to perfect—to regain it. Long suffering had nearly annihilated all my ordinary powers of mind. I was an imbecile—an idiot.

The vibration of the pendulum was at right angles to my length. I saw that the crescent was designed to cross the region of the heart. It would fray the serge of my robe—it would return and repeat its operations—again—and again. Notwithstanding its terrifically wide sweep (some thirty feet or more) and the hissing vigor of its descent, sufficient to sunder these very walls of iron, still the **fraying of my robe** would be all that, for several minutes, it would accomplish. And at this thought I paused. I dared not go farther than this reflection. I dwelt upon it with a pertinacity[32] of attention—as if, in so dwelling, I could arrest *here* the descent of the steel. I forced myself to ponder upon the sound of the crescent as it should pass across the garment—upon the peculiar thrilling sensation which the friction of cloth produces on the nerves. I pondered upon all this frivolity until my teeth were on edge.

Down—steadily down it crept. I took a frenzied pleasure in contrasting its downward with its lateral velocity. To the right—to the left—far and wide—with the shriek of a damned spirit; to my heart with the stealthy pace of the tiger! I alternately laughed and howled as the one or the other idea grew prominent.

28. **What boots it?** means "What good is it?"
29. A **scimitar** is a curved sword.
30. A **bauble** is a cheap but flashy trinket or piece of jewelry.
31. The tiredness caused by a lack of food and water is called **inanition.**
32. **Pertinacity** is strength of purpose.

Down—certainly, relentlessly down! It vibrated within three inches of my bosom! I struggled violently, furiously, to free my left arm. This was free only from the elbow to the hand. I could reach the latter, from the platter beside me, to my mouth, with great effort, but no farther. Could I have broken the fastenings above the elbow, I would have seized and attempted to arrest the pendulum. I might as well have attempted to arrest an avalanche!

Down—still unceasingly—still inevitably down! I gasped and struggled at each vibration. I shrunk convulsively at its every sweep. My eyes followed its outward or upward whirls with the eagerness of the most unmeaning despair; they closed themselves spasmodically at the descent, although death would have been a relief, oh! how unspeakable! Still I quivered in every nerve to think how slight a sinking of the machinery would precipitate that keen, glistening axe upon my bosom. It was *hope* that prompted the nerve to quiver—the frame to shrink. It was *hope*—the hope that triumphs on the rack[32]—that whispers to the death-condemned even in the dungeons of the Inquisition.

I saw that some ten or twelve vibrations would bring the steel in actual contact with my robe, and with this observation there suddenly came over my spirit all the keen, collected calmness of despair. For the first time during many hours—or perhaps days—I *thought*. It now occurred to me that the bandage, or surcingle, which enveloped me, was *unique*. I was tied by no separate cord. The first stroke of the razor-like crescent athwart any portion of the band, would so detach it that it might be unwound from my person by means of my left hand. But how fearful, in that case, the **proximity** of the steel! The result of the slightest struggle how deadly! Was it likely, moreover, that the minions of the torturer had not foreseen and provided for this possibility! Was it probable that the bandage crossed my bosom in the track of the pendulum? Dreading to find my faint, and, as it seemed, my last hope frustrated, I so far elevated my head as to obtain a distinct view of my breast. The surcingle enveloped my limbs and body close in all directions—*save in the path of the destroying crescent.*

Scarcely had I dropped my head back into its original position, when there flashed upon my mind what I cannot better describe than as the unformed half of that idea of deliverance to which I have previously alluded, and of which a moiety[33] only floated indeterminately through my brain when I raised food to my burning lips. The whole thought was now present—feeble, scarcely sane, scarcely definite,—but still entire. I proceeded at once, with the nervous energy of despair, to attempt its execution.

For many hours the immediate vicinity of the low framework upon which I lay, had been literally swarming with rats. They were wild, bold, ravenous; their red eyes glaring upon me as if they waited but for motionlessness on my part to make me their prey. "To what food," I thought, "have they been accustomed in the well?"

Vocabulary

proximity (prok sim′ ə tē) *n.* closeness in space or time; nearness

32. The *rack* was a kind of torture machine that stretched a person's body in different directions.
33. A *moiety* of something is part of it.

---

despair (di spär′) *n.* loss of hope

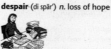
🖋 **Literary Element**

Suspense Reread the text on this page. Why does the reader feel suspense during this part of the story?

The pendulum is only ten or

twelve swings from hitting the

narrator. The reader knows that

the narrator will escape (since

he is telling the story) but does

not know how he will do it.

🖋 **Literary Element**

Suspense Reread the paragraph that begins "For many hours . . ." Why do you think the author includes these details about the rats? How do the rats add to the suspense of the story?

Students may say that the

rats make the situation even

scarier as they look toward the

narrator with hungry eyes.

To Sum Up

➤ The narrator wonders if the steel pendulum will cut through his straps and allow him to escape.

➤ He sees that the straps are not in the path of the blade.

➤ The rats continue to look at the narrator with hunger.

Interactive Question-Response

Content Vocabulary

Have a student read aloud the word and definition of *despair*. Then write on the board the three different ways that the narrator describes his feelings of despair on this page: *the eagerness of most unmeaning despair,* the *collected calmness of despair,* and *the nervous energy of despair.* Explain to students that *eagerness* means "readiness" or "enthusiasm," and *collected* means "in control." **Ask:** *Why might people who feel despair act eagerly, calmly, or nervously?* (They might be eager for a bad thing to be over with. They might calmly accept that bad things are going to happen. Or they might be nervous because they do not know what to do.)

Literary Element Suspense

Ask Early Advanced students to look at the repetition of the word *down.* **Ask:** *How does the repetition of down create a feeling of suspense?* (The reader feels a strong sense of the descending pendulum that will soon hit the narrator. The reader wonders how the narrator will escape.)

Literary Element Suspense

Ask students to review how the rats are described. *(The rats are swarming, wild, bold, and ravenous, and waiting for the narrator to die.)* **Ask:** How do the rats act as a clue about what will happen? *(The rats may play an important role in the narrator's situation as he tries to think of how to escape.)*

Fluency

Expression and Intonation: Punctuation

Intermediate/Early Advanced ▶ Tell students that they will be doing a choral reading of the passage that begins "The first stroke" and ends with "the track of the pendulum?" Remind students to change their voices depending on whether a sentence is a statement, a question, or an exclamation. Model reading the text at a moderate tempo, with appropriate tone for the declarative sentence, the three exclamations, and the question. Then have one student read a sentence. Have another student join in, and a third. Repeat until all students are reading together. When students reach the end of the passage, tell them to go back to the beginning and repeat until every student has been included in the reading. To assess individual fluency, use the Oral Reading Guidelines on page T16.

Beginning/Early Intermediate ▶ Have these students choral read only the three exclamations. Before they begin, model the pronunciation of the text. Then have students practice reading the paragraph in pairs before the choral reading.

Interactive Question-Response

Comprehension Check

Ask students to share what they underlined. **Ask:** *Were you surprised that the narrator escaped from the pendulum? What does the narrator's plan of escape show about him? (Students may express surprise that the narrator escaped after feeling despair that he would die. His plan shows that he is intelligent and can act with reason even when he feels nervous and upset.)*

To Sum Up

Beginning/Early Intermediate ▸ Have students work in pairs to reread all the To Sum Up statements from page 88 forward. Ask students to explain the most important events regarding the pendulum.

The most important events are

when _____.

when _____.

when _____.

(The most important events are when the narrator the narrator sees that he has been trapped beneath a swinging, sharp-edged pendulum; when the narrator learns that the pendulum is descending toward him; and when the narrator uses the rats to escape from the pendulum.)

Comprehension Check

Reread the paragraph that begins "At first the ravenous animals . . . ." How does the narrator escape from the pendulum? Underline the words that tell how the narrator becomes free.

Erred in my calculations means "made a mistake." In this case, the narrator was not mistaken about the rats.

To Sum Up

➤ The narrator rubs the meat juice over his straps.

➤ The rats chew through the straps as the pendulum reaches the narrator's robe.

➤ The narrator escapes from the pendulum.next to him.

92

They had devoured, in spite of all my efforts to prevent them, all but a small remnant of the contents of the dish. I had fallen into an habitual seesaw, or wave of the hand about the platter: and, at length, the unconscious uniformity of the movement deprived it of effect. In their voracity the vermin frequently fastened their sharp fangs into my fingers. With the particles of the oily and spicy viand which now remained, I thoroughly rubbed the bandage wherever I could reach it; then, raising my hand from the floor, I lay breathlessly still.

At first the ravenous animals were startled and terrified at the change—at the cessation of movement. They shrank alarmedly back; many sought the well. But this was only for a moment. I had not counted in vain upon their voracity. Observing that I remained without motion, one or two of the boldest leaped upon the frame-work, and smelt at the surcingle. This seemed the signal for a general rush. Forth from the well they hurried in fresh troops. They clung to the wood—they overran it, and leaped in hundreds upon my person. The measured movement of the pendulum disturbed them not at all. <u>Avoiding its strokes they busied themselves with the anointed bandage.</u> They pressed—they swarmed upon me in ever accumulating heaps. They writhed upon my throat; their cold lips sought my own; I was half stifled by their thronging pressure; disgust, for which the world has no name, swelled my bosom, and chilled, with a heavy clamminess, my heart. Yet one minute, and I felt that the struggle would be over. Plainly I perceived the loosening of the bandage. I knew that in more than one place it must be already severed. With a more than human resolution I lay *still*.

Nor had I **erred in my calculations**—nor had I endured in vain. I at length felt that I was *free*. The surcingle hung in ribands from my body. But the stroke of the pendulum already pressed upon my bosom. It had divided the serge of the robe. It had cut through the linen beneath. Twice again it swung, and a sharp sense of pain shot through every nerve. But the moment of escape had arrived. At a wave of my hand my deliverers hurried tumultuously away. With a steady movement—cautious, sidelong, shrinking, and slow—I slid from the embrace of the bandage and beyond the reach of the scimitar. For the moment, at least, *I was free*.

Word Study

Denotations and Connotations

Point out to students that Poe selects richly connotative words to create the terror the narrator experiences,. Read aloud the paragraph beginning "At first the ravenous animals . . ." on this page. Help students identify words with negative connotations, such as *ravenous, startled, terrified, shrank, alarmedly, heaps, writhed, stifled,* and *disgust.* Then have students locate these words in a dictionary or thesaurus. Help students replace some of these words in the paragraph with synonyms that have less negative connotations, such as *frightened* in place of *terrified* and *aversion* or *displeasure* in place of *disgust.*

Then have students practice analyzing the connotations of other words in the selection by completing the activity on page A16.

Free!—and in the grasp of the Inquisition! I had scarcely stepped from my wooden bed of horror upon the stone floor of the prison, when the motion of the hellish machine ceased and I beheld it drawn up, by some invisible force through the ceiling. This was a lesson which I took desperately to heart. My every motion was undoubtedly watched. Free!—I had but escaped death in one form of agony, to be delivered unto worse than death in some other. With that thought I rolled my eyes nervously around the barriers of iron that hemmed me in. Something unusual—some change which at first I could not appreciate distinctly—it was obvious, had taken place in the apartment. For many minutes in a dreamy and trembling abstraction,[34] I busied myself in vain, unconnected conjecture.[35] During this period, I became aware, for the first time, of the origin of the **sulphurous light** which illuminated the cell. It proceeded from a fissure, about half an inch in width, extending entirely around the prison at the base of the walls, which thus appeared, and were completely separated from the floor. I endeavored, but of course in vain, to look through the aperture.

A *sulphurous light* means "a fiery or hellish light." Sulfur (also spelled *sulphur*) is an element with a foul smell and a yellow color. It is traditionally associated with hell.

34. *Abstraction* means "being deep in thought."
35. A *conjecture* is an opinion or guess.

REFLECT

Identify Sequence
What happens after the narrator discovers the pendulum? Number the following events in the order in which they occur.

_5_ The narrator frees himself from the path of the pendulum.

_2_ The narrator feels despair.

_3_ The narrator rubs his straps with meat.

_4_ The rats jump onto the narrator and eat through his straps.

_6_ The narrator sees fiery light in the dungeon.

_1_ The narrator sees the pendulum's steel edges.

 Talk about your answer with a partner.

To Sum Up

➤ The narrator sees fiery light that comes from a crack in the bottom of the walls.

The Pit and the Pendulum **93**

Interactive Question-Response

Reflect

Partner Talk Have students work in pairs to answer. To help students get started: **Model** *To answer this, I would think about the first thing that happens after the narrator discovers the pendulum. He sees the pendulum's sharp edges and sees that it is descending toward him. So number 1 would be "The narrator sees the pendulum's steel edges."* Write the following sentence frames on the board to help students organize their thoughts.

The first thing that happens is _____.

Then, the next thing that happens is _____.

Interactive Question-Response

Literary Element Suspense

To help students answer the question **Ask:** *What do exclamation points and dashes reveal about a character's emotions? (Exclamation points show excitement, surprise, or fear. Dashes show that a character's thoughts are interrupted or distracted.)*

Literary Element

Suspense Reread the boxed text on this page. Underline the words that end with exclamation marks and dashes. How does the punctuation add to the suspense?

The narrator feels terror at what is happening. The exclamation marks show his fear and surprise. The dashes show that his thoughts are scattered and distracted. The reader wants to learn more about what will happen to him. This seems like it will be the worst terror of all.

To Sum Up

➤ The narrator smells heated iron and struggles to breathe.
➤ The walls seem to glow with fire.
➤ The narrator runs to the edge of the pit but becomes scared and runs back.

As I arose from the attempt, the mystery of the alteration in the chamber broke at once upon my understanding. I have observed that, although the outlines of the figures upon the walls were sufficiently distinct, yet the colors seemed blurred and indefinite. These colors had now assumed, and were momentarily assuming, a startling and most intense brilliancy, that gave to the spectral and fiendish portraitures an aspect that might have thrilled even firmer nerves than my own. Demon eyes, of a wild and ghastly vivacity, glared upon me in a thousand directions, where none had been visible before, and gleamed with the lurid luster of a fire that I could not force my imagination to regard as unreal.

Unreal!—Even while I breathed there came to my nostrils the breath of the vapor of heated iron! A suffocating odor pervaded the prison! A deeper glow settled each moment in the eyes that glared at my agonies! A richer tint of crimson diffused itself over the pictured horrors of blood. I panted! I gasped for breath! There could be no doubt of the design of my tormentors—oh! most unrelenting! oh! most demoniac of men! I shrank from the glowing metal to the center of the cell. Amid the thought of the fiery destruction that impended, the idea of the coolness of the well came over my soul like balm. I rushed to its deadly brink. I threw my straining vision below. The glare from the enkindled roof illumined its inmost recesses. Yet, for a wild moment, did my spirit refuse to comprehend the meaning of what I saw. At length it forced—it wrestled its way into my soul—it burned itself in upon my shuddering reason.—Oh! for a voice to speak! oh! horror!—oh! any horror but this! With a shriek, I rushed from the margin, and buried my face in my hands—weeping bitterly.

Differentiated Instruction

Clarify the Text Support students in understanding the conclusion of the story.

Beginning/Early Intermediate ➤ Read aloud the last two To Sum Up boxes of the selection. Explain that the walls are becoming hot and they are closing in on the narrator. **Ask:** *Do you think the narrator can escape? (No, there does not seem to be a way out.)*

Intermediate ➤ Ask students to reread the paragraph beginning with "The heat rapidly increased…." Use gestures to show the meaning of *acute* (less than 90°) and *obtuse* (between 90° and 180°). **Ask:** *How does the shape of the room change? (The walls take the shape of a flattened diamond.)*

Early Advanced ➤ Explain that the walls are painted with scary figures who seem to glow with fire. Ask students why this would make the situation worse. *(These paintings frighten the narrator even if they do not harm him.)*

The heat rapidly increased, and once again I looked up, shuddering as with a fit of the ague.[36] There had been a second change in the cell—and now the change was obviously in the *form*. As before, it was in vain that I, at first, endeavoured to appreciate or understand what was taking place. But not long was I left in doubt. The Inquisitorial vengeance had been hurried by my two-fold escape, and there was to be no more dallying with the King of Terrors.[37] The room had been square. I saw that two of its iron angles were now acute—two, consequently, obtuse. The fearful difference quickly increased with a low rumbling or moaning sound. In an instant the apartment had shifted its form into that of a **lozenge**. But the alteration stopped not here—I neither hoped nor desired it to stop. I could have clasped the red walls to my bosom as a garment of eternal peace. "Death," I said, "any death but that of the pit!" Fool! might I have not known that *into the pit* it was the object of the burning iron to urge me? Could I resist its glow? or, if even that, could I withstand its pressure? And now, flatter and flatter grew the lozenge, with a rapidity that left me no time for contemplation. Its center, and of course, its greatest width, came just over the yawning gulf. I shrank back—but the closing walls pressed me resistlessly onward. At length for my seared and writhing body there was no longer an inch of foothold on the firm floor of the prison. I struggled no more, but the agony of my soul found vent in one loud, long, and final scream of despair. I felt that I tottered upon the brink—I averted my eyes—

There was a discordant hum of human voices! There was a loud blast of many trumpets! There was a harsh grating as of a thousand thunders! The fiery walls rushed back! An outstretched arm caught my own as I fell, fainting, into the abyss. It was that of General Lasalle.[38] The French army had entered Toledo. The Inquisition was in the hands of its enemies.

36. **Ague** (ā′ gū) is a fever.
37. The King of Terrors could be either the Inquisition or death.
38. **Lasalle** was an officer in the French army of Napoleon Bonaparte, whose army attacked Spain in 1808.

REFLECT

Identify Sequence
How does the repetition of the exclamation point in the final paragraph reinforce that it's the end of the story?

Possible answer: It emphasizes the excitement of the story's ending and signals finality.

 Talk about your answer with a partner.

 Comprehension Check
Reread the boxed text on this page. How are the walls of the dungeon changing? Underline the words that tell how the walls are changing.

To Sum Up

➤ The room gets hotter, and the fiery walls move toward the narrator.
➤ The narrator is about to fall into the pit, but someone catches him.
➤ The walls move back, and trumpets sound. The French army has taken over the city and stopped the Inquisition.

Interactive Question-Response

Comprehension Check

How would you describe this third terror? Why is this terror the most frightening for the narrator? *(The fiery walls are pushing him into the pit. Perhaps the narrator feels as if he is being pushed into the pit of hell.)*

To Sum Up

Beginning/Early Intermediate Have students work in pairs to reread all the To Sum Up statements from page 93 forward. Ask students to explain the most important events in the final part of the story.

The most important events are

when _____.

when _____.

when _____.

(The most important events are when the walls start to glow with fire, when the walls push the narrator toward the pit, and when the narrator is saved by the French army.)

Reflect

Identify Sequence Model reading the sentences ending in exclamation points so that students can hear how the tone signals a change and the story's ending.

Oral Assessment

Provide the following prompts to one student at a time. Observe students' responses. See the Oral Assessment Rubric on page T17 to determine students' levels of language output.

1. Why is the narrator taken to the dungeon?
2. What are some things in the dungeon that scare the narrator?
3. How does the narrator discover the pit?
4. How does the narrator escape from the pendulum?
5. How is the narrator saved at the end of the story?

Vocabulary Check

B. Intermediate

Read each sentence aloud. Encourage students to answer with the correct word. Then turn the sentence into a question and ask students to answer. Some possible questions are: *What else might* impede *your ability to study for a test? What else might you* deduce *from the empty plates and cups? What is another reason that you might feel* ravenous*? If you don't take the elevator, how else could you make a* descent *through a building? How do you comfort your friends when they feel* despair*?*

Academic Vocabulary

Write the following sentence on the board: *In "The Pit and the Pendulum," the* **environment** *of the prison is dark and haunting.*

Tell students that in the above statement about the selection, *environment* means "surroundings," and refers to what the narrator sees around him. Point out that in the sciences, the word *environment* refers to the complex combination of factors (geography, natural resources, plant and animal life, and culture) that affect the life of an individual or community. **Ask** What problem relating to the quality of a community's life concerns environmental scientists? *(pollution)*

The Pit and the Pendulum

Vocabulary Check

A. Circle the picture that best answers the question.

1. Which picture shows a person's **descent**?

3. Which dog is **ravenous**?

2. Which person feels **fatigue**?

4. Which person feels **despair**?

B. Write the correct word for each sentence in the blank.

| deduce   despair   impede   descent   ravenous |

5. Loud music may _____ **impede** _____ my ability to study for my test.

6. From the empty plates and cups, Emilio could _____ **deduce** _____ that the party had ended.

7. Because I forgot to eat breakfast, I felt _____ **ravenous** _____ at lunchtime.

8. The elevator made a _____ **descent** _____ from the fourteenth floor to the second.

9. When Julia felt _____ **despair** _____, she was comforted by her friends.

C. Circle the letter of the sentence that uses the boldface word correctly.

10. a. During the funny movie, the audience was overcome by **lethargy**.
    b. The interesting story brought the students out of their **lethargy**.

11. a. The blue light will **diffuse** a cool glow throughout the room.
    b. The red stoplight will **diffuse** drivers on the road.

12. a. The team felt **despair** when the star player was injured.
    b. The team felt **despair** at winning the tournament.

13. a. If you drive on this road, you should **impede** the fallen tree.
    b. The fallen tree will **impede** the drivers on this road.

Grammar Link   BLM

The Simple Past Tense: Irregular Verbs

Prepare students to complete the activity on page A17. Read the grammar instruction with students, and complete the first item with them to get them started.

The Pit and the Pendulum

Comprehension Check

A. What are three terrors in the dungeon? Write them in the boxes below.

First
the pit in the center of the room

↓

Second
the steel pendulum

↓

Third
the fiery walls that move

B. Think about suspense in "The Pit and the Pendulum." Then complete the sentences below.)

1. I think the most suspenseful moment in the story is Possible response: the moment when the pendulum is about to hit the narrator;

because Possible response: the reader does not know how he will escape.

2. The pendulum adds to the suspense of the story because it Possible response: it slowly descends on the narrator as he tries to figure out how to stop it.

3. The suspense goes away at the end of the story because Possible response: The French army invades Toledo and saves the narrator from the pit.

C. Answer the questions below about the suspense in "The Pit and the Pendulum."

4. Describe one terror that the narrator faces in the dungeon. How does it add to the suspense of the story? How does it make the reader feel?

One terror that the narrator faces is Possible responses: the pit; the pendulum

It adds to the suspense because Possible response for the pit: the narrator almost falls into the pit. He must try to avoid falling in, but the dungeon is dark. Possible response for the pendulum: it is slowly descending on the narrator. The narrator must try to think of a way to escape as he watches the pendulum

The reader feels Possible response for the pit: The reader feels nervous because the narrator could easily fall in the pit in the dark. Possible answer for the response: The reader feels tense because it seems impossible for the narrator to escape

Comprehension Check

B. Intermediate

Encourage students to think about when they felt the most curious or tense during the story. Then ask them to think about why the use of the pendulum is an excellent way to add suspense to the story. Finally, ask students to think about why the suspense goes away at the end of the story.

Writing Link

Interview

Have students imagine they are the narrator and are being interviewed. Write the following on the board and have students fill in the blanks on a piece of paper.

Interviewer: Where were you kept?

Narrator: I was kept in _____. It had in _____ and _____.

Interviewer: What terrified you?

Narrator: Many things, including _____. The most terrifying of all was _____.

Interviewer: How were you rescued?

Narrator: When the walls closed in, I almost _____, but General LaSalle _____

The Pit and the Pendulum

Interview

Imagine that you are a television news reporter. The French army has just invaded Toledo. You are reporting about the horrors of the dungeons of Toledo. You interview the narrator of the story so that people who are watching will understand what the dungeons are like.

Good evening. I am reporting from one of the dungeons of Toledo, where the French army has just freed some prisoners. With me is one of the prisoners.

Interviewer: How long were you in the dungeon?
Narrator: Possible response: I was there for several days, but I am not sure how many.

Interviewer: Why were you sent to the dungeon?
Narrator: Possible response: I was sentenced to death by the court of the Inquisition.

Interviewer: Can you describe what the dungeon was like? How did it look and feel?
Narrator: Possible response: The dungeon was completely dark at first, but some light showed later. The walls were fiery and could move. A large pit was in the center of the dungeon.

Interviewer: What were some of the dangers of the dungeon?
Narrator: Possible response: The pit was dangerous because it was too dark to see, and I almost fell into it. I was also strapped to a piece of wood while a sharp-edged pendulum was lowered toward me.

Interviewer: How did you escape from these dangers??
Narrator: Possible response: I tripped before I fell into the pit, which was very lucky. I escaped from the pendulum by rubbing food on my straps. It attracted rats which bit through the straps and set me free.

Interviewer: What would have happened to you if the French army had not come?
Narrator: Possible response: The fiery walls were pushing me into the pit. I was very scared.

Interviewer: Would you like to say anything to the French army?
Narrator: Possible response: Thank you very much. I am very thankful that you came when you did.

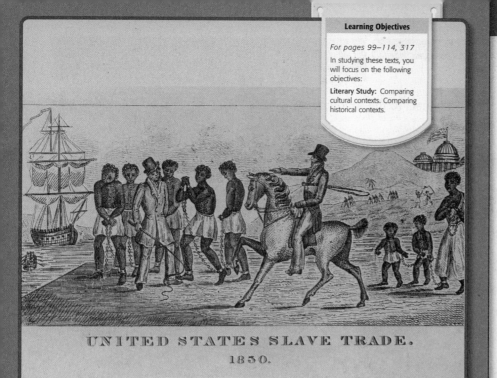

UNITED STATES SLAVE TRADE.
1830.

from MY BONDAGE AND MY FREEDOM
by Frederick Douglass

Frederick Douglass
by Robert Hayden

IN TEXAS GRASS
by Quincy Troupe

from My Bondage and My Freedom/Frederick Douglass/In Texas Grass   **99**

Learning Objectives

For pages 99–114, 317

In studying these texts, you will focus on the following objectives:

Literary Study: Comparing cultural contexts. Comparing historical contexts.

Oral Language

Build Background

Read the titles and authors. Explain that students will read three selections that deal with responses to slavery and how people have reacted to it. **Ask:**

• The word *bondage* means the opposite of *freedom*. What is another word for *bondage*? (*slavery*)

• Based on the titles, which selection is about someone who wrote one of the other selections? (*"Frederick Douglass"*)

Talk About the Autobiography

Explain that the idea of freedom is an important part of each reading.

Beginning/Early Intermediate ▶ Is freedom important to you? (*yes/no*) Work with students to mime the ideas of freedom and constraint.

Intermediate ▶ Explain that Frederick Douglass did not enjoy the freedoms many Americans take for granted because he was a slave. Have students list the kinds of freedom that are most important to them.

A freedom that is important to me is the right to _____. (freedom of religion, free speech, freedom of assembly, a fair trial)

Lesson at a Glance

Oral Language
• Build Background
• Talk About the Autobiography

Vocabulary
• Selection Vocabulary
• Content Vocabulary

Literary Element
• Autobiography

Reading Strategy
• Analyze Cause and Effect

Writing Link
• Mission Statement

Comprehension
BLM

Word Study BLM
Context Meaning BLM

Grammar Link BLM
• Future Time Clauses with *Before, After,* and *When* BLM

Technology
• Student Works™ Plus
• Teacher Works™ Plus
• Listening Library Audio CD
• Classroom Presentation Toolkit
• Glencoe Visual Vocabulary
• Skill Level Up!™ A Skill-Based Language Arts Game

Interactive Question-Response

Connect to the Autobiography

Read aloud Connect to the Autobiography: **Model** / *had a friend who was treated rudely at a restaurant. My friend wrote a letter to the owner of the restaurant, who made an official apology.* Model writing your response in the chart, and have volunteers suggest other responses. Then have individuals fill in their own charts.

Literary Element
Autobiography

Read aloud the Literary Element. Explain, using gestures, that an autobiography tells the story of the author's own life. Have students discuss what events they would include in their own autobiography.

Reading Strategy Analyze Cause and Effect

Read aloud the Reading Strategy. Tell students that analyzing cause and effect means understanding how one thing leads to another. Write on the board: *I was late to school today.* Ask students to provide two possible causes that might lead to the effect of being late. Then ask them to provide two possible effects that being late might cause.

Comparing Literature

Read aloud the Comparing Literature element. Explain to students that a portrayal shows the important qualities of a person or group. Portrayals can be found in movies and television, as well as in readings. Have students describe examples of portrayals that they have seen or read recently. Ask them what qualities or traits made the individuals or groups in those portrayals special.

FROM MY BONDAGE AND MY FREEDOM
Frederick Douglass   **IN TEXAS GRASS**

Connect to the Autobiography

Oppression is the cruel treatment of others. Have you ever known someone who has struggled against oppression? On the lines below, describe the situation. Then tell how the person responded to the oppression. Did he or she fight back? If so, how?

> Possible answer: My brother once had a mean boss at work. He decided to get a new job so he wouldn't have to be treated badly.

Literary Element Autobiography

Authors write autobiographies to tell about their own lives. Frederick Douglass tells about his life during the time of slavery in his **autobiography**.

As you read, ask yourself, Why did Douglass tell about his life in the form of an autobiography?

Reading Strategy Analyze Cause and Effect

An event that brings about another one is a cause. The event that results from a cause is an effect. When you **analyze cause and effect**, you figure out how one event leads to another.

As you read, ask yourself the following questions:

- What are the major events that Douglass writes about?
- What effects were caused by each major event?

Comparing Literature Compare Portrayals of People

When a writer describes a person's important features, it is called a portrayal. A group portrayal shows the important features shared by a group of people. As you read, ask yourself, What makes the individuals and groups described in these readings unique?

Selection Vocabulary

benevolent (b ə nev' ə lənt) *adj.* intending to do good (p. 102)
*The man thanked his friend for the **benevolent** gift.*
➤ Cognate (Spanish) **benévolo**

depravity (di prav' ə tē) *n.* evil (p. 102)
*The newspaper story described the **depravity** of the criminal.*
➤ Cognate (Spanish) **depravación**

induce (in dōōs') *v.* to cause or persuade (p. 103)
*My sister tried to **induce** me to drive her to the movie theater.*
➤ Cognate (Spanish) **inducir**

vanquished (vang' kwisht) *v.* defeated; overcame (p. 106)
*I am sure that our basketball team **vanquished** our opponents.*

censure (sen' shər) *v.* to find fault with; to blame (p. 108)
*Ms. Sarlin will probably **censure** me for losing my book.*
➤ Cognate (Spanish) **censurar**

Content Vocabulary

fury (fyoor' ē) *n.* strong anger (p. 104)
*Mr. Lombardo's red face and loud voice showed his **fury**.*
➤ Cognate (Spanish) **furor**

mirth (murth) *n.* happiness shown by laughter (p. 107)
*The clown at the party caused much **mirth**..*

wreaths (rēaths) *n.* flowers or leaves arranged in a circle (p. 109)
*Many people decorate their doors by hanging **wreaths** on them.*

stretching (strech' ing) *v.* spreading (p. 111)
*Jaime saw the clouds **stretching** across the sky.*

For more practice, see page 317. ➡

Vocabulary Routine

To introduce the vocabulary, read aloud the words and definitions in the student book and have students repeat after you. Discuss how the pictures illustrate the words or sentences. Then follow the vocabulary routine below.

Content Vocabulary

Define: **Fury** is a very strong feeling of anger.
Example: *The coach jumped up and down to show his fury about the referee's decision.* Ask: What word means the opposite of *fury*? ANTONYM

Someone who feels **mirth** is very happy and shows it by laughing. *Everyone enjoyed seeing the mirth of the young singers.* What is an example of someone who feels *mirth*? EXAMPLE

Wreaths are flowers or leaves that are arranged in a circular frame. *Some people put wreaths on their doors as a holiday decoration.* Draw a picture of *wreaths.* DESCRIPTION

Something is **stretching** if it spreads from one place to another. *We looked at the rows of flowers stretching across the park.* What word means about the same as *stretching*? SYNONYM

Vocabulary Practice Have students complete the vocabulary practice activity on page 317.

Selection Vocabulary

Define: A person who volunteers for charities is **benevolent.** Example: Mrs. Auld's *benevolent* nature made her want to teach young Frederick how to read. Ask: What is an example of a benevolent action you have performed? EXAMPLE

Depravity describes a person who is morally evil or corrupt. *By kidnapping people from their homes and families and enslaving them, the slave traders demonstrated their depravity.* How are the words depravity and corruption the same? How are they different? COMPARE AND CONTRAST

When you **induce** someone, you are persuading them. *Douglass tried to induce a dislike for slavery in his friends by contrasting their lives to his.* Describe a time when you induced someone to do something. DESCRIPTION

When you **vanquish** something, you defeat or overcome it. *I vanquished my opponent in the video game to advance to the next level.* What synonyms for vanquish can you think of? What different connotations, or shades of meaning, does each have? SYNONYM

To **censure** means to formally express strong disapproval or to blame someone for a negative outcome. *The United Nations censured the government for humans-rights violations.* Explain what process your school's student government should follow before issuing a censure of one of its members. EXPLANATION

Interactive
Question-Response

Comprehension Check

Ask students to share their answers. **Ask:** *Why do you
think Mrs. Auld's husband might not want Frederick to
learn how to read? (Mr. Auld does not see Douglass
as an equal, and so does not think he needs to know
how to read. Also, it is easier to control someone who
does not know how to read.)*

My condition was variable means
"my life was sometimes good and
sometimes bad."

Mistress here means "teacher."

Comprehension Check
Underline the phrase that explains
why Douglass's mistress stops
teaching him how to read.

To Sum Up

➤ Frederick Douglass lived for
seven years as a slave in
Baltimore.

➤ Douglass's mistress, Mrs. Auld,
began to teach him to read
and write.

➤ She stopped teaching him
because her husband told
her to.

102

I lived in the family of master Hugh, at Baltimore, seven years, during
which time—as the almanac[1] makers say of the weather—**my condition
was variable.** The most interesting feature of my history here, was my
learning to read and write, under somewhat marked disadvantages. In
attaining this knowledge, I was compelled to resort to indirections by
no means congenial to my nature, and which were really humiliating
to me. My **mistress**—who, as the reader has already seen, had begun to
teach me—was suddenly checked in her **benevolent** design, by the strong
advice of her husband. In faithful compliance with this advice, the good
lady had not only ceased to instruct me, herself, but had set her face as a
flint against my learning to read by any means. It is due, however, to my
mistress to say, that she did not adopt this course in all its stringency at
the first. She either thought it unnecessary, or she lacked the **depravity**
indispensable to shutting me up in mental darkness. It was, at least,
necessary for her to have some training, and some hardening, in the
exercise of the slaveholder's prerogative, to make her equal to forgetting
my human nature and character, and to treating me as a thing destitute
of a moral or an intellectual nature. Mrs. Auld—my mistress—was, as I
have said, a most kind and tender-hearted woman; and, in the humanity
of her heart, and the simplicity of her mind, she set out, when I first went
to live with her, to treat me as she supposed one human being ought to
treat another.

It is easy to see, that, in entering upon the duties of a slaveholder,
some little experience is needed. Nature has done almost nothing to

Vocabulary ....
benevolent (b a nev' a lant) *adj.* intending to do good
depravity (di prav' a tē) *n.* evil

1. An *almanac* is a book that is published every year. It has calendars with information
about weather and astronomy.

Comprehension

To support students as they read the selection, have them begin the graphic organizer on
page A18.

prepare men and women to be either slaves or slaveholders. Nothing but rigid training, long persisted in, can perfect the character of the one or the other. One cannot easily forget to love freedom; and it is as hard to cease to respect that natural love in our fellow creatures. On entering upon the career of a slaveholding mistress, Mrs. Auld was singularly deficient; nature, which **fits nobody for such an office,** had done less for her than any lady I had known. It was no easy matter to **induce** her to think and to feel that the curly-headed boy, who stood by her side, and even leaned on her lap; who was loved by little Tommy, and who loved little Tommy in turn; sustained to her only the relation of a chattel.[2] I was *more* than that, and she felt me to be more than that. I could talk and sing; I could laugh and weep; I could reason and remember; I could love and hate. I was human, and she, dear lady, knew and felt me to be so. How could she, then, treat me as a brute, without a mighty struggle with all the noble powers of her own soul. That struggle came, and the will and power of the husband was victorious. Her noble soul was overthrown; but, he that overthrew it did not, himself, escape the consequences. He, not less than the other parties, was injured in his domestic peace by the fall.

When I went into their family, it was the abode of happiness and contentment. The mistress of the house was a model of affection and tenderness. Her fervent piety and watchful uprightness made it impossible to see her without thinking and feeling—*"that woman is a Christian."* There was no sorrow nor suffering for which she had not a tear, and there was no innocent joy for which she had not a smile. She had bread for the hungry, clothes for the naked, and comfort for every mourner that came within her reach. Slavery soon proved its ability to divest her of these excellent qualities, and her home of its early happiness. Conscience cannot stand much violence. Once thoroughly broken down, *who* is he that can repair the damage? It may be broken toward the slave, on Sunday, and toward the master on Monday. It cannot endure such shocks. It must stand entire, or it does not stand at all. If my condition waxed bad, that of the family waxed not better. The first step, in the wrong direction, was the violence done to nature and to conscience, in arresting the benevolence that would have enlightened my young mind. In ceasing to instruct me, she must begin to justify herself *to* herself; and, once consenting to take sides in such a debate, she was riveted to her position. One needs very little knowledge of moral philosophy, to see *where* my mistress now landed. She finally became even more violent in her opposition to my learning to read, than was her husband himself. She was not satisfied with simply doing as *well* as her husband had commanded her, but seemed resolved to better his instruction. Nothing appeared to make my poor mistress—after her **turning toward the downward path**—more angry, than seeing me, seated in some nook or corner, quietly reading a book or a newspaper. I have had her rush at me, with the utmost

Vocabulary

induce (in dōō s′) *v.* to cause or persuade

2. *Chattel* means items of personal property that can be moved, such as furniture or farm animals. Slaves were legally viewed as chattel.

Fits nobody for such an office means that something is not natural.

🖉 **Literary Element**

Autobiography Reread the first sentence in the boxed text at the bottom of this page. What is Douglass saying here about how slavery has affected his life?
- ☐ It took him away from his family.
- ☑ It stopped him from getting an education.
- ☐ It prevented him from making friends.

Turning toward the downward path means deciding to do the wrong thing.

To Sum Up

➤ At first, Mrs. Auld was kind to Douglass.

➤ She became cruel because the system of slavery required people to be cruel.

➤ Slavery causes harm to both slaves and slave owners.

Interactive Question-Response

Literary Element
Autobiography

If students have trouble responding: **Model** *I would begin by reading the sentence. It says that the thing that hurt Douglass was "arresting the benevolence that would have enlightened" his mind. Arresting means stopping,* benevolence *means good will, and* enlightened *means gave knowledge to. From what I've read, I know that Mr. Auld stopped his wife from giving Douglass the knowledge to read. So Douglass is saying here that slavery harmed him in this way: it kept him from learning how to read.* **Ask:** *Why does Douglass say that keeping him from reading is "violence against nature and conscience"? (It is against conscience because it is unfair, and it is against nature because Douglass believes that learning is natural for human beings.)*

Interactive Question-Response

Content Vocabulary

Read aloud the word and definition for *fury*. Ask students when they might expect someone to feel fury: **Model** *I would expect to feel fury if I worked very hard on something and suddenly my work is wasted. For example, suppose I am writing a long document and my computer crashes. If I did not save the document properly, I might feel fury, both at the computer and at myself for not saving my work.*

To Sum Up

Have students work in pairs to reread all the To Sum Up statements from the beginning of the selection on page 102. **Ask:** *What have you learned about Douglass at this point? (He wants to learn how to read.) What have you learned about slavery? (Slavery harms for both slaves and masters.)*

---

fury (fyoor′ ē) *n.* intense anger

To *give an account of myself* is to explain what I have been doing.

Hit upon something means to discover it.

fury, and snatch from my hand such newspaper or book, with something of the wrath and consternation which a traitor might be supposed to feel on being discovered in a plot by some dangerous spy.

Mrs. Auld was an apt woman, and the advice of her husband, and her own experience, soon demonstrated, to her entire satisfaction, that education and slavery are incompatible with each other. When this conviction was thoroughly established, I was most narrowly watched in all my movements. If I remained in a separate room from the family for any considerable length of time, I was sure to be suspected of having a book, and was at once called upon to **give an account of myself.** All this, however, was entirely *too late.* The first, and never to be retraced, step had been taken. In teaching me the alphabet, in the days of her simplicity and kindness, my mistress had given me the "inch," and now, no ordinary precaution could prevent me from taking the "ell."[3]

Seized with a determination to learn to read, at any cost, I **hit upon** many expedients to accomplish the desired end. The plea which I mainly adopted, and the one by which I was most successful, was that of using my young white playmates, with whom I met in the street, as teachers. I used to carry, almost constantly, a copy of Webster's spelling book in my pocket; and, when sent of errands, or when play time was allowed me, I would step, with my young friends, aside, and take a lesson in spelling. I generally paid my *tuition fee* to the boys, with bread, which I also carried in my pocket. For a single biscuit, any of my hungry little comrades would give me a lesson more valuable to me than bread. Not every one, however, demanded this consideration, for there were those who took pleasure in teaching me, whenever I had a chance to be taught by them. I am strongly tempted to give the names of two or three of those little boys, as a slight testimonial of the gratitude and affection I bear them, but prudence forbids; not that it would injure me, but it might, possibly, embarrass them; for it is almost an unpardonable offense to do any thing, directly or indirectly, to promote a slave's freedom, in a slave state. It is enough to say, of my warm-hearted little play fellows, that they lived on Philpot street, very near Durgin & Bailey's shipyard.

To Sum Up

➤ Mr. and Mrs. Auld watched Douglass closely to stop him from reading.

➤ But it was too late. Douglass made up his mind that he would learn to read.

➤ He got white children to teach him by giving them bread.

3. An **ell** is an old English unit of length. It is equal to about 45 inches. Douglass is referring to the saying "give him an inch, and he'll take an ell." It means, "Give him a little bit of freedom, and he'll expect much more."

Differentiated Instruction

Clarify the Text Support students in understanding how Douglass learned to read.

Beginning/Early Intermediate ▶ Read aloud the third bullet in To Sum Up. **Ask:** *How did Douglass learn how to read? (He gave white children bread to teach him to read.)*

Intermediate ▶ Have partners read aloud the boxed text on page 104. Then have them complete these sentence frames: *Mr. and Mrs. Auld believe that slaves should not _____ ____. (be educated) But Douglass learned to read while_____. (playing or doing errands)*

Early Advanced ▶ Point out that Douglass did not have to pay all of the white children who taught him. **Ask:** *Why doesn't Douglass mention the names of the children who were especially kind to him? (He doesn't want them to get into trouble for helping a slave.)*

Although slavery was **a delicate subject,** and very cautiously talked about among grown up people in Maryland, I frequently talked about it—and that very freely—with the white boys. I would, sometimes, say to them, while seated on a curb stone or a cellar door, "I wish I could be free, as you will be when you get to be men." "You will be free, you know, as soon as you are twenty-one, and can go where you like, but I am a **slave for life.** Have I not as good a right to be free as you have?" Words like these, <u>I observed</u>, always troubled them; and <u>I had no small satisfaction</u> in wringing from the boys, occasionally, that fresh and bitter condemnation of slavery, that springs from nature, unseared and unperverted. Of all consciences, let me have those to deal with which have not been bewildered by the cares of life. I do not remember ever to have met with a boy, while I was in slavery, who defended the slave system; but <u>I have often had</u> boys to console me, with the hope that something would yet occur, by which I might be made free. Over and over again, they have told me, that "they believed *I* had as good a right to be free as *they* had"; and that "they did not believe God ever made any one to be a slave." The reader will easily see, that such little conversations with my play fellows, had no tendency to weaken my love of liberty, nor to render me contented with my condition as a slave.

REFLECT

Analyze Cause and Effect

The selection contains many examples of cause and effect. Write two things that have happened in the Cause box. Write the results in the Effect box.

Cause		Effect
Possible answers:	→	Possible answers:
Cause 1: Mr. Auld tells his wife to quit teaching Douglass.		Effect 1: Mrs. Auld stops teaching Douglass to read.
Cause 2: Douglass has lost his teacher, but he still wants to learn how to read.		Effect 2: Douglass convinces his white friends to teach him how to read.

 Talk about your answer with a partner.

---

from **My Bondage and My Freedom**

A *delicate subject* is a topic that makes people uncomfortable.

Someone who is *a slave for life* will be a slave until he dies.

 Literary Element

Autobiography Underline three phrases that show that Douglass is describing his own personal experience.

To Sum Up

➤ Douglass often talked about slavery with his white friends.

➤ None of his friends thought that slavery was fair.

➤ Douglass believed that people are good and fair. Slavery teaches them to be cruel.

Literary Element
Autobiography

If students have trouble responding: **Model** *I would answer this question by looking for phrases that show that Douglass is talking about his own experience, not someone else's. The word* I *is a good signal for this. Phrases such as* I observed *or* I do not remember *show that these events happened to Douglass himself.* **Ask:** *What does Douglass learn from his own experience about the slave system? (That the natural human reaction to slavery is to condemn it.)*

Reflect

Partner Talk Have students work in pairs to answer. To help students get started: **Model** *To answer this question, I would start by looking for sequences of events that lead to other events in the story. For example, at the beginning of the selection it says that Mrs. Auld used to teach Frederick how to read, but then she stopped. Why did she stop? She stopped because her husband told her to. So, one cause is that her husband told her not to teach Frederick, and the effect is that she stopped teaching him to read.*

Write the following sentence frame on the board to help students organize their thoughts:

Another event in the autobiography that causes an effect is _____. The effect that it leads to is _____.

Interactive Question-Response

Comprehension Check

Ask students to share their answers. **Ask:** *Do you think that Douglass will be a slave for life? (No.) What clue suggests that he becomes free eventually? (The selection is taken from a book called* My Bondage and My Freedom.*)*

Comprehension Check

As Douglass became more educated, how did he feel?
- [ ] He felt more powerful than his masters.
- [ ] He felt angry with his friends, because they would not help him.
- [x] He felt worse, because he understood that he was a slave for life.

Brought out here means "fully developed."

To Sum Up

➤ Douglass read about a debate between a slave and his master.

➤ The slave explained why slavery is wrong. He won the debate, and his master set him free.

➤ The book gave Douglass hope.

When I was about thirteen years old, and had succeeded in learning to read, every increase of knowledge, especially respecting the Free States, added something to the almost intolerable burden of the thought—"I am a Slave for life." To my bondage I saw no end. It was a terrible reality, and I shall never be able to tell how sadly that thought chafed my young spirit. Fortunately, or unfortunately, about this time in my life, I had made enough money to buy what was then a very popular school book, viz:[4] the "Columbian Orator." I bought this addition to my library, of Mr. Knight, on Thames street, Fell's Point, Baltimore, and paid him fifty cents for it. I was first led to buy this book, by hearing some little boys say that they were going to learn some little pieces out of it for the Exhibition. This volume was, indeed, a rich treasure, and every opportunity afforded me, for a time, was spent in diligently perusing it. Among much other interesting matter, that which I had perused and reperused with unflagging satisfaction, was a short dialogue between a master and his slave. The slave is represented as having been recaptured, in a second attempt to run away; and the master opens the dialogue with an upbraiding speech, charging the slave with ingratitude, and demanding to know what he has to say in his own defense. Thus upbraided, and thus called upon to reply, the slave rejoins, that he knows how little anything that he can say will avail, seeing that he is completely in the hands of his owner; and with noble resolution, calmly says, "I submit to my fate." Touched by the slave's answer, the master insists upon his further speaking, and recapitulates the many acts of kindness which he has performed toward the slave, and tells him he is permitted to speak for himself. Thus invited to the debate, the quondam[5] slave made a spirited defense of himself, and thereafter the whole argument, for and against slavery, was **brought out.** The master was **vanquished** at every turn in the argument; and seeing himself to be thus vanquished, he generously and meekly emancipates the slave, with his best wishes for his prosperity. It is scarcely necessary to say, that a dialogue, with such an origin, and such an ending—read when the fact of my being a slave was a constant burden of grief—powerfully affected me; and I could not help feeling that the day might come, when the well-directed answers made by the slave to the master, in this instance, would find their counterpart in myself....

Vocabulary

vanquished (vang' kwisht) *v.* defeated; overcame

4. **Viz.** is an abbreviation for the Latin word videlicet. It means namely.
5. **Quondam** means former.

I had now penetrated the secret of all slavery and oppression, and had ascertained their true foundation to be in the pride, the power and the avarice of man. The dialogue and the speeches were all redolent of the principles of liberty, and **poured floods of light** on the nature and character of slavery.... Nevertheless, the increase of knowledge was attended with bitter, as well as sweet results. The more I read, the more I was led to abhor and detest slavery, and my enslavers. "Slaveholders," thought I, "are only a band of successful robbers, who left their homes and went into Africa for the purpose of stealing and reducing my people to slavery." I loathed them as the meanest and the most wicked of men. As I read, behold! the very discontent so graphically predicted by Master Hugh, had already come upon me. I was no longer the light-hearted, gleesome boy, full of <u>mirth</u> and play, as when I landed first at Baltimore. Knowledge had come; light had penetrated the moral dungeon where I dwelt; and, behold! there lay the bloody whip, for my back, and here was the iron chain; and my good, *kind master*, he was **the author of my situation.** The revelation haunted me, stung me, and made me gloomy and miserable. As I writhed under the sting and torment of this knowledge, I almost envied my fellow slaves their stupid contentment. This knowledge opened my eyes to the horrible pit, and revealed the teeth of the frightful dragon that was ready to pounce upon me, but it opened no way for my escape. I have often wished myself a beast, or a bird—anything, rather than a slave. I was wretched and gloomy, beyond my ability to describe. I was too thoughtful to be happy. It was this everlasting thinking which distressed and tormented me; and yet there was no getting rid of the subject of my thoughts. All nature was redolent of it. Once awakened by the silver trump[6] of knowledge, my spirit was roused to eternal wakefulness. Liberty! the inestimable birthright of every man, had, for me, converted every object into an asserter of this great right. It was heard in every sound, and beheld in every object. It was ever present, to torment me with a sense of my wretched condition. The more beautiful and charming were the smiles of nature, the more horrible and desolate was my condition. I saw nothing without seeing it, and I heard nothing without hearing it. I do not exaggerate, when I say, that it looked from every star, smiled in every calm, breathed in every wind, and moved in every storm.

6. *Trump* is a trumpet.

Poured floods of light on here means "made very clear."

mirth (murth) *n.* happiness shown by laughter

The author of my situation here means "responsible for my position."

To Sum Up

➤ Douglass realized that slavery is the result of people's greed, pride, and power.

➤ The more he read, the more he hated slavery and slave owners.

➤ He could not stop thinking about freedom.

Interactive Question-Response

Content Vocabulary

Read aloud the word and definition for *mirth*. Have students reread the two sentences in paragraph one on page 107 beginning with *As I read, behold!* **Ask:** *Which word in these two sentences means the opposite of mirth? (discontent)* Draw a smiling and a frowning face on the board. **Ask:** *Which face should be labeled mirth? (smiling) Which should be labeled discontent? (frowning)*

To Sum Up

Have students work in pairs to reread all the To Sum Up statements from the beginning of the selection on page 102. **Ask:** *What is the most important thing that Douglass has done so far? (He has learned how to read.) What ideas seem most important to Douglass? (Slavery is wrong; freedom is valuable.)*

Word Study   BLM

Context Meaning

"My Bondage and My Freedom" contains words and phrases that may be unfamiliar to modern readers. Point out the word *ascertained* in the first sentence on this page. Demonstrate using context to figure out the meaning of the word for students. Explain that Douglass says he ascertained the things that were the foundation of slavery and oppression. The phrase *figured out* could replace the word *ascertained* and still produce the same meaning.

Then have students practice using context to identify the meaning of words by completing the activity on page A19.

Interactive
Question-Response

Literary Element
Autobiography

If students have trouble responding: **Model** *I would answer the question by rereading the box in the middle of the page. Douglass says that Mrs. Auld and he each had "private thoughts and plans." The word* plans *means the same thing as goals. So the sentence after this one might tell what these goals are. In fact it does. Mrs. Auld's goal is to keep Douglass ignorant, and Douglass's goal is to learn, even if this knowledge is painful. So I would underline "I resolved to know, although knowledge only increased my discontent."* **Ask:** *Why did knowledge increase Douglass's discontent? (It reminded him that he was not free.)*

Reflect

Partner Talk Have students work in pairs to answer. To help students get started: **Model** *To answer this question, I would think about what events led to Douglass's ideas about slavery. Douglass's increased hatred of slavery comes from the new knowledge about it that he has. He has that knowledge because he learned how to read. So one important cause of his feelings about slavery is that he learned how to read.*

Write the following sentence frame on the board to help students organize their thoughts:

Another event that affected Douglass's ideas about slavery is _____. This event made Douglass realize that _____.

A *state of mind* is a way of thinking at a particular time.

Literary Element

Autobiography Reread the boxed text in the middle of this page. Underline the words that describe one of Douglass's most important goals.

Sorrow that dwelt in my young bosom here means "sadness that I felt inside."

Vocabulary

censure (sen' shər) *v.* to blame

7. **An angel stood in the way** refers to a story from the Bible (Numbers 22: 21–35). In the story, a donkey does not move even though its master is beating it. The donkey does not move because it sees an angel standing in its way. His master cannot see the angel.

To Sum Up

➤ Douglass was unable to talk with Mrs. Auld honestly.

➤ They were once friends, but slavery had made them enemies.

➤ If Douglass were free and Mrs. Auld were a slave, she would have acted just like Douglass did.

I have no doubt that my **state of mind** had something to do with the change in the treatment adopted, by my once kind mistress toward me. I can easily believe, that my leaden, downcast, and discontented look, was very offensive to her. Poor lady! She did not know my trouble, and I dared not tell her. Could I have freely made her acquainted with the real state of my mind, and given her the reasons therefor, it might have been well for both of us. Her abuse of me fell upon me like the blows of the false prophet upon his ass; she did not know that an *angel* stood in the way;[7] and—such is the relation of master and slave—I could not tell her. Nature had made us *friends*; slavery made us *enemies*. My interests were in a direction opposite to hers, and we both had our private thoughts and plans. She aimed to keep me ignorant; and I resolved to know, although knowledge only increased my discontent. My feelings were not the result of any marked cruelty in the treatment I received; they sprung from the consideration of my being a slave at all. It was *slavery*—not its mere *incidents*—that I hated. I had been cheated. I saw through the attempt to keep me in ignorance; I saw that slaveholders would have gladly made me believe that they were merely acting under the authority of God, in making a slave of me, and in making slaves of others; and I treated them as robbers and deceivers. The feeding and clothing me well, could not atone for taking my liberty from me. The smiles of my mistress could not remove the deep **sorrow that dwelt in my young bosom.** Indeed, these, in time, came only to deepen my sorrow. She had changed; and the reader will see that I had changed, too. We were both victims to the same overshadowing evil—*she*, as mistress, *I*, as slave. I will not **censure** her harshly; she cannot censure me, for she knows I speak but the truth, and have acted in my opposition to slavery, just as she herself would have acted, in a reverse of circumstances.

REFLECT

Analyze Cause and Effect
At the end of the selection, Douglass dislikes slavery more than ever before. Identify two causes that led to his final view of slavery.

Possible answer: Cause 1: He learns how to read.

Cause 2: He reads the debate between the slave and the

slave owner.

_____

_____

 Talk about your answer with a partner.

Frederick Douglass

When it is finally ours, this freedom, this liberty, this beautiful
and terrible thing, needful to man as air,
usable as earth; when it belongs at last to all,
when it is truly instinct, brain matter, diastole,[1] systole,[2]
5 **reflex action;** when it is finally won; when it is more
than the gaudy **mumbo jumbo** of politicians:
this man, this Douglass, this former slave, this Negro
beaten to his knees, exiled, visioning a world
where none is lonely, none hunted, alien,
10 this man, superb in love and logic, this man
shall be remembered. Oh, not with statues' rhetoric,
not with legends and poems and <u>wreaths</u> of bronze alone,
but with the lives grown out of his life, the lives
fleshing his dream of the beautiful, needful thing.

1. A *diastole* (dī as′ tə lē) is the time between heartbeats when the heart relaxes.
2. A *systole* (sis′ tə lē) is the time when the heart contracts. Diastoles and systoles alternate while the heart beats.

REFLECT

Analyze Cause and Effect
What prediction does Hayden make in this poem? What cause does he give for this prediction?

Possible answer: He predicts that Douglass will be
remembered when all people are free. Douglass will be
remembered because this freedom will be a result of his
own actions.

 Talk about your answer with a partner.

A *reflex action* is something that is done automatically.

Mumbo jumbo is meaningless talk.

wreaths (rēaths) *n.* flowers or leaves arranged in a circle

 Comparing Literature

Which lines in the text contain the speaker's portrayal of Frederick Douglass?
- [✓] lines 7–10
- [ ] lines 1–2
- [ ] lines 3–5

To Sum Up

➤ The speaker imagines a time when all people are free.

➤ He says that Douglass will be remembered then.

➤ Douglass will be remembered because he helped to bring about this freedom.

Comparing Literature

If students have difficulty answering: **Model** *I would answer this question by looking at the poem to see where Douglass is described. Douglass's name is mentioned for the first time in line 7. After that, the poet gives several descriptions of Douglass. This former slave, exiled, and visioning a world where none is lonely are all descriptions of Douglass. So these lines, 7-10, contain the poem's portrayal of Douglass.* **Ask:** *What main points about Douglass are made in this portrayal?* (He had a difficult life, but he had a vision of a better world.)

Reflect

Partner Talk Have students work in pairs to answer. To help students get started: **Model** *To answer this question, I would look first for the prediction. The first eleven lines of the poem are all one complicated sentence. If we leave out the details in the middle, the sentence becomes:* When it is finally ours, this man shall be remembered. *It is freedom, and this man is Douglass. So the poem predicts that Douglass will be remembered when all people are finally free. The last four lines of the poem give the cause for making this prediction.*

Write the following sentence frame on the board to help students organize their thoughts:

The speaker of the poem predicts that _____ because _____.

Differentiated Instruction

Clarify the Text Support students in understanding "Frederick Douglass."

Beginning/Early Intermediate ▸ Read aloud the first and second bullets in To Sum Up. **Ask**: *When will Douglass be remembered?* (when all people are free)

Intermediate ▸ Have partners read the poem aloud. **Ask:** *What is as "needful to man as air"?* (freedom) *Who is "superb in love and logic"?* (Frederick Douglass)

Early Advanced ▸ Point out that Hayden uses extended descriptions and comparisons to make his points in this poem. **Ask:** *What does Hayden contrast with freedom?* (the meaningless talk of politicians.) *What contrast does he use to show how Douglass will be remembered?* (He contrasts statues and poems with real human lives.)

Interactive Question-Response

Comparing Literature

If students have difficulty answering: **Model** *I would look at the answers and try to eliminate wrong answers. First, the portrayal made in this poem is negative. It uses images of decay and death. So it is not correct to say that the poem shows the country taking care of people. On the other hand, the poem doesn't suggest that people have been made slaves again. The people in the poem are ignored, not forced to work. So the best answer is that it shows how the country does not care about former slaves.* **Ask:** *What neglected things does Troupe compare the former slaves to?* (rusting train cars, forgotten African governments, and old race horses.)

To Sum Up

Have students work in pairs to reread the To Sum Up feature. **Ask:** *What does the speaker see?* (old train cars.) *What does he think about?* (race horses and photographs of black people.)

> **Put out to pasture** means no longer allowed to race.

Comparing Literature

Troupe describes scenes of decay and death. He uses these images to portray how the country has treated its former slaves. What do these images say about the country?

- ☐ The country takes care of its former slaves.
- ☑ The country does not care about its former slaves.
- ☐ The country has enslaved the former slaves again.

To Sum Up

- ➤ The speaker sees old train cars on the ground near the railroad tracks.
- ➤ They remind him of race horses who are left to die in the fields.
- ➤ They also remind him of pictures of black men and women sitting on broken porches.

all along the railroad
tracks of texas
old train cars lay
rusted & overturned
5 like new african governments
long forgotten by the people
who built & rode them
till they couldn't run no more
10 & they remind me of old race horses
who've been **put out to pasture**
amongst the weeds
rain, sleet & snow
till they die & rot away
15 like photos fading
in grandma's picture book
of old black men & women, in mississippi
texas, who sit on dilapidated porches
that fall away

20 like dead man's skin
    like white people's eyes
    & inside the peeling photos
    old men sit, sad eyed
    & waiting, waiting for **worm dust**
25 thinking of the master & his long forgotten
    promise of forty acres & a mule
    & even now, if you pass across
    this bleeding flesh
    ever changing landscape
30 you will see the fruited
    countryside, stretching, stretching
    & old black men & young black
    men, sitting on porches, waiting
    waiting for rusted trains
35 silent in texas grass

Worm dust here means "death."

Background Information

General William Sherman
promised freed slaves forty acres
of land and a mule at the end of
the Civil War. This promise was
not widely kept.

---

stretching (strech' ing) *v.* spreading

 Comparing Literature

How would you describe Quincy
Troupe's portrayal of freed African
Americans?

☑ They have been neglected.
☐ They have been appreciated.
☐ They have each received forty
   acres and a mule.

REFLECT

Analyze Cause and Effect
Troupe's poem describes freed African Americans living in poor
conditions. What are some causes these conditions?

Possible answers: broken promises after the end of

slavery; the disregard of the rest of society; continuing

discrimination.

_____

_____

Talk about your answer with a partner.

To Sum Up

➤ The speaker says that freed
   slaves are suffering terribly.

➤ The country did not follow
   through on its promises to
   freed slaves.

➤ You will see freed slaves sitting
   on porches. They are waiting
   for trains that never come.

Oral Assessment

Provide the following prompts to one student at a time. Observe students' responses. See the
Oral Assessment Rubric on page T17 to determine students' levels of language output.

1. Tell me about Mr. and Mrs. Auld.

2. How did Frederick Douglass learn to read?

3. What did Douglass think about slavery?

4. According to the poem "Frederick Douglass," why will Douglass be remembered?

5. In the poem "In Texas Grass," what are freed African Americans compared to?

Interactive Question-Response

Background Information

Read aloud Build Background. Ask students to explain
the purpose of giving freed slaves forty acres and
a mule.

Comparing Literature

If students have difficulty answering: **Model** *I would
answer the question by considering the descriptions
of the freed African Americans. They are certainly
not appreciated, because they are compared to old
abandoned trains. They also did not receive forty acres
and a mule. The promise of forty acres and a mule
is described as* long forgotten. *So the best description
of them is* neglected. **Ask:** *What point do you think
Troupe is trying to make with this portrayal?* (The
United States owed freed African Americans better
treatment than they actually received.)

Reflect

Partner Talk Have students work in pairs to answer.
To help students get started: **Model** *To answer this
question, I would think about the reasons given in
the poem for the poor conditions that it portrays. For
one thing, the poem mentions the promise of forty
acres and a mule. This promise can stand for many
promises about what freedom would be like that were
broken after slavery ended. Also, the poem suggests
that the rest of the society ignores the conditions of
the freed African Americans. So the neglect of society
is another cause for these conditions.*

Write the following sentence frame on the board to
help students organize their thoughts:

*Troupe suggests that one cause of the poor conditions
is _____. Another cause is _____.*

Vocabulary Check

A. Beginning/Early Intermediate

Read each question aloud. Encourage students to point to the correct picture. Then turn the question into a statement and have students repeat as they point to the correct picture.

Vocabulary Check

A. Circle the picture that best answers the question.

1. Which picture shows **wreaths**?

3. Which person is feeling **fury**?

2. Which picture shows **mirth**?

4. Which picture shows **stretching**?

B. Write **T** if the statement is true. Write **F** if it is false.

benevolent	mirth	fury	induce

__T__ 5. A **benevolent** person would help a new student find the lunchroom at school.

__F__ 6. You would probably feel **mirth** after losing an important soccer game.

__T__ 7. One way to deal with **fury** is to take a deep breath and calm down.

__T__ 8. A boss might **induce** her employee to work harder by offering to pay him more.

C. Answer each question below.

9. Give an example of a person or group who has been **vanquished**. Possible answer: an army that is defeated in a battle

10. Give an example of someone acting with **depravity**. Possible answer: the slave owners in Frederick Douglass's autobiography

11. Give an example of a situation that involves **censure**. Possible answer: a writer publishes an editorial that criticizes the government

Grammar Link

Future Time Clauses with *Before, After,* and *When*

Prepare students to complete the activity on page A20. Read the grammar instruction with students, and complete the first item with them to help them get started.

FROM MY BONDAGE AND MY FREEDOM
Frederick Douglass IN TEXAS GRASS

Comprehension Check

A. Answer the following questions about My Bondage and My Freedom.

1. Frederick Douglass's mistress started to teach him how to _____read_____.

2. She stopped teaching when her _____husband_____ told her to.

3. Douglass still wanted to learn, so he asked his _____friends_____ for help.

B. My Bondage and My Freedom is an autobiography about Douglass's life. Robert Hayden's Frederick Douglass is a poem about Douglass's life. Use the chart to describe the similarities and differences in how these two selections describe Douglass and slavery.

	How the Selections Describe Douglass	How the Selections Describe Slavery
Similarities	Both show Douglass as brave and freedom-loving.	Possible answer: Both show slavery as a brutal system.
Differences	Possible answer: The autobiography focuses on Douglass's struggle to read, while the poem gives a more general picture of Douglass	Possible answer: Douglass's autobiography describes how slavery affects him personally. The poem tells how slavery affected an entire group of people.

C. Answer the following questions about portrayals of people in My Bondage and My Freedom and In Texas Grass.

7. What similarities do you see in the way Douglass presents himself in his autobiography and the way Troupe portrays African Americans in In Texas Grass?

Possible answer: Douglass fears that he can never change his life as a slave. The people in Troupe's poems do not seem to believe that their lives can change.

8. What differences do you see in the two portrayals?

Possible answer: Douglass continues to have hope throughout the selection. The people in the poem do not seem to have any source of hope.

9. What might account for the differences in the two portrayals?

Troupe writes at a time long after slavery has ended, so he may be more disappointed and angry than Douglass, who has not yet seen the end of slavery.

Comprehension Check

B. Intermediate

Explain that students should think about the events that are described in the selections to make their comparison. They should also consider what Douglass says in his autobiography about himself and slavery, and what the speaker of the poem says about Douglass and slavery. Encourage students to return to the text for details.

Writing Link

Mission Statement

Point out that the three selections deal with the effects of slavery at different times in our history. Have students work with a partner to talk about how an organization during Douglass's era might have promoted the abolition of slavery or how an organization in the period following the Civil War might have helped freed slaves get an education, find homes, and make a living. Have them imagine such an organization that could have existed during these periods. Then tell students to write a mission statement for their organization.

Students' mission statements should

- provide information on their organization

- convince readers of the importance of their organization

- discuss the purpose of their organization

FROM MY BONDAGE AND MY FREEDOM
Frederick Douglass IN TEXAS GRASS

Conversation

Imagine that Frederick Douglass could have a conversation with one of the characters sitting on the porch in In Texas Grass. Write the conversation that they might have. Use information from Douglass's autobiography and Troupe's poem in your writing.

Douglass: Tell me about your life as a freed man.
Man in poem: My life is ___Possible answer: hard___

My country promised me ___Possible answer: forty___

___acres and a mule___ but they did not fulfill

their promise.

Douglass: Slavery is an evil system. It causes people to

Possible answer: treat each other poorly

___

Man in poem: Yes, but slavery is over. I had hoped that

Possible answer: things would get better

___

Douglass: Things will get better someday. But it might take a long time because ___Possible: slavery taught___

___people to look at slaves as less than human.___

So people will have to realize that freed slaves are

human beings, just like everyone else.

Man in poem: I hope you're right. For now, I spend my time ___Possible answer: sitting on the porch and___

wondering when things will change.

___

Douglass: Try to stay hopeful! I believe that deep down inside, people are ___Possible answer: fair and good.___

Slavery is bad, but human beings are good.

___

Learning Objectives

For pages 115–122, 318

In studying this text, you will focus on the following objectives:

Literary Study: Analyzing oratory.

Reading: Evaluating argument.

And Ain't I a Woman?

by Sojourner Truth

And Ain't I a Woman? **115**

Oral Language

Build Background

Read the title and author. Explain that students will read a speech called "And Ain't I a Woman?" by Sojourner Truth, a former slave who spent her life fighting slavery and working for women's rights. Tell students that *ain't* is a slang word. In the title, *ain't* means "aren't." **Ask:**

- *Is the title a statement or a question? (a question)*

- *Why might a speaker ask her listeners a question? (to get them involved; to get them thinking)*

- *What might the speaker want her listeners to think about? (women; women's rights; what women can do)*

Talk About the Speech

Intermediate Explain that good speakers share certain qualities. For example, a good speaker is lively and cares about his or her ideas. Have students complete the sentence stem to name other qualities of a good speaker.

Most good speakers _____. (speak clearly; tell stories; give examples; use humor; have interesting ideas)

Lesson at a Glance

Oral Language
- Build Background
- Talk About the Speech

Vocabulary
- Selection Vocabulary
- Content Vocabulary

Literary Element
- Oratory

Reading Strategy
- Evaluate Argument

Writing Link
- Speech

Comprehension
BLM

Grammar Link
- Object Pronouns BLM

Technology
- Student Works™ Plus
- Teacher Works™ Plus
- Listening Library Audio CD
- Classroom Presentation Toolkit
- Glencoe Visual Vocabulary
- Skill Level Up!™ A Skill-Based Language Arts Game

Interactive Question-Response

Connect to the Speech

Read aloud Connect to the Speech. Reproduce the sentence stems on the board: **Model** *When I was growing up, my sister and I had to do lots of chores around the house. My parents always gave me more chores than they gave my sister. I thought that was unfair, and I was upset. One day I talked to my parents about it, and they explained that since I was older, I was capable of doing more work.* Model writing your response in the sentence frame, and have volunteers suggest other responses. Then have students fill in their own sentences.

Literary Element   Oratory

Read aloud the Literary Element. Tell students to imagine they wanted to persuade their parents to loan them their car. **Ask:** *What example or story might you tell?* **Model** *I would remind them that the last time I borrowed their car, I took good care of it. I even replaced the gas I used.* Have volunteers share other examples. **Ask:** *What key words or sentences might you include?* **Model** *I would be sure to include the word* responsible *and the sentence "You can trust me."* Have volunteers share other examples.

Reading Strategy
Evaluate Argument

Read aloud the Reading Strategy. Tell students that they probably evaluate arguments every day. For example, they might see a television commercial about a new snack. **Ask:** *How would you decide whether to buy it?* **Model** *I would look for the evidence that it's a good snack. The ad said that it's delicious and good for me.* Point out that you would then evaluate whether the evidence is weak or strong: **Model** *The first point is weak, because we all have different opinions of what tastes good. The second point sounds weak too, because the snack has lots of sugar, and I know that lots of sugar is not good for me. So, I will not buy that snack.*

And Ain't I a Woman?

Connect to the Speech

Think of a time when you felt you were treated unfairly. What happened? How did you react? Explain the situation on the lines below.

I was treated unfairly when **Possible answer: I had to do more chores than my sister did**

When this happened, I **Possible answer: was upset, so I talked to my parents about it**

Literary Element   Oratory

Oratory is the skill of speaking well in front of others. It involves being clear and convincing.

When you speak in a convincing way, you use **persuasive devices** to make your points. Some persuasive devices are
- stories or examples
- repeating important ideas
- short, dramatic sentences

As you read the speech, look for the persuasive devices on the list above.

Reading Strategy   Evaluate Argument

When you **evaluate** something, you form an opinion of it. To evaluate an argument, you decide whether a speaker's point is convincing. Is there enough evidence, or facts to prove the point? Is the evidence weak or strong? Is the argument logical?

In the chart below, write an argument for or against the following idea: Women can be as strong as men. In the second column, give evidence for your argument. Ask a partner to evaluate your argument.

Argument	Evidence
Possible answer: Women can be as strong as men because they often do the same work.	Possible answer: Women are factory workers, bus drivers, athletes, and construction workers.

Selection Vocabulary

racket (rak′ it) *n.* loud noise (p. 118)
*The crowd made such a **racket** that we could not hear the speaker.*
➤ Cognate (Spanish) **raqueta**

borne (bôrn) *v.* past participle of bear; given birth to; produced (p. 118)
*The peach trees have not **borne** any fruit yet.*

oblige (ə blīj′) *v.* to make grateful; to do a service for (p. 119)
*I would be **obliged** if you remove your hat so I can see the stage.*
➤ Cognate (Spanish) **obligar**

Content Vocabulary

rights (rīts) *n.* powers or privileges you have by law (p. 118)
*Men and women should have equal **rights**.*

gathered (gath′ ərd) *v.* collected; brought together (p. 118)
*Students **gathered** in the hallway after class.*

slavery (slā′ vər ē) *n.* ownership of others as property (p. 118)
*After he was sold into **slavery**, he began working in the fields.*

grief (grēf) *n.* a deep feeling of sadness or loss (p. 118)
*Juan felt **grief** when his pet dog died..*

For more practice, see page 318.

Vocabulary Routine

To introduce the vocabulary, read aloud the words and definitions in the student book and have students repeat after you. Discuss how the pictures illustrate the words or sentences. Then follow the vocabulary routine below.

Content Vocabulary

Define: ***Rights*** are powers or privileges you have by law. Example: *You get the right to vote when you turn eighteen.* Ask: What are other examples of *rights* you have in this country? EXAMPLE

If you have ***gathered*** things, you have brought them together. *I gathered the dishes from the table and carried them to the sink.* What word means the opposite of *gathered?* ANTONYM

Slavery occurs when some people own others. *Many people believe that slavery is wrong.* Why might people believe that *slavery* is wrong? EXPLANATION

You feel ***grief*** when something very sad has happened. *She was overcome with grief when her best friend moved away.* What is another word for *grief?* SYNONYM

Vocabulary Practice Have students complete the vocabulary practice activity on page 318.

Selection Vocabulary

Define: A noise that is very loud is a ***racket,*** or clamor. Example: *The racket in the auditorium made it difficult to hear the speaker's answers.* Ask: When have you heard something so loud it caused a racket? EXAMPLE

To have ***borne*** something is to have given birth to or produced something. *The ideals borne during the Civil War affected everyone in America.* How have severe conflicts between countries sometimes borne important new ideas? EXPLANATION

When you ***oblige*** someone, you do them a favor. *The man tried to oblige the woman by helping her carry her groceries.* Describe a time in which you obliged another person. DESCRIPTION

And Ain't I a Woman?

Interactive Question-Response

Background Information

Read aloud the note. Tell students that in the 1850s, women in the United States were not allowed to vote. In addition, African Americans were enslaved in the South. Point out that Truth fought for the rights of both of these groups. Ask students which sentence in the first paragraph addresses the rights of both women and African Americans. ("I think that 'twixt the Negroes of the South and the women at the North, all talking about rights….")

Comprehension Check

Ask students to share what they underlined in the text. Then tell students that the question "And Ain't I a Woman?" means "And aren't I a woman?" **Ask:** *Why do you think Sojourner Truth asks a question rather than using a statement, such as "And I Am a Woman!"* (She wants to get her listeners involved.)

In a fix means "having trouble."

Background Information

Truth gave this speech in 1851 at the Women's Rights Convention. Some of the men there said that women are not strong or smart enough to vote. Truth's speech is her response to the men.

Comprehension Check

Reread the boxed text at the top of the page. Underline the places where Truth repeats an important idea.

To Sum Up

➤ Some people think that women are weaker than men.

➤ Women can work hard. They do not need men's help.

➤ Women have survived slavery, just like men have.

Well, children, where there is so much **racket** there must be something out of kilter.[1] I think that 'twixt[2] the Negroes of the South and the women at the North, all talking about <u>rights</u>, the white men will be **in a fix** pretty soon. But what's all this here talking about? That man over there says that women need to be helped into carriages, and lifted over ditches, and to have the best place everywhere. Nobody ever helps me into carriages, or over mud-puddles, or gives me any best place! <u>And ain't I a woman?</u> Look at me! Look at my arm. I have ploughed and planted, and <u>gathered</u> into barns, and no man could head[3] me! <u>And ain't I a woman?</u> I could work as much and eat as much as a man—when I could get it—and bear the lash as well! <u>And ain't I a woman?</u> I have **borne** thirteen children, and seen them most all sold off to <u>slavery</u>, and when I cried out with my mother's <u>grief</u>, none but Jesus heard me! <u>And ain't I a woman?</u>

Then they talk about this thing in the head; what's this they call it? [Intellect, someone whispers.] That's it, honey. What's that got to do with women's rights or Negroes rights? If my cup won't hold but a pint, and yours holds a quart, wouldn't you be mean not to let me have my little half-measure full?

Then that little man in black there, he says women can't have as much rights as men, 'cause Christ wasn't a woman! Where did your Christ come from? Where did your Christ come from? From God and a woman! Man had nothing to do with Him.

Vocabulary

racket (rak′ it) *n.* loud noise
borne (bôrn) *v.* past participle of *bear;* given birth to; produced

1. The phrase *out of kilter* means "out of order" or "mixed up."
2. *'Twixt* is the shortened form of *betwixt,* an Old English word meaning "between."
3. Here, Truth uses *head* to mean "to do better than" or "to get ahead of."

Comprehension BLM

To support students as they read the selection, have them begin the graphic organizer on page A21.

If the first woman God ever made was strong enough to turn the world upside down all alone, these women together ought to be able to turn it back, and get it right side up again! And now they is asking to do it, the men better let them.

Obliged to you for hearing me, and now old Sojourner ain't got nothing more to say.

Literary Element

Oratory Which persuasive device does Truth use on this page?
- ☑ stories or examples
- ☐ repeating important ideas
- ☐ short, dramatic sentences

Vocabulary

oblige (ə blīj') *v.* to make grateful; to do a service for

REFLECT

Evaluate Argument
In the boxed text on this page, Truth argues that women are strong enough to change the world. Is her argument convincing? Why or why not?

Possible answer: Her argument is convincing because she

gives the example that Eve changed the world.

_____

_____

_____

 Talk about your answer with a partner.

To Sum Up

➤ The first woman God ever made changed the world on her own.

➤ If one woman can change the world, then a whole group of women can make the world a much better place.

Oral Assessment

Provide the following prompts to one student at a time. Observe students' responses. See the Oral Assessment Rubric on page T17 to determine students' levels of language output.

1. Tell me about Sojourner Truth.

2. What do some people in the audience think about women?

3. What does Truth think about women?

4. What are some of Truth's arguments?

5. What is an example of a story that Truth tells?

Interactive Question-Response

Literary Element **Oratory**

If students have difficulty responding: **Model** *I will read the page three times, and each time, I will look for one of the persuasive devices on the list. The first is "stories or examples." This page refers to a story from the Bible. So, I will check the box.* Then have students work with partners to reread the page and check for the other persuasive devices on the list.

To Sum Up

Beginning/Early Intermediate Have students work in pairs to reread all the To Sum Up statements from the beginning of the speech on page 118. Remind students that Truth is trying to convince her listeners that women should have the right to vote. Then have them decide together which of Truth's arguments is the strongest. Have them check the appropriate box below, and then complete the sentence.

☐ Women can work hard, just like men.

☐ Women have survived slavery, just like men.

☐ Women can make the world a better place.

(Answers will vary.)

I think this is Truth's strongest argument because _____. *(Answers will vary.)*

Reflect

Partner Talk Have students work in pairs to answer. To help students get started: **Model** *To answer this, I would think about what makes an argument convincing. I know that convincing arguments have evidence. Truth does provide evidence for her argument that women can change the world. Her evidence is the story of Eve. I would then decide if I think this evidence is strong.* Invite pairs of students to discuss whether they think Truth's evidence is strong.

Vocabulary Check

C. Early Advanced

Tell students that when they read the answer choices, they should think about which one is an example of the vocabulary word. **Ask:** *What is a racket? (a loud noise) Which answer choice is an example of a loud noise? (a thunderstorm)* Have students answer the rest of the questions on their own.

And Ain't I a Woman?

Vocabulary Check

A. Label each picture with the correct word.

| rights | gathered | slavery | grief |

1. slavery
2. rights
3. grief
4. gathered

B. Circle the letter of the word that answers each question correctly.

5. What might make a **racket**?
   a. a large crowd cheering
   b. two people whispering
   c. a cat walking across a rug

6. What might an apple tree have **borne**?
   a. milk
   b. grass
   c. fruit

7. What event might make you feel **grief**?
   a. doing well on a test
   b. saying good-bye to a loved one
   c. winning a soccer game

8. What might make you feel **obliged**?
   a. someone forgets to call you
   b. someone borrows your math book and loses it
   c. someone loans you money for lunch

9. What might someone have **gathered** at the beach?
   a. seashells
   b. pianos
   c. computers

C. Circle the letter of the answer that correctly shows what the word means.

10. **racket**
    a. a loud thunderstorm
    b. a light rain

11. **borne**
    a. a newborn baby
    b. an old man

12. **oblige**
    a. ignore
    b. help

13. **rights**
    a. freedom of speech
    b. no freedom of speech

Grammar Link

Object Pronouns

Prepare students to complete the activity on page A22. Read the grammar instruction with students, and complete the first item with them to help them get started.

And Ain't I a Woman?

Comprehension Check

A. Complete the sentences.

1. The person giving the speech is Sojourner Truth   .

2. She is arguing that women should have equal rights   .

3. She says that women are   Possible answer: strong   .

4. One example she gives is that women   Possible answer: work hard in the fields   .

B. Sojourner Truth uses examples from her own life to show that women are as strong as men. Complete the web with examples she uses.

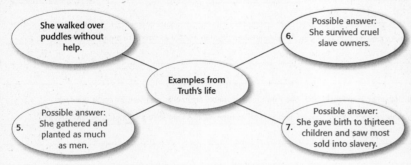

She walked over puddles without help.

6. Possible answer: She survived cruel slave owners.

Examples from Truth's life

5. Possible answer: She gathered and planted as much as men.

7. Possible answer: She gave birth to thirteen children and saw most sold into slavery.

C. Answer the questions about the persuasive devices in "And Ain't I a Woman?"

8. Truth uses examples from her own life to show that women are strong. What are two examples she uses?

   Possible answers: She gathered and planted as much as men. She gave birth to thirteen children
   and saw most sold into slavery.

9. Truth repeats the question "And ain't I a woman?" Why do you think she repeats this question?

   Possible answer: Repeating this question shows that the men's beliefs about women are wrong.

10. Truth uses short, dramatic sentences to make her point. What is an example of a short, dramatic sentence she uses? How does it help her make her point?

    Possible answer: "Where did your Christ come from?" is short and dramatic. It helps the listeners

    realize that Christ came from a woman.

Comprehension Check

B. Intermediate

Remind students that before Sojourner Truth fought for the rights of women and African Americans, she was a slave. Encourage them to reread the first paragraph and look for examples of things that happened to Truth when she was a slave.

Writing Link

Speech

Have students think about an issue they are concerned about, or a group of people who do not have equal rights. Tell them that they are going to write a speech in support of that cause or group. Have them think about the persuasive techniques Truth used in her speech, such as personal experiences, logic, and emotional appeals. Tell them to use the techniques they think would work best in support their cause and would be most persuasive for their audience. Encourage students to give their speeches before the class if they feel comfortable doing so.

And Ain't I a Woman?

Newspaper Article

Imagine that you are writing a newspaper article about Sojourner Truth's speech at the 1851 Women's Rights Convention. You want readers who did not attend the convention to know what happened. You heard the men's arguments and Truth's responses. Now try to make the event come alive for your readers.

Headline: _Possible answer: Debate Rages at Women's Rights Convention_

Yesterday, there was an exciting debate at the Women's Rights Convention.

The topic of the debate was _Possible answer: equal rights for women_
_____

In general, the men argued that _Possible answer: women should not have equal rights_
_____

Some of their reasons were that _Possible answer: women are not as strong or smart as men_
_____
_____

But Sojourner Truth fought back. She made many powerful arguments, and here are some examples. _____
Possible answers: Women work just as hard as men. Women are strong enough to survive slavery.
_____
_____

In the end, _Possible answer: Sojourner Truth really challenged the men and made the audience think._
_____
_____

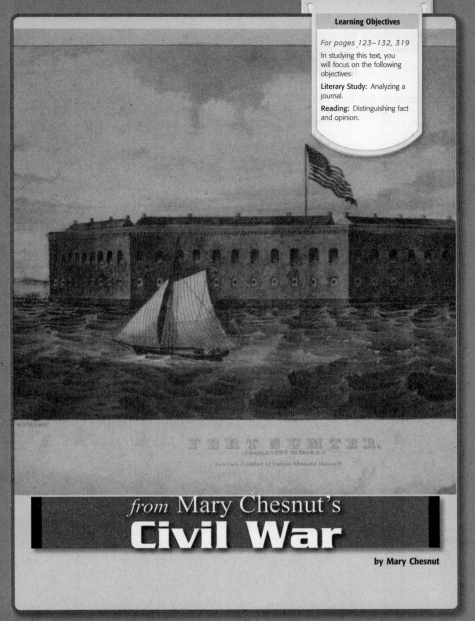

Learning Objectives

For pages 123–132, 319

In studying this text, you will focus on the following objectives:

Literary Study: Analyzing a journal.

Reading: Distinguishing fact and opinion.

FORT SUMTER.
CHARLESTON HARBOR, S. C.

from Mary Chesnut's
Civil War

by Mary Chesnut

Oral Language

Build Background

Read the title and author. Tell students that they will read "from Mary Chesnut's Civil War" by Mary Chesnut, an author who lived in the 1800s. **Ask:**

- Who do you think Mary Chesnut is? *(a writer, a soldier's wife, a soldier, a nurse)*

- What do you think "Mary Chesnut's Civil War" will be about? *(what happened to Mary Chesnut during the war)*

Talk About the Journal

Explain that the journal is about the beginning of the Civil War. Mary Chesnut describes what happens to her and to the people around her.

Beginning/Early Intermediate ▸ Show a map of the United States with a line dividing the North and South. Point out north and south on the map's compass. Tell students that the North and the South fought each other in the Civil War.

Intermediate ▸ Explain that the journal is a personal story about the war. **Ask:** *Would you like to read a history book or a personal story about the Civil War? Why? (I would like to read a personal story. It would be more interesting.)*

Lesson at a Glance

Oral Language
- Build Background
- Talk about the Journal

Vocabulary
- Selection Vocabulary
- Content Vocabulary
- Academic Vocabulary

Literary Element
- Journal

Reading Strategy
- Distinguish Fact and Opinion

Writing Link
- Journal Entry

Comprehension
- BLM

Word Study
- Multiple-Meaning Words BLM

Grammar Link
- Possessive Pronouns BLM

Technology
- Student Works™ Plus
- Teacher Works™ Plus
- Listening Library Audio CD
- Classroom Presentation Toolkit
- Glencoe Visual Vocabulary
- Skill Level Up!™ A Skill-Based Language Arts Game

Interactive Question-Response

Connect to the Journal

Read aloud Connect to the Journal. **Model** *When I graduated from high school, I had many feelings. I was proud and happy. I was also nervous about my future. If I wrote a journal entry about that day, it might have helped me understand my feelings. I think one reason people write journals is to understand their feelings.* Model listing your response on the board. Then have students complete their lists and share them with each other.

Literary Element Journal

Write the following journal entry on the board: *August 5. I went to a party at Alba's house. The food was great. I loved the music. I am glad I went.* Read aloud the Literary Element. Help students identify the parts of the journal entry: the date, the event, a thought, and a feeling. Then, ask students to describe the person who wrote the entry. *(happy, friendly)* Encourage them to explain their answers.

Reading Strategy Distinguish Fact and Opinion

Read aloud the Reading Strategy. Write the following sentence on the board: *Los Angeles is 2,824 miles from New York City.* **Ask:** *How could someone prove that the information is true? (A person could measure the distance.) Does the distance between the two cities change? (no)* Label the statement as a fact. Then, write *Apples taste better than bananas.* **Ask:** *Could someone else think bananas taste better than apples? (yes) Could a person change his or her feeling about apples? (yes)* Label the statement as an opinion. Tell students that recognizing facts and opinions can help them decide which statements are true and which are the writer's personal beliefs. Have students suggest other facts and opinions and explain their answers.

Connect to the Journal

A person who keeps a journal writes down thoughts, feelings, and things that happen each day. Why do you think someone would do that? Think about the reasons a person might write a journal. Then list as many reasons as you can. Share your list with a partner.

Possible answers: to record memories, to reflect on things, to express feelings, to write down things that people

in the future might want to know

_____

_____

_____

Literary Element Journal

Some people write **journals**. They write every day, or almost every day. A journal is also known as a diary.

A journal includes details about
- things that happen to the writer
- things the writer sees happen
- thoughts and feelings about those events

Mary Chesnut saw important things happen. She wrote about her thoughts and feelings. Think about what kind of person Mary Chesnut was as you read her journal.

Reading Strategy Distinguish Fact and Opinion

"The Earth is round" is a **fact**. A fact can be proven. A fact does not change.

"Green is a nicer color than blue" is an **opinion**. An opinion is a belief or feeling. Someone who likes green can start to like blue instead. An opinion can change.

Mary Chesnut wrote about facts and opinions. Look for examples of both as you read.

Selection Vocabulary

allusion (əl ōō' zhən) *n.* a quick mention or hint (p. 126)
*Roberta made an **allusion** to Spain in her report about Mexican food.*
➤ Cognate (Spanish) **alusión**

audaciously (ô dā' shəs lē) *adv.* bravely or rudely (p. 127)
*The young woman spoke **audaciously** to the movie star.*

prostrate (pros' trāt) *adj.* lying face down (p. 127)
*The baby was **prostrate** on the blanket as she slept.*
➤ Cognate (Spanish) **postrado**

delusion (diōō' zh ən) *n.* a belief that is not true (p. 128)
*Carlos had the **delusion** that he could play the flute without practicing.*

pervade (pər vād') *v.* to go through every part (p. 128)
*Loud music and laughter **pervade** the apartment during a party.*

Content Vocabulary

fleet (flēt) *n.* a group of war ships that sail together (p. 126)
*All the ships in the **fleet** sailed home when the war ended.*

intercepted (in' t ər sept' əd) *v.* stopped something on its way somewhere (p. 127)
*Hoang **intercepted** the soccer ball before it reached the goal.*
➤ Cognate (Spanish) **interceptor**

surrender (sə ren' dər) *n.* the act of giving something to someone who demands it (p. 127)
*The chess game ended with the **surrender** of Carla's king.*

escorted (es kort' əd) *v.* went with someone to give help or show honor (p. 129)
*The king **escorted** the queen to the dance.*
➤ Cognate (Spanish) **escoltar**

For more practice, see page 319. ➡

from Mary Chesnut's Civil War **125**

Vocabulary Routine

To introduce the vocabulary, read aloud the words and definitions in the student book and have students repeat after you. Discuss how the pictures illustrate the words or sentences. Then follow the vocabulary routine below.

Content Vocabulary

Define: A ***fleet*** is a group of war ships that sail together. Example: *A flag flew on each ship as the fleet sailed by.* Ask: Describe how a *fleet* might look. DESCRIPTION

A ***surrender*** is the act of giving something to someone who demands it. *The fighting led to the surrender of an important piece of land.* How are a *surrender* and a gift alike? How are they different? COMPARE AND CONTRAST

A person who stopped something from going somewhere ***intercepted*** it. *The teacher intercepted the note Julia passed to Miki.* Give an example of a time you saw something *intercepted*. EXAMPLE

If a group of people ***escorted*** someone, they went with the person to give help or show honor. *The young woman escorted the older man across the street.* Explain how you could *escort* someone. EXPLANATION

Vocabulary Practice Have students complete the vocabulary practice activity on p. 319.

Selection Vocabulary

Define: When someone makes an ***allusion*** to something, they are making a passing reference to a topic. Example: To avoid trouble, he only made a brief *allusion* to his overdue assignment. Ask: When have you made an allusion? EXAMPLE

When someone behaves ***audaciously,*** they are acting in a bold manner. *The bold woman stepped audaciously to the front of the line.* Describe audacious behavior. DESCRIPTION

When someone is ***prostrate,*** he or she assumes a humble position. *The priest was prostrate before the altar.* What is the opposite of prostrate? ANTONYMN

When someone has a ***delusion,*** he or she believes something that is not true. *Mary had a delusion that everyone was out to get her.* How is a delusion different from the truth? COMPARE AND CONTRAST

Something that ***pervades*** is present in each and every part of something. *A sense of dread pervaded the classroom before the final exam.* Explain a time in which you felt a specific emotion pervade a setting. EXAMPLE

Interactive Question-Response

Background Information

Read aloud the note. Tell students that the Civil War was one of the most important events in U.S. history. Explain that people in the South did not agree with President Lincoln and chose Jefferson Davis as their leader. Explain that a fort is an especially strong building used in war. **Ask:** *Do you think the Southern states should have started a war? (yes/no) When do you think people should fight for what they think is right? (Answers will vary.)*

Content Vocabulary

Have a student read aloud the word and definition. Ask students to make a quick drawing of a fleet.

.... **Background Information**

The American Civil War began in 1861. States in the South wanted to leave the country. States in the North wanted to keep the country together. Abraham Lincoln was president. The Civil War began when the Southern army attacked Fort Sumter.
....

fleet (flĕt) *n.* a group of war ships that sail together

April 7, 1861.... Today things seem to have settled down a little. One can but hope still. Lincoln or Seward[1] have made such silly advances and then far sillier drawings back. There may be a chance for peace, after all.

Things are happening so fast.

My husband has been made an aide-de-camp[2] of General Beauregard.[3] Three hours ago we were quietly packing to go home. The convention has adjourned.

Now he tells me the attack upon Fort Sumter may begin tonight. Depends upon Anderson and the fleet outside. The Herald says that this show of war outside of the bar[4] is intended for Texas.[5]

John Manning came in with his sword and red sash. Pleased as a boy to be on Beauregard's staff while the row goes on. He has gone with Wigfall to Captain Hartstene with instructions.

Mr. Chesnut[6] is finishing a report he had to make to the convention.

Mrs. Hayne called. She had, she said, "but one feeling, pity for those who are not here."

Jack Preston, Willie Alston—"the take-life-easys," as they are called—with John Green, "the big brave," have gone down to the island—volunteered as privates.

Seven hundred men were sent over. Ammunition wagons rumbling along the streets all night. Anderson burning blue lights—signs and signals for the fleet outside, I suppose.

Today at dinner there was no **allusion** to things as they stand in Charleston Harbor. There was an undercurrent of intense excitement. There could not have been a more brilliant circle. In addition to our usual quartet (Judge Withers, Langdon Cheves, and Trescot) our two governors dined with us, Means and Manning.

To Sum Up

➤ Mr. Chesnut agrees to help the Southern army fight against the Northern army.

➤ The Southern army plans to attack Fort Sumter.

➤ Colonel Anderson is the Northern leader in the fort.

Vocabulary

allusion (-ōō-zhn) *n.* a quick mention or hint

1. **William Henry Seward** was the U.S. Secretary of State. The U.S. Secretary of State is the person who handles matters between the United States and other countries.
2. An **aide-de-camp** is someone who helps a general or other leader.
3. **General Beauregard** led the Southern army in the attack on Fort Sumter.
4. **Bar** refers to a sand bar. A sand bar is a ridge of sand near the surface of a body of water.
5. **Texas** was one of the Southern states that wanted to separate from the country.
6. **Mr. Chesnut** is the husband of Mary Chesnut. He is also called Colonel Chesnut. He took messages from the Southern army president to Colonel Anderson.

Comprehension

To support students as they read the selection, have them begin the graphic organizer on page A23.

These men all talked so delightfully. For once in my life I listened.

That over, business began. In earnest, Governor Means rummaged a sword and red sash from somewhere and brought it for Colonel Chesnut, who has gone to demand the surrender of Fort Sumter.

— ★ —

And now, patience—we must wait.

— ★ —

Why did that **green goose** Anderson go into Fort Sumter? Then everything began to go wrong.

Now they have <u>intercepted</u> a letter from him, urging them to let him <u>surrender</u>. He paints the horrors likely to ensue if they will not.

He ought to have thought of all that before he put his head in the hole.

April 12, 1861 … Anderson will not capitulate.

— ★ —

Yesterday was the merriest, maddest dinner we have had yet. Men were more **audaciously** wise and witty. We had an unspoken foreboding it was to be our last pleasant meeting. Mr. Miles dined with us today. Mrs. Henry King rushed in: "The news, I come for the latest news—all of the men of the King family are on the island"—of which fact she seemed proud.

While she was here, our peace negotiator—or envoy—came in. That is, Mr. Chesnut returned—his interview with Colonel Anderson had been deeply interesting—but was not inclined to be communicative, wanted his dinner. Felt for Anderson. Had telegraphed to President Davis for instructions.

What answer to give Anderson, &c&c.[7] He has gone back to Fort Sumter, with additional instructions.

When they were about to leave the wharf, A. H. Boykin sprang into the boat, in great excitement; thought himself ill-used. A likelihood of fighting—and he to be left behind!

— ★ —

I do not pretend to go to sleep. How can I? If Anderson does not accept terms—at four—the orders are—he shall be fired upon.

I count four—St. Michael chimes. I begin to hope. At half-past four, the heavy booming of a cannon.

I sprang out of bed. And on my knees—**prostrate**—I prayed as I never prayed before.

There was a sound of stir all over the house—pattering of feet in the corridor—all seemed hurrying one way. I put on my double gown and a shawl and went, too. It was to the housetop.

The shells were bursting. In the dark I heard a man say "waste of ammunition."

Vocabulary

audaciously (ô dā′ shəs lē) *adj.* bravely or rudely
prostrate (pros′ trāt) *adj.* lying face down

7. **&c&c** means "et cetera" or "and others."

Green goose means "foolish person."

intercepted (in′ t ar sept′ əd) *v.* stopped something on its way somewhere

surrender (sə ren′ dər) *n.* the act of giving something to someone who demands it

To Sum Up

➤ Mr. Chesnut asks Anderson to give Fort Sumter to the Southern army.

➤ Anderson does not give the fort to the Southern army.

➤ The Southern army attacks the fort.

Interactive Question-Response

Content Vocabulary

Read aloud the word and definition for *surrender*. Point out that the North owns Fort Sumter. Mr. Chesnut demands the surrender of the fort to the Southern army. **Ask:** *Who would own the fort after the surrender? (the Southern army)*

To Sum Up

Beginning/Early Intermediate ▶ Have students work together to reread the To Sum Up statements from the beginning of the journal. Ask students to explain what Mr. Chesnut and Colonel Anderson each want.

Mr. Chesnut wants _____.

Colonel Anderson wants _____.

(Mr. Chesnut wants Colonel Anderson to give Fort Sumter to the Southern army. Colonel Anderson wants to keep the fort for the North.)

Word Study

Multiple-Meaning Words

Point out the words *paints, maddest,* and *stir* in the selection. Explain to students that these words are examples of **multiple meaning words,** or words that have more than one meaning. Tell them that they should use context clues to determine the new meaning when they encounter words that have more than one meaning.

Then have students practice these skills by completing the activity on page A24.

Interactive Question-Response

Comprehension Check

Have students identify words in the text that support their answers. *("It was a chimney, and the sparks caught my clothes"; "Colonel Chesnut asleep on the sofa in General Beauregard's room")* **Ask:** *Why is Mr. Chesnut tired? (He has been fighting for two nights.) Why is Mary Chesnut tired? (She has been worried.) What can you say about the kind of person Mary Chesnut is? (She loves her husband and wants the fighting to end.)*

Literary Element Journal

If students have difficulty responding, remind them that a person who writes a journal often includes the date of each entry. **Ask:** *What text on the page tells you the day Chesnut wrote a journal entry? (April 15, 1861) Why do you think Chesnut put dates on her entries? (It helped her remember when things happened.)*

✏ Comprehension Check

What details show that the fighting has made the Chesnuts tired? Check each correct answer.
- ☑ Mary Chesnut sits on a chimney and burns her dress.
- ☐ The Chesnuts are too tired to eat..
- ☐ Mr. Chesnut falls asleep on a sofa.

✏ Literary Element

Journal Underline the text that shows when Mary Chesnut wrote a journal entry.

Vocabulary

delusion (dĭ oōo′ zh ən) *n.* a belief that is not true
pervade (par vād′) *v.* to go through every part

To Sum Up

➤ Mary Chesnut worries that people will be hurt in the fighting.
➤ No one is hurt in the fighting.
➤ Fort Sumter starts to burn.

I knew my husband was rowing about in a boat somewhere in that dark bay. And that the shells were roofing it over—bursting toward the fort. If Anderson was obstinate—he was to order the forts on our side to open fire. Certainly fire had begun. The regular roar of the cannon—there it was. And who could tell what each volley accomplished of death and destruction.

The women were wild, there on the housetop. Prayers from the women and imprecations[8] from the men, and then a shell would light up the scene. Tonight, they say, the forces are to attempt to land.

The Harriet Lane[9] had her wheelhouse smashed and put back to sea.

— ★ —

wheelhouse

We watched up there—everybody wondered. Fort Sumter did not fire a shot.

— ★ —

Today Miles and Manning, colonels now—aides to Beauregard—dined with us. The latter hoped I would keep the peace. I give him only good words, for he was to be under fire all day and night, in the bay carrying orders, &c.

— ★ —

Last night—or this morning truly—up on the housetop I was so weak and weary I sat down on something that looked like a black stool. "Get up, you foolish woman—your dress is on fire," cried a man. And he put me out. It was a chimney, and the sparks caught my clothes. Susan Preston and Mr. Venable then came up. But my fire had been extinguished before it broke out into a regular blaze.

— ★ —

Do you know, after all that noise and our tears and prayers, nobody has been hurt. Sound and fury, signifying nothing.[10] A **delusion** and a snare....

— ★ —

Somebody came in just now and reported Colonel Chesnut asleep on the sofa in General Beauregard's room. After two such nights he must be so tired as to be able to sleep anywhere....

April 13, 1861.... Nobody hurt, after all. How gay we were last night. Reaction after the dread of all the slaughter we thought those dreadful cannons were making such a noise in doing.

Not even a battery the worse for wear.

Fort Sumter has been on fire. He has not silenced any of our guns. So the aides—still with swords and red sashes by way of uniform—tell us.

But the sound of those guns makes regular meals impossible. None of us go to table. But tea trays **pervade** the corridors, going everywhere.

Some of the anxious hearts lie on their beds and moan in solitary misery. Mrs. Wigfall and I solace ourselves with tea in my room.

8. ***Imprecations*** are curses.
9. The ***Harriet Lane*** was a ship. The Northern states sent it to help the people at Fort Sumter.
10. ***"Sound and fury, signifying nothing"*** is taken from the play *Macbeth*. William Shakespeare wrote *Macbeth*.

Differentiated Instruction

Clarify the Text Support students in understanding Mary Chesnut's thoughts about the battle.

Beginning/Early Intermediate ➤ Read aloud the To Sum Up box while students follow along. **Ask:** *If someone is worried, does the person feel good or bad? (bad) Do you think Mary Chesnut is happy about the war? (no)*

Intermediate ➤ Read aloud the paragraph that begins "But the sound...." while students follow along. **Ask:** *How does the sound of guns affect Chesnut? (She cannot eat.) Is she the only one who feels that way? How do you know? (No. She says, "None of us go to table.")*

Early Advanced ➤ Draw students' attention to the first paragraph. Explain that *roofing it over* is figurative language that means "flying above." Lead a discussion about the scenes Chesnut imagines and her attitude toward the fighting.

These women have all a satisfying faith....

April 15, 1861.... I did not know that one could live such days of excitement.

They called, "Come out—there is a crowd coming."

A mob indeed, but it was headed by Colonels Chesnut and Manning.

The crowd was shouting and showing these two as messengers of good news. They were <u>escorted</u> to Beauregard's headquarters. Fort Sumter had surrendered.

Those up on the housetop shouted to us, "The fort is on fire." That had been the story once or twice before.

— ★ —

When we had calmed down, Colonel Chesnut, who had taken it all quietly enough—if anything, more unruffled than usual in his serenity— told us how the surrender came about.

Wigfall was with them on Morris Island when he saw the fire in the fort, jumped in a little boat and, with his handkerchief as a **white flag,** rowed over to Fort Sumter. Wigfall went in through a porthole.

When Colonel Chesnut arrived shortly after and was received by the regular entrance, Colonel Anderson told him he had need to pick his way warily, for it was all mined.

As far as I can make out, the fort surrendered to Wigfall.

But it is all confusion. Our flag is flying there. Fire engines have been sent to put out the fire.

Everybody tells you half of something and then rushes off to tell something else or to hear the last news....

escorted (es kort' ǝd) *v.* went with someone to give help or show honor

A **white flag** is a sign of peace.

✏ Literary Element

Journal Reread the boxed text. Which events does Mary Chesnut write about?

- ☑ Mr. Chesnut comes with good news.
- ☐ The Northern army attacks Charleston.
- ☐ The Southern army wins Fort Sumter.

REFLECT

Distinguish Fact and Opinion
Find a fact in Mary Chesnut's journal. Explain what makes it a fact. Then do the same for an opinion.

Possible answer: "Fort Sumter had surrendered" is a fact

because someone could prove it. "How gay we were last

night" is an opinion because it refers to a feeling. No one

can prove that it is true.

_____

 Talk about your answer with a partner.

To Sum Up

➤ A happy crowd brings Mr. Chesnut back from Fort Sumter.

➤ Anderson gives the fort to the Southern army.

Interactive Question-Response

Content Vocabulary

Read aloud the word and definition. Direct students to the fourth and fifth paragraphs. **Ask:** *Who is the crowd escorting? (Colonels Chesnut and Manning) Do you think the crowd escorts the two men to help them or to show them honor? (to show them honor) Why? (The men bring good news that the fort has surrendered.)*

Literary Element Journal

Help students list the major events on the page. *(A crowd comes; Colonels Chesnut and Manning bring good news; the fort surrenders; Colonel Chesnut describes the surrender.)* **Ask:** *In addition to events, what does Chesnut write about? (thoughts, feelings, opinions) Give two examples of feelings or opinions. (excitement, "It is all confusion.")*

Reflect

Partner Talk Have students work in pairs to answer. To help students get started: **Model** *I know that people can prove a fact, and a fact does not change. Let me see if "Seven hundred men were sent over" is a fact. I could prove the statement by reading history books. The number of men who were sent at that time does not change. So that is a fact.* Write the following sentence frames on the board to help students organize their thoughts.

I know that _____ is a fact because _____.

I know that _____ is an opinion because _____.

Oral Assessment

Provide the following prompts to one student at a time. Observe students' responses. See the Oral Assessment Rubric on page T17 to determine students' levels of language output.

1. Who is Mr. Chesnut?

2. Tell me about Colonel Anderson.

3. What does the Southern army do to Fort Sumter?

4. What happens at the end of the journal?

5. What feelings does Mary Chesnut write about in her journal?

Vocabulary Check

B. Intermediate

Write the words *healthy*, *well*, and *sick* on the board. Ask students to define *healthy*. *(strong; not sick)* Have them choose the word that means the opposite of *healthy*. *(sick)* Then, invite volunteers to read the vocabulary words and give their definitions. Remind students that they should match each vocabulary word with the word or words that have the opposite meaning.

---

from Mary Chesnut's
Civil War

Vocabulary Check

A. Match the word with the correct picture.

1. **escorted**   2. **surrender**   3. **intercepted**   4. **fleet**

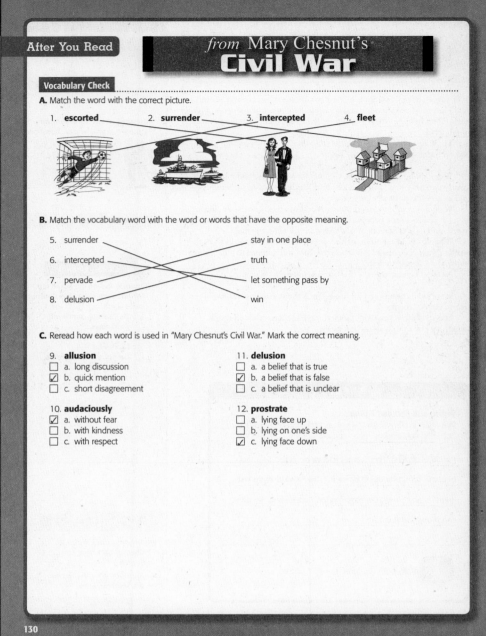

B. Match the vocabulary word with the word or words that have the opposite meaning.

5. surrender   stay in one place

6. intercepted   truth

7. pervade   let something pass by

8. delusion   win

C. Reread how each word is used in "Mary Chesnut's Civil War." Mark the correct meaning.

9. **allusion**
  ☐ a. long discussion
  ☑ b. quick mention
  ☐ c. short disagreement

10. **audaciously**
  ☑ a. without fear
  ☐ b. with kindness
  ☐ c. with respect

11. **delusion**
  ☐ a. a belief that is true
  ☑ b. a belief that is false
  ☐ c. a belief that is unclear

12. **prostrate**
  ☐ a. lying face up
  ☐ b. lying on one's side
  ☑ c. lying face down

Grammar Link

Possessive Pronouns

Prepare students to complete the activity on page A25. Read the grammar instruction with students, and complete the first item with them to help them get started.

from Mary Chesnut's Civil War

Comprehension Check

A. Complete each sentence.

1. Mr. Chesnut meets with Anderson to ask him _Possible answer: to give the fort to the Southern army_.

2. The Southern army attacks the fort because _Possible answer: Anderson will not give it to them_.

3. Anderson agrees to leave the fort after _Possible answer: the fort starts to burn_.

4. The people who bring Mr. Chesnut back from the fort are happy because _Possible answer: Anderson gave them the fort_.

B. Mary Chesnut writes about things that happen. She also writes about her feelings. Use the chart to list events and feelings from her journal.

From Mary Chesnut's Journal	
5. **Events** Possible answers: Mr. Chesnut asks Anderson to surrender Fort Sumter; the Southern army attacks the fort; the fort burns; Anderson surrenders the fort.	6. **Feelings** Possible answers: She enjoys talking to the men, worries about Mr. Chesnut, and is happy no one is hurt.

C. Answer the following questions about Mary Chesnut's journal.

7. List two things you learned about Mary Chesnut from her journal that you could not have learned from a newspaper article.

   Possible answer: She hoped there would be no fighting, and she prayed that Mr. Chesnut and others would be safe.

8. List two opinions Mary Chesnut has about other people.

   Possible answer: John Manning is very happy to help General Beauregard, and Colonel Anderson is foolish.

9. List two events that Mr. Chesnut might have described differently than Mary Chesnut does.

   Possible answer: the attack on Fort Sumter, the surrender of the fort

Comprehension Check

A. Beginning/Early Intermediate

Have students reread all the To Sum Up boxes. Then, check to make sure students know who Mr. Chesnut and Anderson are. **Ask:** *Is Mr. Chesnut in the Southern army or the Northern army? (Southern) Is Anderson in the Southern army or the Northern army? (Northern) At the beginning of the journal, who is in Fort Sumter? (Anderson)* Encourage students to refer to the To Sum Up boxes as they complete the sentences.

Writing Link

Journal Entry

Have students imagine that they are another person living in the same town as Mary Chesnut during the siege of Fort Sumter. Are they a Union soldier inside Fort Sumter, a lower class servant or Colonel Chesnut himself? Have them recreate the same four days Chesnut's journals covered (April 7, 1861; April 12, 1861; April 13, 1861; April 15, 1861) from their character's point of view. Encourage students to share their journal entries with a partner or with the class.

from Mary Chesnut's
Civil War

Journal Entry

Imagine you are Colonel Anderson at Fort Sumter. The fort belongs to the Northern states, but the Southern army wants it. Write journal entries about your two meetings with Mr. Chesnut.

April 7, 1861

Mr. Chesnut came to Fort Sumter today. He wants me to give the fort to the Southern army. When he was here,

I told him __Possible response: I will not give the fort to the Southern army.__

_____

_____

I felt __Possible response: scared that the Southern army would attack the fort.__

_____

_____

April 15, 1861

The Southern army has been shooting at us for days. The fort is on fire. Mr. Chesnut came again today. I told him

__Possible response: I will give the fort to the Southern army.__

_____

_____

I felt __Possible response: bad that I could not keep the fort safe. I am worried about what President Lincoln__

will say.

_____

_____

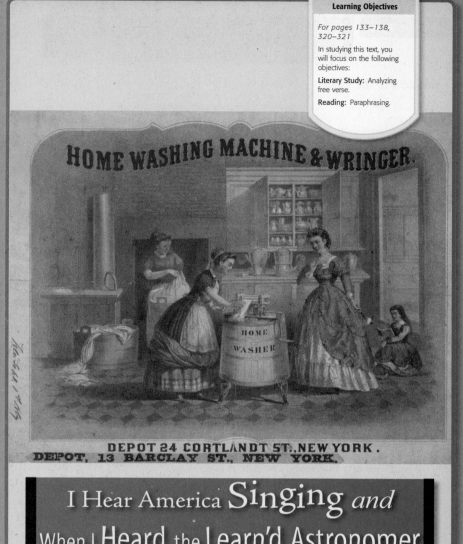

Learning Objectives

For pages 133–138, 320–321

In studying this text, you will focus on the following objectives:

Literary Study: Analyzing free verse.

Reading: Paraphrasing.

HOME WASHING MACHINE & WRINGER.

HOME WASHER

DEPOT 24 CORTLANDT ST., NEW YORK.
DEPOT, 13 BARCLAY ST., NEW YORK.

I Hear America Singing *and*
When I Heard the Learn'd Astronomer

by Walt Whitman

I Hear America Singing *and* When I Heard the Learn'd Astronomer   **133**

Oral Language

Build Background

Read the title and author. Explain that students will read "I Hear America Singing" and "When I Heard the Learn'd Astronomer" by Walt Whitman. **Ask:**

- What word or idea is repeated in the title of both poems? *(hearing)*

- What is an astronomer? *(someone who studies the stars)*

Talk About the Poems

Explain that the poem "I Hear America Singing" is about the songs people sing while they work.

Beginning/Early Intermediate **Ask:** Do you ever hear people singing while they work? *(yes/no)* Work with students to mime singing during work.

Intermediate Ask students for examples of work during which people might sing. Provide this sentence frame to help them answer:

People might sing while they _____. (work on ships, farm, build houses, paint, clean)

Early Advanced **Ask:** *Why do you think people often sing during hard physical work? (Possible answer: to make the time pass more quickly)*

Lesson at a Glance

Oral Language
- Build Background
- Talk About the Poems

Vocabulary
- Content Vocabulary

Literary Element
- Free Verse

Reading Strategy
- Paraphrase

Writing Link
- Poem

Fluency
- Expression and Intonation: Punctuation

Comprehension   BLM
- BLM

Grammar Link   BLM
- *While* and *When* with Past Time Clauses BLM

Technology
- Student Works™ Plus
- Teacher Works™ Plus
- Listening Library Audio CD
- Classroom Presentation Toolkit
- Glencoe Visual Vocabulary
- Skill Level Up!™ A Skill-Based Language Arts Game

Interactive Question-Response

Connect to the Poems

Read aloud Connect to the Poems. Reproduce the sentence frames on the board: **Model** *My friend Andy thinks that work is just something that you have to do to earn money. Someday I want to work as a person who repairs cars or builds bridges and roads. I want to feel happy with my job.* Model writing your response in the sentence frame, and have volunteers suggest other responses. Then have individuals fill in their own sentence frames.

Literary Element   Free Verse

Read aloud the Literary Element. Write a couplet in regular meter on the board, such as *"Shoot if you must this old grey head/ But spare your country's flag!" she said.* Have a student volunteer read the couplet aloud. Point out the regular meter of the lines and the rhyme *head/said.* Explain that free verse is poetry that does not have rhyme and meter, unlike the example on the board. Ask students to rewrite the couplet on the board in free verse.

Reading Strategy   Paraphrase

Read aloud the Reading Strategy. Explain that a successful paraphrase uses different words to state the same meaning as the original. Provide a sample passage to the class, such as: *When Walt Whitman first published Leaves of Grass in 1855, it marked the beginning of a revolution in poetry. At the time, though, few people noticed the young poet's radical work.* Ask students to paraphrase this passage using the questions given in the Reading Strategy.

Connect to the Poems

Much of Walt Whitman's poetry is about work and working people. How do people you know feel about their jobs? What kind of work do you want to do someday? How do you hope to feel about your job?

My friend or family member	Possible answer: Aunt Teresa
thinks that work is	Possible answer: hard but important.
Someday I want to work as	Possible answer: a nurse
I want to feel	Possible answer: satisfied with my job.

Literary Element   Free Verse

Walt Whitman wrote in **free verse**. Free verse is poetry that does not have
- a regular pattern of rhythm
- a regular pattern of rhyme

As you read, ask yourself: How does Whitman use free verse to add meaning to his poems?

Reading Strategy   Paraphrase

When you **paraphrase**, you put something you have read into your own words. Paraphrasing is a good way to check whether you have understood a passage.

Use the following hints to help you paraphrase:
- Think about the meaning of what the author says.
- Break up long and complex sentences into simpler sentences.
- Use words whose meanings are similar to the author's words.
- Change the sentence structure, but don't change the meaning.

As you read, ask yourself, How does Whitman use free verse to add meaning to his poems?

Content Vocabulary

measures (mezh′ ərz) *v.* finds the length or other dimensions of (p. 136)
*The chef **measures** the temperature of the food with a thermometer.*
➤ Cognate (Spanish) **medir**

divide (di vīd′) *v.* to separate (p. 137)
*Ms. Adams decided to **divide** the class into three sections.*
➤ Cognate (Spanish) **dividir**

applause (ə plòz) *n.* approval expressed by clapping the hands (p. 137)
*The actor bowed when he heard the audience's **applause**.*
➤ Cognate (Spanish) **aplauso**

moist (moist) *adj.* slightly wet (p. 137)
*In the morning, the grass is often **moist**.*

For more practice, see page 320. ➡

I Hear America Singing *and* When I Heard the Learn'd Astronomer **135**

Vocabulary Routine

To introduce the vocabulary, read aloud the words and definitions in the student book and have students repeat after you. Discuss how the pictures illustrate the words or sentences. Then follow the vocabulary routine below.

Content Vocabulary

Define: Someone ***measures*** something by finding out one of the object's dimensions, such as length, width, or depth. Example: The carpenter *measures* the length of the board before he cuts it. Ask: What is another example of something else that a carpenter *measures*?
EXAMPLE

You ***divide*** something when you separate it into parts. *Helena used a knife to divide the cake into pieces.* When would you *divide* something into parts?
EXPLANATION

Applause is a demonstration of approval, usually by clapping. *The crowd greeted the hero with applause.* What does *applause* sound like? DESCRIPTION

Something is ***moist*** if it is slightly wet. *Loren's eyes were moist when he watched the sad movie.* What word means about the same as *moist*? SYNONYM

Vocabulary Practice Have students complete the vocabulary practice activity on page 320.

I Hear America Singing

Interactive Question-Response

Literary Element   Free Verse

If students have difficulty responding: **Model** *When I read the first four lines, I don't notice any rhythmic pattern that they share. Each one has its own rhythm. Also, they don't end in rhyming words. On the other hand, each one repeats the word* singing. *So I would say that the poem uses the technique of repetition.* **Ask:** *Why do you think Whitman repeats the word* singing *throughout the poem? (to tie together the idea of many different people working at different jobs and in different places)*

Comprehension   BLM

To support students as they read the selection, have them begin the graphic organizer on page A26.

Makes ready means "prepares."

Leaves off means "stops."

Literary Element

Free Verse What poetic technique does Whitman use in this poem?
- ☐ regular pattern of rhythm
- ☑ repeating words and phrases
- ☐ regular pattern of rhyme

measures (mezh′ərz) *v.* finds the length or other dimensions of

To Sum Up

➤ Whitman celebrates the many voices and songs he hears in America.

➤ He hears many different workers singing songs as they work.

➤ Everyone has his or her own song, and they all sound nice.

136

I hear America singing, the varied carols I hear,
Those of mechanics, each one singing his as it should be blithe[1]
   and strong,
The carpenter singing his as he measures his plank or beam,
The mason singing his as he **makes ready** for work, or **leaves off** work,
5 The boatman singing what belongs to him in his boat,
   the deckhand singing on the steamboat deck,
The shoemaker singing as he sits on his bench, the hatter singing
   as he stands,
The wood-cutter's song, the ploughboy's on his way in the morning,
   or at noon intermission or at sundown,
The delicious singing of the mother, or of the young wife at work,
   or of the girl sewing or washing,
Each singing what belongs to him or her and to none else,
10 The day what belongs to the day—at night the party of young fellows,
   robust, friendly,
Singing with open mouths their strong melodious songs.

1. ***Blithe*** means "without worrying."

Fluency

Expression and Intonation: Punctuation

Intermediate/Early Advanced ➤ Tell students that they will be doing a choral reading of the poem on this page. Remind students to pause when they come to a comma. Model the fluency skill as you read the poem at a moderate tempo. Then have one student read a line. Have another student join in, and a third, and so on. When students reach the end of the poem, have pairs of students reread to each other. To assess individual fluency, use the Oral Reading Guidelines on page T16.

Beginning/Early Intermediate ➤ Have these students choral read only the first four lines of the poem. Before they begin, model the pronunciation of the text. Then have students practice reading the first four lines in pairs before the choral reading.

When I Heard the Learn'd Astronomer

When I heard the **learn'd astronomer,**
When the proofs, the figures, were ranged in columns before me,
When I was shown the charts and diagrams, to add, <u>divide</u>, and
    measure them,
When I sitting heard the astronomer where he lectured with much
    <u>applause</u> in the lecture-room,
5 How soon unaccountable <u>I became tired and sick,</u>
Till rising and gliding out I wander'd off by myself,
In the mystical <u>moist</u> night-air, and from time to time,
Look'd up **in perfect silence** at the stars.

A **learn'd astronomer** is an educated
person who studies the stars.

 Comprehension Check

Underline the words that show
how the speaker feels when he
hears the learn'd astronomer.

In perfect silence means
"completely quietly."

divide (di vīd') *v.* to separate

applause (ə plòz') *n.* approval
expressed by clapping the hands

moist (moist) *adj.* slightly wet

REFLECT

Paraphrase
How would you paraphrase lines 4 and 5?

Possible answer: I became tired and bored while sitting

and listening to the astronomer, who was applauded by

the audience.

_____

_____

Talk about your answer with a partner.

To Sum Up

➤ Whitman hears a scientist talk
about the stars.
➤ The talk makes Whitman feel
tired and sick.
➤ Whitman goes to look at the
stars by himself.

When I Heard the Learn'd Astronomer   **137**

Interactive Question-Response

Comprehension Check

Have students share their answers. **Ask:** *Why do you
think the lecture made Whitman feel tired? (It didn't
have any relationship to the way Whitman feels about
the stars. Whitman is awed by the stars while the
astronomer looks at them scientifically.)*

Reflect

Partner Talk Have students work in pairs to answer.
If students have difficulty responding, help them
paraphrase lines 4 and 5, using the following frame as
a guide.

*I became _____ and _____ while
sitting and_____*

*to the _____, who was _____, by the
audience.*

(bored; tired; listening; astronomer; applauded)

Oral Assessment

Provide the following prompts to one student at a time. Observe students' responses. See the
Oral Assessment Rubric on page T17 to determine students' levels of language output.

1. What does Whitman hear when he travels around America?

2. Give two examples of the different people Whitman sees.

3. What kind of lecture does Whitman hear from the astronomer?

4. How does Whitman react to the lecture?

5. Why does Whitman go out into the night air?

Vocabulary Check

A/B.

Ask: *What is more likely to be damp, a frog or a brick? (a frog) At the end of a performance, does the audience clap or sing? (clap)*

Comprehension Check

C. Early Advanced

If students have difficulty answering the first question:
Model *Free verse means poetry that does not have a regular pattern of rhyme or meter. So one thing I might think about is how Whitman decides to move from line to line, since he doesn't use a definite pattern. When I read the poems, it seems as though each line presents one idea. So I might say that Whitman uses free verse to show the unique song each worker sings. No two workers sing the same song just like no two lines rhyme or follow a set rhythm.*

After Reading

Have students complete the After Reading activity on page 321.

I Hear America Singing and When I Heard the Learn'd Astronomer

Vocabulary Check

A./B. Circle the picture that best answers the question.

1. Which picture shows something **moist**?

2. Which picture shows **applause**?

C. Answer the following questions about the poems.

4. In "I Hear America Singing," the carpenter measures wood. What might he learn about the wood?
   He might learn how wide or high the wood is.

5. In "When I Heard the Learn'd Astronomer," the speaker walks out into the moist night air. How does the air feel? The air feels slightly damp.

Comprehension Check

A./B. Fill in the blanks to complete the passage.

In the first poem, Whitman hears Americans singing while they 6. ____work____. In the second, he listens to a talk by an 7. ____astronomer____. The talk makes him feel 8. ____tired____ He goes outside to see the 9. ____stars____.

C. Answer the questions about Whitman's poems.

10. Why do you think Whitman uses free verse in "I Hear America Singing"? Possible answer: The poem is about people expressing themselves in their own ways. In free verse, you can express yourself in your own way, and you don't have to follow rules about rhythm or rhyme.

11. How would you paraphrase lines 6–7 of "When I Heard the Learn'd Astronomer"? Possible answer: I don't know why, but I didn't feel well until I stood up and walked away on my own.

For more practice, see page 321. ➡

Grammar Link BLM

While and When with Past Time Clauses

Prepare students to complete the activity on page A27. Read the grammar instruction with students, and complete the first item with them to help them get started.

Learning Objectives

For pages 139–146, 322–323

In studying this text, you will focus on the following objectives:

Literary Study: Analyzing rhyme.

Reading: Analyzing sound devices.

If you were coming in the Fall
My **life** closed twice before its **close**
The Soul selects *her* own Society

by Emily Dickinson

If You Were Coming in the Fall/My Life Closed Twice Before Its Close/The Soul Selects Her Own Society **139**

Before You Read

Oral Language

Build Background

Read the title and author. Explain that students will read "If You Were Coming in the Fall," "My Life Closed Twice Before its Close," and "The Soul Selects Her Own Society" by Emily Dickinson. **Ask:**

- Think about the title "If you were coming in the Fall." Do you think that the person addressed is or is not coming in the fall? *(is not)*

- Which of these titles has a puzzle or riddle for the reader? *("My Life closed twice before its close")*

Talk About the Poems

Explain that the poems deal with subjects including love, death, and loss.

Beginning/Early Intermediate **Ask:** *Have you ever felt lonely? (yes/no) What made you feel this way? (a friend moving away)* Work with students to mime loneliness.

Intermediate Ask students whether they enjoy spending time by themselves. Discuss why people might find being alone uncomfortable. **Model** *Some people think that spending time by yourself is boring. But other people might feel that it allows you to think about what really matters in life.*

Lesson at a Glance

Oral Language
- Build Background
- Talk About the Poems

Vocabulary
- Content Vocabulary

Literary Element
- Rhyme

Reading Strategy
- Analyze Sound Devices

Writing Link
- Journal Entry

Fluency
- Pacing: Meaningful Phrases

Comprehension
- BLM

Technology
- Student Works™ Plus
- Teacher Works™ Plus
- Listening Library Audio CD
- Classroom Presentation Toolkit
- Glencoe Visual Vocabulary
- Skill Level Up!™ A Skill-Based Language Arts Game

If You Were Coming in the Fall/My Life Closed Twice Before its Close/The Soul Selects Her Own Society **139**

Interactive Question-Response

Connect to the Poems

Read aloud Connect to the Poems. Reproduce the sentence frames on the board. **Model** *I once lost a close family member.* Model writing your response in the sentence frame, and have volunteers suggest other responses. Then have individuals fill in their own sentence frames.

Literary Element Rhyme

Read aloud the Literary Element. Write on the board: *trouble, bubble, class, cross.* Have a student read the words aloud. **Ask:** *Which pair of words is a full rhyme? (trouble, bubble) Which pair of words is a slant rhyme? (class, cross)* Have students offer full rhymes for *cross* and slant rhymes for *trouble.*

Reading Strategy
Analyze Sound Devices

Read aloud the Reading Strategy. Explain that paying attention to sound devices can help readers understand why poets choose certain words. Write on the board: *The Soul selects her own Society.* **Ask:** *What alliteration is in this line? (soul/selects/society) What assonance is in this line? (soul/own) What consonance is in this line? (soul/selects)* Have students discuss how these different sound devices contribute to the line's rhythm and meaning. If students have difficulty responding: **Model** *I know that many people associate the vowel* o *with feeling alone.* O *is the sound in many related words, such as* alone, lone, lonely, *and* sole. O *can sound like a sigh. So maybe by repeating these sounds, Dickinson wanted to give us the feeling of being alone.*

If you were coming in the Fall
My life closed twice before its close
The Soul selects *her* own Society

Connect to the Poems

Emily Dickinson's short poems raise large questions about the meaning of life. Think about a time that you lost something or someone important to you. How did it feel?

I once lost   Possible answer: a good friend because of an argument.
It made me feel   Possible answer: like I was alone.

Literary Element Rhyme

Rhyme is the repetition of sounds in different words.

- A **full rhyme** occurs when two or more words share the same stressed vowel sound and any sounds that follow the stressed vowel. For example, *science/appliance* is a full rhyme.
- A **slant rhyme** occurs when words share sounds that are similar, although not exactly the same. For example, *bird/card* is a slant rhyme.

Emily Dickinson uses many slant rhymes in her poems. As you read, ask yourself what effect the slant rhymes have on the meaning of the poem.

Reading Strategy Analyze Sound Devices

Sound devices use the sound of language to create interesting effects. Poets use sound devices to show what is important in the poem or to make the poem sound like music. Rhyme is an example of a sound device. Other sound devices include:

- **alliteration**—starting different words with the same consonant sound
- **assonance**—using the same vowel sound in different words
- **consonance**—using the same consonant sound in the middle or end of different words

Pay attention to the sound devices in Dickinson's poems. Think about how they change the rhythm of the poems and emphasize certain words and phrases.

140

Content Vocabulary

brush (brush) *v.* to move lightly (p. 142)
*Trina felt the wind **brush** her cheek.*

separate (sep′ ə r ət) *adj.* kept apart (p. 142)
*The Rosados bought a house with a **separate** garage.*
➤ Cognate (Spanish) **separado**

remains (ri mānz′) *v.* is not yet finished; stays (p. 144)
*The location of the pirate's treasure **remains** unknown.*

ample (am′ pəl) *adj.* more than enough (p. 145)
*We all felt full after the **ample** dinner.*
➤ Cognate (Spanish) **amplio**

For more practice, see page 322. ➡

Vocabulary Routine

To introduce the vocabulary, read aloud the words and definitions in the student book and have students repeat after you. Discuss how the pictures illustrate the words or sentences. Then follow the vocabulary routine below.

Content Vocabulary

<u>Define</u>: To **brush** is to move lightly. <u>Example</u>: Martin heard the leaves *brush* against the window. <u>Ask</u>: What does it feel like to have something *brush* against you?
DESCRIPTION

Things that are **separate** stand apart from one another. *Mrs. Sanchez requested a separate room for her daughter.* What word means the opposite of *separate*? ANTONYM

Something that **remains** is not complete yet. *The full impact of the newspaper story remains uncertain.* How could you fix a problem that *remains* unresolved?
EXPLANATION

Something that is **ample** is more than sufficient. *The students had ample time to finish the project.* The word *enough* has some similarity in meaning to *ample*, but they do not mean the same thing. How are *ample* and *enough* similar, and how are they different?
COMPARE/CONTRAST

Vocabulary Practice Have students complete the vocabulary practice activity on page 322.

Interactive
Question-Response

Background Information

Read aloud the note. Write this opening quatrain from the hymn "Amazing Grace" on the board:

Amazing grace, how sweet the sound

That saved a wretch like me.

I once was lost, but now am found,

Was blind, but now I see.

Have students read the hymn quatrain chorally, and then the first stanza of Dickinson's poem chorally. Ask them to emphasize the rhythm of each stanza so that they see the verses' similarities. If students have difficulty understanding, mark the stressed syllables in the quatrain on the board. Have students clap when they read a stressed syllable, first in the hymn, and then in the Dickinson poem.

Content Vocabulary

Read aloud the word and definition for *brush*. Have students pantomime a leaf brushing against their arm. **Ask:** *If something brushes against you, is it heavy or light? (light)*

Read aloud the word and definition for *separate*. Have a student volunteer read the line from the poem containing *separate*. **Ask:** *Does the speaker put the months into the same drawer or different drawers? (different drawers) What do you think she means by that? (She will keep the months separate so that they will not blend together in her mind. This way, she can count off precisely how much time is left before the person arrives.)*

Literary Element Rhyme

If students have difficulty responding: **Model** *I would answer this by listening at the ends of the lines for words that share sounds. The four words that end the lines in this stanza are* fall, by, spurn, *and* fly. By *and* fly *are the two rhyming words.* **Ask:** *What comparison does this rhyme help to emphasize? (Dickinson would treat the summer the way a housewife treats a fly, as a minor nuisance.)*

Background Information

Dickinson used the meter found in hymns, or religious songs, for the rhythms of her poems. This choice was unusual at the time that she was writing.

Half a smile is a slight smile.

Literary Element

Rhyme Circle the words that rhyme in the first stanza.

brush (brush) *v.* to move lightly

separate (sep′ ə r ət) *adj.* kept apart

To Sum Up

➤ The speaker is addressing another person.

➤ She tells the person that she could easily wait a long time to see him or her again.

If you were coming in the Fall,
I'd brush the Summer by
With **half a smile,** and half a spurn,
As Housewives do, a Fly.

5 If I could see you in a year,
I'd wind the months in balls—
And put them each in separate Drawers,
For fear the numbers fuse—

If only Centuries, delayed,
10 I'd count them on my Hand,
Subtracting, till my fingers dropped
Into Van Dieman's Land.[1]

1. *Van Dieman's Land* is the old name for Tasmania, an island that is part of Australia.

Comprehension

To support students as they read the selection, have them begin the graphic organizer on page A28.

If **certain,** when **this life was out—**
That yours and mine, should be
15 I'd toss it yonder, like a Rind,
And take Eternity—

But, now, uncertain of the length
Of this, that is between,
It goads me, like the Goblin Bee—
20 That will not state—its sting.

If certain here means "if I were certain."

This life was out means "this life has ended."

Interactive Question-Response

Reflect

Partner Talk Have students work in pairs to answer. To help students get started: **Model** *To answer this question, I'm going to look for words that begin with the same letter. One example occurs in line 8. Fear and* fuse *both begin with the letter* f. *Then I would think about the connection between the two words.* Fuse *means "to stick together," but the speaker fears that she will remain apart from the person she loves.* Have students make the *f* sound. **Ask:** *What does the* f *sound suggest to you? (resistance, effort, struggle)* **Model** *I think the repeated* f's *here help to emphasize that the separation is difficult.* Write the following sentence frames on the board to help students organize their thoughts.

Other examples of repeated first letters include _____. These examples show that _____.

REFLECT

Analyze Sound Devices
What examples of alliteration do you see in this poem? How does alliteration affect the poem's meaning?

Possible answer: *fear/fuse* (line 8); *goad/Goblin* (line 19);

state/sting (line 20). These examples of alliteration

emphasize how difficult the separation is for the speaker.

The *g* of *goads/Goblin* may imitate the effect of goading:

_____

 Talk about your answer with a partner.

To Sum Up

➤ The poet says that not knowing when she will see the other person again is very hard.
➤ Waiting to see this person is as painful as being stung by a bee.

Fluency

Pacing: Meaningful Phrases

Intermediate/Early Advanced ➤ Tell students that they will be doing a choral reading of the three stanzas on this page. Have students read the passage ahead of time to decide where students will pause, so that the phrases make meaning. Ask them to notice the meaning of what they read. Model the fluency skill as you read the text at a moderate tempo. Then have one student read a sentence. Have another student join in, and a third, and so on. When students reach the end of the passage, have pairs of students reread to each other. To assess individual fluency, use the Oral Reading Guidelines page T16.

Beginning/Early Intermediate ➤ Have these students choral read only the first stanza of the passage. Before they begin, model the pronunciation of the text. Then have students practice reading the paragraph in pairs before the choral reading.

Interactive
Question-Response

Content Vocabulary

Have a student read aloud the word and definition for *remains*. Have students read the stanza containing *remains*. **Ask:** *What remains to be seen, according to Dickinson? (whether life after death will be as enormous a change as the death-like experiences she has already had) Does she know the answer to this question yet? (She does not. That is why it "remains to see.")*

Comprehension Check

Have students share their answers. **Ask:** *What clues in the poem suggest the events that led to it? ("Parting is all we know of heaven / And all we need of hell.")*

Reflect

Partner Talk Have students work in pairs to answer. To help students get started: **Model** *Assonance means words that share a vowel. So to answer this question, I would look for shared vowels. One example occurs in the first line.* Life *and* twice *both share a long* i *sound. To think about how this affects the meter of the poem, I might compare this line to the first line of the previous poem. "My Life closed twice before its close" and "If you were coming in the Fall" have the same number of syllables. But it takes a little longer to say the first line, because the long vowel sounds draw out the line. The assonance slows the rhythm, which fits with this poem's thoughtful tone.* Write the following sentence frames on the board to help students organize their thoughts.

Other examples of repeated vowels include ___. These repetitions affect the meter by ___.

My life closed twice here means "my life ended twice."

Remains to see here means "remains to be seen." That is, it has not happened yet.

Comprehension Check

What kind of event might have led the speaker of the poem to express these feelings?

losing someone that she loved

_____

_____

_____

_____

remains (ri mānz') *v.* is not yet finished; stays

To Sum Up

➤ The speaker talks about feeling as though her life had ended. She has had this feeling twice.

➤ She is not sure that death will be as powerful as these other experiences.

➤ She compares hell to being apart from someone that you love.

144

My life closed twice before its close—
It yet **remains to see**
If Immortality unveil
A third event to me

5 So huge, so hopeless to conceive
As these that twice befell.
Parting is all we know of heaven,
And all we need of hell.

REFLECT

Analyze Sound Devices
What examples of assonance do you see in this poem? How does assonance affect the poem's rhythm?

Possible answer: There is assonance in the long *i* in

life/twice (line 1) and the long *e* in *we/need* (line 8).

The repeated long vowels slow the rhythm of the poem,

giving it a more thoughtful quality.

_____

 Talk about your answer with a partner.

Differentiated Instruction

Clarify the Text Support students in understanding Dickinson's poem.

Beginning/Early Intermediate ➤ Read aloud the third bullet in To Sum Up. **Ask:** *What is like being apart from someone you love? (hell)*

Intermediate ➤ Have partners read the poem aloud. **Ask:** *What has happened to Dickinson twice? (She has had an experience like death.) What two qualities did these experiences have? (They were huge, or very significant, and hopeless, or depressing.)*

Early Advanced ➤ Have students reread the poem. **Ask:** *What do the last two lines mean? (All that we know about an afterlife in heaven is that we will be separated from our life on earth. All that we need to know about hell is that it will feel like the pain of separation on earth.)*

The Soul selects *her* own Society

The Soul selects her own Society—
Then—shuts the Door—
To her divine Majority—
Present no more—

Unmoved—she notes the Chariots—pausing—   5
At her low Gate—
Unmoved—an Emperor be kneeling
Upon her Mat—

I've known her—from an <u>ample</u> nation—
Choose One—   10
Then—close the Valves of her attention—
Like Stone—

Choose one here means "to choose one."

Literary Element

Rhyme In lines 9 and 11, *nation* and *attention* form an example of:
- [ ] full rhyme
- [x] slant rhyme
- [ ] no rhyme

ample (am′ pəl) *adj.* more than enough

REFLECT

Analyze Sound Devices
Look at lines 10 and 12. How does the length of these lines compare to the length of other lines in the poem? How does the difference in the length change the rhythm? How does the sound of these lines match the meaning of the lines?

Possible answer: These lines are quite short. The words are

single syllables. They have a slant rhyme on the long, heavy

one/stone sounds. The shortness, the change in rhythm,

and the rhyme reinforce the idea of isolation and silence.

_____

 Talk about your answer with a partner.

To Sum Up

➤ The speaker says that the soul carefully chooses who it wants to spend time with.

➤ The soul does not pay attention to the power of chariots or emperors.

➤ The speaker says that the soul closes itself off from others. Its choice cannot be reversed.

The Soul Selects Her Own Society   **145**

Oral Assessment

Provide the following prompts to one student at a time. Observe students' responses. See the Oral Assessment Rubric on page T17 to determine students' levels of language output.

1. How long would the speaker of "If you were coming in the Fall" wait to see the person she is speaking to?

2. How does she feel about their separation?

3. In "My Life closed twice before its close," what is compared to hell?

4. In "The Soul selects her own Society," how does the soul view the powers of chariots and emperors?

5. What happens once the soul has made its choice?

Interactive Question-Response

Content Vocabulary

Have a student read aloud the word and definition for *ample*. Point out that a common phrase using *ample* is *ample warning*. **Ask:** *What does it mean to have* ample *warning? (to have enough warning to prepare) Would you be more likely to have ample warning about a thunderstorm or an earthquake? (thunderstorm)*

Literary Element   Rhyme

If students have difficulty responding: **Model** *I would start answering this question by looking at the stressed syllables of each word. Na-* is stressed in nation, *and* -ten- *is stressed in* attention. *These have different vowel sounds, so the words do not make a full rhyme. On the other hand, both end in* –tion, *so they are similar in sound. So they form a slant rhyme.* **Ask:** *What contrast does this rhyme help to emphasize? (Dickinson contrasts the "ample nation" against the soul's attention on one person.)*

Reflect

Partner Talk Have students work in pairs to answer. To help students get started: **Model** *In order to answer this question, I would start by comparing the lines to other lines in the poem. These lines are significantly shorter than most of the others. Also, there is a slant rhyme in the ends of the lines:* stone *and* one. *I would look next at what the lines are describing to help me think about how the sound affects the meaning. The lines say that the soul chooses one person and then seals itself up as though inside a prison or tomb made of stone. The short lines and the rhyme of* one *and* stone *help to emphasize the idea of solitude or isolation.* Write the following sentence frames on the board to help students organize their thoughts.

Lines 10 and 12 use sound devices including ___. The effect of these sound devices is ___.

Vocabulary Check

A/B. Beginning/Early Intermediate

Ask: *Which picture shows a generous quantity?*
(Picture 3) Which word means "a generous quantity"?
(ample) Which picture shows something staying?
(Picture 1) Which word means "staying"? (remains)
Which picture shows something lightly touching?
(Picture 2) Which word means "to touch lightly"?
(brush)

Comprehension Check

C. Early Advanced

Remind students of the meaning of *alliteration* and *slant rhyme*. Encourage them to consider the meaning of the poems as a whole in answering these questions.

After Reading

Have students complete the After Reading activity on page 323.

After You Read

If you were coming in the Fall
My life closed twice before its close
The Soul selects *her* own Society

Vocabulary Check

A/B. Label each picture using the correct word.

ample	brush	remains

1.

    remains

2.

    brush

3.

    ample

C. In each sentence, choose the word from the list that correctly replaces the underlined word.

ample	separate

4. The poet says she will keep each month in a(n) different drawer. ___separate___

5. She chooses her one friend from a(n) large selection. ___ample___

Comprehension Check

A/B. Answer the questions about Dickinson's poems.

1. What hurts the speaker of "If You Were Coming in the Fall" at the end of the poem? not knowing how long she will be separated from the person she addresses

2. What does parting teach us about, according to "My Life Closed Twice Before Its Close"? heaven and hell

C. Answer the questions about Dickinson's poems.

3. How does Dickinson use alliteration to emphasize her meaning in the first line of "My Life Closed Twice Before Its Close"? the repeated *cl* sound of *closed* and *close* emphasize the poem's idea of ending.

4. In the last stanza of "The Soul Selects Its Own Society," Dickinson forms a slant rhyme using *one* and *stone*. What significance does this rhyme have? The rhyme suggests that the choice of a single companion for the soul hardens into the isolation of stone.

— For more practice, see page 323. ➡

Writing Link

Journal Entry

Have students imagine that they want to leave words of wisdom for generations to come. Ask them to choose a subject from one of Dickinson's poems, such as love or solitude, that they feel strongly about, and create a web or list to generate ideas about it and examples that illustrate it. Then have them write a journal entry expressing their thoughts and feelings on this subject. Encourage them to include relevant advice from themselves as the experts.

An effective journal entry should

- include the student's own thoughts and feelings

- use an appropriately personal style and tone

- follow the conventions of standard English

Learning Objectives

For pages 147–158, 324

In studying this text, you will focus on the following objectives:

Literary Study: Analyzing dialect.

Reading: Analyzing comic devices.

The Celebrated Jumping Frog of Calaveras County

by Mark Twain

The Celebrated Jumping Frog of Calaveras County   **147**

Oral Language

Build Background

Read the title and author. Explain that students will read "The Celebrated Jumping Frog of Calaveras County" by Mark Twain. **Ask:**

- If you *celebrate* something, what do you do? *(You have a party or do something fun with friends or family.)* What do you think *celebrated* means? *(well-known or famous)*

- What can you guess about this story from the title? *(The story will probably be funny since it is about a famous jumping frog.)*

Talk About the Story

Explain that this story is set in a mining camp in California in the 1860s. Mining is what people do to get gold and other things out of the ground.

Early Advanced ▸ Many students will be familiar with the Old West from movies and stories. Ask students to think about how life in the Old West in the 1800s was different from life today. **Model** *I know that people didn't have cars back then, and I have seen movies with people riding horses. So people probably rode horses to get around.* Encourage students to discuss some of the differences between the Old West and modern life. Emphasize that there were no televisions and few leisure activities, so people often told stories for fun.

Lesson at a Glance

Oral Language
- Build Background
- Talk About the Story

Vocabulary
- Selection Vocabulary
- Content Vocabulary
- Academic Vocabulary

Literary Element
- Dialect

Reading Strategy
- Analyze Comic Devices

Writing Link
- Graphic Novel

Fluency
- Expression and Intonation: Dialogue

Comprehension BLM
- BLM

Word Study BLM
- Figurative Language: Idioms and Similes BLM

Grammar Link BLM
- Simple and Compound Sentences BLM

Technology
- Student Works™ Plus
- Teacher Works™ Plus
- Listening Library Audio CD
- Classroom Presentation Toolkit
- Glencoe Visual Vocabulary
- Skill Level Up!™ A Skill-Based Language Arts Game

Interactive Question-Response

Connect to the Story

Read aloud Connect to the Story. Reproduce the list on the board. To help students think about the question: **Model** *My dad is a really good storyteller. He always makes me laugh because his stories are funny.* Write "uses humor or jokes" on the list on the board. Then have the pairs fill in their own lists. When the partners have finished their lists, ask volunteers to add to the list on the board.

Literary Element Dialect

Read aloud the Literary Element. Write the following words on the board:

- *thish-yer* and this here
- *feller* and *fellow* (which means man or boy)
- *reg'lar* and *regular*
- *solitry* and *solitary* (which means single or one)
- *warn't* and *weren't* (or were not)
- *foller* and *follow*

To help students understand the differences in dialect, change your accent and pronunciation as you model these examples. Ask students to repeat them after you. Explain that some of the words in the story are spelled based on how they sound when spoken aloud.

Reading Strategy Analyze Comic Devices

Read aloud the Reading Strategy. Tell students that when they analyze comic devices, they will understand what makes a story funny. **Model** *In movies or television shows, we may laugh at a character's funny actions, such as tripping over or bumping into something, but an author can only use words to be funny.* Give students some examples of how an author might use exaggeration or show other characters reacting humorously to an action. Have students come up with their own humorous situations and share them with a partner.

Connect to the Story

Which of your friends or family members is the best storyteller? What makes this person's stories so good? Discuss these questions with a partner. Together, make a list of what makes a good storyteller.

A good storyteller:
1. Possible answers: uses humor or jokes, speaks with expression
2. imitates different voices and styles, uses details
3. makes you feel like you are in the story

Literary Element Dialect

Dialect is a difference in a language spoken by a group, often within an area and time. For example, dialects may be spoken in different parts of a country.

Dialects may differ from the normal way a language is spoken in

- vocabulary (the words that are used)r
- pronunciation (how the words are spoken)
- grammar (how the words are put together in sentences)

As you read, ask yourself, what are some examples of dialect in this story? How does the dialect add to the humor of the story?

Reading Strategy Analyze Comic Devices

In addition to dialect, Twain uses several other **comic devices**. Comic devices are things that the author uses to make a story funny.

Some of these comic devices include:
- silly situations.
- comic characters.
- ways of speaking.
- exaggerations (when something is made to seem bigger or greater than it is).

As you read, make a list of some of the things in the story that are funny. Then ask yourself, which kinds of comic devices does the author use? What makes these devices so funny?

Selection Vocabulary

garrulous (gar′ ə ləs) *adj.* likes to talk a lot (p. 150)
*My **garrulous** cousin talked for an hour about her vacation.*
➤ Cognate (Spanish) **gárrulo**

conjecture (kən jek′ chər) *v.* to guess (p. 150)
*My sister likes animals, so I **conjectured** that she would like to have a kitten.*
➤ Cognate (Spanish) **conjeturar**

dilapidated (di lap′ ə da′ tid) *adj.* in a bad state or worn down over time (p. 150)
*Birds flew through the holes in the **dilapidated** roof.*

interminable (in tur′ mi nə bəl) *adj.* without end (p. 151)
*Although the boring speech lasted only fifteen minutes, it seemed **interminable**.*
➤ Cognate (Spanish) **interminable**

enterprising (en′ tər prī′zing) *adj.* showing energy for new projects (p. 155)
*To raise money, the **enterprising** students held a car wash on the weekend.*

Content Vocabulary

tranquil (trang′ kwəl) *adj.* calm and quiet (p. 150)
*The empty beach was the perfect place for a **tranquil** vacation.*
➤ Cognate (Spanish) **tranquilo**

gifted (gift′ tid) *adj.* has great ability or is very smart; talented (p. 153)
*After we heard the five-year-old child play the piano, we knew that he was very **gifted**.*

disgusted (dis gus′ tid) *adj.* has a strong dislike for something (p. 154)
*Maggie was **disgusted** by the smell of the trash.*
➤ Cognate (Spanish) **disgustar**

sociable (sō shə bəl) *adj.* friendly; likes to be with others (p. 155)
*On her first day of school, the **sociable** girl talked with many students in her new class.*
➤ Cognate (Spanish) **sociable**

For more practice, see page 324. ➡

Vocabulary Routine

To introduce the vocabulary, read aloud the words and definitions in the student book and have students repeat after you. Discuss how the pictures illustrate the words or sentences. Then follow the vocabulary routine below.

Content Vocabulary

Define: ***Tranquil*** means peaceful and quiet. Example: *The walk through the woods was tranquil.* Ask: What is the opposite of a place that is *tranquil*? ANTONYM

If a person is ***gifted,*** then he or she can do something very well. *The gifted basketball player led his team to win the game.* Who is an example of someone who is *gifted*? EXAMPLE

If you are ***disgusted*** by something, then you strongly dislike it. *Mario's mother was disgusted by his messy room.* What do you think Mario's room must be like? DESCRIPTION

Someone who is ***sociable*** likes to be with others. *Our sociable neighbor is kind to everyone who lives on our street.* How are the words *sociable* and *kind* the same? How are they different? COMPARE AND CONTRAST

Vocabulary Practice Have students complete the vocabulary practice activity on p. 324.

Selection Vocabulary

Define: Someone who is ***garrulous*** talks too much. Example: Mom always says that a *garrulous* person can talk your ears off. Ask: What is the opposite of ***garrulous?*** ANTONYM

Someone may ***conjecture,*** or make an educated guess, when he or she is not sure of an answer or does not have direct evidence. *Scientists may conjecture the results of an experiment before they actually conduct studies to prove their theory.* Explain a good way to conjecture when taking a test. EXPLANATION

Something that is ***dilapidated*** has fallen into ruin because of neglect. *The dilapidated shed looked as if it would blow over in a strong wind.* Give an example of a dilapidated possession that you still find valuable. EXAMPLE

Something that is ***interminable*** is seemingly endless. *Travelers get upset with the interminable delays at airports.* Describe the effects of an interminable school assembly. DESCRIPTION

Someone with an ***enterprising*** spirit shows initiative and willingness to undertake new challenges. *Inventors must be enterprising, coming up with solutions that no one else considers.* What is another word for *enterprising*? SYNONYM

Interactive
Question-Response

Content Vocabulary

Have a student read aloud the word and definition.
Then read aloud the second paragraph of the story up
until "tranquil countenance." **Ask:** *If Simon Wheeler
has a tranquil face, what do you think he is like as a
person? (He is probably calm, peaceful, slow-moving,
thoughtful, and never in hurry.)*

Background Information

Read aloud the note. Explain to students that some
stories, called tall tales, make people and events seem
larger than life. One popular American tall tale is about
Paul Bunyan, a lumberjack (or someone who cuts
down trees) who was very big and strong. Other tall
tale heroes are Pecos Bill, Johnny Appleseed, and Davy
Crockett. Ask students to share some tall tales that they
may know.

---

tranquil (trang′ kwəl) *adj.* calm
and quiet

Gave me good-day means "said a
friendly greeting."

To Sum Up

➤ The speaker finds old Simon
Wheeler in a mining camp.

➤ He asks Wheeler about a man
named Leonidas W. Smiley.

150

In compliance with the request of a friend of mine, who wrote me
from the East, I called on good-natured, **garrulous** old Simon Wheeler,
and inquired after my friend's friend, *Leonidas W. Smiley*, as requested
to do, and I hereunto append[1] the result. I have a lurking suspicion
that *Leonidas W. Smiley* is a myth; that my friend never knew such a
personage; and that he only **conjectured** that, if I asked old Wheeler
about him, it would remind him of his infamous *Jim* Smiley, and he would
go to work and bore me nearly to death with some infernal[2] reminiscence
of him as long and tedious as it should be useless to me. If that was the
design, it certainly succeeded.

I found Simon Wheeler dozing comfortably by the bar-room stove
of the old **dilapidated** tavern in the ancient mining camp of Angel's,[3]
and I noticed that he was fat and bald-headed, and had an expression
of winning gentleness and simplicity upon his tranquil countenance.[4]
He roused up and **gave me good-day.** I told him a friend of mine had
commissioned me to make some inquiries about a cherished companion
of his boyhood named *Leonidas W. Smiley*—*Rev. Leonidas W. Smiley*—a
young minister of the Gospel, who he had heard was at one time a
resident of Angel's Camp. I added that, if Mr. Wheeler could tell me
any thing about this Rev. Leonidas W. Smiley, I would feel under many
obligations to him.

Vocabulary

garrulous (gar′ ə ləs) *adj.* likes to talk a lot
conjecture (kən jek′ chər) *v.* to guess
dilapidated (di lap′ ə da′ tid) *adj.* in a bad state or worn down over time

1. **Append** means "to add" or "to attach."
2. **Infernal** means "awful" or "unpleasant."
3. **Angel's** refers to Angel's Camp.
4. **Countenance** means "face."

Comprehension

To support students as they read the selection, have them begin the graphic organizer on
page A29.

Simon Wheeler backed me into a corner and blockaded me there with his chair, and then sat me down and reeled off the monotonous narrative which follows this paragraph. He never smiled, he never frowned, he never changed his voice from the gentle-flowing key to which he tuned the initial sentence, he never betrayed the slightest suspicion of enthusiasm; but all through the **interminable** narrative there ran a vein of impressive earnestness and sincerity, which showed me plainly that, so far from his imagining that there was any thing ridiculous or funny about his story, he regarded it as a really important matter, and admired its two heroes as men of transcendent[5] genius in finesse.[6]

To me, the spectacle of a man drifting serenely along through such a **queer yarn** without ever smiling, was exquisitely absurd. As I said before, I asked him to tell me what he knew of Rev. Leonidas W. Smiley, and he replied as follows. I let him go on in his own way, and never interrupted him once:

There was a feller here once by the name of *Jim* Smiley, in the winter of '49—or may be it was the spring of '50—I don't recollect exactly, somehow, though what makes me think it was one or the other is because I remember the big flume wasn't finished when he first came to the camp; but any way, he was the curiosest man about always betting on any thing that turned up you ever see, if he could get any body to bet on the other side; and if he couldn't he'd change sides. Any way that suited the other man would suit him—any way just so's he got a bet, he was satisfied. But still he was lucky, uncommon lucky; he most always come out winner. He was always ready and laying for a chance; there couldn't be no solitry thing mentioned but that feller'd offer to bet on it, and take any side you please, as I was just telling you. If there was a horse race, you'd find him flush,[7] or you'd find him busted at the end of it; if there was a dog-fight, he'd bet on it; if there was a cat-fight, he'd bet on it; if there was a chicken-fight, he'd bet on it; why, if there was two birds setting on a fence, he would bet you which one would fly first; or if there was a camp-meeting,[8] he would be there reg'lar, to bet on Parson Walker, which he judged to be the best exhorter[9] about here, and so he was, too, and a good man. If he even seen a straddle-bug[10] start to go anywheres, he would bet you how long it would take him to get wherever he was going to, and if you took him up, he would foller that straddle-bug to Mexico but what he would find out where he was bound for and how long he was on the road. Lots of the boys here has seen that Smiley, and can tell you about him. Why, it never made no difference to *him*—he would bet on *any* thing—the dangdest feller. Parson Walker's wife laid very sick once, for a good while, and it seemed as if they warn't going to save her; but one morning he come in, and Smiley asked how she was, and he said she was considerable better—thank the Lord for his inf'nit mercy—and coming on so smart that, with the blessing of Prov'dence,[11] she'd get well yet; and Smiley, before he thought, says, "Well, I'll risk two-and-a-half[12] that she don't, any way."

A *queer yarn* is a strange story.

Literary Element

Dialect Place a check mark next to the phrases that are examples of Wheeler's dialect. If a phrase is standard English, do not place a check next to it.

- [ ] there was a feller
- [ ] it was the spring of '50
- [x] he was the curiosest man
- [ ] if he could get any body to bet on the other side
- [x] he most always come out winner
- [x] there couldn't be no solitry thing

Vocabulary

interminable (in tur′ mi nə bəl) *adj.* without end

5. **Transcendent** means "better than others."
6. **Finesse** is a smooth skill.
7. Here, **flush** means "has lots of money."
8. A **camp-meeting** is an outdoor religious meeting, sometimes held in a tent.
9. Here, an **exhorter** is a preacher.
10. A **straddle-bug** is a long-legged bug.
11. **Prov'dence** (Providence) is God.
12. **Risk two-and-a-half** means "risk, or bet, $2.50."

To Sum Up

➤ Wheeler begins to tell the speaker a story.

➤ Wheeler tells the story of Jim Smiley, who was once in the mining camp.

➤ Jim Smiley liked to bet, and he almost always won.

The Celebrated Jumping Frog of Calaveras County

Interactive Question-Response

Literary Element Dialect

If students have difficulty responding, have them work with a partner. Encourage them to say the phrases aloud with their partner and listen to how the words sound. Ask students to think about which phrases sound or look normal and which do not. After students have checked the boxes, review the ways that each of the phrases in dialect should be written and pronounced in standard English. Write the correct phrases on the board.

- there was a *fellow*
- he was the *most curious* man
- he *almost* always *came* out *the* winner
- there couldn't be *any solitary* thing

Selection Vocabulary

Have a student read the sentence containing the word *interminable*. **Ask:** *If the narrator says that the narrative, or story, is interminable, then how do you think he feels about it? (He does not like the story. To him, it seems to go on forever.)*

Interactive Question-Response

Comprehension Check

Ask students to share what they underlined in the text.
Ask: *Why do these stories of the horse and the dog belong in a tall tale? (They seem silly and unrealistic. The horse always wins even though she is coughing and sneezing. The dog dies when he has to fight a dog with no back legs.)*

To Sum Up

Have students work in pairs to reread all the To Sum Up statements from the beginning of the story on page 150. Point out that this is a story within another story. Ask students to work together to tell the difference between the two stories. Provide the following sentence frames for students to complete.

One story is about _____. (the narrator who comes to see Simon Wheeler to learn about a friend's friend)

The story within a story is told by _____, and is about _____. (Simon Wheeler; Jim Smiley and how he likes to make bets)

Ornery means "stubborn" or "grumpy."

Throwed up the sponge means "gave up."

Comprehension Check

Reread about the mare and the bull pup in the first and second paragraphs. How did the mare, or horse, do in the races? What happened to the dog? Underline the words that tell the answers to these questions.

Thish-yer[13] Smiley had a mare—the boys called her the fifteen-minute nag, but that was only in fun, you know, because, of course, she was faster than that—and he used to win money on that horse, for all she was so slow and always had the asthma, or the distemper, or the consumption,[14] or something of that kind. They used to give her two or three hundred yards start, and then pass her under way; but always at the fag-end[15] of the race she'd get excited and desperate-like, and come cavorting[16] and straddling up, and scattering her legs around limber, sometimes in the air, and sometimes out to one side amongst the fences, and kicking up m-o-r-e dust, and raising m-o-r-e racket with her coughing and sneezing and blowing her nose—and always fetch up at the stand[17] just about a neck ahead, as near as you could cipher it down.[18]

And he had a little small bull pup, that to look at him you'd think he wan't worth a cent, but to set around and look **ornery,** and lay for a chance to steal something. But as soon as money was up on him, he was a different dog; his under-jaw'd begin to stick out like the fo'castle of a steamboat, and his teeth would uncover, and shine savage like the furnaces. And a dog might tackle him, and bully-rag[19] him, and bite him, and throw him over his shoulder two or three times, and Andrew Jackson—which was the name of the pup—Andrew Jackson would never let on but what *he* was satisfied, and hadn't expected nothing else—and the bets being doubled and doubled on the other side all the time, till the money was all up; and then all of a sudden he would grab that other dog jest by the j'int of his hind leg and freeze to it—not chaw, you understand, but only jest grip and hang on till they **throwed up the sponge,** if it was a year. Smiley always come out winner on that pup, till he harnessed[20] a dog once that didn't have no hind legs, because they'd been sawed off by a circular saw, and when the thing had gone along far enough, and the money was all up, and he come to make a snatch for his pet holt,[21] he saw in a minute how he'd been imposed on, and how the other dog had him in the door,[22] so to speak, and he 'peared surprised, and then he looked sorter discouraged-like, and didn't try no more to win the fight, and so he got shucked out[23] bad. He give Smiley a look, as much as to say his heart was broke, and it was his fault, for putting up a dog that hadn't no hind legs for him to take holt of, which was his main dependence in a fight, and then he limped off a piece and laid down and died. It was a good pup, was that Andrew Jackson, and would have made a name for hisself if he'd lived, for the stuff was in him, and he had genius—I know it, because he hadn't had no opportunities to speak of, and it don't stand to reason that a dog could make such a fight as he could under them circumstances, if he hadn't no talent. It always makes me feel sorry when I think of that last fight of his'n, and the way it turned out.

13. **Thish-yer** is dialect for "this here."
14. **Consumption** is a sickness of the lungs.
15. The **fag-end** is the last part.
16. **Cavorting** means "running and jumping playfully."
17. **Fetch up at the stand** means "come to the finish line."
18. **Cipher it down** means "add it up."
19. **Bully-rag** means "to try to scare."
20. Here, **harnessed** means "set up a fight with."
21. A **pet holt** is a favorite hold.
22. **Had him in the door** means "had him in a weak spot."
23. **Shucked out** means "beaten."

To Sum Up

➤ Jim Smiley had a small dog named Andrew Jackson.

➤ Smiley bet on Andrew Jackson in dog fights.

➤ Andrew Jackson would bite onto another dog's leg and not let go until the other dog gave up.

Word Study BLM

Figurative Language: Idioms and Similes

Point out to students that idioms and similes share a role; both make comparisons so that readers can see something in a new or different way. **Ask:** What image comes to mind when you hear the expression "throwed up the sponge?" *(a person who is dejected and who has given up)* Explain that the idiom comes from the sport of boxing, where at one time a fighter conceded defeat by throwing the sponge or towel used to wipe his face into the ring.

Ask: What other expressions mean the same as "throwed up the sponge"? *(throw in the towel, wave the white flag, have done with, wash one's hands of, call it a day, call it quits, hang up one's fiddle)* After students identify idioms and similes in the activity on page A30, have them discuss how the comparisons involved in both types of expressions provide color and specificity to the story. .

Well, thish-yer Smiley had rat-tarriers,[24] and chicken cocks,[25] and tom-cats, and all them kind of things, till you couldn't rest, and you couldn't fetch nothing for him to bet on but he'd match you. He ketched a frog one day, and took him home, and said he cal'klated[26] to edercate him; and so he never done nothing for three months but set in his back yard and learn[27] that frog to jump. And you bet you he *did* learn him, too. He'd give him a little punch behind, and the next minute you'd see that frog whirling in the air like a doughnut—see him turn one summerset, or may be a couple, if he got a good start, and come down flat-footed and all right, like a cat. He got him up so in the matter of catching flies, and kept him in practice so constant, that he'd nail a fly every time as far as he could see him. Smiley said all a frog wanted was education, and he could do most any thing—and I believe him. Why, I've seen him set Dan'l Webster[28] down here on this floor—Dan'l Webster was the name of the frog—and sing out, "Flies, Dan'l, flies!" and quicker'n you could wink, he'd spring straight up, and snake a fly off'n the counter there, and flop down on the floor again as solid as a gob of mud, and fall to scratching the side of his head with his hind foot as indifferent as if he hadn't no idea he'd been doin' any more'n any frog might do. You never see a frog so modest and straightfor'ard as he was, for all he was so gifted. And when it come to fair and square jumping on a dead level, he could get over more ground at one straddle[29] than any animal of his breed you ever see. **Jumping on a dead level was his strong suit,** you understand; and when it come to that, Smiley would ante up[30] money on him as long as he had a red.[31] Smiley was monstrous proud of his frog, and well he might be, for fellers that had traveled and been everywheres, all said he laid over any frog that ever *they* see.

REFLECT

Analyze Comic Devices

What are two things from the story you find funny? For each, identify the type of comic device, and explain why it is funny. Remember that some types of comic devices are comic characters, silly situations, Wheeler's way of speaking, and exaggeration.

1. Possible answers: Simon Wheeler tells a funny story in a serious way. Wheeler's dialect is often funny because he pronounces words in different ways, such as pronouncing Daniel as Dan'l. Jim Smiley bets on some silly situations, such as two birds on a fence, a straddle-bug, a dog named Andrew Jackson, and his jumping frog.

2. Wheeler also uses funny descriptions such as "whirling in the air like a donut" and "You never see a frog so modest and straightfor'ard."

Talk about your answer with a partner.

---

gifted (gift' tid) *adj.* has great ability or is very smart; talented

Jumping on a dead level was his strong suit means that jumping on flat ground was his strength.

✏ Literary Element

Dialect Place a check mark next to the phrases that are examples of Wheeler's dialect. If a phrase is normal English, do not place a check next to it.

- ☑ he ketched a frog one day
- ☑ he cal'klated to edercate him
- ☑ And you bet you he *did* learn him too
- ☐ He'd give him a little punch behind
- ☐ you'd see that frog whirling in the air like a doughnut
- ☐ Smiley said all a frog wanted was education

24. *Rat-tarriers* are dogs once used for catching rats.
25. *Chicken cocks* are adult male chickens that are trained to fight.
26. *Cal'klated* is dialect for calculated, meaning "planned."
27. Here, *learn* means "teach."
28. *Dan'l Webster* refers to Daniel Webster (1782–1852), a famous speaker who was a U.S. senator and a U.S. secretary of state.
29. Here, *straddle* means "to jump."
30. *Ante up* means "to bet."
31. A *red* refers to a red cent, meaning "any money at all."

To Sum Up

- ➤ Smiley caught a frog and named him Dan'l Webster.
- ➤ For three months, he taught the frog how to jump.
- ➤ Smiley bet on his frog. He was very proud of his frog.

Interactive Question-Response

Content Vocabulary

Have a student read aloud the word and definition of *gifted*. Then read aloud the sentence that begins, "You never see a frog so modest . . ." **Ask:** *Why does Wheeler say that the frog was "so gifted"? (It is a talented jumper.) Why is this sentence funny? (Wheeler is describing the frog as if it is a human being.)*

Literary Element Dialect

If students have difficulty responding, have them work with a partner. Encourage them to say the phrases aloud with their partner and listen to how the words sound. Ask students to think about which phrases sound or look normal and which do not. After students have checked the boxes, review the ways that each of the phrases in dialect should be written and pronounced in standard English. Write the correct phrases on the board. For the phrases which are not dialect, explain to the students why they are not dialect.

- he *caught* a frog one day
- he *calculated* to *educate* him
- And you bet he did *teach* him too

Reflect

Partner Talk Have students work in pairs to answer. To help students get started: **Model** *To answer this, I would think about something in the story that seems funny or silly. It's funny that Jim Smiley will bet on everything, even two birds sitting on a fence. Some of the things that Simon Wheeler says are funny or strange, like "whirling in the air like a doughnut."* Encourage students to explain why these devices are humorous. Write the following sentence frames on the board to help students organize their thoughts.

A silly situation from the story is _____ because _____.

A funny character from the story is _____ because _____.

Interactive Question-Response

Content Vocabulary

Have a student read the sentence containing the word *disgusted*. **Ask:** *What has caused Smiley to become disgusted?* (His prized frog did not move, and he lost his bet.) *What is another way to describe how Smiley feels?* (He feels unhappy, angry, and even offended by what happened.)

Comprehension Check

Ask students to share what they underlined. **Ask:** *What do you think will happen?* (Dan'l Webster will be too heavy to win the race.) *What do you think of the stranger's actions?* (He is smart to think of a way to beat Jim Smiley in a bet.)

 Comprehension Check

Reread the second boxed text on this page. Underline the words that tell what the stranger did to Smiley's frog.

Planted as solid as an anvil means that the frog did not move. An anvil is a heavy iron block.

disgusted (dis gus' tid) *adj.* has a strong dislike for something

To Sum Up

➤ A stranger asks Smiley what he has in the box. Smiley tells him it is a frog that can outjump any frog in the county.

➤ The stranger says he does not have a frog, but would bet Smiley if he did. Smiley asks him to hold his frog while he goes to catch another frog for the stranger.

➤ While Smiley is gone, the stranger fills Dan'l Webster's mouth with small metal balls. When Smiley returns, the two frogs race and Dan'l Webster does not move.

➤ The stranger takes the money and leaves.

154

Well, Smiley kept the beast in a little lattice box, and he used to fetch him down town sometimes and lay for a bet. One day a feller—a stranger in the camp, he was—come across him with his box, and says:

"What might it be that you've got in the box?"

And Smiley says, sorter indifferent like, "It might be a parrot, or it might be a canary, may be, but it an't—it's only just a frog."

And the feller took it, and looked at it careful, and turned it round this way and that, and says, "H'm—so 'tis. Well, what's *he* good for?"

"Well," Smiley says, easy and careless, "He's good enough for *one* thing, I should judge—he can outjump any frog in Calaveras county."

The feller took the box again, and took another long, particular look, and give it back to Smiley, and says, very deliberate, "Well, I don't see no p'ints[32] about that frog that's any better'n any other frog."

"May be you don't," Smiley says, "May be you understand frogs, and may be you don't understand 'em; may be you've had experience, and may be you an't only a amature, as it were. Anyways, I've got *my* opinion, and I'll risk forty dollars that he can outjump any frog in Calaveras county."

And the feller studied a minute, and then says, kinder sad like, "Well, I'm only a stranger here, and I an't got no frog; but if I had a frog, I'd bet you."

And then Smiley says, "That's all right—that's all right—if you'll hold my box a minute, I'll go and get you a frog." And so the feller took the box, and put up his forty dollars along with Smiley's, and set down to wait.

So he set there a good while thinking and thinking to hisself, and then <u>he got the frog out and prized his mouth open and took a teaspoon and filled him full of quail shot[33]</u>—filled him pretty near up to his chin—and set him on the floor. Smiley he went to the swamp and slopped around in the mud for a long time, and finally he ketched a frog, and fetched him in, and give him to this feller, and says:

"Now, if you're ready, set him alongside of Dan'l, with his fore-paws just even with Dan'l, and I'll give the word." Then he says, "One—two—three—jump!" and him and the feller touched up the frogs from behind, and the new frog hopped off, but Dan'l give a heave, and hysted up his shoulders—so—like a Frenchman, but it wan't no use—he couldn't budge; he was **planted as solid as an anvil,** and he couldn't no more stir than if he was an-chored out. Smiley was a good deal surprised, and he was <u>disgusted</u> too, but he didn't have no idea what the matter was, of course.

The feller took the money and started away; and when he was going out at the door, he sorter jerked his thumb over his shoulders—this way—at Dan'l, and says again, very deliberate, "Well, *I* don't see no p'ints about that frog that's any better'n any other frog."

32. *P'ints* is dialect for points, meaning "details" or "characteristics."
33. *Quail shot* is small metal balls used to hunt birds.

Fluency

Expression and Intonation: Dialogue

Intermediate/Early Advanced Tell students that they will be doing a choral reading of some the paragraphs on this page from "What might it be..." to "... any frog in Calaveras county." Remind students to change their voices for different characters and to apply what they know about the character. Model the fluency skill as you read the text at a moderate tempo. Then have one student read a sentence. Have another student join in, and a third, and so on. When students reach the end of the passage, have pairs of students reread to each other. To assess individual fluency, use the Oral Reading Guidelines on page T16.

Beginning/Early Intermediate Have these students choral read up to "... what's *he* good for?". Before they begin, model the pronunciation of the text. Then have students practice reading the paragraph in pairs before the choral reading.

Smiley he stood scratching his head and looking down at Dan'l a long time, and at last he says, "I do wonder what in the nation that frog throw'd off for—I wonder if there an't something the matter with him—he 'pears to look mighty baggy, somehow." And he ketched Dan'l by the nap of the neck, and lifted him up and says, "Why, blame my cats, if he don't weigh five pound!" and turned him upside down, and he belched out a double handful of shot. And then he see how it was, and he was the maddest man—he set the frog down and took out after that feller, but he never ketched him. And—

[Here Simon Wheeler heard his name called from the front yard, and got up to see what was wanted.] And turning to me as he moved away, he said: "Just set where you are, stranger, and rest easy—I an't going to be gone a second."

But, by your leave, I did not think that a continuation of the history of the **enterprising** vagabond *Jim* Smiley would be likely to afford[34] me much information concerning the Rev. *Leonidas W.* Smiley, and so I started away.

At the door I met the <u>sociable</u> Wheeler returning, and he buttonholed[35] me and recommended:

"Well, thish-yer Smiley had a yaller one-eyed cow that didn't have no tail, only jest a short stump like a bannanner, and——"

"Oh! hang Smiley and his afflicted cow!" I muttered, good-naturedly, and bidding the old gentleman good-day, I departed.

REFLECT

Analyze Comic Devices
What are <u>two</u> things you find funny about the frog contest? For each, identify the type of comic device and explain why it is funny. Remember that some types of comic devices are comic characters, silly situations, Wheeler's way of speaking, and exaggeration.

1. Possible answers: The frog competition is silly in itself, but it becomes even sillier when the stranger fills Dan'l Webster's mouth with quail shot. When he learns

2. that Dan'l Webster feels heavy, Smiley uses the funny expression "blame my cats."

Talk about your answer with a partner.

---

sociable (sō′ sha bəl) *adj.* friendly; likes to be with others

✏ Literary Element

Dialect SPlace a check mark next to the phrases that are examples of Wheeler's dialect. If a phrase is in normal English, do not place a check next to it.
- ☑ he 'pears to look mighty baggy
- ☑ Why, blame my cats, if he don't weigh five pound!
- ☐ he was the maddest man
- ☑ Well, thish-yer Smiley
- ☑ a yaller one-eyed cow that didn't have no tail
- ☑ only jest a short stump like a bannanner

Vocabulary
enterprising (en′ tər prī′zing) *adj.* showing energy for new projects

34. **Afford** means "to give."
35. **Buttonholed** means "stopped to talk."

To Sum Up

➤ Smiley is confused about why Dan'l Webster does not win. When Smiley picks up the frog, the metal balls fall out.

➤ Smiley runs after the stranger, but he is gone.

➤ The speaker leaves when Wheeler begins to talk about Smiley's yellow, one-eyed cow.

The Celebrated Jumping Frog of Calaveras County **155**

Oral Assessment

Provide the following prompts to one student at a time. Observe students' responses. See the Oral Assessment Rubric on page T17 to determine students' levels of language output.

1. Why does the narrator talk to Simon Wheeler?
2. What are some things that Jim Smiley places bets on?
3. How does Smiley's dog win fights?
4. Why does Smiley catch a frog?
5. What does the stranger do to win the bet?

Interactive Question-Response

Content Vocabulary

Have a student read the sentence containing the word *sociable*. **Ask:** *How is Wheeler sociable? (He likes to talk with people.) Is the narrator sociable? (Here, the narrator is not sociable, but he may be sociable in another setting.) Is Jim Smiley sociable? (Smiley is sociable when he is trying to get somebody to bet against him.)*

Literary Element Dialect

If students have difficulty responding, have them work with a partner. Encourage them to say the phrases aloud with their partner and listen to how the words sound. Ask students to think about which phrases sound or look unusual. After students have checked the boxes, review the ways that each of the phrases in dialect should be written and pronounced in standard English. Write the correct phrases on the board.

- he *appears* to look *very* baggy
- Why, he *must* weigh five *pounds*!
- Well, *this here* Smiley or Well, Smiley
- a *yellow* one-eyed cow that didn't have *a* tail
- only *just* a short stump like a *banana*

Reflect

Partner Talk Have students work in pairs to answer. To help students get started: **Model** *To answer this question, I would think about what was funny about the frog race. It's funny that the frog was stuck to the ground, not moving, after the stranger filled him with quail shot. It's also funny that Smiley said "blame my cats" when he found out what happened.* Encourage students to explain why these devices are humorous. Write the following sentence frames on the board to help students organize their thoughts.

Something funny in the frog contest is _____ because _____.

A funny line from the frog contest is _____ because _____.

Vocabulary Check

B. Intermediate

Read the questions aloud. After each question, ask students to explain their answers. For example,
Ask: *Why would a sociable person be garrulous? (Someone who likes to be with other people might like to talk to them too.)*

Academic Vocabulary

Remind students that Mark Twain's stories were set in the various regions of the country that he had visited. Tell students that *region* is an academic word that refer to territories or areas of land. Other words that are related in meaning are *regional, regionalism.*

Have students use a map to identify geographic regions of the United States. Challenge students to identify other types of regions they have learned about in their study of history, political science, or even literature.

Vocabulary Check

A. Circle the picture that best answers the question.

1. Which picture shows a **tranquil** setting?

2. Which picture shows a **sociable** boy?

3. Which person is **gifted**?

4. Which picture shows someone who is **disgusted**?

B. Answer yes or no to each of the questions below.

5. Could a **sociable** person be **garrulous**? _____yes_____

6. Might someone be **disgusted** by a **dilapidated** and dirty building? _____yes_____

7. If your friend wanted a lot of excitement, would she plan a **tranquil** vacation? _____no_____

8. Would people admire a **gifted** person? _____yes_____

9. Would students like a class that seemed **interminable**? _____no_____

C. Circle the letter of the sentence that uses the boldface word correctly.

10. a. The **garrulous** boy told his friends about his new cat.
    b. The **garrulous** boy only spoke a few words all day.

11. a. Many visitors admired the **dilapidated** house.
    b. Some workers fixed the **dilapidated** house.

12. a. The **enterprising** young woman planned to start a business selling sandwiches.
    b. When the girl slept all day, she felt **enterprising**.

13. a. We laughed for two hours during the **interminable** movie was 45 minutes long.
    b. Although the movie lasted only two hours, it seemed **interminable**.

Grammar Link BLM

Simple and Compound Sentences

Prepare students to complete the activity on page A31. Read the grammar instruction with students, and complete the first item with them to help them get started.

The Celebrated Jumping Frog of Calaveras County

Comprehension Check

A. "The Celebrated Jumping Frog of Calaveras County" is a story inside of another story. Complete the sentences below about the two stories.

1. In the outside story, the speaker goes to see ___Simon Wheeler___, who tells him a story about Jim Smiley.

2. In the inside story, Jim Smiley is a man who loves to bet. List three things that he bets on.

   a. _Possible answers: birds on a fence, the parson, a straddle-bug, horse races, dog fights,_

   b. _or a jumping frog_

   c. _____

3. The outside story ends when the speaker _leaves because he does not want to hear another story_
   from Simon Wheeler

B. Read the following sentences from "The Celebrated Jumping Frog of Calaveras County." Circle the examples of Simon Wheeler's dialect. Then, rewrite each word or phrase in standard English.

4. "Well, (thish-yer) Smiley" _possible answer: this here_

5. "(ketched) a frog one day, and took him home" _possible answer: caught_

6. "and said he (cal'klated to edercate) him" _possible answer: calculated to educate_

7. "and so he (never done nothing) for three months" _possible answer: did not do anything_

8. "but (set) in his back yard and (learn) that frog to jump." _possible answer: sat and taught_

C. The language used by Wheeler and by the speaker is very different. Complete the sentences below about the characters' use of language.

9. How would you describe Wheeler's use of language? _Possible answer: He uses unusual pronunciations_
   and interesting expressions.

10. How would you describe the speaker's language? _Possible answer: He pronounces words properly and_
    uses big words.

11. Wheeler's language shows that he is _Possible answer: not educated and has learned humorous_
    expressions from living in the mining camp.

12. The speaker's language shows that he is _Possible answer: educated and smart. He has probably read_
    many books.

Comprehension Check

C. Early Advanced

Explain that the way people speak says a lot about who they are, where they are from, and other things about their lives. People's speech can also show if they went to school and if they read books. Give students modern day examples to think about, such as colloquial phrases and slang. Encourage students to think about these things as they answer the questions about the language used by Wheeler and the narrator.

Writing Link

Graphic Novel

If students are unfamiliar with the term *graphic novel*, explain that it is an interaction of text and pictures to tell a story. Like a comic book in format, it generally has a longer, more complex story line. Invite students to work in small groups to create a tall tale, complete with exaggeration, dialect, comic similes and metaphors, and larger than life characters. Some students may want to tell the story of Jim Smiley's yellow one-eyed cow; others may want to create their own tale. Students may split the responsibility between telling the story and illustrating it, or they might share the tasks.

The Celebrated Jumping Frog of Calaveras County

Lesson

Jim Smiley has decided to teach a class on how to train animals. Today's lesson is about how to train a frog to win races. Fill in the sentences below for Smiley's lesson. After you have finished, read your completed lesson to a partner.

The first thing you have to do is _Possible answer: catch a frog_.

A good place to look for a frog is in _Possible answer: a swamp_.

You should give your frog a name, such as _Possible answer: Dan'l Webster_.

Next, you will have to _Possible answers: train, teach, educate, "edercate," "learn"_ your frog to _____
Possible answer: jump

A good way to train your frog is to _Possible answer: use flies to train him to jump_
_____.

When you have trained your frog to jump, you are ready to _Possible answer: have him race against_
other frogs.

A good way to get people to challenge your frog is to _Possible answer: put your frog in a box. If people ask_
what's in the box, tell them that it is frog that can outjump any other frog in the county.

But be careful! Don't ever leave your frog _Possible answer: with a stranger_ and watch out
for people who may _Possible answer: use a trick to win the race_
_____.

A Wagner Matinée

by Willa Cather

Oral Language

Build Background

Read the title and author. Explain that students will read "A Wagner Matinée" by Willa Cather. **Ask:**

- In the title, Wagner refers to Richard Wagner. He was a German composer during the 1800s. Who knows what a composer writes? *(music)*

- A matinée is a show or performance that takes place in the afternoon. What kind of show does the title describe? *(a musical show in the afternoon; an afternoon show of Wagner's music.)*

Talk About the Story

Explain that the story is about a woman who goes to a musical performance for the first time in many years. The music brings back memories and makes her feel strong emotions.

Beginning/Early Intermediate **Ask:** *What things remind you of the place where you used to live?* (certain foods, clothing, music, activities)

Intermediate Explain that the music makes the woman realize what she misses about her past. Have students describe how people usually feel when they miss something.

Learning Objectives

For pages 159–170, 325–326

In studying this text, you will focus on the following objectives:

Literary Study: Analyzing point of view.

Reading: Identifying sequence.

Lesson at a Glance

Oral Language
- Build Background
- Talk About the Story

Vocabulary
- Selection Vocabulary
- Content Vocabulary
- Academic Vocabulary

Literary Element
- Point of View

Reading Strategy
- Identify Sequence

Writing Link
- Advice Column

Fluency
- Expression and Intonation: Punctuation

Comprehension BLM
- BLM

Grammar Link BLM
- Commas before *and, but,* and *or* BLM

Technology
- Student Works™ Plus
- Teacher Works™ Plus
- Listening Library Audio CD
- Classroom Presentation Toolkit
- Glencoe Visual Vocabulary
- Skill Level Up!™ A Skill-Based Language Arts Game

Interactive Question-Response

Connect to the Story

Read aloud Connect to the Story. Reproduce the sentence stems and write-on lines on the board:
Model *Going back to a place can make you feel sad because you miss living there. It can also help you remember what you were like when you lived there.* Model writing your response on a write-on line, and have volunteers suggest other responses. Then have individuals complete the sentences on their own.

Literary Element
Point of View

Read aloud Literary Element. Write on the board:

I walked through the park on my way home from school.

Carmen took her dog for a walk in the park.

Ask *How can you tell which sentence is written in first-person point of view? (It is the sentence that uses the word "I")*. Ask a volunteer to help you change the other sentence to first-person point of view.

Reading Strategy Identify Sequence

Read aloud Reading Strategy. Tell students that when they identify the sequence of events, it helps them to better understand the story. Explain that when they are identifying sequence, it is important to pay attention to time words, such as *before, after, when.* Have students listen carefully to the following sentences and answer the questions: *Before I talked to the class, I said hello to the teachers.* **Ask** *Which did I do first? (I said hello to the teachers).* *I lived in the city after I lived in the country.* **Ask** *Where did I live first? (the country)* Remind students that some events in a story will be told out of order. Make sure to identify when a story is describing events in the past.

A Wagner Matinée

Connect to the Story
How does it feel to go back to a place you have not been in a long time? Think about the question and write down some of your thoughts.

Going back to a place can make you feel ___Possible answer: sad___

because ___Possible answer: you miss living there.___

It can also help you remember ___Possible answer: what you were like when you lived there___

Literary Element   Point of View

Point of view describes how the narrator tells the story. When the narrator is a character in the story, it is told in **first-person point of view**. This narrator refers to himself or herself as "I." A first-person narrator only sees and knows what the character sees and knows. In **third-person limited point of view**, the narrator shows the thoughts and feelings of one character, referred to as "he" or "she." In an **omniscient point of view**, the narrator knows everything about the characters and events.

As you read, look for clues that tell you the point of view. Ask yourself:
- Who is telling the story?
- How does the narrator's point of view affect what I see in the story?

Reading Strategy   Identify Sequence

When you **identify sequence**, you put events or ideas in a logical order. Main events are usually told in the order in which they happened. Sometimes authors show important events and details through flashbacks. Flashbacks stop the present action to show things that happened in the past.

As you read, identify the order in which the events happened. Ask yourself:
- When does the story take place?
- Which events happened before the story takes place?

Selection Vocabulary

legacy (leg′ ə sē) *n.* money that someone gives away after the person dies (p. 162)
*Paul's generous grandmother left him a **legacy** when she died.*
➤ Cognate (Spanish) **legado**

reproaches (ri prōch′ es) *n.* unhappy or angry words toward someone (p. 163)
*Rosa was late again and received another of her mother's **reproaches**.*
➤ Cognate (Spanish) **reproches**

doggedly (dô′gidlē) *adv.* with great effort and without giving up (p. 163)
*The doctor stayed up all night and **doggedly** looked for a cure.*

trepidation (trep′ ə dā′ shən) *n.* a feeling of worry about something in the future (p. 164)
*Anna had not studied very much, so she felt **trepidation** about the test.*

obliquely (ə blēk′ lē) *adv.* in a slanting direction or at an angle (p. 166)
*Her hair covered her left eye as it hung **obliquely** across her face.*
➤ Cognate (Spanish) **oblicuamente**

Content Vocabulary

worn (wôrn) *adj.* damaged by use (p. 162)
*The hat was old and looked **worn**.*

empty (emp′ tē) *adj.* having nothing in it (p. 163)
*When Marcus looked into the box, he could see it was **empty**.*

instrument (in′ strə mənt) *n.* a device that makes musical sounds (p. 163)
*Maria played her flute well, and the **instrument** sounded beautiful.*
➤ Cognate (Spanish) **instrumento**

tears (tērz) *n.* a watery drops that flow from eyes when crying (p. 167)
*Cindy tried not to cry, but you could see the **tears** on her cheeks.*

For more practice, see page 325. ➡

Vocabulary Routine

To introduce the vocabulary, read aloud the words and definitions in the student book and have students repeat after you. Discuss how the pictures illustrate the words or sentences. Then follow the vocabulary routine below.

Content Vocabulary

<u>Define:</u> If something is ***worn,*** you can tell it has been used a lot. <u>Example:</u> *The handle of the cane was worn and smooth.* <u>Ask:</u> How would you describe a coat that is old and *worn*? DESCRIBE

When something is ***empty***, it has nothing in it. *After he took the last cookie, the jar was empty.* How do you make something *empty*? EXPLAIN

An ***instrument*** is used to play music. *She could play almost any song on her instrument.* How are *instruments* and tools similar? How are they different? COMPARE AND CONTRAST

When people cry, they have ***tears*** in their eyes. *She was so upset that tears ran down her face.* What are some different reasons for people's *tears*? EXAMPLE

Vocabulary Practice Have students complete the vocabulary practice activity on page 325.

Selection Vocabulary

<u>Define:</u> When you receive a ***legacy,*** you inherit something, such as money, property, or honor. <u>Example:</u> *The legacy Daniel received from his aunt allowed him to go to college.* <u>Ask:</u> What legacy would you like to leave to your own grandchildren in the future? EXAMPLE

If you are disappointed about something your friend does, you might express ***reproach*** about it. *When Catherine broke her promise to Ann, she suffered Ann's reproach.* What action by your friend might cause you to express reproach? DESCRIPTION

When you do something ***doggedly,*** you keep at it in a stubborn way. *Sara doggedly practiced her dance routine until she knew it by heart.* Compare the results of practicing something doggedly with the results you would get by giving up too early. COMPARE AND CONTRAST

If you feel ***trepidation,*** you are nervous and fearful. *Forrest stopped at the door to the principal's office, filled with trepidation about why he had been called there.* Name an emotion that is the opposite of trepidation. ANTONYM

If you draw a line ***obliquely,*** you draw it in a slanting direction. *Marcie divided her wall obliquely, painting one side blue and the other side yellow.* Give an example of a moment in sports where a player might move obliquely. EXAMPLE

Interactive Question-Response

Background Information

Read aloud the note. Explain that in 1862 there was a government decision called the Homestead Act. Through the Homestead Act, the government allowed people to claim land in places like Nebraska. If they farmed it for five years, then they owned the land.

Literary Element
Point of View

If students make an incorrect choice: **Model** *I know that the story begins with the words "I received one morning a letter..." The word "I" tells me that the narrator is a character in the story.* **Ask:** *If the narrator is a character, what is the point of view? (first-person point of view)*

Content Vocabulary

Read aloud the word and definition for *worn*. Focus students on the first paragraph. **Ask:** *Why does the narrator think the letter is worn? (It had dirt on it. It looked like it was kept in a dirty pocket.) How else could the letter have gotten worn? (It could have traveled a long way. It could have gotten worn in the mail.)*

A Wagner Matinée

A Wagner Matinée

Background Information

The title "A Wagner Matinée" refers to the German opera composer Wilhelm Richard Wagner (1813–1883). This story takes place during the late 1800s. One of the main characters has been living in Nebraska. At that time, most people in Nebraska were settlers who farmed the land.

Literary Element

Point of View In the opening sentence, the narrator's use of "I" tells us that the story is being told in

- [x] first-person point of view
- [ ] third-person limited point of view
- [ ] omniscient point of view

worn (wôrn) *adj.* damaged by use

Settling of the estate refers to the process of giving away someone's money and belongings after they die.

To Sum Up

➤ The narrator gets a letter telling him that his aunt is coming to Boston.

➤ He meets her at the train station the next day.

➤ When they arrive at his home, she is tired and sleeps until morning.

I received one morning a letter, written in pale ink on glassy, blue-lined note-paper, and bearing the postmark of a little Nebraska village. This communication, <u>worn</u> and rubbed, looking as if it has been carried for some days in a coat pocket that was none too clean, was from my uncle Howard, and informed me that his wife had been left a small **legacy** by a bachelor relative, and that it would be necessary for her to go to Boston to attend to the **settling of the estate.** He requested me to meet her at the station and render[1] her whatever services might be necessary. On examining the date indicated as that of her arrival, I found it to be no later than tomorrow. He had characteristically delayed writing until, had I been away from home for a day, I must have missed my aunt altogether.

The name of my Aunt Georgiana opened before me a gulf of recollection so wide and deep that, as the letter dropped from my hand, I felt suddenly a stranger to all the present conditions of my existence, wholly ill at ease and out of place amid the familiar surroundings of my study. I became, in short, the gangling farmer-boy my aunt had known, scourged[2] with chilblains[3] and bashfulness, my hands cracked and sore from the corn husking. I sat again before her parlour organ, fumbling the scales with my stiff, red fingers, while she, beside me, made canvas mittens for the huskers.

The next morning, after preparing my landlady for a visitor, I set out for the station. When the train arrived I had some difficulty in finding my aunt. She was the last of the passengers to alight, and it was not until I got her into the carriage that she seemed really to recognize me. She had come all the way in a day coach; her linen duster[4] had become black with soot and her black bonnet grey with dust during the journey. When we arrived at my boarding-house the landlady put her to bed at once and I did not see her again until the next morning.

Vocabulary

legacy (leg′ ə sē) *n.* money that someone gives away after dying

1. *Render* means "to make available" or "to provide."
2. *Scourged* means "afflicted" or "suffered from."
3. *Chilblains* are red, swollen sores on the skin caused by being in the cold.
4. A *duster* is a long, light coat used to protect a person's clothing from dust.

Comprehension BLM

To support students as they read the selection, have them begin the graphic organizer on page A32.

Whatever shock Mrs. Springer experienced at my aunt's appearance, she considerately concealed. As for myself, I saw my aunt's battered figure with that feeling of awe and respect with which we behold explorers who have left their ears and fingers north of Franz-Joseph-Land,[5] or their health somewhere along the Upper Congo.[6] My Aunt Georgiana had been a music teacher at the Boston Conservatory, somewhere back in the **latter sixties.** One summer, while visiting in the little village among the Green Mountains[7] where her ancestors had dwelt for generations, she had kindled the callow[8] fancy of my uncle, Howard Carpenter, then an idle, shiftless boy of twenty-one. When she returned to her duties in Boston, Howard followed her, and the **upshot** of this infatuation was that she eloped with him, eluding the **reproaches** of her family and the criticism of her friends by going with him to the Nebraska frontier. Carpenter, who, of course, had no money, took up a homestead in Red Willow County, fifty miles from the railroad. There they had measured off their land themselves, driving across the prairie in a wagon, to the wheel of which they had tied a red cotton handkerchief, and counting its revolutions. They built a dug-out in the red hillside, one of those cave dwellings whose inmates so often reverted to primitive conditions. Their water they got from the lagoons where the buffalo drank, and their slender stock of provisions was always at the mercy of bands of roving Indians. For thirty years my aunt had not been farther than fifty miles from the homestead.

I owed to this woman most of the good that ever came my way in my boyhood, and had a reverential[9] affection for her. During the years when I was riding herd for my uncle, my aunt, after cooking the three meals—the first of which was ready at six o'clock in the morning—and putting the six children to bed, would often stand until midnight at her ironing-board, with me at the kitchen table beside her, hearing me recite Latin declensions and conjugations,[10] gently shaking me when my drowsy head sank down over a page of irregular verbs. It was to her, at her ironing or mending, that I read my first Shakespeare, and her old text-book on mythology was the first that ever came into my **empty** hands. She taught me my scales and exercises on the little parlor organ which her husband had bought her after fifteen years, during which she had not so much as seen a musical **instrument**. She would sit beside me by the hour, darning and counting, while I struggled with the "Joyous Farmer."[11] She seldom talked to me about music, and I understood why. Once when I had been **doggedly** beating out some easy passages from an old score of Euryanthe[12] I had found among her music books, she came up to me and, putting her hands over my eyes, gently drew my head back upon her shoulder, saying tremulously,[13] "Don't love it so well, Clark, or it may be taken from you."

5. **Franz-Joseph-Land** is a group of islands in the Arctic Ocean.
6. The **Congo** River in central Africa is also called the Zaire River.
7. The **Green Mountains** reach from western Massachusetts through Vermont and into Canada.
8. **Callow** means "not very experienced."
9. **Reverential** means "with a feeling of deep respect and wonder."
10. **Declensions** are different forms of nouns, pronouns, and adjectives. **Conjugations** are different forms of verbs. Students often memorize these forms when learning a new language.
11. **Joyous Farmer** is a piece of music for children by Robert Shumann (1810–1856).
12. **Euryanthe** (ā ūr i än tā) is an opera by Carl Maria von Weber (1786–1826).
13. **Tremulously** means "in a shaking manner."

Literary Element

Point of View Reread the boxed text at the top of the page. Underline the sentence in which the narrator shares his feelings.

Here, the **latter sixties** means the years of the late 1860s.

Upshot means "the result of."

empty (emp' tē) *adj.* having nothing in it

instrument (in' stra mant) *n.* a device that makes musical sounds

Vocabulary

reproaches (ri prōch' es) *n.* unhappy or angry words toward someone
doggedly (dô'gidlē) *adv.* with great effort and without giving up

To Sum Up

➤ The narrator admires his aunt, because she has had a difficult life.

➤ She was a music teacher in Boston, but she moved to a farm in Nebraska.

➤ When the narrator lived on her farm, she taught him to play the organ.

Interactive Question-Response

Literary Element
Point of View

If students have difficulty responding: **Model** *When the "I" in the story tells us how he feels, that is the narrator telling us his inner thoughts and emotions. He might say "I felt happy" or "I smiled with a feeling of joy."* **Ask:** *Can you see a statement like that in the text? (yes) How does the narrator say he feels about his aunt? (He feels awe and respect.)*

Content Vocabulary

Read aloud the word and definition for *instrument*. **Ask:** *What instrument is being described in the passage? (an organ) What is another instrument like an organ? (a piano) How are they alike? (They both have keys.)*

Fluency

Expression and Intonation: Punctuation

Intermediate/Early Advanced Tell students that they will be doing a choral reading of the boxed text on this page. Remind students to pause when they come to a period. Model the fluency skill as you read the text at a moderate tempo. Then have one student read a sentence. Have another student join in, and a third, and so on. When students reach the end of the passage, have pairs of students reread to each other. To assess individual fluency, use the Oral Reading Guidelines on page T16.

Beginning/Early Intermediate Have these students choral read only the boxed text at the bottom of the page. Before they begin, model the pronunciation of the text. Then have students practice reading the passage in pairs before the choral reading.

Interactive Question-Response

Comprehension Check

Ask students to share their answers. **Ask:** *Think about the description of the Clark's aunt as she sits in the concert hall. Why do you think the narrator chose these comparisons to describe his aunt? (The miners came from the mountains to a big city just like Clark's aunt came from the farm to Boston. The narrator wants to show that a hard life can change people. Clark's aunt has been greatly changed by living in Nebraska for so many years. She has become quiet and withdrawn, like a statue.)*

The world to which she had been dead means "the world that she had not been a part of."

A quarter of a century means "25 years."

Comprehension Check

Reread the boxed text at the bottom of the page. What does Clark compare his aunt sitting in the theatre to? Check two.

- ☑ Rameses
- ☐ Wagner
- ☑ old miners

14. **Semi-somnambulant** (sem′ e som nam′ byə lavnt) means "in a daze, as if sleepwalking."
15. **Huguenots** (hu′ gə nots′) is a French opera by Giacomo Meyerbeer (1791–1864).
16. **Common** refers to Boston Common, a public park.
17. **Rameses** (ram′ ə sez) is the name shared by many kings of ancient Egypt.
18. **[froth and fret . . . flows]** This phrase refers to the general busy activity that would come and go past a museum statue.
19. Here, **bullion** (bool′ yən) is gold.
20. **Yukon** means the Yukon River, a major route to the Klondike gold fields in Canada.

To Sum Up

- ➤ Clark takes his aunt to hear the Symphony Orchestra.
- ➤ On the way there, she mostly worries about her farm.
- ➤ When they arrive, she has a stony look on her face of emotional distance.

When my aunt appeared on the morning after her arrival in Boston, she was still in a semi-somnambulant[14] state. She seemed not to realize that she was in the city where she had spent her youth, the place longed for hungrily half a lifetime. She had been so wretchedly train-sick throughout the journey that she had no recollection of anything but her discomfort, and, to all intents and purposes, there were but a few hours of nightmare between the farm in Red Willow County and my study on Newbury Street. I had planned a little pleasure for her that afternoon, to repay her for some of the glorious moments she had given me when we used to milk together in the straw-thatched cowshed and she, because I was more than usually tired, or because her husband had spoken sharply to me, would tell me of the splendid performance of the Huguenots[15] she had seen in Paris, in her youth.

At two o'clock the Symphony Orchestra was to give a Wagner program, and I intended to take my aunt; though, as I conversed with her, I grew doubtful about her enjoyment of it. I suggested our visiting the Conservatory and the Common[16] before lunch, but she seemed altogether too timid to wish to venture out. She questioned me absently about various changes in the city, but she was chiefly concerned that she had forgotten to leave instructions about feeding half-skimmed milk to a certain weakling calf, "old Maggie's calf, you know, Clark," she explained, evidently having forgotten how long I had been away. She was further troubled because she had neglected to tell her daughter about the freshly-opened kit of mackerel in the cellar, which would spoil if it were not used directly.

I asked her whether she had ever heard any of the Wagnerian operas, and found that she had not, though she was perfectly familiar with their respective situations, and had once possessed the piano score of The Flying Dutchman. I began to think it would be best to get her back to Red Willow County without waking her, and regretted having suggested the concert.

From the time we entered the concert hall, however, she was a trifle less passive and inert, and for the first time seemed to perceive her surroundings. I had felt some **trepidation** lest she might become aware of her queer, country clothes, or might experience some painful embarrassment at stepping suddenly into **the world to which she had been dead** for **a quarter of a century.** But, again, I found how superficially I had judged her. She sat looking about her with eyes as impersonal, almost as stony, as those with which the granite Rameses[17] in a museum watches the froth and fret that ebbs and flows[18] about his pedestal. I have seen this same aloofness in old miners who drift into the Brown hotel at Denver, their pockets full of bullion,[19] their linen soiled, their haggard faces unshaven; standing in the thronged corridors as solitary as though they were still in a frozen camp on the Yukon.[20]

Vocabulary ....
trepidation (trep′ ə dā′ shən) *n.* a feeling of worry about something in the future

---

Differentiated Instruction

Beginning/Early Intermediate Explain that Clark's aunt is far away from her farm and has no way to talk to her family while she is in Boston. Have students think about life on a farm. **Ask:** *Why might Clark's aunt be worried about the farm? (She might think something bad will happen while she is gone. She may think they won't get the work done without her.)*

Intermediate **Ask:** *Why do you think Clark's aunt does not want to visit the Commons? (She doesn't seem to pay much attention to her surroundings. She is not interested in exploring new places. She seems shy or withdrawn.) Why do you think she agrees to attend the concert? (Music is familiar to her. It is something she once loved.)*

Early Advanced **Ask:** *Why does Clark bring his aunt to the Symphony? (to make her happy or to repay her for her kindness when he lived with her in Nebraska)*

The matinée audience was made up chiefly of women. One lost the contour of faces and figures, indeed any effect of line whatever, and there was only the color of bodices past counting, the shimmer of fabrics soft and firm, silky and sheer; red, mauve, pink, blue, lilac, purple, écru,[21] rose, yellow, cream, and white, all the colors that an impressionist[22] finds in a sunlit landscape, with here and there the dead shadow of a frock coat. My Aunt Georgiana regarded them as though they had been so many daubs of tube-paint on a palette.

When the musicians came out and took their places, she gave a little stir of anticipation, and looked with quickening interest down over the rail at that invariable grouping, perhaps the first wholly familiar thing that had greeted her eye since she had left old Maggie and her weakling calf. I could feel how all those details sank into her soul, for I had not forgotten how they had sunk into mine when I came fresh from ploughing forever and forever between green aisles of corn, where, as in a treadmill, one might walk from daybreak to dusk without perceiving a shadow of change. The clean profiles of the musicians, the gloss of their linen, the dull black of their coats, the beloved shapes of the instruments, the patches of yellow light on the smooth, varnished bellies of the 'cellos and the bass viols in the rear, the restless, wind-tossed forest of fiddle necks and bows—I recalled how, in the first orchestra I ever heard, those long bow-strokes seemed to draw the heart out of me, as a conjurer's stick reels out yards of paper ribbon from a hat.

21. *Écru* (ā' kroo) is the color beige, or a light tan.
22. An *impressionist* is a painter who uses a French style of painting. That style focuses on light and color.

REFLECT

Identify Sequence
The narrator has told some of the story in the present and some of it as flashbacks. Number the following events to the order in which they occur in time.

_4_ Aunt Georgiana worries about the calf on the farm.

_2_ Clark's aunt teaches him how to play the organ.

_3_ Clark picks up his aunt at the train.

_5_ Clark and his aunt go to the symphony.

_1_ Aunt Georgiana becomes a music teacher in Boston.

 Talk about your answer with a partner.

Literary Element

Point of View Underline the words that show how Clark feels about music.

To Sum Up

➤ When the musicians come on stage, Clark's aunt becomes alert and interested.

➤ Clark knows how his aunt feels about music.

➤ He remembers how it felt to hear the music at his first concert.

Interactive Question-Response

Literary Element
Point of View

If students have difficulty responding: **Model** *Clark is the narrator of the story. The story is told in first person and the narrator refers to himself as "I." I'll look for words with the word "I" that tell the narrator's feelings about music.* **Ask:** *What comparison does Clark make? (Clark compares the music of the violin bows drawing out his heart to a magician's stick drawing paper ribbons from a hat.) Why is the comparison a good one? Both create a feeling of magic.)*

To Sum Up

Beginning/Early Intermediate Read the statements in the To Sum Up box aloud with students. Then have them complete the following sentence about Clark and his aunt.

The _____ makes Clark and his aunt feel _____ . (music, happy)

Reflect

Partner Talk Have students work in pairs to answer. Explain to students that you are ordering the events according to time, not according to when the events appeared in the text: **Model** *What happened first? It is the event that happened before everything else in time. Aunt Georgiana worked as a music teacher before everything else.* **Ask:** *Which event happened next in time? (Clark's aunt teaches him how to play the organ.)*

The first number was the Tannhauser overture. When the horns drew out the first strain of the Pilgrim's chorus, Aunt Georgiana clutched my coat sleeve. Then it was I first realized that for her this broke a silence of thirty years. I saw again the tall, naked house on the prairie, black and grim as a wooden fortress; the black pond where I had learned to swim, its margin pitted with sun-dried cattle tracks; the rain gullied clay banks about the naked house, the four dwarf ash seedlings where the dish-cloths were always hung to dry before the kitchen door. The world there was the flat world of the ancients;[23] to the east, a cornfield that **stretched to daybreak;** to the west, a corral that reached to sunset; between, the conquests of peace, dearer-bought than those of war.

The overture closed, my aunt released my coat sleeve, but she said nothing. She sat staring dully at the orchestra. What, I wondered, did she get from it? She had been a good pianist in her day, I knew, and her musical education had been broader than that of most music teachers of a quarter of a century ago. She had often told me of Mozart's operas and Meyerbeer's, and I could remember hearing her sing, years ago, certain melodies of Verdi.[24] When I had fallen ill with a fever in her house she used to sit by my cot in the evening—when the cool, night wind blew in through the faded mosquito netting tacked over the window and I lay watching a certain bright star that burned red above the cornfield—and sing "Home to our mountains, O, let us return!" in a way fit to **break the heart** of a Vermont boy near dead of homesickness already.

I watched her closely through the prelude to Tristan and Isolde, trying vainly to conjecture what that seething turmoil of strings and winds might mean to her, but she sat mutely staring at the violin bows that drove **obliquely** downward, like the pelting streaks of rain in a summer shower. Had this music any message for her? Had she enough left to at all comprehend this power which had kindled the world since she had left it? I was in a fever of curiosity, but Aunt Georgiana sat silent upon her peak in Darien.[25] She preserved this utter immobility throughout the number from The Flying Dutchman, though her fingers worked mechanically upon her black dress, as if, of themselves, they were recalling the piano score they had once played. Poor hands! They had been stretched and twisted into mere tentacles to hold and lift and knead with; on one of them a thin, worn band that had once been a wedding ring. As I pressed and gently quieted one of those groping hands, I remembered with quivering eyelids their services for me in other days.

Here, *stretched to daybreak* means that the corn "went all the way to the horizon where the sun rises."

Here, *break the heart* means "fill with sadness and aching."

To Sum Up

➤ Clark's aunt grabs his sleeve when the music starts.

➤ Clark watches his aunt to see how she reacts to the music. He wonders if she remembers it after 30 years on the farm.

➤ Clark's aunt moves her fingers to the music as she listens.

Vocabulary

obliquely (ə blēk′ lē) *adv.* in a slanting direction or at an angle

23. ***The ancients*** refers to those who lived long ago in Greece and Rome.
24. ***Wolfgang Amadeus Mozart*** (woolf′′ gang′ ä′ mə dä′ əs mot′ särt) (1756–1791) was a writer of music from Austria. ***Giuseppe Verdi*** (joo zep′ pe ver′ de) (1813–1901) was from Italy. He wrote operas.
25. The phrase ***"peak in Darien"*** (dar′ e en′) refers to the poem "On First Looking into Chapman's Homer" by John Keats. The poem describes Spanish explorers on a mountain in Darien, now Panama. The explorers stand silently and in wonder at the Pacific Ocean. They were the first Europeans to view the Pacific Ocean.

Differentiated Instruction

Beginning/Early Intermediate ▶ Tell students that the author shows us the aunt's actions so we can tell what she is feeling. **Ask:** *Why do you think Clark's aunt grabbed his sleeve when the music started? (She was so excited to finally hear music again.)*

Intermediate ▶ **Ask:** *Why does the author describe his aunt's farm? (to show how lonely she was there and how she lived without the music she loved.)*

Early Advanced ▶ Have students demonstrate what Clark's aunt was doing with her fingers. *(They should act like they are playing the piano on their legs.)* Explain that *quivering* means shaking. **Ask:** *Why are Clark's eyes quivering when he touches her hand? (He remembers the work she did for him with those hands.)*

Soon after the tenor began the "Prize Song," I heard a quick drawn breath and turned to my aunt. Her eyes were closed, but the <u>tears</u> were glistening on her cheeks, and I think, in a moment more, they were in my eyes as well. It never really died, then—the soul which can suffer so excruciatingly and so interminably; it withers to the outward eye only; like that strange moss which can lie on a dusty shelf half a century and yet, if placed in water, grows green again. She wept so throughout the development and elaboration of the melody.

During the intermission before the second half, I questioned my aunt and found that the "Prize Song" was not new to her. Some years before there had drifted to the farm in Red Willow County a young German, a tramp cowpuncher,[26] who had sung in the chorus at Bayreuth[27] when he was a boy, along with the other peasant boys and girls. Of a Sunday morning he used to sit on his gingham-sheeted bed in the hands' bedroom which opened off the kitchen, cleaning the leather of his boots and saddle, singing the "Prize Song," while my aunt went about her work in the kitchen. She had hovered over him until she had prevailed upon him to join the country church, though his sole fitness for this step, in so far as I could gather, lay in his boyish face and his possession of this divine melody. Shortly afterward, he had gone to town on the Fourth of July, been drunk for several days, lost his money at a faro[28] table, ridden a saddled Texas steer on a bet, and disappeared with a fractured collar-bone. All this my aunt told me huskily, wanderingly, as though she were talking in the weak lapses of illness.

"Well, we have come to better things than the old Trovatore[29] at any rate, Aunt Georgie?" I queried, with a well meant effort at jocularity.[30]

Her lip quivered and she hastily put her handkerchief up to her mouth. From behind it she murmured, "And you have been hearing this ever since you left me, Clark?" Her question was the gentlest and saddest of reproaches.

The second half of the program consisted of four numbers from the Ring, and closed with Siegfried's funeral march. My aunt wept quietly, but almost continuously, as a shallow vessel overflows in a rain-storm. From time to time her dim eyes looked up at the lights, burning softly under their dull glass globes.

The deluge of sound poured on and on; I never knew what she found in the shining current of it; I never knew how far it bore her, or past what happy islands. From the trembling of her face I could well believe that before the last number she had been carried out where the myriad[31] graves are, into the grey, nameless burying grounds of the sea; or into some world of death vaster yet, where, from the beginning of the world, hope has lain down with hope and dream with dream and, renouncing,[32] slept.

26. **Cowpuncher** means "cowboy."
27. **Bayreuth** (bi roit') is a German city famous for its yearly festival of Wagner's music.
28. **Faro** (far' o) is a gambling game played with a deck of cards.
29. **Trovatore** (tro v tor' e) refers to *Il Trovatore*, an opera by Giuseppe Verdi.
30. **Jocularity** means "joking" or "humor."
31. **Myriad** means "countless" or "very many."
32. **Renouncing** means "giving up."

tears (tĕrz) *n.* a watery drops that flow from eyes when crying

✏️ **Literary Element**

Point of View Reread the boxed text at the top of the page. Why can't the narrator tell us the reason his aunt is crying?

☐ because the narrator does not want to tell us.

☐ because the narrator promised to keep it a secret

☑ because the narrator does not know her thoughts

To Sum Up

➤ Clark notices tears on his aunt's cheeks as she listens to the music.

➤ She asks if he had been hearing this music since he left her.

➤ She cries through the rest of the concert.

Interactive Question-Response

Content Vocabulary

Read aloud the word and definition for *tears*. Focus students on the description of the tears. **Ask:** *Think about what tears look like. What do you think it means when the narrator says the tears are glistening on her cheeks"? (They are shining in the light.) What else might glisten under light like tears? (water)*

Literary Element
Point of View

If students make an incorrect choice, remind them that the story is being told from a first person point of view. **Ask:** *In first person point of view, whose inner thoughts and feelings can the narrator share? (only his own) In this story, can the narrator know his aunt's inner thoughts? yes/no (no)*

Interactive Question-Response

To Sum Up

Beginning/Early Intermediate ▶ Have students work in pairs to read all the statements in the To Sum Up boxes from the beginning of the story on page 162. Then have students decide together which three events are the most important events in the story.

The most important events are

when _____,

when _____, and

when _____.

Reflect

Partner Talk Have students work in pairs to answer. To help students to get started: **Model** *To answer this question, I would think about where Clark's aunt will be going now that her visit is over. I would think about what that place is like. I would try to imagine how it might feel for her to go there after hearing the music.* Write the following sentence frames on the board to help students organize their thoughts.

When Clark's aunt leaves the concert hall, she will go _____. This will make her feel _____.

Here, ***find the living level*** means "to go back to normal life."

The concert was over; the people filed out of the hall chattering and laughing, glad to relax and **find the living level** again, but my kinswoman made no effort to rise. The harpist slipped the green felt cover over his instrument; the flute-players shook the water from their mouthpieces; the men of the orchestra went out one by one, leaving the stage to the chairs and music stands, empty as a winter cornfield.

I spoke to my aunt. She burst into tears and sobbed pleadingly. "I don't want to go, Clark, I don't want to go!"

I understood. For her, just outside the concert hall, lay the black pond with the cattle-tracked bluffs; the tall, unpainted house, with weather-curled boards, naked as a tower; the crook-backed ash seedlings where the dish-cloths hung to dry; the gaunt,[33] moulting turkeys picking up refuse about the kitchen door.

33. ***Gaunt*** means "extremely thin."

To Sum Up

➤ The concert ends, but Clark's aunt does not move to leave.

➤ The musicians all leave the stage.

➤ Clark's aunt cries, "I don't want to go!" Clark understands how she feels.

REFLECT

Identify Sequence
What will await Clark's aunt when she leaves the concert hall? Why does she not want to leave?

When Clark's aunt leaves the concert hall, she will have to go

back to the farm. Now that she has heard the music that she

loves so much, she doesn't want to return to the farm where

there are no concerts.

_____

 Talk about your answer with a partner.

Oral Assessment

Provide the following prompts to one student at a time. Observe students' responses. See the Oral Assessment Rubric on page T17 to determine students' levels of language output.

1. Tell me about Aunt Georgiana.

2. What does Clark think of his aunt's life on the farm?

3. Why is Aunt Georgiana special to Clark?

4. How does Aunt Georgiana react during the symphony?

5. What does Clark think about his aunt's reaction to the symphony?

A Wagner Matinée

Vocabulary Check

A. Circle the picture that best answers the question.

1. Which chair looks **worn**?

2. Which person is holding an **instrument**?

3. Which shelf is **empty**?

4. Which face has **tears** on it?

B. Fill in the blank with the correct word.

empty	doggedly	trepidation	legacy	worn

5. The old cardboard box was _____worn_____ around the edges.

6. He slowly walked up to the horse with some ____trepidation____.

7. She looked through the cabinets for food, but they were _____empty_____.

8. He worked ____doggedly____ to finish the project on time.

9. He used the ____legacy____ from his grandmother to open a store.

C. Circle the letter of the sentence that uses the boldface word correctly.

10. a. After he dropped the ball, he feared his team's **reproaches**.
    b. After he hit a home run, he feared he would get his team's **reproaches**.

11. a. The **obliquely** hung curtain was straight and covered the window.
    b. The **obliquely** hung curtain was not straight and covered only half the window.

12. a. The soldier fought **doggedly** against the enemy for many years.
    b. The soldier did not care and fought **doggedly** against the enemy for many years.

A Wagner Matinée **169**

Vocabulary Check

C. Early Advanced

Read each pair of sentences aloud. Encourage students to identify the correct sentence. If students are having difficulty with the choice, repeat the sentences with an easier synonym in place of the vocabulary word. For example:

After he dropped the ball, he feared the coach's scolding.

After he hit a home run, he feared he would get his team's scolding.

After students make the correct choice, read the correct sentence aloud together as a class.

Academic Vocabulary

Write the following sentence on the board: *Aunt Georgiana has an internal response to the **external** stimulus of music.*

Point out to students that *external* is an academic word that has many different meanings. Have them use context clues to figure out the meaning of *external* in each of the following sentences and explain the difference between the two meanings.

1. The skin is the most **external** feature of the human body. (exterior)

2. Despite her **external** composure, Deepali was so on edge she could barely breathe. (superficial or merely appearing as such.)

Grammar Link BLM

Commas before *and, but,* and *or*

Prepare students to complete the activity on page A33. Read the grammar instruction with students, and complete the first item with them to help them get started.

Comprehension Check

C. Early Advanced

Remind students that Clark is the narrator of the story. Explain that means the story is told from his point of view. If students have difficulty with the first question, have them think about the details that Clark includes about him and his aunt in Nebraska. If students have difficulty with the second question, have them think about whose thoughts can and cannot be revealed using first-person point of view. If students have difficulty with the third question, ask them what might the reader know or see if Aunt Georgiana told the story.

After Reading

Have students complete the After Reading activity on page 326.

A Wagner Matinée

Comprehension Check

A. Describe the friendship between Clark and his Aunt Georiana.

1. Clark is thankful to his aunt for _Possible answer: teaching him about books and music_.

2. Aunt Georgiana is thankful to Clark for _Possible answer: bringing her to hear music_

B. In the center oval below, identify the story's narrator and point of view. Fill in the surrounding ovals with answers or examples from the story that tell you about Aunt Georgiana from the narrator's point of view.

Possible answers: Clark says his aunt looks dusty and dirty from her travels. She looks very tired from working hard on the farm for most of her life. She hardly notices the city. She has a distant look on her face.

4. What do you learn about how Aunt Georgiana looks?

Clark; first-person point of view

Possible answers: She treated Clark kindly and cared for him. She taught him to love music and to play the organ.

Possible answers: Aunt Georgiana was once a music teacher. She married a young man and moved to Nebraska. She had a hard life.

3. Who is the narrator? What is the point of view?

6. What do you learn about Aunt Georgiana's personality?

5. What do you learn about Aunt Georgiana's life?

C. Answer the questions about the point of view in "A Wagner Matinee."

7. How does Clark describe his relationship with his aunt?

Possible answer: Clark loves and respects his aunt. He is grateful to her for her kindness when he lived with her on the farm in Nebraska. She taught him to love music. He wants to thank her by taking her to a concert in Boston.

8. During the symphony, what does the point of view keep us from knowing? Explain why.

Possible answer: It prevents us from knowing what Aunt Georgiana is thinking about while she is listening to the music. Because the story is told from Clark's point of view, we can only know what he is thinking.

9. Imagine the story being told with Aunt Georgiana as the narrator. How might the opening of the story have been different?

Possible answer: It might have opened with her on the train to Boston. It also might have shown us why she was so tired. It might have told us what she was thinking about when she traveled to Boston.

For more practice, see page 326. ➡

Writing Link

Advice Column

Have students imagine they are an advice columnist responding to a reader who is contemplating a major move (such as from the city to the country, from the country to the city, from the United States to a foreign country). Have them to create a distinctive persona for their columnist (hard-headed? comforting?) and a well-reasoned response to the reader's situation. Give them a limit of 150–200 words.

An effective advice column should

- create a distinctive persona
- have a clear, well-reasoned position for or against the move
- keep within the space limit

Douglass and
WE WEAR THE MASK

by Paul Laurence Dunbar

Douglass and We Wear the Mask **171**

Oral Language

Build Background

Read the titles and author. Explain that students will read two poems by Paul Laurence Dunbar, one of the first well known African American writers. **Ask: Based on the titles, what do you think the poems will be about?** *(a person named Douglass and the types of masks that people wear)*

Talk About the Poems

Explain that the poem "Douglass" talks directly to Frederick Douglass, a man who escaped from slavery and became a great leader. The poem "We Wear the Mask" talks about the difference between our private feelings and our public face.

Beginning/Early Intermediate ▶ **Ask:** *If you could talk to one person who is no longer living, who would it be?(Students may name a grandparent, a friend, a movie star, an author, or a musician.)*

Intermediate ▶ Have students think of one person from history they admire as a great leader. Have students complete the following sentence frame.

I think _____ was a great leader because _____.

Early Advanced ▶ **Ask:** *Should people say everything they think and feel? (yes/no)* Have students discuss their opinions with a partner.

Lesson at a Glance

Oral Language
• Build Background
• Talk About the Poems

Vocabulary
• Selection Vocabulary
• Content Vocabulary

Literary Element
• Rhyme Scheme

Reading Strategy
• Clarify Meaning

Writing Link
• Blog

Comprehension
• BLM

BLM

Technology
• Student Works™ Plus
• Teacher Works™ Plus
• Listening Library Audio CD
• Classroom Presentation Toolkit
• Glencoe Visual Vocabulary
• Skill Level Up!™ A Skill-Based Language Arts Game

Interactive Question-Response

Connect to the Poems

Read aloud Connect to the Poems. **Model** *One time I found out that someone in my family was very sick. We were expecting friends over for dinner. I was worried inside, but I pretended to have a good time at dinner.* Explain to students that you were disguising your feelings, or "wearing a mask," to show that you were not worried, even though you really were.

Literary Element Rhyme Scheme

Read aloud the Literary Element. Provide examples of rhyming words, such as *cat, sat, hat* and *moon, soon, loon.* Say the words aloud, then have students suggest additional rhyming words. Next, have students preview the rhyme scheme of "Douglass" by looking only at the last word of each line. Have students repeat after you as you read the words aloud, making sure they can pronounce the rhymes correctly. As a class, identify the rhyme scheme for the poem "Douglass."

Reading Strategy Clarify Meaning

Read aloud the Reading Strategy. Tell students that if they are able to clarify the meaning of what they read, it will help them better understand what they are reading. **Model** *Context clues are clues in the text that help you understand a word's meaning. Paraphrasing is stating something in your own words.* Have students preview the poems by scanning them for new words, footnotes, and vocabulary definitions. Encourage them to look up new words in a dictionary before reading the poems.

Douglass *and* WE WEAR THE MASK

Connect to the Poems

Have you ever pretended to be happy when you were feeling sad? Sometimes your face is like a mask that hides your real feelings.

Think-pair-share Think about a time when you hid your real feelings. What was the situation? How did you really feel? What kind of "mask" did you wear? Then share your ideas with a partner.

Literary Element Rhyme Scheme

In many poems, the last words of some lines rhyme. This is called "end rhyme." The **rhyme scheme** of a poem is the pattern of its end rhymes.

- When we talk about the rhyme scheme of a poem, we use letters to stand for rhyming sounds.
- A rhyme scheme of *abab* means the first and third lines rhyme, and the second and fourth lines rhyme.
- The rhyme scheme of Douglass is *abba, abba, cdcdcd.*

As you read, ask yourself, What is the rhyme scheme of We Wear the Mask?

Reading Strategy Clarify Meaning

To clarify something means to make it clear. If you have trouble understanding what you read, you may need to **clarify meaning**.

To **clarify meaning**, you can:
- reread the confusing part.
- read the footnotes and definitions.
- use context clues and a dictionary to define new words.
- paraphrase the text by stating it in your own words.

172

Selection Vocabulary

salient (sāl′ yənt) *adj.* very obvious; easy to notice (p. 174)
*Kindness was a **salient** part of her personality.*
➤ Cognate (Spanish) **saliente**

tempest (tem′ pist) *n.* a violent storm (p. 174)
*The trees shook wildly in the **tempest**.*
➤ Cognate (Spanish) **tempestad**

dissension (di sen′ shən) *n.* disagreement (p. 174)
*There was **dissension** in the drama club over which play to perform.*
➤ Cognate (Spanish) **disentimiento**

guile (gīl) *n.* dishonesty (p. 175)
*She used **guile** to convince the jury that she was innocent.*

vile (vīl) *adj.* disgusting (p. 175)
*The smell of rotten fish is **vile**.*
➤ Cognate (Spanish) **vil**

Content Vocabulary

swarm (swôrm) *v.* to form a large group (p. 174)
*The bees **swarm** around the tree branch.*

shivering (shiv′ ər ing) *v.* shaking slightly (p. 174)
*She was **shivering** from the cold.*

grins (grinz) *v.* smiles (p. 175)
*The boy **grins** as his mother gives him an ice cream cone.*

torn (tôrn) *adj.* ripped apart (p. 175)
*The paper was **torn** into small pieces.*

For more practice, see page 327. ➡

Vocabulary Routine

To introduce the vocabulary, read aloud the words and definitions in the student book and have students repeat after you. Discuss how the pictures illustrate the words or sentences. Then follow the routine below.

Content Vocabulary

<u>Define:</u> To **swarm** is to form a large group. <u>Example:</u> *The ants swarm near our picnic.* <u>Ask:</u> What is another example of something that might *swarm*? EXAMPLE

If a person is **shivering**, he or she is shaking slightly. *The kitten was shivering in the snow.* Why would someone or something be *shivering*? EXPLANATION

When a person **grins**, they smile. *The man grins as his brother tells a joke.* What is the opposite of the word *grins*? ANTONYM

If your homework is **torn**, it is ripped apart. *My math homework was torn, so I taped the pages back together.* Describe a time that something that belongs to you was *torn*. DESCRIPTION

Vocabulary Practice Have students complete the vocabulary practice activity on page 327.

Selection Vocabulary

<u>Define:</u> When something is **salient,** it stands out as important. <u>Example:</u> The *salient* feature of the landscape before us was the lovely snow-covered mountain. <u>Ask:</u> What might be the salient points in an argument that every student should have access to a computer and the Internet? EXPLANATION

If you were caught in a **tempest,** you would be out in a violent wind or storm. *The tempest threatened to uproot the trees on the family's property.* What would be the greatest danger in being out at sea in a tempest? EXAMPLE

If you have **dissension** among your friends, you disagree with them about something. *The dissension about where to have the class picnic was solved when Sara suggested the park.* Describe some dissension you have experienced or that you have heard about in the news. DESCRIPTION

If a person uses **guile** to influence others, he or she is not being quite honest. *We thought Jake was being sincere, but we found out he had used guile to get his own way.* Give an example of the use of guile to get someone to do something. EXAMPLE

Something that is **vile** might smell, look, feel, or seem disgusting or horrifying. *Erin thought the odor left by the skunk was just vile.* Why would food that had mold or maggots on it be considered vile? EXPLANATION

Douglass

Interactive Question-Response

Comprehension Check

If students have difficulty responding: **Model** *The poet uses the words "fall'n on evil days," which means "fallen on unpleasant or troubled times." He also says "not even thou didst know," which means "Douglass did not know days like these."* **Ask:** *Based on the poet's words in these lines, do you think life is better or worse than when Douglass was living? (Life is worse than it was when Douglass was alive.)*

Reflect

Partner Talk Have students work in pairs to answer. To help students get started: **Model** *To answer this, I would reread lines 11 and 12 and the footnote that defines the word "bark," which is a type of boat. Remember that the words "thy" and "thou" refer to Frederick Douglass in this poem.* Write the following sentence frame on the board to help students organize their thoughts.

Douglass's _____ and _____ could _____ through the storm. (voice; arm; guide the boat)

To and fro means "backward and forward."

Comprehension Check

Reread the first two lines. What does the speaker tell Douglass in these lines?
- ☐ Life is better now.
- ☑ Life is worse now.
- ☐ Life is the same now.

swarm (swôrm) *v.* to form a large group

shivering (shiv′ ər ing) *v.* shaking slightly

To Sum Up

➤ The speaker says that life is very hard.
➤ The speaker remembers when Frederick Douglass was a great speaker and leader.
➤ The speaker wishes that Douglass were alive to lead again.

Ah, Douglass,[1] we have fall'n on evil days,
　Such days as thou, not even thou didst know,
　When thee, the eyes of that harsh long ago
Saw, **salient**, at the cross of devious ways,
5 And all the country heard thee with amaze.
　Not ended then, the passionate ebb and flow,[2]
　The awful tide that battled **to and fro**;
We ride amid a **tempest** of dispraise.

Now, when the waves of swift **dissension** swarm,
10 　And Honor, the strong pilot, lieth stark,[3]
Oh, for thy voice high-sounding o'er the storm,
　For thy strong arm to guide the shivering bark,[4]
The blast-defying power of thy form,
　To give us comfort through the lonely dark.

Vocabulary

salient (sāl′ yənt) *adj.* very obvious; easy to notice
tempest (tem′ pist) *n.* a violent storm
dissension (di sen′ shən) *n.* disagreement

1. ***Frederick Douglass*** escaped from slavery. He became a great speaker and leader in the fight against slavery.
2. ***Ebb and flow*** means "fall and rise."
3. ***Stark*** means "stiffly" or "rigidly."
4. A ***bark*** is a type of boat.

REFLECT

Clarify Meaning
Reread lines 11 and 12. Then paraphrase them, or state them in your own words. Use footnotes, definitions, and context clues to define words you don't know.

Possible answer: Your voice and your strength could guide

our boat through the storm.

_____

_____

 Talk about your answer with a partner.

Comprehension [BLM]

To support students as they read the selection, have them begin the graphic organizer on page A34.

WE WEAR THE MASK

We wear the mask that <u>grins</u> and lies,
It hides our cheeks and shades our eyes,—
This debt we pay to human **guile**;
With <u>torn and bleeding hearts</u> we smile,
5 And mouth with myriad[1] subtleties.[2]
Why should the world be overwise,
In counting all <u>our tears and sighs</u>?
Nay, let them only see us, while
    We wear the mask.
10 We smile, but, O great Christ, our cries
To thee from tortured souls arise.
We sing, but oh the clay is **vile**
Beneath our feet, and long the mile;
But let the world dream otherwise,
15   We wear the mask!

Vocabulary

guile (gīl) *n.* dishonesty
vile (vīl) *adj.* disgusting

1. *Myriad* means "too many to count."
2. *Subtleties* are things so small that you can hardly notice them.

REFLECT

Clarify Meaning
Choose one line from the poem that you found confusing.
Explain how you clarified the meaning of that line.

Possible answer: I found line 3 confusing. I looked up *debt*

in a dictionary and read the definition of *guile* below. Then I

tried to paraphrase the line.

_____

_____

 Talk about your answer with a partner.

---

grins (grinz) *v.* smiles

torn (tôrn) *adj.* ripped apart

 Comprehension Check

Reread the first two lines.
Underline the words that show
how people feel inside, behind
their masks.

 Literary Element

Rhyme Scheme What is the
rhyme scheme of lines 10–15 of
this poem?
- [x] aabbac
- [ ] aabbcc
- [ ] ababcc

To Sum Up

➤ The speaker says that we smile
  in order to hide our sadness.
➤ He calls this "wearing a mask."
➤ Our masks cover up the pain
  we feel inside.

Oral Assessment

Provide the following prompts to one student at a time. Observe students' responses. See the
Oral Assessment Rubric on page T17 to determine students' levels of language output.

1. **Tell me about the poem "Douglass."**

2. **How does the speaker of "Douglass" feel about Frederick Douglass?**

3. **Tell me about the poem "We Wear the Mask."**

4. **What kind of mask does the speaker of "We Wear the Mask" wear?**

5. **Why does the speaker wear this mask?**

Interactive Question-Response

Comprehension Check

Ask students to share what they underlined in the text.
Ask: *Do you think the poet is talking about actual
masks, or about what our faces look like when we
hide our feelings? (The poet is talking about what our
faces look like when we hide our feelings. Sometimes
we may smile even when we feel sad or upset.)*

Literary Element Rhyme Scheme

If students have difficulty responding, tell them to write
a small *a* after line 10. Then, have them write an *a* after
every line that ends with a word that rhymes with *cries*.
Have them write a small *b* after line 11, then find the
end rhyme that matches *vile*. Finally, have students
assign a *c* to the final line.

Reflect

Partner Talk Have students work in pairs to answer.
To help students get started: **Model** *To answer this, I
would reread the poem and circle words that I don't
know. Then, I would look up the words in a dictionary
or read the definitions and footnotes in the text to
clarify the meaning of the words. Finally, I would
paraphrase the lines that are confusing in my own
words.* Write the following sentence frame on the
board to help students organize their thoughts.

Some words that are unclear are _____.
*Based on the definitions and footnotes, they
  mean _____.*

Vocabulary Check

C. [Early Advanced]

Read each word aloud. Remind students that a *synonym* is a word that has the same meaning as another word. **Ask:** *Which of the choices has the same meaning as the word salient? (a. obvious)* Encourage students to use a dictionary to look up word choices that are unfamiliar.

Vocabulary Check

A. Label each picture with the correct word.

shivering	grins	swarm	torn

1. grins
2. torn
3. swarm
4. shivering

B. Complete the sentence with the correct word from the word bank.

torn	shivering	tempest	guile

5. The salesman's _____guile_____ made him very successful.

6. The wrapping paper was _____torn_____ to shreds as he opened the package.

7. The _____tempest_____ damaged their home.

8. I was _____shivering_____ with fear during the scary movie.

C. Circle the letter next to the synonym, or word with nearly the same meaning.

9. **salient**
   a. obvious
   b. strange
   c. funny

10. **vile**
    a. pretty
    b. important
    c. disgusting

11. **dissension**
    a. agreement
    b. enjoyment
    c. disagreement

12. **guile**
    a. openness
    b. dishonesty
    c. truthfulness

Douglass and
WE WEAR THE MASK

Comprehension Check

A. Complete the sentences.

1. The speaker in "Douglass" says that life is _____ hard _____.

2. He wishes that Frederick Douglass could _____ lead again _____.

3. In "We Wear the Mask," people wear masks that look _____ happy _____.

4. People hide _____ their real feelings _____ behind a mask.

B. The rhyme scheme of "Douglass" includes four rhyming sounds. In the chart, write words from the poem that rhyme with the listed words.

5. days	6. know	7. swarm	8. stark
ways amaze; dispraise	ago; flow; fro	storm; form	bark; dark

C. Answer the questions about the rhyme schemes of "Douglass" and "We Wear the Mask."

9. What is the rhyme scheme of lines 1–4 of "Douglass"?
   - a. *abba*
   - b. *abab*
   - c. *aabb*

10. How would you describe the end rhyme in lines 9–14 of "Douglass"?
    - a. The end rhymes are paired.
    - b. There is no end rhyme.
    - c. The end rhymes alternate.

11. Which word in "We Wear the Mask" breaks the rhyme pattern?
    - a. lies
    - b. smile
    - c. mask

12. Which line in "We Wear the Mask" is an entirely repeated line, or a refrain?
    - a. It hides our cheeks and shades our eyes
    - b. We sing, but oh the clay is vile
    - c. We wear the mask

Comprehension Check

B. **Intermediate**

Have students work together in groups to read the poem aloud, emphasizing the last word of each line. As they pronounce the end rhymes, students should write the rhyme in the correct column.

Writing Link

Blog

Have students begin a classroom blog to share their reactions to Dunbar's poetry. To create a blog, check your computer program for easy-to-use templates or use an online provider that ensures password-protected access. Emphasize that you will review entries and comments before they are posted.

Tell students that a *blog* is a kind of online journal that writers post on the Internet. Explain that the entries in a blog appear in chronological order, with the most recent entries appearing first. If a reader wants to view entries in chronological order, he or she will have to start at the bottom and read up. Work with students to create topics, or prompts, for them to respond to and set up a secure way for readers to respond to the entries. Remind students to support their opinions with details from the poems.

Douglass and
WE WEAR THE MASK

Friendly Letter

Imagine that you could send Paul Laurence Dunbar a friendly letter about his poems Douglass and We Wear the Mask. In the letter, tell him how you felt when you read both poems.

Dear Mr. Dunbar,

I read your poem "Douglass." It made me feel Possible answer: sad

because Possible answer: Frederick Douglass is not alive anymore .

My favorite line is Possible answer: "To give us comfort through the lonely dark"

I like this line because Possible answer: it is nice to have someone to comfort me .

I also read "We Wear the Mask." This poem made me think about Possible answer: how we hide our true feelings

When I read this poem, I felt Possible answer: excited

because Possible answer: I could identify with it very well .

I wear a mask sometimes. It looks Possible answer: happy even when I am

feeling Possible answer: sad . I wear this mask because

Answers will vary.

 .

Thank you for writing these poems.

Sincerely,

_____

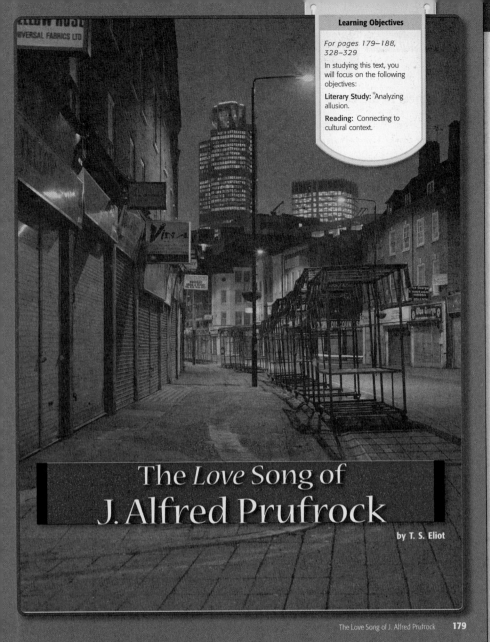

The *Love* Song of
J. Alfred Prufrock

by T. S. Eliot

Oral Language

Build Background

Read the title and author. Explain that authors sometimes use irony in their titles. This poem is titled "The Love Song of J. Alfred Prufrock." **Ask:** *What kind of poem do you think it will be? (an unhappy one)* Tell students to think about other love songs as they read. **Ask:** Is this a typical love poem? *(no)* Why not? *(The narrator does not confess his feelings.)* Tell students to think about what the poem is about, besides love.

Talk About the Poem

Explain that the poem is about upper-class life in London around World War I.

Beginning/Early Intermediate ▶ Discuss students' ideas of how the rich lived in London around 1910. Explain that women could not vote, and that ideals of modesty and politeness were much more conservative than they are today.

Early Advanced ▶ Ask students if they know of people who speak up about things they care about. To stimulate discussion **Ask:** *Do you know people who stay silent? Is it more common to speak up, or to stay silent? Why do you think people are afraid to talk about what they love?*

Lesson at a Glance

Oral Language
- Build Background
- Talk About the Poem

Vocabulary
- Selection Vocabulary
- Content Vocabulary
- Academic Vocabulary

Literary Element
- Allusion

Reading Strategy
- Connect to Cultural Context

Writing Link
- Anecdote

Comprehension
- BLM

Fluency
- Pacing: Phrasing

Grammar Link   BLM
- Word Order of Adjectives

Technology
- Student Works™ Plus
- Teacher Works™ Plus
- Listening Library Audio CD
- Classroom Presentation Toolkit
- Glencoe Visual Vocabulary
- Skill Level Up!™ A Skill-Based Language Arts Game

Interactive Question-Response

Connect to the Poem

Read aloud Connect to the Poem. **Model** *Sometimes it's hard to say something you really care about. You might worry that other people will make fun of you. You might feel as though the moment isn't right, or you need to create a perfect setting. What are some other reasons you don't always show your feelings?* List students' responses on the board. Then have students fill in their own lists.

Literary Element   Allusion

Explain the difference between direct and indirect references. Have students open their books to the first page of the poem. **Model** *This poem begins "Let us go then, you and I." If I were referring directly to the poem, I might say, "As T. S. Eliot says, 'Let us go then, you and I.'" But if I made an **allusion**, an indirect reference, I would just say, "Let us go then, you and I." I would trust you to understand what I was talking about. I might make this allusion to suggest that I feel like the hero of this poem. Or I might think that our city looks like London.* Explain that an allusion isn't just a quote from a literary work. It brings along all that work's meaning and feeling.

Reading Strategy   Connect to Cultural Context

Read aloud the Reading Strategy. Explain that students will be able to understand the poem better if they understand its cultural context. Provide an example of a part of American culture, such as the Internet or fast food. Explain that we behave in certain ways because this is a part of our culture. Remind students to watch for cultural details as they read "The Love Song of J. Alfred Prufrock." Prompt them to think about how the cultural context shapes the characters' actions and words.

The *Love* Song of J. Alfred Prufrock

Connect to the Poem

Have you ever been nervous or afraid to say something to someone? What did you want to say? What made you afraid? Did you decide to speak, or to stay quiet? Why?

Sample answer: I was nervous about asking for help in math class. I was afraid that I would look stupid. I finally

asked, because I decided that getting help was more important than seeming smart.

_____

_____

_____

Literary Element   Allusion

An **allusion** is a reference to a person, a place, or a situation from history, art, music, or literature. Usually an allusion is indirect. That means that the author mentions a character or a quote without naming the source.

For example, this poem begins with an allusion to Dante's *Inferno.* The allusion suggests that Prufrock's journey through London is similar to Dante's journey through hell. In the *Inferno,* Dante is in love with a woman he cannot approach. He also questions the meaning of his life. Prufrock may share these traits.

Reading Strategy   Connecting to Cultural Context

A piece of writing is more meaningful when you think about it from the author's cultural context. **Cultural context** includes:

- the society in which the writer lived.
- the technology of the time.
- what was happening in the world.

All these things influence the way the writer thinks, chooses subjects, and uses language. Ask yourself: Does Prufrock think London is clean or dirty? Are the people friendly, or do they seem to be fake?

Selection Vocabulary

tedious (tē dē əs) *adj.* very long and detailed; boring (p. 182)
*The **tedious** movie could not keep everybody's attention.*
➤ Cognate (Spanish) **tedioso**

presume (pri zōōm') *v.* expect something without a good reason to expect it (p. 183)
*I **presume** I will be promoted, because my boss likes me.*
➤ Cognate (Spanish) **presumir**

digress (di gres') *v.* talk about something other than the main subject (p. 184)
*The children will probably **digress** to talking about video games instead of school.*

malingers (mə ling' gərz) *v.* pretends to be sick to avoid work (p. 184)
*Kelly **malingers** when she has a test at school.*

deferential (def' ə ren' shəl) *adj.* overly polite (p. 186)
*The faithful son was always **deferential** to his father.*
➤ Cognate (Spanish) **deferente**

Content Vocabulary

cheap (chēp) *adj.* costing little money (p. 182)
*Annabelle only had two dollars, so she bought the **cheap** pencils.*

narrow (nar' ō) *adj.* skinny and usually long (p. 184)
*The **narrow** sidewalk did not have enough room for Damien and Sophia to walk next to each other.*

wept (wept) *v.* cried (p. 184)
*Sandra **wept** when her cat died.*

cautious (kô' shəs) *adj.* careful (p. 186)
*Dan is always **cautious** when he climbs trees because he doesn't want to fall out.*
➤ Cognate (Spanish) **cauteloso**

For more practice, see page 328. ➡

Vocabulary Routine

To introduce the vocabulary, read aloud the words and definitions in the student book and have students repeat after you. Discuss how the pictures illustrate the words or sentences. Then follow the vocabulary routine below.

Selection Vocabulary

<u>Define</u>: When something is ***tedious***, it is long, detailed, and boring. <u>Example</u>: A 10-page e-mail about snails is *tedious*. <u>Ask</u>: What is another example of something *tedious*? EXAMPLE

If we ***presume*** something, we are beginning it without knowing we should. *If you presume the experiment before all the directions are given, you might have to redo it.* Describe a time when you have *presumed* something. DESCRIPTION

You ***digress*** when you start to talk about something different from the main topic. *Alicia digressed to talking about ice cream during her health class.* What might you talk about when you *digress*? EXAMPLE

To ***malinger*** is to pretend to be sick to avoid work. *The student had not finished her report, so she malingered on the day it was due.* What punishments could we get if we *malinger*? EXPLANATION

Content Vocabulary

A ***cheap*** item does not cost much money. *A castle costs a lot of money, but an apartment is cheap.* What word means the opposite of *cheap*? ANTONYM

Narrow means "not wide." *A narrow hallway is long and skinny.* What other things can be *narrow*? EXAMPLE

Wept is the past tense of *to weep*, which means to cry. *I wept when I broke my leg.* What emotions could a person have felt when he *wept*? EXAMPLE

People are ***cautious*** when they are being careful. *Construction workers must be cautious around their machinery so they do not hurt themselves.* When are you *cautious*? EXPLANATION

Vocabulary Practice Have students complete the vocabulary practice activity on page 328.

The *Love Song of* J. Alfred Prufrock

Interactive Question-Response

Literary Element Allusion

Explain that Dante's *Inferno* is part of the *Divine Comedy*. The *Divine Comedy* is a long three-part poem. In it, Dante feels as though he has lost his way in life. Accompanied by the poet Virgil, he goes on a journey through the afterlife. He hopes to restore his faith in the order and justice of the world. The *Inferno* is about hell. Eliot may allude to it here to show that city life is like hell. **Ask:** *How does this allusion make you feel about the poem? What does it tell you about the narrator? (The narrator may feel as though he is trapped in hell. He may have lost his faith. It makes me feel as though the poem is dark or hopeless.)*

Content Vocabulary

Read aloud the word and definition. Have students read lines 5–7. **Ask:** *In these lines, what is cheap? (the hotel) What would you expect a cheap hotel to be like? (dirty, dangerous, smelly, stained, seedy)*

Literary Element

Allusion The opening lines are from Dante's *Inferno*. They are spoken by a spirit in hell. The spirit confesses his sins because he thinks no one will ever hear his confession. He still cares about his reputation on earth. What mood does this set for the poem?

Possible answers: doomed,

dark, bleak, sad, hopeless

_____

cheap (chēp) *adj.* costing little money

To Sum Up

➤ Prufrock is on his way to a party where upper-class people will be.

➤ He walks through streets and sees working-class people.

➤ He wants to walk with someone. He wants to ask this person an important question. He will not say what he wants to ask.

S'io credessi che mia resposta fosse
a persona che mai tornasse al mondo,
questa fiamma staria senza più scosse.
Ma per ciò che giammai di questo fondo
non tornò vivo alcun, s'i'odo il vero,
senza tema d'infamia ti respondo.[1]

Let us go then, you and I,
When the evening is spread out against the sky
Like a patient etherised[2] upon a table;
Let us go, through certain half-deserted streets,
5   The muttering retreats
Of restless nights in one-night <u>cheap</u> hotels
And sawdust restaurants with oyster-shells:
Streets that follow like a **tedious** argument
Of insidious intent
10 To lead you to an overwhelming question…
        Oh, do not ask, 'What is it?'
Let us go and make our visit.
In the room the women come and go
Talking of Michelangelo.[3]

Vocabulary
tedious (tē dē əs) *adj.* very long and detailed; boring

1. These lines are from Dante's *Inferno*. They are in Italian. They mean, "If I thought that I was speaking / to someone who would go back to the world, / this flame would shake no more. / But since nobody has ever / gone back alive from this place, if what I hear is true, / I answer you without fear of infamy."
2. ***Etherized*** means "made numb." Patients were once etherized before surgery.
3. ***Michelangelo*** Buonarroti (1475–1564) was an Italian sculptor and painter.

Comprehension   BLM

To support students as they read the selection, have them begin the graphic organizer on page A35.

15 The yellow fog that rubs its back upon the window-panes,
The yellow smoke that rubs its muzzle on the window-panes,
Licked its tongue into the corners of the evening,
Lingered upon the pools that stand in drains,
Let fall upon its back the soot that falls from chimneys,
20 Slipped by the terrace, made a sudden leap,
And seeing that it was a soft October night,
Curled once about the house, and fell asleep.

And indeed there will be time
For the yellow smoke that slides along the street
25 Rubbing its back upon the window-panes;
There will be time, there will be time
To prepare a face to meet the faces that you meet;
There will be time to murder and create,
And time for all the works and days of hands
30 That lift and drop a question on your plate;
Time for you and time for me,
And time yet for a hundred indecisions,
And for a hundred visions and revisions,
Before the taking of a toast and tea.

35 In the room the women come and go
Talking of Michelangelo.

And indeed there will be time
To wonder, 'Do I dare?' and, 'Do I dare?'
Time to turn back and descend the stair,
40 With a bald spot in the middle of my hair—
(They will say: 'How his hair is growing thin!')
My morning coat,[4] my collar mounting firmly to the chin,
My necktie rich and modest, but asserted[5] by a simple pin—
(They will say: 'But how his arms and legs are thin!')
45 Do I dare
Disturb the universe?
In a minute there is time
For decisions and revisions which a minute will reverse.

For I have known them all already, known them all—
50 Have known the evenings, mornings, afternoons,
I have measured out my life with coffee spoons;
I know the voices dying with a dying fall
Beneath the music from a farther room.
So how should I **presume?**

Vocabulary

presume (pri zoom′) *v.* expect something without a good reason to expect it

4. A **morning coat** is a man's dress coat.
5. Here, **asserted** means "made fancier."

Background Information

London was known for its smog in the early 1900s because it had so many factories. Here, Eliot makes the smog seem alive. It rubs "its back along the window-panes" like a cat.

To prepare a face to meet the faces that you meet means to think carefully about your appearance and behavior. Prufrock worries about how other people see him.

Comprehension Check

Why would the women talk of Michelangelo?
- [ ] because they would like to meet him
- [x] to show they are smart and know about art
- [ ] because he is the host of the party

To **measure out one's life** means to have every detail planned. Prufrock says he has measured his life out in coffee spoons. He means his life is full of small, unimportant details.

To Sum Up

➤ The people at the party care about looking beautiful and smart. Prufrock feels as though he is fake.

➤ Prufrock thinks about whether he dares to do something. He decides one thing, and then changes his mind many times.

➤ He worries about what people will think of him.

Interactive Question-Response

Background Information

Read the note aloud. **Model** how a cat rubs its back against something to pet itself. **Ask:** *If the fog is factory smoke rubbing against the windows, is it like a friendly cat or one that will not go away? (will not go away)*

Comprehension Check

Ask students to share their answers. **Ask:** *What might the women be saying about Michelangelo? (His sculptures are amazing. The details are very realistic.)* If students struggle, make sure they understand who Michelangelo is. Mention his famous works, such as the statue of David or the ceiling of the Sistine Chapel.

Fluency

Pacing: Phrasing

Intermediate/Early Advanced Tell students that they will be doing a choral reading of lines 37–48. Remind students to read in phrases or complete sentences for clarity and not word by word. Model the fluency skill as you read the text at a moderate tempo. Then have one student read a sentence. Have another student join in, and a third, and so on. When students reach the end of the passage, have pairs of students reread to each other. To assess individual fluency, use the Oral Reading Guidelines on page T16.

Beginning/Early Intermediate Have these students choral read lines 37–48 of the passage. Before they begin, model the pronunciation of the text. Then have students practice reading the paragraph in pairs before the choral reading.

Interactive
Question-Response

Selection Vocabulary

Have students read the word and definition and then lines 65–66, which contain the word *digress*. Explain that Prufrock is distracted from his topic by the women and their perfume. **Ask:** *What is the difference between* distracted *and* digress? *(A person is distracted when something takes his attention away from the main topic. He digresses if he starts to talk about what is distracting him instead of about the main topic.)*

Content Vocabulary

Explain that many streets of London are *narrow* because they were built before people drove cars. **Ask:** *Would a narrow street be lighter or darker than a wide street? (darker) How would you feel in a narrow street? (crowded, scared, hidden, anonymous)*

Point out that Prufrock has wept, fasted (not eaten), and prayed. **Ask:** *How does he feel? (sad, depressed, nervous, worried, or frustrated)*

---

narrow (nar′ ō) *adj.* skinny and usually long

wept (wept) *v.* cried

To ***bite off a matter with a smile*** is to start talking about something one does not want to talk about and to smile about it anyway.

Vocabulary

digress (di gres′) *v.* talk about something other than the main subject
malingers (mə ling′ gərz) *v.* pretends to be sick to avoid work

To Sum Up

➤ Prufrock wonders how to say what he wants to say. He is distracted by thoughts of a beautiful woman.

➤ He is afraid to disturb the polite, peaceful evening.

➤ He feels weak and unimportant.

184

---

55 And I have known the eyes already, known them all—
The eyes that fix you in a formulated[6] phrase,
And when I am formulated, sprawling on a pin,
When I am pinned and wriggling on the wall,
Then how should I begin
60 To spit out all the butt-ends of my days and ways?
   And how should I presume?
And I have known the arms already, known them all—
Arms that are braceleted and white and bare
(But in the lamplight, downed with light brown hair!)?
65 Is it perfume from a dress
That makes me so **digress?**
Arms that lie along a table, or wrap about a shawl.
   And should I then presume?
   And how should I begin?
70 Shall I say, I have gone at dusk through <u>narrow</u> streets
And watched the smoke that rises from the pipes
Of lonely men in shirt-sleeves, leaning out of windows?…
I should have been a pair of ragged claws
Scuttling across the floors of silent seas.
75 And the afternoon, the evening, sleeps so peacefully!
Smoothed by long fingers,
Asleep…tired…or it **malingers,**
Stretched on the floor, here beside you and me.
Should I, after tea and cakes and ices,
80 Have the strength to force the moment to its crisis?
But though I have <u>wept</u> and fasted, wept and prayed,
Though I have seen my head (grown slightly bald) brought in
   upon a platter[7]
I am no prophet[8]—and here's no great matter;
I have seen the moment of my greatness flicker,
85 And I have seen the eternal Footman[9] hold my coat, and snicker,
And in short, I was afraid.

And would it have been worth it, after all,
After the cups, the marmalade, the tea,
Among the porcelain, among some talk of you and me,
90 Would it have been worth while,
To have bitten off the matter with a smile,
To have squeezed the universe into a ball

---

6. ***Formulated*** means "the same as always." Prufrock feels trapped when other people describe him with formulated words.
7. Prufrock's head upon a platter is an allusion to the prophet John the Baptist from the Bible. King Herod said he would give his step-daughter anything she wanted, and she asked for John's head. Prufrock feels that he has been a victim, but that he is not as important as John the Baptist.
8. A ***prophet*** is someone who tells the future or reveals the truth.
9. The ***eternal Footman*** is death. A footman is a kind of servant.

To roll it towards some overwhelming question,
To say: 'I am Lazarus, come from the dead,[10]
95 Come back to tell you all, I shall tell you all'—
If one, settling a pillow by her head,
    Should say: 'That is not what I meant at all.
    That is not it, at all.'
And would it have been worth it, after all,
100 Would it have been worth while,
After the sunsets and the dooryards and the sprinkled streets,
After the novels, after the teacups, after the skirts that trail
    along the floor—
And this, and so much more?—
It is impossible to say just what I mean!

105 But as if a magic lantern[11] threw the nerves in patterns on a screen:
Would it have been worth while
If one, settling a pillow or throwing off a shawl,
And turning toward the window, should say:
    'That is not it at all,
110   That is not what I meant, at all.'

---

10. This alludes to the Bible, in which Jesus brings his friend **Lazarus** back to life.
11. A **magic lantern** is an old-fashioned light that flashes pictures on a wall.

REFLECT

Connect to Cultural Context
Prufrock lists several things he enjoys about upper-class life, such as the dooryards, novels, and teacups. Why do these things make him cautious? What social rules and expectations seem to keep Prufrock from asking his question? Why might he want to walk in the lower-class streets?

The people around him pay attention to appearances. He

wants to walk in the lower-class streets because that will

let him escape this sense of judgment, and perhaps he will

finally feel comfortable asking his question.

_____

 Talk about your answer with a partner.

To Sum Up

➤ Prufrock does not know if he should ask his question.
➤ He worries that a woman will misunderstand him.
➤ He worries that his question will disrupt this upper-class world.

Interactive Question-Response

Reflect

Partner Talk Have students work in pairs to answer. To help students get started: **Model** *The upper-class life in the poem seems pleasant in lots of small ways. It is orderly and beautiful and polite. I might be afraid of disturbing or ruining such a pleasant life.* Write the following sentence frame on the board to help students organize their thoughts:

When I am around people who _____, I _____.

Differentiated Instruction

Clarify the Text Support students in understanding why Prufrock has trouble saying what he means.

Beginning/Early Intermediate ▶ Explain that Prufrock is part of the upper class. He lives in a world of tea, parties, quiet conversation, and rules. **Ask:** *Do you think people are always honest in this sort of society? Why or why not?*

Intermediate ▶ Have students re-read the boxed selection. Ask them to underline the things Prufrock likes. **Ask:** *Who is the one who settles a pillow by her head? (the woman he loves) Why is he afraid that his effort will not be worth while? (He fears she will misunderstand him or reject him.)*

Early Advanced ▶ **Ask:** *Why does Prufrock say, "It is impossible to say just what I mean"? How do the things he wants compete with each other? (He wants his life to change, but he is afraid of change. He is frustrated because he cannot explain what he wants. He doesn't know how to make his feelings fit within social rules.)*

Interactive Question-Response

Content Vocabulary

Have a student read aloud the word and definition of *cautious*. **Ask:** *How would a person be cautious as an adviser? (be careful to give good advice)*

Literary Element Allusion

If students have difficulty responding, make sure they know that the *Inferno* is a poem and *Hamlet* is a play. **Model** *Prufrock makes a lot of allusions. He seems to be very comfortable with literature. This tells me that he is well educated and he has time to read. What does it tell you about the people he usually talks to? (He expects them to understand these references, so they must also be well-read.) T. S. Eliot expected the readers of this poem to recognize these allusions too. What can you infer about the people Eliot expected to read the poem? (Probably quite a lot of them were like Prufrock.) What do you think Eliot wanted them to do? (to be brave and honest, to break social rules)*

cautious (kô′ shəs) *adj.* careful

 Literary Element

Allusion The allusions in this poem include one to Dante's *Inferno*, two to the Bible, and one to Shakespeare's *Hamlet*. Find them in the text and underline them. Are these allusions to history, art, music, or literature?

literature
_____

Vocabulary ....
deferential (def′ ə ren′ shəl) *adj.* overly polite

12. This reference to **Prince Hamlet** is an allusion to Shakespeare's tragedy *Hamlet*. Prince Hamlet knows the truth about who killed his father, and he must decide what to do about it.
13. **To swell a progress** is to participate in, and thereby increase (swell) the number of people in a royal procession or a play.
14. **Politic** means "prudent or shrewd."
15. An **obtuse** person is slow to understand.

To Sum Up

➤ Prufrock decides not to say anything. He feels he is a follower, not a leader.

➤ He imagines his life quickly passing by as he lives in a world he does not like.

186

No! I am not Prince Hamlet,[12] nor was meant to be;
Am an attendant lord, one that will do
To swell a progress,[13] start a scene or two,
Advise the prince; no doubt, an easy tool,
115 **Deferential,** glad to be of use,
Politic,[14] cautious, and meticulous;
Full of high sentence, but a bit obtuse;[15]
At times, indeed, almost ridiculous—
Almost, at times, the Fool.

120 I grow old…I grow old…
I shall wear the bottoms of my trousers rolled.

Shall I part my hair behind? Do I dare to eat a peach?
I shall wear white flannel trousers, and walk upon the beach.
I have heard the mermaids singing, each to each.

125 I do not think that they will sing to me.

I have seen them riding seaward on the waves
Combing the white hair of the waves blown back
When the wind blows the water white and black.

We have lingered in the chambers of the sea
130 By sea-girls wreathed with seaweed red and brown
Till human voices wake us, and we drown.

Oral Assessment

Provide the following prompts to one student at a time. Observe students' responses. See the Oral Assessment Rubric on page T17 to determine students' levels of language output.

1. What does Prufrock think about the people around him?

2. What person does Prufrock keep thinking about?

3. What does he want to tell this person?

4. Why does he hesitate and change his mind several times?

5. What does Prufrock decide to do?

The *Love Song* of
J. Alfred Prufrock

Vocabulary Check

A. Match each picture with the correct word.

| cheap | wept | narrow | cautious |

1. _____wept_____
2. _____cheap_____
3. _____cautious_____
4. _____narrow_____

B. Unscramble the following vocabulary words.

5. siatuuco ___cautious___
6. seemurp ___presume___
7. merlasgin ___malinger___
8. stodeusi ___tedious___
9. girdses ___digress___

C. Answer the following questions about the vocabulary words in the text.

10. If Prufrock thinks he is **deferential** like a prince's adviser, does he want to lead people to see the world in a new way? Why or why not?

   No, he wants someone else to do it because he does not want to be banished from the upper class.

11. What does Prufrock mean when he says, "Streets that follow like a **tedious** argument"?

   The streets are long and boring. They never seem to end.

12. Prufrock says the evening sleeps. Then, as he decides not to speak, he says it **malingers**. Why might he make this comparison?

   He and the evening are both avoiding effort.

13. When Prufrock starts to **digress** from talking about the change he wants to see, what does he talk about instead?

   Women's bare arms.

14. Does Prufrock ever **presume** to speak? Why or why not?

   No; he does not think he can speak without being ridiculed. He sees himself as unworthy.

Vocabulary Check

C. Advanced Intermediate

Read each question aloud. Ask students to define each vocabulary word and then to find its location in the text. Have the students re-read each passage to answer the questions.

Academic Vocabulary

Write the following sentence on the board: *In "The Love Song of J. Alfred Prufrock," T.S. Eliot* **comments** *on the hopelessness of modern life.*

Point out that *comment* is an academic word. Explain that one way to think about its meaning is to recall how a film critic comments on a new movie.

Have students further explore the meaning of *comment* by discussing the following question in small groups: If you were to write a poem similar to this one about modern life, how would you comment on your world?

Grammar Link BLM

Word Order of Adjectives

Prepare students to complete the activity on page A36. Read the grammar instruction with students, and complete the first item with them to get them started.

Comprehension Check

B. Intermediate

Encourage students to think about what they know about the Inferno and Hamlet. Help them find appropriate, detailed summaries or synopses in the library or online. Encourage students to return to the poem for better understanding.

After Reading

Have students complete the after reading activity on page 329.

The *Love* Song of J. Alfred Prufrock

Comprehension Check

A. Fill in the boxes to explain what happens in the beginning, middle, and end of the poem.

> **1. Beginning**
> Prufrock goes to the party.

↓

> **2. Middle**
> He wants to ask an "overwhelming question," possibly a marriage proposal.
> He thinks he spends too much of his life thinking about trivial things, such as fashions.

↓

> **3. End**
> In the end, he does not say anything.

B. Circle the correct answer to the following questions about allusions in the poem.

4. The streets in London are like Dante's *Inferno* because
   a. Prufrock thinks the city is like hell.
   b. the streets are confusing like a maze.
   c. Prufrock thinks the city is full of sinners.

5. Prufrock says he is not Prince Hamlet. What does he mean?
   a. Unlike a prince, Prufrock can break social rules.
   b. Unlike Hamlet, Prufrock can make a decision.
   c. Prufrock feels like an unimportant character, not a hero.

C. Answer the following questions about allusions in "The Love Song of J. Alfred Prufrock."

6. What are some of the works and people that Prufrock alludes to?
   Michelangelo, Dante's *Inferno*, *Hamlet*, the Bible, "To His Coy Mistress"

7. Choose one of these allusions. Why does Prufrock make this reference? What do you think he means?
   Prufrock alludes to *Hamlet* to point out that his problems are not important. He believes others see
   him as a supporting character instead of a hero. He alludes to the Bible to point out that he has
   no divine inspiration. The allusion to Dante's *Inferno* might suggest that London is like hell or that
   Prufrock, like Dante, feels lost and hopeless. It might also suggest that Prufrock feels like one of the
   nameless multitudes in hell, and that he believes no one will hear his confession. The allusion to
   "To His Coy Mistress" helps the reader understand that the question troubling Prufrock is one of love.

For more practice, see page 329. ➡

Writing Link

Anecdote

Students should think about a time when something happened to them that was like something they read about in a story or saw in a movie. Have them brainstorm words that describe their experience. Then have them think about words they can use as allusions to the story when telling their own story. **Write** these words on the board to guide them: character names, place names, author's name, the main theme, well-known words or phrases. Explain that an anecdote is a short, informal story about personal experience. Ask students to tell their story in two or three paragraphs, using their words and allusions. Encourage students to read their anecdotes aloud.

Learning Objectives

For pages 189–202, 330–331

In studying this text, you will focus on the following objectives:

Literary Study: Analyzing stream of consciousness.

Reading: Drawing conclusions about the protagonist.

The *Jilting* of
Granny Weatherall

by Katherine Anne Porter

The Jilting of Granny Weatherall **189**

Oral Language

Build Background

Read the title and author. Explain that students will read "The Jilting of Granny Weatherall" by Katherine Anne Porter, an author who was born in Texas in the late 1800s. **Ask: What do you think the verb *to weather* means?** *(to survive hard times)* **What do you think of when you hear the name *Weatherall*?** *(someone has come through a lot of hard times)*

Talk About the Story

Explain that the story is about an old woman in the early 1900s who is thinking about her life.

Beginning/Early Intermediate ▸ **Ask:** *Do you think it was hard work to take care of a home in the past? (yes/no)*

Intermediate ▸ Ask students to name things that women did to take care of the home more than a hundred years ago. *(cooked food, washed clothes, cleaned the house, raised children, sewed clothes, and planted gardens.)*

Early Advanced ▸ Ask students to think about the differences between the past and present ways to do things around the house. Write a two-column chart on the board and list some of the differences on the chart.

Lesson at a Glance

Oral Language
- Build Background
- Talk About the Story

Vocabulary
- Selection Vocabulary
- Content Vocabulary
- Academic Vocabulary

Literary Element
- Stream of Consciousness

Reading Strategy
- Draw Conclusions About the Protagonist

Writing Link
- Character Sketch

Fluency
- Expression and Intonation: Punctuation

Comprehension
- BLM

Word Study BLM
- Base Words BLM

Grammar Link BLM
- Sentence Fragments BLM

Technology
- Student Works™ Plus
- Teacher Works™ Plus
- Listening Library Audio CD
- Classroom Presentation Toolkit
- Glencoe Visual Vocabulary
- Skill Level Up!™ A Skill-Based Language Arts Game

Interactive Question-Response

Connect to the Story

Read aloud Connect to the Short Story. Write the sentence frames on the board. **Model** *If I were left alone on my wedding day, I would feel surprised and embarrassed. I would not know what to do or think.* Model writing your response on the board, and have volunteers suggest other responses. Then have individuals fill in their own sentences.

Literary Element Stream of Consciousness

Draw a timeline on the board. Read aloud the Literary Element. Explain that our thoughts do not always follow the order of the timeline. Tell students that someone told you that they liked your sweater or blouse. Then show your thought process: **Model** *This is my favorite sweater. I remember when I got this sweater three years ago on my birthday. The weather was very cold then. I hope that it won't be cold again on my birthday this year. I would like to have a picnic in the park on my next birthday.* Write your thoughts on the timeline. Correlate the events so that "favorite sweater" is with "today," "cold birthday when I got the sweater" is with "three years ago"; "picnic in the park on my next birthday" is with "several months in the future." Ask students to think about the difference between thought order and time order.

Reading Strategy Draw Conclusions About the Protagonist

Read aloud the Reading Strategy. Tell students that if they draw conclusions, then they will better understand Granny Weatherall. Give students an example of a detail from the story, such as: *Granny does not want her children to find her old love letters.* Ask students to use this detail to draw a conclusion about Granny Weatherall. *(She has a secret that she does not want her children to know.)*

The *Jilting* of Granny Weatherall

Connect to the Story

How would you feel if you were left alone on your wedding day? How would you remember that time? Think about these questions, and talk about them with a partner. Then fill in the sentences below.

I would feel Possible answers: sad, angry, or embarrassed	
Later in life, when I remembered that time, I would	
Possible answers: still be very angry or try to forget about it	

Literary Element Stream of Consciousness

Consciousness means a person's thoughts and feelings. A writer uses **stream of consciousness** to show the flow of thoughts, feelings, and memories of a character. In this story, Porter shows Granny's memories as they move back and forward in time. As you read, ask yourself these questions:

- What is the order in which Granny remembers things?
- What is the order in which they happened?

Reading Strategy Draw Conclusions About the Protagonist

To **draw conclusions** means to take your background information and the information from the text to come up with your own idea about something. A **protagonist** is the main character. To draw conclusions about the protagonist means to come up with your own ideas about the main character. As Granny's thoughts move from subject to subject, clues about her past come out. As you read, ask yourself, "What details can I use to draw conclusions about Granny?"

Use a chart like the one below to write details about Granny and to draw conclusions about her.

Details	Conclusions
Granny calls the doctor a brat.	Granny thinks of the doctor as a child.

Selection Vocabulary

tactful (takt' fəl) *adj.* able to say the right things and act the right way around other people (p. 193)
*When she said something nice, the **tactful** woman made the unhappy boy feel better.*

dutiful (dōō' ti fəl) *adj.* careful to obey or do what one should (p. 193)
*The **dutiful** daughter cared for her sick mother.*

vanity (van' i tē) *n.* too much pride (p. 196)
*Because of his **vanity**, the man felt sure he would win first prize.*
➤ Cognate (Spanish) **vanidad**

jilted (jilt' id) *v.* left or rejected a sweetheart (p. 196)
*My sister cried for three days when her boyfriend **jilted** her.*

piety (pī ə tē) *n.* religious devotion; goodness (p. 198)
*The man showed his **piety** when he went to church every week.*
➤ Cognate (Spanish) **piedad**

Content Vocabulary

squeezed (skwēzd) *v.* pressed together (p. 196)
*Marla **squeezed** the tube to get the toothpaste to come out.*

agony (ag' ə nē) *n.* great pain of mind or body (p. 197)
*When he broke his leg, Sam was in terrible **agony**.*
➤ Cognate (Spanish) **agonía**

flimsy (flim' zē) *adj.* without strength (p. 197)
*The frisbee was weak and **flimsy**.*

dwindled (dwind' əld) *v.* became smaller (p. 200)
*The fire from the candle **dwindled**.*

For more practice, see page 330. ➡

Vocabulary Routine

To introduce the vocabulary, read aloud the words and definitions in the student book and have students repeat after you. Discuss how the pictures illustrate the words or sentences. Then follow the vocabulary routine below.

Content Vocabulary

Define: If you **squeeze** something, you press it tightly. Example: *Marie squeezed her favorite coin for good luck.* Ask: Why might Marie *squeeze* her favorite coin? EXPLANATION

When someone is in **agony,** he or she feels a lot of pain. *When Julia burned her arm, she was in agony.* Describe a time when you felt *agony* in your mind or body. DESCRIPTION

Something **flimsy** is thin and weak. *The cheap dress was made of flimsy cloth.* Give an example of something that is *flimsy.* EXAMPLE

Something that **dwindled** became smaller. *The light in the room dwindled in the late afternoon.* What is a word that means the opposite of *dwindled?* ANTONYM

Vocabulary Practice Have students complete the vocabulary practice activity on p. 330.

Selection Vocabulary

Define: Someone who expects to get married but is suddenly abandoned by his or her betrothed has been **jilted.** Example: The groom jilted his bride when he did not arrive at the church for their wedding. Ask: What do you think the relationship is between jilted and the idiom "left (or abandoned) at the altar"? SYNONYM

When someone is **tactful,** they are polite and avoid saying anything insulting or hurtful. *I didn't like the cookies my sister made, but I was tactful and thanked her for her hard work.* What would be the opposite of tactful? ANTONYM

A **dutiful** person does the work that is expected promptly and satisfactorily. *The dutiful girl did her chores without complaining, even though she wished she could play outside instead.* What are some things you have done in a dutiful manner? DESCRIPTION

Someone who is full of **vanity** takes too much pride in his or her appearance or other personal qualities. *Because of the rock star's extreme vanity, he spent several hours each day doing his hair and picking out his clothes.* What is the relationship between *vanity* and *humility*? COMPARE AND CONTRAST

When someone displays **piety,** they do things that show their devotion to their religion. *The priest's piety was evident in the sincere way he read the prayer.* What kinds of actions show a person's piety? EXAMPLE

The *Jilting* of
Granny Weatherall

Interactive Question-Response

Background Information

Explain that a homemaker is someone who takes care of the home. As they read, ask students to think about how Granny has filled the roles of wife, mother, and homemaker during her life. Explain that Granny was also an unusual woman for her time. As they read, ask students to think about the ways that Granny may have been unusual.

Comprehension Check

Ask students to share what they underlined and wrote. **Ask:** *How does Granny's sickness affect the way she sees, hears, and feels? (She sees and hears people, but what she sees and hears is sometimes strange. The doctor seems to float, and her bones feel loose within her.) How does her sickness affect how she understands reality? (She shouts because she sees the doctor float to the ceiling.)*

Background Information

This story is set in the South in the early 1900s. Women of the time were wives, mothers, and homemakers. Their lives depended on who they married. Slavery had ended only a few decades before. Many parts of the South still had great racial inequality.

Respect your elders means "act with kindness to older people."

Comprehension Check

Reread the boxed text. Underline Granny's age. Then answer this question in the space below: What is happening to Granny?

Possible answer: Granny is sick,

and a doctor is treating her.

Because she is sick, things look

strange to her.

To Sum Up

➤ Doctor Harry has come to see Granny Weatherall, who is sick in bed.

➤ Granny feels annoyed with the doctor because he treats her like a child.

➤ Granny sees the doctor float like a balloon.

She flicked her wrist neatly out of Doctor Harry's pudgy careful fingers and pulled the sheet up to her chin. The brat ought to be in knee-breeches. Doctoring around the country with spectacles on his nose. "Get along now, take your schoolbooks and go. There's nothing wrong with me." Doctor Harry spread a warm paw like a cushion on her forehead where the forked green vein danced and made her eyelids twitch. "Now, now, be a good girl, and we'll have you up in no time."

"That's no way to speak to a woman nearly eighty years old just because she's down. I'd have you **respect your elders**, young man."

"Well, missy, excuse me." Doctor Harry patted her cheek. "But I've got to warn you, haven't I? You're a marvel,[1] but you must be careful or you're going to be good and sorry."

"Don't tell me what I'm going to be. I'm on my feet now, morally speaking. It's Cornelia. I had to go to bed to get rid of her."

Her bones felt loose, and floated around in her skin, and Doctor Harry floated like a balloon around the foot of the bed. He floated and pulled down his waistcoat[2] and swung his glasses on a cord. "Well, stay where you are, it certainly can't hurt you."

"Get along and doctor your sick," said Granny Weatherall. "Leave a well woman alone. I'll call for you when I want you . . . Where were you forty years ago when I pulled through milk-leg[3] and double pneumonia? You weren't even born. Don't let Cornelia lead you on," she shouted, because Doctor Harry appeared to float up to the ceiling and out. "I pay my own bills, and I don't throw my money away on nonsense!"

She meant to wave good-bye, but it was too much trouble. Her eyes closed of themselves, it was like a dark curtain drawn round the bed.

1. A ***marvel*** means "something wonderful."
2. A ***waistcoat*** is a vest.
3. ***Milk-leg*** is pain in the leg that can happen after childbirth.

Comprehension BLM

To support students as they read the selection, have them begin the graphic organizer on page A37.

The pillow rose and floated under her, pleasant as a hammock in a light wind. She listened to the leaves rustling outside the window. No, somebody was swishing newspapers: no, Cornelia and Doctor Harry were whispering together. She leaped broad awake, thinking they whispered in her ear.

"She was never like this, *never* like this!" "Well, what can we expect?" "Yes, eighty years old . . ."

Well, and what if she was? She still had ears. It was like Cornelia <u>to whisper round doors</u>. She always <u>kept things secret in such a public way</u>. She was always being **tactful** and <u>kind</u>. Cornelia was **dutiful**; that was the trouble with her. Dutiful and good: "So good and dutiful," said Granny, "that I'd like to spank her." She saw herself spanking Cornelia and making a fine job of it.

"What'd you say, Mother?"

Granny felt her face tying up in hard knots.

"Can't a body think, I'd like to know?"

"I thought you might want something."

"I do. I want a lot of things. First off, go away and don't whisper."

She lay and drowsed, hoping in her sleep that the children would keep out and let her rest a minute. It had been a long day. Not that she was tired. It was always pleasant to snatch a minute now and then. There was always so much to be done. Let me see: tomorrow.

Tomorrow was far away and there was nothing to trouble about. Things were finished somehow when the time came; thank God there was always a little margin over for peace: then a person could spread out the plan of life and tuck in the edges orderly. It was good to have everything clean and folded away, with the hairbrushes and tonic bottles sitting straight on the white embroidered linen; the day started without fuss and the pantry shelves laid out with rows of jelly glasses and brown jugs and white stone-china jars with blue whirligigs[4] and words painted on them: coffee, tea, sugar, ginger, cinnamon, allspice; and the bronze clock with the lion on the top nicely dusted off. The dust that lion could collect in twenty-four hours! The box in the attic with all those letters tied up, well, she'd have to go through that tomorrow. All those letters— George's letters and John's letters and her letters to them both—lying around for the children to find afterwards made her uneasy. Yes, that would be tomorrow's business. No use to let them know how silly she had been once.

Allspice

While she was rummaging round she found death in her mind and it felt clammy and unfamiliar. She had spent so much time preparing for death there was no need for bringing it up again. Let it take care of itself now. When she was sixty she had felt very old, finished, and went round making farewell trips to see her children and grandchildren, with a secret in her mind: This is the very last of your mother, children! Then she made her will and came down with a long fever. That was all just a notion

---

Comprehension Check

Reread the boxed text at the top of the page. Underline the context clues that help you understand the meaning of the vocabulary words *tactful* and *dutiful*.

Literary Element

Stream of Consciousness
Reread the paragraph that begins "Tomorrow was far away . . ." Which of Granny's thoughts comes first? Use the numbers 1–5 to put Granny's thoughts in chronological order.

3 She remembers the box with the letters.

4 She will go through the letters tomorrow.

2 It is good to have everything clean.

5 She does not want her children to find the letters.

1 Tomorrow is far away.

Vocabulary

tactful (takt' fəl) *adj.* able to say the right things and act the right way around other people
dutiful (doo' ti fəl) *adj.* careful to obey or do what one should

4. **Whirligigs** (hwur' li gigz') are circles or twists.

To Sum Up

➤ Doctor Harry and Granny's daughter Cornelia whisper to each other.

➤ Granny feels angry with her dutiful daughter.

➤ Granny does not want her children to find her old letters after she dies. The letters are from George and John.

Interactive Question-Response

Comprehension Check

Ask students to share what they underlined. Then read aloud the definitions for *tactful* and *dutiful*. **Ask:** *Isn't it usually good to be tactful and dutiful? Why does Granny get annoyed with Cornelia because she is tactful and dutiful?* (Granny wants to hear what Cornelia is saying to the doctor. Granny wishes that Cornelia would be more direct and not worry about saying and doing the right thing.)

Literary Element Stream of Consciousness

If students have difficulty responding, ask them to go through the paragraph one sentence at a time. Ask them what the thought is in each sentence. **Ask:** *What do you learn about Granny in this paragraph? How do Granny's thoughts wander to the letters?* (Granny likes to have everything clean and in its place. When she thinks of the things in her house, her thoughts wander to the box of letters.)

The Jilting of
Granny Weatherall

Interactive
Question-Response

To Sum Up

Beginning/Early Intermediate ▶ Have students work in pairs to reread all the To Sum Up statements on pages 192–194. Then have students decide together which events are from the past and which are from the present. Provide the following sentence frames for students to complete.

Some of the events from the past are _____ and _____.

(Granny's hard work over the years and her husband's death.)

Some of the events from the present are _____ and _____.

(Granny gets upset with the doctor and Cornelia because they treat her like a child, and Granny thinks about how she will go through the letters tomorrow.)

To **humor her** means "to do what Granny wants."

Jumped the track means "changed from one action to another."

An **acre** is a measure of land.

To Sum Up

➤ Granny is upset that Cornelia treats her like a child.

➤ Granny remembers all the work she has done over the years.

➤ She thinks about her husband, John, who died long ago.

194

---

like a lot of other things, but it was lucky too, for she had once for all got over the idea of dying for a long time. Now she couldn't be worried. She hoped she had better sense now. Her father had lived to be one hundred and two years old and had drunk a noggin[5] of strong hot toddy[6] on his last birthday. He told the reporters it was his daily habit, and he owed his long life to that. He had made quite a scandal and was very pleased about it. She believed she'd just plague Cornelia a little.

"Cornelia! Cornelia!" No footsteps, but a sudden hand on her cheek. "Bless you, where have you been?"

"Here, mother."

"Well, Cornelia, I want a noggin of hot toddy."

"Are you cold, darling?"

"I'm chilly, Cornelia. Lying in bed stops the circulation. I must have told you that a thousand times."

Well, she could just hear Cornelia telling her husband that Mother was getting a little childish and they'd have to **humor her.** The thing that most annoyed her was that Cornelia thought she was deaf, dumb, and blind. Little hasty glances and tiny gestures tossed around her and over her head, saying, "Don't cross her, let her have her way, she's eighty years old," and she sitting there as if she lived in a thin glass cage. Sometimes Granny almost made up her mind to pack up and move back to her own house where nobody could remind her every minute that she was old. Wait, wait, Cornelia, till your own children whisper behind your back!

In her day she had kept a better house and had got more work done. She wasn't too old yet for Lydia to be driving eighty miles for advice when one of the children **jumped the track,** and Jimmy still dropped in and talked things over: "Now, Mammy, you've a good business head, I want to know what you think of this . . . ?" Old. Cornelia couldn't change the furniture round without asking. Little things, little things! They had been so sweet when they were little. Granny wished the old days were back again with the children young and everything to be done over. It had been a hard pull, but not too much for her. When she thought of all the food she had cooked, and all the clothes she had cut and sewed, and all the gardens she had made—well, the children showed it. There they were, made out of her, and they couldn't get away from that. Sometimes she wanted to see John again and point to them and say, "Well, I didn't do so badly, did I?" But that would have to wait. That was for tomorrow. She used to think of him as a man, but now all the children were older than their father, and he would be a child beside her if she saw him now. It seemed strange and there was something wrong in the idea. Why, he couldn't possibly recognize her. She had fenced in a hundred **acres** once,

5. A **noggin** is a small cup.
6. A **hot toddy** is a drink made with liquor, hot water, sugar, and spices.

digging the **post holes** herself and clamping the wires with just a Negro boy to help. That changed a woman. John would be looking for a young woman with the peaked Spanish comb in her hair and the painted fan. Digging post holes changed a woman. Riding country roads in the winter when women had their babies was another thing: sitting up nights with sick horses and sick Negroes and sick children and hardly ever losing one. John, I hardly ever lost one of them! John would see that in a minute; that would be something he could understand, she wouldn't have to explain anything!

It made her feel like rolling up her sleeves and putting the whole place to rights again. No matter if Cornelia was determined to be everywhere at once, there were a great many things left undone on this place. She would start tomorrow and do them. It was good to be strong enough for everything, even if all you made melted and changed and slipped under your hands, so that by the time you finished you almost forgot what you were working for. What was it I set out to do? she asked herself intently, but she could not remember. A fog rose over the valley, she saw it marching across the creek swallowing the trees and moving up the hill like an army of ghosts. Soon it would be at the near edge of the orchard, and then it was time to go in and light the lamps. Come in, children, don't stay out in the night air.

Lighting the lamps had been beautiful. The children huddled up to her and breathed like little calves waiting at the bars in the twilight. Their eyes followed the match and watched the flame rise and settle in a blue curve, then they moved away from her. The lamp was lit, they didn't have to be scared and hang on to mother any more. Never, never, never more. God, for all my life I thank Thee. Without Thee, my God, I could never have done it. Hail, Mary, full of grace.[7]

Post holes are holes dug in the ground for a fence.

Background Information

The Roman Catholic religion is important in this story. Granny Weatherall has strong religious beliefs and ideas about forgiveness.

7. **Hail, Mary, full of grace** is the beginning of a Roman Catholic prayer to the Virgin Mary.

To Sum Up

➤ Granny remembers how she put up a fence with the help of a Negro (African American) boy.

➤ She thinks that she would look different to her husband now.

➤ She remembers how she cared for the sick.

REFLECT

Draw Conclusions About the Protagonist
What are three things that Granny feels proud of? Use details from the story to draw conclusions about why Granny feels proud.

1. Possible answers: Granny has survived illness; she has worked hard in her life; she kept a clean house; she

2. raised her children well even after her husband died; her children come to her for advice because she has

3. good sense; she cared for the sick; she put up a fence with only the help of a boy.

 Talk about your answer with a partner.

The Jilting of
Granny Weatherall

Interactive
Question-Response

Background Information

Read aloud the note. Ask students to think about the meaning and deeper implications of the word *forgiveness*. (not to blame someone who has done something bad or hurtful) As students read, ask them to think about this question: Does Granny forgive people who have hurt her?

Reflect

Partner Talk Have students work in pairs to answer. To help students get started: **Model** *Granny talks a lot about a clean house, so I think that a clean house is something she is proud of. When she thinks about her husband, she says, "John, I hardly ever lost one of them!" I think this means that she is proud of how she cared for sick people and kept them from dying.* Write the following sentence frame on the board to help students organize their thoughts. Tell students that they will find what comes after the word "because" in the story.

Granny is proud of _____ because _____.

Differentiated Instruction

Clarify the Text Explain to students that much of the action of this story takes place inside Granny's mind.

Beginning/Early Intermediate ➤ Her bedroom is very quiet compared to what is happening inside of her. **Ask:** *What is happening in the bedroom and what is happening in the inner world of her mind?* (Granny is lying in bed sick. Doctor Harry visits Granny, and Cornelia takes care of her. In the inner world, Granny is thinking about her past life, her children, her home, and her husband. She moves between the past and present smoothly in her mind.)

Intermediate ➤ When Granny hears Cornelia whisper, she thinks she hears leaves outside the window. **Ask:** *How are the outer and inner worlds connected in this story?* (Possible answer: Something from the outer world starts a thought or memory in Granny's mind.)

Early Advanced ➤ Ask students whether the inner world can be as active as the outer world. (Yes, because people's imaginations and memories take them to different places.) Have them consider how people use their imaginations and memories. Tell students to think about whether memory is flawed and how it might be flawed.

Interactive
Question-Response

Content Vocabulary

Read aloud the word and definition for *squeezed*. **Ask:**
*What is being squeezed out of Granny? (a memory)
Can a pillow squeeze a memory out of someone?
(No, Granny imagines this.)*

Selection Vocabulary

Read aloud the word and definition of *vanity*. **Ask:**
*Why does Granny say that she shouldn't let her
wounded vanity get the upper hand? (Her pride was
hurt when she was jilted. Her pride prevents her from
forgetting about the jilting.)*

Comprehension Check

Ask students to share what they underlined. **Ask:**
*Why do you think her first name has not been used
earlier? Why didn't the author call the story "The Jilting
of Ellen Weatherall"? (Her role as a grandmother
is very important. Granny is also a funny or homey
name. Ellen might sound more romantic.) Why do
you think she still remembers being jilted? Why is the
memory still painful? (Perhaps George was the great
love of her life. Perhaps she sees her marriage to John
and her family as a reaction to the jilting.) Now why
do you think she doesn't want her children to find
George's letters? (She is ashamed.)*

squeezed (skwēzd) *v.* pressed together

Comprehension Check
Reread the boxed text. Underline Granny's first name. What important event is Granny remembering now? Underline details that tell you about this important event.

Get the upper hand means "win."

To Sum Up

➤ Granny remembers when she was jilted by George on her wedding day sixty years ago.

➤ The memory is painful. She wishes she could stop remembering it.

➤ She thinks someone else is in the room. It is Cornelia, who washes her face.

I want you to pick all the fruit this year and see that nothing is wasted. There's always someone who can use it. Don't let good things rot for want of using. You waste life when you waste good food. Don't let things get lost. It's bitter to lose things. Now, don't let me get to thinking, not when I am tired and taking a little nap before supper…

The pillow rose about her shoulders and pressed against her heart and the memory was being <u>squeezed</u> out of it: oh, push down the pillow, somebody; it would smother her if she tried to hold it. Such a fresh breeze blowing and such a green day with no threats in it. But he had not come, just the same. <u>What does a woman do when she has put on the white veil and set out the white cake for a man and he doesn't come?</u> She tried to remember. No, I swear he never harmed me but in that . . . and what if he did? There was the day, the day, but a whirl of dark smoke rose and covered it, crept up and over into the bright field where everything was planted so carefully in orderly rows. That was hell, she knew hell when she saw it. For sixty years she had prayed against remembering him and against losing her soul in the deep pit of hell, and now the two things were mingled in one, and <u>the thought of him was a smoky cloud from hell</u> that moved and crept in her head when she had just got rid of Doctor Harry and was trying to rest a minute. Wounded **vanity,** <u>Ellen</u>, said a sharp voice in the top of her mind. Don't let your wounded vanity <u>get the upper hand</u> of you. <u>Plenty of girls get **jilted.**</u> <u>You were jilted, weren't you?</u> Then stand up to it. Her eyelids wavered and let in streamers of blue-gray light like tissue paper over her eyes. She must get up and pull the shades down or she'd never sleep. She was in bed again and the shades were not down. How could that happen? Better turn over, hide from the light; sleeping in the light gave you nightmares. "Mother, how do you feel now?" and a stinging wetness on her forehead. But I don't like having my face washed in cold water!

Hapsy? George? Lydia? Jimmy? No, Cornelia, and her features were swollen and full of little puddles. "They're coming, darling, they'll all be here soon." Go wash your face, child, you look funny.

Instead of obeying, Cornelia knelt down and put her head on the pillow. She seemed to be talking but there was no sound. "Well, are you tongue-tied? Whose birthday is it? Are you going to give a party?"

Cornelia's mouth moved urgently in strange shapes. "Don't do that, you bother me, daughter."

"Oh, no, Mother. Oh, no . . ."

Nonsense. It was strange about children. They disputed your every word. "No what, Cornelia?"

"Here's Doctor Harry."

"I won't see that boy again. He just left five minutes ago."

"That was this morning, Mother. It's night now. Here's the nurse."

Vocabulary

vanity (van′ i tē) *n.* too much pride
jilted (jilt′ id) *v.* left or rejected a sweetheart

Fluency

Expression and Intonation: Punctuation

Intermediate/Early Advanced Tell students that they will be doing a choral reading of the boxed text on page 196. Remind students to use correct intonation when they come to a question mark. Model the fluency skill as you read the text at a moderate tempo. Then have one student read a sentence. Have another student join in, and a third, and so on. When students reach the end of the passage, have pairs of students reread to each other. To assess individual fluency, use the Oral Reading Guidelines on page T16.

Beginning/Early Intermediate Have these students choral read only up to "Then stand up to it." Before they begin, model the pronunciation of the text. Then have students practice reading the paragraph in pairs before the choral reading.

"This is Doctor Harry, Mrs. Weatherall. I never saw you look so young and happy!"

"Ah, I'll never be young again—but I'd be happy if they'd let me lie in peace and get rested."

She thought she spoke up loudly, but no one answered. A warm weight on her forehead, a warm bracelet on her wrist and a breeze went on whispering, trying to tell her something. A shuffle of leaves in the everlasting hand of God, He blew on them and they danced and rattled. "Mother, don't mind, we're going to give you a little hypodermic." "Look here, daughter, how do ants get in this bed? I saw sugar ants yesterday." Did you send for Hapsy too?

It was Hapsy she really wanted. She had to go a long way back through a great many rooms to find Hapsy standing with a baby on her arm. She seemed to herself to be Hapsy also, and the baby on Hapsy's arm was Hapsy and himself and herself, all at once, and there was no surprise in the meeting. Then Hapsy melted from within and turned <u>flimsy</u> as gray gauze and the baby was a gauzy shadow, and Hapsy came up close and said, "I thought you'd never come," and looked at her very searchingly and said, "You haven't changed a bit!" They leaned forward to kiss, when Cornelia began whispering from a long way off, "Oh, is there anything you want to tell me? Is there anything I can do for you?"

Yes, she had changed her mind after sixty years and she would like to see George. I want you to find George. Find him and be sure to tell him I forgot him. I want him to know I had my husband just the same, and my children and my house, like any other woman. A good house too and a good husband that I loved and fine children out of him. Better than I hoped for, even. Tell him I was given back everything he took away, and more. Oh, no, O God, no, there was something else besides the house and the man and the children. Oh, surely they were not all? What was it? Something not given back . . . Her breath crowded down under her ribs and grew into a monstrous frightening shape with cutting edges; it bored[8] up into her head, and the <u>agony</u> was unbelievable. Yes, John, get the doctor now, no more talk, my time has come.

When this one was born it should be the last. The last. It should have been born first, for it was the one she had truly wanted. Everything came in good time. Nothing left out, left over. She was strong, in three days she would be as well as ever. Better. A woman needed milk in her to have her full health.

"Mother, do you hear me?"

"I've been telling you—"

"Mother, Father Connolly's here."

"I went to Holy Communion only last week. Tell him I'm not so sinful as all that."

---

8. Here, **bored** means "made a hole."

flimsy (flim' zē) *adj.* without strength

agony (ag' ə nē) *n.* great pain of mind or body

Literary Element

Stream of Consciousness
Reread the boxed text on this page. How does Granny's mind wander? Use the numbers 1–5 to arrange Granny's thoughts in the chronological order.

<u>4</u> She got back everything George took away.

<u>1</u> She remembers Hapsy with a baby.

<u>5</u> One thing was not given back.

<u>3</u> Granny wants to tell George that she has forgotten him.

<u>2</u> Hapsy says, "I thought you'd never come."

To Sum Up

➤ Granny remembers Hapsy with a baby, and she remembers herself with a baby.

➤ She wants Cornelia to find George and tell him that she forgot him. But she secretly thinks about George all the time.

➤ She remembers her last child. Cornelia tells her that Father Connolly has come.

Interactive Question-Response

Content Vocabulary

Have a student read aloud the word and definition of *flimsy*. Explain that *gauze* means a "very thin cloth." Gauze can be so thin that you can see through it. Use the edge of a dress or jacket to demonstrate that gauze is flimsy fabric. **Ask:** *Why is gauze flimsy? (It is thin and weak. You can wave it about and see through it.) Why does Hapsy become as "flimsy as gray gauze"? (Granny's vision of Hapsy with a baby fades as another one takes its place.)*

Content Vocabulary

Have a student read the sentence with the Content Vocabulary word *agony*. **Ask:** *Why does Granny feel agony at this moment? (She is afraid that something was not given back after she was jilted.) Does she feel agony in her mind or body? (Both. Her agony is in her mind, but she imagines a monstrous shape in her body, which causes her pain in her head.)*

Literary Element Stream of Consciousness

If students have difficulty responding, ask them to go through the text one sentence at a time. Ask them what thought is in each sentence. **Ask:** *Who is Hapsy? How does Granny remember her? (Hapsy may have been a child that she loved very much, but this is never stated for certain. Granny remembers Hapsy with a baby. She also joins with her memory of Hapsy so that she becomes the woman who holds Hapsy the baby.)*

Interactive Question-Response

To Sum Up

Beginning/Early Intermediate ▶ Have students work in pairs to reread all the To Sum Up statements on pages 195–198. Then have students write a list of three details about the jilting. Write the following list on the board.

Details about the jilting:

1.

2.

3.

(It happened sixty years ago. Ellen faced the priest alone. The wedding cake was thrown out. She had started to fall, but someone caught her. Her pride was hurt.)

A *teething baby* cries because his or her teeth are coming in.

Vocabulary

piety (pī a tē) *n.* religious devotion; goodness

9. A *confessional* is a place in a Catholic church where a person tells sins to a priest.
10. *Assigns* are people who are given property.
11. *Frippery* is things put out for show.
12. A *nimbus* is a ring of light.

To Sum Up

➤ Granny remembers when she was jilted and the wedding cake was thrown out.

➤ She remembers she had begun to fall and someone caught her.

➤ She remembers when the children woke up with nightmares. She thinks she sees Hapsy next to her bed.

198

"Father just wants to speak to you."

He could speak as much as he pleased. It was like him to drop in and inquire about her soul as if it were a **teething baby,** and then stay on for a cup of tea and a round of cards and gossip. He always had a funny story of some sort, usually about an Irishman who made his little mistakes and confessed them, and the point lay in some absurd thing he would blurt out in the confessional[9] showing his struggles between native **piety** and original sin. Granny felt easy about her soul. Cornelia, where are your manners? Give Father Connolly a chair. She had her secret comfortable understanding with a few favorite saints who cleared a straight road to God for her. All as surely signed and sealed as the papers for the new Forty Acres. For ever . . . heirs and assigns[10] forever. Since the day the wedding cake was not cut, but thrown out and wasted. The whole bottom dropped out of the world, and there she was, blind and sweating, with nothing under her feet and the walls falling away. His hand had caught her under the breast, she had not fallen; there was the freshly polished floor with the green rug on it, just as before. He had cursed like a sailor's parrot and said, "I'll kill him for you." "Don't lay a hand on him, for my sake leave something to God." "Now, Ellen, you must believe what I tell you . . ."

So there was nothing, nothing to worry about any more, except sometimes in the night one of the children screamed in a nightmare, and they both hustled out shaking and hunting for the matches and calling, "There, wait a minute, here we are!" John, get the doctor now, Hapsy's time has come. But there was Hapsy standing by the bed in a white cap. "Cornelia, tell Hapsy to take off her cap. I can't see her plain."

Her eyes opened very wide and the room stood out like a picture she had seen somewhere. Dark colors with the shadows rising towards the ceiling in long angles. The tall black dresser gleamed with nothing on it but John's picture, enlarged from a little one, with John's eyes very black when they should have been blue. You never saw him, so how do you know how he looked? But the man insisted the copy was perfect, it was very rich and handsome. For a picture, yes, but it's not my husband. The table by the bed had a linen cover and a candle and a crucifix. The light was blue from Cornelia's silk lampshades. No sort of light at all, just frippery.[11] You had to live forty years with kerosene lamps to appreciate honest electricity. She felt very strong and she saw Doctor Harry with a rosy nimbus[12] around him.

"You look like a saint, Doctor Harry, and I vow that's as near as you'll ever come to it."

"She's saying something."

"I heard you, Cornelia. What's all this carrying-on?"

"Father Connolly's saying—"

Cornelia's voice staggered and bumped like a cart in a bad road. It rounded corners and turned back again and arrived nowhere. Granny

---

Word Study

Base Words

Point out the word *comfortable* in the highlighted passage. Explain to students that some words have several different forms. Write the base word *comfort* on the board, then write the following sentence: *When you are experiencing comfort, then you feel physically or emotionally at ease.*

Write the derivative *comfortable* on the board. Explain that the suffix *-able* means "able to be." Someone who is comfortable is able to feel comfort. Write the derivative *uncomfortable* on the board. Explain that the prefix *un-* means "not." Someone who is uncomfortable is not experiencing comfort.

Have students practice identifying additional base words and their derivatives by completing the activity on page A38.

stepped up in the **cart** very lightly and reached for the reins, but a man sat beside her, and she knew him by his hands, driving the cart. She did not look in his face, for she knew without seeing, but looked instead down the road where the trees leaned over and bowed to each other and a thousand birds were singing a Mass. She felt like singing too, but she put her hand in the bosom of her dress and pulled out a rosary, and Father Connolly murmured Latin in a very solemn voice and tickled her feet. [13] My God, will you stop that nonsense? I'm a married woman. What if he did run away and leave me to face the priest by myself? I found another a whole world better. I wouldn't have exchanged my husband for anybody except St. Michael [14] himself, and you may tell him that for me, with a thank you into the bargain.

Light flashed on her closed eyelids, and a deep roaring shook her. Cornelia, is that lightning? I hear thunder. There's going to be a storm. Close all the windows. Call the children in . . . "Mother, here we are, all of us." "Is that you, Hapsy?" "Oh, no, I'm Lydia. We drove as fast as we could." Their faces drifted above her, drifted away. The rosary fell out of her hands and Lydia put it back. Jimmy tried to help, their hands fumbled together, and Granny closed two fingers round Jimmy's thumb. Beads wouldn't do, it must be something alive. She was so amazed her thoughts ran round and round. So, my dear Lord, this is my death and I wasn't even thinking about it. My children have come to see me die. But I can't, it's not time. Oh, I always hated surprises. I wanted to give Cornelia the amethyst [15] set—Cornelia, you're to have the amethyst set, but Hapsy's to wear it when she wants, and, Doctor Harry, do shut up. Nobody sent for you. Oh, my dear Lord, do wait a minute. I meant to do something about the Forty Acres, Jimmy doesn't need it and Lydia will later on, with that worthless husband of hers. I meant to finish the altar cloth and send six bottles of wine to Sister Borgia for her dyspepsia. [16] I want to send six bottles of wine to Sister Borgia, Father Connolly, now don't let me forget.

REFLECT

Draw Conclusions About the Protagonist
Draw conclusions about Granny's feelings toward each of the following characters. Write your answers below.

Hapsy: Possible answer: Hapsy may have been Granny's
child who died. Granny misses her very much.

George: Possible answer: George jilted Granny sixty years
ago. Granny is still angry with him.

Talk about your answer with a partner.

A **cart** has two wheels and is pulled by a horse.

Literary Element

Stream of Consciousness
Reread the paragraph that begins "Cornelia's voice staggered" (it starts at the bottom of page 198). How does Granny's mind wander to the subject of the jilting? Use the numbers 1–5 to arrange Granny's thoughts in the correct order.

__1__ Cornelia's voice staggers like a cart.

__5__ Granny remembers how she faced the priest alone.

__3__ Father Connolly speaks Latin.

__4__ Granny thinks the priest is tickling her feet.

__2__ Granny is driving a cart with a man beside her.

13. The priest is giving the Sacrament of the Sick, which is a ritual in the Roman Catholic Church. In this sacrament, the priest says prayers and puts oil on many parts of a person's body.
14. **St. Michael** is an archangel, often shown as a handsome knight.
15. **Amethyst** (am' a thist) is a purple stone used in jewelry.
16. **Dyspepsia** is an upset stomach.

To Sum Up

➤ Granny sees light flash before her eyes.
➤ She thinks that Hapsy has come. Her children Lydia and Jimmy are there instead.
➤ She understands that she is dying.

Interactive Question-Response

Literary Element Stream of Consciousness

If students have difficulty responding, ask them to go through the paragraphs one sentence at a time. Ask them what thought is in each sentence. **Ask:** *Who do you think is the man in the cart? What do the birds sound like they are singing? (The man could be George or it could be death. The birds sound like they are singing a Mass, which reminds Granny of the priest.)*

Reflect

Partner Talk Have students work in pairs to answer. Have students begin by thinking about who each character is. Then: **Model** *Granny says that she wants to see Hapsy and she asks about her a lot. So Hapsy is someone that she loves and cares about.* Write the following sentence frame on the board to help students organize their thoughts.

Granny feels _____ toward Hapsy because _____.

Interactive
Question-Response

Content Vocabulary

Have a student read aloud the word and definition of *dwindled*. **Ask:** *What seems to be dwindling in this last paragraph? (The light from the lamp.) What is really dwindling? (Granny's life, because she is dying.) What does the light symbolize? (The light symbolizes her consciousness.)*

Literary Element Stream of Consciousness

If students have difficulty responding, have them go through the second-to-last paragraph one sentence at a time. Ask them what thought follows the sentences about the light. **Ask:** *Why is Granny unhappy in the last paragraph? Why does Granny say that she'll "never forgive it"? (Granny wants a sign from God that she will be saved. When there is no sign, it makes her think of the time she was jilted. Granny feels like God has jilted her too.)*

Reflect

Partner Talk To expand students' understanding, explain that in the Christian Bible, Christ is referred to as a bridegroom, and that marriage is a metaphor used to describe the spiritual relationship between Christ and his followers. Tell students that some Christians believe that Christ escorts the recently deceased into the afterlife. Porter uses this belief in an ironic way. At the end, Granny is jilted a second time.

dwindled (dwind' əld) *v.* became smaller

 Literary Element

Stream of Consciousness Reread the last two paragraphs. Underline the sentence that shows what Granny thinks about as the light dwindles.

Cornelia's voice made short turns and tilted over and crashed. "Oh, Mother, oh, Mother, oh, Mother . . ."

"I'm not going, Cornelia. I'm taken by surprise. I can't go."

You'll see Hapsy again. What about her? "I thought you'd never come." Granny made a long journey outward, looking for Hapsy. What if I don't find her? What then? Her heart sank down and down, there was no bottom to death, she couldn't come to the end of it. The blue light from Cornelia's lampshade drew into a tiny point in the center of her brain, it flickered and winked like an eye, quietly it fluttered and <u>dwindled</u>. Granny lay curled down within herself, amazed and watchful, staring at the point of light that was herself; her body was now only a deeper mass of shadow in an endless darkness and this darkness would curl round the light and swallow it up. <u>God, give a sign!</u>

For the second time there was no sign. <u>Again no bridegroom and the priest in the house. She could not remember any other sorrow because this grief wiped them all away.</u> Oh, no, there's nothing more cruel than this—I'll never forgive it. She stretched herself with a deep breath and blew out the light.

To Sum Up

➤ Cornelia cries. Granny thinks that she will see Hapsy again.

➤ Granny sees a light dwindle, and she asks for a sign from God.

➤ Just as it happened when she was jilted, she receives no sign from God. Granny blows out the light.

200

REFLECT

Draw Conclusions About the Protagonist
What line in the last paragraph lets you know that Granny was jilted again?

For the second time there was no sign.

_____

_____

 Talk about your answer with a partner.

Oral Assessment

Provide the following prompts to one student at a time. Observe students' responses. See the Oral Assessment Rubric on page T17 to determine students' levels of language output.

1. Tell me about Granny's children.

2. What happened to Granny sixty years ago?

3. How does she feel about it now?

4. Which person does Granny most want to see?

5. What happens at the end of the story?

The *Jilting* of Granny Weatherall

Vocabulary Check

A. Label each picture with the correct word.

agony	dwindled	flimsy	squeezed

1. dwindled

2. squeezed

3. flimsy

4. agony

B. Answer yes or no to each question below.

yes	5. If you were **jilted**, would you feel **agony**?
yes	6. Could someone show **piety** and **vanity** at the same time?
no	7. Would a **tactful** person make fun of someone whose money had **dwindled**?
yes	8. If you were making orange juice, would you need to **squeeze** oranges?
yes	9. Would a **dutiful** person help someone in need?

C. Complete each sentence.

10. Someone who shows **piety** will probably Possible answer: pray often .

11. If a visitor felt uncomfortable, a **tactful** person would Possible answer: say something nice to him or her .

12. If I were **jilted**, I would probably feel Possible answer: hurt and angry .

13. A **dutiful** father would Possible answer: help his kids with their homework .

14. The man's **vanity** appeared when he Possible answer: looked at himself in the mirror for 10 minutes .

Vocabulary Check

B. Intermediate

Read the questions aloud. After each question, ask students to explain their answers. For example, **Ask:** *Why would you feel agony if you had been jilted? Would the agony be in your mind or your body? (I would feel very hurt. The pain would be in the mind and not the body.) How would a tactful person make other people feel? (A tactful person speaks well with other people, so he or she would make others feel good.)*

Academic Vocabulary

Write the following sentence on the board: *Granny Weatherall's **dominant** thoughts are of her children and the man who jilted her.*

Inform students that *dominant* is an academic word. It means "main" or "foremost." Granny's main thoughts are of her children and the man who jilted her.

Have students discuss the following questions.

- **If you are caught outside in a rainstorm, what is your dominant concern?**

- **If there's a big dance coming up in a few weeks, what might be your dominant thoughts?**

Grammar Link

BLM

Sentence Fragments

Prepare students to complete the activity on page A39. Read the grammar instruction with students, and complete the first item with them to help them get started.

Comprehension Check

C. Early Advanced

If students have trouble with the first question, encourage them to look at the text and find examples of times when Granny thinks in the past or present. Ask them to think about how the characters, settings, and language differ between the past and the present. If students have trouble with the second question, ask them to think about what they learned about Granny through stream of consciousness. **Ask:** *If you were on your deathbed like Granny, how might you think?* These thoughts can help them answer the question.

After Reading

Have students complete the after reading activity on page 331.

Comprehension Check

A. Complete these sentences about "The Jilting of Granny Weatherall."

1. Granny feels <u>Possible answers: annoyed;</u> with Doctor Harry because <u>he treats her like a child</u>.

2. Granny feels <u>Possible answers: irritated;</u> with Cornelia because <u>she is so tactful</u>

3. The event that Granny recalls with anger and sadness is <u>the time when she was jilted by George</u>.

4. The person that Granny wishes to see is <u>Hapsy</u>

B. Complete the sentences below about Granny's stream of thoughts and memories in "The Jilting of Granny Weatherall."

5. Who is Hapsy? Hapsy is <u>probably Granny's daughter who died</u>.

6. When Granny sees Hapsy in her mind, Hapsy holds <u>a baby</u>.

7. When the priest comes, Granny remembers the day when <u>she was jilted and the wedding cake was thrown away</u>

8. Granny would like George to know that <u>she has forgotten him</u>

C. Answer these questions about stream of consciousness in "The Jilting of Granny Weatherall."

9. What kind of clues help the reader tell the difference between past and present?

   <u>Possible answer: When Granny thinks about the past, she and other people around her are younger.</u>

   <u>Her language gives a clue to the past, with phrases like "in her day," or "when she was sixty."</u>

   <u>When Granny thinks in the present, she often speaks with or reacts to other characters who are in</u>

   <u>the room with her.</u>

10. Is stream of consciousness a good way to tell the story of someone's death? Why or why not?

   <u>Possible answer: Yes, because a person would probably think back on her life before she died.</u>

   <u>Stream of consciousness helps the reader understand a person's life from her point of view.</u>

For more practice, see page 331. ➡

Writing Link

Character Sketch

Point out that while Granny is the central character, readers have also learned quite a bit about her daughter, Cornelia. Note, for example, that Cornelia obviously loves her mother, but must have noticed how strongly her mother preferred Hapsy. Have students create a web diagram like the one they used to draw conclusions about Granny, and fill it in with what they know about Cornelia. Then have students use the information on their webs to create a character sketch of Cornelia. Have students read their character sketches in small groups, then to discuss and explain their differing interpretations.

Learning Objectives

For pages 203–212, 332–333

In studying this text, you will focus on the following objectives:

Literary Study: Analyzing juxtaposition.

Reading: Analyzing concrete details.

WHEN THE NEGRO WAS IN VOGUE

by Langston Hughes

Oral Language

Build Background

Read the title and author. Explain that students will read "When the Negro Was in Vogue" by Langston Hughes, an African American author who lived in the early 1900s. **Ask:**

- **What do you think the phrase** *in vogue* **means?** *(in style, in fashion, popular)*

- *Negro* was once a common word for African American. How might a group of people be in vogue or in style? *(maybe something like music or art made African Americans stylish or fashionable)*

Talk About the Autobiography

Explain that this autobiography is about the Harlem Renaissance in the 1920s. Many African American artists and writers were creating, performing, and writing during this time.

Beginning/Early Intermediate Remind students about the meaning of an autobiography. Write this sentence frame on the board and ask students to complete it.

An author writes an autobiography about _____. *(himself or herself; his or her life)*

Lesson at a Glance

Oral Language
- Build Background
- Talk About the Autobiography

Vocabulary
- Selection Vocabulary
- Content Vocabulary
- Academic Vocabulary

Literary Element
- Juxtaposition

Reading Strategy
- Analyze Concrete Details

Writing Link
- Blog

Fluency
- Pacing: Phrasing

Comprehension
- BLM

Grammar Link
- Comparative Forms of Adjectives: –er and more BLM

Technology
- Student Works™ Plus
- Teacher Works™ Plus
- Listening Library Audio CD
- Classroom Presentation Toolkit
- Glencoe Visual Vocabulary
- Skill Level Up!™ A Skill-Based Language Arts Game

Interactive Question-Response

Connect to the Autobiography

Read aloud Connect to the Autobiography. Reproduce the sentence frame on the board. **Model** *For a place to be the center of the action, people have to come together and interact with each other. A place that is the center of the action will have many activities or things to do.* Model writing your response on the board, and have volunteers suggest other responses. Then have individuals fill in their own sentences.

Literary Element
Juxtaposition

Read aloud the Literary Element. Explain that juxtaposition happens when different things are placed close together within the same line, sentence, or paragraph. On the board, draw two figures that are side by side. Ask students to think of some examples of different types of people who might be juxtaposed. To help students get started: **Model** *Some examples are a young person and an old person, a lazy person and a hard worker, or a person from a small town and a person from a big city.* Remind students that things, events, ideas, and places can also be juxtaposed.

Reading Strategy   Analyze
Concrete Details

Read aloud the Reading Strategy. Tell students that when they analyze concrete details, they will be able to imagine more easily the times and places they read about. Read aloud an example from the text in which Hughes describes the parties that were held. **Model** *And where the awful bootleg whiskey and good fried fish or steaming chitterling were sold at very low prices. And the dancing and singing and impromptu entertaining went on until dawn came in at the windows."* Ask students to state some concrete details from the passage as you read it a second time. **Ask:** *Which senses do these details appeal to? (sight, hearing, touch, taste, smell)*

WHEN THE NEGRO WAS IN VOGUE

Connect to the Autobiography

Do you like to be where the action is? When Langston Hughes moved to Harlem, he put himself in the center of the art movement. He was in the right place at the right time.

How does a place become the "right place at the right time"? Do people and places of importance usually last a long time? Why or why not? Talk about your answers with a partner. Then, think of a place that is at the center of the action and complete the sentence below.

A place at the center of the action is	Possible answer: the city's downtown
because	Possible answers: there are restaurants to try and theatres to attend;
it is crowded with people every weekend	

Literary Element   Juxtaposition

Juxtaposition is the placing of two or more different things side by side or very close together. Juxtaposition is often used

- to compare or contrast the things
- to cause an emotional response in the reader

In this selection, Hughes juxtaposes the African Americans who live in Harlem with the "Nordics," or white tourists. As you read, ask yourself, What does this juxtaposition tell me about each group?

Reading Strategy   Analyze Concrete Details

Good writers use **concrete**, or specific, **details** to help readers imagine the people and places that they describe. Writers use details that relate to the following senses:

- sight
- sound
- smell
- taste
- touch

Hughes uses concrete details to describe the interesting people and events of Harlem in the 1920s. As you read, ask yourself, What details help me imagine this time and place?

Selection Vocabulary

scintillating (sin′ tə lā′ ting) *adj.* lively; sparkling; exciting (p. 206)
*People listened to Lee's **scintillating** talk at the party.*

vogue (vōg) *n.* fashion; style (p. 206)
*The color black is always in **vogue**.*

patronage (pā′ trə nij) *n.* business; customers (p. 207)
*The shop owner thanked the young couple for their **patronage**.*
➤ Cognate (Spanish) **patrocinio**

millennium (mi le′ nē əm) *n.* a time of great happiness, peace, or good fortune (p. 209)
*When many new businesses opened, the small town enjoyed a **millennium**.*
➤ Cognate (Spanish) **milenio**

impromptu (im′ promp′ tōō) *adj.* without time to prepare (p. 210)
*Jane's uncle made her laugh with his **impromptu** jokes.*
➤ Cognate (Spanish) **improvisado**

Content Vocabulary

orchestra (ôr′ kis trə) *n.* a large group of people playing musical instruments together (p. 206)
*Matt plays the violin in the city **orchestra**.*
➤ Cognate (Spanish) **orquesta**

entertainment (en′ tər tān′ mənt) *n.* an activity that is fun and enjoyable (p. 208)
*The crowd enjoyed the musical **entertainment**.*
➤ Cognate (Spanish) **entretenimiento**

enthusiastic (en thōō′ zē as′ tik) *adj.* full of excitement and interest (p. 209)
*My father was **enthusiastic** while he watched the soccer game.*
➤ Cognate (Spanish) **entusiasta**

refreshments (ri fresh′ mənts) *n.* food or drink, such as snacks or a light meal (p. 210)
*Mona served **refreshments** at her birthday party.*
➤ Cognate (Spanish) **refresco**

For more practice, see page 332. ➡

Vocabulary Routine

To introduce the vocabulary, read aloud the words and definitions in the student book and have students repeat after you. Discuss how the pictures illustrate the words or sentences. Then follow the vocabulary routine below.

Content Vocabulary

<u>Define:</u> An **orchestra** is a group of people who play musical instruments together. <u>Example:</u> *The orchestra played lively music on the Fourth of July.* <u>Ask:</u> What are some musical instruments that might be played in an *orchestra*? DESCRIPTION

An **entertainment** is something fun to see or do. *The comedy show was an enjoyable entertainment.* What kinds of *entertainment* do you like? EXAMPLE

Someone who is **enthusiastic** acts very excited and interested in something. *My sister is enthusiastic about her part in the school play.* How would an *enthusiastic* person act? EXPLANATION

Refreshments are light foods and drinks. *When I visited my aunt yesterday, she served refreshments.* How are *refreshments* like *meals*? How are they different? COMPARE AND CONTRAST

Vocabulary Practice Have students complete the vocabulary practice activity on page 332.

Selection Vocabulary

<u>Define:</u> Something that is **scintillating** is sparkling or brilliant. <u>Example:</u> *The band gave a scintillating performance.* <u>Ask:</u> Who would you describe as a *scintillating* speaker? EXAMPLE

Something in **vogue** is popular or in fashion. *Flared pants are suddenly in vogue this year.* What's currently in *vogue* around our school? EXAMPLE

Patronage refers to the business a store or other commercial operation attracts. *The bakery's patronage increased when it began to open earlier.* How might a nightclub increase its *patronage*? EXPLANATION

An **influx** is a large flow or flood of something. *There was an influx of entries to the contest.* How would you react to an *influx* of responses to an ad you placed? DESCRIPTION

A **millennium** is a time of great happiness. *Our wonderful summer felt like a millennium.* What type of period would be the opposite of a *millennium*? ANTONYM

WHEN THE NEGRO WAS IN VOGUE

Interactive Question-Response

Background Information

Read aloud the note. Explain that even though some African Americans were doing great things in the arts at this time, they were still treated unfairly by white people. Ask students to think about how Hughes writes about this unfairness as they read his autobiography.

Content Vocabulary

Read aloud the beginning of the second paragraph. **Ask:** *What kind of music did the orchestra play? (Danceable and singable tunes; the music must have been fun, lively, and upbeat.) What show was the orchestra a part of? (Shuffle Along)* Explain to students that this show was important to the Harlem Renaissance because it was one of the first big shows to draw attention to African American entertainment.

---

orchestra (ôr′ kis trə) *n.* a large group of people playing musical instruments together

Skyrocketed means "rose very fast."

To Sum Up

➤ In the 1920s, the musical *Shuffle Along* helped to make African American entertainment popular.

➤ Hughes enjoyed many shows, but he remembers *Shuffle Along* the best.

➤ Other African American works became popular too, such as books, sculpture, music, and dancing.

The 1920's were the years of Manhattan's black Renaissance. It began with *Shuffle Along*, *Running Wild*, and the Charleston.[1] Perhaps some people would say even with *The Emperor Jones*, Charles Gilpin, and the tom-toms at the Provincetown. But certainly it was the musical revue, *Shuffle Along*, that gave a **scintillating** send-off to that Negro **vogue** in Manhattan, which reached its peak just before the crash of 1929, the crash that sent Negroes, white folks, and all rolling down the hill toward the Works Progress Administration.[2]

Shuffle Along was a honey of a show. Swift, bright, funny, rollicking, and gay, with a dozen danceable, singable tunes. Besides, look who were in it: The now famous choir director, Hall Johnson, and the composer, William Grant Still, were a part of the orchestra. Eubie Blake and Noble Sissle wrote the music and played and acted in the show. Miller and Lyles were the comics. Florence Mills **skyrocketed** to fame in the second act. Trixie Smith sang "He May Be Your Man But He Comes to See Me Sometimes." And Caterina Jarboro, now a European prima donna,[3] and the internationally celebrated Josephine Baker were merely in the chorus. Everybody was in the audience—including me. People came back to see it innumerable times. It was always packed.

To see *Shuffle Along* was the main reason I wanted to go to Columbia. When I saw it, I was thrilled and delighted. From then on I was in the gallery of the Cort Theatre every time I got a chance. That year, too, I saw Katharine Cornell in *A Bill of Divorcement*, Margaret Wycherly in *The Verge*, Maugham's *The Circle* with Mrs. Leslie Carter, and the Theatre Guild production of Kaiser's *From Morn Till Midnight*. But I remember *Shuffle Along* best of all. It gave just the proper push—a pre-Charleston kick—to that Negro vogue of the 20's, that spread to books, African sculpture, music, and dancing.

Vocabulary

scintillating (sin′ tə lā′ ting) *adj.* lively; sparkling; exciting
vogue (vōg) *n.* fashion; style

1. The **Charleston** is a lively dance to jazz music. The Lindy Hop and the black-bottom, talked about later, are similar dances.
2. The **Works Progress Administration** was formed by the government in 1935 to give jobs to out-of-work people. Many people lost their jobs after the stock market crashed in 1929.
3. A **prima donna** (prē′ mə don′ə) is a lead or featured woman singer.

Comprehension

To support students as they read the selection, have them begin the graphic organizer on page A40.

Put down the 1920's for the rise of Roland Hayes, who packed Carnegie Hall, the rise of Paul Robeson in New York and London, of Florence Mills over two continents, of Rose McClendon in Broadway parts that never measured up to her, the booming voice of Bessie Smith and the low moan of Clara on thousands of records, and the rise of that grand comedienne of song, Ethel Waters, singing: "Charlie's elected now! He's in right for sure!" Put down the 1920's for Louis Armstrong and Gladys Bentley and Josephine Baker.

White people began to come to Harlem in droves.[4] For several years they packed the expensive Cotton Club on Lenox Avenue. But I was never there, because the Cotton Club was a Jim Crow[5] club for gangsters and monied whites. They were not cordial[6] to Negro patronage, unless you were a celebrity like Bojangles. So Harlem Negroes did not like the Cotton Club and never appreciated its Jim Crow policy in the very heart of their dark community. Nor did ordinary Negroes like the growing influx of whites toward Harlem after sundown, flooding the little cabarets and bars where formerly only colored people laughed and sang, and where now the strangers were given the best ringside tables to sit and stare at the Negro customers—like amusing animals in a zoo.

The Negroes said: "We can't go downtown and sit and stare at you in your clubs. You won't even let us in your clubs." But they didn't say it out loud—for Negroes are practically never rude to white people. So thousands of whites came to Harlem night after night, thinking the Negroes loved to have them there, and firmly believing that all Harlemites left their houses at sundown to sing and dance in cabarets, because most of the whites saw nothing but the cabarets, not the houses.

Some of the owners of Harlem clubs, delighted at the flood of white patronage, made the grievous error of barring their own race, after the manner of the famous Cotton Club. But most of these quickly lost business and folded up, because they failed to realize that a large part of the Harlem attraction for downtown New Yorkers lay in simply watching the colored customers amuse themselves. And the smaller clubs, of course, had no big floor shows or a name band like the Cotton Club, where Duke Ellington usually held forth, so, without black patronage, they were not amusing at all.

Some of the small clubs, however, had people like Gladys Bentley, who was something worth discovering in those days, before she got famous, acquired an accompanist, specially written material, and conscious vulgarity. But for two or three amazing years, Miss Bentley sat, and played a big piano all night long, literally all night, without stopping—singing songs like "The St. James Infirmary," from ten in the evening until dawn, with scarcely a break between the notes, sliding from one song to another, with a powerful and continuous underbeat of jungle rhythm. Miss Bentley was an amazing exhibition of musical energy—a

Vocabulary

patronage (păˈ trə nij) n. business; customers

4. **Droves** are large crowds.
5. **Jim Crow** refers to the separation and unfair treatment of African Americans.
6. **Cordial** (kôrˈ jəl) means "warm and friendly."

An *influx* is a constant flow.

A *cabaret* (kabˈ ə räˈ) is a restaurant that has dancing and entertainment.

Comprehension Check

Reread the boxed text. Underline the words that mention the Jim Crow policy, or rule, of places like the Cotton Club.

To Sum Up

➤ Many white people came to Harlem clubs to watch African American entertainment.

➤ African Americans knew that they could not enter clubs for white people in other parts of the city.

➤ Some Harlem club owners stopped letting African Americans enter, but these clubs soon closed.

Interactive Question-Response

Comprehension Check

Ask students to share what they underlined in the text. **Ask:** *What was the effect of this policy? (Most of these clubs lost business and closed.) Why? (The clubs were no longer "in vogue" when they would not allow African Americans to enter. White people wanted to watch African Americans have fun.)*

Fluency

Pacing: Phrasing

Intermediate/Early Advanced ➤ Tell students that they will be doing a choral reading of the five paragraphs on this page. Remind students to read in phrases or complete sentences for clarity and not word by word. Model the fluency skill as you read the text at a moderate tempo. Then have one student read a sentence. Have another student join in, and a third, and so on. When students reach the end of the passage, have pairs of students reread to each other. To assess individual fluency, use the Oral Reading Guidelines on page T16.

Beginning/Early Intermediate ➤ Have these students choral read only the first paragraph of the passage. Before they begin, model the pronunciation of the text. Then have students practice reading the paragraph in pairs before the choral reading

When the Negro Was in Vogue

Interactive Question-Response

Content Vocabulary

Read aloud the word and definition of *entertainment*.
Ask: *What are some examples of entertainment that Hughes likes? (He likes plays, music, dancing, and writing. He especially likes the musical revue Shuffle Along.) What kinds of entertainment do you like? (movies, television, theatre, sports)*

Literary Element
Juxtaposition

If students have difficulty responding: **Model**
Remember that juxtaposition is the placement of two very different things next to each other in a sentence or paragraph. Harold Jackman is a Harlem school teacher "of modest means," which means he does not make very much money. He's sailing to the Riviera for a party thrown by Princess Murat, who is probably very wealthy. **Ask:** *What do you think this juxtaposition shows? (This event seems strange and unnatural because school teachers generally are not acquainted with princesses. This juxtaposition shows that the Harlem vogue created situations that were both unrealistic and over-the-top.)*

To Sum Up

Beginning/Early Intermediate Have students work in pairs to reread all the To Sum Up statements from the beginning of autobiography on page 206. Help students to understand why the 1920s was an exciting time in Harlem. Provide the following sentence frame for students to complete.

Harlem was an exciting place in the 1920s because _____.

(*there was popular entertainment; many African Americans were working as artists, singers, dancers, and writers*)

But everything goes, one way or another means that popular things or trends change as time passes.

entertainment (en' tar tān' mant) *n.* an activity that is fun and enjoyable

Literary Element

Juxtaposition Reread the sentence at the bottom of the page about Harold Jackman. Underline the two things or people that are juxtaposed in this sentence.

To Sum Up

➤ The Harlem Renaissance ended with the 1920s.

➤ Critics say that African American writers tried hard to entertain white people.

➤ Hughes says that good African American writers did not worry about entertaining white people and were true to themselves.

---

large, dark, masculine lady, whose feet pounded the floor while her fingers pounded the keyboard—a perfect piece of African sculpture, animated by her own rhythm.

But when the place where she played became too well known, she began to sing with an accompanist, became a star, moved to a larger place, then downtown, and is now in Hollywood. The old magic of the woman and the piano and the night and the rhythm being one is gone. **But everything goes, one way or another.** The '20's are gone and lots of fine things in Harlem night life have disappeared like snow in the sun—since it became utterly commercial, planned for the downtown tourist trade, and therefore dull.

The lindy-hoppers at the Savoy even began to practise acrobatic routines, and to do absurd things for the entertainment of the whites, that probably never would have entered their heads to attempt merely for their own effortless amusement. Some of the lindy-hoppers had cards printed with their names on them and became dance professors teaching the tourists. Then Harlem nights became show nights for the Nordics.[7]

Some critics say that that is what happened to certain Negro writers, too—that they ceased to write to amuse themselves and began to write to amuse and entertain white people, and in so doing distorted and over-colored their material, and left out a great many things they thought would offend their American brothers of a lighter complexion. Maybe—since Negroes have writer-racketeers, as has any other race. But I have known almost all of them, and most of the good ones have tried to be honest, write honestly, and express their world as they saw it.

All of us know that the gay and sparkling life of the so-called Negro Renaissance of the '20's was not so gay and sparkling beneath the surface as it looked. Carl Van Vechten, in the character of Byron in *Nigger Heaven*, captured some of the bitterness and frustration of literary Harlem that Wallace Thurman later so effectively poured into his *Infants of the Spring*—the only novel by a Negro about that fantastic period when Harlem was in vogue.

It was a period when, at almost every Harlem upper-crust dance or party, one would be introduced to various distinguished white celebrities there as guests. It was a period when almost any Harlem Negro of any social importance at all would be likely to say casually: "As I was remarking the other day to Heywood—," meaning Heywood Broun. Or: "As I said to George—," referring to George Gershwin. It was a period when local and visiting royalty were not at all uncommon in Harlem. And when the parties of A'Lelia Walker, the Negro heiress, were filled with guests whose names would turn any Nordic social climber green with envy. It was a period when Harold Jackman, a handsome young Harlem school teacher of modest means, calmly announced one day that he was

---

7. **Nordics** refers to people of Scandinavia; here, the word means white people in general.

Differentiated Instruction

Clarify the Text Help students to understand the speaker's attitude toward the subject.

Beginning/Early Intermediate Have students work in pairs to reread the To Sum Up statements on page 208. **Ask:** *How did white people affect some Harlem writers? (Harlem writers wrote just to entertain white people.)* Explain that according to some critics, African American writers may have forgotten the true reasons they wanted to write.

Intermediate **Ask:** *What do you think Hughes means when he says "write honestly"? (It means writing about how you truly feel, writing about real life, and writing for yourself, not to impress others or boast.)*

Early Advanced Explain that *tourists* are people who travel to a different place and *commercial* means "useful for making money." **Ask:** *Why does Hughes use the words* tourists *and* commercial *to describe changes in entertainment? (The entertainment of the Harlem Renaissance became more about money than it did about art or feelings.)*

sailing for the Riviera for a fortnight, to attend Princess Murat's yachting party. It was a period when Charleston preachers opened up shouting churches as sideshows for white tourists. It was a period when at least one charming colored chorus girl, amber enough to pass for a Latin American, was living in a pent house, with all her bills paid by a gentleman whose name was banker's magic on Wall Street. It was a period when every season there was at least one hit play on Broadway acted by a Negro cast. And when books by Negro authors were being published with much greater frequency and much more publicity than ever before or since in history. It was a period when white writers wrote about Negroes more successfully (commercially speaking) than Negroes did about themselves. It was the period (God help us!) when Ethel Barrymore appeared in blackface in *Scarlet Sister Mary!* It was the period when the Negro was in vogue.

> I was there. I had a swell time while it lasted. But I thought it wouldn't last long. (I remember the vogue for things Russian, the season the Chauve-Souris first came to town.) For how could a large and enthusiastic number of people be crazy about Negroes forever? But some Harlemites thought the **millennium** had come. They thought the race problem had at last been solved through Art plus Gladys Bentley. They were sure the New Negro would lead a new life from then on in green pastures of tolerance created by Countee Cullen, Ethel Waters, Claude McKay, Duke Ellington, Bojangles, and Alain Locke.

REFLECT

Analyze Concrete Details

Choose an event from the selection, such as the musical *Shuffle Along*, the nightclubs, or the house-rent parties. List three concrete details that Hughes uses to describe the event and complete the sentence about these details.

Event: Possible answer: the nightclubs

Details:

1. Possible answer: White people came to Harlem in droves.
2. Possible answer: White strangers were given the best ringside tables.
3. Possible answer: They stared at African Americans as if they were animals in a zoo.

The details about the nightclubs

help the reader to Possible answer: imagine how the

atmosphere of the clubs began to change when white

people came to watch the African American people

 Talk about your answer with a partner.

---

enthusiastic (en thōō′ zē as′ tik) *adj.* full of excitement and interest

Vocabulary ....

millennium (mi le′ nē əm) *n.* a time of great happiness, peace, or good fortune

To Sum Up

➤ Hughes says that the Harlem Renaissance was fun while it lasted.

➤ Some people thought that the differences in race would no longer matter.

Interactive Question-Response

Content Vocabulary

Read aloud the word and definition of *enthusiastic*. Then read aloud the sentence in which the word appears. **Ask:** *Why were people enthusiastic, or excited, during this time? (They were enthusiastic about the fun and excitement of Harlem entertainment.) What are some things that you are enthusiastic about? (sports, music, books, art, friends, family)*

Reflect

Partner Talk Have students work in pairs to answer. Ask students to choose one event and reread the parts of the autobiography in which they appear. Remind students that concrete details appeal to their senses and help them imagine a scene. To help students get started: **Model** *White people flooded into Harlem after sundown, which is a very specific detail. The white people sat at the best tables and stared at African Americans like they were amusing animals in a zoo, which is very specific also. Details like these help me imagine what it was like to be at the nightclub.* Write the following sentence frame on the board to help students organize their thoughts.

A concrete detail that helps me imagine ____ is ____.

Interactive Question-Response

Content Vocabulary

Read aloud the word and definition of *refreshments*.
Ask: *What were some of the refreshments at the house-rent parties? (awful bootleg whiskey, good fried fish, steaming chitterling, and pig's foot)*

Literary Element
Juxtaposition

If students have difficulty responding: **Model** *Hughes mentions several different kinds of people in the same sentence in this paragraph.* **Ask:** *Why do you think that Hughes juxtaposes these different kinds of people? (He wants to show that people with many different backgrounds and jobs came to the house-rent parties. They had fun together as a group even though their lives were very different.)*

Reflect

Partner Talk Have students work in pairs to answer. To help students get started: **Model** *Hughes mentions that the house-rent parties allowed African Americans to dance without white people watching them, to hear impromptu musical performances, and to have food and drinks for low prices.* Write the following sentence frame on the board to help students organize their thoughts.

The house-rent parties were successful because _____, _____, and _____.

Wages means "money paid for work."

refreshments (ri fresh' mantz) *n.* food or drink, such as snacks or a light meal

Literary Element

Juxtaposition Reread the last paragraph. Underline the things or people that are juxtaposed.

Vocabulary

impromptu (im' promp' too) *adj.* without time to prepare

8. When alcohol was illegal during the 1920s, **speakeasies** were secret clubs where alcoholic drinks were sold.
9. **Augmented** (ôg ment' ad) means "played along with" or "made larger."
10. **Bootleg** means "made or sold illegally."
11. **Whist** is a card game.

To Sum Up

➤ Most African Americans had not heard of the Harlem Renaissance.
➤ African Americans held small house-rent parties without whites.
➤ At these parties, there was food, music, and dancing.

I don't know what made any Negroes think that—except that they were mostly intellectuals doing the thinking. The ordinary Negroes hadn't heard of the Negro Renaissance. And if they had, it hadn't raised their **wages** any. As for all those white folks in the speakeasies[8] and night clubs of Harlem—well, maybe a colored man could find *some* place to have a drink that the tourists hadn't yet discovered.

Then it was that house-rent parties began to flourish—and not always to raise the rent either. But, as often as not, to have a get-together of one's own, where you could do the black-bottom with no stranger behind you trying to do it, too. Non-theatrical, non-intellectual Harlem was an unwilling victim of its own vogue. It didn't like to be stared at by white folks. But perhaps the downtowners never knew this—for the cabaret owners, the entertainers, and the speakeasy proprietors treated them fine—as long as they paid.

The Saturday night rent parties that I attended were often more amusing than any night club, in small apartments where God knows who lived—because the guests seldom did—but where the piano would often be augmented[9] by a guitar, or an odd cornet, or somebody with a pair of drums walking in off the street. And where awful bootleg[10] whiskey and good fried fish or steaming chitterling were sold at very low prices. And the dancing and singing and **impromptu** entertaining went on until dawn came in at the windows.

These parties, often termed whist[11] parties or dances, were usually announced by brightly colored cards stuck in the grille of apartment house elevators. Some of the cards were highly entertaining in themselves.

Almost every Saturday night when I was in Harlem I went to a house-rent party. I wrote lots of poems about house-rent parties, and ate thereat many a fried fish and pig's foot—with liquid refreshments on the side. I met ladies' maids and truck drivers, laundry workers and shoe shine boys, seamstresses and porters. I can still hear their laughter in my ears, hear the soft slow music, and feel the floor shaking as the dancers danced.

REFLECT

Analyze Concrete Details
Write some details that Hughes shares about house-rent parties. What do these details tell you about the reason for their success?

Possible answers: Details that Hughes shares include "to have a get-together of one's own, where you could do the black-bottom with no stranger behind you trying to do it, too," and "dancing and singing and impromptu entertaining went on until dawn came in at the windows." These details show that house-rent parties were successful because African Americans could be free from the watching eyes of whites.

 Talk about your answer with a partner.

Oral Assessment

Provide the following prompts to one student at a time. Observe students' responses. See the Oral Assessment Rubric on page T17 to determine students' levels of language output.

1. Why was the musical *Shuffle Along* important?

2. What happened in Harlem clubs and bars during this time?

3. What happened in the arts during this time?

4. What did Hughes like about the house-rent parties?

5. What did it mean for "the Negro" to be "in vogue"?

WHEN THE NEGRO WAS IN VOGUE

Vocabulary Check

A. Label each picture with the correct word.

entertainment	enthusiastic	orchestra	refreshment

1.   2.   3.   4.

____orchestra____   ____entertainment____   ____refreshment____   ____enthusiastic____

B. Complete each sentence with the best word.

enthusiastic	impromptu	orchestra	refreshments	scintillating

5. During the morning break, the students had some __refreshments__ to give them energy.

6. Emilio is __enthusiastic__ about his new job at the zoo.

7. Many questions were raised in the __scintillating__ article.

8. Phoung plays the flute in the school __orchestra__.

9. When the teacher was sick, the principal gave an __impromptu__ lesson to the class.

C. Complete each sentence.

10. One kind of clothing that is in **vogue** is _Possible answer: tight jeans_____.

11. Your mother might have to serve **impromptu** refreshments if _Possible answer: your friend came to your house and was hungry_____.

12. My family gives its **patronage** to _Possible answer: the pizza restaurant in our neighborhood_____.

13. An example of a **scintillating** movie is _Possible answer: one that is smart and funny_____.

14. I would think a **millennium** had come if _Possible answer: I won the lottery_____.

Vocabulary Check

C. [Early Advanced]

Read each question aloud. If students have trouble thinking of responses, encourage them to rephrase the question in their own words or substitute words that are more familiar to them. **Model** *What kinds of clothes are popular or fashionable? Why would my mother suddenly decide to serve snacks? What restaurant or store does my family go to? What is a movie that is lively or full of energy? What might happen to bring about a time of great happiness?*

Academic Vocabulary

Write the following sentence on the board: *How does Hughes **label** the white tourists who flocked to Harlem for entertainment?*

Explain that *label* is an academic word that has multiple meanings. Other words that are similar in meaning to the way *label* is used in the sentence on the board are *name* and *categorize*.

Divide students into pairs. Have them look up the word *label* in a dictionary. Then have the partners work together to write a definition in their own words of *label* as it is used in the sentence on the board.

Grammar Link   BLM

Comparative Forms of Adjectives: *–er* and *more*

Prepare students to complete the activity on page A41. Read the grammar instruction with students, and complete the first item with them to help them get started.

Comprehension Check

B. Intermediate

If students have trouble responding, point them to pages 208 and 210. Have them reread the paragraphs where these words appear and find the people who are being juxtaposed. To help students understand why these groups are juxtaposed: **Model** *The author calls white people "Nordics," which is kind of funny. It almost seems like white people are strangers in Harlem. It seems they only like going there because it is fashionable. So I think the juxtaposition shows that these two groups of people had a lot of differences during this time. African Americans were still treated unfairly even though Harlem was a popular place to be.*

After Reading

Have students complete the after reading activity on page 333.

WHEN THE NEGRO WAS IN VOGUE

Comprehension Check

A. Complete the sentences below.

1. A musical that was very popular in Harlem in the 1920s was called   Shuffle Along .

2. Some Harlem clubs that had a Jim Crow policy would not   let African Americans enter .

3. Many African Americans held their own parties called   house-rent parties .

B. Complete these sentences about juxtaposition in "When the Negro Was in Vogue."

4. Hughes juxtaposes Nordics, or white tourists, and   Possible answer: African Americans, or Harlem Negroes

5. This juxtaposition shows that   Possible answer: white people still treated African Americans unfairly during this time

6. Hughes juxtaposes ladies' maids, laundry workers, and seamstresses with   truck drivers, shoe shine boys, and porters

7. This juxtaposition shows that   Possible answer: African Americans from different lines of work had fun together at the house-rent parties

C. Answer these questions about "When the Negro Was in Vogue."

8. Why does Hughes juxtapose whites and African Americans at the same Harlem nightclubs? How does this support his theme?

   Possible answer: White people stared at African Americans as if they were animals in the zoo.

   Hughes wants to show that white people felt that the Harlem clubs were just a passing trend.

9. Why does Hughes juxtapose "intellectual" African Americans with "ordinary" Harlem African Americans?

   Possible answer: Hughes wants to show that white acceptance of African Americans was a vogue that

   came and went. It did not bring about long-term change in the lives of African Americans in Harlem.

10. Would you have enjoyed living in Harlem in the 1920s? Explain.

   Possible answer: Students may say that they would have enjoyed the night life and entertainment

   options.

For more practice, see page 333.

Writing Link

Blog

Blogs (short for weblogs) offer a growing record of how individuals respond to the world. Suggest to students that if Langston Hughes were writing today, he might make use of a blog (short for weblog) to write about art, society, and relations between whites and African Americans. Have students meet in small groups to share the blogs that they have read and to discuss the different ways bloggers present their opinions.

Then have students work individually to create a series of blog posts based on the content of "When the Negro Was in Vogue." Before they start, encourage students to discuss the conventions and format of blogs and suggest they brainstorm about how to merge the content of the selection with the format of a blog.

Learning Objectives

For pages 213–226, 334–335

In studying this text, you will focus on the following objectives:

Literary Study: Analyzing a foil character.

Reading: Making generalizations about characters.

The Rockpile

by James Baldwin

The Rockpile   **213**

Oral Language

Build Background

Read the title and author. Explain that students will read "The Rockpile" by James Baldwin, an author who grew up in the New York City neighborhood of Harlem.
Ask:

- Where do you think the story takes place? *(on the rockpile; in a neighborhood; in Harlem; in New York City)*

- What do you think the rockpile looks like? *(smooth rocks stacked on top of each other; sharp rocks jutting out from the ground; a pile of rocks and small stones)*

Talk About the Story

Explain that the story is about two brothers who are not allowed to play on the rockpile across the street from their apartment.

Early Advanced ➤ **Ask:** *What do you think might happen to the boy who goes to play on the rockpile? (he might get hurt; he might get in trouble with his parents) Do you think his brother should tell their parents that he went to the rockpile? Why? (yes, because he might get in trouble for not telling them; no, because he is loyal to his brother and does not want his brother to be mad at him for telling)*

Lesson at a Glance

Oral Language
- Build Background
- Talk About the Story

Vocabulary
- Selection Vocabulary
- Content Vocabulary

Literary Element
- Foil

Reading Strategy
- Make Generalizations About Characters

Writing Link
- Editorial

Comprehension `BLM`
- BLM

Grammar Link `BLM`
- Run-on Sentences BLM

Technology
- Student Works™ Plus
- Teacher Works™ Plus
- Listening Library Audio CD
- Classroom Presentation Toolkit
- Glencoe Visual Vocabulary
- Skill Level Up!™ A Skill-Based Language Arts Game

Interactive Question-Response

Connect to the Story

Read aloud Connect to the Story. Write the sentence frames on the board. **Model** *I once made a promise to a friend. I felt pleased keeping the promise because I knew it was important for my friend to be able to trust me. It was easy for me to keep the promise because I knew how important it was to my friend.* Model writing your response in the sentence frames, and have volunteers suggest other responses. Then have individuals fill in their own sentences.

Literary Element Foil

Read aloud the Literary Element. Explain that the main character of a story is the person whom the story is mostly about. The foil is a lesser character who complements or contrasts with the main character **Ask:** *How do you think a lesser character can show things about a main character? (As the main character responds to and interacts with the lesser character, we learn about the personality of the main character.)*

Reading Strategy Make Generalizations About Characters

Read aloud the Reading Strategy. Tell students that making generalizations about characters will help them understand the differences between characters in a story. Reproduce the chart on the board. **Model** *Suppose that Roy goes to the rockpile, even though he has been told not to. John refuses to go to the rockpile.* **Ask:** *What generalizations can you make about John and Roy? (John obeys his parents; Roy does not.)* Model writing your response in the chart and have students suggest other responses as they read.

Connect to the Story

What would you risk to keep your word to someone? Think about a time when you kept a promise even though it was difficult. Write about your experience and talk about it with a partner.

I kept a promise for	Possible answer: my friend, my brother, my sister
I felt	Possible answer: worried, scared, important, trusted
to be keeping the promise.	
It was	Possible answer: difficult, hard, easy
to keep the promise.	

Literary Element Foil

A **foil** is a lesser character whose contrast with a main character shows traits about that main character. As you read, ask yourself, How is your understanding of the main character improved because the foil's presence?

Reading Strategy Make Generalizations About Characters

A **generalization** is a broad conclusion drawn from details. As you read, ask yourself, What can you conclude about the family members in "The Rockpile"? Write details and generalizations about the main characters in a two-column chart.

Details	Generalizations
Roy gazed at the street, wishing he had wings; John was afraid of the rockpile.	Roy and John have different personalities.

Selection Vocabulary

grappled (grap' əld) *v.* struggled in hand-to-hand combat; wrestled (p. 216)
*The boxers **grappled** with each other in the middle of the ring.*

loitered (loi' tərd) *v.* stood or lingered idly or aimlessly (p. 216)
*The boys **loitered** in the park, looking for something to do.*

intimidated (in tim' ə dāt əd) *adj.* made shy or fearful; scared into not acting (p. 217)
*The large man **intimidated** everyone in the room.*
➤ Cognate (Spanish) **intimidar**

engrossed (en grōst') *adj.* fully attentive to; completely engaged in (p. 218)
*Judy spent all day reading, completely **engrossed** in her book.*

jubilant (jōo' bə lənt) *adj.* extremely happy; successfully joyful (p. 218)
*The girl was **jubilant** when she won the spelling bee.*
➤ Cognate (Spanish) **jubiloso**

Content Vocabulary

acquire (ə kwīr') *v.* to come into possession or control of (p. 216)
*Belinda used cash to **acquire** some groceries.*
➤ Cognate (Spanish) **adquirir**

bathed (bāthd) *v.* washed in a liquid; washed with water or a liquid medicine (p. 220)
*Kristine **bathed** the dog after it ran through the mud.*
➤ Cognate (Spanish) **bañar**

wound (wōond) *n.* an injury to the body (p. 219)
*Paul fell and got a nasty **wound** on his knee.*

bandage (ban' dij) *n.* a strip of cloth used to cover an injury (p. 220)
*The doctor put a **bandage** over the cut.*

For more practice, see page 334. ➡

Vocabulary Routine

To introduce the vocabulary, read aloud the words and definitions in the student book and have students repeat after you. Discuss how the pictures illustrate the words or sentences. Then follow the vocabulary routine below.

Content Vocabulary

Define: When you **acquire** something, you obtain it. Example: The family would like to acquire some furniture for their new house. Ask: What are some other things that you could acquire? EXAMPLE

Sometimes when you hurt yourself, you get a **wound** on your body. *The dog licked the wound on its paw.* Describe a time when you hurt yourself and got a *wound*. DESCRIBE

When something is **bathed**, it is washed and cleaned. *The campers bathed themselves after a week in the woods with no shower.* Why would someone or something need to be *bathed*? EXPLANATION

A **bandage** is a piece of cotton or fabric used to cover a cut. *My mother put a bandage over the scrape on my elbow.* What are some other names for a *bandage*? SYNONYM

Vocabulary Practice Have students complete the vocabulary practice activity on page 334.

Selection Vocabulary

Define: Two people who wrestled **grappled** with each other. Example: The lions *grappled* as they fought for control of the pride. Ask: What word has the same or similar meaning as *grappled*? SYNONYM

A person who is standing around for no useful reason is **loitering**. *Shopping malls are popular places for kids to loiter.* What is the relationship between *loiter* and *linger*? SYNONYM

Someone who is deeply interested in what he or she is doing is **engrossed**. *Sandra was so engrossed in her novel that she was up reading until three in the morning.* Have you ever been so engrossed in something that you lost track of time? How would you describe the feeling of being engrossed? DESCRIPTION

Someone who is **intimidated** is fearful of something else more powerful. *Puolo was intimidated by Andrea's good grades.* What is something that intimidates you? EXAMPLE

When a person feels both triumphant and happy, he or she is **jubilant**. *My dad and I were both jubilant when I scored the game-winning home run.* Give an example of a time you felt jubilant. EXAMPLE

The Rockpile

Interactive Question-Response

Content Vocabulary

Have a student read the sentence containing the Content Vocabulary word, *acquire*, in the second paragraph. **Ask:** *What does Roy want to acquire? (wings) Why do you think he wants to acquire them? (If he had wings, he could fly off the fire escape and join the boys on the rockpile.)*

Literary Element **Foil**

If students have difficulty responding: **Model** *It seems that there are more details about Roy then there are about John on this page. That must mean that Roy is the main character and John is a lesser character.* **Ask:** *What contrast do you see between Roy and John? (Roy is impatient on the fire escape and wants to go to the rockpile. John is quiet and wants to stay away from the rockpile.) What does this contrast tell you about the characters? (John must be Roy's foil.)*

---

acquire (ə kwīr') *v.* to come into possession or control of

  Literary Element

Foil Underline details from the text about Roy and John. Who is the foil based on these details?

The details suggest that John is

Roy's foil in the story.

To Sum Up

➤ The rockpile is in the empty lot across the street from where John and Roy live.

➤ The neighborhood boys play on the rockpile, but John and Roy are not allowed to play there.

➤ John and Roy's mother is afraid they might get hurt if they play on the rockpile.

Across the street from their house, in an empty lot between two houses, stood the rockpile. It was a strange place to find a mass of natural rock jutting out of the ground; and someone, probably Aunt Florence, had once told them that the rock was there and could not be taken away because without it the subway cars underground would fly apart, killing all the people. This, touching on some natural mystery concerning the surface and the center of the earth, was far too intriguing an explanation to be challenged, and it invested the rockpile, moreover, with such mysterious importance that Roy felt it to be his right, not to say his duty, to play there.

Other boys were to be seen there each afternoon after school and all day Saturday and Sunday. They fought on the rockpile. Sure-footed, dangerous, and reckless, they rushed each other and **grappled** on the heights, sometimes disappearing down the other side in a confusion of dust and screams and upended, flying feet. "It's a wonder they don't kill themselves," their mother said, watching sometimes from the fire escape. "You children stay away from there, you hear me?" Though she said "children," she was looking at Roy, where he sat beside John on the fire escape. "The good Lord knows," she continued, "I don't want you to come home bleeding like a hog every day the Lord sends." Roy shifted impatiently, and continued to stare at the street, as though in this gazing he might somehow acquire wings. John said nothing. He had not really been spoken to: he was afraid of the rockpile and of the boys who played there.

Each Saturday morning John and Roy sat on the fire escape and watched the forbidden street below. Sometimes their mother sat in the room behind them, sewing, or dressing their younger sister, or nursing the baby, Paul. The sun fell across them and across the fire escape with a high, benevolent indifference; below them, men and women, and boys and girls, sinners all, **loitered**; sometimes one of the church-members passed and saw them and waved. Then, for the moment that they waved

Vocabulary

grappled (grap' əld) *v.* struggled in hand-to-hand combat; wrestled
loitered (loi' tərd) *v.* stood or lingered idly or aimlessly

---

Comprehension

To support students as they read the selection, have them begin the graphic organizer on page A42.

decorously back, they were **intimidated.** They watched the saint, man or woman, until he or she had disappeared from sight. The passage of one of the redeemed made them consider, however vacantly, the wickedness of the street, their own latent wickedness in sitting where they sat; and made them think of their father, who came home early on Saturdays and who would soon be turning this corner and entering the dark hall below them.

But until he came to end their freedom, they sat, watching and longing above the street. At the end of the street nearest their house was the bridge which spanned the Harlem River[1] and led to a city called the Bronx;[2] which was where Aunt Florence lived. Nevertheless, when they saw her coming, she did not come from the bridge, but from the opposite end of the street. This, weakly, to their minds, she explained by saying that she had taken the subway, not wishing to walk, and that, besides, she did not live in that section of the Bronx. Knowing that the Bronx was across the river, they did not believe this story ever, but, adopting toward her their father's attitude, assumed that she had just left some sinful place which she dared not name, as, for example, a movie palace.

In the summertime boys swam in the river, diving off the wooden dock, or wading in from the garbage-heavy bank. Once a boy, whose name was Richard, drowned in the river. His mother had not known where he was; she had even come to their house, to ask if he was there. Then, in the evening, at six o'clock, they had heard from the street a woman screaming and wailing; and they ran to the windows and looked out. Down the street came the woman, Richard's mother, screaming, her face raised to the sky and tears running down her face. A woman walked beside her, trying to make her quiet and trying to hold her up. Behind them walked a man, Richard's father, with Richard's body in his arms. There were two white policemen walking in the gutter, who did not seem to know what should be done. Richard's father and Richard were wet, and Richard's body lay across his father's arms like a cotton baby. The woman's screaming filled all the street; cars slowed down and the people in the cars stared; people opened their windows and looked out and came rushing out of doors to stand in the gutter, watching. Then the small procession disappeared within the house which stood beside the rockpile. Then, "Lord, Lord, Lord!" cried Elizabeth, their mother, and slammed the window down.

Vocabulary

intimidated (in tim′ ə dāt əd) *adj.* made shy or fearful; scared into not acting

1. The **Harlem River** separates the Bronx and Manhattan, two boroughs, or areas, of New York City.
2. The **Bronx** is actually one of five boroughs, or areas, that make up New York City. It is not a separate city.

Background Information

The story takes place in New York City, which is made up of five boroughs, or areas. The five boroughs are Manhattan, Brooklyn, the Bronx, Queens, and Staten Island. Many different neighborhoods make up the five boroughs. John and Roy live in the neighborhood of Harlem.

To Sum Up

➤ The bridge at the end of the street crosses the Harlem River and leads to the Bronx.

➤ Boys swam in the river in the summer.

➤ One time, a boy named Richard drowned in the river. His mother did not know where he was.

The Rockpile

Interactive Question-Response

Background Information

Read aloud the note. Explain that the neighborhood of Harlem is in the borough of Manhattan. Show students a detailed map of New York City, labeled with the five boroughs, and point out the neighborhood of Harlem. **Ask:** *Do you think you would like living in New York City? Why or why not? (yes, because there are many different places to see and things to do there; no, because it is too big and there are too many people)*

Interactive Question-Response

Comprehension Check

Ask students to share their answer. **Ask:** *Where is John? (on the fire escape) Who is John and Roy's mother having tea with? (Sister McCandless)*

Comprehension Check

Reread the first box of text. Where is John and Roy's mother when Roy decides to go downstairs? Check the box with the correct answer.
- [ ] at the store
- [x] in the kitchen having tea

To Sum Up

➤ One Saturday, Roy and John are sitting on the fire escape when Roy's friends pass by the house and call him.

➤ Roy decides to go downstairs to the rockpile. John warns him not to go.

➤ John worries because he cannot see his brother on the rockpile. Roy appears, laughing.

One Saturday, an hour before his father would be coming home, Roy was wounded on the rockpile and brought screaming upstairs. He and John had been sitting on the fire escape and their mother had gone into the kitchen to sip tea with Sister McCandless. By and by Roy became bored and sat beside John in restless silence; and John began drawing into his schoolbook a newspaper advertisement which featured a new electric locomotive. Some friends of Roy passed beneath the fire escape and called him. Roy began to fidget, yelling down to them through the bars. Then a silence fell. John looked up. Roy stood looking at him.

"I'm going downstairs," he said.

"You better stay where you is, boy. You know Mama don't want you going downstairs."

"I be right back. She won't even know I'm gone, less you run and tell her."

"I ain't got to tell her. What's going to stop her from coming in here and looking out the window?"

"She's talking," Roy said. He started into the house.

"But Daddy's going to be home soon!"

"I be back before that. What you all the time got to be so scared for?" He was already in the house and he now turned, leaning on the windowsill, to swear impatiently, "I be back in five minutes."

John watched him sourly as he carefully unlocked the door and disappeared. In a moment he saw him on the sidewalk with his friends. He did not dare to go and tell his mother that Roy had left the fire escape because he had practically promised not to. He started to shout, Remember, you said five minutes! but one of Roy's friends was looking up at the fire escape. John looked down at his schoolbook: he became **engrossed** again in the problem of the locomotive.

When he looked up again he did not know how much time had passed, but now there was a gang fight on the rockpile. Dozens of boys fought each other in the harsh sun: clambering up the rocks and battling hand to hand, scuffed shoes sliding on the slippery rock; filling the bright air with curses and **jubilant** cries. They filled the air, too, with flying weapons: stones, sticks, tin cans, garbage, whatever could be picked up and thrown. John watched in a kind of absent amazement—until he remembered that Roy was still downstairs, and that he was one of the boys on the rockpile. Then he was afraid; he could not see his brother among the figures in the sun; and he stood up, leaning over the fire-escape railing. Then Roy appeared from the other side of the rocks; John saw that his shirt was torn; he was laughing. He moved until he stood at the very

Vocabulary ....

engrossed (en grōst') *adj.* fully attentive to; completely engaged in
jubilant (joo' bə lənt) *adj.* extremely happy; successfully joyful

top of the rockpile. Then, something, an empty tin can, flew out of the air and hit him on the forehead, just above the eye. Immediately, one side of Roy's face ran with blood, he fell and rolled on his face down the rocks. Then for a moment there was no movement at all, no sound, the sun, **arrested,** lay on the street and the sidewalk and the arrested boys. Then someone screamed or shouted; boys began to run away, down the street, toward the bridge. The figure on the ground, having caught its breath and felt its own blood, began to shout. John cried, "Mama! Mama!" and ran inside.

"Don't fret, don't fret," panted Sister McCandless as they rushed down the dark, narrow, swaying stairs, "don't fret. Ain't a boy been born don't get his knocks every now and again. Lord!" They hurried into the sun. A man had picked Roy up and now walked slowly toward them. One or two boys sat silent on their stoops; at either end of the street there was a group of boys watching. "He ain't hurt bad," the man said, "Wouldn't be making this kind of noise if he was hurt real bad."

Stoop

Elizabeth, trembling, reached out to take Roy, but Sister McCandless, bigger, calmer, took him from the man and threw him over her shoulder as she once might have handled a sack of cotton. "God bless you," she said to the man, "God bless you, son." Roy was still screaming. Elizabeth stood behind Sister McCandless to stare at his bloody face.

"It's just a flesh <u>wound</u>," the man kept saying, "just broke the skin, that's all." They were moving across the sidewalk, toward the house. John, not now afraid of the staring boys, looked toward the corner to see if his father was yet in sight.

REFLECT

Make Generalizations About Characters
Besides worrying about Roy, how do John and his mother, Elizabeth, begin to act in this part of the story? What does this tell you about them?

Possible answer: John and his mother are nervous because

they know that Roy's father, Gabriel, will be coming home

soon. They are worried about how Gabriel will react to Roy's

disobedience and injury.

 Talk about your answer with a partner.

In this sentence, *arrested* means "stopped."

wound (wo͞ond) *n.* an injury to the body

To Sum Up

➤ Someone throws a tin can. It cuts Roy on the forehead above his eyebrow.

➤ John runs inside to tell his mother what happened.

➤ A man picks up Roy and carries him to the house.

Interactive Question-Response

Content Vocabulary

Read aloud the word and definition. **Ask:** *Where is Roy's wound? (on his forehead, just above his eye)*
Ask: *What do you think a "flesh wound" is, based on what the neighbor, who carries Roy, says? (It is not a serious wound because he says "just broke the skin, that's all.")*

Reflect

Partner Talk Have students work in pairs to answer. To help students get started: **Model** *To answer this, I would look for details about what John and Elizabeth are doing and how they are behaving in this part of the story. Then, I would think about what their actions show about how they are feeling.* Write the following sentence frames on the board to help students organize their thoughts.

Elizabeth is _____ (trembling), which shows that she is _____. (nervous or scared)

John is _____ (looking toward the corner to see if his father is coming), which shows that he is _____. (worried about how his father will react)

Interactive Question-Response

Content Vocabulary

Read aloud the words and definitions. **Ask:** *When Elizabeth and Sister McCandless bathed Roy's wound, what did they do? (They washed the blood away.)* **Ask:** *When Elizabeth and Sister McCandless put bandages on Roy's wound, what did they do? (They covered the wound with strips of cloth.) Why do you think they put a bandage on his wound? (to protect it and keep it clean so it can heal)*

Literary Element Foil

If students have difficulty responding: **Model** *Sister McCandless looks sharply at John. She also says that he's the "man of the house," which means that he's responsible for looking after his younger brothers and sisters and keeping them out of trouble. When she turns to Roy, she says "poor little man," which must mean that feels sorry for him.* **Ask:** *What does Sister McCandless's attitude tell you about what she thinks about the two boys? (She thinks that John is irresponsible and that Roy is innocent.)*

---

bathed (bāthd) *v.* washed in a liquid; washed with water or a liquid medicine

bandage (ban' dij) *n.* a strip of cloth used to cover an injury

In this sentence, ***reckon*** means "to think or suppose."

Literary Element

Foil Underline the text that shows Sister McCandless's attitude toward the two brothers. What do these words tell you about her different attitudes toward the two brothers?

Possible answer: Sister

McCandless thinks that John

is irresponsible for letting his

little brother go to the rockpile

and that Roy is innocent in his

actions.

To Sum Up

➤ Roy's mother and a neighbor clean and bandage his wound.

➤ Sister McCandless scolds John for letting Roy go downstairs to the rockpile.

➤ Sister McCandless says that Roy will probably be happy to sit on the fire escape after getting hurt.

Upstairs, they hushed Roy's crying. They <u>bathed</u> the blood away, to find, just above the left eyebrow, the jagged, superficial scar. "Lord, have mercy," murmured Elizabeth, "another inch and it would've been his eye." And she looked with apprehension toward the clock. "Ain't it the truth," said Sister McCandless, busy with <u>bandages</u> and iodine.

"When did he go downstairs?" his mother asked at last.

Sister McCandless now sat fanning herself in the easy chair, at the head of the sofa where Roy lay, bound and silent. <u>She paused for a moment to look sharply at John.</u> John stood near the window, holding the newspaper advertisement and the drawing he had done.

"We was sitting on the fire escape," he said. "Some boys he knew called him."

"When?"

"He said he'd be back in five minutes."

"Why didn't you tell me he was downstairs?"

He looked at his hands, clasping his notebook, and did not answer.

"Boy," said Sister McCandless, "you hear your mother a-talking to you?"

He looked at his mother. He repeated:

"He said he'd be back in five minutes."

"He said he'd be back in five minutes," said Sister McCandless with scorn, "don't look to me like that's no right answer. <u>You's the man of the house, you supposed to look after your baby brothers and sisters—you ain't supposed to let them run off and get half-killed.</u> But I expect," she added, rising from the chair, dropping the cardboard fan, "your Daddy'll make you tell the truth. Your Ma's way too soft with you."

He did not look at her, but at the fan where it lay in the dark red, depressed seat where she had been. The fan advertised a pomade[3] for the hair and showed a brown woman and her baby, both with glistening hair, smiling happily at each other.

"Honey," said Sister McCandless, "I got to be moving along. Maybe I drop in later tonight. I don't **reckon** you going to be at Tarry Service tonight?"

Tarry Service was the prayer meeting held every Saturday night at church to strengthen believers and prepare the church for the coming of the Holy Ghost on Sunday.

"I don't reckon," said Elizabeth. She stood up; she and Sister McCandless kissed each other on the cheek. "But you be sure to remember me in your prayers."

"I surely will do that." She paused, with her hand on the door knob, and <u>looked down at Roy and laughed. "Poor little man," she said, "reckon he'll be content to sit on the fire escape now."</u>

---

3. ***Pomade*** is a perfumed cream, especially one used as a hair dressing.

Elizabeth laughed with her. "It sure ought to be a lesson to him. You don't reckon," she asked nervously, still smiling, "he going to keep that scar, do you?"

"Lord, no," said Sister McCandless, "ain't nothing but a scratch. I declare, Sister Grimes, you worse than a child. Another couple of weeks and you won't be able to see no scar. No, you go on about your housework, honey, and thank the Lord it weren't no worse." She opened the door; they heard the sound of feet on the stairs. "I expect that's the Reverend," said Sister McCandless, placidly, "I bet he going to **raise cain.**"

"Maybe it's Florence," Elizabeth said. "Sometimes she get here about this time." They stood in the doorway, staring, while the steps reached the landing below and began again climbing to their floor. "No," said Elizabeth then, "that ain't her walk. That's Gabriel."

"Well, I'll just go on," said Sister McCandless, "and kind of prepare his mind." She pressed Elizabeth's hand as she spoke and started into the hall, leaving the door behind her slightly ajar. Elizabeth turned slowly back into the room. Roy did not open his eyes, or move; but she knew that he was not sleeping; he wished to delay until the last possible moment any contact with his father. John put his newspaper and his notebook on the table and stood, leaning on the table, staring at her.

> "It wasn't my fault," he said. "I couldn't stop him from going downstairs."
>
> "No," she said, "you ain't got nothing to worry about. You just tell your Daddy the truth."
>
> He looked directly at her, and she turned to the window, staring into the street. What was Sister McCandless saying? Then from her bedroom she heard Delilah's thin wail and she turned, frowning, looking toward the bedroom and toward the still open door. She knew that John was watching her. Delilah continued to wail, she thought, angrily, Now that girl's getting too big for that, but she feared that Delilah would awaken Paul and she hurried into the bedroom. She tried to soothe Delilah back to sleep. Then she heard the front door open and close—too loud, Delilah raised her voice, with an exasperated sigh Elizabeth picked the child up. Her child and Gabriel's, her children and Gabriel's: Roy, Delilah, Paul. Only John was nameless and a stranger, living, unalterable testimony to his mother's days in sin.

To **raise cain** means "to make a great disturbance" or "to lose one's temper."

To Sum Up

➤ John tells his mother that Roy's injury is not his fault.

➤ John's mother tells him not to worry and to tell his father the truth.

➤ The baby, Delilah, starts to cry. The father, Gabriel, comes home.

Interactive Question-Response

To Sum Up

Beginning/Early Intermediate ➤ Have students work in pairs to reread all the To Sum Up statements from the beginning of the story on page 216. Then have students decide together which three events are the most important so far. Provide the following sentence frame for students to complete.

The most important events are

when _____,

when _____,

and when _____.

(The most important events are when Roy decides to go downstairs to the rockpile, when Roy gets hurt on the rockpile, and when John tells his mother that Roy's injury is not his fault.)

Interactive Question-Response

Comprehension Check

Ask students to share their answer. **Ask:** *Is this family rich? (no) How do you know? (They do not have enough money to pay for a doctor.)*

In this sentence, **more'n** means "more than."

Comprehension Check

Reread the second box of text. Underline the words that tell Elizabeth's main reason for not calling a doctor.

To Sum Up

➤ Gabriel asks what happened to Roy. Elizabeth answers that he got hurt on the rockpile.

➤ Gabriel wants to call a doctor for Roy, but Elizabeth says they don't have money for a doctor.

➤ Roy cries as his father tries to look at his bandage.

"What happened?" Gabriel demanded. He stood, enormous, in the center of the room, his black lunchbox dangling from his hand, staring at the sofa where Roy lay. John stood just before him, it seemed to her astonished vision just below him, beneath his fist, his heavy shoe. The child stared at the man in fascination and terror—when a girl down home she had seen rabbits stand so paralyzed before the barking dog. She hurried past Gabriel to the sofa, feeling the weight of Delilah in her arms like the weight of a shield, and stood over Roy, saying:

"Now, ain't a thing to get upset about, Gabriel. This boy sneaked downstairs while I had my back turned and got hisself hurt a little. He's alright now."

Roy, as though in confirmation, now opened his eyes and looked gravely at his father. Gabriel dropped his lunchbox with a clatter and knelt by the sofa.

"How you feel, son? Tell your Daddy what happened?"

Roy opened his mouth to speak and then, relapsing into panic, began to cry. His father held him by the shoulder.

"You don't want to cry. You's Daddy's little man. Tell your Daddy what happened."

"He went downstairs," said Elizabeth, "where he didn't have no business to be, and got to fighting with them bad boys playing on that rockpile. That's what happened and it's a mercy it weren't nothing worse."

He looked up at her. "Can't you let this boy answer me for hisself?"

Ignoring this, she went on, more gently: "He got cut on the forehead, but it ain't nothing to worry about."

"You call a doctor? How you know it ain't nothing to worry about?"

"Is you got money to be throwing away on doctors? No, I ain't called no doctor. Ain't nothing wrong with my eyes that I can't tell whether he's hurt bad or not. He got a fright **more'n** anything else, and you ought to pray God it teaches him a lesson."

"You got a lot to say now," he said, "but I'll have me something to say in a minute. I'll be wanting to know when all this happened, what you was doing with your eyes then." He turned back to Roy, who had lain quietly sobbing eyes wide open and body held rigid: and who now, at his father's touch, remembered the height, the sharp, sliding rock beneath his feet, the sun, the explosion of the sun, his plunge into darkness and his salty blood; and recoiled, beginning to scream, as his father touched his forehead. "Hold still, hold still," crooned his father, shaking, "hold still. Don't cry. Daddy ain't going to hurt you, he just wants to see this bandage, see what they've done to his little man." But Roy continued to scream and would not be still and Gabriel dared not lift the bandage for fear of hurting him more. And he looked at Elizabeth in fury: "Can't you put that child down and help me with this boy? John, take your baby sister from your mother—don't look like neither of you got good sense."

John took Delilah and sat down with her in the easy chair. His mother bent over Roy, and held him still, while his father, carefully—but still Roy screamed—lifted the bandage and stared at the wound. Roy's sobs began to lessen. Gabriel re-adjusted the bandage. "You see," said Elizabeth, finally, "he ain't nowhere near dead."

"It sure ain't your fault that he ain't dead." He and Elizabeth considered each other for a moment in silence. "He came mightly close to losing an eye. Course, his eyes ain't as big as **your'n**, so I reckon you don't think it matters so much." At this her face hardened; he smiled. "Lord, have mercy," he said, "you think you ever going to learn to do right? Where was you when all this happened? Who let him go downstairs?"

"Ain't nobody let him go downstairs, he just went. He got a head just like his father, it got to be broken before it'll bow. I was in the kitchen."

"Where was Johnnie?"

"He was in here?"

"Where?"

"He was on the fire escape."

"Didn't he know Roy was downstairs?"

"I reckon."

"What you mean, you reckon? He ain't got your big eyes for nothing, does he?" He looked over at John. "Boy, you see your brother go downstairs?"

In this sentence, **your'n** means "yours."

REFLECT

Make Generalizations About Characters
Gabriel seems more upset with John than he is with Roy. Based on this information, what generalization can you make about Gabriel? Write quotes from the text to support your answer.

Possible answer: Gabriel likes Roy more than he likes John

because Roy is his own son and John is his step-son. "Didn't

he know Roy was downstairs?" "He ain't got your big eyes

for nothing, does he?"

_____

 Talk about your answer with a partner.

To Sum Up

➤ John takes Delilah from his mother so she and his father can look at Roy's cut.

➤ Gabriel asks where Elizabeth was and who let Roy go downstairs.

➤ Elizabeth says that she was in the kitchen and that no one let Roy go downstairs.

Interactive Question-Response

Reflect

Partner Talk Have students work in pairs to answer. To help students get started: **Model** _To answer this, I would think about the differences in how Gabriel acts toward Roy and how he acts toward John. Gabriel refers to Roy as "his little man," and fusses over him, checking his bandage and asking what happened. Gabriel doesn't seem to take much notice of John, but when he does, he refers to him sternly and calls him "boy." He makes sure to point out that John has Elizabeth's "big eyes," which shows that John is her son, but not his._ Write the following sentence frames on the board to help students organize their thoughts.

_Gabriel treats Roy with _____ because _____. (care, concern, affection; Roy is his own son) Gabriel treats John with _____ because _____. (disrespect, dislike; John is Gabriel's step-son)_

Differentiated Instruction

Clarify the Text Support students in understanding Gabriel's character.

Beginning/Early Intermediate ▶ Read aloud the bullet points in the To Sum Up box. **Ask:** _Do you think Gabriel is mad that Roy got hurt? Why?_ (yes, because he looks at Roy's cut and asks his wife questions)

Intermediate ▶ Have partners read aloud the boxed text on page 223. **Ask:** _Why does Gabriel ask so many questions?_ (because he is trying to figure out what happened to Roy and who to blame for it)

Early Advanced ▶ Explain that Roy is Gabriel's biological son and John is his step-son. Encourage students to reread the complete text on page 223. **Ask:** _What words or phrases tell you that Roy is Gabriel's biological son and John is not?_ (Elizabeth says of Roy, "he got a head just like his father." Gabriel says of John and Elizabeth, "he ain't got your big eyes for nothing.")

Interactive Question-Response

Reflect

Partner Talk Have students work in pairs to answer. To help students get started: **Model** *To answer this, I would think about what Gabriel says and does during the story. I would also think about what other people say about him and how they act toward him.* **Ask:** *What do Gabriel's words and actions tell you about his character? How do you feel about this kind of person?* Write the following sentence frames on the board to help students organize their thoughts.

Gabriel says _____ *and does* _____. *I think that Gabriel is* _____.

Take a strap to you means "hit you with a belt."

---

4. *Perdition* (pər dish′ ən) means "the loss of one's soul and of heavenly salvation" or "eternal damnation."

5. *Propitiation* is a pleasing act intended to calm, soothe, or win favor.

To Sum Up

➤ Gabriel asks John why he did not tell his mother that Roy went downstairs.

➤ Gabriel threatens to hit John, but Elizabeth stops him.

➤ Elizabeth scolds Gabriel for spoiling Roy.

➤ John hurries to pick up his father's lunchbox.

224

"Gabriel, ain't no sense in trying to blame Johnnie. You know right well if you have trouble making Roy behave, he ain't going to listen to his brother. He don't hardly listen to me."

"How come you didn't tell your mother Roy was downstairs?" John said nothing, staring at the blanket which covered Delilah. "Boy, you hear me? You want me to **take a strap to you?**"

"No, you ain't," she said. "You ain't going to take no strap to this boy, not today you ain't. Ain't a soul to blame for Roy's lying up there now but you—you because you done spoiled him so that he thinks he can do just anything and get away with it. I'm here to tell you that ain't no way to raise no child. You don't pray to the Lord to help you do better than you been doing, you going to live to shed bitter tears that the Lord didn't take his soul today." And she was trembling. She moved, unseeing, toward John and took Delilah from his arms. She looked back at Gabriel, who had risen, who stood near the sofa, staring at her. And she found in his face not fury alone, which would not have surprised her; but hatred so deep as to become insupportable in its lack of personality. His eyes were struck alive, unmoving, blind with malevolence—she felt, like the pull of the earth at her feet, his longing to witness her perdition.⁴ Again, as though it might be propitiation,⁵ she moved the child in her arms. And at this his eyes changed, he looked at Elizabeth, the mother of his children, the helpmeet given by the Lord. Then her eyes clouded; she moved to leave the room; her foot struck the lunchbox lying on the floor.

"John," she said, "pick up your father's lunchbox like a good boy." She heard, behind her, his scrambling movement as he left the easy chair, the scrape and jangle of the lunchbox as he picked it up, bending his dark head near the toe of his father's heavy shoe.

REFLECT

Make Generalizations About Characters
Identify Gabriel's character traits. How do you learn about him? Use quotes from the text to support your answer.

Possible answer: We learn about Gabriel through the words and actions of others and through his own words and actions. He threatens to hit John by saying "you want me to take a strap to you?" but Elizabeth stops him by saying "ain't a soul to blame for Roy's lying up there now but you—you because you done spoiled him so that he thinks he can do just anything and get away with it."
How do you feel about him? Why?

Possible answers: Gabriel is not very nice. His children are afraid of him. He doesn't let Roy cry. He threatens to beat John. He yells at Elizabeth.

 Talk about your answer with a partner.

Oral Assessment

Provide the following prompts to one student at a time. Observe students' responses. See the Oral Assessment Rubric on page T17 to determine students' levels of language output.

1. What are Roy and John not allowed to do?

2. What does Roy want to do?

3. What happens to Roy on the rockpile?

4. How does Elizabeth react to Roy getting hurt?

5. How does Gabriel react to Roy getting hurt?

The Rockpile

Vocabulary Check

A. Circle the picture that best answers the question.

1. Which picture shows something that has been **acquired**?

2. Which picture shows a **wound**?

3. Which picture shows something that is being **bathed**?

4. Which picture shows a **bandage**?

B. Match the word on the left with its correct definition on the right. Write the letter on the line provided.

_e_	5. intimidated	a. cloth used to cover an injury
_f_	6. wound	b. stood idly
_d_	7. jubilant	c. washed
_a_	8. bandage	d. extremely happy
_b_	9. loitered	e. made fearful
_c_	10. bathed	f. an injury to the body

C. Write the letter of the phrase that best completes the sentence.

_c_ 11. Someone **engrossed** in doing something is
a. bored by it.
b. not paying attention to it.
c. completely engaged in it.
d. wishes it were finished.

_a_ 12. If you **grappled** with someone, you
a. wrestled with them.
b. danced with them.
c. stood next to them.
d. shook hands with them..

_b_ 13. A person who **loitered**
a. moved around a lot.
b. stayed in one place.
c. was very busy.
d. was very loud.

_d_ 14. Another word for **jubilant** is
a. sad.
b. quiet.
c. angry.
d. happy.

Vocabulary Check

B. Intermediate

Explain to students that they need to match the words to their definitions. Have students try to use the words in their own sentences to help them understand the meaning of each word.

Grammar Link BLM

Run-on Sentences

Prepare students to complete the activity on page A43. Read the grammar instruction with students, and complete the first item with them to help them get started.

Comprehension Check

B. Intermediate

Explain that students can describe not only how the characters look, but also how they act and how they feel. Encourage students to return to the text to find supporting details for each character.

After Reading

Have students complete the after reading activity on page 335.

The Rockpile

Comprehension Check

A. Think about the events in the story. In the first box, write a sentence about what happens at the beginning of the story. In the next box, write two sentences about two events that happen in the middle of the story. In the last box, write a sentence about what happens at the end of the story.

> **Beginning**
> Possible answers: Roy and John's mother tell them not to play on the rockpile.

↓

> **Middle** Possible answers: Roy goes to the rockpile and gets hurt. A neighbor takes Roy upstairs where Elizabeth and Sister McCandless bandage his wound.

↓

> **End**
> Possible answers: Gabriel comes home and gets angry at Elizabeth and John for letting Roy hurt himself.

B. Write three words or phrases that describe each character.

Roy	John	Elizabeth	Gabriel
Possible answers: independent, disobedient, afraid of his father	Possible answers: loyal to his brother, fearful, afraid of his father	Possible answers: tries to protect her children, religious, willing to stand up to Gabriel	Possible answers: big; scary; quick to get angry

C. Answer the questions about "The Rockpile."

1. How does John feel about the rockpile?

   Possible answer: He is afraid of it and he's afraid of the boys who play there.

2. What happens that makes Roy decide to play on the rockpile?

   Possible answer: He is bored and his friends come by and call him.

3. How do Elizabeth, Roy, and John act toward Gabriel?

   Possible answer: They are afraid of him.

4. Why does Gabriel get angry at Elizabeth and John?

   Possible answer: He feels they did not do a good job of keeping Roy out of trouble.

For more practice, see page 335. ➡

226

Writing Link

Editorial

Have students write an editorial for your school newspaper on one of these topics: *Young people must be closely supervised for their own safety* or *Young people must be allowed some unsupervised time to help them mature.*

Remind students that an editorial presents the writer's opinions on a controversial subject. Students should support their opinions with examples from "The Rockpile" and from their own experiences.

Students' editorials should be three to four paragraphs long, and include an introduction and a conclusion. Editorials should use formal language throughout.

Students' essays should

- present a well-reasoned opinion on one of the given topics.

- include examples from the story and examples from the student's experiences.

Learning Objectives

For pages 227–254, 336–337

In studying this text, you will focus on the following objectives:

Literary Study: Analyzing dialogue.

Reading: Drawing conclusions about characters.

THE CRUCIBLE

by Arthur Miller

Oral Language

Build Background

Read the title and author. Explain that students will read Act I of *The Crucible,* a play by Arthur Miller, an American author who died in 2005. Have students look up the definition of *crucible* in the dictionary. **Ask:**

- **What can *crucible* mean?** *(It can mean a container in which metal is melted, or it can mean an ordeal.)*

Talk About the Play

Explain that the play is about the events that brought about the Salem witch trials.

Beginning/Early Intermediate ▶ Work with students to find Salem, Massachusetts, on a map. **Ask:** *What is a trial? (the deciding of a case in a court of law) What is a witch? (Students may mention women in black hats.)* Make sure students understand that people accused other people of being witches out of fear or to hurt them.

Intermediate ▶ **Ask:** *Have you ever heard of the Salem witch trials?* Explain what these trials were and that they took place more than 300 years ago. Have students fill in the following sentence frame:

In the 1600s, people did not have _____. (cars, electricity, televisions)

Lesson at a Glance

Oral Language
- Build Background
- Talk About the Play

Vocabulary
- Selection Vocabulary
- Content Vocabulary
- Academic Vocabulary

Literary Element
- Dialogue

Reading Strategy
- Draw Conclusions About Characters

Writing Link
- Journal Entry

Fluency
- Intonation and Pacing: Smooth Reading

Comprehension `BLM`
- BLM

Word Study `BLM`
- Homophones BLM

Grammar Link `BLM`
- Interrogative Sentences, Exclamatory and Imperative Sentences BLM

Technology
- Student Works™ Plus
- Teacher Works™ Plus
- Listening Library Audio CD
- Classroom Presentation Toolkit
- Glencoe Visual Vocabulary
- Skill Level Up!™ A Skill-Based Language Arts Game

Interactive Question-Response

Connect to the Play

Read aloud Connect to the Play: **Model** *A rumor is a story about someone that is passed from person to person. Usually a rumor is about something bad or embarrassing. Many times the rumor isn't even true, but people may believe it anyway.* Have students think about the results of rumors. Then have them share their thoughts about rumors with a partner.

Literary Element Dialogue

Draw two stick figures on the board, each one with one or two large speech balloons. Ask students for suggestions about what the figures might be saying. Fill in the speech balloons with their suggestions. Explain that what people say to each other is dialogue. Have volunteers come up and model the dialogue between the stick figures.

Reading Strategy Draw Conclusions About Characters

Read aloud the Reading Strategy. Then provide a brief story about a fictional "Uncle Billy." **Model** *Uncle Billy is a fun guy. He always brings plenty of chips and other snacks when he comes over to watch football. Usually he wears some sort of silly hat, or striped socks that don't match the rest of his clothes. One time he did a little dance when his team scored. He cries when the team loses.* Ask students to draw conclusions about Uncle Billy based on details from this story.

THE CRUCIBLE

Connect to the Play

What is a rumor? What happens when a rumor starts? Think about a time when you heard a rumor about someone. With a partner, talk about why rumors start and what can happen as a result of a rumor. Record your thoughts on the lines below.

Literary Element Dialogue

Dialogue is conversation, or talking, between characters. A play is mostly dialogue. In a play, the author has to do many things with dialogue, including

- tell the story (plot)
- show what different characters are like (characterization)
- suggest or tell the main ideas, or themes, of the play

As you read, ask yourself: How does Arthur Miller use dialogue to develop the plot, characterization, and theme?

Reading Strategy Draw Conclusions About Characters

In a play, you know the characters by what they say and do. You can use these details to **draw conclusions**, or form general ideas, about the characters. As you read, ask yourself the following questions:

- What does the character say?
- What does the character do?
- What do other characters say about the character?

_____

_____

_____

_____

Selection Vocabulary

compromise (kom′ prə mīz′) *v.* to expose to suspicion (p. 233)
*Doing business with a criminal may **compromise** the company's good name.*
➤ Cognate (Spanish) **comprometer**

contention (kən ten′ shən) *n.* a verbal argument; quarrel (p. 235)
***Contention** over the new shopping mall caused problems in the town meeting.*
➤ Cognate (Spanish) **contienda**

subservient (səb sur′ vē ənt) *adj.* useful but inferior; submissive (p. 236)
*Jenna resented her **subservient** role in the family.*

pretense (prē′ tens) *n.* a false show or appearance (p. 240)
*He seemed to be working hard, but it was a **pretense**.*
➤ Cognate (Spanish) **pretensión**

evade (i vād′) *v.* to escape or avoid (p. 248)
*The criminal tried to **evade** police.*
➤ Cognate (Spanish) **evadir**

Content Vocabulary

packed (pakt) *adj.* crowded or filled (p. 231) *The park was **packed** with children.* 	**wither** (with′ ər) *v.* to dry up or shrivel (p. 235) *The plant will **wither** if you do not water it..*
leap (lēp) *v.* to jump (p. 246) *The horse tried to **leap** over the fence.* 	**limp** (limp) *adj.* lacking firmness or strength (p. 247) *After several days the flowers became **limp**.*

For more practice, see page 336. ➡

Vocabulary Routine

To introduce the vocabulary, follow the routine below.

Content Vocabulary

Define: If a room is **packed**, it is filled with people. Example: The restaurant was *packed* with hungry customers. Ask: What is one reason a theater might be *packed*? EXPLANATION

If something **withers**, it dries up. *After several weeks, a grape withers into a raisin.* What is something else that *withers* without water? EXAMPLE

If a hiker tries to **leap** across a stream, he tries to jump to the other side. *Try not to fall in the stream as you leap across.* Describe how a dancer would *leap*. DESCRIPTION

If something is **limp**, it is not firm or strong. *Cook the noodles until they become limp.* Give an example of something that is *limp*. EXAMPLE

Vocabulary Practice   Have students complete the vocabulary practice activity on page 336.

Selection Vocabulary

Define: To **compromise** something is to make it seem not as good or worthy as before. Example: If you hang out with known troublemakers, you will probably *compromise* your reputation. Ask: Can you create another sentence that uses *compromise* in this same way? EXAMPLE

Contention means verbal disagreement or argument. *After much contention, we finally agreed never to talk about politics.* What would you call the opposite of a state of contention? ANTONYM

Someone who deliberately acts inferior is being **subservient**. *The woman who waited on us at that restaurant didn't have to be so subservient.* What sorts of behaviors would you expect from someone who is subservient? DESCRIPTION

A **pretense** is a false impression, often conveyed by exaggerated manners or statements. *I suspect that when she says you didn't hurt her feelings it is just a pretense.* What relationship does the word *make-believe* have to *pretense*? SYNONYM

When a person deliberately avoids something, he or she **evades** it. *The escaped criminal evaded capture for more than twenty years.* Have you ever tried to evade something? What and why? EXPLANATION

THE CRUCIBLE

The Crucible

Interactive Question-Response

Background Information

Read aloud Background Information. Explain to students that in the 1950s, people were encouraged to report any suspicious behavior of their neighbors, family, and friends. Tell students that, as they read, they should think about the connection between the Salem witch trials and the 1950s government investigations.

Background Information

This play is set in 1692 in Salem, Massachusetts. But it was written in the 1950s, when the U.S. government was investigating anyone who appeared to have connections with communist groups.

Trouble in this house eventually lands on her back means that Tituba is eventually punished for everything that goes wrong.

To Sum Up

➤ The play takes place in Salem, Massachusetts, in 1692.

➤ As the story begins, Reverend Parris prays by the bed of his daughter.

➤ His daughter Betty is lying on the bed.

230

CHARACTERS
(in order of appearance)

REVEREND PARRIS	MERCY LEWIS	FRANCIS NURSE
BETTY PARRIS	MARY WARREN	EZEKIEL CHEEVER
TITUBA	JOHN PROCTOR	MARSHAL HERRICK
ABIGAIL WILLIAMS	REBECCA NURSE	JUDGE HATHORNE
SUSANNA WALCOTT	GILES COREY	DEPUTY GOVERNOR DANFORTH
MRS. ANN PUTNAM	REVEREND JOHN HALE	SARAH GOOD
THOMAS PUTNAM	ELIZABETH PROCTOR	HOPKINS

(An Overture)

[A small upper bedroom in the home of REVEREND SAMUEL PARRIS, Salem, Massachusetts, in the spring of the year 1692.

There is a narrow window at the left. Through its leaded panes the morning sunlight streams. A candle still burns near the bed, which is at the right. A chest, a chair, and a small table are the other furnishings. At the back a door opens on the landing of the stairway to the ground floor. The room gives off an air of clean spareness. The roof rafters are exposed, and the wood colors are raw and unmellowed.

As the curtain rises, REVEREND PARRIS is discovered kneeling beside the bed, evidently in prayer. His daughter, BETTY PARRIS, aged ten, is lying on the bed, inert.

REVEREND PARRIS is praying now, and, though we cannot hear his words, a sense of his confusion hangs about him. He mumbles, then seems about to weep; then he weeps, then prays again; but his daughter does not stir on the bed.

The door opens, and his Negro slave enters. TITUBA[1] is in her forties. PARRIS brought her with him from Barbados,[2] where he spent some years as a merchant before entering the ministry. She enters as one does who can no longer bear to be barred from the sight of her beloved, but she is also very frightened because her slave sense has warned her that, as always, **trouble in this house eventually lands on her back.**]

1. **Tituba** (ti tōō′ ba).
2. **Barbados** (bär ba′ dōz) is an island in the Caribbean that was, at the time of the play, an English colony.

Comprehension

To support students as they read the selection, have them begin the graphic organizer on page A44.

TITUBA. *[Already taking a step backward.]* My Betty be hearty soon?

PARRIS. Out of here!

TITUBA. *[Backing to the door.]* My Betty not goin' die...

PARRIS. *[Scrambling to his feet in a fury.]* Out of my sight! *[She is gone.]* Out of my—*[He is overcome with sobs. He clamps his teeth against them and closes the door and leans against it, exhausted.]* Oh, my God! God help me! *[Quaking with fear, mumbling to himself through his sobs, he goes to the bed and gently takes BETTY's hand.]* Betty. Child. Dear child. Will you wake, will you open up your eyes! Betty, little one...

[He is bending to kneel again when his niece, ABIGAIL WILLIAMS, seventeen, enters—a strikingly beautiful girl, an orphan, with an endless capacity for dissembling.[3] Now she is all worry and apprehension and propriety.]

ABIGAIL. Uncle? *[He looks to her.]* Susanna Walcott's here from Doctor Griggs.

PARRIS. Oh? Let her come, let her come.

ABIGAIL. *[Leaning out the door to call to SUSANNA, who is down the hall a few steps.]* Come in, Susanna.

[SUSANNA WALCOTT, a little younger than ABIGAIL, a nervous, hurried girl, enters.]

PARRIS. *[Eagerly.]* What does the doctor say, child?

SUSANNA. *[Craning around PARRIS to get a look at BETTY.]* He bid me come and tell you, reverend sir, that he cannot discover no medicine for it in his books.

PARRIS. Then he must search on.

SUSANNA. Aye, sir, he have been searchin' his books since he left you, sir. But he bid me tell you, that you might look to unnatural things for the cause of it.

PARRIS. *[His eyes going wide.]* No—no. There be no unnatural cause here. Tell him I have sent for Reverend Hale of Beverly, and Mr. Hale will surely confirm that. Let him look to medicine and put out all thought of unnatural causes here. There be none.

SUSANNA. Aye, sir. He bid me tell you. *[She turns to go.]*

ABIGAIL. Speak nothin' of it in the village, Susanna.

PARRIS. Go directly home and speak nothing of unnatural causes.

SUSANNA. Aye, sir. I pray for her. *[She goes out.]*

ABIGAIL. Uncle, the rumor of witchcraft is all about; I think you'd best go down and deny it yourself. The parlor's packed with people, sir. I'll sit with her.

PARRIS. *[Pressed, turns on her.]* And what shall I say to them? That my daughter and my niece I discovered dancing like heathen in the forest?

ABIGAIL. Uncle, we did dance; let you tell them I confessed it—and I'll be whipped if I must be. But they're speakin' of witchcraft. Betty's not witched.

3. **Dissembling** means "hiding one's true motives."

Comprehension Check

What does the doctor mean by "unnatural things"?

☐ poison
☑ witchcraft
☐ a virus

packed (pakt) *adj.* crowded or filled

To Sum Up

➤ Tituba, Reverend Parris's slave from Barbados, asks if Betty will be well soon.

➤ Abigail, Reverend Parris's niece, says that Susanna Walcott has come from the doctor.

➤ Susanna says that the doctor wants Reverend Parris to look for unnatural causes of Betty's sickness.

The Crucible **231**

Interactive Question-Response

Comprehension Check

If students have difficulty responding: **Model** *I know "natural" means something that happens or is found in nature. So "unnatural" must mean something that is not found in nature.* **Ask:** *Is poison found in nature? (yes) Is witchcraft found in nature? (no) Is a virus found in nature? (yes)*

Content Vocabulary

Read aloud the word and definition. Ask students to try using the word *packed* to describe an experience: **Model** *I went to a restaurant the other day. It was packed. I had to wait almost an hour to get a table.*

Interactive Question-Response

Literary Element Dialogue

If students have difficulty responding, have them go back and reread only Reverend Parris's lines. Encourage students to underline sentences that reveal Parris's attitude toward Abigail, his enemies, and evil spirits. Then have them share what they underlined.

Ask: *Of these three options–enemies, Abigail, and evil spirits–which does Reverend Parris seem most afraid of? (his enemies) Why? (He mentions "enemies" at least three times and worries abut a "faction" in the church.)*

Literary Element

Dialogue In this conversation between Reverend Parris and Abigail, what does Parris seem afraid of?

- ☑ his enemies
- ☐ Abigail
- ☐ evil spirits

It must come out means "it will not be a secret any more."

Drive me from my pulpit means "remove me from my job in the church."

To Sum Up

- ➤ Reverend Parris and Abigail argue.
- ➤ Reverend Parris saw Abigail with Betty and Tituba in the woods, dancing.
- ➤ Abigail says they did nothing wrong.

PARRIS.   Abigail, I cannot go before the congregation when I know you have not opened[4] with me. What did you do with her in the forest?

ABIGAIL.   We did dance, uncle, and when you leaped out of the bush so suddenly, Betty was frightened and then she fainted. And there's the whole of it.

PARRIS.   Child. Sit you down.

ABIGAIL.   *[Quavering, as she sits.]* I would never hurt Betty. I love her dearly.

PARRIS.   Now look you, child, your punishment will come in its time. But if you trafficked[5] with spirits in the forest I must know it now, for surely my enemies will, and they will ruin me with it.

ABIGAIL.   But we never conjured[6] spirits.

PARRIS.   Then why can she not move herself since midnight? This child is desperate! *[ABIGAIL lowers her eyes.]* **It must come out**—my enemies will bring it out. Let me know what you done there. Abigail, do you understand that I have many enemies?

ABIGAIL.   I have heard of it, uncle.

PARRIS.   There is a faction[7] that is sworn to **drive me from my pulpit.** Do you understand that?

ABIGAIL.   I think so, sir.

PARRIS.   Now then, in the midst of such disruption, my own household is discovered to be the very center of some obscene practice. Abominations[8] are done in the forest—

ABIGAIL.   It were sport,[9] uncle!

PARRIS.   *[Pointing at BETTY.]* You call this sport? *[She lowers her eyes. He pleads.]* Abigail, if you know something that may help the doctor, for God's sake tell it to me. *[She is silent.]* I saw Tituba waving her arms over the fire when I came on you. Why was she doing that? And I heard a screeching and gibberish coming from her mouth. She were swaying like a dumb beast over that fire!

ABIGAIL.   She always sings her Barbados songs, and we dance.

PARRIS.   I cannot blink[10] what I saw, Abigail, for my enemies will not blink it. I saw a dress lying on the grass.

ABIGAIL.   *[Innocently.]* A dress?

PARRIS.   *[It is very hard to say.]* Aye, a dress. And I thought I saw— someone naked running through the trees!

ABIGAIL.   *[In terror.]* No one was naked! You mistake yourself, uncle!

PARRIS.   *[With anger.]* I saw it! *[He moves from her. Then, resolved.]* Now tell me true, Abigail. And I pray you feel the weight of truth upon you, for now my ministry's at stake, my ministry and perhaps your cousin's life. Whatever abomination you have done, give me all of it now, for I dare not be taken unaware when I go before them down there.

ABIGAIL.   There is nothin' more. I swear it, uncle.

---

4. Here, ***have not opened*** means "have not been completely honest."
5. ***Trafficked*** means "dealt or did business with."
6. Here, ***conjured*** means "summoned by using magic spells."
7. A ***faction*** is a small group of people who disagree with the larger group.
8. ***Abominations*** are vile or shameful acts.
9. Here, ***sport*** means "innocent game."
10. Here, ***blink*** means "to deliberately ignore."

PARRIS. *[Studies her, then nods, half convinced.]* Abigail, I have fought here three long years to bend these **stiff-necked** people to me, and now, just now when some good respect is rising for me in the parish, you **compromise** my very character. I have given you a home, child, I have put clothes upon your back—now give me upright answer. Your name in the town—it is entirely white, is it not?

ABIGAIL. *[With an edge of resentment.]* Why, I am sure it is, sir. There be no **blush** about my name.

PARRIS. *[To the point.]* Abigail, is there any other cause than you have told me, for your being discharged from Goody[11] Proctor's service? I have heard it said, and I tell you as I heard it, that she comes so rarely to the church this year for she will not sit so close to something soiled. What signified that remark?

ABIGAIL. She hates me, uncle, she must, for I would not be her slave. It's a bitter woman, a lying, cold, sniveling woman, and I will not work for such a woman!

PARRIS. She may be. And yet it has troubled me that you are now seven month out of their house, and in all this time no other family has ever called for your service.

ABIGAIL. They want slaves, not such as I. Let them send to Barbados for that. I will not black my face for any of them! *[With ill-concealed resentment at him.]* Do you begrudge my bed, uncle?

PARRIS. No—no.

ABIGAIL. *[In a temper.]* My name is good in the village! I will not have it said my name is soiled! Goody Proctor is a gossiping liar! *[Enter MRS. ANN PUTNAM. She is a twisted soul of forty-five, a death-ridden woman, haunted by dreams.]*

REFLECT

Draw Conclusions About Characters
Write a detail about Abigail from the story. Then write what this detail tells you about the type of person she is.

Possible answer: Abigail often lowers her eyes when Parris talks to her. This could mean she doesn't want to look him in the eyes because she is lying.

 Talk about your answer with a partner.

Stiff-necked means "stubborn and arrogant."

Blush, here, means "shame." Abigail claims that her **name**, or reputation, is clean and without sin.

Vocabulary
compromise (kom′ prə mīz′) *v.* to expose to suspicion

11. **Goody** is short for Goodwife, a polite way to refer to a married woman.

To Sum Up

➤ Reverend Parris asks Abigail why she no longer works for Goody Proctor, a woman in the village. Abigail says that Goody Proctor is a liar and has spread rumors about Abigail.

➤ Reverend Parris asks Abigail if she has a good reputation.

➤ Abigail says she does have a good reputation.

The Crucible **233**

The Crucible

Interactive Question-Response

Reflect

Partner Talk Have students work in pairs to answer. To help students get started: **Model** *To answer this, I would scan the play from the beginning and look for the name "Abigail." Then I would make a list of details about her.* Encourage students to talk with their partners about what these details show about Abigail's character. Provide the following sentence frames:

Abigail is described as _____. That means she _____. (dissembling; lies)

Abigail says _____. The truth is that _____. (very little happened in the woods; she seems to be hiding something)

One thing Abigail does is _____. That tells me that she _____. (say nothing when Parris asks her for information that could help Betty; might know something but doesn't want to get in trouble)

Differentiated Instruction

Clarify the Text To support students in understanding the text, discuss the dialogue in the play.

Beginning/Early Intermediate Students may find it helpful to role-play the parts of Abigail and Reverend Parris. Have students work in pairs to improvise simple dialogue based on the To Sum Up statements.

Intermediate Students may encounter unfamiliar words, such as *upright, resentment, apprehension,* and *propriety.* Have students keep a list of words that are new or unfamiliar, and have them pause during their reading to look the words up in a dictionary.

Early Advanced Students may have trouble piecing together the story behind Reverend Parris's questioning of Abigail. **Ask:** *Why is Reverend Parris suspicious? (He heard that Goody Proctor has not come to church often, because she doesn't want to sit by something "soiled." He thinks it is odd that in seven months, no one has asked for Abigail's service.)*

Interactive Question-Response

Comprehension Check

Ask students to share what they underlined. Then have students think about what else the author reveals about Mrs. Putnam. **Ask:** *How does Mrs. Putnam seem to feel about her daughter's illness? (She seems almost pleased and not really worried.)* If students have difficulty responding: **Model** *I think it's strange that Mrs. Putnam is at the Parrises' house at all. If she were really worried about her daughter, she would have stayed home with her. What other clues tell you how she really feels? (She is "shiny-eyed" and "very pleased." She is quick to mention hell, as though these events confirm something she has believed for a long time.)*

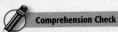

Comprehension Check

Reread the second boxed text. Underline what Mrs. Putnam thinks has caused her daughter's sickness.

Well-to-do means "wealthy" or "rich."

To Sum Up

➤ Mr. and Mrs. Putnam come in.

➤ Their daughter, Ruth Putnam, is also sick.

➤ The Putnams think that both sicknesses are caused by witchcraft.

PARRIS. [As soon as the door begins to open.] No—no, I cannot have anyone. [He sees her, and a certain deference[12] springs into him, although his worry remains.] Why, Goody Putnam, come in.

MRS. PUTNAM. [Full of breath, shiny-eyed.] It is a marvel. It is surely a stroke of hell upon you.

PARRIS. No, Goody Putnam, it is—

MRS. PUTNAM. [Glancing at BETTY.] How high did she fly, how high?

PARRIS. No, no, she never flew—

MRS. PUTNAM. [Very pleased with it.] Why, it's sure she did. Mr. Collins saw her goin' over Ingersoll's barn, and come down light as bird, he says!

PARRIS. Now, look you, Goody Putnam, she never—[Enter THOMAS PUTNAM, a well-to-do, hard-handed landowner, near fifty.] Oh, good morning, Mr. Putnam.

PUTNAM. It is a providence[13] the thing is out now! It is a providence. [He goes directly to the bed.]

PARRIS. What's out, sir, what's—?
[MRS. PUTNAM goes to the bed.]

PUTNAM. [Looking down at BETTY.] Why, her eyes is closed! Look you, Ann.

MRS. PUTNAM. Why, that's strange. [To PARRIS.] Ours is open.

PARRIS. [Shocked.] Your Ruth is sick?

MRS. PUTNAM. [With vicious certainty.] I'd not call it sick; the Devil's touch is heavier than sick. It's death, y'know, it's death drivin' into them, forked and hoofed.

PARRIS. Oh, pray not! Why, how does Ruth ail?

MRS. PUTNAM. She ails as she must—she never waked this morning, but her eyes open and she walks, and hears naught,[14] sees naught, and cannot eat. Her soul is taken, surely.
[PARRIS is struck.]

PUTNAM. [As though for further details.] They say you've sent for Reverend Hale of Beverly?

PARRIS. [With dwindling conviction[15] now.] A precaution only. He has much experience in all demonic arts, and I—

MRS. PUTNAM. He has indeed; and found a witch in Beverly last year, and let you remember that.

PARRIS. Now, Goody Ann, they only thought that were a witch, and I am certain there be no element of witchcraft here.

PUTNAM. No witchcraft! Now look you, Mr. Parris—

PARRIS. Thomas, Thomas, I pray you, leap not to witchcraft. I know that you—you least of all, Thomas, would ever wish so disastrous a charge laid upon me. We cannot leap to witchcraft. They will howl me out of Salem for such corruption in my house.

PUTNAM. [At the moment, he is intent upon getting PARRIS, for whom he has only contempt, to move toward the abyss.] Mr. Parris, I have taken

12. **Deference** is "polite respect."
13. Here, **providence** means "a blessing" or "an act of divine care."
14. **Naught** means "nothing."
15. Here, **conviction** means "certainty."

Differentiated Instruction

Clarify the Text To support students in understanding the text, discuss the dialogue in the play.

Beginning/Early Intermediate **Ask:** *What does Mrs. Putnam think is the cause of Ruth and Betty's illness? (witchcraft)* Provide the following sentence frames:

Mrs. Putnam has heard that _____. (Betty flew)

She thinks Ruth's illness is related to _____. (the deaths of her other seven children)

Intermediate **Ask:** *What is different about the sicknesses of Betty and Ruth? What is similar? (Betty's eyes are closed. She has tried to climb out the window. Ruth seems to be numb. Her eyes are open, but she doesn't see or hear. Both girls may have been involved in suspicious activities in the woods.)*

Early Advanced Have students discuss how these events could have led to hysteria, trials, and death: **Model** *The parents are very concerned about their daughters. They also seem very superstitious. They seem to think the world is full of great evil. The townspeople clearly have old grudges against one another. I think some people may see these events as an excuse to get even with people they don't like.*

your part in all **contention** here, and I would continue; but I cannot if you hold back in this. There are hurtful, vengeful spirits layin' hands on these children.

PARRIS.   But, Thomas, you cannot—

PUTNAM.   Ann! Tell Mr. Parris what you have done.

MRS. PUTNAM.   Reverend Parris, I have laid seven babies unbaptized in the earth. Believe me, sir, you never saw more hearty babies born. And yet, each would <u>wither</u> in my arms the very night of their birth. I have spoke nothin', but my heart has clamored intimations.[16] And now, this year, my Ruth, my only—I see her turning strange. A secret child she has become this year, and shrivels like a sucking mouth were pullin' on her life too. And so I thought to send her to your Tituba—

PARRIS.   To Tituba! What may Tituba—?

MRS. PUTNAM.   Tituba knows how to speak to the dead, Mr. Parris.

PARRIS.   Goody Ann, it is a formidable sin to conjure up the dead!

MRS. PUTNAM.   I take it on my soul, but who else may surely tell us what person murdered my babies?

PARRIS.   [Horrified.] Woman!

MRS. PUTNAM.   They were murdered, Mr. Parris! And mark this proof! Mark it! Last night my Ruth were ever so close to their little spirits; I know it, sir. For how else is she struck dumb now except some power of darkness would stop her mouth? It is a marvelous sign, Mr. Parris!

PUTNAM.   Don't you understand it, sir? There is a murdering witch among us, bound to keep herself in the dark. [PARRIS turns to BETTY, a frantic terror rising in him.] Let your enemies make of it what they will, you cannot blink it more.

PARRIS.   [To ABIGAIL.] Then you were conjuring spirits last night.

ABIGAIL.   [Whispering.] Not I, sir—Tituba and Ruth.

PARRIS.   [Turns now, with new fear, and goes to BETTY, looks down at her, and then, gazing off.] Oh, Abigail, what proper payment for my charity! Now **I am undone.**

PUTNAM.   You are not undone! Let you take hold here. Wait for no one to charge you—declare it yourself. You have discovered witchcraft—

PARRIS.   In my house? In my house, Thomas? They will topple me with this! They will make of it a—

[Enter MERCY LEWIS, the PUTNAMS' servant, a fat, sly, merciless girl of eighteen.]

MERCY.   Your pardons. I only thought to see how Betty is.

PUTNAM.   Why aren't you home? Who's with Ruth?

MERCY.   Her grandma come. She's improved a little, I think—she give a powerful sneeze before.

MRS. PUTNAM.   Ah, there's a sign of life!

Vocabulary

contention (kən ten′ shən) *n.* a verbal argument; quarreling

16. A heart that has **clamored intimations** has nagged its owner with suggestions (of possible witchcraft).

Literary Element

Dialogue Reread the conversation between Mrs. Putnam and Reverend Parris at the top of the page. Why did Mrs. Putnam send Ruth to Tituba?

Possible answer: She wanted

Tituba to talk to the dead

and find out why her babies

keep dying.

wither (with′ ər) *v.* to dry up or shrivel

I am undone means "I am ruined." Parris is certain that Abigail's actions will cause him to lose his job.

To Sum Up

➤ Mrs. Putnam says that seven of her babies died soon after birth.

➤ Mrs. Putnam sent Ruth to Tituba because Tituba claims to be able to contact the dead.

➤ Ruth, Tituba, and Abigail had been trying to contact Mrs. Putnam's babies when they were found dancing.

Interactive Question-Response

Literary Element   Dialogue

Ask students to share their answers to the question. **Ask:** *How does Reverend Parris feel about Mrs. Putnam's actions? (He is shocked.) How do you know? (Reverend Parris says, "To Tituba! What may Tituba—?")*

Content Vocabulary

Read aloud the word and its definition. Have students find the word *withers* on the page. Then ask a volunteer to read aloud the sentence containing the word. **Ask:** *What word in this paragraph has a meaning that is similar to withers? (shrivels) How does this word help you understand Mrs. Putnam's behavior? (She has watched seven babies die inexplicably. She needs to blame someone for their deaths. She cannot bear to blame herself.)*

Interactive Question-Response

Literary Element Dialogue

If students have difficulty responding: **Model** *This conversation shows Mercy and Abigail speaking truthfully to each other. All of the adults have left the room, and the girls are trying to decide what to do. To be believable, the girls must tell the same story. I know Abigail lied to Parris because before she said that no one was naked. Now she says Mercy was naked.*

Strike out against means "attack."

Literary Element

Dialogue Reread the boxed text at the bottom of the page. What does the dialogue between Abigail and Mercy reveal? Check all that apply.

☑ Abigail lied to Parris about what happened in the woods.

☐ Abigail and Mercy put Betty under enchantment.

☑ Mercy was the naked person that Parris saw in the woods.

To Sum Up

➤ Some people from the village have gathered at the Parris's home.

➤ Reverend Parris goes downstairs to lead the people in a psalm.

➤ Abigail talks to another girl, Mercy Lewis, who is the Putnam's servant. Mercy was with Abigail in the woods.

➤ As Mercy and Abigail talk, Mary Warren comes in. She is very scared.

236

MERCY. I'd fear no more, Goody Putnam. It were a grand sneeze; another like it will shake her wits together, I'm sure. [*She goes to the bed to look.*]

PARRIS. Will you leave me now, Thomas? I would pray a while alone.

ABIGAIL. Uncle, you've prayed since midnight. Why do you not go down and—

PARRIS. No—no. [*To* putnam.] I have no answer for that crowd. I'll wait till Mr. Hale arrives. [*To get* MRS. PUTNAM *to leave.*] If you will, Goody Ann…

PUTNAM. Now look you, sir. Let you **strike out against** the Devil, and the village will bless you for it! Come down, speak to them—pray with them. They're thirsting for your word, Mister! Surely you'll pray with them.

PARRIS. [*Swayed.*] I'll lead them in a psalm, but let you say nothing of witchcraft yet. I will not discuss it. The cause is yet unknown. I have had enough contention since I came; I want no more.

MRS. PUTNAM. Mercy, you go home to Ruth, d'y'hear?

MERCY. Aye, mum.

[MRS. PUTNAM *goes out.*]

PARRIS. [*To* ABIGAIL.] If she starts for the window, cry for me at once.

ABIGAIL. I will, uncle.

PARRIS. [*To* PUTNAM.] There is a terrible power in her arms today. [*He goes out with* PUTNAM.]

ABIGAIL. [*With hushed trepidation.*][17] How is Ruth sick?

MERCY. It's weirdish, I know not—she seems to walk like a dead one since last night.

ABIGAIL. [*Turns at once and goes to* BETTY, *and now, with fear in her voice.*] Betty? [BETTY *doesn't move. She shakes her.*] Now stop this! Betty! Sit up now!

[BETTY *doesn't stir.* MERCY *comes over.*]

MERCY. Have you tried beatin' her? I gave Ruth a good one and it waked her for a minute. Here, let me have her.

ABIGAIL. [*Holding* MERCY *back.*] No, he'll be comin' up. Listen, now; if they be questioning us, tell them we danced—I told him as much already.

MERCY. Aye. And what more?

ABIGAIL. He knows Tituba conjured Ruth's sisters to come out of the grave.

MERCY. And what more?

ABIGAIL. He saw you naked.

MERCY. [*Clapping her hands together with a frightened laugh.*] Oh, Jesus! [*Enter* MARY WARREN, *breathless. She is seventeen, a* **subservient**, *naive, lonely girl.*]

MARY WARREN. What'll we do? The village is out! I just come from the farm; the whole country's talkin' witchcraft! They'll be callin' us witches, Abby!

Vocabulary

subservient (səb sur' vē ənt) *adj.* useful but inferior; submissive

17. **Trepidation** means "fear" or "anxiety."

Differentiated Instruction

Clarify the Text Support students in understanding the relationships between characters.

Beginning/Early Intermediate Students may find the family relationships confusing. **Ask:** *Are Abigail and Parris related? How?* (Yes; she is his niece.) *How are Betty and Reverend Parris related?* (She is his daughter.) *Is Parris related to the Putnams?* (no)

Intermediate Students may struggle to keep track of characters. Have students look back at the cast of characters on the first page of the play. Have them write one short sentence about each character they have encountered thus far in their reading.

Early Advanced Students may skim over the stage directions: **Model** *I think it is important to know who is in the room at all times, because some people are keeping secrets.* Encourage students to circle or underline the stage directions that show entrances and exits, or make to sketches or diagrams in the margins.

MERCY. [*Pointing and looking at* MARY WARREN.] She means to tell, I know it.

MARY WARREN. Abby, we've got to tell. Witchery's a hangin' error, a hangin' like they done in Boston two year ago! We must tell the truth, Abby! You'll only be whipped for dancin', and the other things!

ABIGAIL. Oh, we'll be whipped!

MARY WARREN. I never done none of it, Abby. I only looked!

MERCY. [*Moving menacingly toward* MARY.] Oh, you're a great one for lookin', aren't you, Mary Warren? What a grand peeping courage you have!

[BETTY, *on the bed, whimpers.* ABIGAIL *turns to her at once.*]

ABIGAIL. Betty? [*She goes to* BETTY.] Now, Betty, dear, wake up now. It's Abigail. [*She sits* BETTY *up and furiously shakes her.*] I'll beat you, Betty! [BETTY *whimpers.*] My, you seem improving. I talked to your papa and I told him everything. So there's nothing to—

BETTY. [*Darts off the bed, frightened of* ABIGAIL, *and flattens herself against the wall.*] I want my mama!

ABIGAIL. [*With alarm, as she cautiously approaches* BETTY.] **What ails you,** Betty? Your mama's dead and buried.

BETTY. I'll fly to Mama. Let me fly! [*She raises her arms as though to fly, and streaks for the window, gets one leg out.*]

ABIGAIL. [*Pulling her away from the window.*] I told him everything; he knows now, he knows everything we—

BETTY. You drank blood, Abby! You didn't tell him that!

ABIGAIL. Betty, you never say that again! You will never—

BETTY. You did, you did! You **drank a charm** to kill John Proctor's wife! You drank a charm to kill Goody Proctor!

What ails you? means "What is wrong with you?"

Drank a charm means "drank a magic potion."

REFLECT

Draw Conclusions About Characters

Think about Abigail and Mercy. Think about how they are similar. Give one detail about each girl that shows how they are similar.

Abigail shakes Betty, threatens her, and yells at her.

Mercy moves menacingly toward Mary and bullies her.

_____

_____

_____

Talk about your answer with a partner.

To Sum Up

➤ Mary was also with the girls in the woods.

➤ Mary tells the others that people are calling them witches. She tries to claim that she is innocent, but Abigail and Mercy threaten her.

➤ Suddenly Betty gets out of bed and tries to jump out the window. She yells that she is going to fly to her mother, who is dead.

The Crucible **237**

Interactive Question-Response

To Sum Up

Beginning/Early Intermediate ▶ Have students work in pairs to reread all the To Sum Up statements from the beginning of the play. Then have pairs summarize the information that has been revealed in the play so far. Students can use the following sentence frames to organize their thoughts.

Two girls in the village are _____.

People think the problem may be _____.

Ruth, Tituba, and Abigail _____.

(Two girls in the village are very sick. People think the problem may be caused by witchcraft. Ruth, Tituba, and Abigail were dancing in the woods.)

Reflect

Partner Talk Have students work in pairs to answer. To help students get started: **Model** *I'm going to use details about what the characters say to draw conclusions.* Have partners take turns reading aloud the text on pages 236 and 237. Have them pause often and ask each other questions to clarify characters' speech and behavior.

Interactive Question-Response

Comprehension Check

If students are having trouble responding, read aloud the question and each response: **Model** *All of these responses seem like they would make Abigail angry, if they were true. So I need to find out which ones are true and which ones are not. I think Abigail does not want to get in trouble. That's why she tells Mercy what she has told Parris. I think Abigail is in love with John Proctor, but I'm not sure Mary and Betty are in love with him. So I'll leave that answer unchecked.*

Ask: *Why do you think Betty and Mary Warren are so frightened? (They are scared of Abigail, who is vicious. They do not want to get in trouble for what happened in the woods. Mary is genuinely afraid that their activities are going to cause Betty's death.)*

A pointy reckoning is a knife or a dagger. *That will shudder you* means "that will make you shake with fear." Abigail threatens to kill the girls if they ever reveal what they did in the woods.

Comprehension Check

Why is Abigail angry with Mary and Betty? Check all that apply.

- ☑ Abigail does not want to get in trouble.
- ☐ Abigail is in love with John Proctor. So are Mary and Betty.
- ☑ Abigail tried to cast a spell that would kill John Proctor's wife. Betty threatens to reveal this information.
- ☐ Abigail wants the girls to confess.

To Sum Up

➤ Abigail hits Betty in the face. Betty falls on the bed as if she has fainted.

➤ Mary is becoming very frightened. Abigail tells her to "shut it," or keep quiet about what they have done.

➤ Mary and Mercy leave. John Proctor, a farmer, comes in.

ABIGAIL. [*Smashes her across the face.*] Shut it! Now shut it!

BETTY. [*Collapsing on the bed.*] Mama, Mama! [*She dissolves into sobs.*]

ABIGAIL. Now look you. All of you. We danced. And Tituba conjured Ruth Putnam's dead sisters. And that is all. And mark this. Let either of you breathe a word, or the edge of a word, about the other things, and I will come to you in the black of some terrible night and I will bring **a pointy reckoning that will shudder you.** And you know I can do it; I saw Indians smash my dear parents' heads on the pillow next to mine, and I have seen some reddish work[18] done at night, and I can make you wish you had never seen the sun go down! [*She goes to* BETTY *and roughly sits her up.*] Now, you—sit up and stop this! [*But* BETTY *collapses in her hands and lies inert on the bed.*]

MARY WARREN. [*With hysterical fright.*] What's got her? [ABIGAIL *stares in fright at betty.*] Abby, she's going to die! It's a sin to conjure, and we—

ABIGAIL. [*Starting for* MARY.] I say shut it, Mary Warren! [*Enter* JOHN PROCTOR. *On seeing him,* MARY WARREN *leaps in fright.*]

MARY WARREN. Oh! I'm just going home, Mr. Proctor.

PROCTOR. Be you foolish, Mary Warren? Be you deaf? I forbid you leave the house, did I not? Why shall I pay you? I am looking for you more often than my cows!

MARY WARREN. I only come to see the great doings in the world.

PROCTOR. I'll show you a great doin' on your arse one of these days. Now get you home; my wife is waitin' with your work! [*Trying to retain a shred of dignity, she goes slowly out.*]

MERCY LEWIS. [*Both afraid of him and strangely titillated.*][19] I'd best be off. I have my Ruth to watch. Good morning, Mr. Proctor. [MERCY *sidles out. Since* PROCTOR'S *entrance,* ABIGAIL *has stood as though on tiptoe, absorbing his presence, wide-eyed. He glances at her, then goes to* BETTY *on the bed.*]

ABIGAIL. Gah! I'd almost forgot how strong you are, John Proctor!

PROCTOR. [*Looking at* ABIGAIL *now, the faintest suggestion of a knowing smile on his face.*] What's this mischief here?

ABIGAIL. [*With a nervous laugh.*] Oh, she's only gone silly somehow.

PROCTOR. The road past my house is a pilgrimage to Salem all morning. The town's mumbling witchcraft.

ABIGAIL. Oh, posh! [*Winningly she comes a little closer, with a confidential, wicked air.*] We were dancin' in the woods last night, and my uncle leaped in on us. She took fright, is all.

PROCTOR. [*His smile widening.*] Ah, you're wicked yet, aren't y'! [*A trill of expectant laughter escapes her, and she dares come closer, feverishly looking into his eyes.*] You'll be clapped in the stocks[20] before you're twenty. [*He takes a step to go, and she springs into his path.*]

---

18. *Reddish work* means "bloody deeds."
19. To be *titillated* is to be pleasantly excited.
20. The word *stocks* refers to a heavy wooden frame with holes for holding the ankles and wrists of someone who is found guilty of a crime. The stocks exposed the guilty person to public shame.

ABIGAIL. Give me a word, John. A soft word. *[Her concentrated desire destroys his smile.]*

PROCTOR. No, no, Abby. That's done with.

ABIGAIL. *[Tauntingly.]*[21] You come five mile to see a silly girl fly? I know you better.

PROCTOR. *[Setting her firmly out of his path.]* I come to see what mischief your uncle's brewin' now. *[With final emphasis.]* Put it out of mind, Abby.

ABIGAIL. *[Grasping his hand before he can release her.]* John—I am waitin' for you every night.

PROCTOR. Abby, I never give you hope to wait for me.

ABIGAIL. *[Now beginning to anger—she can't believe it.]* I have something better than hope, I think!

PROCTOR. Abby, you'll put it out of mind. I'll not be comin' for you more.

ABIGAIL. You're surely sportin' with me.

PROCTOR. You know me better.

ABIGAIL. I know how you clutched my back behind your house and sweated like a stallion whenever I come near! Or did I dream that? It's she put me out, you cannot pretend it were you. I saw your face when she put me out, and you loved me then and you do now!

PROCTOR. Abby, that's a wild thing to say—

ABIGAIL. A wild thing may say wild things. But not so wild, I think. I have seen you since she put me out; I have seen you nights.

PROCTOR. I have hardly stepped off my farm this sevenmonth.

ABIGAIL. I have a sense for heat, John, and yours has drawn me to my window, and I have seen you looking up, burning in your loneliness. Do you tell me you've never looked up at my window?

PROCTOR. I may have looked up.

ABIGAIL. *[Now softening.]* And you must. You are no **wintry** man. I know you, John. I know you. *[She is weeping.]* I cannot sleep for dreamin'; I cannot dream but I wake and walk about the house as though I'd find you comin' through some door. *[She clutches him desperately.]*

PROCTOR. *[Gently pressing her from him, with great sympathy but firmly.]* Child—

ABIGAIL. *[With a flash of anger.]* How do you call me child!

PROCTOR. Abby, I may think of you softly from time to time. But I will cut off my hand before I'll ever reach for you again. Wipe it out of mind. We never touched, Abby.

ABIGAIL. Aye, but we did.

PROCTOR. Aye, but we did not.

ABIGAIL. *[With a bitter anger.]* Oh, I marvel how such a strong man may let such a sickly wife be—

PROCTOR. *[Angered—at himself as well.]* You'll speak nothin' of Elizabeth!

21. **Tauntingly** means "in a scornful way."

Literary Element

Dialogue Reread the boxed text at the bottom of the page. What does John Proctor mean by "We never touched, Abby"?

He means that he is ending their affair, and that he will not admit to it.

_____

_____

Wintry, here, means "cold or unemotional."

To Sum Up

➤ Abigail flirts with John Proctor. It is clear that they have had an affair.

➤ Abigail used to work for the Proctors. Proctor's wife made Abigail leave because of the affair.

➤ Proctor does not want to continue the affair, but Abigail is in love with him.

Interactive Question-Response

Literary Element Dialogue

If students have difficulty responding, ask them to decide if this statement is literally true. **Ask:** *Did Abigail and John Proctor, in fact, touch? (yes) How do you know? (He says "reach for you again.")* Have students restate John Proctor's dialogue in their own words, focusing on what he really means.

Fluency

Intonation and Pacing: Smooth Reading

Intermediate/Early Advanced ➤ Tell students that they will be doing a choral reading of the dialogue on this page. Have students read the text ahead of time to practice reading smoothly, and not word for word. Model the fluency skill as you read the text at a moderate tempo. Then have one student read a sentence. Have another student join in, and a third, and so on. When students reach the end of the passage, have pairs of students reread to each other. To assess individual fluency, use the Oral Reading Guidelines on page T16.

Beginning/Early Intermediate ➤ Have these students choral read only the boxed text at the bottom of the page. Before they begin, model the pronunciation of the text. Then have students practice reading the paragraph in pairs before the choral reading.

Interactive Question-Response

Comprehension Check

Point out that two things are going on right before Betty covers her ears. Abigail is declaring her love for John Proctor, and people downstairs are singing a psalm. Tell students that they have to read carefully to understand which events the author wants them to connect to. Have students find evidence in the text to support the idea that Betty screams as a result of the psalm. *(Students may suggest that the stage direction implies a connection between the psalm and Betty's distress, or that Abigail reports that Betty is upset because of the singing.)*

Here, **Look for** means "want." Proctor means that he will whip Abigail if she continues to speak this way.

Comprehension Check

What seems to cause Betty to cover her ears and scream?
- ☑ The words "going up to Jesus" are heard.
- ☐ Abigail screams at her and hits her in the face.
- ☐ Proctor and Abigail are having an argument.

22. A covenant is an agreement or promise. Among the Puritans, a **covenanted** person had made a commitment to the church and had signed an agreement testifying to his or her faith.
23. **Prodigious** means "amazing."
24. **Canny** means "clever and careful in one's dealings with others."

To Sum Up

- ➤ As the people downstairs sing the words "going up to Jesus," Betty suddenly wakes and screams.
- ➤ Reverend Parris and the Putnams run in.
- ➤ Mrs. Putnam thinks that Betty cannot bear to hear the Lord's name. The Putnams think this is a sign of witchcraft.

240

ABIGAIL.   She is blackening my name in the village! She is telling lies about me! She is a cold, sniveling woman, and you bend to her! Let her turn you like a—

PROCTOR.   *[Shaking her.]* Do you **look for** whippin'?
[A psalm is heard being sung below.]

ABIGAIL.   *[In tears.]* I look for John Proctor that took me from my sleep and put knowledge in my heart! I never knew what **pretense** Salem was, I never knew the lying lessons I was taught by all these Christian women and their covenanted[22] men! And now you bid me tear the light out of my eyes? I will not, I cannot! You loved me, John Proctor, and whatever sin it is, you love me yet! *[He turns abruptly to go out. She rushes to him.]* John, pity me, pity me!
[The words "going up to Jesus" are heard in the psalm, and BETTY claps her ears suddenly and whines loudly.]

ABIGAIL.   Betty? *[She hurries to BETTY, who is now sitting up and screaming. PROCTOR goes to BETTY as ABIGAIL is trying to pull her hands down, calling "Betty!"]*

PROCTOR.   *[Growing unnerved.]* What's she doing? Girl, what ails you? Stop that wailing!
[The singing has stopped in the midst of this, and now PARRIS rushes in.]

PARRIS.   What happened? What are you doing to her? Betty! *[He rushes to the bed, crying, "Betty, Betty!" MRS. PUTNAM enters, feverish with curiosity, and with her THOMAS PUTNAM and MERCY LEWIS. PARRIS, at the bed, keeps lightly slapping BETTY's face, while she moans and tries to get up.]*

ABIGAIL.   She heard you singin' and suddenly she's up and screamin'.

MRS. PUTNAM.   The psalm! The psalm! She cannot bear to hear the Lord's name!

PARRIS.   No, God forbid. Mercy, run to the doctor! Tell him what's happened here! *[MERCY LEWIS rushes out.]*

MRS. PUTNAM.   Mark it for a sign, mark it!

[REBECCA NURSE, seventy-two, enters. She is white-haired, leaning upon her walking-stick.]

PUTNAM.   *[Pointing at the whimpering BETTY.]* That is a notorious sign of witchcraft afoot, Goody Nurse, a prodigious[23] sign!

MRS. PUTNAM.   My mother told me that! When they cannot bear to hear the name of—

PARRIS.   *[Trembling.]* Rebecca, Rebecca, go to her, we're lost. She suddenly cannot bear to hear the Lord's—
[GILES COREY, eighty-three, enters. He is knotted with muscle, canny,[24] inquisitive, and still powerful.]

REBECCA.   There is hard sickness here, Giles Corey, so please to keep the quiet.

GILES.   I've not said a word. No one here can testify I've said a word. Is she going to fly again? I hear she flies.

PUTNAM.   Man, be quiet now!

Vocabulary ....
pretense (prē' tens) *n.* a false show or appearance

[*Everything is quiet.* REBECCA *walks across the room to the bed. Gentleness exudes*[25] *from her.* BETTY *is quietly whimpering, eyes shut.* REBECCA *simply stands over the child, who gradually quiets.*]

MRS. PUTNAM. [*Astonished.*] What have you done?

[REBECCA, *in thought, now leaves the bedside and sits.*]

PARRIS. [*Wondrous and relieved.*] What do you make of it, Rebecca?

PUTNAM. [*Eagerly.*] Goody Nurse, will you go to my Ruth and see if you can wake her?

REBECCA. [*Sitting.*] I think she'll wake in time. Pray calm yourselves. I have eleven children, and I am twenty-six times a grandma, and I have seen them all through their silly seasons, and when it come on them they will **run the Devil bowlegged** keeping up with their mischief. I think she'll wake when she tires of it. A child's spirit is like a child, you can never catch it by running after it; you must stand still, and, for love, it will soon itself come back.

PROCTOR. Aye, that's the truth of it, Rebecca.

MRS. PUTNAM. This is no silly season, Rebecca. My Ruth is bewildered, Rebecca; she cannot eat.

REBECCA. Perhaps she is not hungered yet. [*To* PARRIS.] I hope you are not decided to go in search of loose spirits, Mr. Parris. I've heard promise of that outside.

PARRIS. A wide opinion's running in the parish that the Devil may be among us, and I would satisfy them that they are wrong.

PROCTOR. Then let you come out and call them wrong. Did you consult the wardens[26] before you called this minister to look for devils?

PARRIS. He is not coming to look for devils!

PROCTOR. Then what's he coming for?

25. *Exudes* means "gives forth" or "gives off."
26. The church *wardens* were members who managed the church's business affairs.

REFLECT

Draw Conclusions About Characters
How are Mrs. Putnam and Rebecca Nurse different? Explain how the women are different using details from the play.

Possible answer: Mrs. Putnam is anxious, while Rebecca

seems calm. Mrs. Putnam is one of the first to be convinced

that witchcraft is the cause of the sickness. Rebecca advises

people to stay calm and not draw hasty conclusions.

 Talk about your answer with a partner.

 Literary Element

Dialogue Paraphrase Rebecca Nurse's advice about how to handle Ruth and Betty.

Possible answer: Don't make

too much out of their actions.

Just stay calm, and wait and

see what happens.

When Rebecca says that children will ***run the Devil bowlegged***, she means that children can get into so much mischief, or misbehavior, that the Devil himself cannot keep up with them.

To Sum Up

➤ An old woman named Rebecca Nurse comes in.

➤ Rebecca thinks that Ruth and Betty are not sick.

➤ Rebecca thinks that the girls are going through a "silly season," as children often do.

The Crucible

Interactive Question-Response

Literary Element Dialogue

If students are having trouble responding, have them read through Rebecca's lines once more. As they do so, have them underline words that explain what Rebecca thinks they ought to do about Betty. Students may find it helpful to look for times when Rebecca addresses the others as "you." (*Students may underline "pray calm yourselves" and "you must stand still, and, for love, it will soon itself come back."*)

Reflect

Partner Talk Have students work in pairs to answer the question. To help students get started: **Model** *What is Mrs. Putnam like? She was very quick to say that witchcraft caused all the trouble. So I know that she is anxious and impulsive. Also, I know she was the one who sent Ruth to Tituba. So she is superstitious, and she is already certain that witches are at work in the village.* Following your example, have students summarize what they know about Rebecca Nurse.

Then provide this sentence frame to help students organize their thoughts:

Mrs. Putnam is _____, but Rebecca Nurse is _____. (vicious; gentle)

Interactive Question-Response

Literary Element Dialogue

Have students share the words they underlined. Help students discuss how they identified these words. **Ask:** *What does Rebecca Nurse have that Mrs. Putnam wants? (many children and grandchildren) In what sentence does Mrs. Putnam talk about this difference? ("You think it God's work …")*

Seed, here, means "offspring."

To **fathom** something is to understand it.

Literary Element

Dialogue Underline the words that show that Mrs. Putnam is jealous of Rebecca Nurse.

To Sum Up

➤ The Putnams do not agree with Rebecca.

➤ The Putnams think that because seven of their babies have died, there must be witchcraft in the village.

242

PUTNAM. There be children dyin' in the village, Mister!

PROCTOR. I seen none dyin'. This society will not be a bag to swing around your head, Mr. Putnam. *[To PARRIS.]* Did you call a meeting before you—?

PUTNAM. I am sick of meetings; cannot the man turn his head without he have a meeting?

PROCTOR. He may turn his head, but not to Hell!

REBECCA. Pray, John, be calm. *[Pause. He defers to her.]* Mr. Parris, I think you'd best send Reverend Hale back as soon as he come. This will set us all to arguin' again in the society, and we thought to have peace this year. I think we ought rely on the doctor now, and good prayer.

MRS. PUTNAM. Rebecca, the doctor's baffled!

REBECCA. If so he is, then let us go to God for the cause of it. There is prodigious danger in the seeking of loose spirits. I fear it, I fear it. Let us rather blame ourselves and—

PUTNAM. How may we blame ourselves? I am one of nine sons; the Putnam **seed** have peopled this province. And yet I have but one child left of eight—and now she shrivels!

REBECCA. I cannot **fathom** that.

MRS. PUTNAM. *[With a growing edge of sarcasm.]* But I must! <u>You think it God's work you should never lose a child, nor grandchild either, and I bury all but one?</u> There are wheels within wheels in this village, and fires within fires![27]

PUTNAM. *[To PARRIS.]* When Reverend Hale comes, you will proceed to look for signs of witchcraft here.

PROCTOR. *[To PUTNAM.]* You cannot command Mr. Parris. We vote by name in this society, not by acreage.

PUTNAM. I never heard you worried so on this society, Mr. Proctor. I do not think I saw you at Sabbath meeting since snow flew.

PROCTOR. I have trouble enough without I come five mile to hear him preach only hellfire and bloody damnation. Take it to heart, Mr. Parris. There are many others who stay away from church these days because you hardly ever mention God any more.

PARRIS. *[Now aroused.]* Why, that's a drastic charge!

REBECCA. It's somewhat true; there are many that quail[28] to bring their children—

PARRIS. I do not preach for children, Rebecca. It is not the children who are unmindful of their obligations toward this ministry.

REBECCA. Are there really those unmindful?

PARRIS. I should say the better half of Salem village—

PUTNAM. And more than that!

PARRIS. Where is my wood? My contract provides I be supplied with all my firewood. I am waiting since November for a stick, and even in November I had to show my frostbitten hands like some London beggar!

27. The expression **wheels within wheels, and fires within fires** means "things are not as simple or innocent as they seem."

28. To **quail** is to hesitate or retreat in fear.

Word Study   BLM

Homophones

Remind students that homophones are words that have different meanings but sound the same. Draw their attention to the word *there* in the highlighted passage and note that homophones for this word often cause writers confusion. **Ask:** Can you think of two homophones for *there*? (*Their,* meaning "belonging to them," and *they're,* meaning "they are.") Write the following three sentences on the board and have students fill the blanks with the correct words.

1. I went to _____ *(their)* house, but they weren't at home.

2. I went to the house, but no one was _____ *(there)*.

3. I knocked on the door, but _____ *(they're)* not home.

Have students practice more with homophones by completing the activity on page A45.

GILES.   You are allowed six pound a year to buy your wood, Mr. Parris.

PARRIS.   I regard that six pound as part of my salary. I am paid little enough without I spend six pound on firewood.

PROCTOR.   Sixty, plus six for firewood—

PARRIS.   The salary is sixty-six pound, Mr. Proctor! I am not some preaching farmer with a book under my arm; I am a graduate of Harvard College.

GILES.   Aye, and well instructed in arithmetic!

PARRIS.   Mr. Corey, you will look far for a man of my kind at sixty pound a year! I am not used to this poverty; I left a thrifty business in the Barbados to serve the Lord. I do not fathom it, why am I persecuted here? I cannot offer one proposition but there be a howling riot of argument. I have often wondered if the Devil be in it somewhere; I cannot understand you people otherwise.

PROCTOR.   Mr. Parris, you are the first minister ever did demand the deed to this house—

PARRIS.   Man! Don't a minister deserve a house to live in?

PROCTOR.   To live in, yes. But to ask ownership is like you shall own the meeting house itself; the last meeting I were at you spoke so long on deeds and mortgages I thought it were an auction.

PARRIS.   I want a mark of confidence, is all! I am your third preacher in seven years. I do not wish to be put out like the cat whenever some majority feels the whim. You people seem not to comprehend that a minister is the Lord's man in the parish; a minister is not to be so lightly crossed and contradicted—

PUTNAM.   Aye!

PARRIS.   There is either obedience or the church will burn like Hell is burning!

PROCTOR.   Can you speak one minute without we land in Hell again? I am sick of Hell!

PARRIS.   It is not for you to say what is good for you to hear!

PROCTOR.   I may speak my heart, I think!

PARRIS.   [In a fury.] What, are we Quakers?[29] We are not Quakers here yet, Mr. Proctor. And you may tell that to your followers!

PROCTOR.   My followers!

PARRIS.   [Now he's out with it.] There is a party in this church. I am not blind; there is a faction and a party.

PROCTOR.   Against you?

PUTNAM.   Against him and all authority!

PROCTOR.   Why, then I must find it and join it.

[There is shock among the others.]

REBECCA.   He does not mean that.

PUTNAM.   He confessed it now!

PROCTOR.   I mean it solemnly, Rebecca; I like not the smell of this "authority."

29. **Quakers** is a term for members of the Society of Friends. They have no creed. They are guided by their doctrine of "inner light."

Comprehension Check

What is the main source of tension between the village men and Reverend Parris?

- [ ] church music
- [x] money
- [ ] witchcraft

To Sum Up

➤ John Proctor and Reverend Parris have an argument.

➤ Proctor thinks Reverend Parris talks about Hell too much.

➤ Proctor is angry that Reverend Parris wanted to own a house.

The Crucible **243**

The Crucible

Interactive Question-Response

Comprehension Check

If students are having trouble, it may be helpful for them to look up the meanings of *deed, salary,* and *mortgage.* **Ask:** *Why did Reverend Parris demand the deed to the house? (He wants to be the owner of the house. The church owns it now. If Parris owns it, the church members won't have the power to take the house away.) Why do you think Proctor did not want to give Parris the deed? (Proctor thinks a minister ought to live a humble life. He feels that handing over the deed to the house is like giving Parris ownership of the church. Proctor feels that the church ought to be the property of the community.)*

Interactive Question-Response

To Sum Up

Beginning/Early Intermediate Have students recall what they have learned by reading the To Sum Up statements from pages 239–244. Working in pairs, have students make a three-column chart by folding a piece of notebook paper in thirds lengthwise. In column 1, have them list each character that has been introduced in this section. In column 2, have them give two details about each character. In column 3, have them make one prediction about what will happen to that character in the rest of the story. Students may evaluate their predictions as they read on.

I never thought you had so much iron in you means "I didn't know you were so tough."

To *clap* someone, here, is to formally accuse that person of a crime. The word also implies that the accusation is quick and sudden. (Today, instead of "clap you with a writ," people might say "hit you with a lawsuit" or "slap you with a lawsuit.")

REBECCA.   No, you cannot break charity[30] with your minister. You are another kind, John. Clasp his hand, make your peace.

PROCTOR.   I have a crop to sow and lumber to drag home. *[He goes angrily to the door and turns to COREY with a smile.]* What say you, Giles, let's find the party. He says there's a party.

GILES.   I've changed my opinion of this man, John. Mr. Parris, I beg your pardon. **I never thought you had so much iron in you.**

PARRIS.   *[Surprised.]* Why, thank you, Giles!

GILES.   It suggests to the mind what the trouble be among us all these years. *[To all.]* Think on it. Wherefore is everybody suing everybody else? Think on it now, it's a deep thing, and dark as a pit. I have been six time in court this year—

PROCTOR.   *[Familiarly, with warmth, although he knows he is approaching the edge of GILES' tolerance with this.]* Is it the Devil's fault that a man cannot say you good morning without you **clap** him for defamation?[31] You're old, Giles, and you're not hearin' so well as you did.

GILES.   *[He cannot be crossed.]* John Proctor, I have only last month collected four pound damages for you publicly sayin' I burned the roof off your house, and I—

PROCTOR.   *[Laughing.]* I never said no such thing, but I've paid you for it, so I hope I can call you deaf without charge. Now come along, Giles, and help me drag my lumber home.

PUTNAM.   A moment, Mr. Proctor. What lumber is that you're draggin', if I may ask you?

PROCTOR.   My lumber. From out my forest by the riverside.

PUTNAM.   Why, we are surely gone wild this year. What anarchy[32] is this? That tract is in my bounds, it's in my bounds, Mr. Proctor.

PROCTOR.   In your bounds! *[Indicating REBECCA.]* I bought that tract from Goody Nurse's husband five months ago.

PUTNAM.   He had no right to sell it. It stands clear in my grandfather's will that all the land between the river and—

PROCTOR.   Your grandfather had a habit of willing land that never belonged to him, if I may say it plain.

GILES.   That's God's truth; he nearly willed away my north pasture but he knew I'd break his fingers before he'd set his name to it. Let's get your lumber home, John. I feel a sudden will to work coming on.

PUTNAM.   You load one oak of mine and you'll fight to drag it home!

GILES.   Aye, and we'll win too, Putnam—this fool and I. Come on! *[He turns to PROCTOR and starts out.]*

PUTNAM.   I'll have my men on you, Corey! I'll clap a writ[33] on you!

[Enter REVEREND JOHN HALE of Beverly. He appears loaded down with half a dozen heavy books.]

HALE.   Pray you, someone take these!

To Sum Up

➤ John Proctor leaves to work on his farm.

➤ Reverend John Hale, an expert on witchcraft, enters.

➤ Hale is carrying many heavy books.

30. For the puritans, **charity** was Christian love. Charity included mercy, forgiveness, kindness, and trust.
31. An act of **defamation** is an attack on a person's good reputation.
32. **Anarchy** is lawless confusion due to a lack of authority. Here, Putnam means "lawlessness."
33. A **writ** is a judge's order.

Differentiated Instruction

Clarify the Text Support students in understanding the dialogue and the unspoken meaning in the play.

Beginning/Early Intermediate **Ask:** *Is witchcraft the only problem in Salem? (no) What other problems are happening? (suspicion, lack of trust, lawsuits, inability to keep a minister, greed, property disputes)*

Intermediate Have students discuss Hale's entrance. **Ask:** *Do you think it is possible for anyone to be an expert on witchcraft? Explain. (No. People's knowledge of witchcraft seems to be mainly superstition and hearsay. So far it seems that anyone can use witchcraft to explain anything odd.)*

Early Advanced **Model** *Giles and Proctor seem to bicker, but I think they're good friends. What other relationships do you see here? (Parris is insecure. He respects the Putnams because they are wealthy. He fears Proctor. Rebecca is a mother to everyone. Mrs. Putnam is jealous of Rebecca's healthy children.)* If students struggle, draw a web diagram on the board to show character relationships.

PARRIS. *[Delighted.]* Mr. Hale! Oh! it's good to see you again! *[Taking some books.]* My, they're heavy!

HALE. *[Setting down his books.]* They must be; they are weighted with authority.

PARRIS. *[A little scared.]* Well, you do come prepared!

HALE. We shall need hard study if it comes to tracking down the Old Boy.[34] *[Noticing REBECCA.]* You cannot be Rebecca Nurse?

REBECCA. I am, sir. Do you know me?

HALE. It's strange how I knew you, but I suppose you look as such a good soul should. We have all heard of your great charities in Beverly.

PARRIS. Do you know this gentleman? Mr. Thomas Putnam. And his good wife Ann.

HALE. Putnam! I had not expected such distinguished company, sir.

PUTNAM. *[Pleased.]* It does not seem to help us today, Mr. Hale. We look to you to come to our house and save our child.

HALE. Your child ails too?

MRS. PUTNAM. Her soul, her soul seems flown away. She sleeps and yet she walks…

PUTNAM. She cannot eat.

HALE. Cannot eat! *[Thinks on it. Then, to PROCTOR and GILES COREY.]* Do you men have afflicted children?

PARRIS. No, no, these are farmers. John Proctor—

GILES COREY. He don't believe in witches.

PROCTOR. *[To HALE.]* I never spoke on witches one way or the other. Will you come, Giles?

GILES. No—no, John, I think not. I have some few queer questions of my own to ask this fellow.

34. **Old Boy** is another name for Satan.

REFLECT

Draw Conclusions About Characters
How does Reverend Parris react to the arrival of Reverend Hale? How do his feelings seem to change?

Possible answer: At first Parris is "delighted" to see Hale.

He is excited and says "it's good to see you again!" as if Hale

is an old friend. Soon, though, Parris begins to be scared

and worried.

 Talk about your answer with a partner.

Literary Element

Dialogue What do you think Reverend Hale means when he says his books are "weighted with authority"?

Possible answers: The books give him the ability to make correct judgments. The books give him the right to carry out punishments.

To Sum Up

➤ Reverend Hale has come to see if Betty's sickness is caused by witchcraft.

➤ Hale is surprised to find out that Ruth Putnam is also sick.

Interactive Question-Response

Literary Element Dialogue

Students may need to look up the words *weighted* and *authority* in the dictionary. **Ask:** *What is Reverend Hale planning to do with the books? (use them to determine if witchcraft is causing Betty's sickness) What will he do if he finds evidence of witchcraft? (He may punish those responsible.) What kind of authority do the books give Reverend Hale? (He uses them to prove that there is witchcraft, and if he finds evidence of witchcraft, he can punish people.) Why would Hale say his authority is heavy? (He believes it has substance and truth.)*

Reflect

Partner Talk Have students work in pairs to answer: **Model** *I know that the bracketed, italicized words are directions to actors. They tell the actors what they do, what their tone of voice should be, and sometimes what their facial expression should be. I'm going to look at these directions for clues about Reverend Parris.* Have pairs discuss how the stage directions and the dialogue work together to show how Reverend Parris reacts to Reverend Hale, and how his feelings change.

Interactive Question-Response

Content Vocabulary

Read aloud the word and its definition. If space permits, have a volunteer demonstrate leaping.
Ask: *Why is it important that Betty tried to leap out of the window? (She is upstairs, so if she could not fly she would die. The adults think this may be evidence that she can fly, or that she believes she can fly.)*

Comprehension Check

Have students share their answers. Ask volunteers to point out the line where each piece of "evidence" can be found on the page. **Ask:** *Which character tells Reverend Hale that Betty tried to jump out the window? (Reverend Parris)* Repeat with the other pieces of evidence. **Ask:** *Why would these things be evidence of witchcraft? (Puritan society clearly does not tolerate difference. It has very strict rules. The townspeople need an explanation for any deviance, or unusual behavior.)*

---

leap (lēp) *v.* to jump

✏️ **Comprehension Check**

What evidence do the adults offer Reverend Hale? Check all correct answers.

- ☑ Betty tried to jump out the window.
- ☑ Betty waved her hands like she was trying to fly.
- ☑ Betty can't bear to hear the Lord's name.
- ☑ The girls were dancing in the woods.
- ☑ Tituba has the ability to conjure the dead.
- ☑ Mrs. Putnam has lost seven children.

To Sum Up

➤ Reverend Hale questions Parris about the girls' dancing in the woods.

➤ Mrs. Putnam confesses that she sent Ruth to Tituba to contact the dead.

PROCTOR. I've heard you to be a sensible man, Mr. Hale. I hope you'll leave some of it in Salem.
[*PROCTOR goes.* HALE *stands embarrassed for an instant.*]

PARRIS. [*Quickly.*] Will you look at my daughter, sir? [*Leads* HALE *to the bed.*] She has tried to <u>leap</u> out the window; we discovered her this morning on the highroad, waving her arms as though she'd fly.

HALE. [*Narrowing his eyes.*] Tries to fly.

PUTNAM. She cannot bear to hear the Lord's name, Mr. Hale; that's a sure sign of witchcraft afloat.

HALE. [*Holding up his hands.*] No, no. Now let me instruct you. We cannot look to superstition in this. The Devil is precise; the marks of his presence are definite as stone, and I must tell you all that I shall not proceed unless you are prepared to believe me if I should find no bruise of hell upon her.

PARRIS. It is agreed, sir—it is agreed—we will abide by your judgment.

HALE. Good then. [*He goes to the bed, looks down at* BETTY. *To* PARRIS.] Now, sir, what were your first warning of this strangeness?

PARRIS. Why, sir—I discovered her—[*Indicating* ABIGAIL.]—and my niece and ten or twelve of the other girls, dancing in the forest last night.

HALE. [*Surprised.*] You permit dancing?

PARRIS. No, no, it were secret—

MRS. PUTNAM. [*Unable to wait.*] Mr. Parris's slave has knowledge of conjurin', sir.

PARRIS. [*To* MRS. PUTNAM.] We cannot be sure of that, Goody Ann—

MRS. PUTNAM. [*Frightened, very softly.*] I know it, sir. I sent my child—she should learn from Tituba who murdered her sisters.

REBECCA. [*Horrified.*] Goody Ann! You sent a child to conjure up the dead?

MRS. PUTNAM. Let God blame me, not you, not you, Rebecca! I'll not have you judging me any more! [*To* HALE.] Is it a natural work to lose seven children before they live a day?

PARRIS. Sssh!
[REBECCA, *with great pain, turns her face away. There is a pause.*]

HALE. Seven dead in childbirth.

MRS. PUTNAM. [*Softly.*] Aye. [*Her voice breaks; she looks up at him. Silence.* HALE *is impressed.* PARRIS *looks to him. He goes to his books, opens one, turns pages, then reads. All wait, avidly.*][35]

PARRIS. [*Hushed.*] What book is that?

MRS. PUTNAM. What's there, sir?

HALE. [*With a tasty love of intellectual pursuit.*] Here is all the invisible world, caught, defined, and calculated. In these books the Devil stands stripped of all his brute disguises. Here are all your familiar spirits—your incubi and succubi;[36] your witches that go by land, by air, and by sea; your wizards of the night and of the day. Have no fear now—we

---

35. **Avidly** means "with intense interest."
36. **Incubi** (ing' kyə bī') and **succubi** (suk' kyə bī') are evil spirits or demons.

shall find him out if he has come among us, and I mean to crush him utterly if he has shown his face! *[He starts for the bed.]*

REBECCA.   Will it hurt the child, sir?

HALE.   I cannot tell. If she is truly in the Devil's grip we may have to rip and tear to get her free.

REBECCA.   I think I'll go, then. I am too old for this. *[She rises.]*

PARRIS.   *[Striving for conviction.]* Why, Rebecca, we may open up the boil of all our troubles today!

REBECCA.   Let us hope for that. I go to God for you, sir.

PARRIS.   *[With trepidation—and resentment.]* I hope you do not mean we go to Satan here! *[Slight pause.]*

REBECCA.   I wish I knew. *[She goes out; they feel resentful of her note of moral superiority.]*

PUTNAM.   *[Abruptly.]* Come, Mr. Hale, let's get on. Sit you here.

GILES.   Mr. Hale, I have always wanted to ask a learned man—what signifies the readin' of strange books?

HALE.   What books?

GILES.   I cannot tell; she hides them.

HALE.   Who does this?

GILES.   Martha, my wife. I have waked at night many a time and found her in a corner, readin' of a book. Now what do you make of that?

HALE.   Why, that's not necessarily—

GILES.   It discomfits[37] me! Last night—mark this—I tried and tried and could not say my prayers. And then she close her book and walks out of the house, and suddenly—mark this—I could pray again!

HALE.   Ah! The stoppage of prayer—that is strange. I'll speak further on that with you.

GILES.   I'm not sayin' she's touched the Devil, now, but I'd admire to know what books she reads and why she hides them. She'll not answer me, y' see.

HALE.   Aye, we'll discuss it. *[To all.]* Now mark me, if the Devil is in her you will witness some frightful wonders in this room, so please to **keep your wits about you.** Mr. Putnam, stand close in case she flies. Now, Betty, dear, will you sit up? *[PUTNAM comes in closer, ready-handed. HALE sits BETTY up, but she hangs limp in his hands.]* Hmmm. *[He observes her carefully. The others watch breathlessly.]* Can you hear me? I am John Hale, minister of Beverly. I have come to help you, dear. Do you remember my two little girls in Beverly? *[She does not stir in his hands.]*

PARRIS.   *[In fright.]* How can it be the Devil? Why would he choose my house to strike? We have all manner of licentious[38] people in the village!

HALE.   What victory would the Devil have to win a soul already bad? It is the best the Devil wants, and who is better than the minister?

GILES.   That's deep, Mr. Parris, deep, deep!

---

37. **Discomfits** means "confuses and frustrates."
38. **Licentious** people do not follow commonly accepted standards of right and wrong.

Keep your wits about you means "Stay calm," or "Don't get so frightened or emotional that you cannot think."

limp (limp) *adj.* without firmness or strength; not rigid

To Sum Up

➤ Rebecca hints that she has doubts about Reverend Hale's ideas. She leaves.

➤ Another villager, Giles Corey, asks Reverend Hale if it strange that Giles's wife secretly reads books.

➤ Reverend Hale is interested. He says they will talk about it later.

Interactive Question-Response

Content Vocabulary

Read aloud the word and its definition. Hold up several objects, such as pencils, rulers, tissue, notebook paper, yarn, or textbooks, and ask students to raise their hands if each object is *limp*. **Ask:** *Is a healthy person usually limp when he or she sits up? (No.)*

Interactive Question-Response

Literary Element Dialogue

Point out that Abigail doesn't have to say, "I accuse Tituba" or "Tituba did it." Instead, she just repeats Tituba's name. **Ask:** *Why do you think people so easily believe that Tituba is to blame? (She is a slave. She is from Barbados. The people don't want to believe one of their own children is to blame.)*

Literary Element

Dialogue Underline the words with which Abigail first begins to blame Tituba for what happened.

Vocabulary ....
evade (i vād′) *v.* to escape or avoid

To Sum Up

➤ Reverend Hale begins to question Abigail.

➤ Abigail confesses that the girls had a kettle with them in the woods.

➤ Reverend Hale thinks this kettle was part of a spell to call the Devil.

➤ Abigail says that Tituba called the Devil.

248

PARRIS. *[With resolution now.]* Betty! Answer Mr. Hale! Betty!

HALE. Does someone afflict you, child? It need not be a woman, mind you, or a man. Perhaps some bird invisible to others comes to you—perhaps a pig, a mouse, or any beast at all. Is there some figure bids you fly? *[The child remains limp in his hands. In silence he lays her back on the pillow. Now, holding out his hands toward her, he intones.]* In nomine Domini Sabaoth sui filiique ite ad infernos.³⁹ *[She does not stir. He turns to ABIGAIL, his eyes narrowing.]* Abigail, what sort of dancing were you doing with her in the forest?

ABIGAIL. Why—common dancing is all.

PARRIS. I think I ought to say that I—I saw a kettle in the grass where they were dancing.

ABIGAIL. That were only soup.

HALE. What sort of soup were in this kettle, Abigail?

ABIGAIL. Why, it were beans—and lentils, I think, and—

HALE. Mr. Parris, you did not notice, did you, any living thing in the kettle? A mouse, perhaps, a spider, a frog—?

PARRIS. *[Fearfully.]* I—do believe there were some movement—in the soup.

ABIGAIL. That jumped in, we never put it in!

HALE. *[Quickly.]* What jumped in?

ABIGAIL. Why, a very little frog jumped—

PARRIS. A frog, Abby!

HALE. *[Grasping ABIGAIL.]* Abigail, it may be your cousin is dying. Did you call the Devil last night?

ABIGAIL. I never called him! <u>Tituba, Tituba…</u>

PARRIS. *[Blanched.]* She called the Devil?

HALE. I should like to speak with Tituba.

PARRIS. Goody Ann, will you bring her up? *[MRS. PUTNAM exits.]*

HALE. How did she call him?

ABIGAIL. I know not—she spoke Barbados.

HALE. Did you feel any strangeness when she called him? A sudden cold wind, perhaps? A trembling below the ground?

ABIGAIL. I didn't see no Devil! *[Shaking BETTY.]* Betty, wake up. Betty! Betty!

HALE. You cannot **evade** me, Abigail. Did your cousin drink any of the brew in that kettle?

ABIGAIL. She never drank it!

HALE. Did you drink it?

ABIGAIL. No, sir!

HALE. Did Tituba ask you to drink it?

ABIGAIL. She tried, but I refused.

HALE. Why are you concealing? Have you sold yourself to Lucifer?

ABIGAIL. I never sold myself! I'm a good girl! I'm a proper girl!
[MRS. PUTNAM enters with TITUBA, and instantly ABIGAIL points at TITUBA.]

---

39. *[In nomine . . . infernos.]* "In the name of the God of the Heavenly Hosts and of His Son, go to hell." Hale is performing an exorcism, a ritual intended to drive out evil spirits.

Differentiated Instruction

Clarify the Text

Beginning/Early Intermediate ➤ Students may miss some of the emotional impact of the scene. Ask students to think about a time they broke the rules and got caught. **Ask:** *How would you feel if you knew someone else had been killed for breaking that same rule? If you could get out of trouble by blaming someone else, would you?*

Intermediate ➤ The dashes on this page may be confusing for some students. Point out that the dashes within a line indicate a pause, or hesitation. When the dash is at the end of a line, it indicates that another person has interrupted. Demonstrate by reading aloud portions of the text, and have students repeat.

Early Advanced ➤ Have students work in small groups to act out the scene that takes place as Reverend Hale questions Abigail. Point out that Reverend Hale's questions are focused on Abigail, even though Reverend Parris interrupts from time to time to offer more information or to react to Abigail's confession.

ABIGAIL.   She made me do it! She made Betty do it!

TITUBA.   *[Shocked and angry.]* Abby!

ABIGAIL.   She makes me drink blood!

PARRIS.   Blood!!

MRS. PUTNAM.   My baby's blood?

TITUBA.   No, no, chicken blood. I give she chicken blood!

HALE.   Woman, have you enlisted these children for the Devil?

TITUBA.   No, no, sir, I don't truck[40] with no Devil!

HALE.   Why can she not wake? Are you silencing this child?

TITUBA.   I love me Betty!

HALE.   You have sent your spirit out upon this child, have you not? Are you gathering souls for the Devil?

ABIGAIL.   She sends her spirit on me in church; she makes me laugh at prayer!

PARRIS.   She have often laughed at prayer!

ABIGAIL.   She comes to me every night to go and drink blood!

TITUBA.   You beg me to conjure! She beg me make charm—

ABIGAIL.   Don't lie! *[To HALE.]* She comes to me while I sleep; she's always making me dream corruptions!

TITUBA.   Why you say that, Abby?

ABIGAIL.   Sometimes I wake and find myself standing in the open doorway and **not a stitch on my body!** I always hear her laughing in my sleep. I hear her singing her Barbados songs and tempting me with—

TITUBA.   Mister Reverend, I never—

HALE.   *[Resolved now.]* Tituba, I want you to wake this child.

TITUBA.   I have no power on this child, sir.

40. **Truck** is another way of saying "to have dealings."

REFLECT

Draw Conclusions About Characters

Why do you think Abigail accuses Tituba? Explain.

Possible answer: She is afraid of being punished, so she

accuses Tituba, knowing that Tituba will take the blame and

Abigail will be seen as a victim.

_____

_____

 Talk about your answer with a partner.

✏️ **Literary Element**

Dialogue Which of the following statements do you think is a lie?

☐ "No, no, sir, I don't truck with no Devil!"

☐ "You beg me to conjure!"

☑ "I always hear her laughing in my sleep!"

Not a stitch on my body means "naked" or "wearing no clothes."

To Sum Up

➤ Abigail accuses Tituba of trying to get the girls to drink blood.

➤ Tituba is brought in. Tituba tries to deny Abigail's accusations.

➤ Abigail says that Tituba makes her have bad dreams.

Interactive Question-Response

Literary Element Dialogue

If students have difficulty responding, have them first explain what really happened (the "facts" of the case). Then have them compare this to what Abigail wants people to think happened. Make a T-chart on the board with headings "What happened" and "Abigail's story." **Model** *I know they danced in the woods. We also heard the girls say that Abigail drank a potion because she wanted to kill John Proctor's wife. We know she is in love with Proctor, and she is ruthless and jealous. We also heard Reverend Parris suggest that other people have heard rumors about Abigail's affair with Proctor. So I think Abigail has many reasons to pretend she is very religious and to blame someone else for her actions. I think what Tituba says is true. Abigail asked Tituba to make the potion. But now Abigail says Tituba forced her to drink it. I think Abigail hopes to get out of trouble by accusing Tituba.*

Reflect

Partner Talk Have students work in pairs to answer the question. To get them started, have volunteers explain what will happen to Abigail if she is found to be the source of the problem. *(Abigail will be punished.)* Then have students explain what will happen to Abigail if Tituba is blamed. *(Abigail will not be punished.)*

Interactive Question-Response

Comprehension Check

If students are having difficulty, have them read the stage directions that correspond to Tituba's lines on the page: **Model** *I see the words* frightened *and* fearfully. **Ask:** *How does Tituba feel as she is questioned by Reverend Hale, Reverend Parris, and Putnam? (She is afraid.)*

To Sum Up

Beginning/Early Intermediate ▶ Have students focus on the last two bulleted To Sum Up statements. **Ask:** *Who first suggests that other people appear with the Devil? (Reverend Hale) Who suggests that these people may be Sarah Good and Goody Osburn? (Putnam)*

Here, *you would be* means "You want to be."

Comprehension Check

Underline the words that explain why Tituba begins to blame other people for what happened.

To Sum Up

➤ Reverend Parris tells Tituba that if she does not confess, she will be whipped.

➤ Putnam threatens Tituba with death by hanging.

➤ Tituba begins to confess.

➤ Hale asks Tituba if the Devil is ever with other people in Salem. Tituba says that when the Devil comes to her, women are with him.

➤ Putnam suggests that Tituba might have seen Sarah Good or Goody Osburn, other women of the village, with the Devil.

HALE. You most certainly do, and you will free her from it now! When did you compact with[41] the Devil?

TITUBA. I don't compact with no Devil!

PARRIS. You will confess yourself or I will take you out and whip you to your death, Tituba!

PUTNAM. This woman must be hanged! She must be taken and hanged!

TITUBA. *[Terrified, falls to her knees.]* No, no, don't hang Tituba! I tell him I don't desire to work for him, sir.

PARRIS. The Devil?

HALE. Then you saw him! *[TITUBA weeps.]* Now Tituba, I know that when we bind ourselves to Hell it is very hard to break with it. We are going to help you tear yourself free—

TITUBA. *[Frightened by the coming process.]* Mister Reverend, I do believe somebody else be witchin' these children.

HALE. Who?

TITUBA. I don't know, sir, but the Devil got him numerous witches.

HALE. Does he! *[It is a clue.]* Tituba, look into my eyes. Come, look into me. *[She raises her eyes to his fearfully.]* **You would be** a good Christian woman, would you not, Tituba?

TITUBA. Aye, sir, a good Christian woman.

HALE. And you love these little children?

TITUBA. Oh, yes, sir, I don't desire to hurt little children.

HALE. And you love God, Tituba?

TITUBA. I love God with all my bein'.

HALE. Now, in God's holy name—

TITUBA. Bless Him. Bless Him. *[She is rocking on her knees, sobbing in terror.]*

HALE. And to His glory—

TITUBA. Eternal glory. Bless Him—bless God…

HALE. Open yourself, Tituba—open yourself and let God's holy light shine on you.

TITUBA. Oh, bless the Lord.

HALE. When the Devil comes to you does he ever come—with another person? *[She stares up into his face.]* Perhaps another person in the village? Someone you know.

PARRIS. Who came with him?

PUTNAM. Sarah Good? Did you ever see Sarah Good with him? Or Osburn?

PARRIS. Was it man or woman came with him?

TITUBA. Man or woman. Was—was woman.

PARRIS. What woman? A woman, you said. What woman?

TITUBA. It was black dark, and I—

PARRIS. You could see him, why could you not see her?

TITUBA. Well, they was always talking; they was always runnin' round and carryin' on—

---

41. **To compact with** is to make an agreement with.

PARRIS. You mean out of Salem? Salem witches?

TITUBA. I believe so, yes, sir.

[Now HALE takes her hand. She is surprised.]

HALE. Tituba. You must have no fear to tell us who they are, do you understand? We will protect you. The Devil can never overcome a minister. You know that, do you not?

TITUBA. *[Kisses HALE's hand.]* Aye, sir, I do.

HALE. You have confessed yourself to witchcraft, and that speaks a wish to come to Heaven's side. And we will bless you, Tituba.

TITUBA. *[Deeply relieved.]* Oh, God bless you, Mr. Hale!

HALE. *[With rising exaltation.]*[42] You are God's instrument put in our hands to discover the Devil's agents among us. You are selected, Tituba, you are chosen to help us cleanse our village. So speak utterly, Tituba, turn your back on him and face God—face God, Tituba, and God will protect you.

TITUBA. *[Joining with him.]* Oh, God, protect Tituba!

HALE. *[Kindly.]* Who came to you with the Devil? Two? Three? Four? How many?

[TITUBA pants, and begins rocking back and forth again, staring ahead.]

TITUBA. There was four. There was four.

PARRIS. *[Pressing in on her.]* Who? Who? Their names, their names!

TITUBA. *[Suddenly bursting out.]* Oh, how many times he bid me kill you, Mr. Parris!

PARRIS. Kill me!

TITUBA. *[In a fury.]* He say Mr. Parris must be kill! Mr. Parris no goodly man, Mr. Parris mean man and no gentle man, and he bid me rise out of my bed and cut your throat! *[They gasp.]* But I tell him, "No! I don't hate that man. I don't want kill that man." But he say, "You work for me, Tituba, and I make you free! I give you pretty dress to wear, and put you way high up in the air, and **you gone** fly back to Barbados!" And I say, "You lie, Devil, you lie!" And then he come one stormy night to me, and he say, "Look! I have white people belong to me." And I look—and there was Goody Good.

PARRIS. Sarah Good!

TITUBA. *[Rocking and weeping.]* Aye, sir, and Goody Osburn.

MRS. PUTNAM. I knew it! Goody Osburn were midwife[43] to me three times. I begged you, Thomas, did I not? I begged him not to call Osburn because I feared her. My babies always shriveled in her hands!

HALE. Take courage, you must give us all their names. How can you bear to see this child suffering? Look at her, Tituba. *[He is indicating BETTY on the bed.]* Look at her God-given innocence; her soul is so tender; we must protect her, Tituba; the Devil is out and preying on her like a beast upon the flesh of the pure lamb. God will bless you for your help.

---

42. Here, *exaltation* means "great enthusiasm."
43. A *midwife* is a woman who assists other women in childbirth.

Literary Element

Dialogue What is Reverend Hale's tone of voice after Tituba begins to confess?

☐ angry and frustrated
☑ kind and understanding
☐ sad and depressed

Tituba speaks in dialect. Here, **you gone** means "you are going to."

To Sum Up

➤ Hale and Parris demand that Tituba tell the names of the women.

➤ Tituba says that one of the women was Goody Good, and another was Goody Osburn.

Interactive Question-Response

Literary Element Dialogue

Remind students that any time they make a statement about a text, they should base their statement on evidence from the text. Have students share their responses as well as their reasoning. Students may find it helpful to use the following sentence frame to organize their thoughts:

I know Reverend Hale's tone is _____ because _____. (gentle; he takes Tituba's hand and she is surprised)

She was probably expecting _____. (punishment)

Interactive Question-Response

Literary Element Dialogue

If students have difficulty making predictions, ask them to summarize what happens on the last page of the selection. They may use the following sentence frames:

First, Abigail _____. (stands up and confesses)

Then, Betty _____. (rises and imitates Abigail)

The men _____. (think they have saved the girls)

Ask: *Do you think the people the girls name will be accused of witchcraft? (yes) What do you think will happen to them? (They will be punished.)* **Model** *We've just seen that Abigail, Betty, and Tituba are willing to accuse other people so that they won't be punished themselves. Do you think some of the people they accuse might do the same thing? (yes/no)* **Ask:** *Of the characters we have seen or heard about, who might be accused? Why?* Provide the following sentence frame:

_____ could be accused because _____. (Proctor, he has contempt for Parris; Mrs. Putnam, she asked Tituba to conjure spirits; Mercy, she danced in the woods; Giles Corey's wife, she reads books; Proctor's wife, Abigail hates her; Rebecca, she showed doubt of Hale's authority)

Reflect

Partner Talk Have students work together in pairs to answer the questions. To help students get started: **Model** *Tituba knows that she is likely to be blamed for any trouble that occurs. Tituba sees that the adults think Betty's sickness is caused by the Devil. She is also afraid of being punished. I think Tituba wants to tell Reverend Hale what he wants to hear. This way, she hopes to avoid being punished.*

Literary Element

Dialogue Based on the final lines of Act One, what would you predict about Act Two?

Possible answer: The women

the girls accuse will be arrested

as witches.

_____

_____

44. **Enraptured** means "filled with intense joy or delight."
45. **Irons** are heavy bands of metal that are fastened around the wrists or ankles of someone who has been arrested.

To Sum Up

➤ Abigail suddenly begins to confess as well.

➤ Abigail claims to have seen several more village women with the Devil.

➤ Betty suddenly joins in, accusing several more women.

➤ The men call for the marshal.

252

[ABIGAIL rises, staring as though inspired, and cries out.]

ABIGAIL. I want to open myself! *[They turn to her, startled. She is enraptured,*[44] *as though in a pearly light.]* I want the light of God, I want the sweet love of Jesus! I danced for the Devil; I saw him; I wrote in his book; I go back to Jesus; I kiss His hand. I saw Sarah Good with the Devil! I saw Goody Osburn with the Devil! I saw Bridget Bishop with the Devil!
[As she is speaking, BETTY is rising from the bed, a fever in her eyes, and picks up the chant.]

BETTY. *[Staring too.]* I saw George Jacobs with the Devil! I saw Goody Howe with the Devil!

PARRIS. She speaks! *[He rushes to embrace BETTY.]* She speaks!

HALE. Glory to God! It is broken, they are free!

BETTY. *[Calling out hysterically and with great relief.]* I saw Martha Bellows with the Devil!

ABIGAIL. I saw Goody Sibber with the Devil! *[It is rising to a great glee.]*

PUTNAM. The marshal, I'll call the marshal!
[PARRIS is shouting a prayer of thanksgiving.]

BETTY. I saw Alice Barrow with the Devil!
[The curtain begins to fall.]

HALE. *[As PUTNAM goes out.]* Let the marshal bring irons![45]

ABIGAIL. I saw Goody Hawkins with the Devil!

BETTY. I saw Goody Bibber with the Devil!

ABIGAIL. I saw Goody Booth with the Devil!
[On their ecstatic cries.]

THE CURTAIN FALLS

REFLECT

Draw Conclusions About Characters
Why do you think Tituba tells the story about seeing the Devil?

Possible answer: She thinks the adults want to hear a

supernatural story; she wants to blame the Devil and not

have to take the blame herself.

Why do you think the other girls also say they saw the Devil?

Possible answer: They also think this is a way to escape

punishment; they may want the attention; they may want to

get back at people they don't like by accusing them.

 Talk about your answer with a partner.

Oral Assessment

Provide the following prompts to one student at a time. Observe students' responses. See the Oral Assessment Rubric on page T17 to determine students' levels of language output.

1. Tell me what happens in Act I of *The Crucible*.

2. What kind of person is Abigail?

3. What really happened the night the girls were caught dancing in the woods?

4. Why does Reverend Hale come?

5. What happens when Reverend Hale questions Abigail?

THE CRUCIBLE

Vocabulary Check

A. Label each picture with the correct word.

packed	wither	leap	limp

1.   wither
2. limp
3. packed
4. leap

B. Circle the letter of the word that means the same as the boldface word.

5. **contention**
   a. suspicion
   b. quarreling
   c. happiness

6. **evade**
   a. every
   b. find
   c. avoid

7. **wither**
   a. grow
   b. shrivel
   c. ask

8. **leap**
   a. jump
   b. walk
   c. run

9. **packed**
   a. wilted
   b. false
   c. crowded

C. Complete the paragraph using words from the word bank.

compromise	evade	pretense	subservient	contention

In "the Crucible," Mary Warren is a ___subservient___ and lonely girl. She wants to ___evade___ any punishment. She is willing to ___compromise___ the other girls by telling the adults what happened in the woods. The other girls want to continue the ___pretense___ that they did nothing but dance. The girls have a ___contention___ about what to tell the adults.

Vocabulary Check

C. Early Advanced

Encourage students to review the words and their definitions before completing the paragraphs and to return to the text for helpful information. When students have completed their paragraphs, have volunteers read them aloud to the class.

Academic Vocabulary

Write this question on the board: What makes the relationships and alliances between characters in the Crucible so **complex?** *(Encourage students to discuss the developing relationships between characters in Act 1, and how these relationships relate to their own experiences or other books or media they have encountered, such as reality-TV programs.)*

Inform students that *complex* is an academic word. Explain that in a more casual conversation, someone might say that counteracting global climate change is a **complex** issue. To further explore the meaning of this word, answer the following question: *What is a* **complex** *issue that American teens face today and why?*

Grammar Link BLM

Interrogative Sentences, Exclamatory and Imperative Sentences

Prepare students to complete the activities on pages A46 and A47. Read the grammar instruction with students, and complete the first item with them to help them get started.

The Crucible

Comprehension Check

B. Intermediate

If students are having difficulty completing the chart, have them work together in pairs. Tell students to skim through the boxed text to find the section in which Reverend Hale is questioning Abigail, and then take turns reading it aloud. As students come to Reverend Hale's questions, have them pause and write them down. Students can repeat this process for the second column of the chart.

After Reading

Have students complete the after reading activity on page 337.

THE CRUCIBLE

Comprehension Check

A. Complete the sentences.

1. The characters in the play think that Betty Parris is sick because __Possible answer: she tried to do witchcraft; a witch made her sick.__ .

2. The girls blame Tituba because __Possible answer: they are afraid of being punished.__ .

B. Much of the dialogue in *The Crucible* depends on questions and their answers. Use the chart to list three questions Reverend Hale asks Abigail, and three questions that he asks Tituba.

Questions that Reverend Hale Asks . . .	
3. Abigail	4. Tituba
Possible answers: Abigail, what sort of dancing were you doing with her in the forest? What sort of soup were in this kettle, Abigail?; What jumped in? Did you call the Devil last night? How did she call him? Did your cousin drink any of the brew in that kettle? Did you drink it? Did Tituba ask you to drink it?	Possible answers: Woman, have you enlisted these children for the Devil? You would be a good Christian woman, would you not, Tituba? When the Devil comes to you does he ever come—with another person? Perhaps another person in the village? You must have no fear to tell us who they are, do you understand? Who came to you with the Devil? Two? Three? Four? How many?

C. Choose the best answer to each question.

5. What does the dialogue between Abigail Williams and John Proctor reveal?
   a. They are working together to accuse women of witchcraft.
   (b.) They had an affair while Abigail was living with the Proctors.
   c. They are planning to run away and get married.

6. What does Rebecca mean when she says "Perhaps she is not hungered yet"? (p. 241)
   (a.) Maybe it is too soon to look for a supernatural cause of Ruth's problem.
   b. Maybe Ruth is not eating because she doesn't like what you made for dinner.
   c. Maybe a loose spirit is the cause of Ruth's problem.

7. After Reverend Hale arrives, Giles tells him that his wife has been secretly reading books. Hale answers, "I'll speak further on that with you." What does this suggest may happen later in the play?
   a. Giles's wife will get rid of her books.
   (b.) Giles's wife will be suspected of witchcraft because of her books.
   c. Giles's wife will use her books to teach children to read.

For more practice, see page 337. ➡

Writing Link

Journal Entry

Ask students to choose one of the characters in the play and to write a one- or two-page journal entry from the point of view of that person. Have them imagine that it is the evening following the events students have just read about, and they are writing just before going to bed. What are that character's impressions of what he or she saw that day? What does the character hope (or fear) will happen tomorrow? Does the character have any secrets, like the one Mrs. Putnam reveals about having sent her daughter to ask Tituba to cast spells? Encourage students to look back over the play to find details that help define the chosen character.

Students' journal entries should

- maintain the first-person point of view of a character in the play
- reflect an understanding of the play

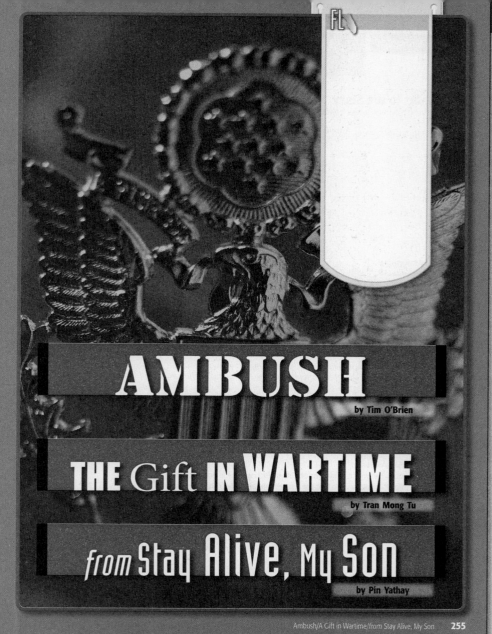

AMBUSH
by Tim O'Brien

THE Gift IN WARTIME
by Tran Mong Tu

from Stay Alive, My Son
by Pin Yathay

Ambush/A Gift in Wartime/from Stay Alive, My Son **255**

Oral Language

Build Background

Read the title and author. Explain that students will read "Ambush" by Tim O'Brien, an American author who fought in the Vietnam War. **Ask:** In an ambush, people hide and wait to attack someone. What do you think the story will be about? *(hiding and fighting)*

Talk About the Story

Explain that the story is about a soldier's memory of the Vietnam War. Tell students that the war lasted from 1965 to 1973.

Beginning/Early Intermediate **Ask:** *Do you know someone who was in an army or navy?* If possible, show pictures of people in military uniform.

Intermediate **Model** *People sometimes lose important things during a war. People may lose a feeling of safety.* **Ask:** *What other things might people lose during a war? (family, homes, friends, money)*

Early Advanced Have students discuss the different feelings people might have during wartime, including soldiers and civilians. **Ask:** *If a family member leaves to fight in a war, how does that affect the family? How do you think a soldier fighting in a war feels?*

Lesson at a Glance

Oral Language
- Build Background
- Talk About the Story

Vocabulary
- Selection Vocabulary
- Content Vocabulary

Literary Element
- Mood

Reading Strategy
- Analyze Concrete Details

Writing Link
- List

Comprehension
- BLM

Grammar Link
- Adjectives and Adverbs BLM

Technology
- Student Works™ Plus
- Teacher Works™ Plus
- Listening Library Audio CD
- Classroom Presentation Toolkit
- Glencoe Visual Vocabulary
- Skill Level Up!™ A Skill-Based Language Arts Game

Interactive Question-Response

Connect to the Story

Read aloud Connect to the Story. Write the sentence frames on the board: **Model** *I have a strong memory of when I moved to a new town when I was ten years old. I remember that I missed my friends but that I made new ones. When I think of that memory, I feel both sad and happy.* Ask students to fill in the sentence frames with their own memories.

Literary Element   Mood

Read aloud the Literary Element note. Write the words *bright, sing,* and *fun*: **Model** *When I read the words bright, sing, and fun, I think of happiness. Those words create a happy mood.* Write *happy mood.* Write the words *fight, yell,* and *dark.* **Ask:** *What mood do the words create? (an angry mood)*

Reading Strategy   Analyze Concrete Details

Read aloud the Reading Strategy note: **Model** *I know that sometimes a writer suggests an idea with a concrete detail. One concrete detail is the sound of children laughing. If I read that detail, I might think the writer was suggesting the idea of being young or having no worries.* Write the phrase *the sound of rain* on the board. **Ask:** *What ideas could a writer suggest with that concrete detail? (sadness; boredom)*

Comparing Literature

Read aloud Comparing Literature. Write the following sentences on the board: *Children who study hard will do well when they grow up. Children who play sports will have a good life.* Point out that each sentence has a different idea, or message, about what is best for children. Provide a sentence frame: **Model** *The message of the first sentence is that children should study hard.*

The message of the second sentence is _____. *(children should play sports)*

Connect to the Story

What strong memory do you have from your past? Write about your memory.

I have a strong memory of Answers will vary. _____

_____

I remember that _____

_____

When I think of the memory, I feel _____

_____

Literary Element   Mood

Mood is a feeling, such as sadness, fear, or happiness. A writer can use details to create a mood. For example, the detail of birds singing could create a happy mood. A writer can also use certain words to create a mood. Words such as *gray, empty,* and *alone* could create a sad mood.

Reading Strategy   Analyze Concrete Details

Writers often include details related to the senses of sight, hearing, smell, taste, and touch. Those details are called **concrete details**. A writer can suggest an idea or feeling with concrete details. The concrete details of a dry mouth and sweaty hands suggest fear. As you read, ask yourself:

• What concrete details does the author use?
• What idea or feeling do the details suggest?

Comparing Literature

War has affected the writers of all the selections. Each writer has an idea, or message, about war. In each selection, look for the writer's message about war. Think about how the messages are the same and how they are different.

Selection Vocabulary

groping (grōp) *v.* feeling about uncertainly with the hands (p. 258)
*Pat was **groping** for the light switch as he walked into the dark room.*

stooped (stoopt) *adj.* bent forward and down (p. 259)
*The old woman carrying heavy grocery bags had **stooped** shoulders.*

ponder (pon' dər) *v.* to think about carefully (p. 259)
*Many people **ponder** the meaning of life.*

gape (gāp) *v.* to stare with the mouth open (p. 259)
*The child at the zoo could only **gape** at the animals.*

dwell on (dwel) *v.* to think about for a long time (p. 259)
*Yi told her friend not to **dwell** on small mistakes.*

Content Vocabulary

weapon (wep' ən) *n.* an object used to fight (p. 258)
*A sword was the common **weapon** of a knight.*

crouched (kroucht) *v.* bent low (p. 259)
*Gabriel dropped a dollar and **crouched** to pick it up.*

escape (es kāp') *n.* a way to get away or get free (p. 263)
*Tina saw smoke and looked for an **escape**.*
➤ Cognate (Spanish) **escapatoria**

separated (sep' ə rāt əd) *v.* set apart (p. 264)
*The boy **separated** the fruit into two bowls.*
➤ Cognate (Spanish) **separar(se)**

For more practice, see page 338. ➡

Vocabulary Routine

To introduce the vocabulary, read aloud the words and definitions in the student book and have students repeat after you. Discuss how the pictures illustrate the words or sentences. Then follow the vocabulary routine below.

Content Vocabulary

<u>Define:</u> A person uses a **weapon**, such as a gun, to fight. <u>Example:</u> The army used a new kind of *weapon* to win the war. <u>Ask:</u> What is another example of a *weapon?* EXAMPLE

If you **crouched**, you would be low to the ground with your knees bent. *The child crouched as she played on the floor.* What is the opposite of *crouched?* ANTONYM

An **escape** is a way to get free. *The rabbit found an escape from the dog under a fence.* How is an *escape* like an exit? SYNONYM

When two things are **separated**, they are set apart from each other. *The teacher separated the class into two groups.* Give an example of something else that can be *separated.* EXAMPLE

Vocabulary Practice Have students complete the vocabulary practice activity on page 338.

Selection Vocabulary

<u>Define:</u> When you are **groping** for something, you are feeling around blindly with your hands. <u>Example:</u> You are groping in a dark room to find the light switch. <u>Ask:</u> What are some other situations when you might be groping? EXAMPLE

A person who is **stooped** is bent forward and downward. *After carrying the heavy boxes, my back was as stooped as that of a hundred-year-old man.* Explain a situation that would leave you stooped. EXPLANATION

To **ponder** is to think about something in a careful, thoughtful way. *A person might ponder a decision about where to go on vacation.* How are the words *ponder* and *think* alike? How are they different? COMPARE AND CONTRAST

When you **gape** at something you stare at it with an open mouth. *People gape when they are surprised or in awe.* What word means the opposite of *gape?* ANTONYM

You **dwell** on something when you think about it for a long time and can't let it go. *People may dwell on a decision they make if they feel it was wrong.* Describe a time when you dwelled on a particular idea for too long. DESCRIPTION

AMBUSH

Interactive Question-Response

Content Vocabulary

Have a student read aloud the last sentence of the first boxed text. Explain that much of the fighting in Vietnam happened in thick jungle growth. The narrator's platoon, or group of soldiers, is moving through the jungle on foot. **Ask:** *What kind of weapon do you think the narrator has? (gun, grenade, knife, machete) What kind of weapon would the narrator probably not have? (bomb, cannon, catapult, slingshot) Why not? (too heavy, too impractical, etc.)* If students have difficulty responding: **Model** *I'm going to have to walk through this hot jungle carrying all my food and my clothes. How much do you think I can carry? Do you think I can carry a cannon?* If necessary, quickly sketch different kinds of weapons on the board.

weapon (wep' an) *n.* a object used to fight

Grenades are small bombs that soldiers usually throw by hand. Before throwing a grenade, a soldier usually pulls out a *pin*, a small piece of metal that activates the fuse. A grenade explodes very soon after its pin is pulled out.

To Sum Up

➤ The narrator is fighting in a war.

➤ The narrator hides with other men near a trail.

➤ The narrator sees a man with a gun walking toward him.

When she was nine, my daughter Kathleen asked if I had ever killed anyone. She knew about the war; she knew I'd been a soldier. "You keep writing these war stories," she said, "so I guess you must've killed somebody." It was a difficult moment, but I did what seemed right, which was to say, "Of course not," and then to take her onto my lap and hold her for a while. Someday, I hope, she'll ask again. But here I want to pretend she's a grown-up. I want to tell her exactly what happened, or what I remember happening, and then I want to say to her that as a little girl she was absolutely right. This is why I keep writing war stories:

He was a short, slender young man of about twenty. I was afraid of him—afraid of something—and as he passed me on the trail I threw a grenade that exploded at his feet and killed him.

Or to go back:

Shortly after midnight we moved into the ambush site outside My Khe. The whole platoon[1] was there, spread out in the dense[2] brush along the trail, and for five hours nothing at all happened. We were working in two-man teams—one man on guard while the other slept, switching off every two hours—and I remember it was still dark when Kiowa shook me awake for the final watch. The night was foggy and hot. For the first few moments I felt lost, not sure about directions, **groping** for my helmet and **weapon**. I reached out and found three **grenades** and lined them up in front of me; the **pins** had already been straightened for quick throwing. And then for maybe half an hour I knelt there and waited. Very gradually, in tiny slivers, dawn began to break through the fog, and from my position in the brush I could see ten or fifteen meters up the trail. The mosquitoes were fierce. I remember slapping at them, wondering if I should wake up Kiowa and ask for some repellent, then thinking it was a bad idea, then looking up and seeing the young man come out of the fog. He wore black clothing and rubber sandals and a gray ammunition belt. His shoulders were slightly stooped, his head cocked to the side as

Vocabulary ....

groping (grōp ing) *v.* feeling about uncertainly with the hands

1. A **platoon** is a small military group.
2. **Dense** means "close together" or "thick."

Comprehension

To support students as they read the selection, have them begin the graphic organizer on page A48.

if listening for something. He seemed at ease. He carried his weapon in one hand, muzzle down, moving without any hurry up the center of the trail. There was no sound at all—none that I can remember. In a way, it seemed, he was part of the morning fog, or my own imagination, but there was also the reality of what was happening in my stomach. I had already pulled the pin on a grenade. I had come up to a crouch. It was entirely automatic. I did not hate the young man; I did not see him as the enemy; I did not **ponder** issues of morality or politics or military duty. I crouched and kept my head low. I tried to swallow whatever was rising from my stomach, which tasted like lemonade, something fruity and sour. I was terrified. There were no thoughts about killing. The grenade was to make him go away—just **evaporate**—and I leaned back and felt my mind go empty and then felt it fill up again. I had already thrown the grenade before telling myself to throw it. The brush was thick and I had to lob it high, not aiming, and I remember the grenade seeming to freeze above me for an instant, as if a camera had clicked, and I remember ducking down and holding my breath and seeing little wisps of fog rise from the earth. The grenade bounced once and rolled across the trail. I did not hear it, but there must've been a sound, because the young man dropped his weapon and began to run, just two or three quick steps, then he hesitated, swiveling to his right, and he glanced down at the grenade and tried to cover his head but never did. It occurred to me then that he was about to die. I wanted to warn him. The grenade made a popping noise—not soft but not loud either—not what I'd expected—and there was a puff of dust and smoke—a small white puff—and the young man seemed to jerk upward as if pulled by invisible wires. He fell on his back. His rubber sandals had been blown off. There was no wind. He lay at the center of the trail, his right leg bent beneath him, his one eye shut, his other eye a huge star-shaped hole.

It was not a matter of live or die. There was no real peril. Almost certainly the young man would have passed by. And it will always be that way.

Later, I remember, Kiowa tried to tell me that the man would've died anyway. He told me that it was a good kill, that I was a soldier and this was a war, that I should shape up and stop staring and ask myself what the dead man would've done if things were reversed.

None of it mattered. The words seemed far too complicated. All I could do was **gape** at the fact of the young man's body.

Even now I haven't finished sorting it out. Sometimes I forgive myself, other times I don't. In the ordinary hours of life I try not to **dwell on** it, but now and then, when I'm reading a newspaper or just sitting alone in a room, I'll look up and see the young man coming out of the morning fog. I'll watch him walk toward me, his shoulders slightly

---

Vocabulary

ponder (pon' dər) *v.* to think about carefully
gape (gāp) *v.* to stare with the mouth open
dwell on (dwel) *v.* to think about for a long time

---

crouched (kroucht) *v.* bent low

To **evaporate**, here, means "to disappear." Literally, *evaporate* means "to change from a liquid or solid into a gas."

Comprehension Check

The narrator throws the grenade at the young man

☐ because the narrator's life is in danger.

☑ because the narrator wants the young man to go away.

☐ because the narrator believes the young man is evil.

To Sum Up

➤ The narrator is afraid of the man with the gun.

➤ The narrator throws a grenade at the man.

➤ The man dies.

Interactive Question-Response

Content Vocabulary

Read aloud the word and definition. Crouch to demonstrate the meaning. **Model** *I might crouch if I needed to pick something up.* **Ask:** *Why else might a person crouch?* (to hide; to talk to a small child; to clean something) *Why does the narrator crouch?* (to hide)

Comprehension Check

Ask students to share their answers. Have students point out the words in the text that support their answers. If students have difficulty responding: **Model** *This is a tough question, because the narrator is saying that he doesn't really have a good reason to kill the young man. I'm going to look back at his description of the thoughts that go through his head.* Have a student read aloud from "I did not hate …" to "telling myself to throw it." **Ask:** *How do you think you would have reacted in this situation?*

To Sum Up

Beginning/Early Intermediate ▶ Have students work in pairs to reread the To Sum Up boxes from the beginning of the story. Then ask students to think about which statements are most important. Have them use those statements to create a summary of the story so far. Provide the following sentence frames for students to complete.

First, the narrator _____.

The narrator feels _____.

Next, the narrator _____.

(First, the narrator sees the young man. The narrator feels afraid. Next, the narrator kills the man.)

Interactive Question-Response

Literary Element Mood

If students have difficulty responding, explain that thinking about the mood of a text can help them understand the author's ideas. **Model** *Two authors could both write about a birthday. One author might write about music, a cake, and dancing. Those details create a happy mood. The other author might write about bad weather and being alone. Those details create a sad mood. Although the authors write about the same topic, they have different ideas about it.* **Ask:** *What words on this page create a different mood or feeling from the rest of the story? (suddenly smile)*

Reflect

Partner Talk Have students work in pairs to answer. To help students get started: **Model** *I know that concrete details are related to the five senses of sight, hearing, taste, touch, and smell. One detail related to sight is that the man on the trail wears black clothes. Black clothes are simple, so the man might have a simple life.* Write the following sentence frame on the board to help students organize their thoughts.

One concrete detail is _____. I think the man _____.

Literary Element

Mood Most of the mood of the selection is frightened or sad. Underline the words that create a different mood.

To Sum Up

➤ The narrator stares at the dead man's body.
➤ Years later, the narrator still thinks about the man he killed.
➤ The narrator imagines that he did not kill the man.

260

stooped, his head cocked to the side, and he'll pass within a few yards of me and <u>suddenly smile</u> at some secret thought and then continue up the trail to where it bends back into the fog.

Vocabulary

stooped (stoopt) *adj.* bent forward and down

REFLECT

Analyze Concrete Details
Write two concrete details about the man on the trail. What sort of person do you think the man is?

Possible answer: He is slender, and he wears rubber sandals.

He is young. He wears a gray ammunition belt. He may not

have much money. He does not seem strong.

_____

_____

 Talk about your answer with a partner.

THE Gift IN WARTIME

I offer you roses
Buried in your new grave
I offer you my wedding gown
To cover your tomb still green with grass

5 You give me medals
Together with silver stars
And the yellow pips[1] on your badge[2]
Unused and still shining

I offer you my youth
10 The days we were still in love
My youth died away
When they told me the bad news

I offer you the smell of blood
From your war dress
15 Your blood and your enemy's
So that I may be moved

I offer you clouds
That linger on my eyes on summer days
I offer you cold winters
20 Amid my springtime of life

You give me your lips with no smile
You give me your arms without tenderness
You give me your eyes with no sight
And your motionless body

1. **Pips** are military badges worn on the shoulder.
2. A **badge** is a mark of someone's job or rank

Comprehension Check

What happens after the speaker's husband dies?

- ☐ The speaker plans to join the army and fight the enemy.
- ☑ The speaker feels that she is older.
- ☐ The speaker marries someone else.

To Sum Up

➤ The speaker talks to her dead husband.

➤ The speaker offers him flowers and her wedding dress.

➤ The speaker takes the badge her husband wore.

Interactive Question-Response

Comprehension Check

Have students identify words in the text that support their answer. *("I offer you my youth," "My youth died away," "I offer you cold winters / Amid the springtime of my life.")* **Ask:** *Why do you think grief might make someone feel older? (The death of someone you love can make you feel that you are closer to your own death. If the person was very important to you, you might feel as though you have lost a reason to live.)*

Differentiated Instruction

Clarify the Text Support students in understanding the poet's language.

Beginning/Early Intermediate Read aloud the To Sum Up box as students follow along. **Ask:** *Does the speaker really talk to her dead husband? (no) How do you think the speaker feels? (sad)*

Intermediate Have students reread the boxed text. Then ask them to complete these sentence frames: *The speaker offers her husband _____. (roses and her wedding dress) The speaker's husband gives her _____. (medals and his lifeless body)*

Early Advanced Ask a volunteer to read aloud the fifth stanza. Explain that the author is using figurative language. Have students discuss possible meanings of "clouds / That linger ... on summer days" *(sadness during happy times)* and "my springtime of life" *(when the speaker is young)*

Interactive Question-Response

Comparing Literature

If students have difficulty responding, explain that comparing authors' messages may help them judge texts. They can think about which message is stronger or which message they agree with more. **Model** *Tim O'Brien and Tran Mong Tu write about similar things. They both write about war, painful memories, and someone dying. So I'm thinking about what is different about their texts. The narrator of "Ambush" is fighting in a war. The man he kills is a stranger. The speaker of "The Gift in Wartime" is the wife of someone fighting in a war. The man who dies is her husband.* **Ask:** *How is Tran Mong Tu's message different from Tim O'Brien's? (She writes about the pain of losing a family member.)*

To Sum Up

Beginning/Early Intermediate ▶ Have students work together to reread the To Sum Up boxes from the beginning of the poem. Check to make sure students understand the phrase *wedding dress*. Ask them to identify things in the poem that are related to war and things that are not. Provide the following sentence frames for students to complete.

Things that remind me of war are _____.

Things that do not remind me of war are _____.

(Things that remind me of war are the badge and shrapnel. Things that do not remind me of war are the flowers and wedding dress.)

Reflect

Partner Talk Have students work in pairs to answer. To help students get started: **Model** *One concrete detail related to sight is "tomb still green with grass." The feeling I get from that detail is sadness.* Model writing the detail and the feeling in the appropriate boxes. Write the following sentence frames on the board to help students organize their thoughts.

Three concrete details are ___. The feeling I get from them is ___.

✏ Comparing Literature

Tim O'Brien has a message about war in "Ambush." Tran Mong Tu has another message about war. How are the messages different?

- ☑ Tim O'Brien writes about dealing with his conscience after killing someone. Tran Mong Tu writes about the pain of losing a family member.
- ☐ Tim O'Brien writes about telling his daughter about war. Tran Mong Tu writes about killing a young man.
- ☐ Tim O'Brien writes about his fear of death. Tran Mong Tu writes about having a strong memory of war.

To Sum Up

➤ The speaker says she will see her husband after she dies.
➤ The speaker will hold shrapnel so her husband will know her.

25 Seriously, I apologize to you
I promise to meet you in our next life
I will hold this shrapnel[3] as a token
By which we will recognize each other

3. **Shrapnel** are small pieces from an exploding bomb.

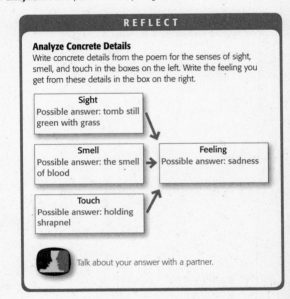

REFLECT

Analyze Concrete Details
Write concrete details from the poem for the senses of sight, smell, and touch in the boxes on the left. Write the feeling you get from these details in the box on the right.

Sight
Possible answer: tomb still green with grass

Smell
Possible answer: the smell of blood

Touch
Possible answer: holding shrapnel

Feeling
Possible answer: sadness

Talk about your answer with a partner.

from Stay Alive, My Son

My first reaction was to give way to despair, to give up, to surrender to my fate. Everything was lost, I was going to die anyway, I knew that. There was no escape.[1] We swelled up[1] and died. It was the law of nature, unalterable. We all died one after another. There was nothing to be done. What did it matter? I would die, and the sooner the better, there in the house with my wife and son.

Then the true enormity[2] of my situation struck me. There would be no such choice. Even that tiny freedom would be taken from me. There would be no gentle, natural passing with my family beside me. **They** were going to slaughter me, like an animal, away in the forest.

At that thought, I felt another sensation, a surge of raw energy that drove out all other feelings. The instinct for self-preservation took over, and I suddenly, desperately, wanted to stay alive. I told myself: "Pull yourself together! Sharpen up! Get out of this! You've always succeeded before! This is your last chance! Do something!"

I began to think. What was to be done? Leave alone? But there was Nawath across the hut, lying prostrate,[3] his limbs swollen. I could hardly bear the thought of leaving him and Any. But neither could I imagine escaping with them. Better they should have a chance to live here than die with me. Better that I should get away, and give myself a chance to live, or at least die on my own terms.

It was all very simple. My mind was made up. I had to tell Any of my decision, that very evening.

After we had eaten, as we sat on the floor opposite each other, with Nawath sleeping behind his cloth partition across the hut, I prepared myself to speak. I was certain of my course, but that did not make me any less nervous. It was a terrible thing to do to us as a family, a terrible thing to impose on Any. But as I glanced up at her, and saw her sweet and wasted[4] features lit dimly by the flickering flames of the cooking fire, I knew there was no other course. It was purposeless to stay on there merely to face death. They would be alone all too soon, anyway.

1. Their bodies **swelled up** because they did not have enough healthy food.
2. **Enormity** is outrageousness or the state of being terrible.
3. **Prostrate** means "flat on the ground."
4. **Wasted**, here, means "weakened, ruined, or made thin." Starvation makes Any appear older than she is.

from Stay Alive, My Son **263**

Background Information

Pin Yathay was born in Cambodia. In 1975, the Khmer Rouge began to rule the country. The Khmer Rouge was a communist political group. The group killed between one and three million people in Cambodia. Many others died from hunger and disease. Most of Pin Yathay's family died during that time. He has shared his story with people around the world.

escape (es kāp') *n.* a way to get away or get free

They, here, refers to the Khmer Rouge. Pin Yathay does not name them, because they are everywhere. The Khmer Rouge are an ever-present, all-powerful force in his life.

To Sum Up

➤ Pin Yathay thinks he will die. He thinks the Khmer Rouge will kill him in a week.

➤ Pin Yathay wants to stay alive.

➤ Pin Yathay plans to leave his wife and his sick son.

Interactive Question-Response

Background Information

Ask students to discuss the feelings and choices a person might have in Pin Yathay's situation in Cambodia. **Model** *I think someone in Cambodia at that time might be very angry at the government.* **Ask:** *What other feelings might someone have? (fear, sadness, hope) What choices do you think people had to make? (whether to stay in the country or leave; whether or not to fight against the government)*

Content Vocabulary

Have a student read aloud the word and definition. **Model** *A person usually needs an escape when something bad happens. For example, if I were locked inside a building, I would need to find an escape.* **Ask:** *Why does Pin Yathay need an escape? (He thinks he will die.)*

Differentiated Instruction

Clarify the Text Support students in understanding Pin Yathay's situation.

Beginning/Early Intermediate ➤ Read aloud the To Sum Up box as students follow along. Draw a man, woman, and boy on the board. Circle the man and draw an arrow away from the woman and boy. Explain that Pin Yathay plans to leave his wife and son. **Ask:** *Why does Pin Yathay plan to leave them? (to stay alive)*

Intermediate ➤ Have students work in pairs to reread the boxed text. **Ask:** *What does Pin Yathay think will happen if he stays at home? (He will die.) What does he plan to do? (leave his wife and son so he can live)*

Early Advanced ➤ Direct students' attention to the last paragraph. Ask them to restate Pin Yathay's thoughts in their own words. Then have them discuss what they think he should do.

Interactive
Question-Response

Comprehension Check

Ask students to share their answers. **Ask:** *Do you think Any's choice to go with her husband is a good one? Why or why not? (Students may say it is a bad choice because she will be safer away from her husband. They may also say she is endangering her son by leaving him behind.)*

Content Vocabulary

Read aloud the word and definition. Demonstrate *separated* by holding two objects close together and then moving them apart. **Ask:** *Why do you think Any does not want to be separated from Pin Yathay? (because she loves him; because she is scared to be alone)*

Comprehension Check

Reread the boxed text. Why is Any unhappy?

- [ ] Her family has no food.
- [ ] Her son has gone away.
- [x] Her husband plans to leave.

separated (sep′ ə rāt əd) *v.* set apart

To Sum Up

➤ Pin Yathay tells his wife, Any, that he plans to leave.

➤ Pin Yathay says that Any and their son, Nawath, will be safe.

➤ Any cries and says she will go with him.

"Any, my dearest," I said, "I have something to tell you." She looked up, without surprise, and I realized she had been expecting a decision of some kind. She too must have known that I could not stay. Speaking softly in order not to wake Nawath—I could see his little bloated[5] face round the edge of the partition—I began to explain. I was doomed, I said. All the former high officials had disappeared. I was trained in the West. I was irredeemable[6] in the eyes of the Khmer Rouge. They would come for me in a week, and that would be that. "But you're a woman, Any, if you were alone with Nawath I don't think they would harm you."

She said nothing, but I saw her gaze turn to one of horror.

"You can live on here with Nawath," I went on. "It's the only answer. I'll take my chances in the forest. If I succeed, we'll meet again. But I have to go soon. In one week, it'll be too late."

"You'll leave?" she said. "Leave me here with Nawath?" And suddenly she began to sob as if she were being torn apart.

"Yes, my dearest. It's the only way," I said, desperately. For the first time, I began to realize that she had not come to the same conclusion as me. "What did you think?"

"Not that. Not that."

I said nothing, for there was only one other course open, the one that was impossible to contemplate. She would see that in a few minutes, I thought, and accept my decision.

But no. With hesitations and bitter sobs, she went on, "It's impossible, my dearest Thay . . . I don't want to be separated from you . . . I prefer to die with you rather than to stay here . . ." As I listened to her in silence, unable to say anything to stem the slow, whispered outpouring of words and sobs and tears, I couldn't believe that she understood what she was saying. Soon, soon, she would see, and know why I had to go alone. "I cannot live without you!" she sobbed. "I prefer to die quickly and cleanly, with you."

She paused, wracked by sobs. I waited for her to say: But if you think it is for the best, of course that is how it must be.

Silence.

To my astonishment, I began to realize she meant what she said. For the first time in our lives, she was refusing to accept my judgment of what was best.

The silence dragged on, broken only by her gasps. She was looking at me. I could see the highlights cast by the fire on her cheeks and in her eyes. Still she said nothing further. I knew then she had understood all along what she was saying.

I felt the strength of her, as well. Once, she had asked my opinion even before buying a dress. Now she had been hardened by experience. She knew what she was doing, knew that in any event she and Nawath

---

5. **Bloated** means "swollen or puffy."

6. **Irredeemable** here means "unable to be changed," especially "unable to be changed into something better." To the Khmer Rouge, Pin Yathay will always be corrupt because of his association with the old government.

would die, knew that we were **in the process** not of choosing life over death, but of choosing different ways of dying.

And she knew that, having chosen, there was one more fearful choice still to make. There seemed nothing I could do or say to help her through it. It was too awful for me to put into words. If I spoke the words, it would turn something that was merely a nightmarish fear into dreadful reality. I could not say them.

"But," she said at last. "But what shall we do with Nawath?"

Yes: those were the words I had refused to utter.

"Tell me, Thay dearest. What shall we do with Nawath?" She broke down again as she struggled to express the thought. "He can't come with us. We can't carry him, and he can't walk far. They would catch us and kill us before . . ." She paused, her face working to control her emotion. "We . . . we have to leave him behind. But . . . what are we going to do with him if we leave him?" She broke off again, overcome by sobs.

Could she really contemplate leaving Nawath? It seemed an extraordinary thing for a mother to do. I realize now that she had made a mother's supreme sacrifice. People say that for a mother the supreme sacrifice is to die with her child. No—if death is inevitable,[7] the mother's supreme sacrifice is to abandon her child, if thereby she can prolong her own life.

I did not understand all that right then and there. But I felt her resolve, and knew there was nothing I could say to make her change her mind. After what we had been through, after being made one body with her by what we had endured together, it never even occurred to me to argue her out of her decision. I don't think I could have done so. I simply had to accept that things were different now.

Any was still sobbing. "What do we do with Nawath?" she asked again, and fell silent. I knew from her tone of voice, and the silence, that she already knew the answer, for there was only one. Knowing it, again neither of us could bring ourselves to express it. Again, expressing it would make it irrevocable.[8]

---

7. If something is **inevitable** (i neva ta bla), it is not possible to avoid.
8. Something **irrevocable** (i rev a ka bla) cannot be undone.

A **process** is a series of changes or actions. To be **in the process** of doing something is to be in the middle of doing it.

Comparing Literature

Tim O'Brien has a message about war in "Ambush." Pin Yathay also has a message about war. How are the messages similar?

- [ ] Both are about being lost in a strange place.
- [ ] Both are about leaving people.
- [x] Both are about making hard choices.

To Sum Up

➤ Pin Yathay knows they must make another hard choice.

➤ Any asks what they will do with their son.

Interactive Question-Response

Comparing Literature

If students have trouble responding: **Model** *"Ambush" is about a soldier who has a problem. He sees a man with a gun and does not know what to do. Should he kill the man or risk being killed? Pin Yathay also has a problem. He does not know what to do, either. His choices are not good ones.* **Ask:** *What do the authors both write about?* (making hard choices) *Explain that comparing authors' messages, or ideas, can help students understand a topic better.* **Model** *In these two stories, we have two different views of war. One narrator is a soldier. The other narrator is a civilian, a person who is not in the army. Because I'm reading both stories, I have a more balanced understanding of war. I see the kind of choices war forces people to make.*

Differentiated Instruction

Clarify the Text Support students in understanding Pin Yathay and Any's dilemma about their son.

Beginning/Early Intermediate ➤ Read aloud the To Sum Up box as students follow along. Then have them complete this sentence frame: *Pin Yathay and Any must choose what to do with their ____.* (son) **Ask:** *Is the choice easy or hard?* (hard)

Intermediate ➤ Have students reread the boxed text. Ask them to identify negative words. *(death, dying, fearful, awful, nightmarish, fear, dreadful)* **Ask:** *Why do you think Pin Yathay uses those words?* (He and Any must make a very hard choice.)

Early Advanced ➤ Write the phrase *supreme sacrifice* on the board. Explain that here *supreme* means "highest." A person makes a sacrifice when he or she gives something away or suffers harm for an important cause. Have students reread the paragraph that contains the phrase. **Ask:** *Which sacrifice do you think is supreme? Why?*

from Stay Alive, My Son

Interactive Question-Response

To Sum Up

Beginning/Early Intermediate ▶ Have students reread the To Sum Up boxes on pages 263–266. Then ask students to explain the decisions Pin Yathay and his wife make. Provide the following sentence frames for students to complete.

Pin Yathay and Any will _____. They will take _____ to the hospital because _____.

(Pin Yathay and Any will leave together. They will take their son to the hospital because he will be safest there.)

Reflect

Partner Talk Have students work in pairs to answer. To help students get started: **Model** *For a drawing, I think the most important concrete details are those related to sight. Pin Yathay describes his son as lying prostrate, which means "lying flat on the ground." His son's limbs, or arms and legs, are swollen.* Model drawing the boy on the board. Write the following sentence frames to help students organize their thoughts.

Concrete details in the story are _____. I should draw _____.

A *morgue* is a place where the bodies of the dead are kept. When Pin Yathay calls the hospital *that morgue of a place*, he does not mean that the hospital is really a morgue. He means that so many people die at the hospital that the hospital is like a morgue.

I glanced at Nawath, still asleep. I felt I wanted to go to him, stroke his head, provide some comfort for him, or myself. But I did not move. I couldn't risk waking him. I glanced back at Any. Her eyes were lowered, as if waiting for me to pronounce sentence.

After another eternal minute, the burden of silence became intolerable. I felt it as an accusation against me for evading[9] responsibility.

"You know there is only one thing to do," I whispered. "We must take him to the hospital."

The hospital, where people went only to die.

I looked into the shadows of her eyes. "We must," I said.

She knew that this time I was right. Nawath's chances were better in **that morgue of a place** than in the forest, while ours were better in the forest than there in the village. We would all die anyway; but to ensure[10] we all lived as long as possible we had to leave him. While we would at least die together, he would die alone, abandoned by the only ones who cared for him.

9. *Evading* means "avoiding," "escaping," or "getting out of."
10. To **ensure** is to make sure.

To Sum Up

➤ Pin Yathay and his wife agree to take their son to the hospital, where many people die.
➤ Pin Yathay thinks the hospital is the safest place for their son.
➤ Pin Yathay and Any are sad that he must leave his son behind.

REFLECT

Analyze Concrete Details
Reread the text, and look for concrete details. Draw the three family members inside the hut. In your drawing, include the concrete details you found in the text.

Students should draw Pin Yathay and Any sitting on the floor near a small fire with their son lying on the floor behind a cloth partition. Any is thin and is crying.

 Talk about your answer with a partner.

Oral Assessment

Provide the following prompts to one student at a time. Observe students' responses. See the Oral Assessment Rubric on page T17 to determine students' levels of language output.

1. Who is the narrator of "Ambush"?

2. What memory does the narrator of "Ambush" describe?

3. Tell me about the speaker of "The Gift in Wartime."

4. What problems does Pin Yathay have in "Stay Alive, My Son"?

5. How does Pin Yathay try to solve his problems?

AMBUSH · THE Gift IN WARTIME · *from* Stay Alive, My Son

Vocabulary Check

A. For each question, circle the correct picture.

1. Which picture shows two people who are **separated**?

2. Which statue is **crouched**?

3. Which picture shows someone using a **weapon**?

4. Which picture shows an **escape** from a ship?

B. Complete each sentence with a vocabulary word.

stooped	dwell on	escape	gape	weapon

5. Many drivers slowed down to _____ gape _____ at the car accident.

6. Though his shoulders are _____ stooped _____, my grandfather is still quite strong.

7. Though the door was blocked, Saki found an _____ escape _____ through a window.

8. An airplane with bombs was an important _____ weapon _____ in World War II.

9. Old age is a time when many people _____ dwell on _____ the past.

C. Reread the parts of the selections where the boldfaced words appear. Mark the correct meaning.

10. The narrator of "Ambush" **gropes** for his gun.
    - ☐ a. looks for without moving
    - ☑ b. feels around without looking
    - ☐ c. takes from someone else

11. The man on the trail had **stooped** shoulders.
    - ☑ a. bent down and forward
    - ☐ b. bent up and backward
    - ☐ c. wide and strong

12. The narrator **gapes** at the dead man's body.
    - ☑ a. stares at with an open mouth
    - ☐ b. turns away with closed eyes
    - ☐ c. looks away and back again

13. Many years later, the narrator **dwells on** his memory of the ambush.
    - ☐ a. does not think about
    - ☐ b. thinks something is not important
    - ☑ c. thinks about for a long time

Vocabulary Check

C. Early Advanced

Encourage students to visualize the action in each sentence before choosing an answer. Especially for *ponder* and *dwell on*, suggest that students return to the text and think carefully about the narrator's responses during and after the ambush. If students are confused by the concept of a phrasal verb such as *dwell on*, write on the board: *Mr. O'Brien dwells in a small house in the suburbs. Mr. O'Brien dwells on a small house in the suburbs.* Explain that *dwell* means something different if *on* does not follow it. **Ask:** *What does* dwells *mean in the first sentence? (lives or resides)* **Model** *The second sentence says "dwells on," so I know he's thinking about that small house. Maybe it was a house that he wanted to buy and couldn't. Maybe something bad happened there.* **Ask:** *How are the two meanings related? (Both of them contain the idea of staying in one place.)*

Grammar Link   BLM

Adjectives and Adverbs

Prepare students to complete the activity on page A49. Read the grammar instruction with students, and complete the first item with them to help them get started.

Comprehension Check

B. [Intermediate]

Remind students that a mood is a feeling such as happiness or fear, and that an author can create a mood through words and details. Ask them to think about how they felt as they read each selection.

After Reading

Have students complete the after reading activity on page 339.

Comprehension Check

A. What happens in "Ambush"? Write numbers to place the events in order.

　3　The narrator kills the young man.

　2　The narrator sees a young man with a gun.

　4　The narrator thinks about the man after the war.

　1　The narrator hides near a trail.

B. Think about the "Ambush" and "The Gift in Wartime." Then answer the questions.

5. What is the mood of "Ambush?" Possible answer: scared; sad

   List three words or details that the author uses to create the mood. Possible answer: *lost*, a foggy morning, holding my breath

6. What is the mood of "The Gift in Wartime?" Possible answer: sad; angry

   List three words or details that the author uses to create the mood. Possible answer: *grave*, the smell of blood, arms without tenderness

C. Compare "The Gift in Wartime" by Tran Mong Tu and "Stay Alive, My Son" by Pin Yathay. How are they alike and different? Complete the sentences."

7. "The Gift in Wartime" and "Stay Alive, My Son" are both about Possible answer: the effects of war on families

8. The message of "The Gift in Wartime" is Possible answer: war causes pain when family members die

9. The message of "Stay Alive, My Son" is Possible answer: war forces people to make hard choices
   Possible answer: He is like his father. He is stubborn and does what he pleases.

For more practice, see page 339. ➡

Writing Link

List

Ask students whether they think war is an inescapable part of the human experience. Is it a part of human nature to go to war? Have them consider this question by making a list of five related questions that they would like to ask and have answered, such as *Are there other effective ways to resolve our differences?* or *Will humans always be in competition over resources?* The questions might be factual, philosophical, historical, or psychological in nature. Have students include at least one *Yes-No* question for which they can think of reasons that support both answers. Then have them write answers to their lists of questions.

Students' lists should

- include thoughtful answers supported by evidence
- include at least one *Yes-No* question with two convincing answers
- reflect the themes of the compared selections

Snow

by Julia Alvarez

Learning Objectives

For pages 269–276, 340

In studying this text, you will focus on the following objectives:

Literary Study: Analyzing indirect characterization.

Reading: Connecting to contemporary issues.

Oral Language

Build Background

Read the title and author. Explain that students will read "Snow" by Julia Alvarez, an author who grew up in the Dominican Republic and moved to New York City when she was ten years old. Help students find the Dominican Republic on a map. **Ask:**

- **Does it snow in warm weather or cold weather?** *(cold)*

- **Do you think it snows a lot in the Dominican Republic?** *(no; it is in a warm part of the world)*

Talk About the Story

Explain that the story is about the first time a young girl sees snow.

Beginning/Early Intermediate ▶ **Ask:** Have you ever lived where it doesn't snow? *(yes/no)* Have students use a globe or map to find places where they think it doesn't snow.

Intermediate ▶ Explain that people who have never seen snow may feel surprised or uneasy when it starts falling from the sky. Have students complete the sentence frame to predict how the girl in the story might feel the first time she sees snow.

I predict that the girl will feel _____. (surprised, afraid)

Lesson at a Glance

Oral Language
- Build Background
- Talk About the Story

Vocabulary
- Selection Vocabulary
- Content Vocabulary

Literary Element
- Indirect Characterization

Reading Strategy
- Connect to Contemporary Issues

Writing Link
- Paragraph

Fluency
- Pacing: Phrasing

Comprehension
- BLM

Technology
- Student Works™ Plus
- Teacher Works™ Plus
- Listening Library Audio CD
- Classroom Presentation Toolkit
- Glencoe Visual Vocabulary
- Skill Level Up!™ A Skill-Based Language Arts Game

Interactive Question-Response

Connect to the Story

Read aloud Connect to the Story. Reproduce the chart on the board. **Model** *When I first saw an apple tree, I felt surprised. I didn't know that apples came from trees.* Model writing your response in the chart, and have volunteers suggest other responses. Then have individuals fill in their own charts.

Literary Element Indirect Characterization

Write the example sentence, "Sue was an outgoing, friendly person," on the board. Tell students that this is direct characterization because the author is telling us what Sue is like. Read aloud the Literary Element. **Ask:** *How could an author use indirect characterization to show that Sue is outgoing and friendly? (show Sue greeting a new student; show Sue with lots of friends)* Then write this sentence on the board: "Jada was a shy person." **Ask:** *Is this direct or indirect characterization? Why? (direct; the author is telling us what Jada is like)* **Ask:** *How could an author use indirect characterization to show that Jada is shy? (show her sitting alone in the lunchroom)*

Reading Strategy Connect to Contemporary Issues

Read aloud the Reading Strategy. Explain that *contemporary* means something that is happening now. Tell students that if they connect what they read to what is happening in the world, they may understand the story better. Tell students that you once read a story about a terrible flood. People lost their homes, and they felt sad and afraid. Then prompt students to answer the questions based on this situation. Help them recognize how they're connecting a story to a contemporary issue.

Sn❄w

Connect to the Story

When you were a child, what things did you see for the first time that surprised you? What feelings or thoughts did you have? Fill in the chart with words that describe these new experiences.

New Things	Thoughts/Feelings
apple tree	I didn't know apples came from trees.
Answers will vary.	

Literary Element Indirect Characterization

Sometimes authors describe a character directly. They might say, "Sue was an outgoing, friendly person." Other times, authors use **indirect characterization** to show the personality of a character.

Indirect characterization may include the following:

- a character's words
- a character's actions
- what others think and say about a character

As you read, look for clues that tell you about the characters. Ask yourself: How does the author show us what Yolanda and Sister Zoe are like?

Reading Strategy Connect to Contemporary Issues

When you **connect to contemporary issues**, you connect what you read to events in the world today. When you think this way, you stay interested in what you are reading. You also see that people often have the same problems today as they did in the past.

As you read, ask yourself the following questions:

- Why are the people in the story afraid?
- Is this problem like another problem in the world today?

Selection Vocabulary

enunciate (i nun′ sē āt′) *v.* to say clearly (p. 272)
*Please **enunciate** the words as you read, so we can understand them.*
➤ Cognate (Spanish) **enunciar**

holocaust (hol′ ə kôst′) *n.* great or complete destruction (p. 272)
*The fire caused a **holocaust** in the forest.*
➤ Cognate (Spanish) **holocausto**

random (ran′ dəm) *adj.* without a pattern (p. 272)
*The painting looked like **random** brushstrokes.*

warily (wâr′ ə lē) *adv.* in a watchful or alert manner; cautiously (p. 273)
*The bird **warily** watched the cat.*

Content Vocabulary

apart (ə pärt′) *adv.* at a distance; separated (p. 272)
*The shy child played **apart** from the other students.*
➤ Cognate (Spanish) **aparte**

daydreaming (dā′ drēm ing) *v.* having pleasant thoughts and images go through the mind while awake (p. 272)
*I was **daydreaming** during class.*

dusty (dus′ tē) *adj.* containing or covered with dust (p. 272)
*The attic was filled with **dusty** furniture.*

faded (fād′ əd) *v.* became gradually fainter and finally disappeared (p. 272)
*The bright colors **faded** when I washed the shirt.*

For more practice, see page 340. ➡

Snow **271**

Vocabulary Routine

To introduce the vocabulary, read aloud the words and definitions in the student book and have students repeat after you. Discuss how the pictures illustrate the words or sentences. Then follow the vocabulary routine below.

Content Vocabulary

<u>Define</u>: If you are **apart** from other people, you are separated from them. <u>Example</u>: *The girls stood three feet apart from each other.* <u>Ask</u>: What is another word for *apart*? SYNONYM

If a glass is **dusty,** it is dirty. *That glass is dusty, so wash it before you drink out of it.* What word means the opposite of *dusty*? ANTONYM

If people are **daydreaming**, pleasant thoughts and images are going through their mind, even though they are awake. *I spent the morning daydreaming about the presents I would get on my birthday.* What do you think about when you *daydream*? DESCRIPTION

When a smile has **faded**, it has slowly gone away. *Her smile faded when the doctor told her she needed to get a shot.* Why might a frown *fade*? EXAMPLE

Vocabulary Practice Have students complete the vocabulary practice activity on page 340.

Selection Vocabulary

<u>Define</u>: When you **enunciate** something, you say it clearly. <u>Example</u>: When you introduce people, you should *enunciate* their names clearly. <u>Ask</u>: What is another situation where you should take care to *enunciate* words? EXAMPLE

A **holocaust** is great destruction, especially by fire. *Because the forest fire destroyed so many homes, it was considered a holocaust.* Describe what the effect of a holocaust would be. DESCRIPTION

When things occur in a *random* order, there is no clear pattern as to why they happen. *Our seats were assigned at random, so I was surprised to be placed near my best friend.* What is the opposite of a random situation? ANTONYM

If you do something in a watchful or alert manner, you do it *warily. The stray dog approached the strange human warily.* What is another word that has a meaning similar to *warily?* SYNONYM

Sn❄w

Interactive Question-Response

Literary Element | Indirect Characterization

If students have difficulty responding: **Model** *I know that indirect characterization includes a character's words and actions. So I will underline places in the text where Sister Zoe says or does something. One thing she says is that Yolanda has a lovely name.* Model underlining that part of the text. **Ask:** *What else does Sister Zoe say or do?* Have students share their answers. **Ask:** *What kind of person is Sister Zoe? (nice thoughtful)*

To Sum Up

Beginning/Early Intermediate ▶ Read the first To Sum Up statement aloud. Tell students that Yolanda is the only student in the class who doesn't know English. **Ask:** *How do you think Yolanda feels as she's learning to speak English? (anxious, out of place)* Encourage students to share experiences in which they have felt like Yolanda might feel.

✏ Literary Element

Indirect Characterization Think about Sister Zoe. Underline the details that show what kind of person she is.

apart (ə pärt') *adv.* at a distance; separated

When something is ***in the air***, everyone is talking and thinking about it.

dusty (dus' tē) *adj.* containing or covered with dust

daydreaming (dā' drēm ing) *v.* having pleasant thoughts and images go through the mind while awake

faded (fād' əd) *v.* became gradually fainter and finally disappeared

To Sum Up

➤ Yolanda is an immigrant who goes to a Catholic school. Sister Zoe teaches her English.

➤ Sister Zoe draws a picture on the chalkboard of a mushroom cloud and radioactive fallout.

➤ Yolanda sees snow falling and thinks it is fallout from a bomb.

272

Our first year in New York we rented a small apartment with a Catholic school nearby, taught by the Sisters of Charity, hefty women in long black gowns and bonnets that made them look peculiar, like dolls in mourning. I liked them a lot, especially my grandmotherly fourth grade teacher, Sister Zoe. I had a lovely name, she said, and she had me teach the whole class how to pronounce it. Yo-lan-da. As the only immigrant in my class, I was put in a special seat in the first row by the window, apart from the other children so that Sister Zoe could tutor me without disturbing them. Slowly, she **enunciated** the new words I was to repeat: *laundromat, cornflakes, subway, snow.*

Soon I picked up enough English to understand **holocaust** was **in the air.** Sister Zoe explained to a wide-eyed classroom what was happening in Cuba. Russian missiles were being assembled, trained supposedly on New York City. President Kennedy, looking worried too, was on the television at home, explaining we might have to go to war against the Communists. At school, we had air-raid drills: an ominous bell would go off and we'd file into the hall, fall to the floor, cover our heads with our coats, and imagine our hair falling out, the bones in our arms going soft. At home, Mami and my sisters and I said a rosary[1] for world peace. I heard new vocabulary: nuclear bomb, radioactive fallout,[2] bomb shelter. Sister Zoe explained how it would happen. She drew a picture of a mushroom on the blackboard and dotted a flurry of chalkmarks for the **dusty** fallout that would kill us all.

The months grew cold, November, December. It was dark when I got up in the morning, frosty when I followed my breath to school. One morning as I sat at my desk **daydreaming** out the window, I saw dots in the air like the ones Sister Zoe had drawn—**random** at first, then lots and lots. I shrieked, "Bomb! Bomb!" Sister Zoe jerked around, her full black skirt ballooning as she hurried to my side. A few girls began to cry.

But then Sister Zoe's shocked look **faded.** "Why, Yolanda dear, that's snow!" She laughed. "Snow."

Vocabulary

enunciate (i nun' sē āt') *v.* to pronounce clearly
holocaust (hol' ə kôst') *n.* great or complete destruction
random (ran' dəm) *adj.* without a pattern

1. For Roman Catholics, a ***rosary*** is a circle of beads. It is also the name for the prayers a Catholic person says while holding these beads.
2. ***Fallout*** is the word for tiny radioactive particles that fall from the sky after a nuclear bomb explodes.

Fluency

Pacing: Phrasing

Intermediate/Early Advanced ▶ Tell students that they will be doing a choral reading of the boxed text in paragraphs 3 and 4 of the story. Remind students to read in phrases or complete sentences for clarity and not word by word. Model the fluency skill as you read the text at a moderate tempo. Then have one student read a sentence. Have another student join in, and a third, and so on. When students reach the end of the passage, have pairs of students reread to each other. To assess individual fluency, use the Oral Reading Guidelines on page T16.

Beginning/Early Intermediate ▶ Have these students choral read only the first paragraph of the passage. Before they begin, model the pronunciation of the text. Then have students practice reading the paragraph in pairs before the choral reading.

"Snow," I repeated. I looked out the window **warily.** All my life I had heard about the white crystals that fell out of American skies in the winter. From my desk I watched the fine powder dust the sidewalk and parked cars below. Each flake was different, Sister Zoe said, like a person, irreplaceable and beautiful.

Literary Element

Indirect Characterization Yolanda thinks the snow is dusty fallout from a bomb. What does this fact tell you about her?

- [x] She has never seen snow.
- [ ] She cannot see very well.
- [ ] She does not like Sister Zoe.

Background Information

This story is set around 1962. That year, President John F. Kennedy ordered the U.S. Navy to stop a shipment of missiles from the Soviet Union to Cuba. People all over the world were afraid that there might be a nuclear war.

Vocabulary

warily (wâr′ a lē) *adv.* in a watchful or alert manner; cautiously

---

REFLECT

Connect to Contemporary Issues
Why are the people in the story afraid?

Possible answer: They are afraid because events in the world

make it seem like there will be a nuclear war.

How is this problem similar to issues in the world today?

Possible answer: People see scary events on the news.

People worry that these events put them in danger.

 Talk about your answer with a partner.

To Sum Up

➤ Yolanda sees that the flakes are snow.

➤ Sister Zoe says that each snowflake is beautiful, like each person.

Snow **273**

Comprehension BLM

To support students as they read the selection, have them begin the graphic organizer on page A50.

Interactive Question-Response

Literary Element
Indirect Characterization

If students have difficulty responding, draw their attention to the part of the story in which Sister Zoe draws "a flurry of chalkmarks" to represent nuclear fallout. Read it aloud, and then draw a flurry of chalkmarks on the board in your classroom. **Ask:** *What do the chalkmarks and snow have in common? (Both are white dots falling from the sky.)* Help students understand that Yolanda makes a mistake because she has seen a picture of nuclear fallout, but she has never seen snow.

Background Information

Read aloud the note. Explain that at the time of the Cuban missile crisis, schools practiced air-raid drills to prepare for a nuclear attack. The problem was that some of these safety measures—such as crouching under desks—would not have protected students from harm. Ask students to think about the description of nuclear fallout in the story. Then ask why crouching under desks would not have protected students. *(Fallout could float around and under desks.)*

Reflect

Partner Talk Have students work in pairs to answer. Help students see that the people in the story are afraid of a nuclear war. Then help them list contemporary issues that make people feel afraid. **Model** *When I listen to news stories about global warming, I feel afraid for the earth's future.* Invite pairs of students to discuss and share their own examples. Then discuss how the fears today are similar to the fears in the story. *(In both cases, people fear for their safety and for the future.)*

Vocabulary Check

B. Intermediate

Remind students that antonyms are opposites, or words with different meanings. Write the following words on the board: *happy, empty.* **Ask:** What is an antonym of *happy? (sad)* **Ask:** What is an antonym of *empty? (full)* Then read each question aloud and have students choose their answers.

After You Read

Sn❄w

Vocabulary Check

A. Circle the word that describes each picture.

1. 2. 3. 4. 5.

1. (daydreaming) / dusty
2. apart / (faded)
3. faded / (dusty)
4. (apart) / daydreaming
5. faded / (holocaust)

B. Match the word to its antonym, or opposite.

d	5. warily	a.	clean
a	6. dusty	b.	bright
b	7. faded	c.	ordered
e	8. holocaust	d.	carelessly
c	9. random	e.	creation

C. Complete the sentences.

10. Sister Zoe **enunciated** English words   Possible answer: for Yolanda to repeat   .

11. Yolanda watched **random** dots fall   Possible answer: from the sky   .

12. Yolanda looked **warily** at   Possible answer: the snow   .

13. Everyone thought a **holocaust** would come from   Possible answer: a nuclear bomb   .

Oral Assessment

Provide the following prompts to one student at a time. Observe students' responses. See the Oral Assessment Rubric on page T17 to determine students' levels of language output.

1. Tell me about Yolanda.

2. Tell me about Sister Zoe.

3. How does Sister Zoe help Yolanda?

4. Why does Yolanda think the snow is fallout from a nuclear bomb?

5. How are snowflakes like people?

Sn❄w

Comprehension Check

A. Complete the sentences.

1. Yolanda and her family just moved to <u>New York</u>.

2. Yolanda thought snow looked like <u>Possible answer: fallout from a bomb</u>.

3. Sister Zoe said snowflakes were like people because <u>Possible answer: each one was different</u> <u>from the others</u>.

B. The author shows Sister Zoe's personality through her words and actions. Write examples of Sister Zoe's words and actions in the chart.

4. Words	5. Actions
Possible answers: She explains about nuclear bombs; "Why Yolanda, dear, that's snow;" She says that each snowflake is different, like a person, irreplaceable and beautiful."	Possible answers: She tutors Yolanda; she teaches Yolanda English words; She draws a picture of a bomb; She laughs.

C. Answer the questions about the characters in "Snow."

6. What details tell you that Sister Zoe wants to help Yolanda?

<u>Sister Zoe says Yolanda's name is beautiful; she teaches Yolanda helpful English words.</u>

7. How do you think Yolanda felt when she learned that the dots in the air were snow?

<u>Possible answer: She probably felt relieved and embarrassed.</u>

8. At the end of the story, how does Sister Zoe describe snow? What do Sister Zoe's words tell you about how she feels about Yolanda?

<u>She says each snowflake is different, like a person, irreplaceable and beautiful. Her words show that</u>

<u>she feels Yolanda is unique, irreplaceable, and beautiful.</u>

Comprehension Check

C. Early Advanced

To help students answer the third question, have them think about how Yolanda feels after mistaking snow for nuclear fallout. *(embarrassed)* **Ask:** How do you think Yolanda feels when Sister Zoe says that all snowflakes are beautiful, just like all people? *(beautiful; special)* Help students see that Sister Zoe likes Yolanda and wants to make her feel better.

Writing Link

Paragraph

Tell students to think of a childhood experience in which they observed a natural occurrence, such as snow, for the first time. Have them write a paragraph in which they describe that thing without actually naming it. Tell them to use details that appeal to the five senses: sight, smell, hearing, taste, and touch. In the last sentence of the paragraph, they should name what they have been describing.

Sn❄w

A Conversation

Imagine that you are Yolanda. You come home from school after seeing snow for the first time. Your mother asks, "How was your day?" Write what Yolanda and her mother might say.

Mother: Hello, Yolanda. How was your day at school?

Yolanda: I was embarrassed, Mami! Remember how Sister Zoe taught us about nuclear bombs? Remember how I told you she drew a picture of a mushroom with

Possible answers: lots of dots; dust
coming out of it?

Mother: I remember. Everyone is afraid of the bombs. What happened today?

Yolanda: I looked outside and saw _____

Possible answer: white stuff falling from the sky.

It looked like   Possible answers: the picture Sister Zoe

made

I was really Possible answers: surprised; afraid
But it was snow, Mami!

Mother: I was afraid when I first saw the snow, too. I am glad it is not dangerous!

Yolanda: Me, too! Sister Zoe says that snowflakes are like people because _____

Possible answer: each one is different.

Mother: Sister Zoe seems like _____

Possible answer: a nice teacher

Yolanda: Possible answer: She is! I was feeling

embarrassed, but she made me feel special.

_____

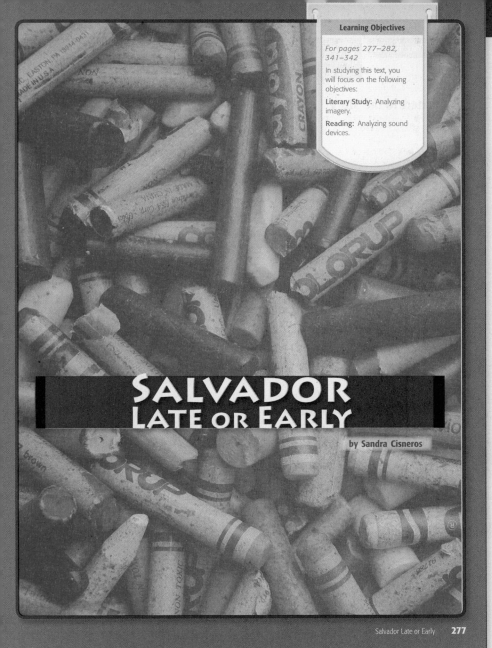

SALVADOR
LATE OR EARLY

by Sandra Cisneros

Oral Language

Build Background

Read the title and author. Explain that students will read a story called "Salvador Late or Early" by Sandra Cisneros. **Ask:**

- What do you think the story will be about? *(a body named Salvador who is sometimes late and sometimes early)*

- What are some reasons a person might be late? *(oversleeping; losing track of time; having too much to do)*

Talk About the Story

Explain that even though this selection is a story, its language is very poetic. The story is like a poem.

Intermediate Students have probably read both stories and poems. Have them name some qualities of each.

A story has _____. *(paragraphs, a plot, characters)*

A poem has _____. *(images, short lines, creative language)*

Point out that Salvador Late or Early has some qualities of a story and some qualities of a poem.

Learning Objectives

For pages 277–282, 341–342

In studying this text, you will focus on the following objectives:

Literary Study: Analyzing imagery.

Reading: Analyzing sound devices.

Lesson at a Glance

Oral Language
- Build Background
- Talk About the Story

Vocabulary
- Content Vocabulary

Literary Element
- Imagery

Reading Strategy
- Analyze Sound Devices

Writing Link
- Song

Comprehension
- BLM

Technology
- Student Works™ Plus
- Teacher Works™ Plus
- Listening Library Audio CD
- Classroom Presentation Toolkit
- Glencoe Visual Vocabulary
- Skill Level Up!™ A Skill-Based Language Arts Game

Interactive Question-Response

Connect to the Story

Read aloud Connect to the Story. Reproduce the sentence stem on the board. **Model** *I think that childhood should be about play. Children should enjoy their childhood and have fun. They can work when they get older. Children are still learning, so they aren't ready to be adults yet.* Model writing your responses on the board. Then have students complete the sentence stems on their own.

Literary Element Imagery

Read aloud the Literary Element. On the board, write the five senses in a row. Point to the word *sight,* say it aloud, and then point to your eyes. Point to the word *sound,* say it aloud, and then point to your ears. Continue with all five senses. Ask students to describe the classroom using words that appeal to each sense. **Ask:** *How does this room sound? (like a library; silent, like bedtime)* **Ask:** *How does this room smell? (like milk; like fresh air)* Continue with the remaining senses. Record students' answers on the board under the appropriate senses.

Reading Strategy Analyze Sound Devices

Read aloud the Reading Strategy. Write the sample sentence on the board: *The simmering stew sizzled.* Help students answer the questions. **Model:** *Alliteration is the repetition of sounds at the beginnings of words, so I am going to underline the first letter of each word in the sentence. Each word starts with s. The s sound is being repeated. This repetition reminds me of the sound of food simmering in the kitchen.* Write another example sentence on the board: *The wind whistles through the willows.* Help students answer the questions using this sentence.

SALVADOR LATE OR EARLY

Connect to the Story

Do you think children should have adult responsibilities? Should childhood be about play, or should it be about learning adult skills?

Partner Talk Complete the sentence below. Then share your ideas with a small group of classmates.

Childhood should be about <u>Possible answer: play</u> because

1. <u>Possible answers: Children should enjoy their childhood.</u>

2. <u>Children aren't ready to be adults yet.</u>

Literary Element Imagery

Imagery is using words to "paint a picture" in the reader's mind. To create imagery, writers use sensory details, or words that appeal to one of the five senses:

- sight
- sound
- touch
- taste
- smell

As you read, ask yourself, Which words and phrases create images?

Reading Strategy Analyze Sound Devices

Sound devices are writing techniques that appeal to the ear. Writers use sound devices to stress certain words or sounds or to help their writing sound musical. When you **analyze sound devices,** you think about how they affect the writing.

A common sound device is called **alliteration**. Alliteration is the repeating of consonant sounds at the beginnings of words. Here is one example: *The simmering stew sizzled.* To analyze alliteration, ask yourself these questions:

- What sound is being repeated?
- What effect does this repetition have?

Content Vocabulary

tumble (tum′ bəl) *v.* to fall in an awkward way (p. 280)
*Be careful where you step, or you might **tumble** to the ground.*

puddles (pud′ əlz) *n.* small, shallow pools of water (p. 280)
*The rain left **puddles** on the street.*

traffic (traf′ ik) *n.* vehicles and people moving along a route (p. 280)
*Main Street always has a lot of **traffic**.*
➤ Cognate (Spanish) **tráfico**

wrinkled (ring′ kəld) *adj.* having creases or small folds (p. 281)
*My shirt was **wrinkled** after I washed it.*

For more practice, see page 341. ➡

Vocabulary Routine

To introduce the vocabulary, read aloud the words and definitions in the student book and have students repeat after you. Discuss how the pictures illustrate the words or sentences. Then follow the routine below.

Content Vocabulary

<u>Define:</u> When you **tumble**, you lose control and fall. <u>Example:</u> If you slip on the ice, you might *tumble* to the ground. <u>Ask:</u> Why might someone *tumble*? EXPLANATION

Puddles are small pools of water. *When snow melts, it creates puddles.* What are some other things that might create *puddles*? EXAMPLES

When a street has a lot of **traffic,** it is filled with people and vehicles. *The highway has lots of traffic in the morning, when people are going to work.* Describe how it might feel to drive on a street that has a lot of *traffic.* DESCRIPTION

Something that is **wrinkled** has creases or small folds. *I ironed my skirt because it was wrinkled.* What is the opposite of *wrinkled?* ANTONYM

Vocabulary Practice Have students complete the vocabulary practice activity on page 341.

SALVADOR LATE OR EARLY

Interactive Question-Response

Literary Element Imagery

Ask students to share their answers. **Ask:** *What do you think "eyes the color of caterpillar" look like? (anno: green and black) What do you think "homes the color of bad weather" look like? (gray, brown, dreary)* Tell students that when you are having difficulty visualizing something, it helps to close your eyes for a moment and think about it.

Comprehension Check

Ask students to share their answers. **Ask:** *How do you think Salvador feels by the time he gets to school? Why? (He is probably tired because he has helped his mother and his brothers all morning.)*

Literary Element

Imagery Underline images in the first paragraph that appeal to the sense of sight.

The business of the baby means "taking care of the baby."

Comprehension Check

Reread the second paragraph of the story. How would you describe Salvador's life?

- ☑ He has lots of chores.
- ☐ He has a few chores.
- ☐ He has no chores.

tumble (tum′ bəl) *v.* to fall in an awkward way

puddles (pud′ əlz) *n.* small, shallow pools of water

traffic (traf′ ik) *n.* vehicles and people moving along a route

To Sum Up

- ➤ Salvador has a very hard life.
- ➤ Salvador takes care of his little brothers.
- ➤ Salvador's many chores make it hard for him to get to school on time.

Salvador with <u>eyes the color of caterpillar</u>, Salvador of the <u>crooked hair</u> and <u>crooked teeth</u>, Salvador whose name the teacher cannot remember, is a boy who is no one's friend, runs along somewhere in that vague direction where <u>homes are the color of bad weather</u>, lives behind a <u>raw wood doorway</u>, <u>shakes the sleepy brothers awake</u>, <u>ties their shoes</u>, <u>combs their hair with water</u>, <u>feeds them milk and corn flakes from a tin cup in the dim dark of the morning.</u>

Salvador, late or early, sooner or later arrives with the string of younger brothers ready. Helps his mama, who is busy with **the business of the baby.** Tugs the arms of Cecilio, Arturito, makes them hurry, because today, like yesterday, Arturito has dropped the cigar box of crayons, has let go the hundred little fingers of red, green, yellow, blue, and nub of black sticks that <u>tumble</u> and spill over and beyond the asphalt <u>puddles</u> until the crossing-guard lady holds back the blur of <u>traffic</u> for Salvador to collect them again.

Comprehension BLM

To support students as they read the selection, have them begin the graphic organizer on page A51.

Salvador inside that <u>wrinkled</u> shirt, inside the throat that must clear itself and apologize each time it speaks, inside that forty-pound body of boy with its geography of scars, its <u>history of hurt</u>, limbs stuffed with feathers and rags, in what part of the eyes, in what part of the heart, <u>in that cage of the chest where something throbs</u> with both fists and knows only what Salvador knows, <u>inside that body too small to contain the hundred balloons of happiness, the single guitar of grief,</u> is a boy like any other disappearing out the door, beside the schoolyard gate, where he has told his brothers they must wait. Collects the hands of Cecilio and Arturito, scuttles off dodging the many schoolyard colors, the elbows and wrists crisscrossing, the several shoes running. Grows small and smaller to the eye, dissolves into the bright horizon, flutters in the air before disappearing like a memory of kites.

---

wrinkled (ring' kald) *adj.* having creases or small folds

Literary Element

Imagery Reread the text on this page. Underline an image that shows how Salvador feels inside.

Comprehension Check

At the end, where do Salvador and his brothers go?
- [ ] home from a restaurant
- [ ] home from the circus
- [x] home from school

REFLECT

Analyze Sound Devices
On the lines below, write down three examples of alliteration in the story. Then choose one example and explain how it affects the story.

1. Possible answer: the color of caterpillar

2. Possible answer: the business of the baby

3. Possible answer: hundred balloons of happiness

Possible answer: The alliteration in "hundred balloons of happiness" makes the phrase stand out. It helps me stop and think about that image.

Talk about your answer with a partner.

To Sum Up

➤ Salvador has a lot of chores, so he doesn't have time for fun and games.
➤ After school, Salvador walks his brothers home.

Oral Assessment

Observe individuals' responses to the following prompts. See the Oral Assessment Rubric on page T17 to determine students' levels of language output.

1. Tell me about Salvador.

2. What are some of Salvador's chores?

3. Why is Salvador sometimes late for school?

4. What does Salvador do after school?

5. How does Salvador feel inside?

Interactive Question-Response

Literary Element **Imagery**

If students have difficulty responding: **Model** *When people talk about feeling things "inside," they are talking about emotions, such as happiness or sadness. I will look for words in the story that describe emotions. "Hurt" is an emotion. "History of hurt" is an image that describes the pain that Salvador feels inside.* Have students underline "history of hurt." Then ask volunteers to share other answers.

Comprehension Check

Have students share their answers. **Ask:** *As Salvador leaves school with his brothers, what else is he doing? (He is looking around the schoolyard and trying to stay out of trouble.) Why is he doing this? (Salvador is trying to keep his brothers safe.)*

Reflect

Partner Talk Have students work in pairs to answer. To help students get started: **Model** *To answer this, I would start rereading the story to find an example of alliteration. As I read, I'm going to look for several words in a row that start with the same letter. When I find them, I'll read the phrase aloud to see if I hear the same sound repeated.* Point out the phrase "busy with the business of the baby," and help students see the repetition of the *b* sound. Then have pairs look for other examples of alliteration in the story. Write the follow sentence frame on the board to help students organize their thoughts:

The phrase _____ contains alliteration because it has repetition of the _____ sound.

Comprehension Check

C. Early Advanced

To answer the last question, encourage students to think about the colors of caterpillars, bad weather, and dark mornings. Ask students whether the colors are bight and cheerful or dark and gloomy. Then have students answer the question.

After Reading

Have students complete the after reading activity on page 342.

SALVADOR
LATE OR EARLY

Vocabulary Check

A/B. Circle the picture that best answers the question.

1. Which picture shows something that might **tumble**?

3. Which picture shows something that might get **wrinkled**?

2. Which picture shows something that might cause **puddles**?

C. Think about the story. Complete each sentence with a vocabulary word from below.

traffic   tumble

4. When Arturito drops the crayons, they ___tumble___ into the street.

5. The crossing-guard stops the ___traffic___ so Salvador can pick up the crayons.

Comprehension Check

A./B. Complete the sentences.

6. Salvador takes care of his brothers .

7. Salvador feeds them breakfast .

8. They try to get to school on time, but Possible answer: there is too much to do .

C. Answer the questions below.

9. What colors are mentioned in the first sentence of the story? What do these colors tell you about Salvador's life?

Possible answer: The first sentence mentions "color of caterpillar," "color of bad weather," and "dim dark of the morning." These colors tell me that Salvador has a dark, dreary life.

For more practice, see page 342. ➡

282

Writing Link

Song

Have students write the lyrics for a song about Salvador. They should focus on the tasks Salvador does throughout the day and how they make him feel. Students should feel free to explore parts of Salvador's day that Cisneros does not discuss in her story. For instance, their songs might show what lunchtime is like for Salvador, or what class is his favorite. Songs should include imagery created using sensory details. The lyrics should also include sound devices such as alliteration, assonance, repetition, rhythm, and rhyme.

Learning Objectives

For pages 283–294, 343

In studying this text, you will focus on the following objectives:

Literary Study: Analyzing essays.

Reading: Determining main idea and supporting details.

Thoughts on the African-American Novel

by Toni Morrison

Oral Language

Build Background

Read the title and author. Explain that students will read "Thoughts on the African-American Novel" by Toni Morrison, the first African American to win the Nobel Prize for Literature. **Ask:**

- What is a novel? *(a long work of fiction; a book)*

- How do you think an African American novel would be different? *(It might deal specifically with the problems of African Americans. Maybe it isn't different at all, but people read it as different because the author is African American.)*

Talk About the Essay

Explain that the essay explores the author's thoughts about writing, novels, and society.

Intermediate ▷ Explain that for a long time, because of slavery, many African Americans were not allowed to read or write. In the late 1800s and early 1900s, African Americans began to challenge societal rules. They wrote books and made art. They also changed American society forever.

People read to _____. (learn, have fun, pass the time)

Lesson at a Glance

Oral Language
- Build Background
- Talk About the Essay

Vocabulary
- Selection Vocabulary
- Content Vocabulary
- Academic Vocabulary

Literary Element
- Essay

Reading Strategy
- Determine Main Idea and Supporting Details

Writing Link
- Essay

Comprehension   BLM
- BLM

Grammar Link   BLM
- Comparative and Superlative Forms of Adverbs BLM

Technology
- Student Works™ Plus
- Teacher Works™ Plus
- Listening Library Audio CD
- Classroom Presentation Toolkit
- Glencoe Visual Vocabulary
- Skill Level Up!™ A Skill-Based Language Arts Game

Interactive Question-Response

Connect to the Essay

Read aloud Connect to the Essay. Reproduce the chart on the board: **Model** *I like Toni Morrison's book* Song of Solomon. *It made me feel as though I knew all the characters and lived in their town.* Model writing your response in the chart, and have volunteers suggest other responses. Then have individuals fill in their own charts.

Literary Element Essay

Read aloud the Literary Element. **Ask:** *Have you ever written an essay? Have you ever read an essay?* Ask students for examples of essays they have read. Ask students to think about topics they believe would be good for an essay: **Model** *I have a complicated problem I need to figure out. I don't think it has one right answer or one wrong answer. But I need to know what is right for me. I'm going to write an essay to explore my thoughts and feelings about this problem. If I have to explain my thoughts to someone else, maybe I will understand my thoughts better.* **Ask:** *What kinds of things should I think about?* (what is right and wrong for other people, why I believe what I believe, whether those things are really true or fair) List students' responses on the board.

Reading Strategy Determine Main Idea and Supporting Details

Read aloud the Reading Strategy. Explain that finding the main idea helps students be sure they have understood what they read: **Model** *If I read an article whose main idea is that dogs are faithful friends, I want to know why the author believes this. I need to look for supporting details. Maybe the author includes facts from a scientific study. Or maybe there is a short story about a dog that got lost, but found its family after a year.* Tell students that one way to determine the main idea is to imagine you are telling a friend about what you are reading. How would you describe a book in one sentence?

Thoughts on the African-American Novel

Connect to the Essay

Think about why you read. With a partner, make a list of your favorite books. Why do you like them?

Book	Why I Like It
Possible answer: *The Red Badge of Courage*	Possible answer: It made me feel like I was right there on the battlefield.

Literary Element Essay

An **essay** is a type of nonfiction. It tells a writer's ideas and opinions. An **informal essay** has a light tone, and its ideas follow a fluid, or flowing, structure. A **formal essay** follows a careful structure of opinions and information. The writer's tone is more serious.

Reading Strategy Determine Main Idea and Supporting Details

To determine a **main idea** is to find the most important thought in what you are reading. As you read, ask yourself, What is the one idea that all of the sentences or paragraphs are about?

Supporting details may include:

- facts that support the idea.
- examples, or real-life instances of the idea.
- reasons, or the author's explanation for his or her beliefs.
- anecdotes, or short stories that illustrate the main idea.

Selection Vocabulary

aristocracy (a' rə sto' krə sē) *n.* people with high social status (p. 286)
*The poor man envied the **aristocracy**.*
➤ Cognate (Spanish) **aristocracia**

exclusively (iks' kloo' siv lē) *adv.* only; without anyone else (p. 286)
*This room is **exclusively** for club members.*
➤ Cognate (Spanish) **exclusivamente**

enlightens (en lī' tənz) *v.* gives knowledge or wisdom to (p. 288)
*A novel **enlightens** readers, showing them how to live.*

meandering (mē an' dər ring) *adj.* following a winding course (p. 288)
*We took a **meandering**, not direct, route.*

unorthodox (un ôr' thə doks') *adj.* not usual or traditional (p. 290)
*The teacher's lessons were **unorthodox**, but successful.*

Content Vocabulary

ceremony (ser' ə mō' nē) *n.* a ritual or formal routine (p. 286)
*The family celebrates Hanukkah with a special **ceremony**.*
➤ Cognate (Spanish) **ceremonia**

didactic (dĭ dak' tik) *adj.* instructive; meant to teach (p. 286)
*My father's stories are **didactic** and always have lessons.*
➤ Cognate (Spanish) **didáctico**

peasants (pez' ənts) *n.* laborers or farmers; people who earn little money or live in the country (p. 286)
*Many **peasants** worked to harvest the crops.*

paradigms (par' ə dīmz') *n.* patterns or examples (p. 290)
*We build cars along certain **paradigms**, such as four wheels and a motor.*
➤ Cognate (Spanish) **paradigma**

For more practice, see page 343. ➡

Vocabulary Routine

To introduce the vocabulary, read aloud the words and definitions in the student book and have students repeat after you. Discuss how the pictures illustrate the words or sentences. Then follow the vocabulary routine below.

Content Vocabulary

Define: A **ceremony** is a ritual or formal routine. Example: The principal gave a speech at the graduation *ceremony*. Ask: Why do you think we have *ceremonies*? EXPLANATION

Peasants are laborers or farmers who earn little money. *The peasants lived in a small group of cottages beside the farm.* What do you think *peasants* look like? DESCRIPTION

Something **didactic** has a lesson. Its goal is to teach you. *Aesop's fables are didactic because they always have morals.* What else is *didactic*? EXAMPLE

Paradigms are patterns or examples. *We have paradigms for how to behave, such as shaking hands when we meet someone.* What is a word that means almost the same thing as *paradigm*? SYNONYM

Vocabulary Practice Have students complete the vocabulary practice activity on page 343.

Selection Vocabulary

Define: The **aristocracy** refers to people of high status or royalty. Example: The Queen of England is part of the English *aristocracy*. Ask: Do you think being part of the aristocracy is easy? Why or why not? EXPLANATION

Something is **exclusively** used when access to it is limited. *She used your computer exclusively.* What is exclusively for your use at home? EXAMPLE

To **enlighten** is to share knowledge or information or offer insights. *The Dalai Lama's speech enlightened me.* What word is similar to *enlighten*? SYNONYMS

Meandering, when used as an adjective, describes something that follows a winding course. *When she ran into her cousins, Jane was following a meandering path through the park.* What word is the opposite of *meandering*? ANTONYM

Anything that is **unorthodox** is out of the norm. *That haircut is very unorthodox.* What is an example of an orthodox and unorthodox way of studying for a test? COMPARE AND CONTRAST

Interactive Question-Response

Content Vocabulary

Have a student read aloud the words and definitions for *ceremony* and *peasants*. **Ask:** *What kind of ceremony might peasants have? (a summer festival, a harvest festival, a wedding, a funeral) How do you think ceremony might fill some of the purposes of art? (It gives people a pattern of behavior. It helps people feel like part of a group.)*

Selection Vocabulary

Have a student read aloud the sentence containing the word *exclusively*. Ask a volunteer to define *exclusively* in his or her own words. Ask students for examples of things that belong exclusively to them or to their cultures. *(language, rituals, traditions, dances, music)* **Ask:** *How do these things make you feel? Do you want to keep these things for yourself, or do you want to share them? Why might a group of people need a new art form if their old one stopped being exclusively theirs?* Have students discuss their responses, using Toni Morrison's example of African American music and the examples students have provided.

ceremony (ser' a mō' nē) *n.* a ritual or formal routine

peasants (pez' ants) *n.* laborers or farmers; people who earn little money or live in the country

Strayed from the fold is a common metaphor. It refers to sheep that have wandered away from the pen that keeps the flock safe. It means "did something different." It can also mean "broke the rules." Someone who **strays from the fold** is being **unorthodox.**

didactic (dī dak' tik) *adj.* instructive; meant to teach

To Sum Up

➤ The author believes that the novel evolved because of the middle class.

➤ Peasants and aristocrats did not need novels, because they already had their own arts.

➤ The industrial revolution changed society. People needed a way to learn how to behave in this new society. Novels showed people how to behave.

The label "novel" is useful in technical terms because I write prose that is longer than a short story. My sense of the novel is that it has always functioned for the class or the group that wrote it. The history of the novel as a form began when there was a new class, a middle class, to read it; it was an art form that they needed. The lower classes didn't need novels at that time because they had an art form already: they had songs, and dances, and ceremony, and gossip, and celebrations. The **aristocracy** didn't need it because they had the art that they had patronized,[1] they had their own pictures painted, their own houses built, and they made sure their art separated them from the rest of the world. But when the industrial revolution[2] began, there emerged a new class of people who were neither peasants nor aristocrats. In large measure they had no art form to tell them how to behave in this new situation. So they produced an art form: we call it the novel of manners, an art form designed to tell people something they didn't know. That is, how to behave in this new world, how to distinguish between the good guys and the bad guys. How to get married. What a good living was. What would happen if you **strayed from the fold.** So that early works such as *Pamela*, by Samuel Richardson, and the Jane Austen material provided social rules and explained behavior, identified outlaws, identified the people, habits, and customs that one should approve of. They were didactic in that sense. That, I think, is probably why the novel was not missed among the so-called peasant cultures. They didn't need it, because they were clear about what their responsibilities were and who and where was evil, and where was good.

But when the peasant class, or lower class, or what have you, confronts the middle class, the city, or the upper classes, they are thrown a little bit into disarray. For a long time, the art form that was healing for Black people was music. That music is no longer *exclusively* ours, we don't

Vocabulary

aristocracy (a' ra sto' kra sē) *n.* people with high social status
exclusively (iks' klōō' siv lē) *adv.* only; without anyone else

1. Here, *patronized* means "given money to or supported."
2. The *industrial revolution* was a great change in society. It happened when factory work and automation began to make the production of food and goods easier and faster. The industrial revolution helped develop a middle class of workers. These workers began to gain some control over where they would work, whom they would work for, and what they would earn.

Comprehension BLM

To support students as they read the selection, have them begin the graphic organizer on page A52.

Note Taking

Reread the text on the left. Then record your answers to the items below.

1. The most interesting word on this page is _____

   because _____ .

2. One word that I didn't know on this page is _____ .

   It means _____ .

3. One thing I read on this page that I already knew is _____

   _____ .

4. One thing I learned on this page that I didn't know is _____

   _____ .

5. Recap, or write in your own words what you learned by reading this page.

   _____

   _____

   _____

   _____

6. Summarize below what you've recorded.

Most Interesting Word	New Word	One Thing I Already Knew	One Thing I Learned

Note Taking

To help students get started, you might want to model your thinking process for completing one of the items.

Interactive Question-Response

Literary Element Essay

Ask students to share the words or phrases they underlined. If students have difficulty responding, say "I think" and state an opinion or belief you hold: **Model** *You can tell that what I just said is something I think, because I said "I think."* **Ask:** *What other phrases could I have used? (in my opinion, it seems to me, I believe, I feel, the way I see it)* Write students' responses on the board. **Ask:** *Do you see any of these words or phrases in the essay?* Point out that while an essay expresses an author's beliefs, not every statement in an essay is an opinion. Authors often use facts to back up their opinions. For example, the statement "That music is no longer exclusively ours" is a statement of fact. Morrison doesn't need to include words such as "I believe."

Comprehension Check

Have students share which responses they checked. If students have difficulty responding: **Model** *I see, at the very beginning of the boxed text the phrase, "things that I try to incorporate into my fiction." So probably the information I need is going to follow that phrase. Yes, the next sentence the author talks about "the ability to be both print and oral literature." So I'm going to check that box.* Have students point out the phrases that tell them what else Morrison tries to put into her fiction.

Literary Element

Essay The author states several of her opinions on this page. Underline the words or phrases that help you recognize them.

A *case study* is a detailed description of an individual situation. Often the writer describes a problem that he or she must solve. For example, a doctor or a social worker might write a case study.

Comprehension Check

Reread the boxed text on this page. What does the author try to put into her fiction? Check all that apply.

- ☑ a combination of print and oral literature
- ☑ the feeling of being in church and responding to the sermon
- ☑ strong emotion
- ☐ African American music
- ☐ characters who are peasants
- ☑ something that enlightens the reader
- ☑ the reader's participation

At my disposal means "available for me to use."

To Sum Up

- ➤ The author believes that novels should help people live.
- ➤ She tries to create the feeling of spoken language in her books.
- ➤ She wants readers to feel as though they participate in her books. People should feel included. Their emotions should be touched.

have exclusive rights to it. Other people sing it and play it; it is the mode[3] of contemporary music everywhere. So another form has to take that place, and it seems to me that the novel is needed by African Americans now in a way that it was not needed before—and it is following along the lines of the function of novels everywhere. We don't live in places where we can hear those stories anymore; parents don't sit around and tell their children those classical, mythological archetypal stories[4] that we heard years ago. But new information has got to get out, and there are several ways to do it. One is in the novel. I regard it as a way to accomplish certain very strong functions—one being the one I just described.

It should be beautiful, and powerful, but it should also *work*. It should have something in it that **enlightens;** something in it that opens the door and points the way. Something in it that suggests what the conflicts are, what the problems are. But it need not solve those problems because it is not a **case study,** it is not a recipe. There are things that I try to incorporate into my fiction that are directly and deliberately related to what I regard as the major characteristics of Black art, wherever it is. One of which is the ability to be both print and oral literature: to combine those two aspects so that the stories can be read in silence, of course, but one should be able to hear them as well. It should try deliberately to make you stand up and make you feel something profoundly in the same way that a Black preacher requires his congregation to speak, to join him in the sermon, to behave in a certain way, to stand up and to weep and to cry and to accede or to change and to modify—to expand on the sermon that is being delivered. In the same way that a musician's music is enhanced when there is a response from the audience. Now in a book, which closes, after all—it's of some importance to me to try to make that connection—to try to make that happen also. And, having **at my disposal** only the letters of the alphabet and some punctuation, I have to provide the places and spaces so that the reader can participate. Because it is the affective and participatory relationship[5] between the artist or the speaker and the audience that is of primary importance, as it is in these other art forms that I have described.

To make the story appear oral, **meandering,** effortless, spoken—to have the reader *feel* the narrator without *identifying* that narrator, or hearing him or her knock about, and to have the reader work *with* the author in the construction of the book—is what's important. What is left out is as important as what is there. To describe sexual scenes in such a way that they are not clinical, not even explicit—so that the reader brings his own sexuality to the scene and thereby participates in it in a very personal way. And owns it. To construct the dialogue so that it is heard. So that there are no adverbs attached to them: "loudly," "softly," "he said menacingly." The menace should be in the sentence. To use, even formally, a chorus. The real presence of a chorus. Meaning the community or the reader at large, commenting on the action as it goes ahead.

Vocabulary

enlightens (en līt' tanz) *v.* gives knowledge or wisdom to
meandering (mē an' dar ring) *adj.* following a winding course

3. Here, **mode** means "a manner of expression." The type of music once considered an art form that belonged only to African Americans is now the form of music that many modern listeners prefer.
4. ***Archetypal stories*** come from ideas inherited through the ages.
5. An ***affective and participatory relationship*** influences your emotions and encourages you to take an active part in the relationship.

Note Taking

Reread the text on the left. Then record your answers to the items below.

1. The most interesting word on this page is _____

   because _____ .

2. One word that I didn't know on this page is _____ .

   It means _____ .

3. One thing I read on this page that I already knew is _____

   _____ .

4. One thing I learned on this page that I didn't know is _____

   _____ .

5. Recap, or write in your own words what you learned by reading this page.

   _____

   _____

   _____

   _____

6. Summarize below what you've recorded.

Most Interesting Word	New Word	One Thing I Already Knew	One Thing I Learned

Note Taking

To help students get started, you might want to model your thinking process for completing one of the items.

Interactive Question-Response

Content Vocabulary

Have students read aloud the word and definition of *paradigms*. **Ask:** *What do you think are some of the paradigms of novels? (Some paradigms are genres, such as science fiction, fantasy, or romance. Some people think that a book must be sad or use big words to be literary or important. Many people think that a novel must have only one or two main characters, and that it tells one main story, perhaps with several related stories.)*

Comprehension Check

Ask students to share what they underlined. **Ask:** *What is very special and identifiable about Black literature? (the things Morrison has just described: the conversational language; the link to traditions of church, music, and oral storytelling; the reader's personal connection to the book)*

Reflect

Partner Talk Have students work in pairs to answer. To help students get started: **Model** *I think one important idea in this essay is that novels should relate to readers' lives. Is that the main idea? Maybe. Toni Morrison says that people turn to art to find out how to behave. That means novels should relate to people. I'm going to talk to my friend about what other ideas are in the essay, and whether they're the main ideas.* Write the following sentence frame on the board to help students organize their thoughts.

Toni Morrison states that novels should _____. She believes this because _____. (connect with readers; she thinks part of the job of art is to show people how to live)

Comprehension Check

Reread the boxed text on this page. Underline the words that tell what the author tries to do in her books.

paradigms (par′ ə dīmz′) *n.* patterns or examples

Just sort of drop g's refers to writing in dialect. Dialect writing mimics, or imitates, everyday speech. In casual speech, people often do not pronounce the *g* at the end of words like *reading*. A dialect writer would write *readin'* or *readin*. To **drop the g** is to leave it out. The words *just sort of* show that the author believes this style of writing is often careless.

Vocabulary

unorthodox (un ôr′ thə doks′) *adj.* not usual or traditional

6. Something *elusive* is difficult to capture or find.

To Sum Up

➤ The author thinks that some people misunderstand her books.

➤ Some people do not understand the way her books are supposed to relate to people's lives.

➤ The author feels joy when she thinks her books connect with people.

In the books that I have written, the chorus has changed but there has always been a choral note, whether it is the "I" narrator of *Bluest Eye*, or the town functioning as a character in *Sula*, or the neighborhood and the community that responds in the two parts of town in *Solomon*. Or, as extreme as I've gotten, all of nature thinking and feeling and watching and responding to the action going on in *Tar Baby*, so that they are in the story: the trees hurt, fish are afraid, clouds report, and the bees are alarmed. Those are the ways in which I try to incorporate, into that traditional genre the novel, **unorthodox** novelistic characteristics—so that it is, in my view, Black, because it uses the characteristics of Black art. I am not suggesting that some of these devices have not been used before and elsewhere—only the reason why I do. I employ them as well as I can. And those are just some; I wish there were ways in which such things could be talked about in the criticism. My general disappointment in some of the criticism that my work has received has nothing to do with approval. It has something to do with the vocabulary used in order to describe these things. I don't like to find my books condemned as bad or praised as good, when that condemnation or that praise is based on criteria from other **paradigms**. I would much prefer that they were dismissed or embraced based on the success of their accomplishment within the culture out of which I write.

I don't regard Black literature as simply books written *by* Black people, or simply as literature written *about* Black people, or simply as literature that uses a certain mode of language in which you **just sort of drop g's.** There is something very special and very identifiable about it and it is my struggle to *find* that elusive[6] but identifiable style in the books. My joy is when I think that I have approached it; my misery is when I think I can't get there.

REFLECT

Determine Main Idea and Supporting Details
Write the main idea of the essay on the top line. Then write some details that support this idea.

Main Idea: Possible answer: Novels should relate to readers' lives

Supporting Details: Possible answer: Novels evolved because the new middle class needed its own art form. Art shows us how to behave. Familiar traditions of music and church influence the author's language. These traditions help readers relate to the author's books. The author judges her own success by whether she thinks readers connect with her books.

 Talk about your answer with a partner.

Oral Assessment

Provide the following prompts to one student at a time. Observe students' responses. See the Oral Assessment Rubric on page T17 to determine students' levels of language output.

1. What do you know about Toni Morrison from this essay?

2. According to Toni Morrison, why did novels develop?

3. Why do people need novels?

4. What traditions are people losing in modern life?

5. What should African American novels try to do?

Note Taking

Reread the text on the left. Then record your answers to the items below.

1. The most interesting word on this page is _____

   because _____ .

2. One word that I didn't know on this page is _____ .

   It means _____ .

3. One thing I read on this page that I already knew is _____

   _____ .

4. One thing I learned on this page that I didn't know is _____

   _____ .

5. Recap, or write in your own words what you learned by reading this page.

   _____

   _____

   _____

   _____

6. Summarize below what you've recorded.

Most Interesting Word	New Word	One Thing I Already Knew	One Thing I Learned

Thoughts on the African-American Novel

Note Taking

To help students get started, you might want to model your thinking process for completing one of the items.

Vocabulary Check

A. Beginning/Early Intermediate

Read each question aloud. Encourage students to point or answer with yes or no. Then turn the question into a statement and have students repeat as you point to the word and picture. For example: *Which picture shows a ceremony? This picture shows a ceremony.*

Academic Vocabulary

Explain that to *create* is to bring something into existence or to be the cause something to happen as a result of one's behavior. Explain that it is an academic word that is used across disciplines. Have students work in small groups to list examples of how they might use the word create in each subject they are studying. Have each group share their examples with the class.

Thoughts on the
African-American Novel

Vocabulary Check

A. Circle the picture that best answers the question.

1. Which picture shows a **ceremony**?

3. Which person is **didactic**?

2. Which picture shows **peasants**?

4. Which picture shows a **paradigm**?

B. Circle the letter of the word that answers each question correctly.

5. What is **unorthodox** behavior?
   a. bringing flowers to your girlfriend
   b. wearing a costume to school
   c. eating a sandwich for lunch

6. Who might be **didactic**?
   a. a younger brother or sister
   b. a stranger on the street
   c. a minister at church

7. What is an example of a **ceremony**?
   a. a school day
   b. a funeral
   c. mail delivery

8. What might move on a **meandering** path?
   a. a downhill skier
   b. a freight train
   c. a river

9. Who are members of the **aristocracy**?
   a. lords, dukes, and earls
   b. you and your classmates
   c. people who work in factories

C. Answer each question.

10. Why is African American music no longer **exclusively** the property of African Americans? Possible answer: It has become popular among many people, not just African Americans.

11. Explain how a novel **enlightens** readers. Possible answer: It shows them how to handle life's problems and conflicts. It tells the truth.

Grammar Link BLM

Comparative and Superlative Forms of Adverbs: *-er* and *More*

Prepare students to complete the activity on page A53. Read the grammar instruction with students, and complete the first item with them to help them get started.

Thoughts on the African-American Novel

Comprehension Check

A. Write what kinds of art and expression each social class has in the chart.

Art Forms that Belong to . . .		
1. Peasants	2. Middle Class	3. Aristocracy
Possible answers: music, dance, ceremony, celebration, gossip	novels	Possible answers: paintings, architecture, patronage

B. Answer the questions about the author's beliefs.

4. African Americans need novels now because __Possible answer: they were the lower class, but they have confronted the middle class__.

5. African Americans need to know __Possible answers: how to behave in their new society, how to deal with life's conflicts__

6. African Americans have lost exclusive rights to __African American music__.

7. African American novels can include __Possible answers: elements of music, church, and spoken language__.

C. Answer the questions about the essay "Thoughts on the African-American Novel."

8. How does the author think people should read books? Why?

   Possible answer: She thinks people should read actively. They should feel as though they participate in the story. Their emotions should be involved. This way, they can learn from the experience of reading.

9. Is this a formal essay or an informal essay? Explain.

   Possible answer: It is an informal essay. It has a flowing structure. The author discusses personal thoughts and feelings. Her language is sophisticated but not formal.

Comprehension Check

B. Intermediate

Remind students to look back at the notes they took while reading. If they cannot answer the questions from their notes, encourage them to return to the text for details.

Writing Link

Essay

Students have selected a topic, created main idea and details, and written an outline for an essay. Now have students write the essay. Encourage them to think about whether they want the essay to be formal or informal. Remind them that they should think about the purpose of the essay—is it intended to persuade, inform, or explain.

Students' essays should

- include a title and thesis statement

- contain an introduction, three body paragraphs, and a conclusion

- have a clearly stated main idea and at least two statements of support in each paragraph

Thoughts on the African-American Novel

Role Play

Prepare an interview that you and a partner will role-play for the class. Pretend that you are Toni Morrison and a reporter is interviewing you. Write your answers to the questions below. Then practice reading the finished interview aloud with your partner. Take turns being the interviewer and Toni Morrison.

Interviewer: What is your name?
Tony Morrison: Toni Morrison

Interviewer: What do you do?
Tony Morrison: I am a writer. I write novels.

Interviewer: What are some of the books you have written?
Tony Morrison: Song of Solomon, Tar Baby, Sula, Beloved

Interviewer: What are some of your proudest moments as a writer?
Tony Morrison: Possible answer: Winning the Nobel Prize made me very proud. I am proud when I write a book that connects with readers.

Interviewer: You've talked about having a chorus in your books. Who does that chorus represent? Why do you have a chorus?
Tony Morrison: Possible answer: It stands for the African American community. In the old days, people sat around and listened to stories, gossiped about them, and interacted with the storyteller. In modern life, that doesn't happen. With a chorus, people can still feel as if they are a part of the storytelling experience.

Interviewer: How do you want people to read your novels?
Tony Morrison: Possible answer: I want them to feel like they are a part of the story. They should participate. They should feel strong emotions. They should question what is happening in the story.

Interviewer: Why do you think people need novels?
Tony Morrison: Possible answer: Novels show people how to deal with life. They show us problems and conflicts that we might face. They might not give us all the answers, but they at least help us understand the problems.

Functional and Workplace

DOCUMENTS

- Letter of Application
- Résumé
- Job Application
- Memo
- Business E-mail
- Travel Directions
- Technical Writing

Oral Language

Build Background

Read the title. Explain that students will learn about practical texts called *functional documents*, such as letters, résumés, and travel directions, which give specific kinds of information for everyday living. **Ask:**

- Have you ever written a functional document, such as a letter or job application? *(yes/no)*

- What purpose do you think functional documents serve in everyday life? *(to help people get where they are going; to give information that others need; to follow a new process; to get work)*

Talk About the Expository Texts

Explain that students will read several types of functional documents. These include a letter of application, résumé, job application, memo, business e-mail, travel directions, and technical writing.

Beginning/Early Intermediate **Ask:** *Have you ever thought about getting a job? (yes/no)* Ask students what they might need to read or write to get a job.

Lesson at a Glance

Oral Language
- Build Background
- Talk About the Expository Texts

Vocabulary
- Content Vocabulary

Reading Strategy
- Analyze Expository Texts

Writing Link
- Job Application

Comprehension
- BLM

Technology
- Student Works™ Plus
- Teacher Works™ Plus
- Listening Library Audio CD
- Classroom Presentation Toolkit
- Glencoe Visual Vocabulary
- Skill Level Up!™ A Skill-Based Language Arts Game

Interactive Question-Response

Connect to the Expository Texts

Read aloud Connect to the Expository Texts. Reproduce the chart on the board: **Model** *One type of application is a job application. The purpose of a job application is to give employers information about the person who wants a job. One feature on a job application is the person's name and how to contact him or her.* Model writing your name and contact information in the chart, and have volunteers suggest other responses for the left column. Then have individuals fill in their own charts.

Reading Strategy Analyze Expository Texts

Read aloud the Reading Strategy. Tell students that knowing the purpose, form, and parts of expository texts will help them both in school and in the world outside of school. **Ask:** *Have you ever read a functional document that taught you how to work something, like a cell phone or video recorder. (yes/no) What type of information did the document contain?* Then prepare students to read the functional documents. Have them keep track of their answers to each question on a sheet of paper as they read.

Connect to the Expository Texts

Think about a time when you filled out a form or application. With a partner, talk about what forms and applications usually look like. Choose one type of form or application. In the chart below, list the features it usually has. Then list the purpose of each feature.

Type of form or application: Possible answer: job application

Feature	Purpose of Feature
1. Lines for name, address, and phone number	1. So the company knows who you are and how to contact you
2. Possible answer: job history	2. Possible answer: So the company can learn about your skills
3. Possible answer: education	3. Possible answer: So the company can find out what you've learned
4. Possible answer: references	4. Possible answer: So the company can talk to your former employers

Reading Strategy Analyze Expository Texts

Expository texts provide information. Functional documents are expository texts that have a specific purpose. They are used often in school, in business, and at home. A functional document should be clear and direct. The person reading the document should be able to get information quickly and easily.

To **analyze expository texts** means to think about the purpose, form, and important information in each one. As you read, ask yourself the following questions:
- What is the purpose of this document?
- What is its form, and why?
- What type of information does it provide?

Content Vocabulary

legible (lej′ ə bəl) *adj.* clear; easy to read (p. 300)
My handwriting is legible because I write carefully.
➤ Cognate (Spanish) **legible**

audience (ô dē əns) *n.* a group of listeners (p. 302)
A large audience listened to the singer.
➤ Cognate (Spanish) **audiencia**

location (lō kā′ shən) *n.* a place or position (p. 303)
The location of the school is marked on the map.

route (rōōt) *n.* a path of travel (p. 303)
Take the direct route from the museum to the park.
➤ Cognate (Spanish) **ruta**

For more practice, see page 344. ➡

Vocabulary Routine

To introduce the vocabulary, read aloud the words and definitions in the student book and have students repeat them after you. Discuss how the pictures illustrate the words or sentences. Then follow the vocabulary routine below.

Content Vocabulary

Define: When something is ***legible,*** it is easy to read. Example: Use *legible* writing when you complete a form. Ask: What is the opposite of *legible* writing? ANTONYM

An ***audience*** is a group of listeners, viewers, or readers. *The audience for that rock group is mainly teenagers.* What is another example of an *audience?* EXAMPLE

A ***location*** refers to a place or position. *The location for the March meeting is the school library.* What is the *location* of one of your activities? EXPLANATION

When I take a certain ***route,*** I use a certain path of travel. *Take Lake Shore Drive for a scenic route into the city.* What is the difference between a *route* and a *location?* COMPARE AND CONTRAST

Vocabulary Practice Have students complete the vocabulary practice activities on page 344.

Functional and Workplace DOCUMENTS

Interactive Question-Response

Comprehension Check

Ask students to share what they underlined in the text. **Ask:** *Why should this sentence appear early in the body of Ann's letter? (It immediately tells Ms. Reyes the purpose of the letter and gives her a reason to keep reading.)* Discuss the form of a business letter and the purpose of each part, including the address blocks, greeting, body, and closing.

To Sum Up

Beginning/Early Intermediate Have students work in pairs to reread the To Sum Up statements and summarize the purpose of application letters. Provide the following sentence frame for students to complete.

A letter of application should tell _____ and _____.

(A letter of application should tell what job you are applying for and why you would be a good person for the job.)

Something that **speaks for itself** is clear or obvious.

Comprehension Check

Underline the part of the letter that tells what the writer is applying for.

A **fan** is a person who likes something a lot.

1. **Accompany** means to go with.
2. A **résumé** is a document that lists a person's qualifications.
3. **Concise** means brief.
4. Here, a **contributor** is a writer.
5. Someone who is **diligent** works hard and steadily.
6. Something **optional** is not required.

❶ The optional[6] subject line indicates the topic of the letter.
❷ In a business letter, the greeting is followed by a colon.
❸ The writer states her purpose directly and immediately.
❹ The writer comments briefly on her qualifications.
❺ The writer makes reference to the accompanying material.

To Sum Up

➤ A letter of application usually goes with a résumé and application form.
➤ The letter should be short and general.
➤ It should tell why you are applying for the job and why you should get it.

Functional documents are specialized forms of expository writing that serve specific purposes. Functional documents are an everyday part of business, school, and even home life. They must be clear, concise, accurate, and correct in style and usage.

Letter of Application

A letter of application is a form of business writing. It can be used when applying for a job, an internship, or a scholarship. In most cases, the letter is intended to accompany[1] a résumé[2] or an application. Because detailed information is usually included in the accompanying form, a letter of application should provide a general overview of your qualifications and the reasons you are submitting an application. A letter of application should be concise.[3] You should clearly state which position you are applying for and then explain whey you are interested and what makes you qualified. The accompanying material should **speak for itself.**

> 32 South Street
> Austin, Texas 78746
> May 6, 2009

Melissa Reyes
City Life magazine
2301 Davis Avenue
Austin, Texas 78764

❶ Re: Internship

❷ Dear Ms. Reyes:

❸ I am a junior at City High School and editor of the City High Herald. I am writing to apply for your summer internship at City Life magazine. As a journalism student and a longtime **fan** of your magazine, I feel that an internship with your magazine would provide me with valuable experience in the field of journalism. I believe that my role with the City ❹ High Herald has given me the skills necessary to be a useful contributor[4] to your magazine this summer. In addition, my enclosed application shows ❺ that I am also a diligent[5] worker.

I thank you for considering my application to your summer internship, and I hope to be working with you in the coming months.

> Sincerely,
>
> *Anne Moris*
>
> Anne Moris

Comprehension BLM

To support students as they read the selection, have them begin the graphic organizer on page A54.

Résumé

The purpose of a résumé is to provide the employer with a comprehensive[7] record of your background information, related experience, and qualifications. Although a résumé is intended to provide a great deal of information, the format is designed to provide this information in the most efficient way possible.

 Jane Wiley
909 West Main Street, Apt. #1
Urbana, Illinois 61802
(217) 555-0489 • jane@internet.edu

Goal
Seeking a position in television news production

② Education
Junior **standing** in the College of Communications at the University of Illinois, Urbana-Champaign.
2005 Graduate of City High School

Honors
Member of National Honor Society

Activities
③ Member, Asian American Association: 2005–present
Environmental Committee Chairperson, Asian American Association:
August 2005–May 2007

Work Experience
④ <u>Radio Reporter,</u> WPGU, 107.1 FM,
Champaign, Illinois: May 2007–Present
⑤ • Rewrote and read stories for afternoon newscasts[8]
• Served as field reporter for general assignments

<u>Cashier,</u> Del's Restaurant,
Champaign, Illinois: May 2006–August 2006
• Responsible for taking phone orders
• Cashier for pickup orders

<u>Assistant Secretary,</u> Office of Dr. George Wright,
Woodstock, Illinois: May 2005–August 2005
• Answered phones
• Made appointments

Comprehension Check

Review the résumé. Underline the jobs that Jane Wiley has had.

Here, **standing** means a rank or position.

---

7. **Comprehensive** means "complete."
8. Here, **newscasts** are radio news programs.
9. Using **parallel structure** means using the same word patterns to express different ideas.

① Header includes all important contact information.
② All important education background is included.
③ Related dates are included for all listed activities
④ Job title is included along with the place of employment
⑤ Job responsibilities are briefly listed, with a parallel structure[9] used in each bulleted item.

To Sum Up

➤ A résumé tells about your past.
➤ It may list your education, activities, and past jobs.
➤ It provides a lot of information in an organized way.

Interactive Question-Response

Comprehension Check

Ask students to share what they underlined in the text. **Ask:** *Where on a resume could an employer find out about a person's job experience? (under the heading* Work Experience) *How does the form of the résumé help employers learn information quickly? (The headings quickly tell the employer what kind of information the person is giving and where it can be found.)*

To Sum Up

Beginning/Early Intermediate ▶ Have students reread the To Sum Up statements. Then have students decide what to include in a résumé and how the form of a résumé helps to communicate significant information quickly. Provide the following sentence frames for students to complete.

Résumés often tell about _____, _____, and _____. (education; activities; jobs)

Although résumés look short, they contain _____. (lot of information about a person.)

Interactive Question-Response

Content Vocabulary

Read aloud the word and definition. Show students some writing that is legible and some that is not legible. Have students focus on the fourth sentence at the top of the page. **Ask:** *What must be legible? (your handwriting) Why? (It makes it easy for the employer to see why you are the right person for the job.)*

Comprehension Check

Ask students to share their answers. **Ask:** *What belongs in the Job History and Personal References sections? (Job History should list previous jobs, along with dates and duties. Personal References should list people to contact for recommendations.)* Explain that people listed as references should be able to speak about a job seeker's abilities and character. Job seekers must first ask a person if they will recommend them.

When you fill out an application *by hand*, you write in ink. You do not use a computer.

legible (lej′ ə bəl) *adj.* clear; easy to read

Comprehension Check

Review the job application. In which section would you list your standing in school?
- [ ] Job History
- [x] Education
- [ ] Personal References

10. If something is **not applicable**, it does not apply or relate.
11. If you fill out something in its **entirety**, you fill it out completely.
12. **Succinctly** means "in a brief and clear way."
13. **Embellishment** means details that are not needed and often not true.

1 The application provides specific instructions.

2 All of the information requested should be provided in its entirety.[11]

3 The information should be provided legibly and succinctly.[12]

4 Experience should be stated accurately and without embellishment.[13]

To Sum Up

➤ Follow the instructions in job applications carefully.

➤ Write neatly.

➤ Make sure that what you write is clear and true.

Job Application

When applying for a job, you usually need to fill out a job application. When you fill out the application, read the instructions carefully. Examine the entire form before beginning to fill it out. If you fill out the form **by hand,** make sure that your handwriting is neat and legible. Fill out the form completely, providing all information directly and honestly. If a question does not apply to you, indicate that by writing *n/a,* short for "not applicable.[10]" Keep in mind that you will have the opportunity to provide additional information in your résumé, in your letter of application, or during the interview process.

1 Please type or print neatly in blue or black ink.

2 Name: _____ Today's date: _____
Address _____
Phone #: _____ Birth date: _____ Sex: __ Soc. Sec. #: _____
****

3 Job History (List each job held, starting with the most recent job.)
1. Employer: _____ Phone #: _____
Dates of employment: _____
Position held: _____
4 Duties: _____
2. Employer: _____ Phone #: _____
Dates of employment: _____
Position held: _____
4 Duties: _____
****

Education (List the most recent level of education completed.)
_____
****

Personal References:
1. Name: _____ Phone #: _____
Relationship: _____
2. Name: _____ Phone #: _____
Relationship: _____

Memos

A memorandum[14] (memo) conveys precise information to another person or group of people. A memo begins with a leading block[15]. It is followed by the text of the message. A memo does not have a formal **closing**.

① TO: All employees
FROM: Jordan Tyne, Human Resources[16] Manager
SUBJECT: New Human Resources Assistant Director
DATE: November 3, 2009

② Please join me in congratulating Daphne Rudy on her appointment as assistant director in the Human Resources Department. Daphne comes to our company with five years of experience in the field. Daphne begins
③ work on Monday, November 10. All future general human resource inquiries should be directed to Daphne.

Please welcome Daphne when she arrives next week.

REFLECT

Analyze Expository Texts
What is the purpose of a memo?

Possible answer: The purpose of a memo is to send people

information in a short, clear format.

Talk about your answer with a partner.

The **closing** of a letter comes at the end. It often includes terms such as "Sincerely" or "From" and the writer's name.

Comprehension Check

Reread the memo. Underline who the memo is to, and who it is from.

14. A **memorandum** is a written note. **Memo** is short for **memorandum**.
15. The **leading block** appears at the top of a memo. It includes lines for *To, From, Subject,* and *Date.*
16. The **human resources** department at a workplace deals with employees' concerns.

① The topic of the memo is stated clearly in the subject line.
② The announcement is made in the first sentence.
③ All of the important information is included briefly in the memo.

To Sum Up

➤ A memo is a short letter that provides information.
➤ A memo can be written to one person or a group of people.
➤ The top of the memo says who it is to and from, the subject, and the date.

Interactive Question-Response

Comprehension Check

Ask students to share what they underlined. Reinforce that in this case the memo is addressed to a group rather than to one person. **Ask:** *Why is the form of a memo effective? (Important information is featured at the top. It quickly states who the memo is from, the topic, and the date.)*

To Sum Up

Beginning/Early Intermediate ▶ Have students reread the To Sum Up statements. Then have students describe the type of information included in the different parts of a memo. Provide the following sentence frames for students to complete.

The top of a memo provides a summary of _____ ___. (the sender, receiver, date, and subject)

The main part of a memo tells _____. (information about the subject)

Reflect

Partner Talk Have students work in pairs to answer. To help students get started: **Model** *To answer this, I would reread the information about memos and think about when I would use a memo. When I write a memo at work, it is usually to announce something important.* Encourage students to think of possible reasons for writing memos and then to generalize an overall purpose. Write the following sentence frame on the board to help students organize their thoughts.

The purpose of a memo is to _____. (briefly give important information to one or more people.)

Interactive Question-Response

Content Vocabulary

Read aloud the word and definition of *audience*. **Ask:** *Why should writers know their audience?* (to write what that group of readers would need or want to know in a format that they can understand) Discuss how e-mails to different audiences would differ.

Comprehension Check

Ask students to share their answers. **Ask:** *Why is the tone of a business e-mail conversational? (An e-mail is a less formal type of writing than a letter or memo.)* Discuss the types of language that are appropriate and inappropriate in a business e-mail.

Reflect

Partner Talk Have students work in pairs to answer. To help students get started: **Model** *Usually I send an e-mail rather than a memo when I know the person well or the situation is casual. For example, I send e-mails to other teachers with updates on work we are doing.* Write the following sentence frame on the board to help students organize their thoughts.

*I would send an e-mail instead of a letter if _____
____. (I was writing to someone I know well or the situation is casual)*

Here, **conventions** are well-known practices or techniques.

audience (ô dē əns) *n.* a group of listeners

Comprehension Check

How would you describe the tone of a business e-mail?
- [x] conversational
- [ ] formal
- [ ] careless

17. **Conversational** speech is informal, as if you are talking to someone you know.
18. **Clarity** means clearness.
19. If sentences are **rambling**, they are too long and wordy.
20. In a **conference call** you can speak with several people at once.
21. **Potential** means possible.

❶ Subject line clearly states the topic.
❷ The purpose is stated immediately and in a conversational tone.
❸ Important details are included in a brief, direct fashion.

To Sum Up

➤ E-mail is a common form of business writing. It has a casual tone.
➤ The subject line of an e-mail tells its purpose.
➤ A business e-mail should be short and direct.

302

Business E-mail

E-mail is quickly becoming the most common form of business communication. While e-mail may be the least formal and most conversational[17] method of business writing, it shouldn't be written carelessly or too casually. The **conventions** of business writing—clarity[18], attention to your <u>audience</u>, proper grammar, and the inclusion of relevant information—apply to e-mail.

An accurate subject line should state your purpose briefly and directly. Use concise language and avoid rambling[19] sentences.

To:	LiamS@internet.com
From:	LisaB@internet.com
CC:	EricC@inernet.com
Date:	January 7, 8:13 a.m.

❶ Subject: New Product Conference Call[20]

Liam,

❷ I just wanted to make sure that arrangements have been made for next week's conference call to discuss our new product. The East Coast sales team has already scheduled three sales meetings at the end of the month with potential[21] buyers, so it's important that our sales team is prepared to talk about the product. Please schedule the call when the manufacturing
❸ director is available, since he will have important information for the sales team.

Lisa

REFLECT

Analyze Expository Texts
When might you send an e-mail instead of a memo?

Possible answer: I would send an e-mail if I am writing to
someone I know well or if I just want to send a friendly
reminder. I would send a memo in a more formal situation.
_____
_____

 Talk about your answer with a partner.

Differentiated Instruction

Clarify the Text Support students in understanding memos and business e-mails.

Beginning/Early Intermediate Read aloud the text in To Sum Up on pages 301 and 302 as students follow along. Gesture as you point out the *To, From, Subject,* and *Date* lines in a memo and business e-mail. Discuss how memos and e-mails are alike in form.

Intermediate Review with students the similarities between a business e-mail and a memo. Discuss how both have similar forms and purposes. Then contrast these types of writing with personal e-mails and notes. **Ask:** *Are personal e-mails and notes more informal or formal than memos and business e-mails? (formal)*

Early Advanced After these students read the text, show how the format of business e-mails and memos helps to fulfill their function. **Ask:** *Which part of these documents help convey information quickly and directly? (the subject line)* Encourage students to write a sample business e-mail.

Travel Directions

When planning an event or a social occasion, it is often necessary to provide people with detailed directions to the <u>location</u>. These directions must be clear enough that anyone who is unfamiliar with the surrounding area can easily find their way. Creating a map that shows the <u>route</u> with clearly labeled streets can also be a great help.

Directions to Darien High School's Graduation Ceremony

From I-95 North, take Exit 11.
Turn Left onto Post Road (Route 1).
At the first light, turn Left onto Samuel Avenue. Travel 2.5 miles.
Turn Right onto Cherry Hill Road.
Turn Left onto High School Lane.
Follow signs to Visitor Parking.

Activity

On a separate sheet of paper, write directions and draw an accompanying map to a location in your town. Be sure to include enough details and give enough clear directions so that even someone who is unfamiliar with the area could find the destination.

REFLECT

Analyze Expository Text
The order of information is important in travel directions. Number the following steps for travel to Darien High School in order.

_5_ Turn onto High School Lane.

_3_ Turn onto Samuel Avenue.

_4_ Take Cherry Hill Road.

_1_ Exit 1-95 North.

_2_ Turn onto Post Road.

_6_ Find Visitor Parking.

 Talk about your answer with a partner.

---

location (lō kā' shən) *n.* a place or position

route (root) *n.* a path of travel

✏️ Comprehension Check

Review the travel directions to Darien High School. Where should you make the second left turn?

☐ Onto Exit 11
☐ Onto Post Road
☑ Onto Samuel Avenue

❶ Begins at a point from which most people will be coming.
❷ Offers travel distances to help travelers locate streets.
❸ Gives the name of each street along the route.

To Sum Up

➤ Travel directions help people find a place.
➤ Travel directions must be clear and easy to follow.
➤ It is helpful to include a map with your travel directions.

Interactive Question-Response

Content Vocabulary

Read aloud the word *location* and its definition. **Ask:** *To what location might you give directions?* (my home, school, a meeting place, a friend's home, a restaurant, a sports arena, a park)

Comprehension Check

Ask students to share their answers. Help students use the map to clarify the correct answer. **Ask:** *Why is order important in giving directions?* (The traveler follows directions step by step. If steps are out of order, the traveler might get lost.) *Do you have any tips for reading directions?* (Read them over ahead of time to get a general idea in your mind.)

Reflect

Partner Talk Have students work in pairs to answer. To help students get started: **Model** *To answer this, I would reread the travel directions. I might label each step in the list of directions with a 1, 2, and so on.* Write the following sentence frame on the board to help students organize their thoughts.

In travel directions, order is important because _____. (travelers follow the directions step by step.)

Differentiated Instruction

Clarify the Text Support students in understanding travel directions.

Beginning/Early Intermediate ▶ Read aloud the second and third bullets in To Sum Up. **Ask:** *What helps people to follow directions?* (The must be clear and easy to follow. A map helps too.) Point out what makes the directions to Darien High School clear and easy to follow.

Intermediate ▶ Have partners read aloud the text. Then have them complete these sentence frames: *The most important goal in writing travel directions is to make the route _____ (as clear as possible). The form of travel directions includes a series of _____ (steps).* Ask students to explain what makes the travel directions to Darien High School clear and easy to follow.

Early Advanced ▶ Ask students what they notice about the format of travel directions. **Ask:** *What does the format of travel directions stress?* (steps along the route) Discuss how maps help make travel directions clear.

Interactive Question-Response

Background Information

Read aloud Background Information. Explain that these are examples of the kind of precise language used in technical writing. **Ask:** *How does the precise language help a reader understand technical instructions? (Understanding the terms makes it easier to follow instructions.)* Discuss the goal of the technical instructions on this page.

To Sum Up

Beginning/Early Intermediate Have students work in pairs to reread the To Sum Up statements. Then have students decide together the purpose of technical writing. Provide the following sentence frame for students to complete.

The goal of technical writing is to _____.
(explain a step-by-step process)

Background Information

A DVD Player plays DVDs, or "digital video discs." *HDTV* stands for "high-definition television." *HDMI* stands for "high-definition multimedia interface."

22. **Cables** are cords that send information electronically.
23. **Jacks** are electrical devices where you can insert plugs.
24. A **port** is a place where one electrical device can be attached to another.
25. **Variations** are different possibilities.
26. To **encounter** means to come upon or experience.

❶ Uses specific language to clearly describe the process.
❷ Lists each step individually.
❸ Directs attention to possible variations[25] the reader may encounter.[26]

To Sum Up

➤ Technical writing is specific and detailed.
➤ Its purpose is to describe a process clearly.
➤ Technical writing explains a process step-by-step.

Technical Writing

Technical writing involves the use of very specific vocabulary and a special attention to detail. The purpose of technical writing is to describe a process clearly enough so that the reader can perform the steps and reach the intended goal, such as installing software, connecting a piece of equipment, or programming a device.

Instructions for Connecting DVD Player to HDTV

❶ Your DVD player can be connected to an HDTV using RCA cables[22] or, for best picture quality, an HDMI cable.

Connecting with RCA Cables:

❷ **Step 1:** Insert the ends of the red, white, and yellow cables into the jacks[23] labeled "AUDIO/VIDEO OUT." Be sure to match the colors of the cable with the color of the jack.

Step 2: Insert the other ends of the RCA cables into the jacks labeled "AUDIO/VIDEO IN" on your HDTV. These are usually located on the side or the back of the television. Again, be sure to match the colors of the cables with the colors of the jacks.

Connecting with HDMI Cable:

Step 1: Insert one end of the HDMI cable into the HDMI port[24] located on the back of the DVD player.

Step 2: Insert the other end of the HDMI cable into the HDMI port on your HDTV.

❸ **Note:** Your HDTV may have more than one HDMI port. If so be sure that you set your HDTV to the correct input when viewing.

Activity

Choose a device that you own or have access to, such as an mp3 player or a cell phone. Write brief step-by-step directions on how to perform a specific function on the device, so that someone else can follow your instructions and perform the function successfully.

Oral Assessment

Provide the following prompts to one student at a time. Observe students' responses. See the Oral Assessment Rubric on page T17 to determine students' levels of language output.

1. Tell me about functional documents.

2. What is the difference between a job application and letter of application?

3. What information is included in a résumé?

4. What is the goal of travel directions?

5. What is the purpose of technical writing?

Functional and Workplace
DOCUMENTS

Vocabulary Check

A. Circle the picture that best answers the question.

1. Which picture shows a **route**?

3. Which picture shows an **audience**?

2. Which picture shows **legible** writing?

 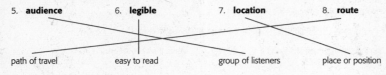

4. Which picture shows a **location**?

B. Match each word with the best phrase below by drawing a line.

5. **audience**   6. **legible**   7. **location**   8. **route**

path of travel   easy to read   group of listeners   place or position

C. Circle the letter of the sentence that uses the boldface word correctly.

9. a. If the old map is **legible**, we will find the treasure easily.
   b. If your paper is **legible**, we will not be able to read it.

10. a. The **audience** told folk tales while the children listened.
    b. We told folk tales to an **audience** of children.

11. a. We drove to the park in our family **route**.
    b. The shortest **route** is not always the fastest.

12. a. What is the **location** of the party: your house or the park?
    b. What is the **location** of the party: 2:00 or 2:30?

For more practice, see pages 345 and 346. ➡

Vocabulary Check

C. Early Advanced

Read each pair of sentences aloud. Review the definition of the vocabulary word. Encourage students to decide if each sentence uses the word correctly. Have students raise their hands if they agree that the word is used correctly. Invite students to explain why.

After Reading

Have students complete the After Reading activities on pages 345 and 346.

Writing Link

Job Application

Direct students to fill out an employment application form. They may use the form in this lesson or find an employment application for a local business and fill that out. Mention that many businesses have online application forms. Make sure that applications are accurate, precise, complete, and neat.

Students' applications should

- provide information in every blank, even if some blanks are filled only with *n/a* for "not applicable"

- contain accurate information

- describe job duties precisely

- be neatly printed or typed

The SKY TREE
How the LEOPARD Got His Claws
Prayer to the Pacific

Vocabulary Practice

A. Label each picture with the correct word.

shelter	soil	waded	salute

1. _____shelter_____
2. _____soil_____
3. _____waded_____
4. _____salute_____

B. Complete each sentence with the best word.

staggered	plots	shelter	seized	contempt

5. The woman _____seized_____ the sharp knife from her little boy.

6. The boy showed _____contempt_____ for his younger brother.

7. A different vegetable grew in each of the farm's _____plots_____.

8. The injured man _____staggered_____ inside the store and asked for help.

9. During the storm, passengers found a _____shelter_____ inside the train station.

C. Fill in each blank with the best word.

salute	staggered	waded	seized	contempt

10. Which word goes with "nearly falling"? _____staggered_____

11. Which word goes with "honor someone"? _____salute_____

12. Which word goes with "grabbed quickly"? _____seized_____

13. Which word goes with "lack of respect"? _____contempt_____

14. Which word goes with "stepped into"? _____waded_____

Upon the *Burning* of Our House *and* To My Dear and Loving Husband

Vocabulary Practice

A. Label each picture with the correct word.

dreadful	consume	sufficient	repay

1.

2.

3.

4.

consume   repay   dreadful   sufficient

B. Write T if the statement is true. Write F if it is false.

_F_ 5. A **sufficient** amount of gas would not be enough to drive somewhere.

_T_ 6. You would probably feel bad at the end of a **dreadful** day.

_T_ 7. If you are **bereft** of apples, then you have no apples to give to your friends.

_T_ 8. You would give someone **recompense** if they worked for you.

C. Unscramble the letters and write the vocabulary word that fits each clue.

bereft	chide	recompense

9. This is what you are when you lose something.

rtebfe   b e r e f t

10. You might do this to someone who did something wrong.

dhcie   c h i d e

11. This is something you would give to someone to thank them for their service.

peneromcse   r e c o m p e n s e

Upon the *Burning* of Our House *and* To My Dear and Loving Husband

A Newspaper Article

Imagine that you could go back in time to see the events from "Upon the Burning of Our House" and talk to Anne Bradstreet about what happened. Then, retell her story for your readers by writing a newspaper article about the poet's experiences.

Headline: <u>Possible responses: Anne Bradstreet's House Burns Down</u>

Last night, Anne Bradstreet's <u>Possible responses: house, home</u> caught on fire.

Bradstreet said that a <u>Possible response: thundering noise</u> woke her up.

When she saw the fire, the first thing Bradstreet did was <u>Possible response: pray to ask God to strengthen her</u>

_____

Then she <u>Possible response: got out of the house</u>.

Today, Bradstreet walked by the ruins of her house to look <u>Possible response: where all things used to be</u>

_____

While she looked, Bradstreet thought about <u>Possible response: the things she had lost</u>.

Later, Bradstreet scolded herself for thinking this way. She said that <u>Possible responses: God, the "mighty</u>

<u>Architect"</u>

had a better home for her in heaven. She said she did not care about her possessions because _____

<u>Possible response: she will have happiness and wealth in heaven</u>.

TIME How They Chose These Words

Vocabulary Practice

A. Label each picture with the correct word.

committee	compose	console	document

1.

____document____

2.

____compose____

3.

____committee____

4.

____console____

B. Complete each sentence with the best word.

committee	compose	console	document

5. The members of the ____committee____ made the rules.

6. All of the rules have been explained in the ____document____.

7. I will ____console____ Marie because she failed her test.

8. The musician will ____compose____ a song for the holiday.

C. Complete each sentence.

9. You might join a **committee** to help Possible answer: plan a school activity
_____.

10. You might **console** your friend who Possible answer: lost his dog.
_____.

11. You might have to sign a **document** if Possible answer: you apply for a job
_____.

12. Something you might **compose** for English class is Possible answer: an essay
_____.

TIME How They Chose These Words

Interview

Imagine that a newspaper reporter wants to interview Thomas Jefferson about his role in writing the Declaration of Independence. Fill in Jefferson's answers to the interview questions below. When you are finished, read the interview aloud with a partner. Take turns reading each part.

Interviewer: What is your name?
Thomas Jefferson: Thomas Jefferson

Interviewer: What role did you play in writing the Declaration of Independence?
Thomas Jefferson: I wrote the first draft.

Interviewer: Who helped you edit your work?
Thomas Jefferson: Benjamin Franklin

Interviewer: How did you feel when the Continental Congress made so many changes to your writing?
Thomas Jefferson: Possible answer: I was upset. I care a lot about my writing.

Interviewer: How would you describe your writing style?
Thomas Jefferson: Possible answer: I try to be very poetic. I also try to use words and ideas that I have read before and admired.

Interviewer: What are some ideas that are important to you?
Thomas Jefferson: Possible answer: I believe that government should be a contract between the people and those who govern them. I also believe that all people have natural rights.

Interviewer: What do you hope Americans will remember you for?
Thomas Jefferson: Possible answer: I hope to be remembered for my ideas about government and for my clear, graceful writing.

Letter to John Adams

Vocabulary Practice

A. Label each picture with the correct word.

defense	passion	generous	dispute

1.
generous

2.
dispute

3.
defense

4.
passion

B. Write **T** if the statement is true. Write **F** if it is false.

_T_ 5. You might end a **dispute** by shaking hands or hugging.

_F_ 6. If you spend time with your friend, you **deprive** him of attention.

_F_ 7. A **generous** boss never lets her workers go on vacation.

_F_ 8. To **foment** change in the way you think, read the same books over and over again.

_T_ 9. If you are on **defense**, you are trying to protect yourself.

C. Complete each sentence.

10. The company's bosses were **tyrants** who mistreated their employees when they _____
    Possible answer: made them work without pay

11. Teachers **foment** change in students when they Possible answer: teach them about new ideas
    .

12. **Vassals** are people who Possible answer: are servants
    .

13. If you **deprive** someone of information, you Possible answer: do not answer his or her questions
    .

Letter to John Adams

Equality Poster

Create a poster that Abigail Adams might send to her husband to share with the Continental Congress. Your purpose is to persuade members of Congress to give women equal rights. Use ideas from "Letter to John Adams" to help make your points inspiring and strong.

Remember the Ladies!

Abigail Adams, wife of John Adams, thinks that women should be treated equally in the new national laws. She thinks women should have equality because

1. Possible answer: if we really care about freedom and equality, we should care about freedom for everyone.

2. Possible answer: women have had to suffer for too long without equality and freedom.

3. Possible answer: laws that treat women as servants are unfair.

"If particular care and attention is not paid to ladies, we are determined to foment a rebellion!"

FROM CIVIL DISOBEDIENCE
On the Eve of Historic Dandi March
FROM LONG WALK TO FREEDOM

Vocabulary Practice

A. Label each picture with the correct word.

illusion	individual	strained	victorious

1.

   illusion

2.

   victorious

3.

   strained

4.

   individual

B. Circle the word or phrase from each pair which gives the best example of the boldfaced word.

5. **authority**
   a. judge
   b. tree

6. **extraordinary**
   a. shooting star
   b. piece of paper

7. **illusion**
   a. magic trick
   b. scientific experiment

8. **individual**
   a. crowd
   b. person

9. **victorious**
   a. losing team
   b. winning politician

C. Complete each sentence.

10. A crossing guard has the authority to _Possible answer: stop traffic_ _____

11. We decided to boycott the television show by _Possible answer: refusing to watch it_ _____

12. One sign that a person has domination over others is that _Possible answer: the others do what that person tells them to do_

13. Sebastian is an extraordinary basketball player because. _Possible answer: he always scores the most points in a game_

14. I strained the mixture by _Possible answer: pouring it through a sieve_ _____

FROM CIVIL **DISOBEDIENCE**
On the Eve of Historic Dandi March
FROM LONG WALK TO FREEDOM

Vocabulary Check

A. Match words from the following word bank to the correct picture.

| authority   illusion   strained   victorious |

1.

illusion

2.

strained

3.

authority

4.

victorious

B. Circle the letter of the word that answers each question correctly.

5. Where is an **individual** most likely to live?
   a. an apartment
   b. a bank
   c. a ship

6. Which place would most likely be the target of a **boycott**?
   a. a public library
   b. a city park
   c. a supermarket

7. What job might lead to **extraordinary** adventures?
   a. accountant
   b. pirate
   c. shoe salesperson

8. What person might have **domination** over an entire country?
   a. king
   b. football player
   c. mayor

C. Circle the letter of the sentence that uses the boldface word correctly.

9. a. The little girl **strained** the large rocks from the sand.
   b. The little girl **strained** the toy trucks from the sidewalk.

10. a. The fans of the **victorious** football team frowned and cried.
    b. The fans of the **victorious** football team smiled and cheered.

11. a. The police have the **authority** to enforce laws.
    b. The citizens have the **authority** to enforce laws.

12. a. The magician performed an **illusion** that the rabbit disappeared.
    b. The rabbit performed an **illusion** that the magician disappeared.

FROM CIVIL DISOBEDIENCE
On the Eve of Historic Dandi March
FROM LONG WALK TO FREEDOM

Interview

Imagine that you are interviewing Thoreau, Gandhi, and Mandela for a magazine article. Write answers that the three men might give to the questions that you ask. Refer to the selection text to support your answers.

Interviewer: What ideas or changes are you fighting for?

Thoreau: I propose that government ___Possible___ answer: should be made better. Government must "recognize the individual as a higher and independent power, from which all its own power and authority are derived."

Gandhi: I would like to see ___Possible answer: an___ independent India, free from British rule. We will march ___Possible answer: and "utilize all our___ resources in the pursuit of an exclusively nonviolent struggle" to attain this freedom.

Mandela: I have worked and pledged ___Possible___ answer: "to liberate all our people from the continuing bondage of poverty, deprivation, suffering, gender, and other discrimination."

Interviewer: What reasons support your argument or purpose?

Thoreau: Even in ancient times, it was recognized by ___Possible answer: the Chinese philosopher, Confu-___ cius, that the "individual is the basis of the empire."

Gandhi: In order to attain Swaraj, or "home rule" ___Possible answer: we must "withdraw cooperation"___ from the unfair British laws, such as "paying taxes, keeping titles, or sending children to official schools, etc. in all or as many ways possible."

Mandela: I discovered as a young man ___Possible___ answer: "that my freedom had already been taken from me … I slowly saw that not only was I not free, but my brothers and sisters were not free."

Interviewer: How or why do you think you will succeed?

Thoreau: I believe that an improved government will ___Possible answer: "be just to all men, and treat the___ individual with respect as a neighbor." This will make for a "more perfect and glorious State."

Gandhi: I believe that the people of India can ___Possible answer: "complete the work begun by me.___ I have faith in the righteousness of our cause and the purity of our weapons."

Mandela: I know that in my country ___Possible___ answer: "we have not taken the final step of our journey, but the first step on a longer and even more difficult road."

The Pit and the Pendulum

Vocabulary Practice

A. Label each picture with the correct word.

descent	despair	fatigue	ravenous

1. ravenous
2. despair
3. descent
4. fatigue

B. Choose the correct antonym for each of the following words.

descent	despair	lethargy	proximity	ravenous

lethargy   5. energy   proximity   8. far away

ravenous   6. full   descent   9. rise

despair   7. hope

C. Put a checkmark next to the sentence that is a good example of the vocabulary word.

10. **deduce**
    ___ The boys were hungry after school and wanted a piece of cake.
    ✓ From the smell in the kitchen, the boys knew that their mother had baked a cake.

11. **ravenous**
    ✓ The brothers were very hungry after school and wanted something to eat.
    ___ One brother liked chocolate cake, but the other liked apple pie.

12. **proximity**
    ___ Maria's best friend moved to another city.
    ✓ Maria's best friend lives in the same neighborhood.

13. **lethargy**
    ✓ Cindy felt sleepy after she watched too much television.
    ___ After she watched television, Cindy went outside to play baseball.

14. **despair**
    ✓ Nathan didn't think he would ever finish his homework.
    ___ Nathan finally finished his homework at three in the morning..

FROM MY BONDAGE AND MY FREEDOM
Frederick Douglass IN TEXAS GRASS

Vocabulary Practice

A. Match each word to the correct picture.

<u>B</u> 1. **fury**

<u>D</u> 2. **mirth**

<u>A</u> 3. **wreaths**

<u>C</u> 4. **stretching**

A.

B.

C.

D.

B. Circle the best example of the vocabulary word in each pair.

5. **depravity**
   a. stealing
   b. hiking

6. **mirth**
   a. funeral
   b. party

7. **benevolent**
   a. selfishness
   b. kindness

8. **wreaths**
   a. olive leaves
   b. aluminum cans

C. Complete each sentence.

9. The new government showed that it was **benevolent** by <u>Possible answer: building houses for homeless people</u>

10. Tomorrow's newspaper will **censure** the mayor for <u>Possible answer: taking bribes</u>

11. A person in history who showed great **depravity** <u>Possible answer: Adolf Hitler</u>

12. The teacher tried to **induce** the students to <u>Possible answer: study harder</u>

13. My fear of the dark was finally **vanquished** when I was able to <u>Possible answer: spend the night alone</u>

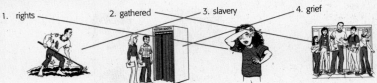

Vocabulary Practice

A. Label each picture with the correct word.

1. rights   2. gathered   3. slavery   4. grief

B. Unscramble the underlined word to complete the sentence.

5. Her hard work has <u>erbno</u> great results. _____borne_____

6. During the sad movie, Jose felt <u>firge</u>. _____grief_____

7. I would be <u>dlogbei</u> if you would help me with my homework. _____obliged_____

8. Freedom of speech is one of our most important <u>gtsrih</u>. _____rights_____

9. When the train passes by, it makes a <u>tcarek</u>. _____racket_____

C. Complete each sentence.

10. I would be obliged if you _Possible answer: would help me carry my suitcase_____.

11. Eduardo's mother has borne _Possible answer: two children_____.

12. Please don't make a racket because _Possible answer: the baby is trying to sleep_____.

13. After school, Rosa gathered _Possible answer: her books and walked home_____.

from Mary Chesnut's
Civil War

Vocabulary Practice

A. Label each picture with the correct word.

escorted	fleet	intercepted	surrender

1.
   intercepted

2.
   escorted

3.
   surrender

4.
   fleet

B. Complete each sentence with the best word.

intercepted	delusion	pervade	surrender

5. The war ended with the ____surrender____ of the city to the enemy.

6. Good smells ____prevade____ the house when my grandfather cooks.

7. The detective ____intercepted____ the message before it could reach the spies.

8. Yan had the ____delusion____ that she could pass the test without studying.

C. Unscramble the letters and write the vocabulary word that fits each clue.

9. Chesnut makes one of these to the Harriet Lane.

   lnulaiso a l l u s i o n

10. The Southern army acted this way when it attacked Fort Sumter.

    alusuaocydi a u d a c i o u s l y

11. Chesnut prayed in this position.

    stetraorp p r o s t r a t w

12. Chesnut realizes that her worries were this when no one was hurt.

    uledsoni d e l u s i o n

I Hear America Singing *and* When I Heard the Learn'd Astronomer

Vocabulary Practice

A. Label each picture with the correct word.

applause	divide	measures	moist

1.
2.
3.
4.

1. measures
2. moist
3. applause
4. divide

B. Unscramble the vocabulary words.

5. **veidid**   d i v i d e
6. **stomi**   m o i s t
7. **semeraus**   m e a s u r e s
8. **ulsapape**   a p p l a u s e

C. Complete each sentence.

9. Audiences use **applause** after performances to show Possible answer: that they liked what they saw

10. I will **divide** this cake into eight slices by using Possible answer: a knife

11. To keep the plant's soil **moist**, I Possible answer: water it daily

12. A smart decorator **measures** a room before Possible answer: buying a rug

I Hear America Singing *and* When I Heard the Learn'd Astronomer

Friendly Letter

Imagine that you are Walt Whitman, writing a letter to your friend. Tell your friend what you've been hearing and seeing, as described in your poems.

Dear Friends,

I have heard and seen a lot in the last few days! First, I heard America singing. I heard _____

Possible answer: a carpenter
_____.

I also heard   Possible answer: a shoemaker
_____.

All that singing made me feel Possible answer: very happy _____ because _____

Possible answer: each voice was different and beautiful
_____.

Then, yesterday, I went to hear the learn'd astronomer. The astronomer talked about _____

Possible answer: proofs, figures, charts, and diagrams
_____.

During the lecture, I Possible answer: started feeling tired and sick. So, I got up and left the room

_____.

I went Possible answer: out into the moist night air, where I watched the stars by myself. I felt a lot better

_____.

I hope you're seeing and hearing interesting things as well!

Your friend,

Walt

If you were coming in the Fall
My life closed twice before its close
The Soul selects *her* own Society

Vocabulary Practice

A. Match each word to the correct picture.

__D__ 1. **ample**

__B__ 2. **brush**

__A__ 3. **remains**

__C__ 4. **separate**

A.   B.

C.   D.

B. Fill in the blanks in the sentences using the words listed below.

| ample | brush | remains | separate |

5. A single coat _____remains_____ in the closet.

6. The wood pile will give us _____ample_____ fuel for winter.

7. Each class formed a _____separate_____ line in the hall.

8. I felt a butterfly _____brush_____ by my face.

C. Complete each sentence.

9. People eating together at a restaurant may ask for **separate** checks so that Possible answer: they can pay
   individually _____ .

10. The teacher gave us **ample** time for the test, so everyone Possible answer: finished it without rushing
    _____ .

11. The job **remains** open because no one Possible answer: has applied for it _____ .

12. When you hike, you can avoid having poison ivy **brush** against your legs by Possible answer: wearing ____.
    long pants _____ .

If you were coming in the Fall
My life closed twice before its close
The Soul selects *her* own Society

Journal Entry

Suppose that Emily Dickinson keeps a journal in which she works out the ideas for her poems. Complete the entries below to see what Dickinson writes in her journal.

Date: May 12, 1862

I wish my friend were coming in the fall. In that case, Possible answer: I would brush away the summer like a housewife brushes away a fly.

But since I don't know when I will see my friend again, I feel Possible answer: like I'm being stung by a bee.

Date: June 30, 1862

I wonder what death will be like. I don't know whether actual death will be worse than Possible answer: the two times in my life when I felt like I had died.

Date: August 15, 1862

Everyone cares so much about what other people think! But more and more I feel that the soul has to choose Possible answer: its company carefully.

Being true to yourself is the most important thing, even if it sometimes feels as though Possible answer: you are sealed off behind a stone door.

Possible answer: It doesn't matter whether your friends have wealth or status. It doesn't matter how other people view your friendship. All that matters is that you understand each other.

The Celebrated Jumping Frog of Calaveras County

Vocabulary Practice

A. Label each picture with the correct word.

disgusted	gifted	sociable	tranquil

1. sociable
2. tranquil
3. disgusted
4. gifted

B. Choose the correct antonym for each word.

dilapidated	garrulous	interminable	sociable	tranquil

tranquil	5. loud	dilapidated	8. new
sociable	6. unfriendly	interminable	9. a short time
garrulous	7. quiet		

C. Put a checkmark next to the sentence that is a good example of the vocabulary word.

10. **interminable**
    - ✓ The test seemed to last forever.
    - ___ The test was very difficult.

11. **dilapidated**
    - ✓ The visitors thought the house was old and worn down.
    - ___ The visitors thought the house should be painted a different color.

12. **enterprising**
    - ___ The young man never saved money.
    - ✓ The young man started his own business.

13. **conjecture**
    - ___ Maria did not do well on the test.
    - ✓ Maria guessed the answer to a test question.

14. **garrulous**
    - ✓ The lady enjoyed talking with her friends in the park.
    - ___ The lady enjoyed walking her dogs in the park.

A Wagner Matinée

Vocabulary Practice

A. Label each picture with the correct word.

worn	instrument	empty	tears

1.

   empty

2.

   tears

3.

   worn

4.

   instrument

B. Write each vocabulary word on the line beside the antonym.

worn	empty	doggedly	trepidation	obliquely

trepidation   5. confidence   _worn_   8. new

obliquely   6. straightly   _empty_   9. full

doggedly   7. lazily

C. Complete the following sentence starters.

10. From her grandmother, Monica received a _legacy_ of five hundred dollars and a gold ring.

11. The police officer _doggedly_ chased the bank robber down the block.

12. The teacher gave James several _reproaches_ for his late homework.

13. In the dark forest I felt _trepidation_ when I heard a sudden noise.

A Wagner Matinée

Postcard

Imagine that you are a cousin of the narrator in the story. You traveled with Aunt Georgiana from Nebraska to Boston. Write a postcard to send to your friends in Nebraska. Tell your friends about Boston and the symphony. Explain how you feel about being away from home.

Hello Everyone!

My trip is almost over, but I have seen interesting things in my time here. When we got here I felt Possible responses: very tired because Possible responses: the train ride was very long and I did not sleep well.

The next day we went to the symphony. The people there were Possible responses: mostly very dressed up. The music Possible responses: was the most beautiful sound I had ever heard. We did not want it to stop.

It feels like I've been gone a long time. I miss _____ Possible responses: all the open space and the animals. Boston is not as pretty. I am Possible responses: ready to come back now. Boston was exciting, but there is nothing like home.

Friends Always, _____

To:
My Friends

At:
My Town, Nebraska

Douglass and WE WEAR THE MASK

Vocabulary Practice

A. Label each picture with the correct word.

swarm	shivering	grins	torn	vile

1.
   shivering

2.
   torn

3.
   swarm

4.
   grins

5.
   vile

B. Unscramble the underlined word to complete the sentence.

6. A **ilve** smell reached her nose. _____vile_____

7. The **mtetsep** shook the small boat. _____tempest_____

8. The woman **nrgis** at the joke. _____grins_____

9. The wet dog was **vishrenig** in the rain. _____shivering_____

C. Complete each sentence.

10. There was **dissension** in our family over _Possible answer: what to watch on television_____.

11. The boy's **guile** _Possible answer: kept him from getting caught_____.

12. A **salient** part of my personality is that I am _Possible answer: opinionated_____.

13. A **vile** thing I once ate was _Possible answer: raw oysters_____.

14. During the **tempest**, the ocean was _Possible answer: filled with big waves_____.

The *Love* Song of J. Alfred Prufrock

Vocabulary Practice

A. Label each picture with the correct word.

narrow	cautious	wept	cheap

1. cautious
2. wept
3. narrow
4. cheap

B. Match each vocabulary word to its antonym. Remember that antonyms are words that have opposite meanings.

5. tedious — exciting
6. deferential — rude
7. cheap — expensive
8. narrow — wide
9. cautious — reckless

C. Complete each sentence.

10. If I **presume** to ask the teacher questions, she might think Possible answer: I did not do my homework

11. When people **digress** from talking about science, they could talk about _____

12. A salesperson might **malinger** if he Possible answer: does not want to go to work.

13. You might be **deferential** in a conversation with Possible answers: my parents, a teacher, the principal.

14. In a **tedious** class, you might Possible answer: doodle or yawn.

The *Love Song* of
J. Alfred Prufrock

Advice Column

Work with a partner to write an advice column in a newspaper. In your advice column, tell people how to approach someone they love. Some examples would be to tell people to work to earn someone's love, or to be honest about their feelings.

Be sure to include
- details about what people should do
- reasons why people should follow your advice
- allusions to literature, philosophy, or history that support your advice. Some examples of allusions you could use are quotes from famous people, cultural sayings, and characters or lines from literature.

If you care about someone, <u>Possible answers: be sure to tell them how you feel</u>

because <u>otherwise they might never know the truth about your feelings</u>.

Some easy ways to show your love are <u>by writing notes or showing affection by holding their hand or</u>

<u>kissing them</u>

But don't ever <u>lie to them or abuse their trust</u>

Dishonesty can only lead to <u>heartache</u>

As <u>Lao-Tzu</u> says, <u>kindness in words</u>

<u>creates confidence; kindness in thinking creates profoundness; kindness in giving creates love</u>

That's good advice. If you want to be happy in love, <u>be kind in word, thought, and deed. The rest will follow.</u>

The *Jilting* of
Granny Weatherall

Vocabulary Practice

A. Circle the picture that best answers the question.

1. Which person's money has **dwindled**?

3. Which girl is **squeezing** something?

2. Which person is in **agony**?

4. Which table is **flimsy**?

B. Match each word to its correct synonym.

A 5. **agony**   A. pain

D 6. **dutiful**   B. weak

E 7. **dwindle**   C. pride

B 8. **flimsy**   D. well-behaved

C 9. **vanity**   E. get smaller

C. Put a checkmark next to the sentence that is a good example of the vocabulary word.

10. **tactful**
   ✓ When the student gave the wrong answer, the teacher gently corrected him.
   ___ When the student gave the wrong answer, another student laughed at him.

11. **piety**
   ___ The children took care of their sick grandmother.
   ✓ The grandmother prayed every day for her grandchildren.

12. **jilted**
   ✓ The girl left her boyfriend at the dance.
   ___ The girl left her purse at the dance.

13. **vanity**
   ___ Lisa believed that many beautiful women were at the party.
   ✓ Lisa believed that she was the most beautiful woman at the party.

The *Jilting* of Granny Weatherall

Granny's Response

Imagine that George comes to Granny's house or calls her on the phone before she dies. What does Granny say to George? Write Granny's response, or answer, to George. Then read the finished response aloud to a partner.

I have had something to say to you for _____sixty; many_____ years.

When you _____jilted_____ me on our wedding day, I felt __Possible answer: angry and hurt__ .

You left me alone to face __the priest_____

and the wedding cake was __Possible answer: thrown away and wasted_____ .

But after you left, I got married to _____John_____ and had many fine __children__ .

Even though you hurt me, __Possible answer: I still had a good life. I got back everything you took from me.__
_____ .

I have many things to be proud of. I am proud of __Possible answer: how I raised my kids, kept a clean house,__

__took care of the land, and took care of the people around me. My children still come to me for advice.__

_____

Even though what you did to me was __Possible answer: mean and hurtful_____ ,

I want you to know that __Possible answer: I have forgotten you, and my life was better without you.__

_____ .

WHEN THE NEGRO WAS IN VOGUE

Vocabulary Practice

A. Circle the picture that best answers the question.

1. Which person might play in an **orchestra**?

3. Which is an example of **refreshments**?

2. Which person is **enthusiastic**?

4. Which is an example of an **entertainment**?

B. Write the correct synonym on the line next to its vocabulary word.

5. **scintillating** ____exciting____   a. not prepared

6. **millennium** __a peaceful time__   b. excited

7. **impromptu** ___not prepared___   c. style

8. **enthusiastic** ____excited____   d. exciting

9. **vogue** _____style_____   e. a peaceful time

C. Put a checkmark next to the sentence that is a good example of the meaning of the vocabulary word.

10. **scintillating**
   ✓ Jeannie could not stop reading the interesting book.
   ___ Jeannie checked out a new book from the library.

11. **vogue**
   ___ Mark likes to wear orange because it is his favorite color.
   ✓ Mark always dresses in the latest style.

12. **patronage**
   ___ The toy store is owned by a mother of two children.
   ✓ Many young mothers shop at the baby store.

WHEN THE NEGRO WAS IN VOGUE

Party Invitation

Imagine that you lived in Harlem during the 1920s. You are having a house-rent party this Saturday. Complete this invitation that you will give to your friends. After you have finished, read your invitation to a partner.

House-Rent Party!

A house-rent party will be held on _____ Saturday _____ night.

The party will be held at my apartment in Harlem.

Come and get away from all of the tourists in the clubs and cabarets.

Come and hear lots of great music! Some instruments that will be played are _____ the piano, the guitar, the cornet, and the drums.

Refreshments will be served, including bootleg whiskey, fried fish, steaming chitterling, and pig's feet.

People from all different lines of work will be at the party, including ladies' maids, truck drivers, laundry workers, shoe shine boys, seamstresses, and porters.

You will be entertained with lots of music, dancing, and card games.

You won't want to miss this party because Possible answer: you can dance the night away and have a great time.

See you there!

The Rockpile

Vocabulary Practice

A. Label each picture with the correct word.

| acquire | wound | bathed | bandage |

1.
2.
3.
4.

bathed   bandage   acquire   wound

B. Write T if the statement is true. Write F if it is false.

F   5. If someone **bathed** a dog, he or she kept the dog dry.

F   6. It is not good to put a **bandage** on a cut.

T   7. If you **grappled** with someone, you might wrestle with him or her to the ground.

F   8. A **wound** never hurts.

T   9. If someone **intimidated** you, you were afraid of him or her.

C. Circle the word or phrase that means the same as the boldfaced word.

10. We were **jubilant** when our team scored the final goal.
    a. very angry
    b. very happy
    c. very sad

11. Lucy was **intimidated** by the loud noise.
    a. made brave
    b. surprised
    c. frightened

12. Tim was **engrossed** by the movie he saw last night.
    a. completely engaged in
    b. totally disgusted by
    c. very unhappy with

13. The wrestlers **grappled** on the mat during the wrestling match.
    a. stood
    b. danced
    c. struggled

14. The street was crowded with people who **loitered** for hours.
    a. shouted
    b. remained
    c. ran around

The Rockpile

Letter

Imagine that you are John. Write a letter to your father, telling him about what happened and about how you feel. Explain that you are sorry that Roy got hurt and that you will try harder to keep him out of trouble.

Dear Dad,

I know that Roy and I are ___Possible answer: not allowed to play on the rockpile because it is dangerous___

_____.

I tried to warn Roy and stop him ___Possible answer: from going downstairs to play with the boys___

but he ___Possible answer: would not listen to me.___

Roy promised he would ___Possible answer: be back in five minutes___ and even

though I ___Possible answer: was worried about him, I could not stop him from going___.

I was ___Possible answer: afraid when Roy got hurt___ and I did

not want ___Possible answer: to see him bleed or cry___

_____.

I know that you ___Possible answer: are angry with me___ but I tried ___Possible answer: to stop

Roy from going downstairs___. It is not my ___Possible answer: fault that

he got hurt___.

I am sorry ___Possible answer: that Roy got hurt___

and I promise I will ___Possible answer: try harder next time to keep my little brother out of trouble___

_____.

Your son,

John

THE CRUCIBLE

Vocabulary Practice

A. Circle the correct word for each picture.

1.	2.	3.	4.
limp	packed	(wither)	(packed)
(leap)	(limp)	leap	wither

B. Unscramble the words to complete the sentences.

5. The cupboard was **apkedc** with cans. _____packed_____

6. The flowers will **twihre** once they are picked. _____wither_____

7. I try to **devae** my sister when she is in a bad mood. _____evade_____

8. Her false smile was only a **netserep.** _____pretense_____

9. In the summer heat, we felt tired and **plim.** _____limp_____

C. Complete each sentence with a phrase from the box.

> **angry and resentful   may go to jail   reputation as an honest person**
> **very happy   different opinions**

10. **Contention** can be caused by _different opinions_

11. If a person is forced to be **subservient**, he or she may feel _angry and resentful_ .

12. Lying can **compromise** your _reputation as an honest person_

13. If you **evade** your taxes, you _may go to jail_ .

14. Don't be fooled by her **pretense** of anger, because she is really _very happy_ .

THE CRUCIBLE

A Newspaper Article

Imagine that you are writing a newspaper article about the events in this play. You want people who live outside Salem to know what happened.

Headline: Possible answer: Women Accused of Witchcraft!

It all began when Betty Parris, Reverend Parris' ten-year-old daughter, Possible answers: became sick; was not able to move; fainted

Reverend Parris had seen Betty, his niece Abigail, and some other girls Possible answer: dance in the woods

Many people thought that Betty's sickness Possible answer: was caused by witchcraft

Reverend Hale, an expert on witchcraft, came to Salem to Possible answers: find out what happened; question the girls

After many questions, the girls confessed that they had Possible answer: tried to speak to the dead

The girls did not want to get in trouble, so they Possible answer: said it was all Tituba's idea

Tituba, Reverend Parris's slave from Barbados, was then questioned. She confessed that Possible answer: she had tried to conjure the dead

She also said that Possible answer: she saw some women from the village with the Devil

Look for another article tomorrow with details about the upcoming trials!

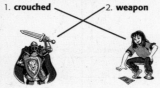 

AMBUSH **THE** Gift **IN WARTIME**
from **Stay Alive, My Son**

Vocabulary Practice

A. Match each word with the correct picture.

1. **crouched**   2. **weapon**   3. **escape**   4. **separated**

B. Write the answer to each question.

5. Do you **dwell on** something you **ponder** about? yes

6. If you **gape**, are your lips together or **separated**? separated

7. If someone **crouched**, would he be standing up straight, or in a **stooped** position? stooped

8. Would you try to find an **escape** from someone who had a **weapon**? yes

9. If you were **groping** for something under the bed, would you **crouch**, or stand on your toes?

   crouch

C. Use each word in a sentence.

groping	stooped	ponder	gape	dwell

10. Sample answer: I was groping blindly for my glasses.

11. Sample answer: Tom had a stooped posture from the years he spent bent over his desk.

12. Sample answer: I like books that make me ponder the meaning of life.

13. Sample answer: It's rude to gape at someone who is different.

14. Sample answer: I try not to dwell on arguments with my friends.

AMBUSH · THE Gift IN WARTIME
from Stay Alive, My Son

A Conversation

Imagine that Any, from in "Stay Alive, My Son," meets the speaker of "The Gift in Wartime." The two women talk about what happens to them during war. They also talk about their feelings. Write the conversation they might have.

Speaker of "The Gift in Wartime": War is not easy for families.

Any: The war in Cambodia makes it hard to get food and medicine. Because of that, my son

Possible answer: is very sick

Speaker: I miss my husband. He _____

Possible answer: died in a war

Any: My husband is afraid he will die. He plans to hide in the forest.

Speaker: I wish my husband had not gone away to fight. All I have from him is _____

Possible answer: his medals and badge

Any: My husband planned to leave alone, but I

Possible answer: told him that I would go with him

_____

Speaker: People need to make hard choices during a war.

Any: Yes. My son is not strong enough to go with us. We have to _____

Possible answer: take him to the hospital;

leave him behind

Speaker: I feel   Possible answer: sad without my

husband

Any: I feel   Possible answer: sad about my son;

scared about the future

Now, complete the conversation.

Speaker: _____

_____

Any: _____

_____

Speaker: _____

_____

_____

Any: _____

_____

_____

Speaker: _____

_____

_____

Any: _____

_____

_____

Sn❄w

Vocabulary Practice

A. Label each picture with the correct word.

apart	dusty	faded	daydreaming

1. daydreaming

2. dusty

3. faded

4. apart

B. Complete each sentence with the best word.

dusty	apart	daydreaming	random	warily

5. Lupe threw her dirty clothes in _____random_____ piles on her bedroom floor.

6. The sick puppy sat in a cage _____apart_____ from its brothers.

7. No one cleaned the house, so the counters were very _____dusty_____.

8. The little girl _____warily_____ watched the big dog as it came toward her.

9. Jorge was ___daydreaming___ about playing baseball when the teacher called on him.

C. Choose the sentence that uses the vocabulary word correctly.

10. (a.) Actors must **enunciate** their lines.
    b. Actors rehearse for months before they **enunciate** a play.

11. a. I **warily** cheered for the winning team.
    (b.) I stepped **warily** into the dark house.

12. (a.) All the people were afraid of a **holocaust**.
    b. The people celebrated the **holocaust**.

13. (a.) The numbers seemed **random** at first, but then I could see a pattern.
    b. The numbers were organized in a **random** pattern.

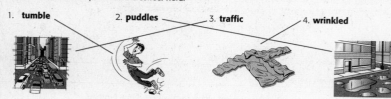

SALVADOR
LATE OR EARLY

Vocabulary Practice

A. Draw a line from each picture to the correct word.

1. **tumble**　　2. **puddles**　　3. **traffic**　　4. **wrinkled**

B. Circle the correct answer to each question.

5. Where would you find **traffic**?
   a. on a busy street
   b. on an empty street
   c. on a map

6. If something is **wrinkled**, what does it look like?
   a. it is smooth
   b. it has many colors
   c. it has creases

7. When would you most likely see **puddles**?
   a. before it rains
   b. after it rains
   c. when it is very hot

8. After you **tumble**, where would you most likely be?
   a. in the air
   b. on a bus
   c. on the ground

C. Unscramble the letters and write the vocabulary word that fits each clue.

9. A dollar bill that has been in your pocket might be **lewkrind**. _____wrinkled_____

10. When snow melts, it might make **ledpuds**. _____puddles_____

11. Something slippery could make you **lutbem**. _____tumble_____

12. A lot of cars, trucks, and buses can create **fratfci**. _____traffic_____

SALVADOR
LATE or EARLY

Letter

Imagine that you are Salvador. Write a letter to your teacher explaining why you are late to school so often. Help her understand why it's hard for you to get to school on time. Ask for her understanding.

Dear Teacher,

I'm sorry for coming to school _Possible answer: late_____. I do not mean to _Possible answer: cause trouble_____.

I come to school late because _Possible answer: I have to take care of my brothers_____. I have to do many things for them, such as helping them _Possible answers: wake up, tie their shoes, comb their hair, and eat breakfast_____.

Sometimes my brothers cause trouble, like when _Possible answer: Arturito spilled his crayons all over the street_____.

This makes us even later.

My mother is busy taking care of the baby, so I _Possible answer: have to help her as much as I can_____.

I am only a child, but sometimes I feel _Possible answer: like I have as many responsibilities as an adult_____.

I hope you can _Possible answer: understand that I try my hardest to get to school on time. But it can be very hard_____.

Sincerely,

Salvador

342

Thoughts on the African-American Novel

Vocabulary Practice

A. Label each picture with the correct word.

peasants	ceremony	paradigms	didactic

1. __didactic__   2. __peasants__   3. __paradigms__   4. __ceremony__

B. Write **T** if the statement is true. Write **F** if it is false.

_F_ 5. A **didactic** book is written to entertain readers.

_T_ 6. A wedding is one kind of **ceremony**.

_F_ 7. A member of the **aristocracy** probably has very little money.

_F_ 8. A **meandering** story would be short and direct.

_T_ 9. We can learn what to do by following **paradigms**.

C. Answer each question with a word from the list.

enlighten	aristocracy	unorthodox	meandering	exclusively	ceremony

10. Which word goes with "members only"? ___exclusively___

11. Which word goes with "unusual" or "not traditional"? ___unorthodox___

12. Which word goes with "high rank" or "wealth"? ___aristocracy___

13. Which word goes with "winding" or "indirect"? ___meandering___

14. Which word goes with "show wisdom to someone"? ___enlighten___

Before You Read

Functional and Workplace
DOCUMENTS

Vocabulary Practice

A. Label each picture with the correct word.

audience	legible	location	route

1.

2.

3.

4.

   route   audience   legible   location

B. Complete each sentence with the best word.

audience	legible	location	route

5. The band played songs that the _____audience_____ liked.

6. Highway 1 is the _____route_____ along the California coast to San Francisco.

7. The teams held their game at a _____location_____ between their two towns.

8. My teacher said he could not read my essay because the writing is not _____legible_____.

C. Complete each sentence.

9. The best **route** from my home to my school is _Possible answer: south on First Avenue and then west on Main Street_.

10. If the directions are not **legible**, we will not be able to _Possible answer: find the station_.

11. The **audience** for cartoon shows is mainly _Possible answer: young children_.

12. You can find out the **location** of the nearest gas station by _Possible answer: asking your neighbor_.

Functional and Workplace
DOCUMENTS

Comprehension Check

A. Write the name of each functional document described in the chart below.

Functional Document	Description
résumé	a complete record of your background information
travel directions	explanation of how to get somewhere
technical writing	step-by-step description of a process
business e-mail	casual way to share information

B. Complete each sentence.

5. When you fill out a job application, it is important to _Possible answer: be accurate and neat_ .

6. When you give travel directions, it is helpful to _Possible answer: provide a map with the route labeled_ .

7. Technical writing tells people how to _Possible answer: perform a process_ .

8. Some sections you should include on a résumé are _Possible answer: goal, education, honors, activities,_ and work experience .

C. Answer these questions.

9. What is important to say in a letter of application? _Possible answer: It is important to say why you want_ the job and why you would be good at it. .

10. Why is a résumé arranged like an outline? _Possible answer: It is a way of providing a lot of information_ in a form that's easy to read. .

11. Why is it helpful to fill in the subject line in a business e-mail? _Possible answer: It tells the reader what_ the e-mail will be about. .

12. What can you include on a map to help people follow it? _Possible answer: You can include landmarks,_ street names, scale, and a compass rose. .

Functional and Workplace DOCUMENTS

Letter of Application

Write a letter of application for a summer job at a place where you would like to work. Assume that you will submit an application form and résumé along with this letter.

[your address] _____

[your city and state] _____

[date] _____

Jorge Valdez

[business name] _____

[address] _____

[city and state] _____

Re: Summer Job

Dear Mr. Valdez:

Recently I learned that you might have a job opening at Possible answer: Town Video Store .

I am writing to apply for Possible answer: a summer job as a clerk .

I am interested in this job because Possible answer: I love movies, and I enjoy talking to other people about movies .

I am qualified for this job because Possible answers: I know a lot about movies, and I am very hard-working .

I also have experience at Possible answer: customer service. I worked in a convenience store last summer .

If you hire me, Possible answer: you will not regret it. I will be an excellent employee .

Thank you for your time and consideration. I hope to hear from you soon.

Sincerely,

_____

This glossary lists the vocabulary words found in the selections in this book. The definition given is for the word as it is used in the selection; you may wish to consult a dictionary for other meanings of these words. The key below is a guide to the pronunciation symbols used in each entry.

Pronounciation Key

a	at	ō	hope	ng	sing
ā	ape	ô	fork, all	th	thin
ä	father	oo	wood, put	th	this
e	end	ōō	fool	zh	treasure
ē	me	oi	oil	ə	ago, taken, pencil,
i	it	ou	out		lemon, circus
ī	ice	u	up	′	indicates primary stress
o	hot	ū	use	ˌ	indicates secondary

English

A

acquire (ə kwīr′) *v.* to come into possession or control of; (p. 216)

agony (ag′ ə nē) *n.* great pain of mind or body; (p. 197)

allusion (ə lōō′ zhən) *n.* a quick mention or hint; (p. 126)

ample (am′ pəl) *adj.* more than enough; (p. 145)

apart (ə pärt′) *adv.* at a distance; separated; (p. 272)

applause (ə plòz′) *n.* approval expressed by clapping the hands; (p. 137)

aristocracy (a′ rə sto′ krə sē) *n.* people with high social status; (p. 286)

Espanõl

A

acquire/adquirir *v.* llegar a poseer o controlar; (p. 216)

agony/agonía *s.* gran dolor de la mente o del cuerpo; (p. 197)

allusion/alusión *s.* una mención rápida o pista; (p. 126)

ample/amplio *adj.* más que suficiente; (p. 145)

apart/aparte *adv.* a distancia; separado; (p. 272)

applause/aplauso *s.* aprobación expresada con un golpeteo de las manos; (p. 137)

aristocracy/aristocracia *s.* personas de alto estado social; (p. 286)

audaciously (ô dā′ shəs lē) *adv.* bravely or rudely; (p. 127)

audience (ô′ dē əns) *n.* a group of listeners; (p. 302)

authority (ə thôr′ ə tē) *n.* power to tell someone what to do; (p. 58)

B

bandage (ban′ dij) *n.* a strip of cloth used to cover an injury; (p. 220)

bathed (bāthd) *v.* washed in a liquid; washed with water or a liquid medicine; (p. 220)

benevolent (bə nev′ ə lənt) *adj.* intending to do good; (p. 102)

bereft (bi reft′) *adj.* without something needed or wanted; (p. 20)

borne (bôrn) *v.* past participle of *bear*; given birth to; produced; (p. 118)

boycott (boi′ kot) *v.* to protest by refusing to participate; (p. 62)

brush (brush) *v.* to move lightly; (p. 142)

C

cautious (kô′ shəs) *adj.* careful; (p. 186)

censure (sen′ shər) *v.* to find fault with; to blame; (p. 108)

ceremony (ser′ ə mō′ nē) *n.* a ritual or formal routine; (p. 286)

cheap (chēp) *adj.* costing little money; (p. 182)

chide (chīd) *v.* to find fault with or to blame; (p. 21)

committee (kə mit′ ē) *n.* a group of people who work together on a project; (p. 28)

audaciously/audazmente *adv.* valientemente o atrevidamente; (p. 127)

audience/audiencia *s.* un grupo de oyentes; (p. 302)

authority/autoridad *s.* poder de decirle a alguien qué hacer; (p. 58)

B

bandage/venda *s.* una tira de tela que se usa para cubrir una herida; (p. 220)

bathed/bañó *v.* lavó con un líquido; lavó con agua o un medicamento líquido; (p. 220)

benevolent/benévolo *adj.* que quiere hacer el bien; (p. 102)

bereft/privado *adj.* sin algo que se necesita o quiere; (p. 20)

borne/rendido *s.* participio pasado de *rendir*; dado a luz; producido; (p. 118)

boycott/boicot *v.* protestar al negarse a participar; (p. 62)

brush/rozar *v.* mover ligeramente; (p. 142)

C

cautious/cauteloso *adj.* cuidadoso; (p. 186)

censure/censurar *v.* echar la culpa; regañar; (p. 108)

ceremony/ceremonia *s.* un ritual o rutina formal; (p. 286)

cheap/barato *adj.* que cuesta poco dinero; (p. 182)

chide/reprender *v.* echar la culpa o regañar; (p. 21)

committee/comité *s.* un grupo de personas que trabajan juntas en un proyecto; (p. 28)

compose (kəm pōz′) *v.* to create, such as a piece of writing or music; (p. 28)

compromise (kom′ prə mīz′) *v.* to expose to suspicion; (p. 233)

conjecture (kən jek′ chər) *v.* to guess; (p. 150)

console (kən sōl′) *v.* to comfort someone who feels sad; (p. 34)

consume (kən sōōm′) *v.* to eat up; (p. 20)

contempt (kən tem(p)t′) *n.* disliking something because you think it is worthless; (p. 11)

contention (kən ten′ shən) *n.* a verbal argument; quarrel; (p. 235)

crouched (kroucht) *v.* bent low; (p. 259)

D

daydreaming (dā′ drēm ing) *v.* having pleasant thoughts and images go through the mind while awake; (p. 272)

deduce (di dōōs′, dūs′) *v.* to come to a conclusion; (p. 84)

defense (di fens′) *n.* ability to resist an attack; (p. 40)

deferential (def′ ə ren′ shəl) *adj.* overly polite; (p. 186)

delusion (di lōō′ zhən) *n.* a belief that is not true; (p. 128)

depravity (di prav′ ə tē) *n.* evil; (p. 102)

deprive (di prīv′) *v.* to take away from; to stop someone from having or enjoying; (p. 40)

descent (di sent′) *n.* movement from a higher level to a lower level; (p. 83)

despair (di spār′) *n.* loss of hope; (p. 91)

compose/componer *v.* crear algo, como una obra escrita o musical; (p. 28)

compromise/comprometer *v.* exponer a la sospecha; (p. 233)

conjecture/conjeturar *v.* adivinar; (p. 150)

console/consolar *v.* alentar a alguien que se siente triste; (p. 34)

consume/consumir *v.* comerse todo; (p. 20)

contempt/desprecio *s.* rechazar algo porque pensamos que no tiene valor; (p. 11)

contention/contienda *s.* discusión verbal; pelea; (p. 235)

crouched/agacharse *v.* inclinarse; (p. 259)

D

daydreaming/soñar *(despierto)* *v.* tener pensamientos e imágenes agradables en la mente al estar despiertos; (p. 272)

deduce/deducir *v.* llegar a una conclusión; (p. 84)

defense/defensa *s.* capacidad de resistir un ataque; (p. 40)

deferential/deferente *adj.* muy cortés; (p. 186)

delusion/ilusión *v.* creencia que no es verdadera; (p. 128)

depravity/depravación *s.* maldad; (p. 102)

deprive/privar *v.* quitar; impedir que alguien tenga o disfrute de algo; (p. 40)

descent/descenso *s.* movimiento de un nivel alto a un nivel bajo; (p. 83)

despair/desesperanza *s.* pérdida de esperanza; (p. 91)

didactic (dī dak′ tik) *adj.* instructive; meant to teach; (p. 286)

digress (di gres′) *v.* talk about something other than the main subject; (p. 184)

dilapidated (di lap′ ə da′ tid) *adj.* in a bad state or worn down over time; (p. 150)

disgusted (dis gus′ tid) *adj.* has a strong dislike for something; (p. 154)

dispute (dis pūt′) *n.* argument; difference of opinion; (p. 42)

dissension (di sen′ shən) *n.* disagreement; (p. 174)

divide (di vīd′) *v.* to separate; (p. 137)

document (dok′ yə mənt) *n.* something written or printed that gives information about a subject; (p. 28)

doggedly (dô′gid lē) *adv.* with great effort and without giving up; (p. 163)

domination (dom′ ə nā′ shən) *n.* the state of controlling someone or something; (p. 68)

dreadful (dred′ fəl) *adj.* very bad; (p. 20)

dusty (dus′ tē) *adj.* containing or covered with dust; (p. 272)

dutiful (doo′ ti fəl) *adj.* careful to obey or do what one should; (p. 193)

dwell on (dwel) *v.* to think about for a long time; (p. 259)

dwindled (dwind′ əld) *v.* became smaller; (p. 200)

E

empty (emp′ tē) *adj.* having nothing in it; (p. 163)

---

didactic/didáctico *adj.* instructivo; dedicado a enseñar; (p. 286)

digress/divagar *v.* hablar acerca de algo que no es el tema principal; (p. 184)

dilapidated/deteriorado *adj.* en mal estado o desgastado por el tiempo; (p. 150)

disgusted/repugnado *adj.* siente un fuerte rechazo hacia algo; (p. 154)

dispute/disputa *s.* discusión; diferencia de opiniones; (p. 42)

dissension/disentimiento *s.* desacuerdo; (p. 174)

divide/dividir *v.* separar; (p. 137)

document/documento *s.* algo escrito o impreso que da información acerca de un asunto; (p. 28)

doggedly/tenazmente *adv.* con mucho esfuerzo y sin rendirse; (p. 163)

domination/dominación *s.* el estado de controlar a alguien o algo; (p. 68)

dreadful/espantoso *adj.* muy malo; (p. 20)

dusty/polvoriento *adj.* que contiene o que está cubierto de polvo; (p. 272)

dutiful/obediente *adj.* cuidadoso de respetar o hacer lo correcto; (p. 193)

dwell/reflexionar *v.* pensar por mucho tiempo; (p. 259)

dwindled/disminuyó *v.* se hizo más pequeño; (p. 200)

E

empty/vacío *adj.* que no tiene nada dentro; (p. 163)

engrossed (en grōst′) *adj.* fully attentive to; completely engaged in; (p. 218)

enlightens (en lī′ tənz) *v.* gives knowledge or wisdom to; (p. 288)

enterprising (en′ tər prī′ zing) *adj.* showing energy for new projects; (p. 155)

entertainment (en′ tər tān′ mənt) *n.* an activity that is fun and enjoyable; (p. 208)

enthusiastic (en thoo′ zē as′ tik) *adj.* full of excitement and interest; (p. 209)

enunciate (i nun′ sē āt′) *v.* to say clearly; (p. 272)

escape (es kāp′) *n.* a way to get away or get free; (p. 263)

escorted (es kort′ əd) *v.* went with someone to give help or show honor; (p. 129)

evade (i vād′) *v.* to escape or avoid; (p. 248)

exclusively (iks′ kloo′ siv lē) *adv.* only; without anyone else; (p. 286)

extraordinary (iks trôr′ də ner′ ē) *adj.* very unusual; (p. 66)

F

faded (fād′ əd) *v.* became gradually fainter and finally disappeared; (p. 272)

fatigue (fə tēg′) *n.* weakness due to tiredness; (p. 86)

fleet (flēt) *n.* a group of war ships that sail together; (p. 126)

flimsy (flim′ zē) *adj.* without strength; (p. 197)

foment (fō′ ment′) *v.* to help grow or develop; (p. 41)

fury (fyoor′ ē) *n.* strong anger; (p. 104)

engrossed/absorto *adj.* muy concentrado; totalmente abstraído; (p. 218)

enlightens/ilumina *v.* da conocimiento o sabiduría; (p. 288)

enterprising/emprendedor *adj.* con energía para nuevos proyectos; (p. 155)

entertainment/entretenimiento *s.* una actividad que es divertida y agradable; (p. 208)

enthusiastic/entusiasta *adj.* lleno de emoción e interés; (p. 209)

enunciate/enunciar *v.* decir con claridad; (p. 272)

escape/escapatoria *s.* una forma de salir o escaparse; (p. 236)

escorted/escoltó *v.* fue con alguien para ayudarlo o para honrarlo; (p. 129)

evade/evadir *v.* escapar o evitar; (p. 248)

exclusively/exclusivamente *adv.* sólo; sin nadie más; (p. 286)

extraordinary/extraordinario *adj.* muy poco común; (p. 66)

F

faded/atenuarse *v.* perder gradualmente intensidad y al final desaparecer; (p. 272)

fatigue/fatiga *s.* debilidad debido al cansancio; (p. 86)

fleet/flota *s.* grupo de buques de guerra que navegan juntos; (p. 126)

flimsy/frágil *adj.* sin fuerza; (p. 197)

foment/fomentar *v.* ayudar a crecer o a desarrollar; (p. 41)

fury/furor *s.* enfado fuerte; (p. 104)

G

gape (gāp) *v.* to stare with the mouth open; (p. 259)

garrulous (gar′ ə ləs) *adj.* likes to talk a lot; (p. 150)

gathered (gath′ ərd) *v.* collected; brought together; (p. 118)

generous (jen′ ər əs) *adj.* very giving; (p. 41)

gifted (gif′ tid) *adj.* has great ability or is very smart; talented; (p. 153)

grappled (grap′ əld) *v.* struggled in hand-to-hand combat; wrestled; (p. 216)

grief (grēf) *n.* a deep feeling of sadness or loss; (p. 118)

grins (grinz) *v.* smiles; (p. 175)

groping (grōp) *v.* feeling about uncertainly with the hands; (p. 258)

guile (gīl) *n.* dishonesty; (p. 175)

H

holocaust (hol′ ə kôst′) *n.* great or complete destruction; (p. 272)

I

illusion (i lōō′ zhən) *n.* something that misleads or deceives; (p. 72)

impede (im pēd′) *v.* to slow or block action; (p. 85)

impromptu (im promp′ tōō) *adj.* without time to prepare; (p. 209)

individual (in′ də vij′ ōō əl) *n.* a single person; (p .58)

G

gape/mirar *(boquiabierto) v.* observar con la boca abierta; (p. 259)

garrulous/gárrulo *adj.* le gusta hablar mucho; (p. 150)

gathered/reunió *v.* agrupó, convocó; (p. 118)

generous/generoso *adj.* muy bondadoso; (p. 41)

gifted/dotado *adj.* tiene gran habilidad o es muy inteligente; talentoso; (p. 153)

grappled/forcejeó *v.* peleó mano a mano; luchó; (p. 216)

grief/pena *s.* profundo sentimiento de tristeza o pérdida; (p. 118)

grins/sonríe *v.* ríe; (p. 175)

groping/tentar *v.* tocar de manera insegura con las manos; (p. 258)

guile/engaño *s.* deshonestidad; (p. 175)

H

holocaust/holocausto *s.* destrucción grande o completa; (p. 272)

I

illusion/ilusión *s.* algo que confunde o engaña; (p. 72)

impede/impedir *v.* retrasar u obstruir una acción; (p. 85)

impromptu/improvisado *adj.* sin tiempo para prepararse; (p. 209)

individual/individuo *s.* una sola persona; (p. 58)

induce (in do͞os′) v. to cause or persuade; (p. 103)

instrument (in′ strə mənt) n. a device that makes musical sounds; (p. 163)

intercepted (in′ tər sept′ əd) v. stopped something on its way somewhere; (p. 127)

interminable (in tur′ mi nə bəl) adj. without end; (p. 151)

intimidated (in tim′ ə dāt əd) adj. made shy or fearful; scared into not acting; (p. 217)

J

jilted (jilt′ id) v. left or rejected a sweetheart; (p. 196)

jubilant (jo͞o′ bə lənt) adj. extremely happy; successfully joyful; (p. 218)

L

leap (lēp) v. to jump; (p. 246)

legacy (leg′ə sē) n. money that someone gives away after the person dies; (p. 162)

legible (lej′ ə bəl) adj. clear; easy to read; (p. 300)

lethargy (leth′ ər jē) n. not moving; the state of being slow or tired; (p. 88)

limp (limp) adj. lacking firmness or strength; (p. 247)

location (lō kā′ shən) n. a place or position; (p. 303)

loitered (loi′ tərd) v. stood or lingered idly or aimlessly; (p. 216)

M

malingers (mə ling′ gərz) v. pretends to be sick to avoid work; (p. 184)

---

induce/inducir v. provocar o convencer; (p. 103)

instrument/instrumento s. un mecanismo que emite sonidos musicales; (p. 163)

intercepted/interceptó v. paró algo en su camino; (p. 127)

interminable/interminable adj. sin fin; (p. 151)

intimidated/intimidado adj. asustado o acobardado; atemorizado de actuar; (p. 217)

J

jilted/abandonó v. dejó o rechazó a su novio o novia; (p. 196)

jubilant/jubiloso adj. muy feliz; extremadamente alegre; (p. 218)

L

leap/brincar v. saltar; (p. 246)

legacy/legado s. dinero que alguien deja después de morir; (p. 162)

legible/legible adj. claro; fácil de leer; (p. 300)

lethargy/letargo s. no moverse; el estado de sentirse desganado o cansado; (p. 88)

limp/flojo adj. sin firmeza o fuerza; (p. 247)

location/ubicación s. un lugar o posición; (p. 303)

loitered/merodeó v. rondó o deambuló ociosamente o sin propósito; (p. 216)

M

malingers/finge (enfermedad) v. se hace el enfermo para no trabajar; (p. 184)

meandering (mē anʹ dər ing) *adj.* following a winding course; (p. 288)

measures (mezhʹ ərz) *v.* finds the length or other dimensions of; (p. 136)

millennium (mi leʹ nē əm) *n.* a time of great happiness, peace, or good fortune; (p. 208)

mirth (murth) *n.* happiness shown by laughter; (p. 107)

moist (moist) *adj.* slightly wet; (p. 137)

N

narrow (narʹ ō) *adj.* skinny and usually long; (p. 184)

O

oblige (ə blīj́ʹ) *v.* to make grateful; to do a service for; (p. 119)

obliquely (ə blēkʹ lē) *adv.* in a slanting direction or at an angle; (p. 166)

orchestra (ôrʹ kis trə) *n.* a large group of people playing musical instruments together; (p. 206)

P

packed (pakt) *adj.* crowded or filled; (p. 231)

paradigms (parʹ ə dīmzʹ) *n.* patterns or examples; (p. 290)

passion (pashʹ ən) *n.* strong liking of or desire for something; (p. 40)

patronage (pāʹ trə nij) *n.* business; customers; (p. 207)

meandering/serpenteante *adj.* que sigue un camino sinuoso; (p. 288)

measures/mide *v.* averigua la longitud u otras dimensiones; (p. 136)

millennium/milenio *s.* período de mil años; (p. 208)

mirth/júbilo *s.* felicidad expresada con risa; (p. 107)

moist/húmedo *adj.* ligeramente mojado; (p. 137)

N

narrow/estrecho *adj.* delgado y generalmente largo; (p. 184)

O

oblige/agradecer *v.* mostrar gratitud; realizar un servicio; (p. 119)

obliquely/oblicuamente *adv.* en dirección inclinada o en ángulo; (p. 166)

orchestra/orquesta *s.* un gran grupo de personas que tocan juntas instrumentos musicales; (p. 206)

P

packed/atestado *adj.* abarrotado o lleno; (p. 231)

paradigms/paradigmas *s.* patrones o ejemplos; (p. 290)

passion/pasión *s.* fuerte interés o deseo de algo; (p. 40)

patronage/patrocinio *s.* negocio; clientes; (p. 207)

peasants (pez′ ənts) *n.* laborers or farmers; people who earn little money; (p. 286)

pervade (pər vād′) *v.* to go through every part; (p. 128)

piety (pī′ ə tē) *n.* religious devotion; goodness; (p. 198)

plots (pläts) *n.* small areas of land; (p. 6)

ponder (pon′ dər) *v.* to think about carefully; (p. 259)

presume (pri zo͞om′) *v.* expect something without a good reason to expect it; (p. 183)

pretense (prē′ tens) *n.* a false show or appearance; (p. 240)

prostrate (pros′ trāt) *adj.* lying face down; (p. 127)

proximity (prok sim′ ə tē) *n.* closeness in space or time; nearness; (p. 91)

puddles (pud′ əlz) *n.* small, shallow pools of water; (p. 280)

R

racket (rak′ it) *n.* loud noise; (p. 118)

random (ran′ dəm) *adj.* without a pattern; (p. 272)

ravenous (rav′ ə nəs) *adj.* very hungry; (p. 89)

recompense (rek′ əm pens′) *n.* something given in return for something else; (p. 22)

refreshments (ri fresh′ məntz) *n.* food or drink, such as snacks or a light meal; (p. 210)

remains (ri mānz′) *v.* is not yet finished; stays; (p. 144)

peasants/campesinos *s.* obreros o agricultores; personas que ganan poco dinero; (p. 286)

pervade/saturar *v.* llenar por completo; (p. 128)

piety/piedad *s.* devoción religiosa; bondad; (p. 198)

plots/terrenos *s.* pequeñas áreas de tierra; (p. 6)

ponder/considerar *v.* pensar con cuidado; (p. 259)

presume/presumir *v.* esperar algo sin una buena razón; (p. 183)

pretense/pretensión *s.* falsa muestra o apariencia; (p. 240)

prostrate/postrado *adj.* acostado boca abajo; (p. 127)

proximity/proximidad *s.* cercanía en el espacio o en el tiempo; inmediación; (p. 91)

puddles/charcos *s.* hoyos pequeños y de poca profundidad, llenos de agua; (p. 280)

R

racket/alboroto *s.* fuerte ruido; (p. 118)

random/aleatorio *adj.* sin un patrón; (p. 272)

ravenous/hambriento *adj.* con mucha hambre; (p. 89)

recompense/recompensa *s.* algo que se da a cambio de alguna otra cosa; (p. 22)

refreshments/refrigerios *s.* alimentos o bebidas, como una merienda o comida ligera; (p. 210)

remains/permanece *v.* todavía no está terminado; continúa; (p. 144)

repay (ri pā′) *v.* to pay back or give back; (p. 22)

reproaches (ri prōch′ es) *n.* unhappy or angry words toward someone; (p. 163)

rights (rīts) *n.* powers or privileges you have by law; (p. 118)

route (rōōt) *n.* a path of travel; (p. 303)

S

salient (sāl′ yənt) *adj.* very obvious; easy to notice; (p. 174)

salute (sə lūt′) *v.* to honor someone with a gesture of respect; (p. 10)

scintillating (sin′ tə lā′ ting) *adj.* lively; sparkling; exciting; (p. 206)

seized (sēzd) *v.* took away suddenly; grabbed; (p. 8)

separate (sep′ ə rət) *adj.* kept apart; (p. 142)

separated (sep′ ə rāt′ əd) *v.* set apart; (p. 264)

shelter (shel′ tər) *n.* something that provides protection from the weather, such as a building; (p. 7)

shivering (shiv′ ər ing) *v.* shaking slightly; (p. 174)

slavery (slā′ vər ē) *n.* ownership of others as property; (p. 118)

sociable (sō′ shə bəl) *adj.* friendly; likes to be with others; (p. 155)

soil (soi(-ə)l) *n.* dirt; (p. 4)

squeezed (skwēzd) *v.* pressed together; (p. 196)

repay/devolver *v.* reponer o regresar; (p. 22)

reproaches/reproches *s.* palabras de descontento o enfado hacia alguien; (p. 163)

rights/derechos *s.* poderes o privilegios que tenemos por ley; (p. 118)

route/ruta *s.* un itinerario de viaje; (p. 303)

S

salient/prominente *adj.* muy claro; fácil de notar; (p. 174)

salute/saludar *v.* honrar a alguien con un gesto de respeto; (p.10)

scintillating/brillante *adj.* vivo; centelleante; emocionante; (p. 206)

seized/agarró *v.* tomó repentinamente; sujetó; (p. 8)

separate/separado *adj.* que está apartado; (p. 142)

separated/separó *v.* dividió; (p. 264)

shelter/refugio *s.* algo que ofrece protección del clima, como un edificio; (p. 7)

shivering/tiritar *v.* temblar ligeramente; (p. 174)

slavery/esclavitud *s.* posesión de otras personas; (p. 118)

sociable/sociable *adj.* amistoso, le gusta estar con los demás; (p. 155)

soil/tierra *s.* suelo; (p. 4)

squeezed/exprimió *v.* apretó; (p. 196)

staggered (sta′ gərd) *v.* walked unsteadily, nearly falling; (p. 12)

stooped (sto͞opt) *adj.* bent forward and down; (p. 259)

strained (strānd) *v.* pressed or poured through a device with holes for filtering; (p. 52)

stretching (strech′ ing) *v.* spreading; (p. 111)

subservient (səb sur′ vē ənt) *adj.* useful but inferior; submissive; (p. 236)

surrender (sə ren′ dər) *n.* the act of giving something to someone who demands it; (p. 127)

swarm (swôrm) *v.* to form a large group; (p. 174)

T

tactful (takt′ fəl) *adj.* able to say the right things and act the right way around other people; (p. 193)

tears (tērz) *n.* a watery drops that flow from eyes when crying; (p. 167)

tedious (tē′ dē əs) *adj.* very long and detailed; boring; (p. 182)

tempest (tem′ pist) *n.* a violent storm; (p. 174)

torn (tôrn) *adj.* ripped apart; (p. 175)

traffic (traf′ ik) *n.* vehicles and people moving along a route; (p. 280)

tranquil (trang′ kwəl) *adj.* calm and quiet; (p. 150)

trepidation (trep′ ə dā′ shən) *n.* a feeling of worry about something in the future; (p. 164)

staggered/tambalearse *v.* caminar inestablemente, casi cayéndose; (p. 12)

stooped/encorvado *adj.* doblado hacia adelante y abajo; (p. 259)

strained/escurrió *v.* apretó o vertió a través de un aparato con agujeros para filtrar; (p. 52)

stretching/extender *v.* desplegar; (p. 111)

subservient/servil *adj.* útil pero inferior; sumiso; (p. 236)

surrender/rendición *s.* la acción de dar algo a alguien que lo exige; (p. 127)

swarm/aglomerar *v.* formar un grupo grande; (p. 174)

T

tactful/discreto *adj.* capaz de decir las cosas correctas y actuar de la manera correcta alrededor de los demás; (p. 193)

tears/lágrimas *s.* gotas que fluyen de los ojos cuando lloramos; (p. 167)

tedious/tedioso *adj.* muy largo y detallado; aburrido; (p. 182)

tempest/tempestad *s.* una tormenta violenta; (p. 174)

torn/arrancado *adj.* separado con violencia; (p. 175)

traffic/tráfico *s.* vehículos y personas que se mueven por una ruta; (p. 280)

tranquil/tranquilo *adj.* calmado y silencioso; (p. 150)

trepidation/turbación *s.* sentimiento de preocupación por algo en el futuro; (p. 164)

tumble (tum′ bəl) *v.* to fall in an awkward way; (p. 280)

tyrants (tī′ rənts) *n.* rulers who use power in an unfair way; (p. 41)

U

unorthodox (un ôr′ thə doks′) *adj.* not usual or traditional; (p. 290)

V

vanity (van′ i tē) *n.* too much pride; (p. 196)

vanquished (vang′ kwisht) *v.* defeated; overcame; (p. 106)

vassals (va′ səlz) *n.* servants or slaves; (p. 40)

victorious (vik tôr′ ē əs) *adj.* winning; (p. 64)

vile (vīl) *adj.* disgusting; (p. 175)

vogue (vōg) *n.* fashion; style; (p. 206)

W

waded (wād′ ed) *v.* walked in shallow water; (p. 13)

warily (wār′ ə lē) *adv.* in a watchful or alert manner; cautiously; (p. 273)

weapon (wep′ ən) *n.* an object used to fight; (p. 258)

wept (wept) *v.* cried; (p. 184)

wither (with′ ər) *v.* to dry up or shrivel; (p. 235)

worn (wôrn) *adj.* damaged by use; (p. 162)

wound (wo͞ond) *n.* an injury to the body; (p. 219)

tumble/desplomarse *v.* caer de manera embarazosa; (p. 280)

tyrants/tiranos *s.* gobernantes que usan el poder de manera injusta; (p. 41)

U

unorthodox/inusitado *adj.* poco usual o tradicional; (p. 290)

V

vanity/vanidad *s.* demasiado orgullo; (p. 196)

vanquished/derrotó *v.* venció; superó; (p. 106)

vassals/vasallos *s.* criados o esclavos; (p. 40)

victorious/victorioso *adj.* ganador; (p. 64)

vile/vil *adj.* asqueroso; (p. 175)

vogue/boga *s.* moda; estilo; (p. 206)

W

waded/vadeó *v.* caminó en agua poco profunda; (p. 13)

warily/cautelosamente *adv.* de manera cuidadosa o prudente; precavidamente; (p. 273)

weapon/arma *s.* un objeto que se usa para luchar; (p. 258)

wept/lloró *v.* derramó lágrimas; (p. 184)

wither/marchitarse *v.* secarse o arrugarse; (p. 235)

worn/desgastado *adj.* dañado por el uso; (p. 162)

wound/herida *s.* lesión al cuerpo; (p. 219)

wreaths (rēths) *n.* flowers or leaves arranged in a circle; (p. 109)

wrinkled (ring′ kəld) *adj.* having creases or small folds; (p. 281)

wreaths/corona *s.* flores u hojas arregladas en un círculo; (p. 109)

wrinkled/arrugado *adj.* que tiene pliegues o pequeños dobleces; (p. 281)

Comprehension, Word Study, and Grammar Blackline Masters

The SKY TREE
How the LEOPARD Got His Claws
Prayer to the Pacific

Name _____ Date _____

Directions: Use this graphic organizer as you read "The Sky Tree," "How the Leopard Got His Claws," and "Prayer to the Pacific." Write your questions in column 1. When you know an answer, write it in the second column.

Questions	Answers
1. Why did Aataentsic cut down the tree that gave everyone food?	1. She did not want her husband to die.

The SKY TREE
How the LEOPARD Got His Claws
Prayer to the Pacific

Name _____ Date _____

Word Study Synonyms and Antonyms

Synonyms are words that have the same or nearly the same meanings. **Antonyms** are words that have the opposite or nearly the opposite meanings. Both synonyms and antonyms must be the same part of speech.

Sickness and *disease* are synonyms; both mean the same thing and both are nouns. *Sickness* and *ill* are not synonyms because one is a noun and the other is an adjective.

Sickness and *health* are antonyms; they have opposite meanings and both are nouns. *Sickness* and *well* are not synonyms; one is a noun, the other an adjective.

Practice A On the first blank following each of the boldfaced words from the selections write a synonym for the word. On the second blank, indicate what part of speech the synonyms are. Use a dictionary or thesaurus if you need help.

EXAMPLE: **scattered**   _____dispersed_____   _____verb_____

1. **toppled**   _____   _____

2. **soil**   _____   _____

3. **claws**   _____   _____

4. **excitement**   _____   _____

5. **humming**   _____   _____

Practice B On the blank following each of the italicized words write an antonym that changes the meaning of the sentence.

EXAMPLE: The ruler of the country was very *wise* _____foolish_____.

1. The athlete looked at her opponent with *contempt* _____.

2. The hot air balloon came down to earth very *gently* _____.

3. All the students *immediately* _____ filed out of the auditorium.

4. In his review, the critic said that the lead actor's performance was *terrible* _____.

5. We all *laughed* _____ at the news of the election results.

Name _____ Date _____

Grammar Link Irregular Verbs: *Have*, *Do*, and *Go*

Kathy's classes finish at 4:00 every day.
Then she **goes** home.
She **has** a cup of coffee and **does** her homework.

The third person forms of *have, go,* and *do* are irregular.

	He She **has** a problem. It
I **have** a job.	
I **do** the work.	He She **does** the work. It
I **go** to work.	
	He She **goes** outside. It

Practice Complete the sentences with the correct forms of the verbs in parentheses.

1. The Sky Tree (go) _____ through the hole in Sky Land.

2. Turtle (have) _____ a good idea.

3. The dog and the duck (go) _____ away from the other animals.

4. The animals (do) _____ the work to build their shelter.

5. The leopard (go) _____ on a journey.

6. The leopard (have) _____ new claws and a loud voice.

7. Now, the dog (do) _____ work for the hunter.

8. Both "the Sky Tree" and "How the Leopard Got His Claws" (have) _____ talking animals.

Upon the *Burning* of Our House *and*
To My Dear and Loving Husband

Name _____   Date _____

Directions: As you read "Upon the Burning of Our House" and "To My Dear and Loving Husband," write down lines you don't understand in the left column. In the right column, rewrite the lines in your own words.

Line from Poem   **Rewrite**

"When by the ruins oft I past"	→	I walked by the ruins a lot
	→	
	→	

Upon the *Burning* of Our House *and*
To My Dear and Loving Husband

Name _____ Date _____

Grammar Link Past Time Expressions

Yesterday, last, and *ago* tell us when an action happened in the past. We use these words in the following ways.

yesterday	morning, afternoon, and evening
last	night, periods of time (week, month, year), days of the week, and seasons (summer, winter, spring, fall)
ago	lengths of time, for example, *five minutes ago*

Time expressions usually come at the beginning or at the end of a sentence. When they come at the beginning of a sentence, we use a comma after the time expressions.

Yesterday morning, I walked to school.

When a time expression comes at the end of a sentence, we do not use a comma before the expression.

I walked to school **yesterday morning.**

Practice Fill in the blanks with *yesterday, last,* or *ago.*

Anne: Where have you been? My house caught on fire two days _____!

Ben: Oh no! I didn't know that. I was on vacation from _____ Tuesday until _____ evening. Are you okay?

Anne: Yes, I'm okay. But I lost my beautiful house. It was very old. It was built fifty years _____.

Ben: I'm so sorry.

Anne: I walked by the ruins _____ afternoon. It made me think about the party we had _____ April. And it made me think about the wedding we had here _____ year.

Ben: That was your daughter's wedding, wasn't it? I saw her _____ evening when I got back. Three years. . . . That was a long time _____.

Anne: It was hard to sleep _____ night. I was thinking about the fire. Oh, I have to go. I was supposed to meet my daughter ten minutes _____.

Ben: Yes, I have to do some things I should have done _____.

TIME How They Chose These Words

Name _____ **Date** _____

Directions: As you read "How They Chose These Words," use the boxes below to write the main idea of the article and the supporting details. Write down at least one supporting detail for each of the four sections of the article. Write the details first. When you have finished with the details, determine the main idea.

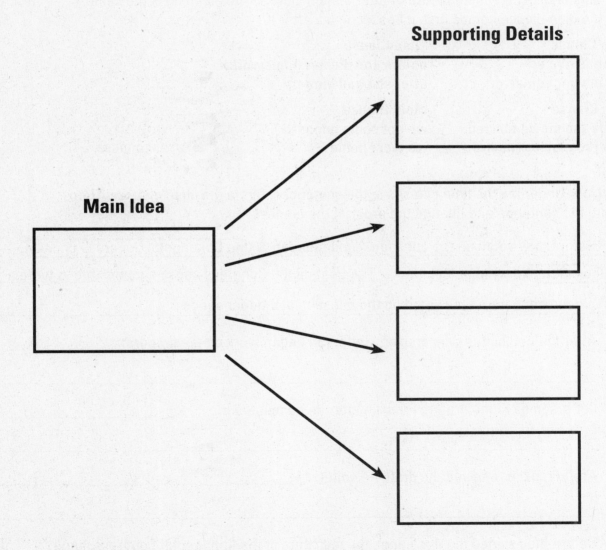

Supporting Details

Main Idea

TIME How They Chose These Words

Name _____ Date _____

Grammar Link The Simple Past Tense:
Time Clauses with *Before* and *After*

1. A time clause begins with a conjunction such as *before* or *after*.
2. A time clause has a subject and a verb, but it is not a complete sentence.
3. A time clause must be used with a main clause to form a complete sentence.
4. A time clause can come before or after a main clause. The meaning is the same. If the time clause comes first, it has a comma after it.

Main Clause	Time Clause
Amy had dinner	**before she did her homework.**
Amy did her homework	**after she had dinner.**

Time Clause	Main Clause
Before the movie started,	we got some popcorn.
After the movie was over,	we went home.

Practice Underline the time clauses in the sentences. Circle the main clauses. Then rewrite the sentence and change the order of the clauses.

1. Before they voted on the question of independence, (the Continental Congress chose a committee) to write a document.   The Continental Congress chose a committee to write a document before they voted on the question of independence.

2. After the committee was chosen, Jefferson began work on the first draft. _____

_____

3. Jefferson gave the draft to Franklin after he completed it. _____

_____

4. After Franklin received the draft, he edited it. _____

_____

5. Before they signed the document, the members of the Continental Congress made some cuts. _____

_____

Letter to John Adams

Name _____ **Date** _____

Directions: As you read "Letter to John Adams," think about the author's purpose. Use the chart below to list the descriptions she includes and the opinions she expresses.

Descriptions	Opinions
1. She describes the people fighting against America as "savage and bloodthirsty."	1. You cannot truly love freedom if you deprive some people of their liberties.
2.	2.
3.	3.
4.	4.
5.	5.

Letter to John Adams

Name _____ Date _____

Grammar Link The Present Perfect Tense of Be: *For* and *Since*

Affirmative Statement			
Subject	**Have/Has**	**Past Particle of *Be***	
I You	**have**		
He She It	**has**	**been**	here **for** two hours. **since** 10 o'clock.
We You They	**have**		

Practice Complete the sentences with the present perfect form of the verb be.

Abigail: I miss you! I _____ waiting for your letter for a month.

John: I'm sorry. I _____ trying to write for a long time, but I have been busy here.

Abigail: Dr. Crane _____ to our house since the soldiers left.

John: Please tell me how the house looks! I _____ wondering about it for weeks.

Abigail: The house _____ okay since we left. It is dirty, but not badly damaged.

John: That's good news. I _____ feeling well for the last few weeks. How about you?

Abigail: I am full of hope! Everything _____ better since the British left Boston.

John: I _____ feeling hopeful since the British left, too.

Abigail: I believe you _____ writing new laws since the last time we spoke.

John: We _____ working hard since then. I think we are making progress.

Abigail: As you work, please remember the ladies! They _____ treated unfairly for many years.

John: You are right. The law _____ unfair for too long. We will try to give women and men equal rights.

CIVIL DISOBEDIENCE
On the Eve of Historic Dandi March
FROM LONG WALK TO FREEDOM

Name _____ Date _____

Directions: As you read the essays, think about the main arguments made by each author. Use the chart below to keep track of each essay's main idea and the reasons that support it.

from Civil Disobedience	On the Eve of Historic Dandi March	*from* Long Walk to Freedom
Main Idea: Thoreau believes _____ _____ _____ Reasons: 1. 2. 3.	Main Idea: Gandhi believes _____ _____ _____ Reasons: 1. 2. 3.	Main Idea: Mandela believes _____ _____ _____ Reasons: 1. 2. 3.

CIVIL DISOBEDIENCE
On the Eve of Historic Dandi March
FROM LONG WALK TO FREEDOM

Name _____ Date _____

Word Study Negative Prefixes: *un-, im-, in-, il-, dis-, a-,* and *ir-*

Negative prefixes are word parts added to the beginnings of base words. Negative prefixes change the meaning of a word to its antonym.

The following chart shows common negative prefixes:

Prefix Meaning "Not" or "Opposite Of"	Example Word
un-	unacceptable
dis-	displace
il-, im-, in-, ir-	irreversible
a-	amoral

Practice A Select the correct negative prefix from the list above that turns each of the following words into its antonym.

_____ **1.** convenient   _____ **4.** regular

_____ **2.** fair   _____ **5.** logical

_____ **3.** honest   _____ **6.** possible

Practice B In the following sentences, add a negative prefix to the root word in parentheses.

1. The court order was (typical). _____

2. Considering the blunder was his fault, the judge was surprisingly (apologetic). _____

3. The investigation showed the mayor had been (honest) about his past. _____

4. Thoreau believes that many government actions are (expedient). _____

5. Several (responsible) people placed an obstacle on the railroad track. _____

CIVIL DISOBEDIENCE
On the Eve of Historic Dandi March
FROM LONG WALK TO FREEDOM

Name _____ Date _____

Grammar Link   Spelling of Regular Past Tense Verbs: Pronunciation of –*ed*: /t/, /d/, and /id/

Verb Ending	Spelling Rule	Examples
Most regular verbs	Add –*ed*	*rain, rained*
Verb ends in *e*	Add –*d*	*arrive, arrived*
Verb ends in consonant plus *y*	Change *y* to *i* and add –*ed*	*cry, cried*
Verb ends in vowel plus *y*	Add –*ed*	*enjoy, enjoyed*
Verb ends in one consonant plus vowel plus consonant (one-syllable verbs)	Double the consonant and add –*ed*	*stop, stopped*
Verb ends in *x, w*	Add –*ed*	*show, showed*
Verb ends in vowel plus consonant and stress is on first syllable (two-syllable verb)	Add –*ed*. Do not double the consonant.	*visit, visited*
Verb ends in vowel plus consonant and stress is on second syllable (two-syllable verb)	Double the consonant and add –*ed*.	*prefer, preferred*

Practice Write the correct spelling of the simple past tense form.

1. call _____

2. hurry _____

3. follow _____

4. fix _____

5. hunt _____

6. chase _____

7. swat _____

8. worry _____

9. tie _____

10. drop _____

11. carry _____

12. bait _____

13. fray _____

14. try _____

15. drip _____

16. study _____

17. waste _____

18. work _____

The Pit and the Pendulum

Name _____ **Date** _____

Directions: As you read "The Pit and the Pendulum," keep track of the order of events in a flowchart.

The court of the Inquisition sentences the hero to death.

↓

↓

↓

↓

↓

↓

↓

↓

The Pit and the Pendulum

Name _____ **Date** _____

Word Study   Root Words and Word Origins

Word origins, also called **etymologies,** describe the history and development of words. They can be found in dictionary word entries, usually at the beginning or end of the entry. A typical word entry might look like this:

im pede (im pēd´) *v.* **im ped ed; im ped ing** [L *impedire,* fr *in-* + *ped* foot] to slow or block progress or action; to obstruct

The word origin is the portion of the entry enclosed in brackets. The word origin for *impede* indicates that it comes from the Latin word *impedire,* which has the same meaning as impede. *Impedire,* in turn, is made up of the prefix *in-* and the root *ped,* which means "foot." Some other words that share the root *ped* are *expedite,* "perform quickly"; *expedition,* "journey for a special purpose"; *pedestrian,* "a person on foot"; and *pedometer,* "instrument for recording how far one walks."

Root words, or base words, are words to which prefixes and suffixes can be added to form other words. You can often use your knowledge of roots, prefixes, and suffixes to figure out the meaning of an unfamiliar word.

Practice A Match each vocabulary word from "The Pit and the Pendulum" with the word that has the same origin. Use a dictionary if necessary.

1. deduce
2. impede
3. lethargy
4. proximity

a. expedient _____
b. approximate _____
c. introduce _____
d. lethe _____

Practice B Use your knowledge of word parts and word origins to answer the following questions. Put a check next to the correct definition of the italicized word. Use a dictionary to check your answers.

1. An *abduction* is the act of
   a. taking something away. _____
   b. granting a favor. _____

2. A *profusion* of flowers is
   a. a small quantity of flowers. _____
   b. a large display of flowers. _____

3. *Proximo* means occurring
   a. from time to time. _____
   b. once a month. _____

4. A *lethargic* pet is
   a. active. _____
   b. lazy. _____

The Pit and the Pendulum

Name _____ Date _____

Word Study Denotations and Connotations

Denotation is the literal, or dictionary, meaning of a word. **Connotation** is the implied, or cultural, meaning of a word. For example, *alarm* and *terror* both have the same denotation: "fear"; but *alarm* suggests a sudden shock of fear whereas *terror* suggests the most extreme degree of fear.

Practice A Each word listed below is followed by two synonyms. Circle the synonym that has the more negative connotation. Use a dictionary to check your answers.

EXAMPLE: fat   overweight, (obese)

1. odd   bizarre, grotesque
2. trivial   unimportant, petty
3. die   perish, pass away
4. agitation   disturbance, excitement
5. unsatisfactory   unacceptable, intolerable

Practice B Each of the sentences below is followed by two synonyms for the italicized word in the sentence. Fill in the blanks with the appropriate synonym. Use a dictionary to check your answers.

1. A _____ is a meaner *laugh* than a _____. (guffaw, cackle)

2. _____ is a more intense form of *trembling* than _____ is. (shuddering, quivering)

3. When you *endeavor* to do something, _____ suggests a more serious, concentrated effort than _____ does. (attempt, strive)

4. If you wanted to replace the word *shocking* in a sentence, _____ would be a more precise choice than _____. (hideous, offensive)

5. A _____ is a *frown* that suggests the possibility of pain and is less threatening than a _____. (scowl, grimace)

The Pit and the Pendulum

Name _____ Date _____

Grammar Link   Simple Past Tense: Irregular Verbs

Many verbs do not use the *–ed* verb form. The past form of these verbs is irregular.

Subject	Past Form of Verb (*to go*)	
I		
You		
He/She/It	went	to Africa last year.
We		
They		

Here are some common irregular verbs.

Base Form	Past Form	Base Form	Past Form
be	was/were	give	gave
come	came	have	had
do	did	hear	heard
eat	ate	make	made
feel	felt	tell	told
get	got	think	thought

Practice Fill in the blanks with the simple past tense of the irregular verbs in parentheses.

The hero of "The Pit and the Pendulum" (come) _____ before the court of the

Inquisition. The court punished him for something he (do) _____. The court

(tell) _____ him he must die for his crime. He fainted.

He woke up in a dark dungeon. He (feel) _____ around the walls. A deep pit

(be) _____ in the center of the dungeon.

The next time he woke up, the jailers (have) _____ tied him to a board. A heavy,

sharp pendulum hung over him. The jailers also (give) _____ him food, but rats

(eat) _____ most of it.

The hero (think) _____ carefully. He rubbed food on his straps. The rats chewed

the straps. The hero (be) _____ free!

Then he saw that the walls were moving. The walls (make) _____ the shape of

a diamond to push him into the pit. Just when the hero was about to fall, the French army arrived.

from MY BONDAGE AND MY FREEDOM
Frederick Douglass   IN TEXAS GRASS

Name _____ Date _____

Directions: As you read the selections, think about the main points made by each author about slavery and its effects. Use the chart below to keep track of each selection's main idea about freedom and slavery, and the reasons that support it.

from My Bondage and My Freedom	Frederick Douglass	In Texas Grass
Main Idea: Douglass thinks that slavery _____ _____ _____ Reasons: 1. 2. 3.	Main Idea: Hayden believes _____ _____ _____ Reasons: 1. 2. 3.	Main Idea: Troupe believes _____ _____ _____ Reasons: 1. 2. 3.

FROM MY BONDAGE AND MY FREEDOM
Frederick Douglass   IN TEXAS GRASS

Name _____   Date _____

Word Study Context Meaning

Context refers to the parts of a text just before and after a word that determine its meaning. The following chart shows some types of context clues.

Type of context clue	Example
Contrast	Unlike her former *kindly* manner, Mrs. Auld's behavior was now **dour.**
Example	The **rhetoric** of slavery included *speeches* and *essays* proclaiming that slave owners were caring for people unable to care for themselves.
Restatement	I used many **expedients** to continue my reading—any *method* or *device* that would keep my actions from my masters.

Practice Use the chart and the context clues in each sentence to figure out the meaning of the boldfaced word. Write your explanation in the space provided.

EXAMPLE: Douglass says that slavery **divested** his mistress from her good qualities. She was no longer sweet and kind.

> **Explanation:** Divested means to take away, because the next sentence describes how she was after slavery affected her.

1. The dialogue and the speeches were as **redolent** of the principles of liberty as the first leaves in May are suggestive of spring.

    _____

2. The increase of knowledge was **attended** with bitter, as well as sweet results.

    _____

3. I **loathed** them as the meanest and the most wicked of men.

    _____

4. I was no longer the light-hearted, **gleesome** boy, full of mirth and play.

FROM MY BONDAGE AND MY FREEDOM
Frederick Douglass IN TEXAS GRASS

Name _____ Date _____

Grammar Link Future Time Clauses with *Before, After,* and *When*

1. A future time clause can begin with *before, after,* or *when*.
2. When a time clause refers to the future, the verb is in the simple present tense.

Time Clause Simple Present	Main Clause Future
Before Douglass **goes** home,	he **will study** spelling.
When he **learns** to read,	he **will know** about slavery.
After the slaves **are** freed,	they **will receive** forty acres and a mule.

EXAMPLE: Before Douglass goes home, he will study spelling.

3. We can put the time clause before or after the main clause. They both have the same meaning.

    He will know about slavery **when he learns to read.**
    When he learns to read, he will know about slavery.

4. When the time clause comes first, we put a comma (,) after the time clause.

Practice Underline the time clauses in the sentences about Frederick Douglass.

1. Frederick Douglass will learn Latin and Greek before he becomes free.

2. Before she teaches Frederick to read, Mrs. Auld will talk to her husband.

3. Frederick Douglass will ask his friends before he buys the book.

4. When Mrs. Auld sees Frederick with a book, she will yell at him.

5. When Douglass feels discontented, he will read about the debate.

6. After he becomes a free man, Frederick Douglass will receive forty acres and a mule.

7. Douglass will dislike his master after he learns about slavery.

8. When all people are free, they will remember Frederick Douglass.

And Ain't I a Woman?

Name _____ Date _____

Directions: Sojourner Truth's speech includes many informal words and expressions. As you read "And Ain't I a Woman?" use the chart below to record examples of Truth's unique diction, or word choice. Then use context clues to help you figure out what each example means.

Unique Word Choice	Meaning
"all this here talking"	all of the discussion

And Ain't I a Woman?

Name _____ **Date** _____

Grammar Link Object Pronouns

Many sentences in English have a subject, a verb, and an object.

Noun Subject	Verb	Noun Object	Pronoun Subject	Verb	Pronoun Object
John	likes	rice.	He	likes	it.

The subject can be a noun (John). The subject can also be a pronoun (He). The object can be a noun (rice). The object can also be a pronoun (it).

We often use a pronoun in place of a noun. Here are the subject and object pronouns.

Subject Pronouns	Object Pronouns
I	me
you	you
he	him
she	her
it	it
we	us
they	them

Practice Replace the underlined words with a subject or object pronoun.

1. <u>Sojourner Truth</u> is a former slave. _____

2. In 1851, she gave <u>a speech</u> about women's rights. _____

3. She told <u>the men in the crowd</u> that women are strong. _____

4. <u>Women</u> are as strong as men, in Truth's opinion. _____

5. For example, men do not need to help <u>women</u> get into carriages. _____

6. Women have worked hard planting <u>crops</u>. _____

7. <u>A female slave</u> might have to be strong enough to give up her child. _____

8. Truth shared <u>bible stories</u> with the crowd. _____

9. "<u>Christ</u> came from a woman," she reminded them. _____

10. A woman named Eve changed <u>the world</u> on her own! _____

from Mary Chesnut's
Civil War

Name _____ **Date** _____

Directions: As you read "from Mary Chesnut's Civil War," look for important events. Write the events in the correct order.

1.

2.

3.
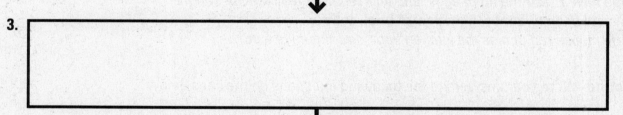

4.
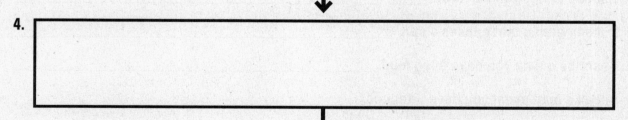

5.

from Mary Chesnut's
Civil War

Name _____ Date _____

Word Study Multiple-Meaning Words

The same word often has more than one meaning. Note the different meanings of the words *paint, mad,* and *stir.*

paint
1. to produce in lines and colors on a surface by applying colors
   *He **paints** portraits of his friends any chance he gets.*
2. to give a description of
   *The mayor **painted** a happy picture of the city's success.*

mad
1. having intense anger
   *The mother was very **mad** after the little boy ate all the cookies.*
2. marked by wild merriment
   *The birthday party was the **maddest** event I'd ever attended.*

stir
1. to mix
   *You have to **stir** the flour, eggs, and milk together to make the dough.*
2. a state of disturbance, agitation, or brisk activity
   *The mouse ran across the kitchen floor, causing quite a **stir**.*

Practice Write your answers to the following questions on the lines below.

1. List two things you can **stir**. _____

2. List something that causes a **stir**. _____

3. Describe a time you have been **mad**. _____

4. Recall a **mad** event you have attended. _____

5. List two things you can **paint**. _____

6. How would you **paint** an exciting story? _____

from Mary Chesnut's
Civil War

Name _____

Date _____

Grammar Link Possessive Pronouns

Possessive Pronouns	Possessive Adjectives
mine	me
yours	your
hers	her
his	his
its	its
ours	our
yours	your
theirs	their

A possessive adjective comes before a noun. A possessive pronoun stands alone. Both show that something belongs to someone.

Mary Chesnut wrote in **her** journal. The journal is **hers**.
That is **their** boat. The boat is **theirs**.
Mr. Jones, is this **your** hat? Mr. Jones, is this **yours?**

Practice Circle the correct form.

1. Mrs. Wigfall: Is that (your / yours) coat?

   Mr. Preston: No, it is not. (My / Mine) is green.

2. Mary Chesnut: Are the people from the North here?

   Mr. Chesnut: Yes, they are.

   Mary Chesnut: Is (their / theirs) fort strong?

   Mr. Chesnut: Yes, (theirs / their) is strong.

3. Mrs. Smith: Is that (your / yours) book?

   Mrs. King: No, it is not (my / mine). I thought it was (yours / your).

4. Mr. Manning: Where is (theirs / their) army?

   Mr. Miles: (Their / Theirs) is inside the fort.

   Mr. Manning: Is (our / ours) army inside the fort, too?

   Mr. Miles: No, (ours / our) is on the island.

5. Mr. Chesnut: Is that Mrs. Wigfall's horse?

   Mr. Wigfall: Yes, it is (her / hers).

   Mr. Chesnut: It looks like (your / yours) horse.

   Mr. Wigfall: No, it does not look like my horse. (My / Mine) has spots.

I Hear America Singing *and*
When I Heard the Learn'd Astronomer

Name _____   Date _____

Directions: As you read "I Hear America Singing" and "When I Heard the Learn'd Astronomer," use the chart below to visualize details from the poems.

Detail	What I Pictured
"I Hear America Singing" 1. "The boatman singing what belongs to him in his boat, the deckhand singing on the steamboat deck" 2. "The delicious singing of the mother, or of the young wife at work, or of the girl sewing or washing" 3. "When I Heard the Learn'd Astronomer" 4. "When the proofs, the figures, were ranged in columns before me" 5. "When I sitting heard the astronomer where he lectured with much applause in the lecture-room" 6.	

I Hear America Singing and
When I Heard the Learn'd Astronomer

Name _____ Date _____

Grammar Link *While* and *When* with Past Time Clauses

1. *While* can begin a time clause.
2. The verb in a *while* clause is often in the past progressive tense.

WHILE

Main Clause	**Time Clause**
A man crossed the street	**while he was driving.**
Time Clause	**Main Clause**
While he was driving,	a man crossed the street.

3. *When* can begin a time clause.
4. The verb in a *when* clause is often in the simple past tense.

WHEN

Main Clause	**Time Clause**
Jenny was working in the office	**when Tony called.**
Time Clause	**Main Clause**
When Tony called,	Jenny was working in the office.

Practice Match the sentence parts below to find out what Walt Whitman did.

____ 1. Whitman was walking by the river when

a. he noticed a hole in his shoe.

____ 2. He was listening to the boatman when

b. the audience started to applaud.

____ 3. The shoemaker was singing when

c. the astronomer began his lecture.

____ 4. Walt was leaving the shoemaker when

d. he heard the boatman singing.

____ 5. Walt was sitting in a lecture-room when

e. he looked up at the stars.

____ 6. The astronomer was showing charts when

f. he decided to leave the lecture.

____ 7. Walt was feeling tired when

g. he heard the hatter singing.

____ 8. Walt was walking by himself when

h. Walt brought in his shoes.

If you were coming in the Fall
My life closed twice before its close
The Soul selects *her* own Society

Name _____ **Date** _____

Directions: As you read "If you were coming in the Fall," "My Life closed twice before its close," and "The Soul selects her own Society," use the chart below to keep track of the main ideas and supporting details for each poem.

"If you were coming in the Fall"	"My Life closed twice before its close"	"The Soul selects her own Society"
Main Idea: Parting is especially painful when it is uncertain how long it will last. **Supporting Details:** 1. The speaker is willing to wait months or even years without complaining. 2. 3.	**Main Idea:** **Supporting Details:** 1. 2. 3.	**Main Idea:** **Supporting Details:** 1. 2. 3.

The Celebrated Jumping Frog of Calaveras County

Name _____ **Date** _____

Directions: As you read "The Celebrated Jumping Frog of Calaveras County," use the web below to list different examples of comic devices from the story.

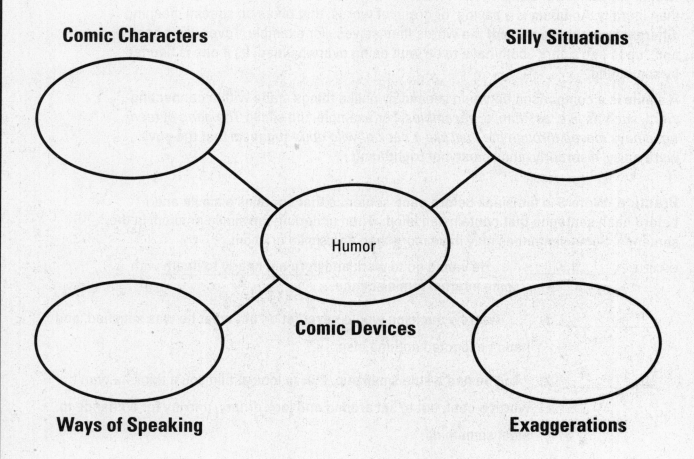

Comic Characters

Silly Situations

Humor

Comic Devices

Ways of Speaking

Exaggerations

The Celebrated Jumping Frog of Calaveras County

Name _____ Date _____

Word Study Figurative Language: Idioms and Similes

Idioms and similes are expressions meant to be understood imaginatively rather than literally. An **idiom** is a saying, or group of words, that takes on special meaning different from the meaning of the words themselves. For example, "over one's head" and "up to one's ears" both have to do with being overwhelmed, as if one is flooded by something.

A **simile** is a comparison between seemingly unlike things made with a connecting word, such as *like, as, than,* or *resembles*. For example, the simile *The gang of teen-aged boys moved through the mall like a pack of wild dogs* suggests that the boys were noisy, disorderly, and somewhat frightening.

Practice Write *S* in the blank before each sentence that contains a simile and *I* before each sentence that contains an idiom. Then underline the simile or idiom in the sentence. Some sentences may have more than one simile or idiom.

EXAMPLE: _____I_____ ". . . He would go to work and <u>bore me nearly to death</u> with some infernal reminiscence. . . ."

_____ **1.** ". . . Andrew Jackson would never let on but what he was satisfied, and hadn't expected nothing else. . . ."

_____ **2.** "And he had a little small pup, that to look at him you'd think he wan't worth a cent, but to set around and look ornery, and lay for a chance to steal something."

_____ **3.** ". . . He was a different dog; his under-jaw'd begin to stick out like the fo'castle of a steamboat.

_____ **4.** ". . . He saw in a minute how he'd been imposed on, and how the other dog had him in the door, so to speak, and he 'peared surprised. . . ."

_____ **5.** "Jumping on a dead level was his strong suit, you understand; and when it came to that, Smiley would ante up money on him."

_____ **6.** ". . . the next minute you'd see that frog whirling in the air like a doughnut. . ."

The Celebrated Jumping Frog of Calaveras County

Name _____ Date _____

Grammar Link   Simple and Compound Sentences

A **simple sentence** has one subject and one predicate.

SUBJECT	PREDICATE
Jason	**told** several tall tales.
Leanne and Greg	**laughed** at the stories.
The class **members**	**chose** a hero and **wrote** a tale.

A **compound sentence** contains two or more simple sentences joined by a comma and *and, but,* or *or.* They can also be joined by a semicolon (;).

Eli wrote the dialogue, **and** Erica was responsible for the plot.
Eli wrote the dialogue; Erica was responsible for the plot.

Practice   Write *S* in the blank before each simple sentence and *C* before each compound sentence. An example is provided.

EXAMPLE: _____S_____ You and I can probably summarize the story in a few sentences.

_____ **1.** The mare in the story wins her races, but the dog loses his last fight.

_____ **2.** The mare got excited and desperate, and she cavorted, kicked up dust, and charged ahead.

_____ **3.** Mark Twain and Bret Harte became friends when both lived in San Francisco.

_____ **4.** Twain lived in the West before settling in Connecticut.

_____ **5.** Twain was forced to quit school and become a printer's apprentice.

_____ **6.** I like *The Adventures of Tom Sawyer,* but everyone I know prefers *The Adventures of Huckleberry Finn.*

_____ **7.** His plan to travel to the Amazon fell through, but Twain happily became a riverboat pilot instead.

_____ **8.** Twain went West and took a job as a reporter.

_____ **10.** Twain was a product of the Mississippi Valley and the receding frontier.

A31

A Wagner Matinée

Name _____   **Date** _____

Directions: As you read "A Wagner Matinée," identify the story's main events. Use the chart below to record the story's main events in the sequence in which they happen. Focus on what Clark does with his aunt during the visit. Be careful not to confuse the main events with the flashbacks.

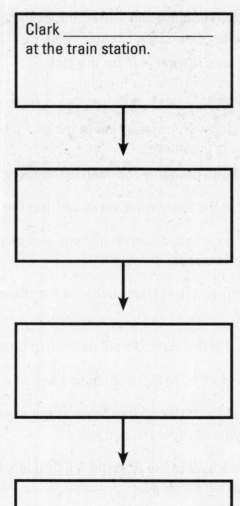

Beginning of story

Clark _____
at the train station.

End of story

A Wagner Matinée

Name _____ Date _____

Grammar Link Commas Before *and, but,* and *or*

Use a comma to separate two main clauses that are joined by *and, but,* or *or.* How do you know if you have two main clauses? A main clause is a group of words with a subject and a predicate. It can stand on its own and make sense.

Each underlined part in this sentence is a main clause:

<u>Aunt Georgiana had received a legacy</u>, and <u>she had to go to Boston to get it.</u>

Notice that when the two main clauses are joined by *and*, a comma goes before the word *and.*

If either part of the sentence is not a main clause, do not use the comma.

EXAMPLE: Aunt Georgiana had received a legacy and had to go to Boston to get it.

Notice that the second part of the sentence does not have a subject. It cannot stand on its own and make sense.

Practice Write *OK* on the line if the sentence is correct as written. If it is not correct, rewrite it correctly.

1. Aunt Georgiana had traveled all day and was very tired. _____

   _____

2. Clark wanted to take his aunt to the matinée but he was not sure how she would react.

   _____

3. They could have stayed in Boston, or they could have gone west. _____

   _____

4. Aunt Georgiana listened to the music and tears streamed down her face.

   _____

5. The music ended but Aunt Georgiana did not want to leave. _____

   _____

Douglass and WE WEAR THE MASK

Name _____ **Date** _____

Directions: Use this graphic organizer as you read the poems "Douglass" and "We Wear the Mask." When you come to a confusing part, write it in the first column under the poem's title. In the second column under the poem's title, write how you could clarify the meaning of the confusing part.

"Douglass"		"We Wear the Mask"	
Confusing Things	Ways to Clarify	Confusing Things	Ways to Clarify

The *Love* Song of
J. Alfred Prufrock

Name _____   Date _____

Directions: As you read "The Love Song of J. Alfred Prufrock," use the chart below to list T. S. Eliot's descriptions of life in London in the early 1900s.

Descriptions of Place	Descriptions of Clothing	Descriptions of People
1. The streets are almost empty.	1. Prufrock wears a dress coat.	1. The women think Michelangelo is important.
2.	2.	2.
3.	3.	3.
4.	4.	4.
5.	5.	5.

The *Love* Song of
J. Alfred Prufrock

Name _____   Date _____

Grammar Link   Word Order of Adjectives

When we use two or more adjectives, we use this general order.

	1. Opinion	2. Size	3. Age	4. Color	5. Material	6. Nationality	
	beautiful						
	beautiful	large					
It's a	beautiful	large	old				box.
	beautiful	large	old	red			
	beautiful	large	old	red	wooden		
	beautiful	large	old	red	wooden	Chinese	

Note: We do not usually use more than two or three adjectives with one noun.

Practice   Circle a or an and put the adjectives in the correct order.

1. yellow/heavy   a / an _____ fog

2. new/tedious   a / an _____ book

3. trailing/satin   a / an _____ skirt

4. small/pleasant   a / an _____ party

5. red/new/silk   a / an _____ necktie

6. wooden/comfortable   a / an _____ chair

7. dark/old   a / an _____ street

8. silver/antique   a / an _____ pitcher

9. French/charming/new   a / an _____ song

10. brick/tall   a / an _____ house

The *Jilting* of Granny Weatherall

Name _____ Date _____

Directions: As you read "The Jilting of Granny Weatherall," write details about the things that happened during the different times of Granny's life.

On the day she was jilted

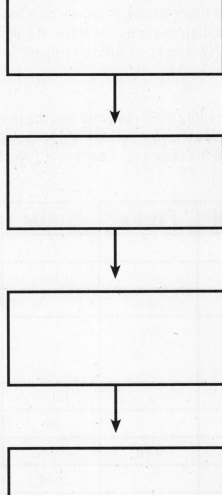

As a young mother

After her husband died

As an old woman

The *Jilting* of Granny Weatherall

Name _____   Date _____

Word Study   Base Words

One good way of understanding the meaning of a word is to look at its parts. For example, the word *uneasy* is formed from the **base word** *ease,* the prefix *un-* and the suffix *-y.* A prefix is a word part that is added to the beginning of a base word. A suffix is a word part that is added to the end. (Often it is necessary to adjust the spelling of the base word to fit the prefix and suffix onto it.) A word can have both a prefix and a suffix (*uneasy*), or just one of those (*easy*), or simply be a base word alone (*ease*). A word can also have more than one prefix or suffix at a time. An example is *unfavorably*, which has one prefix (*un-*) and two suffixes (*-able* and *-ly*) attached to the base word *favor.*

Practice For each word below, identify the base word and the prefix or suffix. The word will have an asterisk beside it if you should change the spelling of the base word when the suffix is added. Use the meaning of each word part to figure out the meaning of the entire word.

Word	Base Word	Prefix	Suffix	Meaning
morally	moral		ly	in a moral way
tactful	tact		ful	full of tact
unfamiliar	familiar	un		not familiar
twilight	light	twi		two lights (the light that consists of both daylight and night)
carefully	care		ful, ly	in a way full of care
* vanity	vain		ity	the quality of being vain
forehead	head	fore		front part of the head
* monstrous	monster		ous	like a monster
* unbelievable	believe	un	able	not able to be believed
* enlarged	large	en	ed	made larger

The *Jilting* of Granny Weatherall

Name _____ **Date** _____

Grammar Link Sentence Fragments

A **sentence fragment** is an incomplete sentence. A sentence fragment might lack a subject or a verb. Or it might be a subordinate clause.

Granny Weatherall.	Missing a subject
Thinks about George.	Missing a verb
Because he jilted her on their wedding day.	Subordinate clause
Granny Weatherall thinks about George.	Complete sentence
He jilted her on their wedding day.	Complete sentence

Writers sometimes use sentence fragments to create a special effect. Often, writers use sentence fragments in dialogue to imitate the sound of speech. Usually, however, complete sentences are clearer than sentence fragments.

Practice Write whether each sentence fragment needs a subject, needs a verb, or is a subordinate clause. Then, rewrite each sentence fragment as a complete sentence.

EXAMPLE: Feels great pain. ____Needs subject.____ *Granny Weatherall feels great pain.*

1. Is on her deathbed. _____

    _____

2. Her daughter Cornelia. _____

    _____

3. Doctor Harry. _____

    _____

4. Because she remembers her child, Hapsy. _____

    _____

5. Wants to clean the house. _____

    _____

6. Wishes she could throw away her old love letters. _____

    _____

WHEN THE NEGRO WAS IN VOGUE

Name _____ **Date** _____

Directions: In "When the Negro Was in Vogue," Langston Hughes uses details that appeal to the five senses. As you read, make notes of details that appeal to the senses of sight, hearing, touch, taste, and smell in the boxes below.

Sight

Hearing

Touch

Taste

Smell

WHEN THE NEGRO WAS IN VOGUE

Name _____ Date _____

Grammar Link   Comparative Forms of Adjectives: –er and *more*

When we compare things, we use a comparative adjective + *than*.

1. Short adjectives (one syllable): Add –er.

Adjective	Comparative Adjective
old	older **than**
hot	hot**ter*** **than**

   *If an adjective ends in one vowel and one consonant, double the consonant.

2. One and two syllable adjectives ending in *y:* Change *y* to *i* and add –er. If you are unsure of which form is correct, use a dictionary.

Adjective	Comparative Adjective
happy	happ**ier than**
friendly	friendl**ier than**

3. Long adjectives (two syllables or more): Use the word *more* in front of the adjective.

Adjective	Comparative Adjective
difficult	**more** difficult **than**
beautiful	**more** beautiful **than**

4. Irregular adjectives:

Adjective	Comparative Adjective
good	**better than**
bad	**worse than**

Practice A Write the comparative form of the adjective.

1. small _____

2. bad _____

3. interesting _____

4. funny _____

Practice B Complete the sentences about Monica and Olivia. Use the comparative form of the words in parentheses.

1. Olivia is (young) _____ Monica.

2. Monica is (tall)_____ Olivia.

3. Olivia's hair is (dark) _____ Monica's hair.

4. Monica is (friendly)_____ Olivia.

The Rockpile

Name _____ **Date** _____

Directions: As you read "The Rockpile," write details about the characters. Write things that the characters do or say in the correct column. Think about what generalizations can be made about the characters.

Roy	John	Elizabeth	Sister McCandless	Gabriel

The Rockpile

Name _____ Date _____

Grammar Link   Run-on Sentences

A **run-on sentence** is two or more already complete sentences written as if they are one sentence. You can fix this problem in different ways.

1. Break the run-on into separate sentences.
2. Separate the individual sentences with a semicolon.
3. Add the correct coordinating conjunction (usually *and, but,* or *or*).
4. Rewrite the sentences to present the same information in a different way.

Run-on Sentence

Roy wants to play outside on the rockpile John is afraid to.

Possible Corrections

1. Roy wants to play outside on the rockpile. John is afraid to.
2. Roy wants to play outside on the rockpile; John is afraid to.
3. Roy wants to play outside on the rockpile, but John is afraid to.
4. Although Roy wants to play outside on the rockpile, that idea frightens John.

When deciding which method to use, think about what best conveys the meaning you intend. Also, consider sentence length. Many short sentences in a row can make your writing seem immature; however, many long and sophisticated sentences in a row can make your writing confusing.

Practice   Nearly all run-on sentences are mistakes. However, very occasionally—and very carefully—an author might use them on purpose, for dramatic effect. In dialogue a run-on can make it sound as if the person is speaking very quickly, without stopping for breath. In "The Rockpile," Baldwin uses run-ons at the moment Roy is injured, to give the reader a sense of how fast things seem to be moving. The two-sentence passage below comes from page 000 of "The Rockpile." How could you revise the passage to avoid the two run-ons? Write your answer on the lines provided.

Immediately, one side of Roy's face ran with blood, he fell and rolled on his face down the rocks. Then for a moment there was no movement at all, no sound, the sun, arrested, lay on the street and the sidewalk and the arrested boys.

_____

_____

THE CRUCIBLE, ACT 1

Name _____ Date _____

Directions: In *The Crucible,* it can be hard to figure out what really happened. Imagine you are a detective. As you read, write the facts of the case in column 1. Write people's opinions about what happened in column 2.

Fact	Opinion
Abigail, Betty, and the other girls danced in the woods.	Parris thinks dancing is evil.
Ruth is sick.	Mrs. Putnam thinks Ruth's sickness is caused by the Devil.

THE CRUCIBLE, ACT 1

Name _____ **Date** _____

Word Study Homophones

Homophones are words that sound the same but mean something different (in fact the word *homophone* literally means "of the same sound"). Usually homophones also have different spellings (like *see* and *sea*).

Practice Each of the lines below is from *The Crucible*. Each also contains an underlined word that is a homophone. Figure out the homophone and then write a sample sentence using it in the space provided.

1. Why, <u>it's</u> sure she did.

   homophone: _____

   sample sentence: _____

2. Why, how does Ruth <u>ail</u>?

   homophone: _____

   sample sentence: _____

3. Her <u>soul</u> is taken, surely.

   homophone: _____

   sample sentence: _____

4. He has indeed; and found a <u>witch</u> in Beverly last year, and let you remember that.

   homophone: _____

   sample sentence: _____

5. . . . I am certain there be no element of witchcraft <u>here</u>.

   homophone: _____

   sample sentence: _____

THE CRUCIBLE, ACT 1

Name _____ **Date** _____

Grammar Link   Interrogative Sentences

An **interrogative sentence** is a sentence that asks a question. Interrogatives are easy
to spot because they end with a question mark. They often begin with a question
word, such as *who, what, where, when, why,* or *how.* They may also start with
the main verb of the sentence, as, for example, *Did you hear something just now?*
Heard out loud, an interrogative sentence is also fairly easy to identify, because the
speaker's voice goes up in pitch at the end of the sentence.

Practice All the sentences below come from *The Crucible.* Some are interrogative
sentences and some are not. Read each one aloud. Does it sound like a question?
Place a check in the box beside each interrogative sentence.

☐ **1.** What does the doctor say, child

☐ **2.** Go directly home and speak nothing of unnatural causes

☐ **3.** Your name in the town—it is entirely white, is it not

☐ **4.** I will not have it said my name is soiled

☐ **5.** Why, that's strange

☐ **6.** Why aren't you home

☐ **7.** Mercy, you go home to Ruth, d'y'hear

☐ **8.** Do you mean to tell me you've never looked up at my window

☐ **9.** I never spoke on witches one way or the other

☐ **10.** Will it hurt the child, sir

THE CRUCIBLE, ACT 1

Name _____ Date _____

Grammar Link   Exclamatory and Imperative Sentences

Exclamatory sentences are sentences that express strong feelings, such as surprise or anger. They always end with an exclamation mark.

Imperative sentences express commands. They end with an exclamation mark or a period. Usually, the subject of the sentence is understood to be *you,* but the word itself might be omitted.

Practice A   Each sentence below is from *The Crucible*. Each one is also an exclamation, an imperative, or both. Circle the correct designation for each one.

1. Betty, you never say that again!
   Exclamation   Imperative   Both

2. There be children dyin' in the village, Mister!
   Exclamation   Imperative   Both

3. Clasp his hand, make your peace.
   Exclamation   Imperative   Both

4. That's deep, Mr. Parris, deep, deep!
   Exclamation   Imperative   Both

Practice B   Emotions run high in *The Crucible*, so there are many exclamations in the dialogue. For each exclamation below, circle the emotion that you think the person is feeling as he or she says the line.

1. I am writing since November for a stick, and even in November I had to show my frostbitten hands like some London beggar! (spoken by Reverend Parris when he is complaining about his treatment by the villagers)
   Joy   Shock   Outrage   Surprise

2. And then she close her book and walks out of the house, and suddenly—mark this—I could pray again! (spoken by Giles Corey when he's talking about how his wife reads books that she won't show him)
   Amazement   Delight   Amusement   Boredom

3. Oh, God bless you Mr. Hale! (spoken by Tituba after Hale tells her she'll be forgiven now that she has confessed to witchcraft)
   Nervousness   Hilarity   Horror   Relief

AMBUSH   THE Gift IN WARTIME
from Stay Alive, My Son

Name _____ **Date** _____

Directions: As you read the selections, think about the concrete details each author includes. Use the chart below to list concrete details from each selection. Then, note whether the detail is related to the sense of sight, hearing, smell, taste, or touch. Finally, write an idea or feeling the detail suggests.

Detail	Sense	Idea or Feeling
"The night was foggy."	sight	the narrator cannot see and may be scared

AMBUSH THE Gift IN WARTIME
from Stay Alive, My Son

Name _____ **Date** _____

Grammar Link   Adjectives and Adverbs

Adverbs and adjectives look similar, but they do different things.

An adjective describes a noun. It usually answers the question *what*.

An adverb often answers the question *how*. Adverbs describe verbs, adjectives, or other adverbs.

FORM

Adjective		Adverb		Rules for Forming Adverbs
stow beautiful	quick bad	slow**ly** beautiful**ly**	quick**ly** bad**ly**	For most adverbs, we add *-ly* to an adjective.
happy	easy	happ**ily**	eas**ily**	If the adjective ends in *y*, we change the *y* to *i* and then add *-ly*.
hard late	fast early	hard late	fast early	Some adverbs are the same as the adjective.
good		well		The adverb form of *good* is *well*.

FUNCTION

Adjectives and adverbs look similar, but they do different things.

1. An adjective describes a noun and usually answers the question *what*.
   What color is the car? The car is **red**.
2. An adverb often answers the question *how*. Adverbs describe verbs, adjectives, and other adverbs.
   How does she dance? She dances **beautifully**. She dances **very beautifully**.

Practice   Pin Yathay has many strengths. Here are some of them. Underline the correct form of the adjective or adverb.

1. He is a (good / well) writer.

2. He remembers the past (clear / clearly).

3. He solves problems (careful / carefully).

4. He is often (helpful / helpfully) to people.

5. He speaks (good / well).

Snw

Name _____ **Date** _____

Remember, when authors use indirect characterization, they tell you what a character is like by showing
- the character's words
- the character's actions
- what others think and say about the character

Directions: As you read, use the charts below to list examples of indirect characterization of Yolanda and Sister Zoe. Then write down what each example tells you about the character.

Sister Zoe	
Example of Indirect Characterization	**What It Tells Me About the Character**
Sister Zoe tells Yolanda she has a lovely name.	Sister Zoe is nice. She is trying to make Yolanda feel comfortable.

Yolanda	
Example of Indirect Characterization	**What It Tells Me About the Character**

SALVADOR
LATE OR EARLY

Name _____ **Date** _____

Directions: What kind of person is Salvador? As you read, complete the chart below. On the left, write details from the story about Salvador. On the right, explain what each detail tells you about him.

Detail About Salvador	What the Detail Tells Me About Salvador
1. Salvador has crooked hair and crooked teeth.	1. Salvador may not have time to take care of his hair and teeth. He is probably a very busy person.

Thoughts on the African-American Novel

Name _____ **Date** _____

Directions: As you read, practice finding the main idea and supporting details. Write down the main idea of each paragraph. Then write down one detail that supports it.

Paragraph 1

Main Idea: The novel serves a purpose for the class of people that write it.

Supporting Detail: "early works such as *Pamela,* by Samuel Richardson, and the Jane Austen material provided social rules and explained behavior"

Paragraph 2

Main Idea: _____

Supporting Detail: _____

_____

Paragraph 3

Main Idea: _____

Supporting Detail: _____

_____

Paragraph 4

Main Idea: _____

Supporting Detail: _____

_____

Paragraph 5

Main Idea: _____

Supporting Detail: _____

_____

Thoughts on the African-American Novel

Name _____ Date _____

Grammar Link **Comparative and Superlative Forms of Adverbs: *–er* and *More***

A snail moves **more slowly** than a tortoise.
In fact, a snail moves the **most slowly** of all animals.
A duck walks **less easily** than it swims.

Adverb	Comparative	Superlative	
easily	more/less easily	the most/least easily	We compare adverbs ending in *–ly* with *more* and the *most*, or *less* and the *least*.
slowly	more/less slowly	the most/least slowly	
carefully	more/less carefully	the most/least carefully	
fast	faster	the fastest	For adverbs that have the same form as adjectives, we use *–er* and *–est*.
hard	harder	the hardest	
early	earlier	the earliest	
well	better	the best	*Well* is an irregular adverb.

Practice Complete each sentence using the comparative or superlative form of the adverb in italics. Follow the example.

1. I read Morrison's essay *carefully* the first time, and then I read it again <u>more carefully</u>.

2. Society can change *fast,* but during the Industrial Revolution it changed _____ than ever before.

3. Some forms of music once belonged *exclusively* to African Americans, but now that music belongs _____ to African Americans.

4. African Americans *likely* needed a new form of expression, and they _____ needed a guide to using their new social status.

5. Any novel can connect *intimately* with readers, but a novel rooted in the oral tradition can connect _____.

6. Many writers write *thoughtfully* about race. Morrison writes _____ of all.

Functional and Workplace
DOCUMENTS

Name _____ **Date** _____

Directions: As you read "Functional Documents," list each type of functional document in column 1. Then write the purpose for each type of document in column 2. The first one is completed for you as an example.

Type of Document	Purpose of Document
1. Letter of Application	To show your interest in and qualifications for a job
2.	
3.	
4.	
5.	
6.	
7.	

During Reading

The SKY TREE
How the LEOPARD Got His Claws
Prayer to the Pacific

Name _____ **Date** _____

Directions: Use this graphic organizer as you read "The Sky Tree," "How the Leopard Got His Claws," and "Prayer to the Pacific." Write your questions in column 1. When you know an answer, write it in the second column.

Questions	Answers
1. Why did Aataentsic cut down the tree that gave everyone food?	1. She did not want her husband to die.

During Reading

The SKY TREE
How the LEOPARD Got His Claws
Prayer to the Pacific

Name _____ **Date** _____

Word Study | Synonyms and Antonyms

Synonyms are words that have the same or nearly the same meanings. **Antonyms** are words that have the opposite or nearly the opposite meanings. Both synonyms and antonyms must be the same part of speech.

Sickness and *disease* are synonyms; both mean the same thing and both are nouns. *Sickness* and *ill* are not synonyms because one is a noun and the other is an adjective.

Sickness and *health* are antonyms; they have opposite meanings and both are nouns. *Sickness* and *well* are not synonyms; one is a noun, the other an adjective.

Practice A On the first blank following each of the boldfaced words from the selections write a synonym for the word. On the second blank, indicate what part of speech the synonyms are. Use a dictionary or thesaurus if you need help.

EXAMPLE: **scattered** _____ dispersed _____ _____ verb _____

1. **toppled** _____ tumbled _____ _____ verb _____
2. **soil** _____ earth _____ _____ noun _____
3. **claws** _____ nails _____ _____ noun _____
4. **excitement** _____ enthusiasm _____ _____ noun _____
5. **humming** _____ buzzing _____ _____ adjective _____

Practice B On the blank following each of the italicized words write an antonym that changes the meaning of the sentence.

EXAMPLE: The ruler of the country was very *wise* _____ foolish _____

1. The athlete looked at her opponent with *contempt* _____ admiration _____
2. The hot air balloon came down to earth very *gently* _____ roughly _____
3. All the students *immediately* _____ eventually _____ filed out of the auditorium.
4. In his review, the critic said that the lead actor's performance was *terrible* _____ wonderful _____
5. We all *laughed* _____ grieved _____ at the news of the election results.

The Sky Tree/How the Leopard Got His Claws/Prayer to the Pacific

Upon the *Burning of Our House* and *To My Dear and Loving Husband*

Name _____ Date _____

Directions: As you read "Upon the Burning of Our House" and "To My Dear and Loving Husband," write down lines you don't understand in the left column. In the right column, rewrite the lines in your own words.

Line from Poem		Rewrite
"When by the ruins oft I past"	→	I walked by the ruins a lot
	→	
	→	

Upon the Burning of Our House *and* To My Dear and Loving Husband

A5

The SKY TREE
How the LEOPARD Got His Claws
Prayer to the Pacific

Name _____ Date _____

Grammar Link Irregular Verbs: *Have, Do,* and *Go*

Kathy's classes finish at 4:00 every day.
Then she **goes** home.
She **has** a cup of coffee and **does** her homework.

The third person forms of *have, go,* and *do* are irregular.

	He	
	She	**has** a problem.
	It	
I **have** a job.	He	
I **do** the work.	She	**does** the work.
I **go** to work.	It	
	He	
	She	**goes** outside.
	It	

Practice Complete the sentences with the correct forms of the verbs in parentheses.

1. The Sky Tree (go) _____goes_____ through the hole in Sky Land.

2. Turtle (have) _____has_____ a good idea.

3. The dog and the duck (go) _____go_____ away from the other animals.

4. The animals (do) _____do_____ the work to build their shelter.

5. The leopard (go) _____goes_____ on a journey.

6. The leopard (have) _____has_____ new claws and a loud voice.

7. Now, the dog (do) _____does_____ work for the hunter.

8. Both "the Sky Tree" and "How the Leopard Got His Claws" (have) _____have_____ talking animals.

A4

A57

During Reading

Upon the Burning of Our House and *To My Dear and Loving Husband*

Name _____ Date _____

Grammar Link Past Time Expressions

Yesterday, last, and *ago* tell us when an action happened in the past. We use these words in the following ways.

yesterday	morning, afternoon, and evening
last	night, periods of time (week, month, year), days of the week, and seasons (summer, winter, spring, fall)
ago	lengths of time, for example, *five minutes ago*

Time expressions usually come at the beginning or at the end of a sentence. When they come at the beginning of a sentence, we use a comma after the time expressions.

Yesterday morning, I walked to school.

When a time expression comes at the end of a sentence, we do not use a comma before the expression.

I walked to school **yesterday morning.**

Practice Fill in the blanks with *yesterday, last,* or *ago.*

Anne: Where have you been? My house caught on fire two days _____ ago _____!

Ben: Oh no! I didn't know that. I was on vacation from _____ last _____ Tuesday until _____ yesterday _____ evening. Are you okay?

Anne: Yes, I'm okay. But I lost my beautiful house. It was very old. It was built fifty years _____ ago _____.

Ben: I'm so sorry.

Anne: I walked by the ruins _____ yesterday _____ afternoon. It made me think about the party we had _____ last _____ April. And it made me think about the wedding we had here _____ last _____ year.

Ben: That was your daughter's wedding, wasn't it? I saw her _____ yesterday _____ evening when I got back. Three years.... That was a long time _____ ago _____.

Anne: It was hard to sleep _____ last _____ night. I was thinking about the fire. Oh, I have to go. I was supposed to meet my daughter ten minutes _____ ago _____.

Ben: Yes, I have to do some things I should have done _____ yesterday _____.

During Reading

TIME How They Chose These Words

Name _____ Date _____

Directions: As you read "How They Chose These Words," use the boxes below to write the main idea of the article and the supporting details. Write down at least one supporting detail for each of the four sections of the article. Write the details first. When you have finished with the details, determine the main idea.

Supporting Details

Main Idea

Panel 1 (During Reading — Letter to John Adams)

Name _____ Date _____

Letter to John Adams

Directions: As you read "Letter to John Adams," think about the author's purpose. Use the chart below to list the descriptions she includes and the opinions she expresses.

Descriptions	Opinions
1. She describes the people fighting against America as "savage and bloodthirsty."	1. You cannot truly love freedom if you deprive some people of their liberties.
2.	2.
3.	3.
4.	4.
5.	5.

Letter to Adams

A9

Panel 2 (Grammar Link)

Name _____ Date _____

TIME How They Chose These Words

Grammar Link The Simple Past Tense:
Time Clauses with *Before* and *After*

1. A time clause begins with a conjunction such as *before* or *after*.
2. A time clause has a subject and a verb, but it is not a complete sentence.
3. A time clause must be used with a main clause to form a complete sentence.
4. A time clause can come before or after a main clause. The meaning is the same. If the time clause comes first, it has a comma after it.

Main Clause   **Time Clause**
Amy had dinner   before she did her homework.
Amy did her homework   after she had dinner.

Time Clause   **Main Clause**
Before the movie started,   we got some popcorn.
After the movie was over,   we went home.

Practice Underline the time clauses in the sentences. Circle the main clauses. Then rewrite the sentence and change the order of the clauses.

1. Before they voted on the question of independence, the Continental Congress chose a committee to write a document. _____ The Continental Congress chose a committee to write a

   document before they voted on the question of independence. _____

2. After the committee was chosen, Jefferson began work on the first draft. _____

   Jefferson began work on the first draft after the committee was chosen. _____

3. Jefferson gave the draft to Franklin after he completed it. _____

   After he completed it, Jefferson gave the draft to Franklin. _____

4. After Franklin received the draft, he edited it. _____

   Franklin edited the draft after he received it. _____

5. Before they signed the document, the members of the Continental Congress made some cuts. _____ The members of the Continental Congress made some cuts before they

   signed the document. _____

A8

A59

A60

Left page (A10)

During Reading

Name _____   Date _____

Letter to John Adams

Grammar Link The Present Perfect Tense of Be: *For and Since*

Affirmative Statement

Subject	Have/Has	Past Participle of *Be*	
I You	have		
He She It	has	been	here **for** two hours. **since** 10 o'clock.
We You They	have		

Practice Complete the sentences with the present perfect form of the verb be.

Abigail: I miss you! I __have been__ waiting for your letter for a month.

John: I'm sorry. I __have been__ trying to write for a long time, but I have been busy here.

Abigail: Dr. Crane __has been__ to our house since the soldiers left.

John: Please tell me how the house looks! I __have been__ wondering about it for weeks.

Abigail: The house __has been__ okay since we left. It is dirty, but not badly damaged.

John: That's good news. I __have been__ feeling well for the last few weeks. How about you?

Abigail: I am full of hope! Everything __has been__ better since the British left Boston.

John: I __have been__ feeling hopeful since the British left, too.

Abigail: I believe you __have been__ writing new laws since the last time we spoke.

John: We __have been__ working hard since then. I think we are making progress.

Abigail: As you work, please remember the ladies! They __have been__ treated unfairly for many years.

John: You are right. The law __has been__ unfair for too long. We will try to give women and men equal rights.

Copyright © by The McGraw-Hill Companies, Inc.

Right page (A11)

During Reading

Name _____   Date _____

CIVIL DISOBEDIENCE
On the Eve of Historic Dandi March
FROM LONG WALK TO FREEDOM

Directions: As you read the essays, think about the main arguments made by each author. Use the chart below to keep track of each essay's main idea and the reasons that support it.

from Civil Disobedience	On the Eve of Historic Dandi March	*from* Long Walk to Freedom
Main Idea: Thoreau believes _____	Main Idea: Gandhi believes _____	Main Idea: Mandela believes _____
Reasons: 1. Possible answer: Majority rule is not always just. 2. 3.	Reasons: 1. Possible answer: Going to prison will draw more followers. 2. 3.	Reasons: 1. Possible answer: South Africa's racial government was changed through courage. 2. 3.

from Civil Disobedience/On the Even of Historic Dandi March/*from* Long Walk to Freedom

A11

Name _____ Date _____

CIVIL DISOBEDIENCE
On the Eve of Historic Dandi March
FROM LONG WALK TO FREEDOM

Grammar Link Spelling of Regular Past Tense Verbs: Pronunciation of –ed: /t/, /d/, and /id/

Verb Ending	Spelling Rule	Examples
Most regular verbs	Add –ed	*rain, rained*
Verb ends in e	Add –d	*arrive, arrived*
Verb ends in consonant plus y	Change y to i and add –ed	*cry, cried*
Verb ends in vowel plus y	Add –ed	*enjoy, enjoyed*
Verb ends in one consonant plus vowel plus consonant (one-syllable verbs)	Double the consonant and add –ed	*stop, stopped*
Verb ends in x, w	Add –ed	*show, showed*
Verb ends in vowel plus consonant and stress is on first syllable (two-syllable verb)	Add –ed. Do not double the consonant.	*visit, visited*
Verb ends in vowel plus consonant and stress is on second syllable (two-syllable verb)	Double the consonant and add –ed.	*prefer, preferred*

Practice Write the correct spelling of the simple past tense form.

1. call — called
2. hurry — hurried
3. follow — followed
4. fix — fixed
5. hunt — hunted
6. chase — chased
7. swat — swatted
8. worry — worried
9. tie — tied
10. drop — dropped
11. carry — carried
12. bait — baited
13. fray — frayed
14. try — tried
15. drip — dripped
16. study — studied
17. waste — wasted
18. work — worked

Name _____ Date _____

CIVIL DISOBEDIENCE
On the Eve of Historic Dandi March
FROM LONG WALK TO FREEDOM

Word Study Negative Prefixes: *un-, im-, in-, il-, dis-, a-,* and *ir-*

Negative prefixes are word parts added to the beginnings of base words. Negative prefixes change the meaning of a word to its antonym. The following chart shows common negative prefixes:

Prefix Meaning "Not" or "Opposite Of"	Example Word
un-	unacceptable
dis-	displace
il-, im-, in-, ir-	irreversible
a-	amoral

Practice A Select the correct negative prefix from the list above that turns each of the following words into its antonym.

in-	1. convenient	ir-	4. regular
un-	2. fair	il-	5. logical
dis-	3. honest	im-	6. possible

Practice B In the following sentences, add a negative prefix to the root word in parentheses.

1. The court order was (typical). atypical
2. Considering the blunder was his fault, the judge was surprisingly (apologetic). unapologetic
3. The investigation showed the mayor had been (honest) about his past. dishonest
4. Thoreau believes that many government actions are (expedient). inexpedient
5. Several (responsible) people placed an obstacle on the railroad track. irresponsible

The Pit and the Pendulum

Name _____ Date _____

Word Study Root Words and Word Origins

Word origins, also called **etymologies,** describe the history and development of words. They can be found in dictionary word entries, usually at the beginning or end of the entry. A typical word entry might look like this:

im pede (im pēd') v. **im ped ed; im ped ing** [L *impedire,* fr *in-* + *ped* foot] to slow or block progress or action; to obstruct

The word origin is the portion of the entry enclosed in brackets. The word origin for *impedire* indicates that it comes from the Latin word *impedire,* which has the same meaning as impede. *Impedire,* in turn, is made up of the prefix *in-* and the root *ped,* which means "foot." Some other words that share the root *ped* are *expedite,* "perform quickly"; *expedition,* "journey for a special purpose"; *pedestrian,* "a person on foot"; and *pedometer,* "instrument for recording how far one walks."

Root words, or base words, are words to which prefixes and suffixes can be added to form other words. You can often use your knowledge of roots, prefixes, and suffixes to figure out the meaning of an unfamiliar word.

Practice A Match each vocabulary word from "The Pit and the Pendulum" with the word that has the same origin. Use a dictionary if necessary.

1. deduce   a. expedient   **2**
2. impede   b. approximate **4**
3. lethargy   c. introduce   **1**
4. proximity d. lethe   **3**

Practice B Use your knowledge of word parts and word origins to answer the following questions. Put a check next to the correct definition of the italicized word. Use a dictionary to check your answers.

1. An *abduction* is the act of
   a. taking something away. ✓
   b. granting a favor.

2. A *profusion* of flowers is
   a. a small quantity of flowers.
   b. a large display of flowers. ✓

3. *Proximo* means occurring
   a. from time to time. ✓
   b. once a month.

4. A *lethargic* pet is
   a. active.
   b. lazy. ✓

The Pit and the Pendulum

Name _____ Date _____

Directions: As you read "The Pit and the Pendulum," keep track of the order of events in a flowchart.

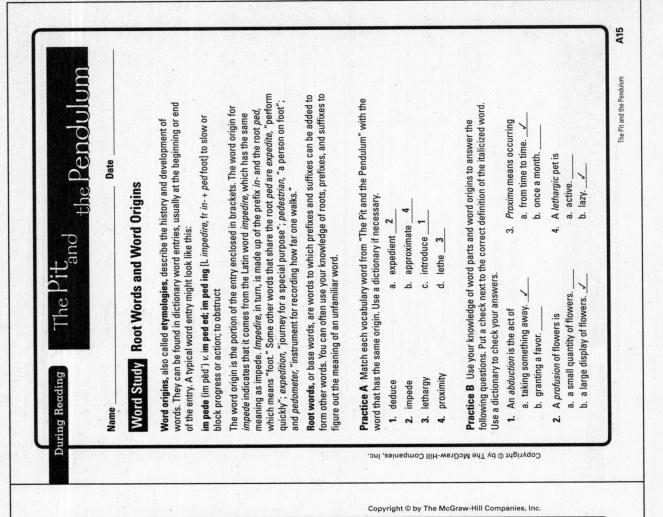

The court of the Inquisition sentences the hero to death.

→

The hero faints and wakes up in a dungeon.

→

The hero finds a deep pit in the middle of the dungeon. He thinks he is meant to fall into it.

→

He sleeps and wakes up strapped to a board. A razor-sharp pendulum swings above him. Some food is nearby. Rats swarm over it.

→

The pendulum descends slowly. It is within inches of the hero's chest.

→

The hero rubs food on his straps. The rats gnaw through them.

→

The hero is free, but his jailers have watched him escape.

→

The walls begin to move. The whole dungeon is fiery hot.

→

The walls push the hero toward the pit. He is going to fall in.

→

The French army arrives in the city. They defeat the Inquisition and free its prisoners. Just in time, a French general saves the hero.

The Pit and the Pendulum

Name _____ Date _____

Word Study Denotations and Connotations

Denotation is the literal, or dictionary, meaning of a word. **Connotation** is the implied, or cultural, meaning of a word. For example, *alarm* and *terror* both have the same denotation: "fear", but *alarm* suggests a sudden shock of fear whereas *terror* suggests the most extreme degree of fear.

Practice A Each word listed below is followed by two synonyms. Circle the synonym that has the more negative connotation. Use a dictionary to check your answers.

EXAMPLE: fat   overweight, (obese)

1. odd   bizarre, (grotesque)
2. trivial   unimportant, (petty)
3. die   (perish), pass away
4. agitation   (disturbance), excitement
5. unsatisfactory   unacceptable, (intolerable)

Practice B Each of the sentences below is followed by two synonyms for the italicized word in the sentence. Fill in the blanks with the appropriate synonym. Use a dictionary to check your answers.

1. A ___cackle___ is a meaner *laugh* than a ___guffaw___. (guffaw, cackle)

2. ___Shuddering___ is a more intense form of *trembling* than ___quivering___ is. (shuddering, quivering)

3. When you *endeavor* to do something, ___strive___ suggests a more serious, concentrated effort than ___attempt___ does. (attempt, strive)

4. If you wanted to replace the word *shocking* in a sentence, ___hideous___ would be a more precise choice than ___offensive___. (hideous, offensive)

5. A ___grimace___ is a *frown* that suggests the possibility of pain and is less threatening than a ___scowl___. (scowl, grimace)

The Pit and the Pendulum

Name _____ Date _____

Grammar Link Simple Past Tense: Irregular Verbs

Many verbs do not use the *—ed* verb form. The past form of these verbs is irregular.

Subject	Past Form of Verb (*to go*)
I	
You	
He/She/It	went
We	to Africa last year.
They	

Here are some common irregular verbs.

Base Form	Past Form	Base Form	Past Form
be	was/were	give	gave
come	came	have	had
do	did	hear	heard
eat	ate	make	made
feel	felt	tell	told
get	got	think	thought

Practice Fill in the blanks with the simple past tense of the irregular verbs in parentheses.

The hero of "The Pit and the Pendulum" (come) ___came___ before the court of the Inquisition. The court punished him for something he (do) ___did___. The court (tell) ___told___ him he must die for his crime. He fainted.

He woke up in a dark dungeon. He (feel) ___felt___ around the walls. A deep pit (be) ___was___ in the center of the dungeon.

The next time he woke up, the jailers (have) ___had___ tied him to a board. A heavy, sharp pendulum hung over him. The jailers also (give) ___gave___ him food, but rats (eat) ___ate___ most of it.

The hero (think) ___thought___ carefully. He rubbed food on his straps. The rats chewed the straps. The hero (be) ___was___ free!

Then he saw that the walls were moving. The walls (make) ___made___ the shape of a diamond to push him into the pit. Just when the hero was about to fall, the French army arrived.

The Pit and the Pendulum

FROM MY BONDAGE AND MY FREEDOM
Frederick Douglass IN TEXAS GRASS

Name _____ Date _____

Word Study **Context Meaning**

Context refers to the parts of a text just before and after a word that determine its meaning. The following chart shows some types of context clues.

Type of context clue	Example
Contrast	Unlike her former *kindly* manner, Mrs. Auld's behavior was now **dour**.
Example	The **rhetoric** of slavery included *speeches* and *essays* proclaiming that slave owners were caring for people unable to care for themselves.
Restatement	I used many **expedients** to continue my reading—any *method* or *device* that would keep my actions from my masters.

Practice Use the chart and the context clues in each sentence to figure out the meaning of the boldfaced word. Write your explanation in the space provided.

EXAMPLE: Douglass says that slavery **divested** his mistress from her good qualities. She was no longer sweet and kind.

Explanation: Divested means to take away, because the next sentence describes how she was after slavery affected her.

1. The dialogue and the speeches were as **redolent** of the principles of liberty as the first leaves in May are suggestive of spring. Possible answers follow practice items.

   filled with or suggestive; redolent and suggestive used in parallel ways

2. The increase of knowledge was **attended** with bitter, as well as sweet results.

   "was present"; both bitter and sweet results were present

3. I **loathed** them as the meanest and the most wicked of men.

   hated or strongly disliked; men described as meanest and most wicked

4. I was no longer the light-hearted, **gleesome** boy, full of mirth and play.

   as light-hearted; described full of play and mirth

from My Bondage and My Freedom/Frederick Douglass/In Texas Grass

---

FROM MY BONDAGE AND MY FREEDOM
Frederick Douglass IN TEXAS GRASS

Name _____ Date _____

Directions: As you read the selections, think about the main points made by each author about slavery and its effects. Use the chart below to keep track of each selection's main idea about freedom and slavery, and the reasons that support it.

from My Bondage and My Freedom	Frederick Douglass	In Texas Grass
Main Idea: Douglass thinks that slavery _____	Main Idea: Hayden believes _____	Main Idea: Troupe believes _____
Reasons: 1. _____	Reasons: 1. _____	Reasons: 1. _____
2. _____	2. _____	2. _____
3. _____	3. _____	3. _____

And Ain't I a Woman?

Name _____ Date _____

Directions: Sojourner Truth's speech includes many informal words and expressions. As you read "And Ain't I a Woman?" use the chart below to record examples of Truth's unique diction, or word choice. Then use context clues to help you figure out what each example means.

Unique Word Choice	Meaning
"all this here talking"	all of the discussion

Name _____ Date _____

FROM MY BONDAGE AND MY FREEDOM
Frederick Douglass IN TEXAS GRASS

Grammar Link Future Time Clauses with *Before, After,* and *When*

1. A future time clause can begin with *before, after,* or *when.*
2. When a time clause refers to the future, the verb is in the simple present tense.

	Time Clause			Main Clause	
	Simple Present			**Future**	
Before	Douglass	**goes**	home,	he **will study**	spelling.
When	he	**learns**	to read,	he **will know**	about slavery.
After	the slaves	**are**	freed,	they **will receive**	forty acres and a mule.

EXAMPLE: Before Douglass goes home, he will study spelling.

3. We can put the time clause before or after the main clause. They both have the same meaning.
   He will know about slavery **when he learns to read.**
   When he learns to read, he will know about slavery.
4. When the time clause comes first, we put a comma (,) after the time clause.

Practice Underline the time clauses in the sentences about Frederick Douglass.

1. Frederick Douglass will learn Latin and Greek before he becomes free.
2. Before she teaches Frederick to read, Mrs. Auld will talk to her husband.
3. Frederick Douglass will ask his friends before he buys the book.
4. When Mrs. Auld sees Frederick with a book, she will yell at him.
5. When Douglass feels discontented, he will read about the debate.
6. After he becomes a free man, Frederick Douglass will receive forty acres and a mule.
7. Douglass will dislike his master after he learns about slavery.
8. When all people are free, they will remember Frederick Douglass.

Name _____ Date _____

And Ain't I a Woman?

Grammar Link   Object Pronouns

Many sentences in English have a subject, a verb, and an object.

Noun Subject	Verb	Noun Object	Pronoun Subject	Verb	Pronoun Object
John	likes	rice.	He	likes	it.

The subject can be a noun (John). The subject can also be a pronoun (He). The object can be a noun (rice). The object can also be a pronoun (it).

We often use a pronoun in place of a noun. Here are the subject and object pronouns.

Subject Pronouns	Object Pronouns
I	me
you	you
he	him
she	her
it	it
we	us
they	them

Practice Replace the underlined words with a subject or object pronoun.

1. Sojourner Truth is a former slave. _____ She
2. In 1851, she gave a speech about women's rights. _____ it
3. She told the men in the crowd that women are strong. _____ them
4. Women are as strong as men, in Truth's opinion. _____ They
5. For example, men do not need to help women get into carriages. _____ them
6. Women have worked hard planting crops. _____ them
7. A female slave might have to be strong enough to give up her child. _____ She
8. Truth shared bible stories with the crowd. _____ them
9. "Christ came from a woman," she reminded them. _____ He
10. A woman named Eve changed the world on her own! _____ it

---

from Mary Chesnut's Civil War

Name _____ Date _____

Directions: As you read "from Mary Chesnut's Civil War," look for important events. Write the events in the correct order.

1. Mr. Chesnut agrees to help the Southern army fight against the North.
2.
3.
4.
5.

from Mary Chesnut's Civil War

Name _____ Date _____

from Mary Chesnut's
Civil War

Word Study Multiple-Meaning Words

The same word often has more than one meaning. Note the different meanings of the words *paint*, *mad*, and *stir*.

paint
1. to produce in lines and colors on a surface by applying colors
   *He **paints** portraits of his friends any chance he gets.*
2. to give a description of
   *The mayor **painted** a happy picture of the city's success.*

mad
1. having intense anger
   *The mother was very **mad** after the little boy ate all the cookies.*
2. marked by wild merriment
   *The birthday party was the **maddest** event I'd ever attended.*

stir
1. to mix
   *You have to **stir** the flour, eggs, and milk together to make the dough.*
2. a state of disturbance, agitation, or brisk activity
   *The mouse ran across the kitchen floor, causing quite a **stir**.*

Practice Write your answers to the following questions on the lines below.

1. List two things you can **stir**. Possible answers: **dough, sauces**

2. List something that causes a **stir**. Possible answer: a controversial book

3. Describe a time you have been **mad**. Possible answer: after losing a game

4. Recall a **mad** event you have attended. Possible answer: a friend's birthday party

5. List two things you can **paint**. Possible answers: mural, portrait

6. How would you **paint** an exciting story? Possible answers: using hand gestures, speaking in a louder voice

---

Name _____ Date _____

from Mary Chesnut's
Civil War

Grammar Link Possessive Pronouns

Possessive Pronouns	Possessive Adjectives
mine	me
yours	your
hers	her
his	his
its	its
ours	our
yours	your
theirs	their

A possessive adjective comes before a noun. A possessive pronoun stands alone. Both show that something belongs to someone.

Mary Chesnut wrote in **her** journal. The journal is **hers.**
That is **their** boat. The boat is **theirs.**
Mr. Jones, is this **your** hat? Mr. Jones, is this **yours?**

Practice Circle the correct form.

1. Mrs. Wigfall: Is that (your / yours) coat?
   Mr. Preston: No, it is not. (My / Mine) is green.

2. Mary Chesnut: Are the people from the North here?
   Mr. Chesnut: Yes, they are.

   Mary Chesnut: Is (their / theirs) fort strong?
   Mr. Chesnut: Yes, (theirs / their) is strong.

3. Mrs. Smith: Is that (your / yours) book?
   Mrs. King: No, it is not (my / mine). I thought it was (yours / your).

4. Mr. Manning: Where is (theirs / their) army?
   Mr. Miles: (Their / Theirs) is inside the fort.
   Mr. Manning: Is (our / ours) army inside the fort, too?
   Mr. Miles: No, (ours / our) is on the island.

5. Mr. Chesnut: Is that Mrs. Wigfall's horse?
   Mr. Wigfall: Yes, it is (her / hers).
   Mr. Chesnut: It looks like (your / yours) horse.
   Mr. Wigfall: No, it does not look like my horse. (My / Mine) has spots.

from Mary Chesnut's Civil War

Name _____ Date _____

I Hear America Singing *and*
When I Heard *the* Learn'd Astronomer

Grammar Link *While* and *When* with Past Time Clauses

1. *While* can begin a time clause.
2. The verb in a *while* clause is often in the past progressive tense.

WHILE

Main Clause	Time Clause
A man crossed the street	while he was driving.
Time Clause	**Main Clause**
While he was driving,	a man crossed the street.

3. *When* can begin a time clause.
4. The verb in a *when* clause is often in the simple past tense.

WHEN

Main Clause	Time Clause
Jenny was working in the office	when Tony called.
Time Clause	**Main Clause**
When Tony called,	Jenny was working in the office.

Practice Match the sentence parts below to find out what Walt Whitman did.

d 1. Whitman was walking by the river when   a. he noticed a hole in his shoe.

a 2. He was listening to the boatman when   b. the audience started to applaud.

h 3. The shoemaker was singing when   c. the astronomer began his lecture.

g 4. Walt was leaving the shoemaker when   d. he heard the boatman singing.

c 5. Walt was sitting in a lecture-room when   e. he looked up at the stars.

b 6. The astronomer was showing charts when   f. he decided to leave the lecture.

f 7. Walt was feeling tired when   g. he heard the hatter singing.

e 8. Walt was walking by himself when   h. Walt brought in his shoes.

A27

Name _____ Date _____

I Hear America Singing *and*
When I Heard *the* Learn'd Astronomer

Directions: As you read "I Hear America Singing" and "When I Heard the Learn'd Astronomer," use the chart below to visualize details from the poems.

Detail	What I Pictured
"I Hear America Singing"	
1. "The boatman singing what belongs to him in his boat, the deckhand singing on the steamboat deck"	
2. "The delicious singing of the mother, or of the young wife at work, or of the girl sewing or washing"	
3.	
"When I Heard the Learn'd Astronomer"	
4. "When the proofs, the figures, were ranged in columns before me"	
5. "When I sitting heard the astronomer where he lectured with much applause in the lecture-room"	
6.	

A26

A68

Name _____ Date _____

The Celebrated Jumping Frog of Calaveras County

Directions: As you read "The Celebrated Jumping Frog of Calaveras County," use the web below to list different examples of comic devices from the story.

Silly Situations

Exaggerations

Comic Devices

Humor

Comic Characters

Ways of Speaking

Name _____ Date _____

If you were coming in the Fall
My life closed twice before its close
The Soul selects her own Society

Directions: As you read "If you were coming in the Fall," "My Life closed twice before its close," and "The Soul selects her own Society," use the chart below to keep track of the main ideas and supporting details for each poem.

"If you were coming in the Fall"	"My Life closed twice before its close"	"The Soul selects her own Society"
Main Idea: Parting is especially painful when it is uncertain how long it will last.	**Main Idea:** Parting is the worst pain that we know.	**Main Idea:** Our choice of friends is not rational. Often we want only one intimate friend.
Supporting Details:	**Supporting Details:**	**Supporting Details:**
1. The speaker is willing to wait months or even years without complaining.	1. The speaker has twice experienced a pain like death.	1. The soul may reject multitudes of people, even emperors.
2. The speaker will wait centuries, or until the end of this lifetime.	2. The speaker does not know if she will experience such a pain again.	2. The soul may "shut the door" or "close the Valves of her attention" to people who seek her company.
3. The speaker compares uncertainty to the sting of a bee.	3. "Parting is . . . all we need of hell."	3. The soul can be "like Stone" to unwanted company.

The Celebrated Jumping Frog of Calaveras County

Name _____ Date _____

Word Study   Figurative Language: Idioms and Similes

Idioms and similes are expressions meant to be understood imaginatively rather than literally. An **idiom** is a saying, or group of words, that takes on special meaning different from the meaning of the words themselves. For example, "over one's head" and "up to one's ears" both have to do with being overwhelmed, as if one is flooded by something.

A **simile** is a comparison between seemingly unlike things made with a connecting word, such as *like*, *as*, *than*, or *resembles*. For example, the simile *The gang of teenaged boys moved through the mall like a pack of wild dogs* suggests that the boys were noisy, disorderly, and somewhat frightening.

Practice *Write S in the blank before each sentence that contains a simile and I before each sentence that contains an idiom. Then underline the simile or idiom in the sentence. Some sentences may have more than one simile or idiom.*

EXAMPLE: __I__   " . . . He would go to work and bore me nearly to death with some infernal reminiscence. . . ."

__I__   1. " . . . Andrew Jackson would never let on but what he was satisfied, and hadn't expected nothing else. . . ."

__I__   2. "And he had a little small pup, that to look at him you'd think he wan't worth a cent, but to set around and look ornery, and lay for a chance to steal something."

__S__   3. " . . . He was a different dog; his under-jaw'd begin to stick out like the fo'castle of a steamboat.

__I__   4. " . . . He saw in a minute how he'd been imposed on, and how the other dog had him in the door, so to speak, and he 'peared surprised. . . ."

__I__   5. "Jumping on a dead level was his strong suit, you understand; and when it came to that, Smiley would ante up money on him."

__S__   6. " . . . the next minute you'd see that frog whirling in the air like a doughnut. . . ."

The Celebrated Jumping Frog of Calaveras County

Name _____ Date _____

Grammar Link   Simple and Compound Sentences

A **simple sentence** has one subject and one predicate.

SUBJECT	PREDICATE
Jason	**told** several tall tales.
Leanne and Greg	**laughed** at the stories.
The class members	**chose** a hero and **wrote** a tale.

A **compound sentence** contains two or more simple sentences joined by a comma and *and*, *but*, or *or*. They can also be joined by a semicolon (;).

Eli wrote the dialogue, **and** Erica was responsible for the plot.
Eli wrote the dialogue; Erica was responsible for the plot.

Practice *Write S in the blank before each simple sentence and C before each compound sentence. An example is provided.*

EXAMPLE: __S__ You and I can probably summarize the story in a few sentences.

__C__   1. The mare in the story wins her races, but the dog loses his last fight.

__C__   2. The mare got excited and desperate, and she cavorted, kicked up dust, and charged ahead.

__S__   3. Mark Twain and Bret Harte became friends when both lived in San Francisco.

__S__   4. Twain lived in the West before settling in Connecticut.

__S__   5. Twain was forced to quit school and become a printer's apprentice.

__C__   6. I like *The Adventures of Tom Sawyer*, but everyone I know prefers *The Adventures of Huckleberry Finn.*

__C__   7. His plan to travel to the Amazon fell through, but Twain happily became a riverboat pilot instead.

__S__   8. Twain went West and took a job as a reporter.

__S__   10. Twain was a product of the Mississippi Valley and the receding frontier.

A Wagner Matinée

Name _____ Date _____

Grammar Link Commas Before *and, but, and or*

Use a comma to separate two main clauses that are joined by *and, but, or,* or *or.* How do you know if you have two main clauses? A main clause is a group of words with a subject and a predicate. It can stand on its own and make sense.

Each underlined part in this sentence is a main clause:

Aunt Georgiana had received a legacy, and she had to go to Boston to get it.

Notice that when the two main clauses are joined by *and,* a comma goes before the word *and.*

If either part of the sentence is not a main clause, do not use the comma.

EXAMPLE: Aunt Georgiana had received a legacy and had to go to Boston to get it.

Notice that the second part of the sentence does not have a subject. It cannot stand on its own and make sense.

Practice Write *OK* on the line if the sentence is correct as written. If it is not correct, rewrite it correctly.

1. Aunt Georgiana had traveled all day and was very tired. OK

   _____

2. Clark wanted to take his aunt to the matinée but he was not sure how she would react.

   Clark wanted to take his aunt to the matinée, but he was not sure how she would react.

3. They could have stayed in Boston, or they could have gone west. OK

   _____

4. Aunt Georgiana listened to the music and tears streamed down her face.

   Aunt Georgiana listened to the music, and tears streamed down her face.

5. The music ended but Aunt Georgiana did not want to leave.

   The music ended, but Aunt Georgiana did not want to leave.

A33

A Wagner Matinee

A Wagner Matinée

Name _____ Date _____

Directions: As you read "A Wagner Matinée," identify the story's main events. Use the chart below to record the story's main events in the sequence in which they happen. Focus on what Clark does with his aunt during the visit. Be careful not to confuse the main events with the flashbacks.

Beginning of story

| Clark _____ at the train station. |

→

| |

→

| |

→

| |

End of story

A32

A71

During Reading

Douglass and
WE WEAR THE MASK

Name _____ Date _____

Directions: Use this graphic organizer as you read the poems "Douglass" and "We Wear the Mask." When you come to a confusing part, write it in the first column under the poem's title. In the second column under the poem's title, write how you could clarify the meaning of the confusing part.

"Douglass"		"We Wear the Mask"	
Confusing Things	**Ways to Clarify**	**Confusing Things**	**Ways to Clarify**
Possible answer: Who is Douglass?	Possible answer: Read the footnotes to learn that the "Douglass" refers to Frederick Douglass.	Possible answer: What does the line "mouth with myriad subtleties" mean?	Possible answer: Read the footnotes and paraphrase the line in my own words: Say many things that are so slight that they are hard to notice.

During Reading

The *Love Song of*
J. Alfred Prufrock

Name _____ Date _____

Directions: As you read "The Love Song of J. Alfred Prufrock," use the chart below to list T. S. Eliot's descriptions of life in London in the early 1900s.

Descriptions of Place	Descriptions of Clothing	Descriptions of People
1. The streets are almost empty.	1. Prufrock wears a dress coat.	1. The women think Michelangelo is important.
2. It is evening.	2. The women wear trailing skirts and perfume.	2. People talk about literature and art.
3. A dark, heavy fog hangs in the air.	3. Prufrock parts his hair to hide his bald spot.	3. People eat toast, marmalade, and tea off fancy dishes.
4. The streets are narrow and winding.	4. Prufrock wears a necktie with a pin.	4. People chat and listen to music.
5. It is October.	5. The women wear bracelets and shawls.	5. People have servants.

The Love Song of J. Alfred Prufrock

Name _____ **Date** _____

The *Jilting* of Granny Weatherall

Directions: As you read "The Jilting of Granny Weatherall," write details about the things that happened during the different times of Granny's life.

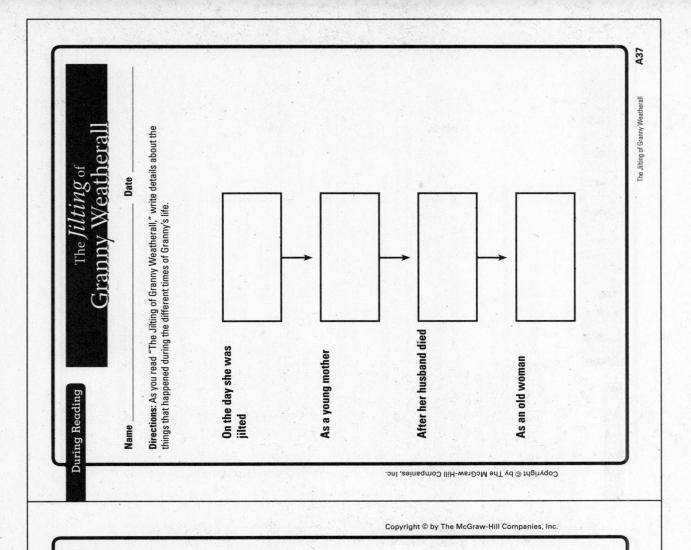

On the day she was jilted → ☐

As a young mother → ☐

After her husband died → ☐

As an old woman → ☐

Name _____ **Date** _____

The *Love* Song of J. Alfred Prufrock

Grammar Link Word Order of Adjectives

When we use two or more adjectives, we use this general order.

	1. Opinion	2. Size	3. Age	4. Color	5. Material	6. Nationality	
	beautiful	large					
	beautiful	large	old				
	beautiful	large	old	red			
	beautiful	large	old	red	wooden		
It's a	beautiful	large	old	red	wooden	Chinese	box.

Note: We do not usually use more than two or three adjectives with one noun.

Practice Circle a or an and put the adjectives in the correct order.

1. yellow/heavy   (a) an   heavy yellow _____ fog
2. new/tedious   (a) an   tedious new _____ book
3. trailing/satin   (a) an   trailing satin _____ skirt
4. small/pleasant   (a) an   pleasant small _____ party
5. red/new/silk   (a) an   new red silk _____ necktie
6. wooden/comfortable (a) an   comfortable wooden _____ chair
7. dark/old   a /(an)   old dark _____ street
8. silver/antique   a /(an)   antique silver _____ pitcher
9. French/charming/new (a) an   charming new French _____ song
10. brick/tall   (a) an   tall brick _____ house

The *Jilting* of Granny Weatherall

Name _____ Date _____

Word Study Base Words

One good way of understanding the meaning of a word is to look at its parts. For example, the word *uneasy* is formed from the **base word** *ease*, the prefix *un-* and the suffix *-y*. A prefix is a word part that is added to the beginning of a base word. A suffix is a word part that is added to the end. (Often it is necessary to adjust the spelling of the base word to fit the prefix and suffix onto it.) A word can have both a prefix and a suffix (*uneasy*), or just one of those (*easy*), or simply be a base word alone (*ease*). A word can also have more than one prefix or suffix at a time. An example is *unfavorably*, which has one prefix (*un-*) and two suffixes (*-able* and *-ly*) attached to the base word *favor*.

Practice For each word below, identify the base word and the prefix or suffix. The word will have an asterisk beside it if you should change the spelling of the base word when the suffix is added. Use the meaning of each word part to figure out the meaning of the entire word.

Word	Base Word	Prefix	Suffix	Meaning
morally	moral		ly	in a moral way
tactful	tact		ful	full of tact
unfamiliar	familiar	un		not familiar
twilight	light	twi		two lights (the light that consists of both daylight and night)
carefully	care		ful, ly	in a way full of care
* vanity	vain		ity	the quality of being vain
forehead	head	fore		front part of the head
* monstrous	monster		ous	like a monster
* unbelievable	believe	un	able	not able to be believed
* enlarged	large	en	ed	made larger

The *Jilting* of Granny Weatherall

Name _____ Date _____

Grammar Link Sentence Fragments

A **sentence fragment** is an incomplete sentence. A sentence fragment might lack a subject or a verb. Or it might be a subordinate clause.

Granny Weatherall.	Missing a subject
Thinks about George.	Missing a verb
Because he jilted her on their wedding day.	Subordinate clause
Granny Weatherall thinks about George.	Complete sentence
He jilted her on their wedding day.	Complete sentence

Writers sometimes use sentence fragments to create a special effect. Often, writers use sentence fragments in dialogue to imitate the sound of speech. Usually, however, complete sentences are clearer than sentence fragments.

Practice Write whether each sentence fragment needs a subject, needs a verb, or is a subordinate clause. Then, rewrite each sentence fragment as a complete sentence.

EXAMPLE: Feels great pain. _____   *Granny Weatherall feels great pain.*

1. Is on her deathbed. _____ Needs subject _____
   Granny Weatherall is on her deathbed.

2. Her daughter Cornelia. _____ Needs verb _____
   Her daughter Cornelia is helping around the house.

3. Doctor Harry. _____ Needs verb _____
   Doctor Harry comes to see her.

4. Because she remembers her child, Hapsy. _____ subordinate clause
   She remembers her child, Hapsy.

5. Wants to clean the house. _____ Needs subject _____
   Granny wants to clean the house.

6. Wishes she could throw away her old love letters. _____ Needs subject _____
   She wishes she could throw away her old love letters.

Name _____ Date _____

WHEN THE NEGRO WAS IN VOGUE

Grammar Link **Comparative Forms of Adjectives:** *—er* and *more*

When we compare things, we use a comparative adjective + *than*.

1. Short adjectives (one syllable): Add *—er*.

Adjective	Comparative Adjective
old	older **than**
hot	hotter* **than**

*If an adjective ends in one vowel and one consonant, double the consonant.

2. One and two syllable adjectives ending in *y*. Change *y* to *i* and add *—er*. If you are unsure of which form is correct, use a dictionary.

Adjective	Comparative Adjective
happy	happier **than**
friendly	friendlier **than**

3. Long adjectives (two syllables or more): Use the word *more* in front of the adjective.

Adjective	Comparative Adjective
difficult	more difficult **than**
beautiful	more beautiful **than**

4. Irregular adjectives:

Adjective	Comparative Adjective
good	better **than**
bad	worse **than**

Practice A Write the comparative form of the adjective.

1. small _____ smaller than _____   3. interesting _____ more interesting than _____

2. bad _____ worse than _____   4. funny _____ funnier than _____

Practice B Complete the sentences about Monica and Olivia. Use the comparative form of the words in parentheses.

1. Olivia is (young) _____ younger than _____ Monica.

2. Monica is (tall) _____ taller than _____ Olivia.

3. Olivia's hair is (dark) _____ darker than _____ Monica's hair.

4. Monica is (friendly) _____ friendlier than _____ Olivia.

Name _____ Date _____

WHEN THE NEGRO WAS IN VOGUE

Directions: In "When the Negro Was in Vogue," Langston Hughes uses details that appeal to the five senses. As you read, make notes of details that appeal to the senses of sight, hearing, touch, taste, and smell in the boxes below.

Sight

Hearing

Touch

Taste

Smell

During Reading

The Rockpile

Name _____ Date _____

Grammar Link   Run-on Sentences

A **run-on sentence** is two or more already complete sentences written as if they are one sentence. You can fix this problem in different ways.

1. Break the run-on into separate sentences.
2. Separate the individual sentences with a semicolon.
3. Add the correct coordinating conjunction (usually *and, but,* or *or*).
4. Rewrite the sentences to present the same information in a different way.

Run-on Sentence

Roy wants to play outside on the rockpile John is afraid to.

Possible Corrections

1. Roy wants to play outside on the rockpile. John is afraid to.
2. Roy wants to play outside on the rockpile; John is afraid to.
3. Roy wants to play outside on the rockpile, but John is afraid to.
4. Although Roy wants to play outside on the rockpile, that idea frightens John.

When deciding which method to use, think about what best conveys the meaning you intend. Also, consider sentence length. Many short sentences in a row can make your writing seem immature; however, many long and sophisticated sentences in a row can make your writing confusing.

Practice Nearly all run-on sentences are mistakes. However, very occasionally—and very carefully—an author might use them on purpose, for dramatic effect. In dialogue a run-on can make it sound as if the person is speaking very quickly, without stopping for breath. In "The Rockpile," Baldwin uses run-ons at the moment Roy is injured, to give the reader a sense of how fast things seem to be moving. The two-sentence passage below comes from page 000 of "The Rockpile." How could you revise the passage to avoid the two run-ons? Write your answer on the lines provided.

Immediately, one side of Roy's face ran with blood, he fell and rolled on his face down the rocks. Then for a moment there was no movement at all, no sound, the sun, arrested, lay on the street and the sidewalk and the arrested boys.

Possible answer: Immediately, one side of Roy's face ran with blood. He fell and rolled on his face down the rocks. Then for a moment there was no movement at all, and no sound; the sun, arrested, lay on the street and the sidewalk and the arrested boys.

During Reading

The Rockpile

Name _____ Date _____

Directions: As you read "The Rockpile," write details about the characters. Write things that the characters do or say in the correct column. Think about what generalizations can be made about the characters.

Roy	John	Elizabeth	Sister McCandless	Gabriel
Possible answers: "Roy shifted impatiently," "Roy felt it to be his right, not to say his duty, to play there," "Roy began to fidget"	Possible answers: "John said nothing… he was afraid of the rockpile and the boys who played there."	Possible answers: "'You children stay away from there, you hear me?' Though she said 'children,' she was looking at Roy."	Possible answers: "She paused for a moment to look sharply at John."	Possible answers: "He stood, enormous, in the center of the room…"

The Rockpile

THE CRUCIBLE, ACT 1

Name _____ Date _____

Word Study Homophones

Homophones are words that sound the same but mean something different (in fact the word *homophone* literally means "of the same sound"). Usually homophones also have different spellings (like *see* and *sea*).

Practice Each of the lines below is from *The Crucible*. Each also contains an underlined word that is a homophone. Figure out the homophone and then write a sample sentence using it in the space provided.

1. Why, <u>it's</u> sure she did.

   homophone: _____ its _____

   sample sentence: I got ink all over the inside of my bag when my pen lost its cap somehow. _____

2. Why, how does Ruth <u>ail</u>?

   homophone: _____ ale _____

   sample sentence: At the tavern, people ordered mugs of ale. _____

3. Her <u>soul</u> is taken, surely.

   homophone: _____ sole _____

   sample sentence: I have a hole in the sole of my shoe. _____

4. He has indeed; and found a <u>witch</u> in Beverly last year, and let you remember that.

   homophone: _____ which _____

   sample sentence: I am trying to decide which of these three shirts to wear today. _____

5. . . . I am certain there be no element of witchcraft <u>here</u>.

   homophone: _____ hear _____

   sample sentence: It's so loud in this room, I can't hear what you're saying. _____

THE CRUCIBLE, ACT 1

Name _____ Date _____

Directions: In *The Crucible*, it can be hard to figure out what really happened. Imagine you are a detective. As you read, write the facts of the case in column 1. Write people's opinions about what happened in column 2.

Fact	Opinion
Abigail, Betty, and the other girls danced in the woods.	Parris thinks dancing is evil.
Ruth is sick.	Mrs. Putnam thinks Ruth's sickness is caused by the Devil.

During Reading

THE CRUCIBLE, ACT 1

Name _____ Date _____

Grammar Link Interrogative Sentences

An **interrogative sentence** is a sentence that asks a question. Interrogatives are easy to spot because they end with a question mark. They often begin with a question word, such as *who, what, where, when, why,* or *how.* They may also start with the main verb of the sentence, as, for example, *Did you hear something just now?* Heard out loud, an interrogative sentence is also fairly easy to identify, because the speaker's voice goes up in pitch at the end of the sentence.

Practice All the sentences below come from *The Crucible.* Some are interrogative sentences and some are not. Read each one aloud. Does it sound like a question? Place a check in the box beside each interrogative sentence.

1. ☑ What does the doctor say, child
2. ☐ Go directly home and speak nothing of unnatural causes
3. ☑ Your name in the town——it is entirely white, is it not
4. ☐ I will not have it said my name is soiled
5. ☐ Why, that's strange
6. ☑ Why aren't you home
7. ☑ Mercy, you go home to Ruth, d'y'hear
8. ☑ Do you mean to tell me you've never looked up at my window
9. ☐ I never spoke on witches one way or the other
10. ☑ Will it hurt the child, sir

During Reading

THE CRUCIBLE, ACT 1

Name _____ Date _____

Grammar Link Exclamatory and Imperative Sentences

Exclamatory sentences are sentences that express strong feelings, such as surprise or anger. They always end with an exclamation mark.

Imperative sentences express commands. They end with an exclamation mark or a period. Usually, the subject of the sentence is understood to be *you,* but the word itself might be omitted.

Practice A Each sentence below is from *The Crucible.* Each one is also an exclamation, an imperative, or both. Circle the correct designation for each one.

1. Betty, you never say that again!
   Exclamation Imperative (Both)

2. There be children dyin' in the village, Mister!
   (Exclamation) Imperative Both

3. Clasp his hand, make your peace.
   Exclamation (Imperative) Both

4. That's deep, Mr. Parris, deep, deep!
   (Exclamation) Imperative Both

Practice B Emotions run high in *The Crucible,* so there are many exclamations in the dialogue. For each exclamation below, circle the emotion that you think the person is feeling as he or she says the line.

1. I am writing since November for a stick, and even in November I had to show my frostbitten hands like some London beggar! (spoken by Reverend Parris when he is complaining about his treatment by the villagers)
   Joy Shock (Outrage) Surprise

2. And then she close her book and walks out of the house, and suddenly—mark this—mark this—I could pray again! (spoken by Giles Corey when he's talking about how his wife reads books that she won't show him)
   (Amazement) Delight Amusement Boredom

3. Oh, God bless you Mr. Hale! (spoken by Tituba after Hale tells her she'll be forgiven now that she has confessed to witchcraft)
   Nervousness Hilarity Horror (Relief)

The Crucible, Act 1

AMBUSH · THE Gift IN WARTIME · from Stay Alive, My Son

Name _____ Date _____

Grammar Link Adjectives and Adverbs

Adverbs and adjectives look similar, but they do different things.

An adjective describes a noun. It usually answers the question *what*.

An adverb often answers the question *how*. Adverbs describe verbs, adjectives, or other adverbs.

FORM

Adjective		Adverb		Rules for Forming Adverbs
stow	quick	slowly	quickly	For most adverbs, we add -*ly* to an adjective.
beautiful	bad	beautifully	badly	
happy	easy	happily	easily	If the adjective ends in *y*, we change the *y* to *i* and then add -*ly*.
hard	fast	hard	fast	Some adverbs are the same as the adjective.
late	early	late	early	
good		well		The adverb form of *good* is *well*.

FUNCTION

Adjectives and adverbs look similar, but they do different things.

1. An adjective describes a noun and usually answers the question *what*.
   What color is the car? The car is **red**.

2. An adverb often answers the question *how*. Adverbs describe verbs, adjectives, and other adverbs.
   How does she dance? She dances **beautifully**. She dances **very beautifully**.

Practice Pin Yathay has many strengths. Here are some of them. Underline the correct form of the adjective or adverb.

1. He is a (good / well) writer.

2. He remembers the past (clear / clearly).

3. He solves problems (careful / carefully).

4. He is often (helpful / helpfully) to people.

5. He speaks (good / well).

A49

AMBUSH · THE Gift IN WARTIME · from Stay Alive, My Son

Name _____ Date _____

Directions: As you read the selections, think about the concrete details each author includes. Use the chart below to list concrete details from each selection. Then, note whether the detail is related to the sense of sight, hearing, smell, taste, or touch. Finally, write an idea or feeling the detail suggests.

Detail	Sense	Idea or Feeling
"The night was foggy."	sight	the narrator cannot see and may be scared

A48

A79

SALVADOR LATE OR EARLY

Name _____ Date _____

Directions: What kind of person is Salvador? As you read, complete the chart below. On the left, write details from the story about Salvador. On the right, explain what each detail tells you about him.

Detail About Salvador	What the Detail Tells Me About Salvador
1. Salvador has crooked hair and crooked teeth.	1. Salvador may not have time to take care of his hair and teeth. He is probably a very busy person.

Snow

Name _____ Date _____

Remember, when authors use indirect characterization, they tell you what a character is like by showing
• the character's words
• the character's actions
• what others think and say about the character

Directions: As you read, use the charts below to list examples of indirect characterization of Yolanda and Sister Zoe. Then write down what each example tells you about the character.

Sister Zoe

Example of Indirect Characterization	What It Tells Me About the Character
Sister Zoe tells Yolanda she has a lovely name.	Sister Zoe is nice. She is trying to make Yolanda feel comfortable.

Yolanda

Example of Indirect Characterization	What It Tells Me About the Character

Thoughts on the African-American Novel

Name _____ Date _____

Grammar Link Comparative and Superlative Forms of Adverbs: *–er* and *More*

A snail moves **more slowly** than a tortoise.
In fact, a snail moves the **most slowly** of all animals.
A duck walks **less easily** than it swims.

Adverb	Comparative	Superlative	
easily	more/less easily	the most/least easily	We compare adverbs ending in *–ly* with *more* and the *most*, or *less* and the *least*.
slowly	more/less slowly	the most/least slowly	
carefully	more/less carefully	the most/least carefully	
fast	faster	the fastest	For adverbs that have the same form as adjectives, we use *–er* and *–est*.
hard	harder	the hardest	
early	earlier	the earliest	
well	better	the best	*Well* is an irregular adverb.

Practice Complete each sentence using the comparative or superlative form of the adverb in italics. Follow the example.

1. I read Morrison's essay *carefully* the first time, and then I read it again more carefully.

2. Society can change *fast*, but during the Industrial Revolution it changed faster _____ than ever before.

3. Some forms of music once belonged *exclusively* to African Americans, but now that music belongs less exclusively to African Americans.

4. African Americans *likely* needed a new form of expression, and they _____ more likely needed a guide to using their new social status.

5. Any novel can connect *intimately* with readers, but a novel rooted in the oral tradition can connect more intimately .

6. Many writers write *thoughtfully* about race. Morrison writes the most thoughtfully of all.

Thoughts on the African-American Novel

A53

Thoughts on the African-American Novel

Name _____ Date _____

Directions: As you read, practice finding the main idea and supporting details. Write down the main idea of each paragraph. Then write down one detail that supports it.

Paragraph 1
Main Idea: The novel serves a purpose for the class of people that write it.
Supporting Detail: "early works such as *Pamela*, by Samuel Richardson, and the Jane Austen material provided social rules and explained behavior"

Paragraph 2
Main Idea: _____

Supporting Detail: _____

Paragraph 3
Main Idea: _____

Supporting Detail: _____

Paragraph 4
Main Idea: _____

Supporting Detail: _____

Paragraph 5
Main Idea: _____

Supporting Detail: _____

A52

A81

During Reading

Name _____ **Date** _____

Functional and Workplace
DOCUMENTS

Directions: As you read "Functional Documents," list each type of functional document in column 1. Then write the purpose for each type of document in column 2. The first one is completed for you as an example.

Type of Document	Purpose of Document
1. Letter of Application	To show your interest in and qualifications for a job
2. Possible answer: Résumé	Possible answer: To provide your background information, education, and work experience to an employer
3. Possible answer: Job application	Possible answer: To provide a brief and accurate overview of your experience to an employer
4. Possible answer: Memos	Possible answer: To give specific information to another person or a group of peopl
5. Possible answer: Business E-mail	Possible answer: To communicate with coworkers quickly and concisely using correct grammar
6. Possible answer: Travel Directions	Possible answer: To provide people with detailed and clear directions to the location of your event
7. Possible answer: Technical Writing	Possible answer: To describe a process clearly and in the correct order so that a reader can complete a task

Notes

Notes

Notes

Notes

Notes

Notes

Notes

Notes

Notes

Notes

Notes

Notes